Forms of Local Government

FORMS OF LOCAL GOVERNMENT

A Handbook on City, County and Regional Options

Edited by Roger L. Kemp

McFarland & Company, Inc., Publishers
Jefferson, North Carolina, and London

The present work is a reprint of the library bound edition of Forms of Local Goverment: A Handbook on City, County and Regional Options, *first published in 1999 by McFarland.*

Acknowledgments: Grateful acknowledgment is made to the following organizations and publishers for granting permission to reprint the material contained in this volume: American Planning Association; Congressional Quarterly, Inc.; Georgia Municipal Association; Government Finance Officers Association; Institute of Community and Area Development; International City/County Management Association; National Association of Counties; National Association of Regional Councils; National Civic League; National League of Cities; State of California; The Council of State Governments; University of Baltimore; University of Cincinnati; University of North Carolina; University of South Florida; U.S. Advisory Commission on Intergovernmental Relations; West Group.

LIBRARY OF CONGRESS CATALOGUING-IN-PUBLICATION DATA

Forms of local government: a handbook on city, county and regional options / edited by Roger L. Kemp.
    p. cm.
    Includes index.

    ISBN-13: 978-0-7864-3100-7
    softcover : 50# alkaline paper ∞

    1. Local government — United States.   I. Kemp, Roger L.
JS331.F67   2007
352.14'0973 — dc21   99-20785

British Library cataloguing data are available

Cover photograph: Town Hall in Wisconsin ©2007 Digital Vision

Manufactured in the United States of America

McFarland & Company, Inc., Publishers
  Box 611, Jefferson, North Carolina 28640
  www.mcfarlandpub.com

To Jill,
my traveling companion and soul mate

CONTENTS

PREFACE

Within the American federal system of government, cities and counties are creatures of the state, and are established consistent with each state's constitution and statutes. Each state provides for the creation of local governments and determines the amount of authority that cities and counties may exercise. In some states, local governments are established by legislation (e.g., through charters granted by the state). Most states, however, are authorized by state enabling statutes that permit the citizens of an area desiring local services to form their own unit of local government.

There are actually several types of local government, including counties, cities, towns and townships, school districts, and special districts. Regional forms of government have evolved over the years to cope with a variety of urban problems that transcend the traditional political boundaries of cities and counties. The focus of this book is on forms of government for cities, counties, and regions. The term "cities" includes similar municipal political entities such as municipalities, towns, townships, and boroughs. The "county" designation includes boroughs in Alaska and parishes in Louisiana. Regional government structures also go by a variety of names too numerous to mention here. This work, however, focuses on sub-state regional governments, formed either by cities, by cities together with their counties, or in some cases by cities and counties separately, typically in highly urbanized areas.

States vary greatly in the methods by which they regulate local government structures. One of the principal methods involves restrictions on the forms of local government that citizens may use and the degree, if any, to which they may exercise home-rule powers.

In some states, forms of local government are set by the state constitution and laws. In most cases, this power is delegated to communities with home-rule privileges, empowering citizens to select the form of government of their choice, perhaps with a few state-imposed limits on their options. This volume sets forth various forms of local government that citizens may consider when deciding upon the form that best serves their needs. The typical forms of local government for each level of government examined in this work — cities, counties, and regions — are briefly highlighted below.

Cities

The three basic forms of municipal (city) government include the mayor-council, council-manager, and commission plans. Under the mayor-council plan, the duties of the mayor vary greatly, typically depending upon the size of the city. Generally, larger cities are most likely to have the strong mayor-council plan of government. Under the council-manager plan, a separation of powers exists between the legislative and executive functions of government. The commission plan, on the other hand, involves the direct election of legislators and executives to lead the various functions of municipal government. This form of government, which merges the legislative and executive functions, remains in only a few communities in America.

Counties

There are also three primary forms of county government, including the commission,

commission-administrator, and council-executive plans. The commission plan allows for the direct election of administrators. Under the commissioner-administrator form, the powers of the "administrator" may vary depending upon which plan is used — council-manager (strong executive), chief administrative officer (weak executive), and county administrative assistant (supervisor/coordinator). Under the council-executive plan, the county executive is directly elected by voters and performs specific executive functions.

Regions

There are five main forms of regional government agencies. These include the regional planning commission, council of governments, regional advisory committee, regional allocation agency, and special purpose regional agency. Regional planning commissions may encompass a single county, multiple counties, or multiple jurisdictions. Councils of governments may include cities, cities and a single county, or cities and multiple counties. Regional advisory committees are created by states to oversee the planning function of portions of land within the state. Regional allocation agencies are typically responsible for allocating certain federal funds within selected geographic areas. Special purpose regional agencies have the authority to plan and control development in selected areas of a state.

The purpose of this volume is to sort through and make sense out of the complex assortment of local government forms. To accomplish this, and to facilitate reader reference to individual topics, this book has been organized into the following sections: a general introduction to the subject of local governments; three sections examining, in turn, the different forms of city, county, and regional government; three sections reviewing city, county, and regional government studies and trends; and a final section comprising thoughts about the future of all three levels of government.

The most important purpose of this volume is to educate local public officials and citizens as to the various forms of local government, their main characteristics, and their ramifications. The goal of all forms of government should be to provide elected leaders and citizens with sound political and administrative processes to ensure the nonpartisan and professional operations of their governmental structure. To this end, the form of government used should be determined by a plurality of the voters in any given political jurisdiction. This volume should enable both political leaders and citizens to make more informed decisions concerning the form of government they select.

Most published works on local forms of government focus on only one level — either city, county, or regional government. This is one of the few volumes dealing with *all* forms of government for all three levels. For this reason, this book represents an important codification of knowledge in this field.

ROGER L. KEMP
June 1999
Meriden, Connecticut

PART I
Introduction

CHAPTER 1

OVERVIEW OF LOCAL GOVERNMENTS

John Kincaid

In the American federal system, local governments are legal creatures of the states, established in accordance with state constitutions and statutes. All states provide for the establishment of local governments and determine how much authority may be exercised by each type of government. Some local governments are created by direct state action (e.g., through charters granted by the state). Most, however, are authorized by state enabling statutes that allow citizens of an area needing or desiring local services to create their own unit of local government.

This chapter examines the extent to which states regulate municipalities and county governments in the conduct of their business or, conversely, the extent to which states allow local governments to manage their own affairs. This chapter gives a brief overview of the types of local government in the United States.[1]

Types of Local Governments

States have established five major types of local government either by constitutional provision or statute: (1) counties, (2) cities, (3) towns and townships, (4) school districts, and (5) special districts.

COUNTIES

Counties are administrative arms of the state that provide general government services, such as courts, jails, law enforcement, land records, vital statistics, public health, welfare, and roads. Many counties also provide municipal-type services, such as hospitals, airports, streets and highways, parks, libraries, and environmental protection.[2]

County governments exist in 48 states (Connecticut and Rhode Island abolished counties as governmental units). Parts of Alaska, Montana, and South Dakota also are not contained within counties. The county designation includes boroughs in Alaska and parishes in Louisiana.

The number of recognized county governments varies dramatically among the states. For example, Texas has 254 counties, while Hawaii has only 4 (Honolulu is a city-county). County populations also differ tremendously, with 96 counties having less than 2,500 residents and 22 having more than one million.[3]

Counties are governed by an elected body, usually a board of supervisors or a board of commissioners. More than two-thirds of the county boards consist of three to five members. They may be elected by district or at large and typically are part-time officials. The board chair may be selected by the members or may be elected directly by the voters.[4] About 400 counties have an appointed county manager or administrator, and about 70

Originally published as "Local Governments in the United States," Chapter 1 of *State Laws Governing Local Government Structure and Administration*, Report No. M-186, March 1993. Published by the U.S. Advisory Commission on Intergovernmental Relations, Washington, D.C.

counties have a separately elected county executive.

Many counties also have additional independently elected officials, such as sheriff, prosecuting attorney, or clerk. The trend in recent years, however, has been to make these positions appointive by the county board.

In many states, counties have a dual role, serving both as subunits (or arms) of state government and as local governments in their own right. The role of counties in Maine, Massachusetts, New Hampshire, and Vermont is greatly circumscribed. Vermont counties, for example, exist primarily to maintain the court house and county jail. Only a few more functions (i.e., some road maintenance and police responsibilities) are performed by Maine's counties.[5]

Property tax receipts accounted for 73.3 percent of county tax revenues nationally in 1990. Another 18.8 percent of revenues came from general and selective sales and gross receipts taxes. Individual and corporate income taxes accounted for only 3.0 percent of county tax funding in 1990.[6]

MUNICIPALITIES

Municipal governments provide public services, in addition to those provided by counties and special districts, "for a specific concentration of population in a defined area."[7] All 50 states have units of municipal government. As with counties, the number of municipalities per state varies greatly. Hawaii, for example, has only one, while Illinois has 1,282 municipalities.

Each state has enacted statutory requirements for municipal incorporation. The criteria for incorporation vary among the states and among different classes of municipalities. Generally, an area must have a minimum population or density before it is eligible for incorporation. Alabama, for example, sets a 300-person population minimum for incorporation. Florida requires an average of 1.5 persons per acre before a community may incorporate. Georgia requires that any new community seeking incorporation be at least three miles from any existing municipality.[8]

Procedures for incorporation typically include: (1) presentation of a petition from the community describing the boundaries and the population of the proposed municipality, (2) an election to ascertain popular support for the incorporation, and (3) certification by the secretary of state that the election results support creation of the municipality and that all legal requirements for incorporation have been met.

There are three basic forms of municipal government: mayor-council, council-manager, and commission.[9] Under the mayor-council form, the council is the legislative body. Typically consisting of five to seven members, councils may be elected at large or by district, or a combination. In most communities, council membership is a part-time responsibility.

Mayors may be characterized as either strong or weak. In the strong mayor-council plan, commonly found in large cities, the mayor is the chief executive, is popularly elected, and possesses broad budgetary, administrative, and appointive powers, including veto power over ordinances enacted by the council. Mayors in a weak mayor-council system typically possess few independent powers.

Conceived in 1908, the council-manager form calls for an elected city council (usually nonpartisan) and a professional city manager hired by the council. The council sets tax rates, decides on the budget, and makes policy, and the manager implements policy and administers city affairs. Council-manager municipalities also have mayors, who are members of the council but do not perform executive functions. The mayor is the chief political and policy leader of the city, and may be selected by the council or elected by the voters. Approximately 2,500 municipalities operate under council-manager government.

The commission form, used by less than 5 percent of municipalities, consists of a nonpartisan elected commission of three to five members who perform legislative and executive duties.

Municipal revenues in 1990 came from the following sources: property taxes, 50.9 percent; general and selective sales and gross receipts taxes, 27.9 percent; and individual and corporation income taxes, 13.3 percent.[10]

TOWNSHIPS

Township governments serve the inhabitants of areas of land "without regard to population concentration."[11] As used in this report, the term township includes towns in Connecticut, Maine (including organized plantations), Massachusetts, Minnesota, New Hampshire (including organized locations), New York, Rhode Island, Vermont, and Wisconsin, and townships in Kansas, Illinois, Indiana, Michigan, Missouri, Nebraska, New Jersey, North Dakota, Ohio, Pennsylvania, and South Dakota.

In seven states — Indiana, Massachusetts, New Hampshire, New Jersey, Pennsylvania, Rhode Island, and Wisconsin — townships comprise all areas of the state, except in Indiana, where they are coextensive with cities and have no governmental functions and, in the other states, where municipalities have been incorporated.

Town government in its classic form is distinguished from township government. The New England town is governed by an annual town meeting in which all residents are eligible to participate. Large towns in Connecticut and Massachusetts, however, conduct town meetings using approximately 100–150 representatives elected by the residents. Maine towns commonly hire a town manager, supervised by the selectmen, to administer local government.[12]

During town meetings, residents enact ordinances and establish the budget. Part-time officials, usually called selectmen, supervise daily operations.

Township governments, if similar to municipalities, utilize a municipal form of government. Otherwise, townships commonly are governed by an elected board of usually three to five part-time supervisors or trustees. Additional township officials, such as the clerk or treasurer, may be elected by the voters.

New England, New Jersey, and Pennsylvania townships have relatively broad powers and perform functions similar to municipalities. Some New England townships run schools. Midwestern townships typically perform limited government functions.[13]

Townships rely almost exclusively on the property tax for tax revenues. In 1990, 92.4 percent of township tax revenues nationwide came from the property tax. Individual and corporate income taxes contributed only 2.4 percent of revenue, and only 0.3 percent came from general and selective sales and gross receipts taxes.[14]

SCHOOL DISTRICTS

As defined by the Census Bureau, independent school districts are "organized local entities providing public elementary, secondary, and/or higher education which, under state law, have sufficient administrative and fiscal autonomy to qualify as separate governments."[15] There are 14,556 independent school districts, which are distinguished from the 1,488 dependent public school systems that operate as an arm of county, municipal, township, or state government. Dependent systems are found in 17 states and the District of Columbia.[16]

More than 80 percent of all school districts are governed by a nonpartisan elected board. Commonly composed of 5 to 15 members, the board sets education policy and oversees administration of the schools by a professional superintendent of schools.[17]

Of all types of local government, in 1990, school districts placed the heaviest reliance (97.5 percent) on property tax revenue.[18]

SPECIAL DISTRICTS

Special districts are generally "authorized by state law to provide only one or a limited number of designated functions and with sufficient administrative and fiscal autonomy to qualify as separate governments." They may be known by a variety of titles, such as "districts, authorities, boards, [or] commissions ... as specified in the enabling state legislation."[19]

Special districts are the most numerous units of local government. They are created either directly by state legislation or by local action, pursuant to state law. Special districts often overlie county and municipal units or may cross state lines. Only one-fourth of all special districts serve an area whose boundaries are coterminous with either a city, county, or a township.[20]

In 1964, the U.S. Advisory Commission on Intergovernmental Relations (ACIR) identified a list of factors promoting creation of special districts.[21] Among the financial reasons are: (1) debt and tax limitations on general local units; (2) the district's suitability for financing services through service or user charges, as opposed to general tax revenues; and (3) the more suitable financial base that may be available to support a particular service by resort to special boundaries.

Limitations on the powers of general governments also stimulate the creation of special districts. Such limitations include: (1) strict construction of local government powers, (2) lack of power for those governments to establish differential taxing areas within their boundaries, and (3) lack of authority to contract with other local units or to undertake joint responsibility for providing services.

Closely related to these limitations are those imposed by the territorial scope of existing units of government. City and county areas may be too small for efficient and effective management of certain functions (e.g., air pollution control), they may not conform to the natural boundaries needed for a function (e.g., water basins), or they may not match the area in which beneficiaries have agreed to pay more for special services.

Political factors often are involved in the creation of special districts. Citizens may believe that providing a service through a special district removes that service from possible partisan influence. In some other cases, the federal government stimulated the development of special districts, particularly conservation, drainage, flood control, and irrigation districts. A few types of special districts existed before general local governments (e.g., fire protection).

Like counties, special districts are governed by a board. In some districts, the board may be elected by the public. More commonly, however, board members are appointed by officials of the state, counties, municipalities, and/or townships that have joined to form the special district.[22]

In 1992, almost 92 percent of special districts performed a single function. More than a third (36 percent) of all special districts provide sewer and water services, 16 percent are fire districts, 11 percent provide housing services, 6 percent provide education and library services, 4 percent are health and hospitals districts, and 4 percent are transportation related.[23]

Based on financial data, transportation districts dominate the "top 50" list (18 of 50), followed closely by power districts (14) and water and sewer districts (10). The remainder of the top 50 includes port authorities, housing finance agencies, and an airport authority, a park district, and a bridge and tunnel authority.[24]

Special districts have several sources of revenue, and some districts have more than one source. Forty-three percent have the authority to levy property taxes (e.g., districts providing libraries, hospitals, health, highways, airports, fire, natural resources, parks and recreation, and cemeteries, and districts with multiple functions). Close to 25 percent of districts may impose service charges (e.g., sewerage, solid waste disposal, water supply, and other utility districts). Slightly more than 30 percent rely on grants, shared taxes, rentals, and reimbursement from governments (e.g., education, soil and water conservation, and housing and community development districts). Other districts rely on special assessments or other taxes.[25]

Those without taxing authority include some of the largest special districts, such as the Port Authority of New York and New Jersey and the Chicago Transit Authority. Districts may have more than one source of revenue.

The Overall Pattern of Local Governments

NUMBERS OF LOCAL GOVERNMENTS

According to the U.S. Bureau of the Census, Americans receive services from 3,043 counties, 19,296 municipalities, 16,666 townships, 14,556 independent school districts and 33,131 special districts.[26]

Frequently, these local jurisdictions overlap (i.e., occupy the same territory), although towns and townships do not overlie municipalities. Towns and townships, as well as most municipalities and special districts, generally lie within counties, although municipalities and special districts sometimes cross county boundaries. There are some exceptions, however.

In Virginia, cities are independent entities, separate from the counties. In Maryland, the constitution makes the city of Baltimore a separate entity. Consolidated city-county governments have been created in several places (e.g., Jacksonville-Duval County, Florida; Nashville-Davidson County, Tennessee; and San Francisco, California).

LOCAL GOVERNMENT STRUCTURE

The states vary markedly in their methods of regulating local government structure. One of the principal methods involves restrictions on the forms of local government that citizens may use and the degree, if any, to which they may exercise home rule (i.e., self-government or autonomy over internal affairs).

In many cases, local government structures and the specific duties of local officials are set by the state constitution and laws. In other cases, this power is delegated to communities with home rule privileges, empowering them to select a form of government of their choice, perhaps with a few state-imposed limits on their options.

Montana took a unique approach in its 1972 state constitution. The legislature provides optional or alternative forms of government that the citizens of a local government may adopt, amend, or abandon by majority vote. Within four years of the ratification of the 1972 constitution, each local government was required to review its structure and submit one alternative form to the voters. Thereafter, a local government review was mandatory every ten years. The provision was amended effective in 1979 to require an election once every ten years to determine if a local government will undertake a review procedure.[27]

Previous studies by ACIR have shown that home rule powers may be exercised in four primary areas: structure, function, fiscal, and/or personnel.[28] Structural home rule allows localities to determine their own form of government. Functional home rule enables entities to exercise powers of local self-government. Fiscal home rule authorizes local governments to determine their revenue sources, set tax rates, borrow funds, and engage in other related actions.

Home rule regarding personnel matters allows localities to set rules governing employment, the rates of remuneration, the conditions of employment, and collective bargaining, among other factors. These grants of power usually are limited by general state law.

Local governments that possess discretionary authority may not always use it. Previous ACIR research revealed that the power to draft and adopt a charter frequently is not utilized by local governments, nor do governments amend their charters often. Knowledgeable observers reported that a number of factors contribute to this phenomenon, including federal and state court decisions, federal and state grant-in-aid conditions, and fiscal constraints.[29]

Notes

1. For additional information on local governments, see U.S. Advisory Commission on Intergovernmental Relations (ACIR), *State and Local Roles in the Federal System* (Washington, DC, 1982); Parris N. Glendening and Mavis Mann Reeves, *Pragmatic Federalism: An Intergovernmental View of American Government* (Pacific Palisades, California: Palisades Publishers, 1984); International City/County Management Association (ICMA), *The Municipal Year Book* (Washington, DC, annual); and U.S. Department of Commerce, Bureau of the Census (Census), *Government Organization, 1987 Census of Governments, Volume 1, Number 1* (Washington, DC, 1988), and *Government Organization, 1992 Census of Governments*, Volume 1, Number 1 (Washington, DC, forthcoming 1993).

2. See also "Counties," *Intergovernmental Perspective*, 17 (Winter 1991): entire issue.

3. ICMA, *The Municipal Year Book 1992*, p. xvi.

4. See John Kincaid, "Federalism and State and Local Government," in Godfrey Hodgson, ed., *The United States, Handbooks to the Modern World*, Volume 2 (New York: Facts on File, 1992), p. 1053.

5. See Census, *Government Organization, 1987*, pp. A-97, A-105, A-141, and A-212

6. ACIR, *Significant Features of Fiscal Federalism, 1992 Edition, Volume 2, Revenues and Expenditures* (Washington, DC, 1992), p. 127

7. According to the Census Bureau, the term includes all cities, villages, boroughs (except in Alaska),

and towns outside the New England states, Minnesota, New York, and Wisconsin.

8. See Census, *Government Organization, 1987*, p. B-3.

9. See ibid., pp. A-3, A-44, and A-53.

10. See Kincaid, "Federalism and State and Local Government," pp. 1055–1056.

11. These governmental units are called towns in the six New England states, New York, and Wisconsin. They may or may not be incorporated. Twenty states, located primarily in the northeast and north central regions, have established towns or townships.

12. See Kincaid, "Federalism and State and Local Government," p. 1054.

13. See Census, *Government Organization, 1987*, p. ix.

14. ACIR, *Significant Features 1992*, p. 128.

15. See Census, *Government Organization, 1987*, p. xii.

16. Of that number, Alaska, Hawaii, Maryland, North Carolina, and Virginia rely solely on dependent systems. A majority of schools in Connecticut, Maine, Massachusetts, Rhode Island, and Tennessee are dependent systems. The vast majority of dependent school systems in North Carolina, Tennessee, and Virginia are run by counties. Counties also run some schools in Alaska, Arizona, California, Maryland, Massachusetts, Mississippi, New Jersey, New York, and Wisconsin. In New Jersey and New England, dependent schools are arms of township government.

17. See Kincaid, "Federalism and State and Local Government," p. 1056.

18. ACIR, *Significant Features 1992*, p. 127.

19. See Census, *Government Organization, 1987*, p. xii.

20. See ibid., p. x.

21. ACIR, *The Problem of Special Districts in American Government* (Washington, DC, 1964).

22. See Kincaid, "Federalism and State and Local Government," p. 1057.

23. See Census, *Government Organization, 1992* (Preliminary Report), pp. 7–8.

24. Amy Lamphere, "Top 50 Special Districts: 3rd Annual Financial Report," *City & State*, March 23, 1992, p. 8.

25. See Census, *Government Organization, 1987*, p. xvi.

26. See ibid., p. B-1, and *Government Organization, 1992* (Preliminary Report), p. 1.

27. Montana Constitution, Article XI, Section 9 (2).

28. ACIR, *Measuring Local Discretionary Authority* (Washington, DC, 1981). See also ACIR, *State Constitutional and Statutory Restrictions Upon the Structural, Functional, and Personnel Powers of Local Government* (1962), and *State Law Foundations of Local Self-Government: Constitutional, Statutory, and Judicial Issues* (forthcoming 1993).

29. See ACIR, *Measuring Local Discretionary Authority*, pp. 7–8.

CHAPTER 2

THE STRUCTURE
OF LOCAL GOVERNMENTS

James H. Svara

From its earliest days one hundred years ago, the National Civic League has emphasized structural reform in government as an important — indeed the central — strategy for strengthening democracy in the United States. This is significant when one considers the alternatives. At various times over the last century, some have argued that promoting social or economic change would be more efficacious than focusing on structural change, or that stimulating citizen activism would be a more direct way to expand the influence of citizens than changing governmental institutions. Throughout this time, however, the National Municipal League/National Civic League has stressed that governmental form and practices create the foundation on which other change is based and influences whether citizen participation will be more or less successful in impacting governmental action. The "model charters" have at once been the best known products of the League and symbolized the League's commitment to improving the structure and legal process of government.

As the National Civic League enters its second century, it is unclear how much emphasis should be placed on structural reform as part of an agenda for promoting change in local government. The relevance of continuing to recommend that local government adopt certain institutions depends on whether these proposals have addressed and continue to address the problems confronted by American cities and counties and the citizens who live in them. What were the unique problems in several distinct periods over the past century? How were reform proposals articulated and what values did they reflect? And, what is the degree of fit between the problems and the proposals? These periods are labeled Innovation (1894–1919), Expansion and Orthodoxy (1920–1945), Consolidation of Reform (1966–1988), and Reaffirmation and Renewal, or the End of Reform (1989–Present). The reform proposals will not be reviewed in detail. Rather, the central ideas in reform arguments, as incorporated in the Model Charters and contemporary statements to promote reform, will be examined.

Period I: Innovation, 1894–1919

The original municipal program — the first model charter approved in 1899 — established the approach of emphasizing structural change as the primary response to problems with government performance and defects in the practice of local democracy. Although some have criticized the reformers for ignoring social reform and failing to attack underlying problems of economic inequality and political powerlessness,[1] the reformers of the Progressive Era believed that structural and legal change

From *National Civic Review,* Vol. 83, No. 3, Summer-Fall 1994. Published by the National Civic League, Denver, Colorado. Reprinted with permission of the publisher.

(e.g., changing governmental form, reorganizing and professionalizing departments and establishing home rule), were pre-conditions for other changes. Rather than proposing a program of substantive policies for local officials — and the early leaders of the League included many social reformers — the approach was to change the structure and process of government to enable new leaders with greater accountability to the public to undertake innovations in policies and services. A historian commenting on the nature of reform argues that the reformers believed that institutions and practices had to be thoroughly modernized "if urban government were to move effectively into the field of social welfare and were to ride herd on economic interests."[2]

The root of many of the problems in government performance was structural. Authority within government was highly fragmented with direct election of a wide range of officials — including some department heads and commission members — and extensive checks and balances. There was an absence of clear lines of administrative authority, and personnel systems were haphazard. Commentators at the beginning of the century identified the "prerequisites of local self-government."[3] They included the legal power to act, local autonomy, local campaigns dealing with local issues, a simple governmental structure with few elected officials, and selection of staff based on merit. It was difficult to formulate a substantive program of reform without first ensuring the organizational capacity for democratic government and effective implementation of policies.

The first model charter organized the governmental form around the principle of the strong elected executive. This approach accomplished the objectives of concentrating authority and strengthening executive leadership, but reformers recognized limitations in this approach from the beginning. Durand, in his review of the *Municipal Program* in 1900, would have preferred to see greater council control over the executive and asked whether it would be possible to create a form akin to the cabinet system "in which close harmony, rather than separation, of executive and legislature should be sought?"[4] Goodnow observed in 1904 that, with an elected chief executive, "it is difficult if not impossible to prevent politics from affecting administration, not only in its action but also its organization, with the result that qualifications of even clerical and technical positions in the public service soon become political in character."[5] Deming looked with favor on English local government which had a strong council — including a mayor without executive authority — that directed the city administration.[6]

There was a continuing concern about the problems produced by separation of powers as well as a desire to strengthen the city council. Deming observed that division of power between the mayor and council was an obstacle to effective governmental performance not found in English cities "in which neither the check and balance system nor numerous elective offices hindered the steady evolution and intelligent application of the representative principle to municipal government."[7] To Goodnow, the creation of the "council system" of city government "has the great advantage that it avoids all possibility of conflict between municipal authorities. The council being absolutely supreme in the city there is really no authority with which conflicts may arise."[8] Goodnow, who favored a "rehabilitation" of the city council, feared that vesting all executive powers in the mayor limited the role of the council, but he supported concentrating authority in the office of a strong mayor as a step toward increasing the council's importance. Woodruff supported the new commission form because it eliminated "needless checks and balances" and simplified government, even though he recommended that the Staunton, Virginia, and Lockport, New York, practice of using a full-time manager to take over the administrative load of the commissioners be considered.[9] Although it might appear that the reformers were flitting from one approach to another,[10] there is consistency in the qualities they sought to incorporate in government. The reformers were looking for a structural approach that would reconcile their support for representative democracy with the principles of hierarchy and merit while avoiding the undemocratic features of the commission form.

With the Second Model Charter adopted in 1916 (published with commentary in *A New Municipal Program* in 1919[11]), the reformers established an original and comprehensive model for reorganizing government to meet the pressing problems of the time. They broadened the base of leadership through reliance on representative rather than executive democracy. In the second "Model Charter," the council was the "pivot of the municipal system."[12] The reformers stressed the importance of a smaller council whose members would have a perspective that was greater than that of a particular neighborhood or small section of a city. At the same time, proportional representation from the city at-large or from multi-member districts in "great" cities, was included to ensure that the governing body provide "fair representation of all large minorities" and be "truly representative of all elements and groups of opinion."[13] The council was given investigatory powers and authority to appoint the city manager. This latter provision, reflecting the concept of the "controlled executive," strengthened both the council and the executive without either jeopardizing the role of the council or perpetuating separation of powers.[14] Thus, the council-manager form was integral to the democratic aspirations of the reformers in the National Municipal League as well as being intended to advance the administrative performance of cities. By 1918, one observer characterized the council in this form as a "restored and powerful representative body."[15]

To improve administrative performance and elevate the level of policy making, the reformers stressed professionalism, administrative reorganization, and the insulation of administrators from interference by elected officials. The Model Charter distinguished "legislation" from "administration," naturally assigning the former to the council and the latter to the manager, but the theoreticians and early practitioners of the council-manager plan did not adhere to a fundamental dichotomy between policy and administration. The council would exercise regular and comprehensive supervision, so there was no presumption that the manager would handle the administration affairs of the city in isolation

from the council. According to the commentary, "administration is given a place apart, but it is not an independent place. It is subject to control but not to factious interference."[16]

Conversely, the manager was called upon to offer policy advice and recommendations to the council in its enactment of legislation. The commentary on the *New Municipal Program* contains numerous references to the manager's policy role. Overall, the manager must "show himself to be a leader, formulating policies and urging their adoption by the council."[17] The reformers did not intend to simply add an administrative technician who would take charge of implementation of policies. They sought to strengthen leadership, and they were successful. An observer at the time remarked that the manager is "an active and influential factor in legislation" whose "judgment will rarely be considered lightly."[18] Adrian concludes that "by the 1920s, the city manager had become a firmly established community leader."[19]

Early managers also were concerned about maintaining positive relations with the citizenry. At the 1918 meeting of the City Management Association, Henry Waite, the first city manager in Dayton (who would serve as president of the National Municipal League from 1921–1923), advised his colleagues to "keep in touch with people" and avoid a tendency "to be cold and efficient." Another speaker warned that "mere efficiency will never solve the problem of municipal government" and reminded the managers that the council-manager form is an "attempt to harmonize efficiency with democracy."[20]

Relevance of reforms to conditions of period. The major problems of this period included fragmented authority, complexity and conflict within government, limits to democratic accountability, corruption, low-level and poor-quality services, and a lack of competence and public service commitment among municipal staff. The solution promoted by reformers was change in the structure of government to create representative democracy and integrated authority in government.

The council-manager form was seen as an advance over the strong mayor form originally endorsed by the National Municipal League because it was based on the unitary model rather than separation of powers, enhanced the role of the council, and strengthened the executive at the same time that it controlled the executive. Other provisions promoted city-wide interests and weakened small neighborhood and partisan interests, while preserving representativeness through proportional representation and districts in large cities. The professional values advanced by this program were honesty, integrity, expertise, competence, and commitment to providing services based on need. The reformers and early practitioners of the council-manager form of government sought to advance efficiency, but they expressed concern that the pursuit of efficiency not distance officials from citizens. Accounts of activities in early council-manager cities commonly refer to the expanded services and results achieved by efficiently using resources. The overarching goal of the reformers was the creation of "a civic culture of integrity and informed accomplishment."[21]

Through 1919, 144 cities with populations over 2,500 had adopted the council-manager form, although less is known about the use of other elements of the *Model City Charter*.[22]

Period II: Expansion and Orthodoxy, 1920–1945

The early part of this period was the time of popularizing the model plan and moving out from the pioneer cities. By the early 1920s, marketing of the plan and simplification of its features were commonplace in the arguments used to support it. In addition, the Progressive Era had ended, and attitudes about the plan became more narrowly focused on administrative advantages. Richard Childs, "godfather" of the council-manager form, lamented in the early 1930s that the form was being adopted for the "wrong reasons."[23] The advantage of the plan was that it permitted the people to directly control their council, which in turn hired a professional manager without having to depend on the intervention of a political machine. Arguments about the efficiency and economy of the form, in Child's

opinion, reflected "shallow and meretricious reasoning."

Confusion over the manager's policy role — in contrast to the original straight-forward recognition of the manager's influence in the legislative sphere — became evident during the 1920s and was compounded by the conditions of the Great Depression.[24] Restricted interpretations of the manager's role in community affairs were emerging. A.R. Hatton, professor and field representative of the National Municipal League in the early 1920s, advised managers to refrain from any involvement in "politics," including promoting public acceptance of policies adopted by the city council. Although he recognized that the manager is hired for working on "the solution of the problems of the city" and "thinking out far and wide constructive plans for the city," the manager "has no part in a fight for municipal policy."[25] Some observers warned that the manager was assuming too much power. Reformers were chagrined by the explicit advocacy of programs and public disagreement with the council by William R. Hopkins, the first city manager in Cleveland.[26] Even a highly respected manager like Waite in Dayton was criticized after leaving office for being too visible — "the outstanding figure in the government" — and his successor was praised for having greater appreciation of the proper role of the city manager. Any activity in policy was viewed by some as a violation of the plan.[27]

Perhaps to allay suspicions that the council-manager form would lead to administrative dominance, popularizers of the plan reinforced the idea that the manager should be simply an administrative technician. The manager may offer advice, Fassett suggested in 1922, "but if he is wise he will seldom advise except when so requested, and will leave to them [the council members] their specific functions as completely as they must leave administrative work to him."[28] The leadership role explicitly justified by the authors of the *New Municipal Program* was being defined out of existence (even though it never disappeared in practice). A new orthodoxy emerged that diminished the policy role of the manager and hardened the line of separation between the council and the manager in a way not intended by the drafters of the second *Model City Charter*.

These shifts were reinforced by the impact of the Depression. In a time of desperate shortage in local government resources and widespread taxpayer revolts,[29] the manager was given a very low profile — in no way responsible for the policy decisions or their attendant costs. The belief that taxes could be contained by the presence of a manager caused the form of government to be even more strongly associated with efficiency.[30] One observer pointed out that the council-manager form would not be able to secure a popular base of support if it continued to stress the money it saved rather than the improved services it provided.[31]

As a consequence of this change in thinking, the strongest advocacy of strict adherence to the dichotomy model came during the orthodoxy of the 1930s and early 1940s.[32] As an issue of philosophy with the city management profession, the matter was stated clearly by Ridley and Nolting in *The City Management Profession*. The manager should not "let himself be driven or led into taking the leadership or responsibility in matters of policy."[33] In general, the manager should stay "out of the limelight as much as possible." The 1938 Code of Ethics of the International City Management Association (ICMA) stated unequivocally that "the city manager is in no sense a political leader." The preamble asserts that, in the council-manager form, "policy shall be determined exclusively by the council." The manager offers advice and information, but policy decisions are to be made and defended by the city council. The commentary accompanying the fifth edition of the *Model City Charter* in 1941 omitted reference to any roles for the manager other than administrative.

Although the manager's policy role was eliminated by the dichotomy model, the accompanying emphasis on the manager's autonomy in the administrative realm served to expand the manager's importance. The ICMA code asserted that "the city manager, in order to preserve his integrity as a professional administrator, resists any encroachment on his control of personnel" and "insists on the exercise of his own judgment in accomplishing council policies."[34] Vieg observed in the mid-thirties that the form was commonly referred to as the "city manager plan," a term which implied that the mayor and council were of little consequence and was "tantamount to exalting administration in a way that neither Wilson nor Childs had ever dreamed of."[35] He advised paying "far more attention to the council (including the mayor) side of the council-manager plan" in the future.

Relevance of reforms to conditions of period. This simplification and narrowing of the reform message was a response to the perceived problems of the period. The concern for fighting corruption and improving the performance of government was carried over from Period I. As the national government launched large-scale relief efforts, attention was focused on Washington as the leader in measures to combat the Depression,[36] while at the local level managers looked inside the organization for ways to increase economy and efficiency. The concept of the controlled executive who assisted the council in the legislative sphere and directed the administrative sphere with council oversight was recast as the dichotomy model. This approach — expressed simply as the separation of policy and administration — ignored the manager's role in formulating policy and helping to shape priorities, but at the same time promoted greater freedom for the manager to streamline administrative practices without political interference. The dominant values were efficiency, economy and fairness, and these obscured the wider range of values important in the first period.

Adoptions of the council-manager form were brisk during the 1920s. The number of cities with populations over 2,500 using the form increased from 144 in 1920 to 369 in 1933. Adoptions slowed during the Depression when the formation of suburbs stopped, and picked up only moderately during the war years. In 1945, 455 cities with over 2,500 residents employed the council-manager form. Approximately one-quarter of the cities over 25,000 in population used the council-manager plan. Despite the association of the council-manager plan with small towns, the form was less commonly used in cities under 25,000 in population than in those that exceeded 25,000.[37]

Period III: Consolidation of Reform, 1946–1965

This period is characterized by unprecedented economic growth and development and the social transformation of the United States after World War II. Two great revolutions reshaped America—the rise of the suburbs and the sunbelt and the expansion of the middle class to incorporate skilled trade and service workers whose income supported a middle-class life-style.[38] City managers directed the large-scale construction of new infrastructure, expanded the range and reach of local services, and oversaw large-scale residential development.[39] They offered the background and orientation that residents of growing urban areas were looking for.

In a "wave of political reform and municipal revitalization" sparked initially by returning young veterans, "the common goal was to replace the small-time politics of cronyism with administrations composed of growth-oriented businessmen and bureaucrats."[40] Besides removing entrenched officials, these new politicians "promised to crack down on vice and clean up police departments, and argued for planning and efficient city bureaus." Acceptance of the council-manager form grew tremendously during this period. The number of cities with populations over 2,500 using the form doubled in the first ten years after the war from 455 to 1,001, and over 1,600 cities used the form by 1965. (The number of cities using the council-manager form has continued to grow since that time to exceed 2,700 in 1994.) The percentage of cities increased as well, with the most dramatic change occurring between 1945 and 1955. In that year, half the cities with between 25,000 and 100,000 residents used the council-manager form, as did two-fifths of the cities between 10,000 and 25,000 and one-third of the cities over 100,000. The council-manager form of government had become solidly established.

During this period, city managers emerged from the shadows of the Depression years. ICMA president C.A. Harrell identified the city manager as a "community leader." The "ideal manager" is a "positive, vital force in the community" who "visualizes broad objectives, distant goals, far-sighted projects."[41] The 1952 ICMA Code of Ethics included this tenet: "The city manager as a community leader submits policy proposals to the council and provides the council with facts and advice on matters of policy to give the council a basis for making decisions on community goals." A commentator concluded in the 1953 *Municipal Year Book*'s review of the previous year that "the debate over whether a city manager should be a leader in policy formation seems to have died down, with the weight of evidence indicating that a successful manager inevitably performs such a function in one way or another." Though a departure from the attitudes of the previous period, this position did not, as the commentator indicated, "modif[y] appreciably the original theory behind the council-manager plan."[42] By viewing the manager's policy role as one that was not originally intended, the city manager was denied legitimacy as a leader who served the council and the public.

Furthermore, the wall of protection around the manager's sphere which was erected during the period of orthodoxy when government activity was severely restricted remained in place when the manager was working on an agenda of growth and development. City managers became insulated and claimed dominance within their sphere. Newland observes that, by the 1950s,

> Structures of executive power became inviolate in "The Plan." The manager's budget became a bastion of executive power, barely subject to council modification. The manager came to have a near monopoly of information, subject only to inquiry by the council as a whole.... Appointed managers prospered in power, but the old politics of reform gradually withered and, by the late 1960s, that greatly expanded executive power lacked the authority of popular support.[43]

The actual freedom displayed by local government managers on the job should not be overstated. City councils were relatively homogeneous — over-representing white businessmen. They were able to achieve consensus regarding the broad goals the manager would pursue and were comfortable delegating broad authority to the manager. The manager could be a low-profile policy leader because of the ease of communicating with a cohesive council. Still, the values stressed by professional managers reinforced executive dominance and over-shadowed the contributions of the council.

Change was occurring in the electoral practices used by cities, but the National Civic League continued to support "old" institutions in the sixth edition of *Model City Charter*, published in 1964.[44] Although the sixth edition provided for the option of a directly elected mayor, the debate over how to select the mayor was not resolved. Richard Childs' book *The First Fifty Years*, published in 1965, continued to raise objections to mayoral election. Childs warned that his "alternative, meaning second choice" method would threaten the tenure and status of the manager.[45] Although the sixth edition included a mixed election system option, the at-large seats outnumbered district seats 4–3. Furthermore, the district council members were only nominated from districts but then chosen by the voters at-large. ICMA also listed at-large elections as among the "main features" of the council-manager plan.[46] Although the at-large method was not integral to the reform plan (as ICMA itself would conclude in 1973), it had been a convenient feature from the manager's perspective because it produced councils which were likely to work smoothly internally and with the manager.

Relevance of reforms to conditions of period. The major new problems of this period were population growth, shortages in services, and inadequate infrastructure. The central-city population increased 50 percent between 1940 and 1970, and the population in the metropolitan suburban fringe almost quadrupled.[47] The solutions provided by the council-manager form of government were planning, professional project development and service delivery, sound fiscal management, and modernization of the local government organization. The reform model applied equally well to the conditions faced by growing urban counties.

The expansion of the use of the reform model in this period was integrally related to the changing population patterns in post-war America. Although it was common from the earliest days of the *New Municipal Program* to argue whether reform — and particularly council-manager government — was appropriate for large cities, the experience in this period linked the reform model to the dynamic urban areas in the country where growth was occurring, including 13 cities with populations over 250,000, plus five that exceeded 500,000 people in 1965. Its features were well suited for the challenges of growth, just as the model had adapted to the retrenchment of the 1930s. The reform model did not, however, directly replace pre-existing governmental institutions in large, older cities that continued to be characterized by strong partisan and ethnic politics.[48] Rather, the reform model provided an approach for improving government responsiveness and performance in cities (and increasing counties) that sought such change. This option was especially attractive in jurisdictions that needed to cope with the pressures of growth and whose populations incorporated new residents who were not resistant to revising established institutions. Elements of the reform model, such as appointed administrative officers, were also increasingly incorporated in the mayor-council plan.

The meaning and record of the reform movement, however, was subject to question as the period ended. Banfield and Wilson in their path-breaking *City Politics* describe the council-manager form at this time as a combination "of the values sought by the plan's inventors (to make easier the effectuation of the popular will) with that sought by its later promoters and supporters (to economize)."[49] Although the reform plan in their opinion has provided government that "is honest, impartial, and efficient 'in the small,' it is not clear it has always accomplished what its inventors mainly intended — namely by centralizing authority to make local government an effective instrument for carrying out the popular will." Although this might happen in cities where "good government" and business interests provide a strong political base, the reform plan is unlikely to "deal boldly with a city's larger problems" in bigger, more heterogeneous cities. This assessment might be disputed on historical grounds, but it points to issues that would be salient in the succeeding periods.

Period IV: Maturity and Challenge, 1966–1988

The 1960s represent a time of fundamental transition. The civil rights movement was transforming the political agenda at the local, state, and national levels and changing the nature of political activism by minorities throughout the United States. Over the next two decades, other groups expanded their participation as well. Specific interest groups, often with very narrow agendas, mobilized supporters and acquired the capacity to focus intense pressure on public officials. Increasingly, representatives of "single-interest groups" were able to secure elected office.

The Great Society and other legislative initiatives of the Johnson administration greatly expanded the federal role in local government, creating direct relationships between national- and local-level administrators in policy initiation and implementation. As a consequence of incentives or requirements from the federal government, local governments broadened the array of programs in which they were involved and the influence of administrators as implementors of federal programs expanded. Most cities would retain many of the new programs even when federal funds were reduced or eliminated under the Carter and Reagan administrations. By this time, however, cities — whether reformed or unreformed, sun-belt or cold-belt — were much more similar in the range of services they provided than they had been prior to this period.

Innovative mayors in mayor-council cities of the 1960s represented a new breed of programmatic politicians.[50] Unlike the "pols" who made a career in the party organization and public office, this new group incorporated professional values and approaches in their po-

litical style. They were supported in their efforts by the politically-oriented professional assistants we associate with the Kennedy White House, McNamara's Pentagon, or the mayoralty of John Lindsay. In the 1980s, "professional politicians," interested in both policy initiatives and a career in public office, increasingly won seats on local councils.[51] The connections between professionalism and politics became increasingly complex. Reform governments were no longer the exclusive locus of professionalism in local government.

City councils increasingly utilized district elections or a combination of district and at-large seats to fill gaps in representation, and the membership of the council became increasingly diverse. Council members were more likely to view themselves as representing neighborhoods as well as the city as a whole and sought to speak for a wider range of groups in the community. By the late 1980s, council members in council-manager cities reported spending at least as many hours on the job as their counterparts in mayor-council cities. They spent slightly less time on constituency services than their mayor-council counterparts, but nonetheless devoted a great deal of attention to the ombudsmanic role and linking citizens to government.[52] Common features of council organization and process in mayor-council cities — the use of committees and the presence of council staff — appeared frequently in council-manager cities.[53] These features increased the likelihood that the council and manager did not operate in a coordinated way and broadened the points of contact between council members and staff other than the manager.

At the same time, non-partisan professionals were becoming more overtly political. The "New Public Administration" provided a rationale for active pursuit of equity by professional administrators. City managers, who had always been policy leaders, as the founding reformers had intended, became more visible and vocal in this role. Mulrooney called for greater leadership from managers to deal with the social crises of the early 1970s.[54] Banovetz advocated activism by managers to correct the lack of representativeness on city councils.[55] Once again, the manager was "discovered" to be a policy leader in the scholarly literature, although there was recognition that managers provide policy leadership within a framework of mission goals that are shaped by elected officials with the assistance of the manager.[56] Over the period, managers were more vulnerable to attack, in part because they lost the protective cover of apparent neutrality which survived through Period III, and in part because the policy issues in which their governments were involved were more complex and less likely to receive consensus support from increasingly diverse councils.

"Official" responses to these changing conditions from ICMA through reports and policy statements during this period were mixed. In some of this material, greater flexibility and forward thinking is displayed while other parts reflect a continuation of the attitudes established in previous periods. The work did provide the foundation, however, for changes that would be solidified in the next period.

In new criteria established in 1969, ICMA sought to support the development of "overall professional management" by recognizing a general management position in governments with an elected executive. The approach reflected a realization that "professional local government management is not synonymous with the council-manager form of government." But no rejection of the council-manager plan, implicit or explicit, was intended by these new criteria.[57] The policy-making role of city managers was included explicitly in recognition criteria for first time. The recognition criterion for both types of positions stated that "the position should have direct responsibility for policy formulation on over-all policy problems." The 1969 Code of Ethics reflected this new emphasis on professional management in all settings by omitting explicit reference to the city manager. At the time, it might have appeared, as Stillman concluded, that "the city management profession, long wed to the reform ideals of the council-manager plan, had now parted company with that plan,"[58] but subsequent developments clearly indicated that this was not the case.

ICMA created committees, in 1973 and 1975 and again in 1983, to examine ways to increase support for the council-manager plan. The committees revealed a continuation of manager-centered attitudes from the previous period by referring to the form as "the effective management form" of government (1973) and to their cities as "professionally managed communities," as opposed to council-governed communities (1983). The reports demonstrated flexibility, however, by arguing that the council-manager form can flourish with district elections, direct election of the mayor and extensive citizen participation, and stressed the needs of elected officials. The 1975 report included the recommendation that the National Municipal League rewrite the *Model City Charter* to address the need to enhance political leadership and reflect the growing importance of the mayor.

The Future Horizons Committee report, "New Worlds of Service," published in 1979, was appropriately far-sighted.[59] It identified representative democracy as one of the profession's ideals and suggested ways for the manager to support the council. The report recognized that both the council and manager have "a shared stake in both policy and administration" and anticipated that "political frustration" among elected officials will make them "much less comfortable with delegations of authority of any significance." The manager in the community leadership role as well as in dealings with elected officials was expected to increasingly fill the role of "broker/negotiator." Shared power and authority within the organization and in dealings with the community also were recognized.

The Declaration of Ideals published in 1984 gave explicit expression to the values that were salient during the 1970s, including support for citizen participation, clarification of community values, promotion of equity, concern for conserving resources, and development of a responsive, dynamic organization. Although the declaration expressed support for representative democracy, however, it said nothing about the council or the manager's responsibilities to the council.

Relevance of reforms to the conditions of period. The major problems in this period included the need to expand civil rights and access for minority groups, open the public process to wider participation, expand opportunities for social and economic development (first with federal governmental assistance and then without), and accommodate expanding needs and demands with declining resources. The values underlying the reform program in this period reflected a new commitment to advancing equity, promoting openness and involvement in the governmental process, and supporting elected officials. Managers were recognized as political, not only in their involvement in policy formulation but also in their role as brokers among elected officials and community groups. The manifestation of these values is evident in the record of council-manager governments during this period.

Although there is a widely held impression that council-manager governments are less attentive to persons of low-income and minority residents, there is no systematic difference between the performance of council-manager and mayor-council governments in this arena. In fact, there is evidence that council-manager governments are *more* likely to identify need and develop programs to respond to need — as opposed to responding to the demands of select groups.[60] When change did occur in the governmental process because of shifts in political power in the community and use of district elections to increase the diversity of council membership, the council-manager form readily accommodated the reorientation of government.[61] Council-manager governments were innovative at introducing citizen participation mechanisms in the 1970s and responding to challenges arising from increased population diversity in the 1980s.

By the end of the period, managers were attempting to reconcile advocacy of positions to promote equity with accommodation to the new direction and orientation of changing councils and shifting community politics. The tendency at the start of the period to view the manager as the central feature of the council-manager plan had been checked by the end, but the new orientation of professional managers and supporters of reform had not been fully expressed.

Period V: Reaffirmation and Renewal, or the End of Reform, 1989–Present

The 1990s can be viewed in two ways, either as part of the period that began in the mid–1960s and continues to the present, or alternatively as part of a new period that began in the late 1980s. In the former view, the traditional reform effort is sufficiently established that it is no longer "reform." It has been observed that distinguishing "reformed" and "unreformed" governments is difficult because of the "hybridization" of governmental institutions.[62] Furthermore, some would argue that the program of local government reform is no longer relevant to the 1990s. The alternate view is that the local government institutional reform program has been reaffirmed and renewed.

The renewal interpretation is supported by several measures that have been taken to reassess the content of the reform program and the values advanced by it. The revision of the *Model City Charter*, revision of the recognition criteria used by ICMA, and the report of a new ICMA task force on the council-manager plan reflect a rethinking of the meaning as well as the program of reform. These steps seek to link the reform movements both to the concepts and idealism of the *New Municipal Program* and the political conditions of the 1990s.

The seventh edition of the *Model City Charter* was published in 1989 after five years of review and study with special emphasis on issues of representation and leadership. The representation issue was resolved by developing an array of choices for cities to choose among depending on their circumstances. The commentary emphasizes "the importance of the at-large principle" and recommends it for small communities or ones in which minority representation is not an issue, but it also recognizes the need for representation of minorities through the use of districts or proportional representation.[63]

Direct election of the mayor was provided as an option equal in status to election by and from within the council. The introduction indicates that each community should consider which method would be "most conducive to the development of strong political leadership." The revised charter attempts to crystallize in the mayor a new leadership position for the council-manager plan. The authority to appoint advisory board members and the responsibilities for representing the city in external relations and preparing a summary statement of the city's conditions, needs, and direction are designed to enhance the mayor's leadership role without diminishing the authority of either the council or the manager. There is the clear intent to make the office a source of coordination among officials in city government and a guiding force in policy development. The recommendation that the mayor or chairperson be directly elected when the council is chosen from districts reflects the hope that the mayor will exert a centralizing and coalescing impact on council members with diverse perspectives.

The concept of a model with alternatives reflects a shift in the attitudes of those interested in structural reform. The limited alternatives in the sixth edition were labeled as departures from the preferred practices. The acceptance of alternatives in council selection and choice of the mayor indicate that contemporary structural reformers are not wedded to a fixed program of institutional changes. Although the first generation of reformers had used structural changes to promote certain attributes in city government — not as ends in themselves — the constancy of the Model Charters after the second made it difficult to determine whether the structure or the substance of the governmental process was the primary concern of the later reformers. The seventh edition abandoned some old positions and adopted new ones to achieve certain ends. There is continuity in support for the appointed executive form of government and the staff functions that promote professionalism in local government.

In 1989, ICMA introduced new recognition criteria which incorporated greater flexibility into the standards and supported greater interaction with the council. The key change in the criteria was to recognize as a council-manager government jurisdictions in which the council confirms or ratifies personnel actions by the manager. In addition, guidelines

were added for other criteria that acknowledge input from the council in "administrative" matters. For example, it is recognized "that many parties often participate in the budget process and may contribute to the development of the manager's recommended budget." Even when there is no formal approval of appointments, the manager "may choose to consult with and seek consensus from council" regarding appointments and dismissals. The local government management profession was recognizing the integral role of the council and the contributions — formal and informal — of elected officials to functions once viewed as the exclusive province of the manager.

Since 1992, another Task Force on the Council-Manager Plan appointed by ICMA has focused on the council-manager form as an approach to governance and management which combines the efforts of elected officials and professional administrators.[64] While previous groups had emphasized the status of the manager, the authority of the position, and factors that impact professionalism, the current task force in its draft report identifies representative democracy as a central and distinctive feature of the form and directs attention to the contributions and characteristics of elected officials as well as those of the manager. The chief elected official — mayor or chairperson — is recognized as an important figure in the government who can contribute to cohesion within the council, open communication between the council and the manager, and more effective goal setting and policy making. The manager's role is described in terms of its responsibilities vis-à-vis the council — including the expectation that the manager will provide policy advice, promote team building, and support council oversight of organizational performance and appraisal of the manager. The manager's responsibility to direct the organization, appoint staff, and prepare the budget are considered important means of assuring the manager's accountability, not broad grants of authority to be exercised in isolation.

Taken together, these redefinitions of the program of local government reform have stressed the concepts of representative democracy and managerial accountability and have cast off adherence to a fixed package of institutions and a manager-centered view of local government. In the past five years, there has been a clear restatement of a progressive philosophy of reform.

Relevance of reforms to conditions of period. If one examines the problems currently facing local government as emphasizing governmental process rather than substantive policy problems — as the first generation of reformers did — there is a need for governments to be purposeful, customer-driven, open and inclusive, and productive. Confusion, drift, fragmentation, and dysfunctional contentiousness stand in the way of achieving these qualities. When the problems in local governments are viewed in this way, council-manager government with a directly elected mayor or chairperson and district representation — one of the optional reform packages of the seventh *Model City Charter* and revised *Model County Charter*— represents an appropriate institutional response. It provides a representative council whose democratic function is not diminished by a legally powerful elected executive, a mayor or chairperson who promotes cohesion and purpose, and a professional manager who offers policy, process and organizational leadership under the control of the council.

The structure reinforces the cooperative pursuit of the public interest and the development of goals and policies that reflect the long-term needs of the entire community. It promotes inclusion of citizens. It represents a blending of democracy and professionalism that is ideal in the sense that this approach, more than others, promotes the simultaneous and mutually supportive fulfillment of the values associated with both concepts. Reformers would argue that professionalism is an essential complement to democracy in local government if professionalism is understood to encompass the values of social responsibility, accountability, responsiveness, equity, effectiveness, equal access and openness, and efficiency and innovation.[65]

The mayor-council model of government is viewed by some as conceptually superior, but its characteristics limit how well it responds to current conditions.[66] Separation of powers, with its attendant conflict between the executive and legislature, affects the governance of the community, as bargaining among contending interests weakens the search for a common vision based on shared interests. Involving citizens is colored by the need to secure political allies, which entails exclusion as well as inclusion. Service delivery is affected by the need to develop constituencies as well as to serve citizens according to principles of equality and equity. Improving management practices must be balanced with the concern for maintaining political support and organizational resources.

Some contend that changing characteristics of elected officials and new conditions in the governmental process produce strains that challenge the council-manager form. There is the impression that mayors who seek a larger role for themselves are antagonistic to city managers. In fact, there is evidence to the contrary — effective mayors work well with and strengthen city managers as well as expanding the contributions of the city council. The real strain comes from increasingly factious councils — wherein the members can not work together. There are certainly instances of assertive council members, particularly the new professional politicians, who wish to displace the manager and have a direct hand in resolving service complaints from citizens. The greater threat, however, is that no one — least of all the manager — can force a fragmented council to work collaboratively. In this situation, proponents of cohesion advocate an elected executive who can use the powers of the office to gain leverage over recalcitrant council members. The conditions of the 1990s, according to his view, require reliance on executive rather than representative democracy.

The alternate view is that council performance can be improved by effective facilitative leadership on the part of the mayor. The potential for political leadership by the mayor in council-manager governments has received too little attention because of a strong tendency to equate leadership by the mayor with the exercise of formal and informal powers that are not available to the chief elected official in this form. The facilitative model of leadership, which stresses empowering others and fostering commitment to a shared vision, is available in the council-manager form with no separation of powers. When the chief elected official provides facilitative leadership — promoting cohesion, communication, and commitment to goals arrived at through an open process that finds common ground and overcomes differences — the leadership needs of the government are met in a way that promotes a purposeful and inclusive governmental process.[67]

As a model for local government which stresses the importance of promoting representative democracy, supporting political leadership, engaging citizens, and creating open, productive organizations, the council-manager form still is more likely to produce effective governance and management than the elected executive form. The common argument that the mayor-council form of government produces stronger leadership must be reexamined. The success of that form depends on the presence of a mayor who provides certain leadership traits and capabilities — those associated with the innovator/entrepreneur model of leadership. Such executives create conditions that approximate the normal qualities of the council-manager form by achieving a unity of purpose that overcomes the typical consequences of separation of powers. Unfortunately, the form cannot be counted on to produce such leadership, because it is a very difficult style to achieve and maintain in a context of institutionally induced conflict. The council-manager form, on the other hand, has multiple sources of leadership — both political and professional. When the mayor provides effective facilitative leadership, the form works better. But when this is absent, other council members and the manager can offset the effects of an ineffective mayor and the form *still* can function well.

Conclusion: Is Structural Reform Still Important and Relevant?

The issue of the relevance of reform must be periodically reassessed to determine whether the values promoted by the reform movement are in tune with the changing conditions in local governments. Although the central institutional feature of the reform package has remained the same for almost 80 years, the values articulated or emphasized in practice have shifted over time. Accomplishments have also varied. Although we tend to think of reform governments in terms of achievements in "efficiency and economy," this was the central thrust of reform institutions only in Period II. Hallmark features of the periods might be summarized as follows:

- Period I — staff accountability to council, competence, and accomplishment
- Period II — efficiency, economy, and fairness
- Period III — service provision and development
- Period IV — equity and accommodation to changing political forces
- Period V — coherence, responsiveness, inclusiveness, and productivity

It is not appropriate to promote — or attack — reform institutions today on the grounds of efficiency and economy as dominant emphases, even though they remain secondary or instrumental objectives. The tradition of reform was not rooted in these values, despite their centrality in Period II and beyond. If the American urban experience had somehow jumped from 1919 to 1969, the *New Municipal Program* — shaped by the idealism of the Progressive era — would have been readily recognized as the appropriate starting point for dealing with the political, social and economic challenges of the later period. The experience of Periods II and III, however, obscured the continuing relevance of reform.

The program of reform has continued to stress the unique advantages of the council-manager form while it has abandoned support for specific electoral institutions. Although in the earlier days supporting reform was often accompanied by an attack on established institutions and practices, this has changed. Advocating the use of the council-manager form is not intended to denigrate the elected executive forms in cities and counties, many of which have included appointed chief administrative officers who embody professional values. The pursuit of reform values can and does occur in these jurisdictions as well. Reformers should be concerned with making all governments work well and incorporate democracy and professionalism to the fullest extent possible.

If there is recognition that positive accomplishments can be achieved in other forms of government, why continue to state a preference for the council-manager form? First, the program and values of reform provide a reference point for assessing the performance of governments and offer guidance for making improvements in all communities, regardless of their form. Second, a preferred approach is the one which is judged conceptually and empirically to be more likely to produce positive characteristics and achieve positive results than alternative approaches. As an organizing concept, separation of powers has serious drawbacks at the local level compared with the unitary model's potential for cooperative relationships between governing board and appointed executive. The supposed advantage of having an elected executive with extensive power who can focus political leadership is offset by three factors: limiting the role of the council, the possibility of debilitating conflict over the prerogatives of office between the mayor and the council, and the difficulty of finding mayors who can provide the wide range of political and organizational leadership required by the office. Thus, from the perspective of one who seeks to use structural features as one tool to enhance government performance (i.e., a reformer), it makes sense to identify and promote a "model." The alternative to advocating reform is neutrality on questions of structure. Without a reform model, structural choices are equal options. Advice about dealing with performance problems is *ad hoc*. The conceptual grounding for local government improvement is lost.

The continuing relevance of reform is based on the premise that the recommended institutions still are superior to other approaches in addressing shortcomings in local governments and in promoting effective performance. The council-manager form of government offers advantages in meeting the problems of cities and counties today because the continuing strengths of the form have been reviewed and renewed in light of current conditions. It must be acknowledged that in very large cities with a highly complex political process (and in very small places where first-person familiarity predominates), it is difficult for institutions to achieve their desired intent, but this is true of the mayor-council as well as the council-manager form. In local governments of any size, the realities of the situation can undermine the purposes intended by the institutional arrangement. The issue is whether one should abandon the attempt to use institutions to influence government performance. The basic question regarding the relevance of reform is still the same as it has been for the last century: How well does a governmental model promote desired ends and values in the governmental process?

In conclusion, an emphasis on institutional reform has been appropriate in the past. Despite continuity in the institutions included in the *Model City Charter* from the second through the sixth editions, the relative emphasis given to values supporting reform has shifted over time as conditions in local government have changed.

The reform program has not had the static quality that is sometimes attributed to it. In the last five years, attitudes about preferred electoral institutions have changed, but the council-manager form remains as the centerpiece. The reform package included in the seventh *Model City Charter* still promotes the values of earlier periods: accountability, competence, accomplishment, efficiency, economy, service, development, and equity. Its central benefits in light of current conditions are to promote purposeful democracy; inclusive, citizen-oriented policy making and service delivery; and creative, adaptive management of resources. As such, it warrants support as the model approach to organizing local government. The reform impulse is still relevant in the 1990s.

Notes

1. For a complete discussion of differing historical interpretations of the reform movement, see James H. Svara, "Progressive Roots of the Model Charter and the Manager Profession: A Positive Heritage,"

National Civic Review, 78:5, September-October 1989, pp. 339–355.

2. Otis A. Pease, "Urban Reformers in the Progressive Era," *Pacific Northwest Quarterly*, April 1971, p. 53.

3. Horace E. Deming, *The Government of American Cities: A Program of Democracy* (New York: G.P. Putnam's Sons, 1909), pp. 9–10, ch. 11.

4. E. Dana Durand, "Review of a Municipal Program," *Political Science Quarterly*, Vol. XV (1900), p. 330. In "Council Government versus Mayor Government I," *ibid.*, pp. 427–451 and "II," pp. 675–709, he advocated the move to council-centered government in the United States.

5. Frank J. Goodnow, *City Government in the United States* (New York: The Century Co., 1910 [copyright, 1904]), p. 153. Reprinted by Arno Press, 1974.

6. Deming, pp. 15–20.

7. Deming, pp. 56–57.

8. Goodnow, p. 180.

9. Clinton Rogers Woodruff, ed., *City Government by Commission* (New York: D. Appleton and Company, 1911), pp. 311 and 317.

10. Jon C. Teaford, *The Twentieth-Century American City*, second edition (Baltimore: The Johns Hopkins Press, 1993), pp. 38–39.

11. Clinton Rogers Woodruff, ed., *A New Municipal Program* (New York: D. Appleton and Company, 1919).

12. Ibid., p. 153.

13. Ibid., pp. 100–101.

14. See Richard S. Childs, "The Theory of the New Controlled-Executive Plan," *National Municipal Review*, 2:1, January 1913, pp. 76–81.

15. Russell McCulloch Story, *The American Municipal Executive* (Urbana: University of Illinois, 1918), p. 218. Reprinted by Johnson Reprint Corporation, New York, 1970.

16. *A New Municipal Program*, p. 155.

17. Ibid., p. 130. For a complete discussion of the views of the early reformers on the manager's policy role, see Svara, "Progressive Roots," pp. 345–346.

18. Story, p. 220.

19. Charles Adrian, *A History of American City Government* (New York: University Press of America, 1987), p. 452.

20. City Manager's Association, *Fourth Year-Book* (1918), comments by Waite, p. 92, and W.P. Lovett, Executive Secretary, Detroit Citizens League, pp. 94–95.

21. Chester Newland, "The Future of Council-Manager Government," in H. George Frederickson, ed., *Ideal and Practice in City Management* (Washington: International City Management Association, 1989), p. 259.

22. This includes cities in which the plan was put in effect through June of 1920. See *Seventh Year-Book* (City Managers' Association, 1921), pp. 241–246.

23. Richard S. Childs, "What to Expect of Political Reform," *National Municipal Review*, 21:6, June, 1932, pp. 350, 353.

24. For a review of the historical debate over the manager's policy role, see James H. Svara, "Policy and Administration: City Managers as Comprehensive Professional Leaders," in George Frederickson, ed., *Ideal and Practice in City Management* (Washington: International City Management Association, 1989), pp. 70–77.

25. A.R. Hatton, "The Manager — The Greatest Problem of City Manager Government," *Seventh Year-Book* (City Managers' Association, 1921), pp. 200–201. A number of managers including Waite from Dayton, pp. 207–208, disagreed with his position and argued that the manager should both help to sell ideas to the council and, once adopted, support them before the public.

26. Citizens League of Cleveland, "Five Years of City Manager Government in Cleveland: An Impartial Estimate of Cleveland's Experience," *National Municipal Review*, 18:3 (Supplement, March 1929), pp. 212–213. The editors of *National Municipal Review* (19:2, February 1930, p. 73), commented that Hopkins saw himself as a "glorified mayor."

27. See Svara, "Progressive Roots," pp. 345–346.

28. Charles M. Fassett, *Handbook of Municipal Government* (New York: Thomas Y. Crowell Co., 1922), p. 42.

29. David T. Beito, *Tax Resistance During the Great Depression* (Chapel Hill: University of North Carolina Press, 1989), p. xii. Bieto has observed that tax strikes and anti-tax measures during the Depression were more numerous than in the 1970s and 1980s.

30. Adrian, p. 327.

31. John Albert Vieg, "Advice for Municipal Reformers," *The Public Opinion Quarterly*, October 1937, pp. 89–91.

32. Richard J. Stillman II, *The Rise of the City Manager* (Albuquerque: University of New Mexico Press, 1974), p. 51, pp. 43–53.

33. Clarence C. Ridley and Orin Nolting, *The City Manager Profession* (Chicago: University of Chicago Press, 1934), p. 30.

34. The first code of ethics in 1924 indicated that it is the council "who primarily determine public policy" and referred more generally to "declin[ing] to submit to dictation in matters for which the responsibility is solely" the manager's.

35. John Albert Vieg, "The Manager Plan and the Metropolitan Community," *The American Political Science Review*, 1937, pp. 76–77. The author refers to Woodrow Wilson and his pathbreaking article, "The Study of Administration," which was published in 1887.

36. Adrian, p. 327. Ironically, the council-manager city of Cincinnati received considerable attention at the start of the Depression for its early efforts to combat unemployment.

37. The percentage breakdown in 1945 was as follows: 1000–2500, 2.1 percent; 2500–5000, 6.7 percent; 5000–10,000, 13.0 percent; and 10,000–25,000, 19.9 percent.

38. Kenneth Fox, *Metropolitan America* (Jackson: University Press of Mississippi, 1986), pp. 50–54.

39. James M. Banovetz, ed., *Managing the Modern City* (Washington: International City Management Association, 1971), p. 84.

40. Carl Abbott, *Urban America in the Modern Age: 1920 to the Present* (Arlington Heights, Ill.: Harlan Davidson, Inc., 1987), p. 79.

41. C.A. Harrell, "The City Manager as a Community Leader," *Public Management*, October 1948, pp. 290–294.

42. Edward W. Weidner, "Municipal Highlights of 1952," *The Municipal Year Book* (Washington, D.C.: International City Management Association, 1953), p. 3.

43. Newland in Frederickson, p. 259. In a survey of city managers in the San Francisco Bay Area of California conducted in 1966–67, only 31 percent of the managers agreed that they should consult with the council before drafting their own budget. Ronald O. Loveridge, *City Managers in Legislative Politics* (Indianapolis, Ind.: Bobbs-Merrill Co., 1971), p. 49.

44. For a discussion of the differences between the Sixth and Seventh Editions of the *Model City Charter*, see James H. Svara, "The Model City and County Charters: Innovation and Tradition in the Reform Movement," *Public Administration Review*, November-December 1990, pp. 688–692.

45. Richard S. Childs, *The First Fifty Years* (New York: National Municipal League, 1965), pp. 39–47.

46. Edward C. Banfield and James Q. Wilson, *City Politics* (Cambridge, Mass.: Harvard University Press, 1963), p. 172.

47. Fox, *Metropolitan America*, p. 51. The metropolitan population outside the central city increased from 20.2 to 75.6 million. The central city population was 63.8 million in 1970.

48. Banfield and Wilson, *City Politics*, ch. 11.

49. Banfield and Wilson, *City Politics*, pp. 172, 186.

50. See, for example, James V. Cunningham, *Urban Leadership in the Sixties* (Cambridge, Mass.: Schenkman Publishing Co., 1970).

51. Alan Ehrenhalt, *The United States of Ambition* (New York: Random House, 1991).

52. James H. Svara, *Continuity and Change in America's City Councils: 1979–1989* (Washington, D.C.: National League of Cities, 1991).

53. Newland in Frederickson, pp. 263–264; Svara, *Continuity and Change in America's City Councils*.

54. Keith Mulrooney, "Prologue: Can City Managers Deal Effectively with Major Social Problems?" *Public Administration Review*, January-February 1971, pp. 6–14.

55. James M. Banovetz, "Environment and Role of the Administrator," in Banovetz, ed., *Managing the Modern City* (Washington, D.C.: International City Management Association, 1971), pp. 83–84.

56. David N. Ammons and Charldean Newell, "'City Managers Don't Make Policy:' A Lie; Let's Face It," *National Civic Review*, 77:2, March-April 1988, pp. 124–132; James H. Svara, "Dichotomy and Duality: Reconceptualizing the Relationship Between Policy and Administration in Council-Manager Cities," *Public Administration Review*, January-February 1985, pp. 221–232.

57. Quotes from issue devoted to new recognition criteria in *Public Management*, March 1973.

58. Stillman, *Rise of the City Manager*, p. 67.

59. International City Management Association Committee on Future Horizons, *New Worlds of Service* (Washington, D.C.: International City Management Association, 1979).

60. James H. Svara, *Official Leadership in the City: Patterns of Conflict and Cooperation* (New York: Oxford University Press, 1990), ch. 3.

61. Rufus P. Browning, Dale Rogers Marshall, and David H. Tabb, *Protest Is Not Enough* (Berkeley: University of California Press, 1984), ch. 4; Lyndon Baines Johnson School of Public Affairs, "Local Government Election Systems," *Policy Research Report No. 62* (Austin: University of Texas, 1984).

62. Elaine Sharp, "City Management in an Era of Blurred Boundaries," in Frederickson, ed., *Ideal and Practice*, pp. 4–6. It should be noted that most of the overlap in the use of election institutions does not directly diminish the distinction between forms of government.

63. National Civic League, *Model City Charter*, Seventh Edition (Denver, Colo.: National Civic League Press, 1989), p. 20. Second quote is from pp. xvi–xvii.

64. The author is a member of the task force.

65. For a discussion of the values of local government managers, see John Nalbandian, *Professionalism in Local Government* (San Francisco, Calif.: Jossey-Bass, 1991).

66. For arguments being put forward to support the mayor-council form, see Ronald Gurwitt, "The Lure of the Strong Mayor," *Governing*, August 1993, pp. 36–41. For criticisms of the form summarized in this paragraph, see Svara, *Official Leadership in the City*, ch. 3; Newland in Frederickson, p. 267; and Terrell Blodgett, "Beware the Lure of the 'Strong Mayor,'" *Public Management*, January 1994, pp. 6–11.

67. James H. Svara and Associates, *Facilitative Leadership in Local Government: Lessons of Successful Mayors and Chairpersons* (San Francisco: Jossey-Bass, 1994).

CHAPTER 3

EVOLUTION OF NATIONAL CIVIC LEAGUE POLICIES

William N. Cassella, Jr.

As National Civic League policies and programs have evolved over more than 100 years, they have continued to reflect historic objectives rooted in the circumstances of the organization's origins, while experiencing modification in response to an ever-changing civic scene.

NCL's constitution (Article II, Chapter 2) asserts that the organization "is established in order to multiply the number, harmonize the methods and combine the forces of citizens who know how to work together for progressive improvement of our system of government with special attention to the need for more vigorous and responsible state and local institutions."

That assertion harks back to the call for the first National Conference for Good City Government at which steps were taken to found the National Civic League (then known as the National Municipal League). This call, issued by the Municipal League of Philadelphia and the City Club of New York in December of 1893, expressed belief that the conference would "accomplish much in arousing public interest, in raising popular standards of political morality, and in securing for the advocates of municipal reform that feeling of brotherhood and cooperation, and that unity of actions and methods, which will multiply their strength and enthusiasm, and inspire the people with the hope and confidence essential to final success."[1]

Consequently, the National Civic League (NCL) has sought to discover, perfect, explain — and keep up to date — systems and methods to help its members and other citizens in efforts to improve our system of government and its underlying democratic practices. What are often thought of as the "policies" or, as some would have it, "doctrines" of the National Civic League are simply means to the end of helping people to be more effective practicing citizens. Thus, NCL's central purpose is neither more nor less than practical civic education, largely in the form of in-service training for participating citizens and citizen-officials.

One reason why it is difficult to describe NCL, its program or its methods is that, while holding to its integrity of purpose, it is pragmatic and highly adaptable to the needs of different people in different communities at different times. Perhaps this is another way of saying that it is characteristically and bafflingly American.

NCL owes much to its lay leaders, past and present. It necessarily depends heavily on the day-to-day work of its professional staff. But its resources and its power flow mainly from its ability to marshall the force of hundreds of "experts," including a distinguished roster of current and former public officials, and thousands of citizens in a continuing process of mutual encouragement, education and assistance.

From *National Civic Review,* Vol. 83, No. 3, Summer-Fall 1994. Published by the National Civic League, Denver, Colorado. Reprinted with permission of the publisher.

NCL's "campus" extends throughout the United States, and often beyond. Its "students" are all persons who, whether they know it or not, are aided or influenced by an NCL-inspired or NCL-communicated idea. And most of its "faculty," at any given moment, are those of its "students" who are in the process of passing on to anyone else anything they have learned.

To be sure, there is a relatively small number of experienced civic and governmental hands, technicians and scholars who contribute, out of proportion to their number, to the development and exposition of the techniques and procedures that constitute NCL's "program." The National Civic League is the communications agency for the transfer of the best and latest thinking of these experts to citizens and officials on the front lines. It is important to note, however, that the group of creative thinkers upon whom NCL depends is always open — both to new people and new ideas.

The annual National Conference on Governance (until 1990 called the National Conference on Government) has from the start been NCL's most spectacular educational forum. It is also a recurring synthesis of virtually all the elements that make up the organization itself. It brings together the many kinds of persons who are, in truth, the National Civic League, whether they hold membership or not. And at the conference, as they do in their daily civic, political or professional activities, many of these persons play several roles — as teachers, students and practitioners, and sometimes as civic innovators or inventors. Many long-recognized improvements in governmental and civic techniques have been refined and molded, if not actually generated, in the give-and-take discussions at the NCL's annual meeting. Various activities, engaging different groups of people with differing levels of sophistication, are always occurring at the same time.

NCL has many facets. Groups of highly experienced persons wrestle with such tough problems as how to adjust home-rule concepts to the needs of government in metropolitan regions, how to get action on constitutional revision or charter change, how to reorganize the executive and staff the legislature, what is needed to modernize fiscal procedures and controls at both the state and local levels, how to assure genuine representation of both majority and minority interests in public decision making, how to improve election administration, and guidance for ethical standards in the public service. Other groups, meanwhile, are exchanging and comparing experiences and ideas for meeting current practical problems in their respective states, metropolitan areas or cities and towns. Still others may be receiving guidance, face to face or at long distance, on techniques of citizen organization.

This picture of the National Civic League in operation reflects certain basic and wholesome characteristics of American society: its pluralism, the readiness of its members to help themselves to new ideas and useful information upon which to act, and its reliance on voluntary cooperation among individuals and groups who choose their own areas of specialization.

This explains in part why people who have known the National Civic League favorably for a long time often have quite different views of the organization. Each one naturally emphasizes the aspects of the program in which he or she personally is most involved, or from which the greatest benefit has been derived. To one, NCL may mean the council-manager plan. To another, it may be the source of ideas on constitutional revision. To a third, it is the inspiration and the know-how for the maintenance of an effective local citizens organization for good government. To others it stands for sound standards and procedures for local budgeting and debt management, or for permanent personal voter registration and honest election administration. More generally, NCL may stand for the demonstration of the notion that sound governance is worth fighting for. And for many others, the National Civic League is simply the organization from whose publications — the National Civic Review, the *Model City Charter* and others — or from whose central office it is possible at any time to get helpful civic information or the answer to an urgent question.

Each of these views is correct. Taken together they contribute to but do not complete the picture of the National Civic League. The history of our system of government has demonstrated that its soundness depends on many things, but especially the following:

- A system of elections that makes the process of voting as easy and effective as possible;
- Legislative bodies that fairly represent the voters and respond accurately to the public need for government;
- A responsible chief executive at the head of a manageable administrative structure;
- A proper system of controls over the raising and expenditure of public resources;
- A system of inter-governmental relations that conserves the values of local self-government while recognizing the need for some central government standards and controls, as well as the growing need for political and administrative coordination in both mature and expanding communities, particularly metropolitan regions;
- The practice of bringing foresight — based on deliberate, fact-supported planning — to bear on formulation of both long-range public policies and quick decisions made in response to emergency or crisis situations; and
- An alert, informed and participating citizenry, collaborating freely with the responsible officials of their governments.

NCL's program includes policies relating to all seven of these essentials for good government. This fact, as much as any other, distinguishes NCL from other civic organizations, most of which concentrate on one or two specific elements such as the merit system, planning, getting out the vote, civil liberties, or other social, economic or service issues. This means that NCL is the one organization to which concerned and engaged citizens can turn with a real but vaguely defined need for substantive guidance and a reasonably sure prospect of getting help. How does NCL help? First, by clarifying the nature of the inquiry; and second, by supplying comprehensive, customized assistance or referring

the party to a more specialized organization, individual or information source.

Model Charters and Laws: Practical Guides

NCL models provide tools and guides for injecting foresight into the self-governing system. For practical purposes, NCL's "practices" have been packaged in various ways, especially in the "models": the *Model City Charter* and *Model County Charter*, the *Model State Constitution*, and various model laws in the fields of finance, election administration, planning, public ethics, and a range of others. Some "policies," such as those relating to elections, representative bodies, the responsible executive, and fiscal controls, are embodied in a number of these models as well as in other NCL publications. NCL is constantly reviewing and reappraising its "policies," carefully cautioning citizens against slavish acceptance of the letter of any "model." No NCL model has ever been represented as an absolute rule, but as a guide to help reform-minded citizens find their own solutions to governance problems. Users of NCL models, as a matter of course, are advised that any standard or "precut" solution must be fitted to their own circumstances.

"Foresight is an essential ingredient of good government as it is of good business. But foresight is not achieved without effort. Any large-scale modern enterprise, whether public or private, calls for special organs or agencies of a staff nature to inform and advise top policy makers." The foregoing assertion underscores NCL's interest in encouraging state and local governments to be equipped to take a forward look as they develop public policies. Responsibility in government is much more than reacting to the needs and desires of the moment; it also must include anticipating difficulties and making adequate preparations to cope with them. These preparations may be preventive measures or solutions standing ready to meet problems as they arise.

NCL's concern for foresight in the development of public policy pervades many aspects of its program. Of course, fiscal planning is intended to be fiscal foresight. Local physical planning has been a feature of NCL models since 1913. Legislative research agencies are really planning agencies of the legislature — devices whereby legislative proposals are developed on the basis of competent studies and research, not simply by the impulse of individual legislators. A well conceived public personnel program must express foresight in all of its aspects or it can become a stagnating element in public administration. For sure, charter and constitution drafting are critical exercises in foresight, because the charter is the basic plan of local government, as indeed the state constitution is of state government. In these and other ways NCL's policies encourage citizens and governments to look ahead.

Over its history, NCL has seen a special duty to exercise foresight in the face of particular emergency situations — to supply guidance to states and localities in facing new and unanticipated difficulties. For example, with the repeal of national "prohibition," NCL developed a *Model Liquor Control Law*. During the depression crisis of the 1930s, when communities were facing unparalleled financial difficulties, NCL supplied emergency tools in the form of "citizen councils for constructive economy" and "pay your taxes" campaigns which prevented indiscriminate stoppage of vital public services and panic-induced tax delinquency. At the beginning of World War II, NCL published a study, *Rent Control in War and Peace*, to assist policy makers in dealing with this difficult problem.

Recognizing a problem of scandalous proportions, NCL acted as both innovator and convener in the effort, now marked with notable success, to place post-mortem medical examinations on a sound scientific basis removed from the shabbier side of politics. The organization exercised foresight in tactical as well as substantive terms, by bringing together specialists whose professional involvement was necessary to attack the problem.

Publication of the *Model State and Regional Planning Law* in 1955 anticipated a specific need for guidance, but NCL had already pioneered with various reports on the governance of metropolitan areas, including landmark publications in 1922 and 1930.[2]

NCL's compendia on legislative apportionment, published in 1959 and 1962, anticipated the U.S. Supreme Court's rulings on "one man, one vote" in *Baker v. Carr* and *Reynolds v. Syms*. Actually, institutional reforms embodied in NCL models, notably the council-manager plan, have been included as basic items in the reform agendas later promulgated by virtually all other national and local organizations committed to strengthening the state and local elements of the federal system.

The extent to which NCL is able to demonstrate the relevance of its program of institutional reform to the most pressing issues of the moment will vary with the issue. For example, one annual conference theme, "The Total Environment: Planning and Paying for Quality," illustrated the importance of relating a current issue with enormous popular appeal to the necessity of adapting government to face that issue. There is a fondness in our society for stating problems but a tendency to neglect the institutional means for achieving solutions.

Building Responsible Governance: Reciprocal Responsibility

The ultimate emphasis of all NCL policies is responsibility. Responsibility, broadly acknowledged and exercised by both public officials and citizens, is the key to democratic self-government. NCL policies have not been developed on the basis of theory alone, but as a result of experience with and understanding of the practical working of responsible government. With the constant cooperation of the best informed and best qualified people, these policies have been formalized as usable models.

NCL has learned that informed citizens, if they can only find out how to begin, will be responsible, participating citizens. Proof of this is reflected in the All-America City Award Program which NCL has presented since 1949. These annual awards recognize citizen efforts to strengthen self-government and promote overall community improvement, and their stories are valuable lessons in stimulating and spreading innovative ideas, as well as inspiring collaborative and constructive citizen action.

It is evident that the issues citizens face in public affairs grow increasingly complex and the diverse appeals to their sense of duty become more and more confusing. Thus, citizens have a greater need than ever to help in focusing on *essential* issues and investing their efforts in projects and procedures that hold promise for strengthening the basic elements of our formal and informal systems of governance.

Beyond *general* civic education — and beyond the *specific* civic education that NCL carries on through the models, guides, and responses to queries from charter commissions, legislators, mayors, managers, council members, and others — NCL assists citizens to organize for and win important civic victories. The guidance, both formal and informal, supplied by the National Civic League to organizers and leaders of community-based groups is a vital part, if not a central feature, of NCL's program for developing more responsible government through the activities of responsible citizens.

The present article constitutes the first in a series intended to review the theoretical basis and practical contribution of NCL policies, programs and activities to the various phases of political and social reform throughout the 20th century. Below, we discuss NCL's work to strengthen the structure and reform the practice of representative government.

REPRESENTATIVE GOVERNMENT

Representative government depends in the first instance on people who care enough to work for it and know enough to maintain it. It also depends on workable election machinery and legislative bodies that are truly representative.

It depends further on setting the elected governing body in an overall governmental structure that provides for the carrying out of its policies by a responsible executive whose strategic position incorporates cooperation with the legislature in policy development.

In the United States, moreover, representative government depends on the existence of an impartial and reasonably independent judicial branch, the performance of which has much to do with the popular attitude toward government, not only because of the way it dispenses justice but also because it is relied upon to enforce the rule of law upon all other organs and units of government.

It is with these basic aspects of the form and structure of government — the system of elections, the construction of a representative legislature, the position of the chief executive, and the organization and role of the judiciary — that American constitutions and charters are principally concerned. Likewise, these aspects of form and structure — particularly in state and local governments — historically have influenced a large part of the agenda of the National Civic League.

NCL's policies with respect to the form and structure of government flow directly from its commitment as expressed in its charter to "the proposition that informed, competent citizens, participating fully in public affairs in their home communities are the key to good local, state and national government." Consequently, goals for citizens interested in improving their government must be developed with two basic considerations in mind: (1) they must be related to the solution of a particular problem or series of problems, and (2) they must find an organization or procedure to be used in the solution of a problem that will enhance the responsibility of government to the citizens.

Horace E. Deming, New York attorney and civic leader and chairman of NCL's first Municipal Program Committee, said in 1899,

> No proposition for the improvement of city government in the United States is worth consideration that does not provide for the full, free and deliberate expression of the wishes of the voters and for the carrying of their wishes into effect. No scheme of city government will give promise of much improvement which will not develop an effective and general interest among the voters themselves in the actual conduct of the public affairs of the city.
>
> One of the problems which the proposed Municipal Program undertakes to solve is to provide a form of city government which will compel the development of this interest, and upon which the public opinion of the voters, when deliberately expressed, will be effective.[3]

One of the reasons for the establishment of the National Civic League was the widespread debauchery of local politics and elections by corrupt, monopolistic and collusive political machines. Consequently, NCL has been deeply concerned with parties, politics and election machinery from the day it was founded.

Out of the situation that then existed developed the emphasis in early NCL conferences, written into the first *Municipal Program.* (The *Municipal Program*, published in 1900, contained proposed state constitutional amendments on elections and state-municipal relations, and a "Municipal Corporations Act," which was the first *Model City Charter.*) It fostered the idea expressed by Professor Frank J. Goodnow, that "city government must, to be efficient, be emancipated from the tyranny of the national and state parties and from that of the legislature — the tool of the party."[4] From this thought stemmed NCL's early advocacy of so-called "nonpartisan" local elections, which were to be promoted by various devices including the separation of municipal from national and state elections, nomination by petition and a blanket ballot listing candidates for each office alphabetically. In the intervening years, nonpartisan municipal elections have become the rule rather than the exception, and are now provided for in more than 60 percent of U.S. municipalities with populations over 5,000.

NCL's interest in nonpartisan local elections never was and certainly is not now an indication of hostility to the basic principle that the political process, through which citizens maintain direct control over their government, is generally most healthy when it operates through a vigorous two-party system. If our municipalities had, 100 years ago, enjoyed a genuine competition between two parties popularly controlled, there would probably never have been any demand for nonpartisan local elections. The fact is, as has frequently been pointed out in NCL publications, that introduction of so-called nonpartisan local elections in many communities has prompted the development of *genuine* two-party politics, geared to local issues, in cities previously held in the apparently immovable grip of a corrupt, one-party or bipartisan machine. Spokespersons for NCL also have pointed out on occasion that, by weakening the hold on local patronage machines of the state and national parties, the moral climate of politics generally has been improved in many areas so that state-wide contests can be conducted with more reference to genuine issues than was possible before.

NCL has never advocated nonpartisan elections for state purposes. To the contrary, it has in many cases, through the National Civic Review and other publications, urged upon citizens the duty of being active in the national parties of their choice. A roster of NCL leaders, past and present, indicates that most of them have discharged their civic obligations through both nonpartisan community action and participation in one or the other of the major parties.

NCL's models for the conduct of elections testify not only to a concern for the purity of elections and for the protection of the right of every qualified citizen to cast a meaningful vote that is fairly counted, but also to a genuine interest in responsive politics. It has published materials on party organization and encouraged and assisted groups working to secure amendments to the primary laws that permit the omission of primary elections where no candidates file petitions in opposition to party organization slates.

We already have noted that a central feature of government geared to the will of the people is a representative policy-making or legislative body. All governments in the United States purport to have some such body, although in many cases their representative character continues to be open to serious question.

During the 1960s, as the legislative apportionment in virtually every state was subjected to litigation, NCL provided analytical data on the representativeness (or unrepresentativeness) of the legislatures for both sides in this constitutional struggle. The Supreme Court of the United States affirmed that population is the basis of equitable representation, the position consistently endorsed by National Civic League models. Although malapportionment has been removed as the principal indictment of legislative bodies, both at the state and local levels, debate continues on the relative merits of single-member and multi-member districts, arrangements that combine the two, and cumulative voting and other so-called "modified at-large" systems designed to assure minority party representation.

Additional problems are caused by the common practice of gerrymandering legislative districts to favor the dominant political party or faction. Recent editions of NCL's model charters provide mechanisms for redistricting on a fair and equal basis, and a policy statement adopted by NCL's board in 1991 outlines criteria for use in developing districting plans, as well as standards for public access to and involvement in the exercise of political boundary drawing.

While NCL's *Model State Constitution* long provided for a single-house state legislature, it now includes alternative provisions for representative bicameral and unicameral legislatures.[5]

The fundamental basis of the U.S. political system is that ultimate political power is placed in the hands of the directly elected representatives of the people in the legislative branch. This flows from the legislature's control of the purse, power to override an executive veto, and primary control over the process of constitutional amendment.

In addition to the structure of representation in state and local governing bodies, the procedures, organization and staffing of these bodies is of the utmost importance if they are to respond adequately to the will of the people. NCL recognized early on the particularly critical need for state legislatures to adapt their organization and procedures to perform more effectively in developing state policy and allocating fiscal resources to state programs.

It is essential that all state legislatures be provided with a permanent staff that can develop information on state programs independent of that supplied by the special advocates in the executive bureaucracy. In the last analysis, the legislature provides the most important vehicle for balancing the conflicting demands being made upon the state for its limited resources. Observing this critical need, NCL has provided information and guidance on the restructuring of state legislatures.

During the days of the muckrakers, the unrepresentativeness and unresponsiveness of many large, bicameral, ward-elected city councils were notorious. Gradually, NCL "doctrine," as reflected in the Models and other literature, came to favor relatively small councils elected at-large and, in communities prepared to adopt it, the Hare System of Proportional Representation (commonly known today as the single-transferable vote, proportional representation, or simply "P.R."). These arrangements, in sharp contrast with those they replaced, automatically eradicated the evils associated with gerrymandered and unequal districts and the subordination of the wide interests of the whole city to the parochialism of ward politics.

For a time, NCL models expressed a preference for proportional representation as a means for ensuring the representation of significant minorities, the best way to enable each voter to cast an effective ballot, and the surest — if not the only way in some situations — to guarantee majority rule while assuring a genuinely pluralistic dialogue.

With the publication of the most recent editions of the models it was recognized that P.R. enjoyed very limited support, and it was no longer presented as the preferred method for electing legislative bodies. Thus, the sixth and seventh editions of the *Model City Charter* have included the option of "mixed" representation, where some council members are elected at large and some from single-member districts. This option recognizes the fact that in some communities election at large of all members of the policy-making body would leave significant segments of the local population unrepresented. In recent years, of course, interest in P.R. and other, semi-proportional electoral systems has reasserted itself, as communities have acknowledged that the geographic distribution of "protected minorities" as defined by the Voting Rights Act no longer follows traditional patterns of ghettoization. Recognizing this trend, the National Civic Review restored its "Proportional Representation" department in 1993.

Other issues concerning the representative character of local government extend beyond the structure of municipal governing bodies to embrace the decentralization of certain aspects of public decision making to the neighborhood level through advisory agencies and commissions. All such advisory bodies must be considered as NCL's policies experience ongoing refinement.

Among the devices developed by reformers to assist in determining the "will of the people" are the instruments of so-called "direct democracy" — the initiative, referendum and recall. NCL's policy on these tools has been somewhat ambivalent. If used properly they can enhance governmental responsibility. If misused they may have disastrous consequences. They may completely upset the workings of representative government. Thus, NCL no longer includes the "recall" in any of its models, but endorses the initiative and referendum if they are to be used as the "gun behind the door," in response to extreme circumstances. The commentaries to the sixth and seventh editions of the *Model City Charter* and the revised edition of the *Model County Charter* state that they are "more valuable in their availability than their use." That the citizen initiative in some regions of the United States has assumed the status of "first resort" for influencing public policy — in many cases among small but influential minorities — is an issue to be addressed by emerging generations of reformers.

In the early days of its history, NCL absorbed the National Short Ballot Organization, which had been developed by Richard S. Childs with Woodrow Wilson's support. That organization had been calling attention to the various deleterious effects on representative government of the popular election of too many separate officers, especially administrative and judicial. Among these effects are the dissipation of the attention of the voters and the erosion of legitimate executive and legislative responsibility, as well as the fragmentation of administrative and electoral responsibility triggered by the maintenance of independently elected officials.

The "short ballot" principle supplied part of the impetus for the spread of the commission form of government and later of the council-manager and mayor-council forms, which have reduced the use of the long ballot in local elections. However, most states, all but a few counties, and too many municipalities still suffer from this anachronism. Even where the short ballot principle is applied in the election of public officers, the excessive use of the initiative and referendum increasingly crowds state and local ballots. The effects are felt not only in the weaknesses of the governments immediately affected, but also in the distraction of voter attention to the detriment even of national politics. Thus, the further spread of the short ballot is an important piece of unfinished business for reform-minded citizens interested in improving representative government.

Notes

1. Frank Mann Stewart, *A Half Century of Municipal Reform* (Berkeley and Los Angeles, Calif.: The University of California Press, 1950), p. 15.

2. See Chester C. Maxey, *The Political Integration of Metropolitan Communities* (published as the entire issue of the *National Municipal Review*, August 1922); and Committee on Metropolitan Government of the National Municipal League, *The Government of Metropolitan Areas in the United States* (New York, National Municipal League, 1930).

3, 4. *Proceedings of the Columbus Conference for Good City Government*, November 16, 17, 18, 1899, Clinton Rogers Woodruff, ed. (Philadelphia, Penn.: National Municipal League, 1899).

5. See National Municipal League, *Model State Constitution*, sixth edition (New York: National Municipal League, 1965).

CHAPTER 4

SHARING THE LOAD
OF GOVERNANCE

James H. Svara

The roles and responsibilities of the local government manager are subjects of continuing fascination to practitioners and scholars. In recent publications from ICMA, there is increased recognition that the manager's role is broader than that of an administrative technician, yet the boundaries of that role are not clearly identified. The local government management profession is exploring new territory in its search for effectiveness, excellence, and ideals.[1] The effort falls short, however, because of a tendency to cling to the simplistic view that policy and administration are the separate spheres of the council and the manager. In order to better understand the responsibilities of the manager in American cities, we must find an alternative to the "dichotomy" model.

One example illustrates the problem. The recently announced City Management Declaration of Ideals is a challenging statement of the high aspirations of the profession. The first ideal is to promote the "existence and effectiveness of representative local government." An interpretation of the declaration (*Public Management*, August 1984) from the perspective of Peters and Waterman's principles of excellence suggested that managers could accomplish that ideal by "simple form and lean staff." How can an administrative strategy be sufficient to achieving the broad-ranging ideal of making "representative democratic government work?" The answer is to fall back upon

the dichotomy model of responsibilities. As William H. Hansell put it,

> Elected officials perform the task for which they are best qualified — making policy and moderating the level and the standards of service and commitment in the community. A professional manager is responsible for the day-to-day operations of the government and for the delivery of services.

A realistic and workable outline of the manager's responsibilities must recognize that the chief executive officer is a full-fledged participant in the governance of his or her community and not simply responsible for the administration of its services. Furthermore, like it or not, the council is far more involved in administration and even in day-to-day operations than the simple dichotomy model would suggest. The facts belie the dichotomy model, and neither the manager's policy role nor the council's administrative activities are necessarily inappropriate.

In order to better understand how responsibilities are and should be divided, the first step is to revise our conceptualization of council-manager relations. This is not an exercise in iconoclasm. A city manager observed to me in a recent interview that the mythical symbols of council-manager government are important, and that harm could be done by "exposing" the deviations from them. On the contrary, the proposed revision builds upon

From *Public Management*, Vol. 67, No. 7, July 1985. Published by the International City/County Management Association, Washington, D.C. Reprinted with permission of the publisher.

the traditional divisions and incorporates the symbols of this form of government, while at the same time acknowledging the realities of official interactions in the governmental process. Put simply, the approach recognizes that some responsibilities are separate and some are shared.

The Dichotomy-Duality Model

After extensive interviewing with councilmembers and administrators, I became convinced that the root of the problem in assigning responsibilities is an inadequate definition of the major governmental functions. It is commonplace to divide the work of government between policy determination and policy execution, yet each of these can be further subdivided. The determination of policy involves defining purpose and setting broad goals — the formulation of *mission* — as well as the specification of detailed middle-range *policy*, such as the content of the budget or formulas for service delivery.

Execution involves the implementation of policy, i.e., the transition of policies into operating programs, which shall be referred to as *administration*, and the creation and maintenance of personnel, budgeting, informational, and other systems which sustain but are independent of policy and administration. These latter activities are *management*. There is a conceptual dichotomy between mission and management, which represent activities that come close to being "pure" policy, on the one hand, and "pure" operations, on the other. Policy and administration, in contrast, are a duality, distinct but inseparable aspects of the process of developing and delivering government programs.

The division of responsibility for these functions, illustrated in Figure 1, is based on typical patterns observed first in the five cities over 100,000 in population in North Carolina and since confirmed through research in a number of large manager cities outside the state. Furthermore, it is normatively tenable because it provides both for democratic control and for insulation of staff from inappropriate political interference.

The council dominates mission formulation, although the manager plays a major advisory role through administrative planning, analyzing conditions and trends, and developing proposals. The principle of political supremacy is protected by the control of elected officials over decisions that create the framework for specific policy choices, whether these choices are made by council or staff. In policy, the manager has a slightly larger space than the council because of the large amount of policy advice and policy setting by administrators, but the greater "quantity" of managerial policy making does not alter the council's ultimate responsibility for all policy.

The staff has the much larger role in administration, although the council makes a substantial contribution to this sphere. The most common form of intervention in administration accompanies councilmember handling of citizen complaints about services. In addition, councils frequently make specific decisions that serve to implement general policies or programs. Although the congressional veto of administrative actions was prohibited by the courts, city councils, especially through their committees, commonly step in to check and alter program implementation. Councils may also engage in formal and informal administrative oversight.

Management is the sphere of the manager, with the council's role limited to approving management "policy," such as the nature of the pay plan, suggestions about management improvement, support of managerial initiatives, and assessment through appraisal of the manager. The manager presumably has final authority over most operational questions, and, therefore, the insulation of administrators from interference by elected officials is secured. Unlike the details of administration, in which councilmembers take an active interest, the details of management are usually handled by the manager. This interpretation of management is not intended to diminish its importance. This function encompasses the development and operation of the organization that does the work of city government. Good management is a precondition for effective governance.

To summarize, the dichotomy-duality

Figure 1
Dichotomy-Duality Model

**Mission-Management Separation with Shared
Responsibility for Policy and Administration**

ILLUSTRATIVE TASKS FOR COUNCIL	DIMENSIONS OF GOVERNMENTAL PROCESS	ILLUSTRATIVE TASKS FOR ADMINISTRATORS

COUNCIL'S SPHERE

ILLUSTRATIVE TASKS FOR COUNCIL		ILLUSTRATIVE TASKS FOR ADMINISTRATORS
Determine "purpose," scope of services, tax level, constitutional issues.	MISSION	Advise (what city "can" do may influence what it "should" do); analyze conditions and trends.
Pass ordinances, approve new projects and programs, ratify budget.	POLICY	Make recommendations on all decisions, formulate budget, determine service distribution formulas.
Make implementing decisions, e.g., site selection, handle complaints, oversee administration.	ADMINISTRATION	Establish practices and procedures and make decisions for implementing policy.
Suggest management changes to manager; review organizational performance in manager's appraisal.	MANAGEMENT	Control the human, material, and informational resources of organization to support policy and administrative functions.

MANAGER'S SPHERE

The curved line suggests the division between the council's and the manager's spheres of activity, with the council to the *left* and the manager to the *right* of the line.

The division presented is intended to roughly approximate a "proper" degree of separation and sharing. Shifts to either the left or right would indicate improper incursions.

From "Dichotomy and Duality: Reconceptualizing the Relationship between Policy and Administration in Council-Manager Cities," *Public Administration Review* 45 (1985).

---

model is based on the separation of responsibility for mission and management and shared responsibility for policy and administration. There is an unavoidable mixing of authority and activity in policy and administration that coexists with the more clearly divisible responsibilities for mission and management, although in these latter functions the manager and council, respectively, fill a supportive role.

The Manager's Responsibilities

The dichotomy-duality model can be used to develop a list of the manager's responsibilities that encompasses his extensive contributions to the governance of the community and provides the basis for effective interaction with the council. A working relationship obviously involves two parties, but the manager can induce a positive response from elected officials by adopting roles that enhance the position of the council while protecting his professional prerogatives. The manager, in his relationship with the council, must be both assertive and supportive at the same time. Assertiveness is required to clarify his role and to tell the council what it must do, and supportiveness is needed to help the council discharge its responsibilities.

With regard to mission, the council needs help with decisions that it must make. The manager should conduct comprehensive administrative planning in order to identify trends and emerging problems and to frame issues for the council. Ironically, the most important task of councilmembers is probably the hardest and least natural for them, given a tendency toward short time perspective and piecemeal solutions to immediate problems. Professional administrators, on the other hand, by temperament and training, tend to adopt a proactive stance to community problems. Studies of council decision making, as reported in *The Effective Local Government Administrator* (page 61), conclude that major choices about future development constitute 80 percent of the importance among decisions but account for only 5 percent of the time spent by the council. The manager should provide councilmembers with the information and encouragement they need to chart a course for their jurisdiction.

If mission is clear, the manager can more easily fill his policy function. As Henry Mintzberg (*The Nature of Managerial Work*, page 95) has observed about private sector chief executive officers, the basic reasons why organizations need managers are to ensure, first, that the organization "serves its basic purpose," and, second, that it "serves the ends of those persons who control it." The public manager can be expected to operate according to the same premises, keeping in mind that the public indirectly controls the organization, and provide policy leadership that is consistent with basic purpose.

In administration, managers can be more supportive in responding to the council and providing information for oversight. Increasingly, councilmembers see themselves as ombudsmen and are very interested in constituent complaints. The manager can respond to this concern by regularizing the process of complaint handling, as several managers in the study cities have done. A designated staff member, acting for the manager, receives complaints from councilmembers, refers the matter to the appropriate office, and provides a follow-up report to the councilmember of the action taken. The manager should insist that response to inquiries or complaints coming directly from citizens be equal to that given to councilmember transmitted complaints. A method of tracking complaints and using them to measure responsiveness and to identify systematic problems in service delivery also can be established, with periodic reports given to councilmembers to lessen their

fear that they will miss out on important indicators of staff performance. Despite administrative procedures for complaint handling and reporting, however, the manager should recognize that elected officials need to provide constituency services and will continue to be involved in administration in this way.

The other major change in this area is to help structure and provide the information required for systematic oversight. As administrators incorporate more objectives and performance measures in their work plans and budgets, they are creating elements that will be useful in an oversight process that examines accomplishments in terms of objectives. Most cities, however, need to further develop effectiveness measures, such as those proposed by The Urban Institute and the ICMA (*How Effective Are Your Community Services*), and to strengthen their capacity to conduct evaluation research.

The whole approach to oversight will need to be developed in consultation with the council. This may appear to be a formidable new task for practitioners, yet improved oversight can be defended not only on the grounds of improving performance and promoting comprehensive assessment of services, but also as a process that will lessen burdens in other areas. With formalized oversight, need would be reduced for specific inquiries into administrative performance and for pursuing individual complaints. Therefore, the existing workload created by council checking activities would ideally be lessened, and the attention of council and staff alike would be directed toward the general rather than the random specifics of administration.

The manager should insist on the freedom to manage the organization, while helping the council to organize its appraisal activities more thoroughly and systematically. The manager is obligated to protect the staff from arbitrary or callous actions that impair performance and damage morale. The extent of the manager's control over council behavior is, of course, limited, unless he resorts to potentially self-destructive threats. It seems, however, that the likelihood of disruptive council actions is minimized if the manager has maintained the highest standards of management practice and

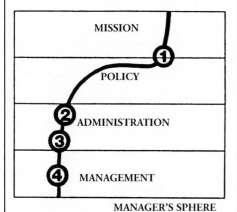

**Figure 2
Key Points in Interaction
in Council-Manager Relations**

COUNCIL'S SPHERE

MISSION

①

POLICY

② ADMINISTRATION

③

④ MANAGEMENT

MANAGER'S SPHERE

1. Goal setting activities
2. Council oversight administration
3. Complaint handling by staff with reports to the council
4. Council appraisal of the manager and organizational performance

The Likelihood of Change by Managers ... and Councils

Is it realistic to expect city administrators to behave in the ways described? These responsibilities are consistent with two major streams in thought about professional standards, both of which have received support in the past. Put together, the ethical requirements can be called the Neo-Traditional Public Administration. The approach recognizes the role of the manager as a policy shaper who is concerned about equity, openness, participation, and responsiveness — qualities stressed in the New Public Administration movement of the late sixties and early seventies. In addition, the standards implicit in the responsibilities reassert the importance of the long-standing values of efficiency, economy, and respect for the political authority.

The Declaration of Ideals asserts the same ethical imperatives. Strengthening representative government requires that administrators help elected officials meet their responsibility to determine the direction of community development and provide accountability to the public. Support for citizen participation, integration of the community, equitable service delivery, and a responsive and productive organization are all present among the ideals. The declaration advances the proposition that strong, conscientious professionals strengthen rather than threaten democratic government, a conclusion consistent with the dichotomy-duality model.

It is a bigger question whether the council will want or be able to change its tendencies, particularly a predilection for the particular over the general and for short-term over long-term action. As a collective body of equals, a council does not readily make rational choices concerning organization or behavior. Perhaps there is hope for change, however, if councilmembers realize that they are not only policy makers and that their interest in administration is legitimate but can be satisfied in more constructive ways than is commonly done.

Using the dichotomy-duality model as a guide, councilmembers can better recognize their unique roles and responsibilities. Interviews with councilmembers sometimes reveal

if the council is fully aware of the quality of management. The council that raids departmental budgets to make cuts or threatens job reductions to wring out more savings presumably does not believe that the manager has maintained adequate control over budgeting or personnel. Therefore, it is in the interests of the manager to promote appraisal of the whole organization and to encourage the council to provide critical review, so as to expand support for improved management and to strengthen his prerogatives.

The changes are summarized in Figure 2, with the key points of interaction superimposed on the dichotomy-duality model. Managers need to help the council with (1) goal setting, (2) oversight, (3) complaint handling, and (4) appraisal of the manager and the organization. Doing so strengthens the manager's hand as a policy maker, implementer, and manager.

a sense of malaise that they are not accomplishing anything in spite of (or because of) the sometimes frantic pace they maintain. They should feel more positive about what they contribute, especially as the formulators of mission for the organization. They can ease their anxiety about the activity and influence of manager and staff in policy by accepting the legitimacy and necessity of staff contributions, as long as they make decisions within the framework of goals set by the council. Furthermore, the council can acknowledge its interest in administration and move toward more systematic, rather than specific and episodic, involvement in it. Finally, the council can organize and broaden its appraisal of the manager and organizational performance. By so doing, it is in a better position to support the manager in making management changes, on the one hand, and to answer citizen queries about organizational efficiency, on the other.

The manager will benefit as well from a closer match between the council's perception of the manager's role and his actual behavior. The manager will have a stronger, more aware council with which to work. He will also have a clearer and broader mandate of responsibilities with expanded discretion, greater accountability, and more freedom to manage. The result can be higher involvement by both council and manager and more effective governance and administration in council-manager cities.

Notes

1. See *The Effective Local Government Administrator* and *Public Management* in April and May 1984 for applications of *In Search of Excellence* to local government; *PM* in August for the City Management Declaration of Ideals.

CHAPTER 5

THE RESPONSIBLE PUBLIC EXECUTIVE[1]

William N. Cassella, Jr.

If public opinion is to be effective, there must be some visible point within the governmental structure upon which it may focus either praise or blame, as well as a representative or legislative channel through which its desires are made known and policies and programs developed in response to those desires.

The National Civic League program has stood from the very beginning four-square behind the principle of a responsible, accountable chief executive, presiding over an integrated administrative structure. Upon this principle have been built NCL's model charters and state constitution — in fact, all aspects of its program as it relates to administrative organization. In this connection, NCL has endorsed both elected and appointed chief executives — the two representing different ways in which the executive may be held responsible — recognizing that both arrangements are valid depending on the circumstances involved.

Mayor and Manager

Initially, NCL favored the "strong mayor," or elected chief executive. This was such a drastic departure from prevailing practice that it gained relatively little acceptance. Few were willing to entrust extensive powers to a single local executive. Nineteenth-century reformers, as well as machine politicians, had been responsible for fragmenting the executive dimension of government. Each separately elected department head saw in a single elected chief executive a threat to his patronage. The reformers were unwilling to trust either an elected chief executive or a department head. They wanted and often secured "a board of public works of three heavily bonded members appointed by the mayor for six-year terms in rotation, the mayor's own term being two years." The board, not the mayor, would select a superintendent of public works. The goal was to prevent a scandal in public works, but the result was to create a situation where no one was really responsible — certainly not the mayor, who likely had not appointed all the members of the board of public works. Similar boards were set up as the "protectors" of health, parks, recreation, and planning departments.

The realization that there seemed little likelihood that American communities would be willing to buy the strong mayor idea encouraged a search for other means of assuring executive responsibility. NCL did not question the validity of the strong elected chief executive, if indeed strong, but it has insisted that the diffused executive responsibility that has continued to be characteristic of many mayor-council cities does not permit citizens to hold their government accountable in an orderly

Originally published at "The Responsible Executive," *National Civic Review,* Vol. 83, No. 4, Fall-Winter 1994. Published by the National Civic League, Denver, Colorado. Reprinted with permission of the publisher.

fashion. Moreover, NCL has maintained that the strong elected chief executive form does not generally encourage a well balanced, properly integrated, and efficiently managed governmental program, despite the notable exceptions.

It should be noted that some of the problems arising with an elected executive arrangement are inherent in the "separation" of the legislative and executive branches with a crippling scheme of "checks and balances." In NCL's 1900 model city charter, which embodied a strong mayor-council system, appointments of department heads were by the mayor without the "advice and consent" of the council. This so-called "uncontrolled" appointing power prompted fears that the elected mayor would have too much power.

Adherence to the principle of an integrated, responsible executive has always led NCL to reject the commission form of government. Even in the early part of the 20th century, when the commission plan was popular among reformers, NCL refused to endorse commission government. It has often been said that a city commission is too small to be a legislative body and too large to administer. However, the fact that the early popularity of the commission plan established a precedent for shortening the ballot, eliminating a whole string of elected officials and independent boards, and centering all powers — legislative and executive alike — in the same body did have considerable influence upon NCL policy makers. In the commission plan, the "short ballot" principle had been accepted along with a small policy-making body not elected from traditional wards. The question, then, was how to combine the organizational achievements of commission government with an integrated, responsible executive.

The answer took shape in the mind of Richard S. Childs. In one of his earliest writings on the "manager plan," he stated, "Upon a state legislature or a city legislature (i.e., a *group* of men who act in group) we willingly confer greater power than we dare give *one* man, and all these large powers can, without diminution, be boldly and flexibly administered through a *controlled* executive." Childs noted, in describing the first adoption of what

later become known as the council-manager plan, "This little city modifies the commission plan by making the commissioners act as a board, never singly, and perform all executive work through an appointed city manager, who holds office subject to their pleasure."

Thus, Childs's great contribution to governmental theory and practice was an ingenious combination of experience in commission-governed cities and the basic organizational experience of private business.

In 1915 the council-manager plan was made part of the *Model City Charter*. Although subsequent revisions of the *Model* have modified details, its basic features have remained unchanged, providing for a professional executive appointed by the legislative body, who in turn grant the manager responsibility for the appointment of all administrative department heads and supervision of their performance.[2]

Unquestionably, this important shift in NCL's "municipal program" was brought about largely as a result of the conviction that in the council-manager plan was found the most practical arrangement for securing a responsible chief executive. In the commentary published with the new model charter, known as *The New Municipal Program*, this point was stressed:

> ...The distinguishing characteristic of the form of city government advocated in *The New Municipal Program* is to be found in the concentration of administrative powers and responsibilities in the hands of a city manager. ...Indeed, the initial sentence of this portion [of the charter] strikes the keynote of the entire administrative organization by declaring that the city manager shall be *the chief executive officer of the city*. It is true that this declaration in and of itself may mean much or nothing. Similar declarations are to be found, for instance, in nearly all our state constitutions, and in many city charters of the mayor-and-council type. ...
>
> The trouble ... has been in the past that the constitutions and charters, after making a declaration of a sound principle of governmental organization, have nullified that declaration by the distribution of functions actually made in the organic law. Fortunately, ... *The New Municipal Program* lives up to its confession of faith in this regard and the opening declaration

as to the position of the city manager is a promise that is fulfilled in the working out of the details of organization.

It was also clearly recognized that the new *Model* rejected the "separation of powers" concept that characterized the national and state governments. It was stated, "The dominant note in our new *Model City Charter* is elimination of the system of checks and balances in the organization of our cities and the substitution therefor of responsible government under a small legislative chamber which in turn selects a single administrative head. The city manager plan not merely represents the type in common use in business corporations but also in parliamentary government."

The ever-increasing popularity of council-manager government in all but extremely small or extremely large cities has demonstrated without doubt the continued belief that this plan provides an effective and responsible instrument for the formulation and execution of public policy. The *Model City Charter* has been the guide for municipal reorganization which has resulted in an astonishing improvement in the quality of public administration at the municipal level and generally in more responsible and professionally competent local government. NCL staff continue to aid those in communities who are pressing for the adoption of the council-manager plan, but in recent years just as many requests for assistance have come from those endeavoring to improve details of council-manager charters that have been in effect for some time.

NCL does not campaign for the universal adoption of its *Model City Charter*. Although the inspiration for seeking local government reorganization may come from NCL's efforts, the initiative for change in a specific community must come from the locality itself. Indeed, there are numerous occasions when NCL staff members, aware of the local political climate and stated preferences of the local officials and civic leadership, provide assistance to charter-review bodies that are preparing a document quite at variance with the *Model*.

Were NCL doctrinaire in its advocacy of council-manager organization, this practice would be heresy. However, such is not the case; form of government is not viewed by the National Civic League as an end in itself, but a means to secure more responsible governance. In fact, the latest revisions of the *Model City Charter* have expanded the optional provisions to assist communities favoring an elected chief executive.

County Executive and County Administrator

The National Civic League's position with respect to county government reorganization has been similar to that for cities. The *Model County Charter*, like the *Model City Charter*, provides for an appointed executive responsible to the legislative body. There is strong historical precedent for assigning both the executive and legislative powers to county governing bodies. Characteristically, American counties have operated with the "commission" plan, which does combine these powers in one body. Despite the substantial persistence of independently elected county administrative officials, one by one their powers are being assigned to an appointed official responsible to the county governing body.

The tendency among cities to establish independent boards and commissions also has haunted counties, but this practice has diminished gradually, accompanied by greater willingness to centralize powers in a single body. Thus, the establishment of an arrangement whereby a chief executive (manager) is appointed by the board seems the logical next step for many counties. A variety of appointed county executives have been set up under various names and with various combinations of powers. All of these move a part of the distance toward a responsible executive.[3] NCL's position has been one of encouraging even the modest moves in this direction, while calling attention to the formula for a truly integrated, responsible executive provided by the *Model County Charter*.[4]

A number of counties have adopted charters with substantial powers in the hands of an elected executive. The attitude of NCL board and staff members toward these experiments has been one of encouragement with the feeling that if counties are to be equipped to comply with the responsibilities of modern government they must have at least a partially integrated executive structure. When NCL is consulted by those drafting elected executive charters, it is often necessary to discourage the inclusion of language in the document that limits the power of the executive and makes it more difficult to establish clear lines of executive responsibility.

One of the most difficult problems arising from the use of an elected chief executive, with its attendant separation of powers, is the matter of securing "advice and consent" from the legislative body for executive appointments. Sometimes there are efforts to require similar approval for removals. Unless the elected chief executive is an extraordinarily strong political leader, the problem of securing council approval of appointments may act not only to check executive abuse, but also to dilute executive responsibility.

The Governor

Since publication of the first *Model State Constitution* in 1921, the National Civic League has consistently supported the idea of strengthening the office of governor as a state-level counterpart of the American presidency. According to the *Model* arrangement, the governor would be the only elected executive officer of the state and thereby clearly responsible to the electorate for administration. The host of lesser elected officials and administrative boards would be eliminated.[5]

The explanatory essays and commentary published with successive editions of the *Model State Constitution* stress the principle of concentration of administrative power in a single, popularly elected chief executive. Nonetheless, the reluctance to provide for an integrated executive and the confusion regarding the American doctrine of "separation of powers" have made progress toward a strong state executive discouragingly slow. The *Model*

provides a pattern for untangling that confusion and giving both the executive and legislative departments clearer lines of responsibility. NCL also has endeavored to stress the need for a strong state executive in its advocacy of various efforts toward state administrative reorganization and the development and staffing of the gubernatorial office.

Conclusion

To hold their leaders accountable while in office or when seeking election — as well as to assess the various and inevitable claims and promises of candidates — citizens must possess a sound understanding of the roles, responsibilities and performance expectations of their elected officers. Governmental form, when rationally structured and respected by responsible officials, constitutes a sure standard for evaluation.

NCL policies have sought to locate responsibility clearly in the legislative and executive arenas, in the context of both the unitary model and the separation-of-powers system, not only to improve the function of government, but also to assist individuals in the exercise of informed citizenship.

Notes

1. This article is the second in a series on the evolution of National Civic League policies, which commenced with the Summer-Fall 1994 issue and will conclude in 1995.

2. See National Civic League, *Model City Charter*, Seventh Edition (Denver, Colo.: National Civic League Press, 1989, 1992).

3. See National Civic League, *Modern Counties: Professional Government— The Non-Charter Route* (Denver, Colo.: National Civic League Press, 1993).

4. See National Civic League, *Model County Charter*, Revised Edition (Denver, Colo.: National Civic League Press, 1990).

5. See National Municipal League (National Civic League), *Model State Constitution*, Sixth Edition (New York: National Municipal League, 1963, Revised 1968).

PART II
Cities

CHAPTER 6

FORMS OF LOCAL GOVERNMENT IN AMERICAN HISTORY

Charles R. Adrian

Poets, politicians, journalists, and sociologists have ridiculed form as an insignificant factor in the kind of government we experience. Political scientists and reformers have not been so certain. The most familiar comment on the subject is probably that of the great British poet of the Augustan age, Alexander Pope: "For forms of government let fools contest. Whatever is best administered is best."[1] True, public administration was not exactly Pope's strong suit, but he was not alone in his viewpoint. Edmund Burke, Lincoln Steffens, and many others agreed with him. Burke subscribed to a theory of history holding that the quality of leadership determined the quality of life. "Great men are the guideposts and landmarks in the state," he observed in 1774. In 1904 Steffens argued that corrupt leaders, and especially those who corrupted them, were responsible for bad government.[2]

The Significance of Structure

Though political scientists have studied city government and politics for many years, they are unable to make definitive statements about any autonomous effects of form or structure on the political system, especially about administrative considerations.

Some scholars, without clear evidence, have rejected the possibility of an autonomous influence coming from the structure itself.

Some find the question uninteresting or unimportant. Although sociologists often picture structure as inhibiting function to one degree or another, some of them have expressed serious doubt about the effect of formal rules. Practicing politicians sometimes give short shrift to the idea,[3] especially reform opponents who do not wish to prepare a more substantial defense of the status quo. Marxians argue that power in the city is grounded only in the control over the means of production. This kind of analysis can lead to a dismissal of form as irrelevant,[4] as can a conviction that informal political organizations outside the provisions of the charter, such as the boss-and-machine structure, are the dominating forces in allocating power.[5]

In addition to the traditional weak mayor-council forms, which served as the structural base for dozens of political machines, other forms of local government rarely hampered the bosses. Thus, bosses ruled under the strong mayor-council plan (Boston under James Michael Curley), the commission plan (Jersey City under Frank Hague and Memphis under Edward H. Crump), and the council-manager plan (Kansas City under Thomas J. Pendergast). Indeed, political machines could themselves be reformed or modified to allow the party to increase its efficiency or modernity or to give the boss greater control, without much affecting the way the governmental structure itself operated. Anton J. Cer-

Reprinted with permission from *Municipal Year Book* 1998. Published by the International City/County Management Association, Washington, D.C.

mak, a brilliant administrator, reorganized the Chicago machine in the early 1930s in order to concentrate power in the boss but without creating a new governmental system of operation.[6] Under George W. Olvany, Tammany Hall in Manhattan looked carefully at a modernization plan in the late 1920s.[7] It failed to adopt one for short-sighted reasons unrelated to the question of whether the machine structure was independent of that of the city government, but the machine, not the city charter, was the subject under study.

Despite other viewpoints, some political scientists have reached the conclusion that the structure of city government is important in helping to determine the content of policy, access to decision making, the image of the city held by outsiders, and the accomplishments of the goals of major interest groups.[8] Certainly reformers have long believed this or they would not have devoted, as many of them have, years of effort and thousands of their own dollars in efforts to secure the adoption of new charters, to oust old machines, or to reach other difficult-to-achieve goals. (Some reformers have certainly been sophisticated enough to recognize that at least a part, and possibly a very large part, of their efforts have involved symbolic activities. But interviews with reformers virtually always reveal assumptions concerning the efficacy of structure itself.)

The question of the impact of structure on form upon government cannot be settled here. To some extent, participants in the debate have talked past one another, not actually discussing the same issues. Furthermore, too many variables exist to say anything definitive about their interaction patterns or about causality. Certainly some aspects of structure have been statistically measurable. The use of professional management, merit personnel systems, the executive budget, the initiative and referendum, nonpartisan elections, and quite a number of other reform goals or policies have surely not varied randomly among the various forms of city government. And the relative influence of specific interest groups or access to decision makers is certainly not the same for citizens generally or to certain categories of citizens from one structure to another.

Although it cannot be demonstrated formally, it seems eminently reasonable to assume that structure affects the policy processes and outcomes in some way. The question is not one of its existence but of the extent, form, and character of such effects. The 1986 *Form of Government* survey sheds some additional light on this.[9]

Unlike administration and policy-making, form undoubtedly affects *elections*. To a much greater degree than we may care to concede democracy as expressed through voting is a matter of *faith* in the process. No ideal election system exists; all involve, to some degree, arbitrary rules by which winners are determined. All have some "slippage" or inaccuracy in the counting process, although this is usually a result of inadequate financing or deliberate or accidental human error that the system permits though strictly speaking does not cause.

The growth of elections, suffrage, and ballot forms is reported in textbooks and monographs and need not be dwelt upon here.[10] In general, the beginning of modern democracy dates from the Glorious Revolution of 1688–89 in the United Kingdom, where the theory of parliamentary supremacy replaced the Stuart concept of the "divine right of kings." Subsequent developments spread to the 13 colonies that became the United States about 90 years later.

In this incipient democracy, the eligibility rules were derived primarily from two principles: (1) *The possession of a certain amount of property*. This supposedly ensured that the voter had a sufficient stake in an election to behave responsibly. The basic minimum rule was ownership of a 40 shilling freehold. (2) *The voter must have attained adulthood*. Originally restricted to an upper middle-class electorate with adult status based on the common-law rule of age 21, eligibility to vote was broadened gradually but inexorably. Merchants first assaulted the freehold rule and got it changed to property of a specific value, but the Jacksonians succeeded in abolishing most property requirements altogether in the 1820s and 1830s.

Court action in quite recent decades gradually eliminated late nineteenth-century rules designed to restrict voting to those who could read English. Rules in the South designed to disenfranchise blacks (and the white poor as well) were not finally overcome until the federal Voting Rights Act of 1965. The voting age was left at the traditional 21 until four states reduced it to 18 or 19 in the 1950s. In the late 1960s, as a by-product of the social conflict surrounding the Vietnam war, the figure was dropped to 18, which corresponds to the age most people leave high school, take a job, or go to college, thus becoming more nearly autonomous from their parents. It was also the age of military draft eligibility. The Twenty-sixth Amendment to the United States Constitution (1971) established this as the universal voting age in the United States, and there seems little likelihood of its changing in the future.

The form of the ballot and rules for voting procedures have caused, and probably always will continue to cause, problems in elections. The voters' choices were given orally in early democracies, a time when even persons of considerable wealth might be illiterate. While our British friends were still voting *viva voce*, Americans introduced the written ballot, which became the standard practice by the 1780s. One need not dwell long on why an oral vote imposed strong pressures to conform to social expectations. But the ballot was not truly secret even with the adoption of the written form. As the political parties increased in importance in the early Republic, they aided those who identified with them (and the illiterate) by printing distinctive ballots, even pre-marking them with the "X" in the "right" places and perhaps with only the party's candidates listed so that one could not "split" the ticket. The Australians devised a truly secret ballot, uniform in size, color, and content, printed by the government at its expense, and available only at the polling booth from election officials, to be marked and folded in secret but deposited in public. This ballot was first used in the United States in Louisville, Kentucky, in 1888 and was rapidly accepted across the nation, though the last state to adopt it, South Carolina, held out until the 1950s.

The outcome of elections may also be, or

once have been, altered by rules concerning citizenship, legal insanity, felony conviction, pauperism, literacy, and registration. In the era when property was an essential requirement, owners need not necessarily have lived in the locality or even city in which they voted, but residency rules were created and became universal after property ownership ceased to be a requirement. (The rule then became that each person was entitled to one legal domicile, with which he or she had some personal identification, though actual residence might be somewhere else for years, such as while one was away at college.) Registration was introduced in some large cities in the mid–nineteenth century and gradually became almost universal. Its stated and often actual purpose was, and still is, to reduce fraud in elections. But many forms of registration exist, and it is quite easy to devise one that will either maximize or minimize potential participation by the citizen who has low political information and a low interest level. The rules on registration as well as other rules may deliberately or fortuitously affect the pattern of participation in elections.

Problems of ballot form are compounded in the United States because since early in the twentieth century we have nominated by primary election. Every ballot has a built-in set of biases that potentially influence each election outcome. For practical purposes, some rules must be arbitrary. A common example of built-in biases may be found in the run-off primary common in the South, and the nonpartisan "primary" election, used in thousands of local elections. In these, numerous persons may file for the first vote. The common result is that no candidate achieves a required majority (50 percent of the votes cast plus one). The candidate with a plurality, the most votes, could simply be declared the winner, as is common enough in ordinary partisan primary contests, even though more votes were cast against than for that person. The arbitrariness involved does not seem to trouble the voting public, probably because a final outcome is not involved: a general, interparty election follows. Although the South is changing, voting rules from one-party days still are largely in use, in part because many offices continue to be settled as Democratic contests. In the traditional southern primary, the fact that a majority of votes were not cast for the candidate finishing first seemed wrong because it was in fact a final result. The first vote in non-partisan elections has always been considered to be a primary election (although technically, it is not). A second election in each case could easily produce a majority result. The obvious — but by no means necessarily most equitable — "solution" would be to have the two candidates with the highest number of votes compete in a second election. One's "common sense" says that this is fair. But it may be no more equitable than the first result if we make two assumptions about election conditions: (1) individual voters have an order of preference among two or more of the candidates, and (2) one of the two highest vote getters, although the first choice of many, is the second choice of very few. This could happen, for example, if one candidate were an extremist on certain matters, an eccentric, or an avowed ethnic-group candidate.

With one position to be filled, the result might look like this:

Candidate	Primary election	General election	Winner
A	37%	57%	A
B	28	43	
C	25	—	
D	10	—	

But suppose that instead of eliminating anyone at the primary, we were to consider all second choices, such as the following (third and fourth choices would also be possible):

Candidate	First Choice	Second Choice
A	37%	24%
B	28	16
C	25	44
D	10	3

Viewed from this aspect of voter choice, the elimination of candidate "C" (and conceivably both "C" and "D" in another possible illustration that readers can easily construct for themselves) is arbitrary and contrary to popular will, if we assume that the winner should be preferred by more than one-half of the voters in the election, if not as a first choice, then by cumulative subsequent choices. This weakness in the structure of the ordinary ballot led to the adoption from its British origins of the use in some cities of proportional representation (PR) in the 1920s and 1930s. Several types of PR plans were already known, but the most accurate one was the Hare single transferable vote system, with Droop quota.[11] This approach, sparing the reader the details, would sidestep the problem some will have spotted in the above scenario of having to weight second choices without again being arbitrary.

PR received much publicity when it was made a part of the Cincinnati reform charter of 1925. New York City adopted the plan (with a different quota system) in the "La-Guardia" charter (effective in the 1937 election), and PR seemed to be on its way, but it was adopted by a total of only about 25 cities. It ran into trouble precisely because it did what it was designed to do — it distributed council seats on a proportional basis to various political parties or other discernible interests. In New York, this meant that after World War II, two council seats went to Communist party members and two more to fellow travelers. Growing opposition from newspaper editors and the major parties forced abandonment of the plan in 1947, with a subsequent return to an all–Democratic party city council.[12] In Cincinnati, the plan continued in use although it was opposed for many reasons, including its distribution of a proportionate share of council seats to blacks. Its representational strength was its political weakness. After much controversy, PR was abolished by charter amendment in Cincinnati in 1952. Within a little more than a decade, it had disappeared in all American cities.[13] It had been opposed consistently by those who could gain from its elimination and by others because its operation was not easy to understand. It required esoteric rules of centralized counting to determine the winners. Many people would not trust a system that complex. Others saw no beauty in making democracy so precise as to produce what they saw as unwanted council factions creating chronic conflict.

The rules of the game and the structure of the contest may have important effects in many ways. Although one of the enduring myths of democracy holds the simple majority sacred, it is often an elusive thing. That, perhaps, works to reinforce its symbolic value. Yet, the majority must often be constructed artificially. At the local level, the actual majority commonly consists of the registered nonvoters. The majority, however generated, is not always accepted as adequate for decision purposes. Although the practice is coming under increasing court scrutiny, we sometime demand an extraordinary majority, especially for adopting charters, charter amendments, tax overrides, or bond issues. By requiring some extraordinary vote, we may sometimes defeat the majority preference, an irony that apparently is often accepted without much hesitation. (In the cases of demands for extraordinary majorities, advocates are seeking to achieve the closest approximation to total community consensus — unanimity, the community ideal. But the idea is often impractical.)

The Primary Election

The most important and a unique structural innovation in the United States is the primary election, used generally for nomination purposes now for about 75 years. Its origin can be found in limited use in Pennsylvania in the 1840s. Its revival came about in the 1890s in an effort to break up the monopoly political control of the Bourbon aristocracy in the South. Use spread rapidly in the early years of the twentieth century and especially in connection with the popularity of Progressivism before the outbreak of World War I. Prior to this time, caucuses and conventions were the standard method for nomination. The rules sometimes required an extraordinary majority. As an example at the national level, James Knox Polk became the first dark-horse candidate to win the presidency, in 1844, because the leading candidate, Martin Van Buren (who had been defeated for reelection four years earlier) could muster a majority, but not two-thirds of the delegates at the Democratic

National Convention. So Polk, a compromise, was nominated on the ninth ballot and later elected president.

The arbitrary rule (it was designed to give the South a veto over the nomination) probably made an important difference historically. Polk was ready to fight Mexico over Texas and California; Van Buren opposed prompt annexation because he wanted to avoid the war that began two years later in April 1846. Franklin D. Roosevelt easily put together a majority of delegates in 1932 but scrambled to get the two-thirds vote needed for the nomination. (In 1936, at the height of his popularity, FDR persuaded the convention to adopt a simple majority rule. This abolition of the southern veto over the Democratic presidential nomination contributed later to the destabilization of the "Solid South" in presidential and congressional politics.)

The Early Years

The forms of government with which we as a nation began were, of course, inherited from England.[14] With the nation 97 percent rural by the first census in 1790, its leaders did not yet see forms of city government as a major concern, but experimentation and change soon began. The earliest American city governments possessed characteristics most of which are still familiar to us today, though there are a few surprises. Cities were legally public corporations, possessing what we would call special charters, but they were granted by the governor or proprietor acting in the name of the Crown, not by Parliament or the colonial legislatures. These few urban places were usually called *boroughs*, the traditional English term. A few were *cities*, in England an honorary title granted by the Crown, usually because the borough possessed a cathedral. (New York was a city from its first charter in 1686.) They had the right to exist in perpetuity, to sue and to be sued, to use a corporate seal, and to own property.

As in England, there was a unicameral council manned by aldermen and common councillors or assistant aldermen sitting together (the alderman sometimes also had judicial duties). Presiding was the mayor, who was a full voting member (except in Philadelphia). The mayor and recorder (corporation counsel or city attorney) were chosen annually, either by the council or the governor, but they were never elected as they were in England. There was no separation of powers. In addition to the aldermen, the mayor and recorder, or a combination of them, usually had more judicial powers, hence the "mayor's" and "recorder's" courts that still survive in some states. Several boroughs were "close" corporations, Philadelphia being the largest. In these, vacancies on the council were filled by the remaining members, and terms of office were for life. But in most of the boroughs, council members were elected by the freemen, freeholders of sufficient property, or other taxpayers who qualified as voters.

In colonial or revolutionary America, none of the urban places as yet provided municipal utilities or other services. The councils appointed officers to regulate trade and occupations (to supervise the fixed price of bread or to guard against the sale of very low quality pork, for example), to oversee the common land (and to lease some of it out to individuals), to manage the municipal markets and fairs, and to organize other activities.

The first two boroughs created in what became the United States were Maine coastal places, Agamenticus (1641) and Kittery (1647). Neither was ever organized, and all of New England operated under the town government system at the time of Independence and until long afterward.[15] New York, as Niew Amsterdam, was organized by the Dutch in 1656, taken over by the English nine years later, and operated as a municipal corporation. It received a charter upon local petition (the standard English procedure) in 1686. Philadelphia was chartered in 1691. About 20 other municipalities, many of them very small, were also incorporated between then and 1746, after which no additional charters were executed until after Independence, perhaps an indication of a growing reluctance on the part of the royal governors and the proprietors to grant more autonomy to the increasingly recalcitrant colonials.

A New Set Decision Makers

With the coming of independence, decision about municipal governments were no longer made in London. The new leaders in the state capitals immediately asserted their claims to power. The legislatures quickly assumed control over municipal corporations, preempting the rights of the governors that would have existed by precedent. The practice of limiting legislative power over local government developed quickly, for in Massachusetts the new state constitution prohibited the legislature from imposing a municipal charter on a town without its own consent. (Such a charter could have been used to increase legislative influence as compared with the autonomy of the towns.)

The English model had never in fact existed in exactly the same form in the colonies as it did at home. In particular, the mayor was weaker in the colonies. Being appointed by the governor or proprietor, he was less trusted by local residents than were the council members, who kept the corporate powers in their hands, restricting the mayor to his vote and to presiding over the council. The governor, in naming the mayor, had potential influence over the municipality. But in England, there was no central government intervention possible, for the mayor was elected by the same electors as were council members.

Changes in the status and structure of cities began promptly after the Declaration was issued. Pennsylvania set aside the Philadelphia charter of 1701, ending the "close" corporation and providing for the election of council members, although a completely new charter did not go into effect until 1789. Close corporations in all states were soon abolished. Except for their necessary alterations to allow for elections, charter changes at first were small in scope.

A sharp new direction was taken, however, in the Baltimore charter of 1797, which introduced for the first time at the local level the concept of separation of powers and checks and balances. This was borrowed, of course, from the new Maryland and United States constitutions. In the bicameral Baltimore council, the lower house consisted of two members from each of eight wards, elected for one-year terms. In the upper house, each ward elected one member (the at-large idea came later). The wards also chose members of an electoral college, which then selected the mayor. The most significant long-term provision, however, gave the mayor a *veto* power, which could be overridden by a two-thirds vote in each house.

There appear to have been no traumatic experiences or obvious threats to local government to inspire the establishment of these derivative institutions. They were no doubt thought of, however, as thoroughly American. At first the veto spread slowly, but it became a commonplace power of the mayor from the 1830s, with the Jacksonian-era charters. The electoral college idea, by contrast, never gained in popularity. This approach was perhaps just an imitation that produced no apparent benefits, or perhaps it reflected a general discontent with the manner in which the mayor had been chosen in colonial times and still was being chosen nearly a generation after Independence. After all, civic leaders were aware of the British precedent of election. Other changes soon took place. In 1821, selection of New York's mayors was shifted from gubernatorial appointment to choice by the council, but this did not produce a groundswell of demand for limitation. The Detroit (1806) and New Orleans (1815) charters, for example, had still left selection to the governors. Then in 1822, a great change occurred. Boston became the first New England town to give up its status and ask the state legislature for a charter. The result was to provide the settled, tradition-bound hub city with an elected mayor. And in that same year, out on the frontier, the St. Louis mayor was made subject to popular vote. Other cities followed in short order: Detroit (1824), Philadelphia (1826), Baltimore (1833), New York (1834), and then a flood of others. Jacksonian democracy, in the temper of the times, was carried from rural America into the cities.[16] It called for keeping government "close to the people," believing that almost anyone of goodwill could govern. By 1840, almost all mayors were chosen by popular vote.

Still more changes in form followed: The elected mayor in many cities continued to preside over the council and now, in addition, appointed some or all of the committees, sometimes making himself chair of the important ones and thus in a position to lead in shaping policy development. The mayor was reaching the level of policy leader at the very time that the functions and activities of cities were rapidly expanding. By the 1850s, there was a strong trend toward the separation of the mayor from the council.

Jackson called for further extension of the ballot. Administrators should be chosen not by the now-elected mayor but by the voters directly. This approach was first seen in the Detroit charter of 1824. The ward assessors, tax collectors, and constables were made elective. This idea spread rapidly and soon encompassed the clerk, treasurer, and corporate counsel or city attorney. Before long it included in some places the city engineer and the chief of police. Jacksonianism continued to spread. It appeared in full fig, Wild West style, in the San Francisco charter of 1851, which provided for the election of the mayor, assessors (three of them), city attorney, comptroller, marshal, recorder, street commissioner, tax collector, and treasurer. The powers of both the council and the mayor were being weakened, but decentralized power appealed to Jacksonians, and focusing administrative responsibility was not yet perceived as a problem.

Another development, essential to bringing frontier government "close to the people," was the loosening of the suffrage rules, which had not changed much since the late seventeenth century. Municipal suffrage was in some cases even more restrictive than was the general, which was determined by the amount of taxes paid or the amount of land owned. The rules were based on the firm and logical belief that property ownership generated in an individual a serious interest in community welfare, while a transient, propertyless population, if enfranchised, would be free to act irresponsibly. The rules remained in effect for two generations after Americans had been told that "all men are created equal." Suffrage eligibility was not yet seen as a human right that should be extended to all males, much less to females.

Nevertheless, the ideas of American democracy seemed, from the beginning, to call for a broad suffrage. Jefferson saw education, not property, as the sound basis for participation in government. Even before the Jacksonians, voting rights began to broaden. Universal white manhood suffrage was first extended by two rural New England states, Vermont (1791) and New Hampshire (1792), along with Kentucky (1792), on the frontier. The campaign for extending the vote to women got underway in the late 1840s, and the Wyoming Territory gave women full voting rights in 1869, but only three other states, all in the West, followed this path in the nineteenth century. However, 15 states had extended full voting rights before adoption of the Nineteenth Amendment in 1920, when 19 others, mostly in the Southeast, still allowed no female suffrage at all.

Free blacks owning property could generally vote with whites in the early years of the Republic, but this privilege was gradually withdrawn as the Civil War approached, and in some states this was done much earlier. Kentucky allowed "all free male" adult citizens to vote in 1792 but withdrew this privilege from blacks seven years later. For white males, the removal of property requirements generally came a generation or so after the three pioneering states, mostly in the 1830s, but sometimes later. Chicago, in its original village charter of 1833, had full traditional taxpayers' requirements, for example. These were reduced to $3.00 in annual taxes in the city charter of 1837. Universal manhood suffrage was not authorized for Chicagoans until 1841.

The Expansion of Services

From early times, city governments controlled the common land used for pasture and recreation, operated ferry boats, maintained cemeteries, graded streets, controlled use of public firewood and timber, fixed the price for bread and beer, licensed restaurants, taverns, and liquor stores, operated public markets and fairs, and occasionally performed other tasks. Cities relied upon fees, land rents, and income from businesses, rarely upon taxes. After

Independence, the power to tax was gradually bestowed. Modern functions of government had their beginning in early America with elementary police and fire protection, the operation of public schools (beginning in New England in the seventeenth century), and some basic welfare ("relief") under the Poor Law of 1601. Water supply (though sometimes privately owned) was the first municipal utility. After about 1830, other functions were added with increasing frequency.

Charles W. Eliot, president of Harvard for 40 years, was born in Boston in 1834. He once said that as a boy he had lived in that city and remembered that it had no public water supply, no sewers anywhere in town (even when the population had reached 50,000), no street lights "to speak of," and only basic police and fire protection.[17] Yet when he died in 1926, Boston and other American cities had a line of services and functions virtually as complete, if not of the same quality, as those of today. It had all happened within the lifetime of one man (though it was a long lifetime).

Trends in Structure

By the 1840s, full-time municipal employees became necessary. The patronage system of personnel administration had always existed and had been tied to political parties at least since Jefferson's election in 1800. The simple, nontechnical tasks of the day really did make it possible to change personnel with each election. But this practice, together with the use of full-time employees, which became commonplace in the 1850s (a tumultuous and often lawless time in American cities) set the stage for the coming of the boss-and-machine system that flourished between the Civil War and World War I.

Early in the nineteenth century, the tasks of government were overseen by council committees. But as the population increased and city responsibilities expanded, council members had too little time or ability to serve as administrators, or their interests were in other things, like patronage. The New York charter of 1830 required the council to appoint administrators or boards to head various functions.

This was the beginning of departments. (Today boards and commissions are interchangeable terms, but originally commissions were established on an *ad hoc* basis, for example, to build a new city hall or install a water-supply system.) This plan was followed elsewhere, and soon the boards were made elective: in New York in 1849, in Cleveland in 1852, and then elsewhere during the remainder of the century. The extreme decentralization of city government that resulted together with the inability of the best-intentioned voters to identify able administrators, among other weaknesses in the rapidly growing cities, led to increasing dissatisfaction. The need for better administrative skills, coordinated programs and policies, sufficiently skilled employees, and less waste in government, was rapidly developing and becoming increasingly clear.

The one development in city government structure that supported better democracy during the last half of the nineteenth century was the growth in the size of councils as urban populations grew and the ethnic makeup of the nation became more complex. In cities with bicameral systems, more of them in the East than the West or South, the upper house was normally elected at large and represented *de facto* the downtown merchants, bankers, and developers. It brought citywide businesses and other economic interests into the political arena. The lower house was chosen by wards, which often were drawn along ethnic-group residential lines. Representation was more direct and specific than it is today. Council members did not, however, always simply satisfy themselves with being effective representatives of their constituents' interests as combined into an overall set of community values and goals. By seeking to gain narrow, short-range personal goals, pursue nepotism, and aid friends and neighbors by exploitation of municipal wealth, council members in many cities often demonstrated the characteristic interests that Americans had come to refer to contemptuously as "politics." Many persons, taught about democracy but not civic responsibility, had discovered that it was fun to spend other people's money for their own advantage. During this degenerate period,

council members fouled the environment in which the councils existed. They provided one instead in which corruption and pettiness thrived, and they left behind an unwanted inheritance that is still with us.

As the century waned, reformers turned to the executive for leadership. The first charters using versions of the strong-mayor plan went into effect in Brooklyn (then a separate city) in 1880 and Boston in 1885. Gradually the idea spread, in large cities at first, then into others. The centralization of bureaucratic responsibility with the coordination of activities was a result. The plan helped overcome the waste and lack of focus or purpose of the old headless system, especially when the mayor was given full appointive powers, the item veto, and from early in the twentieth century, responsibility for the executive budget. But there were problems, too. The political role of the mayor as policy developer and as the person responsible for selling a program to the public was not always compatible with carrying responsibility for day-to-day operations. The voting public could not identify a candidate with the needed administrative skills, and there was nothing to keep the candidate with the fewest such qualifications from making the strongest claims of possessing them. In large cities, the mayor lacked the needed time for some tasks. And the plan was found to be less than a copy of the corporate model of decision making that many reformers sought. Something else was needed.

With the beginning of the twentieth century came first the commission plan, introduced at Galveston, Texas, in 1901, though there were precedents for it in America.[18] The council-manager plan followed, with the first manager in 1908 and the full plan in 1911, though again there were precedents.[19] Both plans called for small councils with typically seven or fewer members. Both bicameralism and the large, representative ward council were suddenly and almost completely rejected everywhere. Subcommunity representation was not an important consideration of reformers; some were hostile to the very idea. The stories of these developments, the general failure of the former plan, and the success of the latter, which finally was the long-sought reflection of the corporation's formal model, will be well known to most readers. They can, in any case, be reviewed quickly in textbooks and other writings.[20] The commission idea, with the populistic initiative, referendum, and recall added, became the "Des Moines plan." Commission government spread rapidly at first, extending to some 500 cities by 1917. It then went into a long, permanent decline, with very few adoptions after that and with 90 percent of all adoptions being eventually abandoned. The council-manager plan, on the other hand, started a climb on the popularity charts in a trend that still has not ended. Adoptions came particularly on three large waves: First it attracted the efficiency-and-economy reformers. Next came those who hoped to save tax dollars during the Great Depression. (The plan was designed for professional administration from top to bottom, which discourages waste but not necessarily at bargain-basement prices.) Then it became the model of choice for the great suburban movement after 1945. And still today it attracts reformers seeking professionalism and efficiency, as well as most of those who are dissatisfied with the current lot of their city.[21]

In the more than two centuries during which America has been developing its own forms of local governments, we have not sought to create a large number of fundamentally different approaches to government. Rather small differences are commonplace within what are in essence two systems.

The Later Mayor-Council Plan

The mayor-council plan has carried many Jeffersonian and Jacksonian traditions into the present day, including emphasis upon the political aspects of government, separation of powers, and in the early years, a large, often bicameral council featuring easy citizen access to a member, the representation of many ethnic, social, and economic groups, dependence on grass-roots management skills, and the political party as the coordinating agent with other governments at all levels.

Through the years, the plan has followed a definitive pattern of change: From the 1880s onward, the earlier deterioration of the executive structure was gradually halted and the mayor's administrative power increased, but only a few cities have ever accepted the truly powerful mayor that we find, for example, in Boston and Detroit. Something further toward the midrange of the weak-strong continuum is the rule, and in the largest cities, the voters (and sometimes the state legislatures as well) have generally kept the mayors quite weak.[22] The "strong" (or at least strengthened) mayor was expected to provide political and policy leadership, negotiated settlements among the many council members, and at least some degree of coordinated administration among the various departments.

Later, another trend that strengthened the mayor as administrator allowed the appointment of a chief administrative officer (CAO). (Sometimes council approval was required.) This allowed the elected mayor to serve as chief executive officer of the city, to concentrate on political leadership, to maintain morale among officers and employees, and to plan policy and development. The CAO, a professional administrator, served as the chief operations officer, responsible for the daily management of the city. In practice, the powers of the CAO vary greatly from one city to another, but all adoptions recognized the unsuitability of reliance upon grass-roots administrations. The first use of this modification appears to have occurred in San Francisco in 1931, but it did not spread until after World War II. Los Angeles and Philadelphia added CAOs by charter in 1951, and gradually most large and many smaller cities did so, too.[23]

Political parties were the institution by which the Jacksonians believed they could coordinate the "bedsheet" ballot they had created. Gradually the need for leadership and coordinated policy became greater while the executive, because of the use of elective administrations, boards, and commissions, became ever weaker. The boss-and-machine system grew rapidly after the Civil War, and in the cities where it existed, the party did serve as a coordinating device. But where machines were weak or absent, the party never was effective for this purpose, and no substitute approach was found or devised. Furthermore, the possible cleansing action of party competition and turnover did not function because cities, especially machine cities, increasingly came under one dominant party. Two-party competition, except at the national level and in a few states, has always been a myth in this country.

The mighty machines, along with the capital-accumulating "robber barons," arose together with the urbanization that accompanied industrialization. The machines were villains to the middle classes, but to journalists, historians, and political scientists, they have always been glamorous, worth studying because they offered perhaps the ultimate in the pure exercise of power, at least within a democracy. But their history was short — about 80 years or three generations in all, by which time they had been defeated, not by middle-class righteousness, but because the need for them passed as the result of social change. By the mid–1950s, they were all gone except for the anomalies in Chicago and Albany, and these could not survive the deaths of their last leaders in the mid–1970s. Nonpartisanship, which spread rapidly in the early twentieth century, affected mayor-council cities but not to the extent it did the reformed cities. In 1986, 60 percent of them had nonpartisan elections, compared to 74.6 percent in commission and 81.9 percent in council-manager cities.

The councils changed greatly through time. With the beginning of bicameralism in 1797, councils began to increase in size. Although it never extended to as many as 50 percent of the cities, bicameralism suited the central business district elite, and the small, at-large upper house (usually called the select council) continued throughout its history to be dominated by community leaders. The lower house (usually called the common council) was elected by wards. The common council could expand indefinitely, indeed tended to do so, and especially along ethnic lines. Thus, as a city's population became more complex socially, its lower house grew in size.[24] Even quite small cities might have large common councils, especially those that had once been New England towns. The lower house had lit-

tle incentive to concern itself with citywide problems, and its members frequently were parochial, selfish, wasteful of the city's resources, patronage oriented, and often enough, venal. Except for parochialism, the select councils were sometimes no better. Late in the century, James Bryce, in disgust, called cities dominated by such councils the "one conspicuous failure" in American democracy.[25]

Mutterings of discontent began to make themselves heard by the 1880s. Even in cities where "reform" did not become a war cry, the council came under sharp criticism. Change started slowly, first in attempts to strengthen the office of the mayor. Then the reformers of the second decade of the new century sought to change the structure to the new forms, and this was accompanied in the cities retaining the mayor-council form with a drastic reduction in the size of the councils. Often, though not always, with the resistance of the machines, change came slowly at first, but it had been an avalanche by the 1920s. By the end of the decade, the large councils were almost all gone. Bicameralism came under vigorous attack at the same time. Today, with 50 aldermen, Chicago has the only really good-sized council. (Even it had dropped from 70 members in 1921.) By the mid–1950s, bicameralism had disappeared, unless one counts the unusual arrangement in New York.[26] Today, in mayor-council cities, the mean size of the council is 6.88 members, barely larger than council-manager cities, with 6.13.[27] There was also a rush to abandon alignment with the political parties, although never with the same eagerness as in the reformed cities. With most all cities under the partisan ballot at the turn of the century, the figure dropped rapidly in the second and third decades and continued on its path until today's figure reads but 39 percent partisan elections in mayor-council cities. In some of these cases, state law rather than local preference established the partisan ballot.

Haste, in council reform, may have had, in some cities at least, its proverbial result. In the urgent desire (1) to eliminate corruption, parochialism, and the squandering of resources, (2) to replace the "errand runner" with the "community regarding councillor," and (3) to discourage the revival of faltering machines, access and representation were undervalued as part of the currency of democracy. The efficiency-and-economy reformers, people of influence and affluence, had no need to fear lack of access and representation, but the poor and members of ethnic groups did, and it was they who paid much of the cost in establishing the new councils. They were often excluded from direct access or representation on the council, and this was true whatever the form of government put into or kept in effect.

The Changing Council-Manager Plan

The beginning-of-the-century search for a new structure of government for cities was, in effect, an effort to return to the simplicity of the American colonial system, a system in which there was no separation of powers. More directly, however, the reformers wanted to emulate the highly successful corporate structure, thinking the form would help produce the same much-admired results. The first effort, the commission plan of the beginning of the century, was a false start. It was a serious effort at reform, but its initial use in Galveston evoked the familiar "Hawthorne effect"; its encouraging results led to false hopes. Its many weaknesses are well known and need not be discussed here.[28] Use of the plan is slowly disappearing today, with only about 185 cities still clinging to it. In some of these, attempts have been made to modernize it by using professional budget and personnel officers hired on a merit basis, but for some of the deficiencies, there is no solution.

The council-manager plan finally brought to cities a form that paralleled that of the private corporation. It seems surprising that it was not developed somewhat earlier, for the essence of it was also the basis for modern school administration (except that the school superintendent traditionally has had a written contract). In its conceptualization, the plan was Hamiltonian rather than Jeffersonian, and it sought professional efficiency over political leadership and subgroup representation. It consists of a small council (most commonly five or seven members) elected at-large on a nonpartisan ballot. The council hires (and fires) a professional manager who carries out policies through a professional staff. The plan has been so widely accepted that it is in effect in about 73 percent of all the nation's cities today. Its stability and its reflection of the American mainstream is shown in the slowly aging, largely middle-class councils it produces, the increasing number of women serving on councils, the increasing educational levels of council members (nationally, more than one-fourth are college graduates), and an increasing understanding of the theory of the plan, an understanding that was often lacking in earlier days.[29]

Though successful in terms of adoptions, continued support, rarity of abandonments,[30] and compatibility with modern expectations of local government, the council-manager plan is subject to some criticisms and continues to see some changes in its role and, to some degree, its form. The same is also true, of course, of the mayor-council plan. Most interesting of all, perhaps, is that the two urban forms are slowly converging, not with a collision the likely result but with excellent prospects for the further interchange of aspects of structure and function.

The Merging Forms

The organizational needs of one city are much the same as those of another if one controls roughly for size. It is to be expected, then, that cities might drift toward one another in structural pattern. Modern methods of transportation and communication especially make this the case. Today we can point to five distinct trends toward the convergence of the two primary forms:

1. Intergovernmental relations among bureaucrats at the three levels in a federal system and including both urban forms continue on a daily basis to provide coordination of functions and activities. This task was once considered to be that of the political parties, which never did it very well, and the administrators, with their shared values, standards,

goals, and procedures, have taken over this job, resulting in the further diminution of the functional utility of parties.

2. With the success and continuing expansion of the office of CAO and the ever-wider use of the merit system, differences in professionalism between the two forms continue to diminish. Andrew Jackson could argue in 1829 that public positions could be made "so plain and simple that men of intelligence may readily qualify themselves for their performance," but training is more complex and time-consuming today. The reformed structures once featured better-trained employees, but this is no longer so in relation to well run mayor-council cities. Suitable qualifications do not differ by form of government.

3. As the role of the CAO expands, that of the city manager becomes somewhat more focused, (a) moving away from nonconsensual functions that lack agreed-upon "solutions," or means of resolution, and concentrating upon those functions for which an efficiency expert is needed,[31] and (b) serving as the city's expert on the problems and opportunities of intergovernmental relations. The manager and CAO can both act within the federal government's version of local government, which is seen primarily as an administrative structure implementing policy after its principal characteristics have been delineated in Washington. The manager and CAO have another broad and important intergovernmental task — serving as negotiators and fund finders in hunting expeditions among state and federal agencies. Despite efforts by the Reagan administration to reorient federalism, demanding and expecting the availability of funds for various purposes from Washington will remain important to cities simply because the marginal cost of raising additional funds is cheapest at that level. That economic fact of life will not change so long as the national government controls its own credit.

4. While the chief executive in mayor-council cities has always had some opportunity to function as a policy initiator or developer, this has not been the case with most mayors in council-manager cities. The indefinite responsibility for leadership other than by the manager had occasionally been a subject for criticizing the plan, especially in larger cities. Then in the late 1960s, or even a little earlier in some places, city governments came under pressure to broaden their activities into areas involving social issues having indeterminant modes of resolution, with a resulting lack of local consensus. In these areas, no experts exist (though there may be plenty of community volunteers for the role) and involvement in them can be risky for a manager because there are no likely professional payoffs and no assured peer support. But a mayor who seeks approval in the political realm rather than from peers in ICMA might find political profit in emerging as a leader on such issues, even if the problem has no known means of satisfactory resolution.[32] In cities in which this pattern of action has appeared, leadership has been divided along consensual and dissentual lines, contrary to the original conception of the plan. But this approach — we shall have to observe results for a time before deciding — may prove a strengthening factor, especially in larger cities lacking social homogeneity and values and thus make it more appropriate for today. Success will surely depend in part, however, upon the mayor's ability and willingness to recognize the areas in which the manager can act as a professional or technical expert and accept the rule that these belong to the manager. The mayor-with-CAO plan is especially well suited, at least potentially, for the assignment of functions along the lines of local value consensus or conflict. The hierarchical lines are not so clear in the council-manager plan, but developments in recent years again show the tendency toward a common approach.

5. Originally, the council-manager approach was conceived of as having a council of amateurs, representing citywide interests, making broad policy that would be carried out in a disinterested manner by professionals. The founding father, Richard S. Childs, thought one of the plan's greatest features allowed for the elimination of the errand-runner councillor.[33] But at-large, nonpartisan elections also reduced the prospects for ethnic-group or dissenting representation. As small council-manager cities with socially homoge-

neous populations grew into large cities that were much more heterogeneous, problems of representation increased. With the social unrest of the 1960s, the broadening of the local agenda, the politicization of blacks, Hispanics, and others, agitation for change became effective.[34] Unfortunately minorities have needed to resort again to the federal courts in order to achieve fair representation, possibly at the further cost of local autonomy and control. Still, even though proposed changes call for a wider use of the ward system and, in some cases, the enlargement of the council, changes that threaten a return of the errand runner and parochial councillors, they also increase opportunities for better access and representation. These are matters of no small importance when one considers that the local level is the last remaining one in which "democracy" can have any real direct, participatory meaning for the ordinary citizen.

Today, the council-manager plan is used in almost one-half of all cities of 2,500 or more population. The reform cities still are revealed in the statistics, even though the convergence trend I discuss exists. The council-manager cities lack the separation of powers characteristics of the older mayor-council model. They are more likely to make use of the initiative, referendum, and recall. They are far less likely to have a partisan ballot. The mid-nineteenth century movement to remove the mayor from the council was so successful that today only one-third of the mayor-council mayors (most of them in weak-mayor cities) still are members, far fewer than in other forms. Their right to vote (except in case of ties) is therefore greatly restricted, but they are much more likely to have the power of veto.

The mayor in mayor-council cities, given the logic of the separation of powers and the tradition since the 1820s, would logically be elected, and 98 percent of them are. On the other hand, in council-manager cities with the mayor ordinarily a member of the council and not an independent executive, greater variety may correctly be expected, with only 61.8 percent directly elected as mayor, 35.5 percent selected by the council, and the others chosen on a rotation basis or by getting the highest vote in the general election. Sim-

ilarly, with the emphasis on sharing the mayoralty, 9.3 percent of council-manager cities have limits on the number of consecutive terms that can be served in that office. Only 3.6 percent of mayor-council cities have such limits.

That most politically active persons in council-manager cities now understand the general theory of the plan can be determined, at least indirectly. Only 13.4 percent of mayors in council-manager cities have a veto power, and of these it happens that the same percentage can vote on all issues before the council. Thus, only 1.8 percent of the mayors in responding council-manager cities have what amounts to the powers of a mayor in a weak-mayor city. About three-fourths of the mayors having a veto power can vote only to break ties.

It is unlikely that one would find today a situation like that in Jackson, Michigan, in the 1930s. The city had been a pioneer in the council-manager plan, having adopted it in 1914, but much of the time the council had used local, nonprofessional managers, occasionally hiring a professional to build public works. In 1935, an unsatisfactory manager was dismissed, and his successor was hired as chauffeur for the council. (The mayor had wanted to dispense with the position altogether and use the money to build public toilets.) A reform slate, chosen in 1937, hired a professional manager who explained the theory of the plan to the council. Although council-managership had, at least formally, been in effect in Jackson for 23 years not one council member had ever before heard it explained.[35] We have come a long way from such times, at least.

Conclusion

The story of the struggle for the most desirable form of city government is a long and complicated one. It began with a simple, direct form, though one using a highly restricted suffrage. It grew more varied and complex through the nineteenth century as various new factors and pressures entered the picture. Then the trend reversed. It began to simplify and unify in the present century, though variation in detail continued to exist and perhaps always will.

As we near the beginning of another century, further convergence of the two forms seems likely, and further efforts will surely be made both to improve further the quality of the daily work of urban governments and to preserve the meaning for citizens of the democratic experience. State and national governments, except for the act of voting alone, have become for the vast numbers of people, spectator events to be witnessed on television screens. The task remaining for us all is to make certain that the opportunity is kept open for local government always to remain something more than that, something special.

Notes

1. Alexander Pope, *Essay on Man* (1734), various editions.

2. Lincoln Steffens, *Autobiography of Lincoln Steffans* (New York: Harcourt, Brace & World, Inc., 1931).

3. See Charles R. Adrian's *Governing Urban America*, 1st ed. (McGraw-Hill Books Company, Inc., 1955), pp. 172–73.

4. Robert S. Lynd and Helen M. Lynd, *Middletown* (New York: Harcourt, Brace & World, Inc., 1925) and their *Middletown in Transition* (New York: Harcourt, Brace & World, Inc., 1937).

5. Charles R. Adrian, *A History of American City Government, 1920–1945* (Lanham, Md.: University Press of America, 1987).

6. Alice Gottfried, *Boss Cermak of Chicago* (Seattle: University of Washington Press, 1962).

7. Adrian, *History*, Chapter 8.

8. As partial evidence, see Robert L. Lineberry's and Edmund P. Foster's "Reformism and Public Policies in American Cities," *American Political Science Review* 61 (September 1967): 714–17.

9. The data used in this article were collected from the survey "Forms of Government—1986," conducted by ICMA.

10. Two classic sources are Joseph P. Harris' *Election Administration in the United States* (Washington, D.C.: The Brookings Institution, 1934) and Kirk H. Porter's *A History of Suffrage in the United States* (Chicago: University of Chicago Press, 1918).

11. George H. Hallet, Jr. *Proportional Representation: The Key to Democracy*, 2nd ed. (New York: National Municipal League, 1940).

12. Belle Zeller and Hugh A. Bone, "The Repeal of P.R. in New York City: Ten Years in Retrospect," *American Political Science Review* 42 (December 1948): 1127–48.

13. Adrian, *History*, Chapter 9.

14. See William Anderson's *American City Government* (New York: Henry Holt and Co., 1925) and W.B. Munro's *Municipal Government and Administration* (New York: Macmillan Company, 1923).

15. See John F. Sly's *Town Government in Massachusetts* (Cambridge: Harvard University Press, 1930).

16. Arthur M. Schlesinger, Jr., *The Age of Jackson* (Boston: Little Brown and Company, 1945).

17. The story is repeated in Munro's *Municipal*, 99n.

18. See E.B. Schulz's, *American City Government* (Pittsburgh: Stackpole and Hack, 1949), pp. 319–21 and also Charles R. Adrian's and Ernest S. Griffith's *A History of American City Government, 1775–1870* (Lanham, Md.: University Press of America, 1976), p. 161.

19. Charles R. Adrian, *Governing Urban America*, 1st ed. (New York: McGraw-Hill Book Co., Inc., 1955), pp. 195–206.

20. See Bradley R. Rice's, *Progressive Cities: The Commission Government Movement in America* (Austin: The University of Texas Press, 1977).

21. Heywood T. Sanders, "Governmental Structure in American Cities," in *The Municipal Year Book* (Washington, D.C.: International City Management Association, 1979).

22. See Sunder's "Government Structures," Tables 4/7 and 4/8.

23. Charles R. Adrian, *Governing Urban America*, 2nd ed. (New York: McGraw-Hill Book Company, Inc., 1961), pp. 210–14.

24. Adrian and Griffith, *City Government*, Chapter 9.

25. James Byron, *The American Commonwealth* (New York: McMillan Company, 1888).

26. Charles R. Adrian, *Governing Urban America*, 1st ed. (New York: McGraw-Hill Book Company, Inc.), p. 233.

27. Heywood T. Sanders, "The Government of American Cities: Continuity and Change in Structure," in *The Municipal Year Book* (Washington, D.C.: International City Management Association, 1982), Table 3/7.

28. Rice, *Progressive*.

29. Mary A. Schellinger, "Council Profile," *Baseline Data Report*, vol. 15, no. 5 (Washington, D.C.: International City Management Association, May 1983).

30. Arthur W. Bromage, *Manager Plan Abandonments*, 5th ed. (New York: National Municipal League, 1959).

31. Charles R. Adrian and James F. Sullivan, "The Urban Appointed Chief Executive, Past and Emergent," *The Urban Interest* 1 (Spring 1979): 3–9. It is worthwhile to contrast Clarence B. Ridley's, *The Role of the City Manager in Policy Formulation* (Washington, D.C.: International City Management Association, 1958) with Keith F. Mulrooney's "Can City Managers Deal Effectively with Major Social Problems?" *Public Administration Review* 31 (January 1971): 7–9; and R.J. Stillman's *The Rise of the City Manager* (Albuquerque: University of New Mexico Press, 1974).

32. See James H. Svara's "The Mayor in Council-Manager Cities: Recognizing Leadership Potential," *National Civic Review* 75 (September-October 1986): 271–83; David A. Booth's "Are Elected Mayors a Threat to Managers?" *Administrative Science Quarterly* 12 (March 1968): 572–89; and Robert P. Boynton's and Deil S. Wright's "Mayor-Manager Relationships in Large Council-Manager Cities," *Public Administration Review* 31 (January 1971): 35–42.

33. Richard S. Childs, *Civic Victories* (New York: Harper & Row, Publishers, 1952) and his *The First Fifty Years of the Council-Manager Plan of Municipal Government* (New York: National Municipal League, 1965).

34. See Tari Renner's "Municipal Election Processes: The Impact of Minority Representation," *Baseline Data Report*, vol. 19, no. 6 (Washington, D.C.: International City Management Association, November-December, 1987); Howard D. Neighbor's "The Case Against Non-partisanship: A Challenge from the Courts," *National Civic Review* 66 (October 1977): 447–51; and his "The Supreme Court Speaks, Sort of, on the 1982 Voting Rights Act Amendments," *National Civic Review* 75 (November-December 1986): 346–53.

35. Charles R. Adrian, *A History of American City Government, 1920–1945* (Lanham, Md.: University Press of America, 1987), pp. 477–79.

CHAPTER 7

CONTEMPORARY CHOICES FOR CITIZENS

Julianne Duvall

The structure of municipal government — how it is organized — refers to the way in which the powers and responsibilities of the government are divided among the elected and the appointed city officials. The manner in which a local government is structured is important, as the operation of local government is directly affected by its organizational structure.

There are currently four basic forms of municipal government in the United States: Mayor-Council, Council-Manager, Commission, and Town Meeting. This chapter will describe each of the four forms of government, trace the history of each, present the perceived advantages and disadvantages of each form, and illustrate the division of responsibilities characteristic to each form. This chapter then discusses usage trends and illustrates the proportions of American cities operating under each form in selected years from 1950 to present.

This chapter also documents the historical changes in the forms of government used by U.S. municipalities with populations of over 5,000 for the years 1952 to 1987 (Table 1, page 64). A thumbnail reference guide to the pros and cons of each form of government described in this chapter is also provided (Table 2, page 65).

Forms of Local Governance

MAYOR-COUNCIL FORM OF GOVERNMENT

The use of the mayor-council form of government was imported from England during the colonial period. At that time, the colonial council was all powerful and the mayor was appointed by the colonial governor. The functions of city government were few and the citizens of the newly-formed states, having overthrown the British king, were afraid to give powers to a single executive. The popular feeling prevailed that an official with few powers could do relatively little damage.

Under this "weak mayor" form, the mayor's administrative powers were very limited in proportion to the powers of the council, especially in the areas of budget-making and the appointment and removal of subordinate officers and employees; the mayor was chief executive in name only.

As time passed, American city government underwent many changes: general control over cities became the responsibility of state legislatures; popular election of city councils was established, though with a restricted electorate; and bicameral councils became a common characteristic of city government that continued into the 20th century. During this time, the mayor was not an independent official elected by the people, but rather he

Originally published as "Choices of the Citizenry: Forms of Municipal Government in the U.S.," *Issue Brief,* May 1989. Published by the National League of Cities, Washington, D.C. Reprinted with permission of the publisher.

Table 1
Form of Government in U.S. Cities Over 5,000 Population

Year	Total Cities	Mayor-Council No.	Percent	Council-Manager No.	Percent	Commission No.	Percent	Town Meeting/RTM No.	Percent
1952	2,525	1,388	55.0	658	26.1	390	15.3	89	3.6
1957	2,653	1,297	48.9	834	31.4	328	12.3	94	3.5
1962	3,087	1,622	52.5	1,130	36.6	259	8.4	33	1.1
1967	3,155	1,600	50.7	1,245	39.5	243	7.7	66	2.1
1972	1,875	825	44.0	886	47.2	111	5.9	53	2.8
1977	3,881	1,803	46.4	1,704	43.9	161	4.1	213	5.4
1982	4,318	2,054	47.5	1,847	42.7	140	3.2	277	6.4
1987	4,360	2,082	47.9	1,866	42.8	135	3.0	277	6.3

Source: ICMA *Municipal Yearbook* for years indicated.

was selected by the council for a one-year term of largely ceremonial duties.

In 1797, Baltimore, Maryland, became the first major city to give its mayor the power to veto council ordinances. In 1822, Boston, Massachusetts, adopted direct election of the mayor by the people. In 1830, New York's mayor received an absolute veto power. By 1850, the mayor had become the chief administrative officer in many American municipalities. Despite these tendencies to strengthen the mayor, 19th century local government was dominated by the council and the weak mayor form of government was the almost universal system of local government in the United States.

Weak Mayor Form of Government

Characteristics. The weak mayor form of government is characterized by a powerful, relatively large council which carries out administrative functions such as budget preparation, makes all major appointments, and approves the hiring and dismissal of lower level employees. Under this form, there are many council committees, administrative boards, and commissions which exist and operate with considerable independence of the regular city government. These boards are generally created either to remove a particular municipal function from the political setting or because there is little confidence that city government can administer the service in a business-like way.

In addition to the position of mayor, there are many elective offices, including some department heads. The mayor has very restricted powers: limited or no veto power, limited or no appointment and removal power, and no important administrative functions.

Advantages and Disadvantages. Those favoring the weak mayor form argue that this is the original approach to municipal government and that there is a long historical tradition and much experience upon which to build. It has worked well in many small communities, particularly in rural areas. Proponents conclude that this form's representative council, with maximum authority, has a real potential to meet the needs of its constituents. The city of Minneapolis is an example of the weak mayor form of municipal government.

Opponents of the weak mayor form argue that under this plan responsibility, as well as power, are diffused. There is a lack of strong leadership, and the form makes no provision for professional administration. Particularly in larger cities, the political vacuum caused by adherence to this form invites "machine" politics, and various types of political manipulation. Cooperative working agreements are of great importance in the weak mayor form of government; if these informal agreements break down, the local government is unable to accomplish its tasks.

Table 2
Summary of Advantages and Disadvantages of Each Form of Municipal Government

Advantages	Disadvantages
Weak Mayor	
• Long historical tradition • Elected representative council to meet constituents' needs • Has worked well in small and rural localities	• Power and responsibility diffused • Lack of strong leadership • Political vacuum may lead to "boss-ism" and "machine" politics
Strong Mayor	
• Strong leadership with centralized responsibility • Facilitates policy formulation and implementation	• Too much responsibility for one person • Mayor may not be a professional administrator
Council-Manager	
• Professional manager in charge of managing city • Council retains policy control • City run in business-like manner	• No strong, effective political leadership • Tendency for manager to usurp policy functions • Manager may be a stranger to the city, seeking only to advance his/her career
Commission	
• Has worked well in emergency situations • Simple organizational structure • Swift direct implementation of policy	• Legislative and policy functions held by one body • No checks and balances • No one person with overall administrative responsibility • Difficult to elect legislators with administrative abilities
Town Meeting/Representative Town Meeting	
• "Purest" form of democracy • Allows all voters a say in how town is run • Deep historical tradition • Has worked well in small localities	• Difficult to do long-range planning • Challenging to educate all citizens adequately • Preparing warrant may be cumbersome process • Annual meetings poorly attended

Strong Mayor Form of Government

In the latter part of the 19th century, larger American cities sought to simplify their organizational structure, to strengthen the office of the mayor, and to eliminate some or all of the separately elected municipal officials. Thus, the "strong mayor" form of municipal government emerged.

In 1880, the city of Brooklyn, New York, adopted the strong mayor form, and in 1898, New York City followed. The citizens of large cities looked to embrace a strong and honest administration. The strong mayor, a responsible leader politically accountable to all the people, could act in many cases as a foil to the "machine."

Characteristics. The strong mayor plan takes the executive power away from the council and vests it in the mayor. It rejects the widespread scattering of administrative responsibilities, provides for an executive budget, and enables the mayor to assume direction of an integrated and administrative structure. The strong mayor does not hold membership in the council but does exercise veto power over council actions. As chief executive of the city, the strong mayor is granted authority to appoint and to remove department heads and other officials. The city council is charged with legislative functions and the plethora of boards and commissions found under the weak mayor form is often absent in the strong mayor structure.

Advantages and Disadvantages. Proponents of the strong mayor form contend that it provides strong political and administrative leadership for the city. It does away with the broad division of responsibilities which is one perceived defect of the weak mayor system. The strong mayor has both the responsibility for running the city and the authority necessary to carry out this task. Policy formulation and implementation are often facilitated by this form. The council, relieved of day-to-day administrative tasks, can focus on the major public needs of the city.

Opponents of the strong mayor plan contend that one person is handling both political and administrative functions and that there is no assurance that the mayor will have professional administrative capabilities. Many cities, particularly larger ones, have overcome this argument by permitting the mayor to appoint a professional administrator. The mayor remains the center of government leadership and public responsibility.

Council-Manager Form of Government

The council-manager plan traces its roots to Staunton, Virginia, where, in 1908, the bicameral city council enacted an ordinance creating the office of "general manager." Dayton, Ohio, was the first relatively large city to put the manager form into operation; in 1914, a commission-manager form was installed to help the city cope with damages caused by a major flood. In the 20th century, the council-manager form of municipal government has been the fastest growing form.

Characteristics. The council-manager form is similar in structure to a private corporation, with the voters, council, and manager being organizationally similar to the stockholders, board of directors, and corporate general manager. There are few elective officers — usually only the council — with the mayor generally selected by and from the council to serve as a titular and ceremonial leader and to preside at council meetings. The policy-making legislative body is the council. The manager is a full-time professional executive charged with the administration of municipal affairs, appointed by, responsible to, and subject to dismissal by the council. The manager's tenure is based solely on performance.

Advantages and Disadvantages. Proponents of the council-manager plan point out that the presence of a professional manager in charge of the city allows the city to be run in a businesslike way. As the people's representatives, the council retains control of policy.

Opponents of the plan cite the lack of strong, effective political leadership, that the manager is not directly accountable to the electorate, who have only indirect control over their council-appointed administrator. They argue that the manager may be only a transitory stranger in charge of municipal affairs, using the city only as a rung on his career ladder.

Commission Form of Government

Between 1870 and 1891, several southern cities, such as New Orleans, Louisiana, and Mobile, Alabama, had a commission form of government, but subsequently abandoned it. In 1901, Galveston, Texas, adopted the commission form with three commissioners to be appointed by the governor and two to be elected by the voters. Within three years, all five commissioners' positions were made elective by judicial decision. Galveston's successful rebuilding of its hurricane-devastated city under this new form led to its adoption in Des Moines, Iowa, in 1907. Innovations were added, resulting in what became known as the Des Moines Plan, a commission form of government plus the initiative, referendum, recall petitions, non-partisan election, and civil service merit system.

Characteristics. Commission government provides for the election of a small number of commissioners (typically three, five or seven) who hold all legislative and executive powers of city government. Collectively, sitting as a single body, the commissioners perform the duties of the city council — pass resolutions, enact ordinances, levy taxes, and appropriate funds. Individually, each commissioner is the administrative head of a major city department, such as public works, police, fire, health, or finance. Each city activity is thus under the authority of only one commissioner.

In its role as city council, the commission is presided over by one of its members who is usually titled as mayor. The mayor may be elected directly by the people or selected by the commission. The mayor has no power of veto and no administrative powers beyond the city department which he oversees.

This form of municipal government is currently in decline. A number of cities, including Birmingham, Alabama; Topeka, Kansas; and Tulsa, Oklahoma; have all recently changed their city charters to adopt the Mayor-Council form of government.

Advantages and Disadvantages. Proponents of the commission form of municipal government point out that historically this plan has worked extremely well in emergency situations and that city government is simplified by the centralization of power and authority. Commission government gives to a few people the power and authority to run city government, avoiding possible abuses inherent in giving all powers to one person. The commission plan usually includes methods for direct public intervention in government — initiative, referendum, and recall.

Opponents of the plan point out that there is both too much and too little centralization: too much in placing both the legislative and administrative powers in the same hands, and too little because the whole city administration is neatly divided into a part for each commissioner. Opponents also cite a lack of effective leadership, with no one having overall administrative responsibility and the difficulty of selecting a person who is qualified to both represent the voter's interests on the city council and be a competent professional administrator to head up a city government department.

Town Meeting

The town meeting form of government, almost exclusively found in the New England states, is a form of local government that also has its roots in colonial America. It is the pure form of direct democracy, as every voter in the community has the opportunity to participate in the law-making process by expressing his or her own views, trying to convince other citizens, and voting on public matters.

In New England, the town is the principal kind of rural or noncity government. The town is an area of government that includes whatever villages there may be, plus the open country. Except where a municipality has been incorporated, the town performs most of the functions a county does elsewhere.

As the population of a community increases, a modification of this form may be instituted. Known as the Representative Town Meeting, this newer plan features town voters choosing a number of citizens (usually one hundred or more) to represent them at meetings. Any voter may still attend and participate in the discussions, but only the representatives may vote. In localities operating under the Representative Town Meeting, selectmen and other officers also are elected to supervise the administration of the local laws.

Characteristics. Town meeting assemblies usually choose a board of selectmen, generally consisting of three to five members, who carry on the business of the town between meetings, have charge of town property, grant licenses, supervise other town officials, and call special town meetings. A town clerk, treasurer, assessor, constable, school board, and other officers are elected by the voters or appointed by the selectmen. The town meeting participants often elect a finance committee to prepare the town budget.

Town meetings, both regular and special, must be preceded by a warrant, an official document that gives notice of the date, time, and location of the meeting, specifies the items to be discussed at the meeting, and authorizes the meeting. The preparation and issue of the warrant is primarily a duty of the selectmen.

Advantages and Disadvantages. Proponents of the town meeting form of government point out that this structure represents a pure form of democracy, in that all registered voters may participate fully in any meeting. Outside of the structure for annual meetings, the town meeting form of organization resembles the Weak Mayor-Council form, except there is no mayor, only a president of the council, and no one has veto power. More and more commonly, the selectmen choose a manager and assign routine administrative tasks to him/her.

There are also some difficulties with this form of government. It is difficult for the town government to do much long-range planning, meeting attendance is often very low because citizens cannot or will not spend the time (often more than a day) that the meeting occupies. It is also difficult to ensure that citizens understand the complex issues and have sufficient background to vote responsibly on issues placed before them. Preparation of the warrant announcing the meeting can become a laborious task, especially regarding the budget: each line item of the budget becomes a separate article of business on the agenda.

Despite these difficulties, town meeting is still a viable form of local government in many municipalities. Some have overcome the challenges of this form by appointing a town manager or an administrative assistant to handle day-to-day operations of their communities.

Trends in Form Usage

The form of municipal government utilized by a locality is a tool; it makes a difference as to how a community is governed and as to which groups and interests in the municipality are most influential. Local cultural circumstances help determine the type of structure that is utilized and how the form is modified to fit the local situation. For these reasons, there is no one form of government that is appropriate to all municipalities.

In the 23 very large cities with populations of 500,000 or more (based on 1986 Bureau of the Census estimates), 19 have Mayor-Council form of government, while the remaining four have Council-Manager government. Among all 182 cities with a population of 100,000 or more, 77 (42.3 percent) are organized under the Mayor-Council form, 102 (56.0 percent) employ the Council-Manager form, and only 3 (1.6 percent) use the Commission form. None of these cities has a Town Meeting form of government.

The percentage of large cities employing the various forms do not hold when examining cities of smaller size. A report of 4,360 cities with populations of 5,000 or more contained in the 1987 *Municipal Yearbook* finds that 2,082 (47.9 percent) have Mayor-Council form, 1,866 (42.8 percent) have Council-Manager form, 135 (3 percent) have Commission form, and 277 (6.3 percent) have Town Meeting form of municipal government.

Over the past 35 years, these figures have varied somewhat due to two readily identifiable factors: 1) an increasing number of municipalities whose populations reach the 5,000 mark; and 2) municipal changes in the form of government employed. Table 1 illustrates the historical changes in forms of government used by U.S. municipalities.

CHAPTER 8

THE COUNCIL-MANAGER
FORM OF GOVERNMENT

Roger L. Kemp

Businessmen have been convinced for many years that professional managers are essential to their organizations. Professional managers are trained for their jobs through formal education and experience. The professional manager uses analytical skills to solve business problems in the best long-term interests of the company, and is guided by a code of professional ethics that avoids conflicts-of-interest. These attributes apply to business managers as well as to the managers of local governments.[1]

Business firms spend substantial amounts of money for training and educational programs to foster the development of their professional managers. Unfortunately, the need for professional managers and their continuing development and training is not always recognized in local governments.[2] Certainly, city governments are big businesses. Usually, they are the largest employers in the city, have expenditure levels comparable to large private sector companies, and have borrowings of an equal scale.

We want our city governments to be run by our elected representatives. Because of this, we frequently have difficulty reconciling the need for professional management with the role of the elected officials. The council-manager form of government provides the best answer to effective leadership by the mayor and city council, and a professional approach to solving the city's problems. The record of Amer-

ican cities and their accomplishments attests to this form of government.[3]

This chapter will set forth the different forms of local government in the United States, outline the history of the council-manager form of municipal government, including its success and popularity, examine the duties of a typical city manager, and analyze the factors that should be taken into consideration before implementing a desirable plan to manage a city — regardless of what form it takes. Any plan of government, naturally, should be in keeping with the wishes of the people as expressed through their publicly elected representatives.

Different Forms
of Local Government

There are several workable forms of local government. They usually depend upon the role of the central government, and the degree of home-rule powers given to cities in running the affairs of communities. The typical types of local governments in the United States include — strong mayor, commission, mayor-council, and council-manager plans. The characteristics of each are highlighted below.

Strong Mayor. In many large cities in America, the mayor is elected to "lead" the city. This typically includes running the municipal

---

Reprinted with permission of the publisher from *Current Municipal Problems,* published by West Group, 155 Pfingsten Road, Deerfield IL 60015.

organization through city employees, with the top management being selected by the mayor. This plan has its obvious advantages and disadvantages, depending upon the qualifications of the person elected as the mayor. A good political leader is sometimes not a good municipal administrator. Hiring trained administrators has served to overcome this shortcoming.[4]

Commission. This form of government, which usually employs nonpartisan, at-large elections, includes a board of commissioners. Collectively they serve as the legislative body. Individually, each commissioner serves as the head of one or more administrative departments. The municipal reform movement in the United States has all but led to the demise of this type of local government. Its weaknesses are obvious, since few elected leaders possess the necessary requirements to operate large portions of a municipal organization.[5]

Mayor-Council. This form has a legislative body that is elected either at-large, by ward or district, or by some combination of the two (e.g., some at-large and others by district). The distinguishing characteristics of this plan are two. One, the mayor is elected separately, and two, the official designation of the Office of the Mayor is the formal head of the city government. Depending upon local laws, the powers of the mayor may vary greatly, from limited ceremonial duties to full-scale authority to appoint and remove department managers. The mayor sometimes has veto power over the city council.[6]

Council-Manager. This form of government has a legislative body elected by popular vote. They are responsible for policymaking, while the management of the organization is under the direction of a city manager. The council appoints and removes the manager by majority vote. The mayor is a member of the council, with no special veto or administrative powers. The mayor is, however, the community's recognized political leader and represents the city at official ceremonies, as well as civic and social functions.[7]

The strong mayor form is limited to some large cities in most states. It is seldom the form used in small and medium-sized communities. The commission plan, while still in existence in a few cities in selected states, is not in widespread use. Because of its inherent limitations, it is not perceived as a model of municipal organization. The mayor-council plan exists primarily in larger cities. The city manager, or chief administrative officer, is appointed by the entire city council. The duties of the administrator vary from city to city. This plan works well when implemented properly, but is not increasing in number among local governments.

The council-manager plan, the topic of this article, is the most successful and popular model of local government in most communities across America. Some facts about this plan are summarized below.[8]

- Nearly 2,500 cities in the United States operate under this plan.
- Almost 80 percent of cities recognized by the International City Management Association operate under this form of government.
- It is the single most popular form of government in cities over 10,000 in population.
- Dade County, Florida (pop. 1,625,979) is the largest council-manager jurisdiction in the United States.
- Larger council-manager cities in America include Dallas, Texas; San Diego, California; San Jose, California; and Rochester, New York.
- 77 counties in the United States operate under this plan.
- This form of government represents over 100 million citizens in America.
- The council-manager plan is adopted more than once each week by a city or county, on the average, since 1945 (75 local governments adopt this plan each year).
- This form of government is growing faster than any other form of local government because of its popularity.

History and Growth of the Council-Manager Plan

The council-manager plan of local government has been called one of the few original

American contributions to political theory. Half a century after the first city manager experiment in Staunton, Virginia, one out of four Americans live in a city organized under this plan, and nearly 2,500 in the United States are run by city managers, with the political leadership and policymaking being provided by locally elected representatives. The council-manager plan was a product of the Progressive reform era in local politics and is now three-quarters of a century old. The various factors leading to the growth and popularity of this form of municipal government are examined in the following paragraphs.

While the plan developed slowly, it was the product of several ideas and forces that shaped political management thought in America. Among those factors that affected its development most significantly were the growth of urbanization, the popularity of business and corporate ideals, the Progressive reform movement, and the professional public administration movement. These ideological and social roots of the council-manager plan are highlighted below.

Growth of Urbanization. Urbanization at the turn of the century dramatically changed the landscape of cities across the nation. During this time, towns and cities experienced rapid growth. While the rural population doubled, the urban population grew seven times its previous size. Urbanization quickly converted villages to towns, towns into cities, and cities into metropolitan centers. The rise of cities during this era was attributable to numerous social and economic forces, including the decline of agricultural industry, the rise of modern industries, the expansion of the economy generally, positive governmental and financial incentives for industrial growth, and a massive influx of overseas immigrants. Urbanization placed unprecedented demands on local governments throughout the country for additional public facilities and services. These factors led to the need for specialized expertise to manage the various facets of local governments.[9]

Popularity of Business and Corporate Ideals. Businessmen and the public concept of the corporation have been instrumental in determining public values. The success of corpora-

tions in the private sector had a significant influence on American political and administrative thought. Probably no political or administrative philosophy reflects business practices and corporate ideals more clearly than the growth of the council-manager plan. Many citizens still compare the operation of local government with that of the private corporation. The elected representatives are the board of directors, the city manager is the general manager, and the citizens of the community are the stockholders of the government.[10] Economy and efficiency, two primary values of the business community, are foundations of the council-manager plan.[11]

Progressive Reform Movement. Many of the effects of rapid urbanization, particularly the early political machines and large monopolistic corporations, met with disfavor among many citizens, who were known as Progressives. These individuals, who formed a significant movement because of their large numbers, felt that the best interests of the public were frequently not being served by the existing political processes and some large corporations that were perceived as being too strong and having too much power over common people. One of the most significant municipal reforms developed and supported by the Progressives was the council-manager plan. The management concepts embodied in this plan ideally suited the Progressive political philosophy of the time — a competent professional manager and public policy established by nonpartisan elected representatives. The manager's apolitical qualities suited the Progressive values, which favored impartiality and looked down upon personality politics and favoritism. Two key Progressive ideals, equality of participation in the political process and centralized administrative authority, were well balanced in the council-manager plan.[12]

Public Administration Movement. The modern city management profession also fits with the emerging "modern" concepts of public management in the early 1900s. Many administrative scholars espoused a sharp division between policy determination and policy implementation. Many scholars of the time drew a sharp distinction between "politics" and "administration."[13] The council-manager plan incorporated the ideals of the separation of policymaking and the implementation of public policy. The elected representatives are responsible for setting public policy; the city manager is concerned with its implementation. The separation of these two tasks formed the basis of the emerging council-manager form of local government.[14]

As the Progressive movement emerged and spread, the public administration thought of the time, together with the growth of urbanization, and the increasing popularity of business and corporate ideals, provided the positive background against which the council-manager plan blossomed into national popularity. All of these ideological and social forces provided the positive environment in which the council-manager plan spread from city to city across the landscape of America's local governments.

The City Manager's Role

The council-manager plan emphasizes the separation of the roles of policymaking and the administration of operating a city. The public officials, elected by the people, set the policy of the municipal organization. The city manager, appointed by the elected officials, is responsible for the implementation of the policy, as well as running the daily duties of the ongoing organization. The city manager is solely responsible to the elected representatives, and can normally be terminated at will if he or she does not perform the job properly. The typical duties of the city manager include, but are not limited to, the following tasks[15]:

- The administration of the management affairs of the city.
- Appointing and removing (for cause) all employees of the municipal organization.
- All employees, including the management staff, are hired based on their professional qualifications and experience in municipal affairs.
- Preparation, along with the financial staff, of the annual budget. While the budget is approved by the elected

officials, it is implemented by the management staff.
- Keeping the elected officials informed about the financial condition of the city, including revenue and expenditure projections.
- Recommends salary and pay schedules for each appointive position. While competitive salaries and wages are desirable, the ability to pay also enters into the picture.
- In addition to implementing policies, the city manager makes policy recommendations to the elected officials consistent with sound management practices.
- Recommends the organizational structure, all reorganizations and consolidations, for the efficient and effective operation of the municipal organization.
- Attends all meetings of the city council, except when excused in advance. The manager is also required to advertise and post public notices of all such meetings.
- Supervise the acquisition of all materials, supplies, and equipment that are in the approved budget. The manager also supervises the awarding of all contracts for services within the amounts specified by the elected officials.
- All contracts above a specified amount are subject to competitive bidding procedures, usually by receiving "sealed" bids by a specified date. Contracts are awarded to the lowest responsible bidder.
- When services or contracts are necessary, and not in the approved budget, an additional approval is needed from the elected officials prior to awarding the contract.
- Rules governing the purchase of goods and services, and the awarding of contracts, are normally recommended by the city manager and approved by the elected officials. All such policies must be consistent with applicable laws.
- The city manager ensures that all laws and policies approved by the elected officials are enforced equally throughout the city. Old and outdated laws are

periodically revised or eliminated as appropriate.

- Investigates all citizen complaints, and problems in the administrative organization. The manager recommends changes, as necessary, to the elected officials for their approval.
- The city manager is required to devote his or her entire time to the discharge of all official duties. Any outside employment is usually approved in advance by the elected representatives to ensure that no conflict-of-interest exists.

The Future of the Council-Manager Plan

There are several different forms of governmental structure that cities can adopt including, among others, the strong mayor form, the commission type, the mayor-council plan, as well as the council-manager model. Each structure's strengths and weaknesses lie in the eyes of the constituent, the political office holder, the professional government manager, or the employees of the municipal organization. The particular form to select is not an easy decision to make. Certainly, elected leaders, above all, want to be responsive to their constituents. For many communities in America, the council-manager plan has a proven track record of success.

Nearly 2,500 cities in the United States operate under the traditional council-manager plan, with its separation between the policy-making role of elected officials and the implementation of the policy being left to the professional government manager. This is the most successful and popular form of government in cities over 10,000 in population. Some of the larger cities in America have also been successful in implementing the council-manager plan. The fact that this form of government has been adopted on the average of once each week by a city or county in the United States since 1945 attests to the desirability of this model of municipal government representation. Because of its popularity among citizens, it is the fastest growing form of local government in America.

The form of local government a city selects should best serve the needs of the people. Voters elect their representatives, based on their confidence, not only to set public policies, but also to see to it that policies are implemented into programs and services to serve the community. If the council-manager plan best serves this goal, it may be the most desirable form of local government. If another form of governmental structure is utilized, be it the strong mayor form, the commission type, the mayor-council model, or some other combination of these, it should embody the representational needs of citizens. The form of government best suited for a particular city should be determined through the electoral process. No system of government is perfect, nor can any single system represent the wishes of all of the people all of the time. When the form of local government selected represents the wishes of the majority of the people, this is the form that best serves the democratic process and the will of the people.

Notes

1. Jonathon Justin, Professional Management and Responsive Government 267, *National Civic Review*, National Municipal League, Inc., New York, New York, June 1978.

2. Ibid.

3. Ibid.

4. Charles R. Adrian, Governing Urban America 214, McGraw Hill Pub. Co., Inc., New York, NY, 1977.

5. Ibid.

6. Ibid.

7. Ibid.

8. International City Management Association, Facts on the Council-Manager Plan 1, International City Management Assn., Washington, D.C., Sept. 1982.

9. Stillman, Richard J., *The Rise of the City Manager* 6, 7, University of New Mexico Press, Albuquerque, New Mexico, 1974.

10. Ibid., page 8.

11. Several early books on city managers include a discussion on the business values of the council-manager plan, for example: Harry A. Toulmin, *The City Manager*, D. Appleton & Co., New York, New York, 1915, and Robert Rightor, *The City Manager in Dayton*, National Municipal League, Inc., New York, New York, 1919.

12. Stillman, note 9 supra, at 8,9.

13. For example, see Frank J. Goodnow, *Politics and Administration*, 16, Macmillan Co., New York, New York, 1900.

14. Stillman, note 9 supra, at 10,11.

15. International City Management Association, Ordinance for Establishing Council-Manager Plan 2, 3, International City Management Association, Washington, D.C., undated.

Bibliography

Adrian, *Governing Urban America*, McGraw Hill Pub. Co., New York, New York, 1977.

Banfield & Wilson, *City Politics*, Harvard University Press, Cambridge, Massachusetts, 1963.

Booth, *Council-Manager Government in Small Cities, Public Management*, International City Management Assn., Washington, D.C., November 1973.

Boynton, *The Council-Manager Plan: A Historical Perspective, Public Management*, International City Management Assn., Washington, D.C., October 1974.

International City Management Association, *The Council-Manager Plan: Answers to Your Questions*, International City Management Assn., Washington, D.C., February 1980.

_____, *Citizens' Guide to Council-Manager Plan: An Annotated Bibliography*, International City Management Assn., Washington, D.C., 1975.

_____, *Facts on the Council-Manager Plan*, International City Management Assn., Washington, D.C., September 1982.

Justin, "Professional Management and Responsive Government," *National Civic Review*, National Municipal League, Inc., New York, New York, June 1978.

Kennedy, "Should Your Town Have a Professional Manager?," *The Massachusetts Selectman*, Vol. XXXVI, No. 1, Massachusetts Municipal Assn., Boston, Massachusetts, Winter 1977.

Mosher, *Democracy and the Public Service*, Oxford University Press, New York, New York, 1968.

Mardis & Heisel, *When the Manager Plan Comes to Town*, Nation's Cities, National League of Cities, Washington, D.C., May 1971.

National Municipal League, *Questions and Answers About the Council-Manager Plan*, National Municipal League, Inc., New York, New York, 1974.

Nolting, *The Mayor's Right Hand*, Nation's Cities, National League of Cities, Washington, D.C., May 1974.

Stene, *Selecting a Professional Administrator: A Guide for Municipal Councils*, International City Management Assn., Washington, D.C. 1972.

Stillman, *The Rise of the City Manager*, University of New Mexico Press, Albuquerque, New Mexico, 1974.

Waldo, *The Administrative State*, Ronald Press, New York, New York, 1948.

CHAPTER 9

UNDERSTANDING THE ROLE OF THE MAYOR'S OFFICE

James H. Svara

In November of odd-numbered years, cities throughout North Carolina hold elections to choose their mayor. Nearly a third of them — virtually all cities with over 5,000 population — use the council-manager form of government. The office of mayor in those cities — that is, council-manager cities — is probably the most misunderstood leadership position in government. Some of us may think of a mayor in North Carolina as being comparable with mayors of cities in certain other states, who occupy a true executive office (most visibly, the big-city mayors of the North). Others of us may dismiss the mayor as a figurehead. North Carolina's nonexecutive mayors are commonly perceived either to be doing less than they actually are or to have more power to act than state law and the municipal charter give them. Mayors in council-manager cities are not mere ribbon-cutters and gavel-pounders, nor are they the driving force in city government. What they are — somewhere between the two stereotypes — is an important leader who can strongly influence how well city government performs.

It is difficult for voters to know how to assess candidates for mayor. Those who seek and hold the office may also need to know more about the position and the realistic potential inherent in it. Mayoral candidates, borrowing a page from the campaign book of the executive mayor, often present themselves as the leader who will take charge of city government and propose bold solutions to the city's problems. Once elected, however, they will have difficulty in following through. Although he or she has the title of mayor and some of the popular expectations for leadership associated with the title, the North Carolina mayor has no powers on which to base true executive leadership and must depend on other officials, elected and appointed, for most of what he accomplishes. He lacks both the ability to initiate policies on his own and the legal authority to implement those policies.

Let's look at the office of council-manager mayor in order to help voters know what qualities to look for in a candidate and to suggest to officeholders and candidates how they can best fill that post.

The Nature of the Office

The council-manager mayor is analogous to a company's chairman of the board, important but not crucial to the organization's operation. The government may operate adequately with minimal leadership from the mayor, since the plural executive organization provided by the council spreads out the responsibility for policy initiation. In addition, the manager has considerable informal influence, based on expertise and staff support, over the generation of proposals, and he has formal authority to direct implementation.

Originally published as "Understanding the Mayor's Office in Council-Manager Cities," *Popular Government*, Vol. 51, No. 2, Fall 1985. Reprinted by permission of the Institute of Government, University of North Carolina at Chapel Hill.

Still, the "chairman" mayor can have an impact on governmental performance through contributions to the governing process that, though different from those of the "executive" mayor, are still important.

The elements of leadership can be organized in two categories. One category is a coordinative function in which the mayor is more or less active at pulling together the parts of the system to improve their interaction. The parts are the council, manager/staff, and public; the mayor has a special and close relationship with each. By virtue of his favored position, the mayor can tap into various communication networks among elected officials, governmental staff, and community leaders. Although they can and do interact with each other independently, the mayor — if he has done his homework — can transmit messages better than anyone else in the government because of his broad knowledge. He therefore has a unique potential to expand the level of understanding and improve the coordination among the participants in city government.

The second element is guidance in the initiation of policy, which may be done as part of the coordinating function or separately. The mayor not only channels communication but may also influence and shape the messages being transmitted. He can also use more dramatic techniques to raise issues and put forth proposals, but these must be used cautiously because he runs the risk of alienating the council, whose support he needs to be effective.

Variety of Roles

It is a testament to the diffuseness of the mayor's job that there is such variation in how the job is perceived, once one goes beyond formal responsibilities.[1] In a series of interviews with and about the mayors of North Carolina's five largest cities (Charlotte, Winston-Salem, Greensboro, Raleigh, Durham) the mayors, council members, and community leaders were asked to describe the mayor's responsibilities and roles in their city. The responses revealed ten roles, which can be grouped into four dimensions of leadership —

i.e., major areas in which a mayor may contribute to the functioning of city government. Whether he engages in the roles and how well he handles them are questions that provide the basis for distinguishing among types of mayoral leadership, which are addressed in the next section. The dimensions and roles of leadership are listed in Table 1 page 77.

Ceremony and presiding. The *ceremonial* function is the dimension of leadership that observers of city government typically see. The mayor is in heavy demand for appearances at many and various meetings, dinners, and other special occasions. He also serves as *spokesman for the council*, enunciating positions taken, informing the public about coming business, and fielding questions about the city's policies and intentions. In these two activities, the mayor builds an extensive contact with the public and the media, which can be a valuable resource. In addition, the mayor *presides* at meetings. In so doing, he sets the tone for meetings and may exert mild influence over outcomes by guiding the debate, by drawing more from some witnesses and limiting the contributions of others, and by determining the timing of resolution of issues. Councils often face difficult choices and, like small groups generally, depend to some extent on the resolve of the leader either to decide or to delay.

Communication and facilitation. Beyond simply transmitting council views to the public, the mayor may also serve as an *educator*. In his relations with the council, the public, the media, and or the manager and staff, the mayor identifies issues or problems for consideration, promotes awareness of important concerns, and seeks to expand citywide understanding by providing information. In this activity, he is not primarily promoting an idea, as in the activities discussed below, but informing and educating. For example, the mayor who systematically speaks to the press and groups about the increasing imbalance between needs and revenues helps to prepare the public for a tax increase at budget time.

As *liaison* person with the manager, he links the two major components of the system — the legislative body and administrative apparatus — and can facilitate communication

Table 1
Dimensions and Roles of Mayoral
Leadership in Council-Manager Cities

— Roles are identified by letters A–J.
— Dimensions are indicated by numbers I–IV.

I. Ceremony and Presiding: the typically perceived type of leadership
  A. Ceremonial tasks
  B. Spokesman for council
  C. Presiding officer
II. Communication and Facilitation
  D. Educator: informational and educational tasks vis-a-vis the council, manager, and/or public.
  E. Liaison with manager: promotes informal exhange between the council and the manager and staff.
  F. Team leader: coalescing the council, building consensus, and enhancing group performance.
III. Organization and Guidance
  G. Goal-setter: setting goals and objectives for council and manager; identifying problems; establishing tone for the council.
  H. Organizer: stabilizing relationships; guiding the council to recognition of its roles and responsibilities; defining and adjusting the relationship with the manager.
  I. Policy advocate: developing programs; lining up support for or opposition to proposals.
IV. Promotion
  J. Promoter: promoting and defending the city; seeking investment; handling external relationships; securing agreement among parties to a project.

and understanding between elected and appointed officials. The mayor increases the manager's awareness of council preferences and can predict how the council will react to administrative proposals. Although the manager must maintain positive relations with each member of the council, the mayor-manager interaction is an efficient way to exchange information. For the mayor to hold up his end of the relationship, he must be sensitive to the concerns of all council members, accurately convey their sentiments, and share with them what he learns from the manager.

Finally, as *team-builder* the mayor works to coalesce the council and build consensus. In this regard, he promotes cohesion without trying to guide the council in any particular direction. Council members do not automatically work well together, and the larger the council the less harmony there is likely to be. The goal here is not agreement or likemindedness, but rather to approach city business as a common enterprise. The mayor as team leader seeks to promote full expression, help the council work through differences expeditiously, and encourage it to face issues and resolve them decisively.

Organization and policy guidance. In the roles considered so far, the mayor has stressed communication and coordination, whereas the group of roles to be discussed here involves influencing the direction of city government affairs and the content of policy. As *goal-setter*, the mayor establishes goals and objectives for council and manager, identifies problems, and sets the tone for the council. Some mayors keep track of a set of key objectives so that the council and the manager orient themselves to accomplishing these priority items.

The mayor may also be active as an *organizer* and stabilizer of the key relations within city government. He guides the council to recognition of its role and responsibilities. He helps to define the pattern of interaction between council and manager, monitors it, and makes adjustments. The sharing and separation of responsibilities between the council and manager in this form of government is a complex relationship.[2] The mayor is uniquely situated to control it and better able than any other official to correct it, if change is needed. For example, the mayor may advise the manager to bring more matters to the council or fewer; he may intervene with a council member who is intruding into operational matters; or he may seek to alleviate tension between the council and staff before a serious rift develops. The mayor often handles these efforts in organization and stabilization privately. Indeed, his ability to make such adjustments out of the spotlight is one of his greatest advantages.

Finally, the mayor may be a *policy advocate*. As an active guide in policy-making, he develops programs and lines up support or organizes opposition to proposals. In these activities, the mayor most closely resembles the executive mayor's public persona as the city's problem-solver. The chairman mayor has a potential for policy leadership that is not sufficiently recognized.[3] Still, the mayor should be aware that advocating policies must be balanced with the other roles, not pursued to the exclusion of others. He must proceed subtly and more indirectly than the executive mayor, who can launch a new proposal with a press conference and has extensive resources for building coalitions. Still, the chairman mayor can influence the perspectives and decisions of the council and the manager. Especially if he is a mayor elected directly by the voters rather than a member of the council who has been elected to the mayorship by his council colleagues (as some mayors are), the mayor has a vague mandate to lead, but he must take care not to alienate the council and isolate himself by moving too far away from it as an assertive advocate of new policies.

Promotion. Conceptually distinct from the functions already discussed is the mayor's role in promoting and defending the city. He may be involved in external relations and help secure agreement among parties to a project. For some mayors, the *promoter* role is a simple extension of ceremonial tasks. Others are active initiators of contacts and help develop possibilities for the city. As official representative, the mayor has extensive dealings with officials in other governments and may serve as a key participant in formulating agreements with state or federal officials, developers, and others who seek joint ventures with city government. The mayor may also take the lead in projecting a favorable image of the city and seek to "sell" others on investment in it.

Types of Leadership

The kind of mayoral leadership an incumbent provides depends on which roles he performs and how well. The combinations of activities pursued by individual mayors is varied, but certain general types are clear.[4] Mayors develop a leadership type for themselves by the way they combine the four dimensions of leadership. (See Table 2, page 79.)

The mayor could invest so little in the office and define its scope so narrowly that he is simply a *caretaker*—a uniformly underdeveloped type of leadership. For most mayors, the presiding and ceremonial tasks are inescapable because they are legally required or inherent parts of the job. Mayors who perform no other roles may be called *symbolic heads* of their government. Such narrowly defined leadership will not meet the needs of the modern governmental system. Although he serves as presiding officer, ceremonial head, and spokesman, such a mayor makes no effort to unify the council members, keep them informed, communicate with the public, intervene between the council and manager, and so forth. As a consequence, the council is likely to be divided, confused, and disorganized, and the manager's influence will expand.

If he does undertake the unifying, informing, communicating and intervening tasks, the mayor becomes a *coordinator*. Pursuing these

Table 2
Performance Levels in Various Leadership Functions by Types of Mayors in Council-Manager Cities

Type	Ceremony and presiding	Communication and facilitation	Organization and guidance	Promotion
Caretaker	Low	Low	Low	Low
Symbolic leader	High	Low	Low	Low
Coordinator	High	High	Low	Low
Activist/Reformer	High	Low	High	Variable Low
Promoter	High	Low	Low	High
Director	High	High	High	High

activities effectively is essential to a smoothly functioning council-manager government with strong elected leadership. Council members do not always work together well; nor do the council, manager, and public necessarily interact smoothly. The coordinator is a team leader; he keeps the manager and council in touch and interacts with the public and outside agencies in order to improve communication. He helps to achieve high levels of shared information. But since he is weak in policy guidance, he contributes little to policy formulation (at least, no more than any other member of the council). The coordinator is not a "complete" type of leader, since the organizing and guidance roles are not part of his repertoire.

There are two other incomplete types of leader. One of them has two variations — the activist and the reformer. This type emphasizes policy guidance and advocacy but neglects coordinative activities, especially team-building. The *activist* wants to get things accomplished quickly and succeeds by force of his personality and the presence of a working majority on the council. Although influential, the activist is viewed by some members of the council (perhaps even his own supporters) as abrasive and exclusionary in his leadership. The tenure of this type of mayor is marked by successful policy initiatives along with friction and disgruntlement among the council members. The *reformer* launches

noble campaigns that have little prospect of success because he has limited support on the council. The reformer is more concerned with enunciating ideas about what the city should do than working with the council and maintaining coordination. As a result, he is likely to be ineffective as a policy leader because he is isolated from the rest of the council.

Another incomplete form of leadership found occasionally is the mayor who specializes in promotion. The *promoter* role may be combined with any of the other types and is becoming increasingly important for all mayors. The mayor who is excessively involved in promotion, however, may devote so much time to traveling and selling the city that he gives little attention to other aspects of the job. This type of leader may be more successful at negotiating agreement among developers, financial institutions, and government agencies for a major project than he is at welding a majority within the council. The specialized promoter leaves a vacuum of responsibility for tasks involving coordination, organization, and policy guidance, and others must try to fill it.

The *director* is a complete type of mayor who not only contributes to smooth functioning but also provides a general sense of direction. A primary responsibility of the council is to determine the city government's mission and its broad goals. The director contributes significantly to consideration of broad questions of purpose. One mayor suggested that "my toughest job was keeping the council's attention on the horizon rather than on the potholes."

This type of mayor stands out as a leader in the eyes of the council, the press, and the public, but he must use that recognition as a source of leverage rather than control. He can enhance the influence of elected officials by unifying the council, filling the policy vacuum that can exist on the council, and guiding policy toward goals that meet the community's needs. Furthermore, he is actively involved in monitoring and adjusting relationships within city government to maintain balance, cooperation, and high standards. No one else can attack the causes of friction between the council and manager (which may be produced by failings of either party) or promote the constructive interaction that is needed for effective performance. This mayor does not usurp the manager's prerogatives or diminish his leadership. In fact, in the organizer role, the mayor seeks to enhance the manager's ability to function as the chief executive officer. In sum, although the director does not become the driving force as the executive mayor can be, he is the guiding force in city government.

Conclusion

The council-manager form of government needs certain contributions from the mayor in order to function smoothly. At a minimum, the mayor should accept the coordinator type of leadership in order to facilitate exchange of information among public, council, and staff and to help the council operate more effectively. This attention to the internal dynamics of city government and relationships with the public is crucial for complete leadership. If a mayor is to shape both the process and the direction of city government, he cannot ignore the coordinative dimension; he can achieve victories over the short run but may become an isolated reformer. The mayor who defines the job as simply symbolic leadership is ignoring many important roles that are needed for effective city government.

Voters will have difficulty assessing whether a candidate has the qualities and intentions needed to be a good mayor for their city. In meetings with candidates, it is important to find out how they conceive the office and how they would relate to other officials. Priorities and ideas about policy are important, because they are likely to be manifested in the intricate details of interaction handled by the mayor. It is also important to know how the prospective mayor will work with others to accomplish his policy goals. The media should try to find out how the candidates perform as leaders in small groups. The performance of incumbents can be assessed against the checklist of roles outlined in Table 1. The standards for assessing performance must be grounded in the conditions of that community and in what kind of mayor the city needs. Given the ambiguous nature of the mayor's office, these efforts by citizens to learn about candidates take on a special importance. In the process, voters not only assess the candidates but also help shape expectations for the office itself.

For candidates and incumbents, it is time to abandon the notion that the mayor's office is "what one chooses to make of it." This oft-heard statement is misleading in two important respects. First, the activities of a good mayor are not matters of choice. The increasing demands on city governments mean that these governments need strong leadership from the mayor, at least as a coordinator and preferably as a director. If the mayor does not undertake these activities, a serious vacuum exists in council-manager government. Therefore, a good mayor *must* perform certain roles.

Second, the statement fosters the misconception that mayors who seek to define the responsibilities of their post broadly are on an "ego trip." They could, it would seem, just as well "choose" to be the first among equals on the council rather than make a big deal of being the mayor. That position is not consistent with this study's analysis of leadership in the large North Carolina cities. The nature of the office in council-manager government requires that the mayor be prepared to accept certain responsibilities reflected in the ten roles. He does so not because of inflated self-esteem but because the position calls for assumption of responsibility. Indeed, the mayor who provides complete leadership has accepted restraints on his freedom and the obligation to be an invisible leader within the council as well as a public advocate. The same logic applies to similar positions, such as the chairman or chairwoman of the county board of commissioners or the school board. Whoever occupies such offices should be expected to assert leadership across a wide range of roles and should not be faulted for doing so.

In conclusion, the council-manager mayor can contribute substantially to the performance of his government and the betterment of his community. The position is not a pale imitation of the executive mayor's office in mayor-council city but rather a unique leadership position that requires distinctive qualities. Council-manager cities ask the mayor not to run the show but to bring out the best in council and staff and to foster a common sense of purpose.

Notes

1. David M. Lawrence and Warren J. Wicker, eds., *Municipal Government in North Carolina* (Chapel Hill: Institute of Government, 1982), pp. 51–52.

2. James H. Svara, "Dichotomy and Duality: Reconceptualizing the Relationship Between Policy and Administration in Council Manager Cities," *Public Administration Review*, 45 (January/February 1985), 221–32.

3. Nelson Wikstrom, "The Mayor as a Policy Leader in the Council-Manager Form of Government: A View from the Field," *Public Administration Review* 39 (May/June 1979), 270–76.

4. A review of the literature and typology of roles in mayor-council and council-manager cities is presented in James H. Svara and James W. Bohmbach, "The Mayoralty and Leadership in Council-Manager Government," *Popular Government* 42 (Winter 1976), 1–6.

CHAPTER 10

THEORY V. REALITY WITH THE COUNCIL-MANAGER PLAN

B. J. D. Rowe

Today better than three-quarters of the population of the United States live and or work in cities and counties. Growth in the number, size, and complexity of these governments has been a function of temporal responses to six primary factors: improved agricultural practices, growth in commerce and trade, changes and improvements in production and engineering, advances in medical science and technology, changes in methods of transportation, and transformation from the industrial/manufacturing era to an information-processing one.

From the 1900s to the 1960s, the growth of municipalities resulted from the translation of these factors into increased employment opportunities, higher birth and lower death rates, speedier ways of transporting people and goods, and cleaner and more effective waste removal. Accompanying these advances were also such maladies as urban blight, deteriorating housing stock, crime and vandalism, and overcrowding. Together, these advances and maladies have mandated the delivery of new and the improvement of traditional public services.

To address this mandate, each city and county charter provides for one of three basic forms of municipal government: mayor-council, commission, and council-manager. Although variations of each form are seen, the council-manager form of government is touted as the "best" approach to promote the effective and efficient delivery of municipal services. That imperative is more compelling with the decline of central cities and the concomitant escalating growth of suburban areas. While central cities must adjust to a decreased tax base, smaller cities and counties must cope with increased demands on resources and services. Since the council-manager form of government is not without its critics, a review of contemporary research reveals the extent to which the council-manager form of municipal government adheres to two key principles of public administration that form its conceptual base. Moreover, what the research reveals about the appropriateness of these principles is equally important.

The Council-Manager Form: Bases in Administrative Theory

As students and practitioners of municipal government know, the prototype for the council-manager (C-M) plan was inaugurated in Staunton, Virginia, in 1908. In this instance, however, the C-M plan was grafted onto the mayor-council form and a bicameral council retained.

It was not until 1912 that Sumter, South Carolina, adopted, by charter amendment, the C-M form of government. This new form of municipal government gained some notoriety when, the following year, Dayton, Ohio,

Originally published as "Theory and Myth v. Practice: Council-Manager Form of Government," *Public Management*, Vol. 69, No. 2, February 1987. Published by the International City/County Management Association, Washington, D.C. Reprinted with permission of the publisher.

became the first large city to adopt this structure. Today, 2,558 cities and 87 counties in the United States, as well as 124 cities and/or townships and 6 counties in Canada, operate under this form of government.[1]

The formation of C-M government is based on two underlying principles of public administration: the separation of politics and administration and the promotion of economy and efficiency in government. The development and expansion of the C-M form paralleled that period in modern administration known formally as the "scientific management period." Embracing the tenets of classical theory, the school of scientific management, also known as "Taylorism," attracted the attention of scholars and practitioners in both business and government from 1900 to 1935.[2] Indeed, it was during this period (1904) that Richard Childs, considered the father of C-M government, graduated from Yale and embarked on a career in business.[3]

Taylor's theory of scientific management marked the introduction of new managerial and administrative practices designed to help private sector management adapt production practices to the needs of the burgeoning industrial economy of the 1900s. The theory's framework rested on four key values: efficiency, rationality, productivity, and profit. Methods and practices employed in business were transferred to the public sector in the interest of promoting, if not efficiency and profit, then efficiency and economy. Emphasis was on efficiency as a primary goal of both private and public management. Key to the attainment of this end in the public sector was the separation of politics from administration. This could be accomplished by putting "business in government" via the professionalization of local governance.

Textbook descriptions of the C-M form of municipal government generally reflect this theoretically based conceptualization. Thus, ideally the C-M form is characterized by:

- A small (five to nine members) city council, generally elected at large on a nonpartisan ballot, with responsibility for policymaking via legislation and the overall supervision of the administration of city government;

- A full-time professionally trained city administrator who serves at the behest of the council but with full responsibility for the implementation of policy through day-to-day city operations, including, for example, the hiring/firing of department heads and the preparation and administration of the executive budget;

- A popularly elected or council-selected mayor who serves as political leader and ceremonial official.

This conceptualization sought to divorce politics and policymaking from administration. Hence, the collective provision of city council initiative and leadership in policy formulation cojoined with the professionally and technically based conduct of daily administrative activities by a city manager under the overall guidance of the council.

The Separation of Politics from Administration

As with most social and behavioral research, scholarly attention has been directed at those aspects of the C-M plan seen as most problematic and controversial.

By far the bulk of the research on C-M government has focused on some aspect of the separation of politics and administration principle. Included among writings concerning the division of responsibility between the council and the manager are those addressing leadership and decisionmaking, council-manager relations, and role conflicts. A second and related series of popular topics for scholarly attention concerns manager selection and tenure and manager behavior.

Basic to council-manager government is the division of responsibility between the council and the manager. While this separation may be clear in theory, in practice it may be difficult to maintain. Councils tend to interfere in administrative matters, while managers become involved in major policy decisions. This is sometimes due to the indecisiveness of the council. Studies have noted that, when faced with controversial alternatives, councils tend to shun acts that may prove politically controversial. When action that might engender controversy must be taken, selected policy alternatives generally emanate from administrative officials like the manager who are more removed from direct public scrutiny. Even early proponents were aware of the need for managerial involvement in policymaking. The manager "was meant to exercise broad discretion in the administration of policies and to help formulate new policies of social welfare and municipal enterprise."[4] Adrian's study of three middle-sized council-manager cities in Michigan revealed that though the manager avoided a "public posture" of policy leadership, the manager as well as administrative departments were the principal sources of policy innovation and leadership.[5]

The policy role of the manager was confirmed in another early study by Kammerer and DeGrove, who concluded that the manager is a political figure of considerable importance.[6] By 1975, Huntley and Macdonald reported that 90 percent of the managers participating in an ICMA survey either always or nearly always participated in the formulation of municipal policy.[7]

Research not only has clarified the extent of that political importance, but has documented a concomitant conflict in role expectations as well. In one of the more comprehensive early studies of the manager's role in the policy process, Loveridge found considerable divergence in manager and council-member views regarding the extent to which managers should be involved in policymaking. Managers tended to see themselves as policy activists exerting policy leadership on most issues on the city agenda. Councilmembers, on the other hand, saw the manager as a staff assistant or advisor.[8] Loveridge concluded that considerable potential for conflict exists between manager and council because of these divergent views. As a result, situational factors influenced the extent to which managers assumed policy roles. Managers were found to actively advocate policy in less controversial policy issue areas, when policy proposals already had the implicit approval of the council, and in policy areas consonant with community values and or the perceived desires of powerful interest groups and leadership cliques in the community.[9]

In his 1969 study of 45 managers in cities of 100,000 or more, Wright found that, although managers generally viewed themselves chiefly as administrators, their actual duties could be grouped into three role categories: managerial, policy-related, and political. Executing policy, budgeting, and controlling bureaucratic functions were seen as the key tasks of the managerial role, while the policy-related role involved manager relationships with the council and mayor. The political role had two dimensions. The horizontal dimension involved manager relations and contacts with nongovernmental individuals and groups in the community. The second or vertical dimension described intergovernmental relations as it incorporates manager relations with officials at higher levels of government. According to Wright, managers desired expansion of both their policy and political roles.[10]

Lyden and Miller's longitudinal study of managers in the Pacific Northwest documents the expansion of manager desires noted by Wright. They found an increase in the percentage of managers willing to initiate policy in 1974 from what had been seen in 1966.[11]

Recent research has expanded our understanding of the dynamics of the policy role controversy in council-manager governments. In a 1982 nationwide study, Lewis addressed methodological deficiencies of previous studies (Wright, Loveridge, etc.) on the subject by developing a comprehensive multidimensional typology through which the behavior of local government managers could be categorized and "explained." He found that 24 percent of his total sample could be characterized as "traditional/cooperative." These managers were less inclined to consult with the council, more inclined to become involved in policymaking, avoided extraofficial contacts and community issues, and exhibited moderate resistance to council involvement in administration.

This "majority" was followed closely by the 21 percent (of total sample) who were characterized as "team/moderate" managers. More than any other grouping, these managers consulted with the council regarding administrative matters, though they clearly saw themselves as productive in these consultations rather than reactive. Team/moderate managers had a substantial role in policymaking, extraofficial contacts, and community issues. Only 17 percent of Lewis's sample were characterized as "textbook traditional administrators." As might be expected, while these managers did not particularly consult with council over administrative matters such as hiring/firing and budgeting, they were not particularly resistant to council involvement in administrative matters. This group tended to avoid policymaking as well as extraofficial contacts and community issues.[12]

While Lewis's findings provide a more precise grouping of manager role behavior, thereby substantiating manager participation in politics and policymaking, more recent research suggests that traditional views of council-manager relations, characterized by conflict over the proper roles of each in politics and administration, may not be as adversarial as suggested by early investigations. Fannin contends, for example, that differences in the way managers and councilmembers define policy affect their responses to role behavior questions. Moreover, situational role expectation questions yield very different results than do general role expectation questions. To Fannin, then, methodological inconsistencies may account for much of the early fervor over council-manager relations in general and the proper roles of each in policymaking, in particular.[13]

Svara, on the other hand, does not debate the definition of policy but sees the preoccupation with conflict as due to the use of an inappropriate model: the separation of policy and administration. In response, Svara proposes a new model, based in part on field observations in five North Carolina cities, that allocates responsibility for defining "mission" to elected officials and the management of programs to administrators. To Svara, then, policy and administration fall between mission and management and are thus the shared responsibility of both elected officials and managers.[14]

Several observations may be made about these findings. First, the separation of politics and administration may not be as compelling a principle for municipal governance as once presumed. As previously noted, some early proponents of the C-M plan saw the two not as separate but as inextricably intertwined components of a larger process. The American political system with its electoral process naturally thrusts politics into the realm of administration, and vice versa. A pluralist-democratic system compels constituent groups to influence policy by electing presidents, congressional representatives, state legislators, and a city council to serve their political interests and demands. The production and distribution of public goods and services via administrative practices is a response to the articulation of those interests and demands.

Second, situational factors significantly influence the extent to which the politics/policy-administration controversy is an issue in council-manager jurisdictions. These factors include, for example, council proclivity toward policy advocacy and innovation, council-mayor relations, the size and level of political sophistication of the citizenry, manager personality, and political astuteness.

Third, the traditional politics/policy versus administrative role controversy is related to the devolution of managerial authority. This may, on the surface, appear obvious. Yet the nature of the relationship remains in question. That is, is the increased politicization of managers a "cause" or an "effect" of the politics/policy-administration dichotomy?

Economy and Efficiency in Government

The principle of economy and efficiency in government attempts to promote rationality in policymaking and reflects the application of business ideals to public management of the 1900s. Assuming the "one best way" edict of scientific management, the economy-efficiency principle as a goal was supported by the notion that politics is and should be separate from administration. Expanding governmental policy responsibilities from the 1920s to the 1960s increased the significance of efficiency. Increases in public business subject to the efficiency criterion would result in rational and thrifty administrative products. The principle holds that in implementing policy, public officials, particularly administrators, eliminate waste and enhance productivity by maximizing the value of product per unit of cost (or at least minimize the cost per unit of product).

In light of the previously noted relationship between politics and administration and the inevitable involvement of administrators in politics, the economy-efficiency criterion can cause considerable concern for public administrators, including city managers. Very often, the policy aspects of administration emphasize high-quality output(s) in lieu of economy and or efficiency.

This is increasingly a source of stress in municipal governance. Several studies have noted increased stress in the manager profession. Kammerer et al., Lyden and Miller, Henry, and Stillman, for example, have documented increased stress associated with the manager profession as due to one or more of the following: council-manager conflicts and resultant effects on manager tenure; manager dissatisfaction with salary, location, and community interest; personal issues such as the restrictions of dual careerism; challenging of administrative authority; and reconciling increased responsibility and accountability with decreased resources.[15]

In the 1980s, the most telling of these sources of stress might well be the delivery of programs and services with decreasing resources. Local budget austerity due to federal retrenchment, a decreasing tax base, assumption of new services, etc., makes the economy and efficiency criterion more compelling.

To this criterion should be added the criterion of effectiveness (a program's performance relative to specified objectives). Assuming program or service goals and objectives are specified, cost-effectiveness is measurable; that is, the relationship between program/service costs and outcomes can be determined. Program and budgetary adjustments can then be made.

Under conditions of fiscal austerity, these adjustments may mean the elimination of whole programs, reductions in services, and

or reassessment of objectives and outcome criteria. Based on a study by the Organization for Economic Cooperation and Development, Schick reports that several adjustments have reoriented the public budgeting of many nations from a growth process to one that focuses on the conservation of resources. Primary adjustments have been: fiscal norms and targets that constrain agency budget requests, the conversion of multiyear budgeting from a planning to a control process, the use of baselines to compute cutback objectives, and preparation techniques that strengthen the conservation function of budgeting.[16]

These international findings have import for local government. In their study of mayors and managers of 90 municipalities in Pennsylvania, McGowan and Stevens found that local government officials were insecure about the future and continued to react to adverse fiscal conditions by making marginal adjustments while hoping for a restoration of resources and services.[17] This decremental approach to fiscal adversity is not seen as a nationwide trend, however. In a subsequent 1982 nationwide study of 456 municipalities, McGowan and Poister learned that in municipal governments between 25,000 and one million in population the use of sophisticated management practices increased dramatically between 1976 and 1982. These included techniques: (1) focusing on resource and expenditure control (e.g., program budgeting, zero-base/target-base budgeting); (2) used to set broad-based goals and objectives (e.g., management by objectives [MBO]); (3) providing information and administrative support (e.g., management information systems [MIS] and performance monitoring systems); (4) aimed at raising the level of efficiency and effectiveness (e.g., productivity improvements programs); and (5) focusing on individual and group performance.[18]

MBO and the combination of productivity improvement programs were used by a majority of the cities. Encouraged by these findings, McGowan and Poister note that fiscally healthy as well as fiscally stressed cities saw the efficacy of these tools for improved productivity as a means of coping with fiscal constraints. This is particularly insightful for council-manager governments. Of the 456 municipalities participating, 314 (68.9 percent) were of the C-M form. Moreover, C-M governments represented 69 percent of the cities employing program budgeting, MIS, performance monitoring, and productivity improvement techniques. The C-M form represented 60 percent of the cities utilizing MBO and 53 percent of those using some type of management incentive program.[19]

Conclusion

Although the findings of the aforementioned study are encouraging, the overall paucity of research literature specifically addressing the coping techniques of C-M governments is discouraging. Even where innovative techniques are known, little is known about how well these efforts work, what variations are used, who the primary actors are in efficiency-oriented innovations, or whether their use translates into effective service delivery as seen by the citizenry.

Indeed, only cursory attention is directed at the managers' role in the effective and efficient delivery of programs and services under new fiscal mandates. Weiland and Fullington acknowledged in their survey of 20 small towns in Kansas that the employment of a city manager had a significant bearing on a town's success in attracting increasingly scarce federal funds. Likewise, Sink chronicled the leadership of a city manager who used the nontraditional political role to develop a redevelopment machine consisting of the city and private-sector organizations.[20] More such documentation is needed.

Given new and compelling mandates for productivity, effectiveness, and efficiency, concern should be redirected from the more prescriptive dimensions of council-manager role behavior seen in the early literature to a more descriptive dimension. Research describing variations in form, role assignments and behaviors, and innovations in management that work would contribute not only to the inevitable dissolution of destructive aspects of the myth of separation but to the spread of positive alternatives, strategies, and techniques as well.

The primary strength of the C-M plan is the unification of powers in an elected body and the professional administration of public business. Forces of contemporary governance have altered the theoretical conception from one of separateness to one of the interrelatedness of politics and administration for the sake of effectiveness and efficiency.

Notes

1. Recognized Municipalities by ICMA Region," in *The Municipal Year Book* (Washington, D.C.: The International City Management Association, 1986), p. xiii.

2. See Frederick W. Taylor, *The Principles of Scientific Management* (New York: W.W. Norton, 1967, first published 1911).

3. For an account of the history of the council-manager movement by one who helped shape it, see Richard S. Childs, *The First 50 Years of the Council-Manager Form* (New York: National Municipal League, 1965). For a discussion of the political philosophy of Childs, see John Porter East, *Council-Manager Government: The Political Thought of Its Founder, Richard S.Childs* (Chapel Hill, N.C.: University of North Carolina Press, 1965).

4. Harold Stone, Don K. Price, and Kathryn Stone, *City Manger Government in the United States* (Chicago: Public Administration Service, 1940), p. 17. See also Leonard D. White, *The City Manager* (Chicago: University of Chicago Press, 1927), and the symposium "Leadership and Decision-Making in Manager Cities," *Public Administration Review*, 17 (Summer 1958), pp. 208–38.

5. Charles R. Adrian, "Leadership and Decision-Making in Manager Cities: A Study of Three Communities," *Public Administration Review* 18 (Summer 1958), pp. 208–13. See also Charles R. Adrian, *Four Cities* (Philadelphia: University of Pennsylvania Press, 1963); Clarence Ridley, *The Role of the City Manager in Policy Formation* (Chicago: International City Managers Association, 1958); Robert Paul Boynton and Deil S. Wright, "Mayor-Manager Relationships in Large Council-Manager Cities: Reinterpretation," *Public Administration Review* 31 (January-February 1971), pp. 28–35.

6. Gladys M. Kammerer and John M. DeGrove, *Florida City Managers: Profile and Tenure* (Gainesville: Public Administration Clearinghouse, University of Florida, 1961).

7. Robert J. Huntley and Robert J. MacDonald, "Urban Managers Organizational Preferences, Managerial Styles, and Social Policy Roles," in *Municipal Year Book* (Washington, D.C.: International City Management Association, 1975), pp. 149–59.

8. Ronald O. Loveridge, "The City Manager in Legislative Politics," *Polity* 1 (Winter 1968), pp. 214–36.

9. Ibid.

10. Deil S. Wright, "The City Manager as a Development Administrator," in Robert T. Daland, ed., *Comparative Urban Research* (Beverly Hills: Sage Publication, 1969), pp. 203–48.

11. Fremont J. Lyden and Ernest G. Miller, "Policy Perspectives of the Northwest City Manager, 1966–1974: Continuity or Change?" *Administration and Society* 8 (4) (February 1977), pp. 469–80.

12. Edward B. Lewis, "Role Behavior of U.S. City Managers: Development and Testing of a Multidimensional Typology," *International Journal of Public Administration* 4 (2) (1982), pp. 135–65.

13. William R. Fannin, "City Manager Policy Roles as a Source of City Council/City Manager Conflict," *International Journal of Public Administration* 5 (4) (1983), pp. 381–99.

14. James H. Svara, "Dichotomy and Duality: Reconceptualizing the Relationship Between Policy and Administration in Council-Manager Cities," *Public Administration Review* 45 (1) (January/February 1985), pp. 221–32. See also William P. Browne, "Municipal Managers and Policy: A Partial Test of the Svara Dichotomy-Duality Model." *Public Administration Review* 45 (5) (September/October 1985), pp. 620–22.

15. Writings represent three decades of the profession. See Gladys M. Kammerer, Charles D. Farris, John M. DeGrove, and Alfred B. Clubok, *City Manager in Politics: An Analysis of Manager Tenure and Termination* 13 (Winter 1962), University of Florida Social Sciences Monographs; Fremont J. Lyden and Ernest G. Miller, "Why City Managers Leave the Profession: A Longitudinal Study in the Pacific Northwest," *Public Administration Review* 36 (2) (March/April 1976), pp. 175–81; and Charles T. Henry, "Trends in City Management Careers 1970–1980: A Profession Under Stress," *Urban Data Service Report* 14 (3) (March 1982), pp. 1–6, and 10–13; and Richard J. Stillman II, "Local Public Management in Transition: A Report on the Current State of the Profession," in *The Municipal Year Book* (Washington, D.C.: International City Management Association, 1982), pp. 161–71.

16. Allen Schick, "Macro-budgetary Adaptations to Fiscal Stress in Industrialized Democracies," *Public Administration Review* 46 (2) (March/April 1986), pp. 124–34.

17. See Robert P. McGowan and John M. Stevens, "Local Government Initiatives in a Climate of Uncertainty," *Public Administration Review* 43 (2) (March/April 1983), pp. 127–36.

18. Robert P. McGowan and Theodore H. Poister, "Municipal Management Capacity: Productivity Improvement and Strategies for Handling Fiscal Stress," in *The Municipal Year Book* (Washington, D.C.: International City Management Association, 1984), pp. 206–13. See also McGowan and Poister, "Personnel-Related Management Tools in Municipal Administration," *Review of Public Administration* 4 (1) (Fall 1983), pp. 78–96.

19. Ibid., 1984, p. 208.

20. J. Weiland and M. Fullington, "The Small Town's Search for Federal Funds: Do Managers Make a Difference?" *Municipal Management* 4 (1) (Summer 1981), pp. 28–31; and David Sink, "The Political Role of City Managers in Economic Redevelopment Programs: Theoretical and Practical Implications," *State and Local Government Review* 15 (1) (Winter 1983), pp. 10–15.

CHAPTER 11

AN ASSESSMENT OF THE COUNCIL-MANAGER PLAN

Karl F. Johnson and C. J. Hein

The council-manager form of government has been for so long the standard against which other forms of local government are measured that, when an occasional flurry of challenges arises, supporters of council-manager government become concerned. While there is a record of continued growth and solid achievement, in recent years the academic literature has contained considerable criticism of city managers and the form of government. What is perhaps the most successful governmental reform in the United States finds itself challenged by a new group of reformers who regard it as failing in some important respects.

The arguments have been that city managers are (1) not fiscally responsible (i.e., city manager cities spend more than other cities); (2) not responsive to the city council; and (3) not responsive to citizen needs. The proposed alternative is to abolish the professional manager position and replace it with a mayor-council cum neighborhoods system of government, sometimes in effect replacing the manager with the "professional amateur government officials," a full-time mayor often with full-time councilmembers, all paid full-time salaries and supplied with full-time paid staff. Other reformers prefer a more formal role for neighborhoods (with full-time staffs) in the governmental system.

C-M Research

In some recent research (Johnson and Hein, 1984), we used ICMA recognition of cities as one variable in a regression analysis of city revenues, expenditures, and selected other factors. Some of our findings reflect favorably on the performance of city manager cities and run counter to the criticisms noted.

As part of the reform movement, local government management has been expected to adhere to the principles of good business practice, efficiency, and neutrality (Banfield and Wilson 1963; Stillman 1977). In contrast, Morgan and Pelissero (1980) compared a few council-manager cities with a "matched" group of control cities over an 11-year period and found that the council-manager cities spent more money, on the average, thereby refuting the reason for reforming a city with a city manager. Even setting aside Morgan and Pelissero's small sample size, Hofferbert (1981) made the cogent point that the finding may reflect only some short-term fluctuations and, therefore, merely fall into the "cumulative-marginality fallacy." Our findings, in contrast to those of Morgan and Pelissero, suggest that manager cities currently tend to operate as originally suggested by reform advocates; ICMA-recognized cities tend to raise less revenue and spend less than nonrecognized cities. On the other hand, this relationship might lead some to the conclusion that the council-

Originally published as "Assessment of the Council-Manager Form of Government Today," *Public Management,* Vol. 67, No. 7, July 1985. Published by the International City/County Management Association, Washington, D.C. Reprinted with permission of the publisher.

manager form of government is too fiscally conservative.

Some authors push further and argue that the council-manager form is not very open to the needs of deprived groups in the community, as may be evidenced by a manager's alleged lack of interest in citizen participation. For example, Almy (1977) pointed out that city managers tended not to involve citizen participation in the decisions related to revenue-sharing funds. Further, Huntley and MacDonald (1975) found that one of the activities city managers prefer least was to speak on controversial issues to civic groups, church groups, and so on. The decision to avoid citizen participation in policymaking about revenue sharing may thus have been concerned with avoiding controversy. Walking a fine line between politics and professional expertise is one aspect of the manager's job. While being discreet about the use of power, the manager has more latitude in fiscal decision making when there is polarization among citizen groups (Huntley and MacDonald, 1975).

Critics charge that the council-manager form of government stifles the give and take of interest positions in the community, forcing the council to take a back seat and even threatening democracy (Wood, 1959; Lineberry and Fowler, 1967). The analysis in our study showed significant participation by the ICMA city management variable in implementing revenue and spending. But the findings can represent a manager and council working together within a normal interplay of interest groups in the community, along with instances of greater influence by the managers and their staffs.

Local government officials have expressed concerns about fiscal problems (McGowan and Stevens, 1982), and tighter budget control was one solution increasingly followed by city managers (Stillman, 1982). But this does not mean that managers are moving to usurp the council's or mayor's roles in the political arena. The manager's participation in the more political aspects of city affairs was one of those activities least favored by city managers (Stillman, 1982). If anything, managers found that a good deal of their time and activity was spent resisting attempts by the mayor and

council to intrude in administrative affairs (Huntley and MacDonald, 1975; Stillman, 1982).

Where conflict and transition are occurring, the city manager may be expected to be drawn further into the policy affairs of city government, while such elected officials as the mayor may continue to receive the benefits "of public exposure with little political risk" (Sanders, 1982). Thus as resources become more scarce, the threat to a professional city manager and this form of government becomes more acute; scapegoats are needed to handle the frustration of having no resources to deliver to the citizens who provide electoral support.

The major effect shown in our study between the ICMA management variable and revenue and expenditure patterns was at the link with conventional revenue sources like property taxes (Johnson and Hein, 1984). Substantial concern with state and federal revenues is shown by city management (McGowan and Stevens, 1982). What we feel might be taking place is that city managers are having to offset declining funds, due to program cuts at the federal and state levels, with traditional city revenues and revenue-sharing funds, if possible.

Critics attack city managers from both sides. Sometimes the complaint is that city managers have thwarted democracy by being too conservative, because the empirical findings indicate a lower response to certain ethnic or implied community demands (Lineberry and Fowler, 1967). Or perhaps managers have been too liberal by increasing revenues and expenditures, as indicated by Morgan and Pelissero (1980). But there is some evidence in the literature that they are balanced in their approach to social issues.

Managers have initiated significant changes in social policy within their administrations. Over 80 percent of those cities with populations greater than 25,000 that have adopted affirmative action plans for minorities and women have done so at the initiation of their ICMA-recognized city management (Huntley and MacDonald, 1975). At the same time, these managements were cautious about participating in employment programs that legally committed them to provide employ-ment opportunities and quotas (Huntley and MacDonald 1975).

Thus, the commitment is to move, at least symbolically, partially toward social equity and concern. Yet the manager must be cau-tious about the administration's fiscal response to the community consensus. The future roles of the manager have been seen as a balance between "back to the fundamentals" pure management and the "forward to the new horizons" broker/negotiator, change agent, fa-cilitator of new innovations (Stillman 1982). The successful blend of these roles in relation to the future consequences of the fiscal picture for local governments warrants careful study.

Another major concern of the critics of the council-manager form of government, espe-cially among political scientists who are wor-ried about the deterioration of the political party system in the United States, is that the city management form contributes to the weakening of local party organizations, thus making it possible for national political orga-nizations and one-issue groups to gain dis-proportionate control over our political par-ties. Other institutional changes such as the increasing influence of electronic media in elections also contribute to the deterioration of local party organizations.

There may not be a Democratic or Repub-lican way to pave a street, as supporters of the council-manager form often say, but if strong, active local Republican and Democratic party organizations are a needed counterweight to such things as media dominance of our polit-ical system, we may need to consider ways to encourage local party organizations to help frame the issues and debate the policies of our city governments. The issue, of course, is non-partisanship or partisanship of the electorate and the governing body, not the continuing nonpartisanship of the city manager. It may be more difficult to be nonpartisan in a partisan environment, but if that is an important ele-ment in our democracy, city managers may have to try to work in a more partisan gov-erning system.

Increased partisanship, however, does not seem to fit in very well with another solution offered by the critics of the council-manager system, namely, to give an increased role in policy and spending decisions to neighbor-hood organizations. None of these proposals envision Republicans and Democrats com-peting for control of the neighborhood coun-cil. The neighborhood is viewed as a small, nonpartisan element representing the views of the residents, presumably arrived at by demo-cratic give and take. Perhaps a potential al-liance exists between supporters of nonparti-san neighborhoods and nonpartisan city managers. In any case, critics of the council-manager system sometimes present conflict-ing demands, such as nonpartisan neighbor-hoods vs. strong local party organizations.

Current Trends

Probably the growth rate of the council-manager form of government has been grad-ually slowing down, and naturally there is concern about whether it has reached its peak. Some people also may be concerned about whether we can expect more cities to abandon the form and move to some other form such as the strong mayor plan.

Sanders (1982) reported that from 1970 to mid–1981, some 3.5 percent of cities with the council-manager form had discontinued it. In the same period, about 10 percent of cities with the mayor-council form of government shifted to the council-manager form. We would expect that, in the period of tight finances since 1981, the change rate will have slowed down, because campaigns to change the form of government may have been viewed as an unnecessary expense.

One imponderable for the future is whether the "lean and mean" budget posture adopted by some city managers these past few years is viewed positively or negatively by cit-izens and their elected representatives. May-ors and councilmembers seemed to like hav-ing the city manager propose spending cuts. Citizens whose programs were cut were often not pleased. To the extent that managers have an internal drive to cut expenditures, it may come into conflict with citizen desires for ad-ditional services. Very few cities are now pro-viding an optimum level of services. To the extent that this is blamed on (credited to?) the city manager, there may be further citizen discontent with the form of government.

Our view is that, over the long haul, the professionalism of the council-manager form of government will find support from citizens. Most people want fair, effective, and efficient government. When the information needed to make reasoned comparisons is made available, the sense of balance conveyed by the council-manager form of government will prevail.

References

Almy, T.A., 1977, "City managers, public avoidance, and revenue sharing," *Public Administration Review* 37 (January/February): 19–17.

Banfield, E.C. and J.Q. Wilson, 1963, *City Politics*, New York, N.Y.: Vintage Books.

Hofferbert, R.I., 1981, "Communication on 'Morgan and Pelissero,'" *American Political Science Review* 75 (September): 722–725.

Huntley, R.J. and R.J. MacDonald, 1975, "Urban managers: Organizational preferences, managerial styles, and social policy roles," *Municipal Year Book* 1975 (Washington, D.C.: ICMA): 149–159.

Johnson, K.F. and C.J. Hein, 1984, "Reform, suburban cities and public opinion policy in relation to municipal revenues and expenditures: A first look," Prepared for the Western Social Science Association meetings, San Diego, Calif.: April 1984.

Lineberry, R.L. and E.P. Fowler, 1967, "Reformism and public policies in American cities," *American Political Science Review* 61 (September): 701–716.

McGowan, R.P. and J.M. Stevens, 1982, "Survey of local government officials: Analysis of current issues and future trends," *Urban Interest* 4 (Spring): 49–56.

Morgan, D.R. and J.P. Pelissero, 1980, "Urban policy: Does political structure matter?" *American Political Science Review* 74 (December): 999–1006.

Sanders, H.T., 1982, "The government of American cities: Continuity and change in structure," *Municipal Year Book* 1982 (Washington, D.C.: ICMA): 178–186.

Stillman, R.J. II, 1977, "City manager — professional helping hand or political hired hand," *Public Administration Review* 37 (November/December): 659–670.

_____, 1982, "Local public management in transition: A report on the current state of the profession," *Municipal Year Book* 1982 (Washington, D.C.: ICMA): 161–173.

Wood, R.C., 1959, *Suburbia*, Boston, Mass.: Houghton-Mifflin.

PART III
Counties

CHAPTER 12

OVERVIEW OF COUNTY GOVERNMENTS

Tanis J. Salant

Discussion of the American county typically generates diverse views on the usefulness and role of county government that range from praise as the regional government of the 21st century to ambivalence as the sleeping giant of the 1990s to judgments of obsolescence. Opinion has often reflected misconceptions and outdated perceptions; indeed, county government has endured a barrage of jaundiced assessments for decades. Attempts to reform counties have been occurring since the beginning of the century, and home rule and consolidation movements continue today.

Until recently, however, little was actually known about county government. Academic research tended to focus on the federal, state, and municipal governments or to lump counties together with municipalities as "local governments."

This chapter traces the origins and development of county government from an administrative arm of the state into a vital and integrated unit of the intergovernmental system.

Origins

County government's lineage can be traced to the English shire of a thousand years ago. Throughout its development in England, two opposing traditions unfolded and were later transported to this country: the county as an administrative arm of the national government and the county as a local government.[1] Primitive counties delivered the principal services of the royal government through justices of the peace who were appointed by the king, but local officials, particularly the sheriff, also were important. Early responsibilities included judicial, military, and public works functions.

The English county remained as the leading unit of local government, but the parish and borough also became providers of local services. Parishes generally were formed in small rural areas as a unit of church and civil government to furnish elementary education, poor relief, and highways, while boroughs were established in more urban areas to provide police and judicial services.

Early settlers in North America crafted a host of adaptations to conform to their own economic and geographic needs. In Virginia, initial jurisdictions were modeled after the parish, but because the state was agricultural with a dispersed population, larger areas were called for, and eight counties were superimposed to serve as election, judicial, and military districts.[2] These first counties were governed by a plural executive form called the county court, a model replicated extensively in other counties, especially those in the South.

New York and New Jersey adopted a third form of local government. These states were divided into counties, but elected township

Originally published as "County Governments: An Overview," *Intergovernmental Perspective*, Vol. 17, No. 1, Winter 1991. Published by the U.S. Advisory Commission on Intergovernmental Relations, Washington, D.C.

officials automatically became members of the county board of supervisors, and a penchant for large county governing boards commenced. In Pennsylvania, the county became the primary unit of local government because of the state's widely dispersed population, and county governing bodies, called boards of commissioners, were elected at large.

These colonial origins show the diversity of rationales for counties, but the dual tradition of the county as an arm of the state and as a local government persisted. Virginia's strong county form was followed throughout much of the South. Massachusetts' form, which provided fewer services, spread throughout New England. The county supervisor form originating in New York and New Jersey surfaced in parts of Illinois, Michigan, and Wisconsin, while Pennsylvania's county commissioner form was transported to many midwestern and western states.

Historical Development of County Government

Colonial counties were not altered significantly by the American Revolution, and in the quest for a balance of power between the federal government and the states, the framers of the new Constitution did not include provisions specifically for local governments. Early state constitutions generally conceptualized county government as an arm of the state, declaring it to be "nothing more than certain portions of the territory into which the state is divided for more convenient exercises of the powers of government,"[3] and left the prime responsibility of serving local constituencies to municipalities.

By the Civil War, however, counties were assuming more responsibilities. Many states fashioned them into election districts, paving the way for their becoming a significant political unit for party machines and placing them in the center of the "spoils system." County governing bodies also were gaining more elective positions, and the potential for corruption increased along with the expansion in their political power, planting seeds that eventually resulted in a deeply tarnished image and subsequent cries for reform.

Following the Civil War, populations grew, and both cities and counties experienced greater demands for urban services. After World War I, three trends helped strengthen the secondary role of counties as units of local government: (1) population growth, (2) suburbanization, and (3) the reform movement to streamline governmental structure.[4] By World War II, urbanization and the reform movement were bringing changes to county government that broadened its role further: changes in organization, more autonomy from the state, a greater number of intergovernmental linkages, more resources and revenues, better political accountability, and a "cleaner image."[5] Newer services joined the more traditional ones, such as responsibility for libraries, airports, hospitals, other health services, planning, zoning, and fire protection.

Diversity in Size, Governance and Authority

There are 3,042 county governments in the United States, with another 22 city-county consolidations and 44 "independent cities" that perform county activities. Forty-eight states are divided into functional county governments (called "boroughs" in Alaska and "parishes" in Louisiana). Connecticut and Rhode Island are divided into "unorganized areas" for the purpose of elections, but they have no functional county governments. The number of counties per state ranges from 3 in Delaware to 254 in Texas. Eight states have fewer than 20 counties, and 7 have 100 or more; the average number is 64. Counties range in area from 26 to 159,099 square miles, and the average is between 400 and 599 square miles. County populations range from as low as 164 in Loving County, Texas, to 8 million in Los Angeles County; the average is between 10,000 and 25,000 residents.

Counties, like cities, are created by the state, but primarily for the purpose of providing state services. As such, counties are considered quasi-corporations. Their powers are derivative, but counties have always been recognized as units of local government as well. With few exceptions, the county governing body and most line officers are elected locally, and some authority to provide optional local services and raise additional revenues makes local autonomy a reality, though limited. Many observers point out, however, that counties often have huge responsibilities but little real authority beyond local police powers, an anomaly often frustrating to county officials.

All counties were created originally as general law units of government subject to almost unlimited state control. Since the home rule movement was launched in California with passage of a state constitutional amendment in 1911, 35 other states have given counties the option of having discretionary authority through home rule.[6] Home rule provisions vary from state to state, but typically focus on changes in governmental structure as the avenue for modernization and autonomy. A few states also grant additional authority in functional and fiscal areas, and even some of the 12 states without home rule have granted extra authority through special legislation.

The most common type of home rule is charter government, offered to counties by 24 states. Charter home rule permits counties to frame and adopt their own charter and generally brings greater autonomy than other types of home rule, particularly in functional and fiscal domains. In 1988, Iowa became the most recent state to provide for charter adoption, while Texas remains the only state to have repealed such a provision.

Of the 1,307 counties eligible to adopt a charter, 117 have succeeded in doing so. Charter adoption tends to have more appeal in urban counties and in areas with reform-minded constituencies. The failure of charter adoption has been attributed to lack of a compelling need for structural change, little interest among voters in reform issues, or the opposition of county constitutional officers, whose elective positions are often transformed into appointive ones or consolidated with other offices.[7]

Approximately 2,924 counties, or 95 percent, remain general law counties. The others operate under charter, as city-county consolidations, or as variations attained through special legislation. Regardless of status, however,

all counties are still obliged to perform traditional state services, and their original rationale as administrative arms of the state survives intact.

All functional county governments are governed by locally elected executive bodies. The composition and title vary greatly across states and sometimes within, but boards of commissioners and boards of supervisors with three to five members are the most common. There are about 17 different titles, and board size ranges from one member to over fifty in New York.[8] Titles often reflect their origins, such as "Judge Executives" in Kentucky, reflecting that state's initial emphasis on delivering judicial services.

In most counties, board members serve in both legislative and executive capacities. Boards have overall fiscal responsibility for the county, approving the budget, and setting the property tax rate as well as levying other types of taxes. Most counties elect additional officers to head constitutionally mandated departments, such as the sheriff, attorney, recorder, assessor, and treasurer. Often referred to as "row officers," constitutional officers are elected countywide and have functional authority independent of the governing board.

County Government Today

In addition to traditional duties and other programs mandated by the state, counties perform a growing list of optional services once largely reserved for municipalities. Despite the limits and controls imposed by the state, many counties now enjoy a large measure of autonomy. Yet, in spite of dramatic changes in scope, authority, and level of resources, many scholars and "reformists" still hold that county government is anachronistic, rigid, and ill-equipped to meet the needs of a rapidly changing society. This position perpetuates the view of counties as an arm of the state and further obscures the real changes that have been occurring. Laments are frequently heard in state legislatures that county government is difficult to understand. Confusion and ambivalence on the part of taxpayers as well as legislators have hurt the efforts of county officials to secure tax increases from voters and to plead their case in state capitols.

A more contemporary view recognizes the county as a major provider of local services as well as an arm of the state. This view is an outgrowth of urbanizing and suburbanizing trends and dwindling federal support to states and localities, where counties are called on to deliver more services both within and outside of municipal boundaries. Recent research has led to the development of a *quadruple* role concept of county government, an amplification designed to reflect its growing importance in the intergovernmental system.[9] These roles can be defined as follows:

Administrative Arm of the State. Under this role, counties deliver services that are state programs, typically client- or formula-driven and beyond the control of counties. Indigent services are in this category, and state mandates under this role are generally the most onerous.

Traditional Government. These services also are (constitutionally) mandated and are performed generally by elected constitutional officers. Usually, however, counties have discretion in the level of service provided. These include countywide services performed by such officers as assessor and treasurer, and traditional services in unincorporated areas, such as law enforcement. Other services can include the county hospital, the superior court, and road construction and maintenance.

Local Government. These functions can be divided into three categories: municipal-type services in the unincorporated area, such as planning and zoning, libraries, and parks and recreation; services provided jointly with cities and towns (or for them) through intergovernmental agreements; and responses to individual constituent requests by elected supervisors or commissioners (a function that can consume more time than their "formal duties").

Regional Government. This role is perhaps the fastest growing, and includes such functions as transportation, air quality, conservation, landfill and toxic sites, growth management, and economic development. These functions are typically environmental or "quality of life" issues that address long-range problems. Rural and medium-size counties also play this role, especially in landfill siting, growth management, and economic development. In this role, counties often become the dominant government in the region.

Contemporary Issues

Traditional government roles likely claim the greatest portion of county budgets today, particularly because of escalating expenditures for law enforcement, corrections, and courts. But new roles as "local" and "regional" governments are not likely to diminish, and recognizing this trend would help state legislatures address county issues, particularly the financial ones. Legislators frequently point to the diversity among counties as problematic in crafting uniform legislation, but while the nature of county government has changed dramatically since its inception and demographic shifts continually place new strains on existing structures and resources, diversity should not be overemphasized or cited as an obstacle to problem solving. Recent research concludes that, with respect to "major" problems, there are more similarities than differences among counties.[10] Special circumstances, such as demography, geography, economy, and spending traditions, determine more the *severity* of problems and the way they are handled than the *type*.

Recent surveys of county officials, legislative hearings in state capitols, and a growing body of literature point to the relationship with the state as the most critical component of county viability. Insufficient revenues have become the biggest headache for county officials, and the spiraling costs of state-mandated programs, particularly those for indigent services and long-term health care, are cited as the primary cause. These mandates are handed down without accompanying funds, or sufficient funds, to finance them, and client-driven state formulas keep costs beyond the control of counties. Unfunded state mandates are now widely recognized as unworkable, especially in light of the restricted revenue-raising capacity of counties, and many states are searching for alternatives.

Urban problems are no longer confined to communities with population concentrations. Environmental concerns and the shift of indigent populations from inner cities to outlying areas have superimposed urban problems on rural structures. Urban, suburban, and rural counties alike are grappling with common concerns. Affordable housing, solid waste management, clean air, water quality, AIDS, refugee resettlement, juvenile justice, hazardous material transportation, energy alternatives, cable TV, urbanizing parks systems, and managing natural disasters are just a few of the concerns of county officials — concerns that reflect intergovernmental complexity and a greater role for counties in societal problem solving.

It should be in the best interests of both the federal and state governments to have healthy county governments, particularly since economic development and urban growth issues have become so prominent. The state of counties across the nation is only now beginning to receive more attention, and the double jeopardy of spiraling mandated costs and revenue and expenditure caps makes the fiscal future of all but the wealthiest counties look grim. Counties have assumed and been given a multiplicity of roles, however, even in less populated areas of the country, and the performance of these roles will require authority, resources, energy, and creativity.

Basic Forms of County Government

1. **Commission Form.** An elected county commission or board of supervisors, which is the most common form of county government, has legislative authority (e.g., to enact ordinances, levy certain taxes, and adopt budgets) as well as executive and administrative authority (e.g., to administer local, state, and federal policies, appoint county employees, and supervise road work). Typically, however, administrative responsibilities are also vested in independently elected constitutional officers, such as a county sheriff, treasurer, coroner, clerk, auditor, assessor, and prosecutor.

2. **Commission-Administrator.** There are three basic types of this form, some of which also have additional, independently elected constitutional officers. About 786 counties have one type of this form.

   A. **Council-Manager.** The county council or board, which is the legislative body, appoints a county manager who performs executive functions, such as appointing department heads, hiring county staff, administering county programs, drafting budgets, and proposing ordinances.

   B. **Chief Administrative Officer.** The county board or commission, as the legislative and quasi-executive body, appoints a chief administrative officer to supervise and coordinate county departments, but not appoint department heads, and to prepare budgets, draft ordinances, and oversee program implementation.

   C. **County Administrative Assistant.** The county board or commission, as the legislative and executive body, appoints an administrative assistant to help carry out the commission's responsibilities.

3. **Council-Executive.** A county executive is independently elected by the people to perform specific executive functions. The county board or commission remains the legislative body, but the county executive may veto ordinances enacted by the commission, with the commission having override power by an extraordinary majority vote. The county executive's authority and responsibilities are much like those of a mayor in a strong mayor-council municipality. About 383 counties have this form.

Notes

1. Laura Kaifez, John Stuart Hall, and Albert K. Karnig, "Counties in the National Context," in *County Government in Arizona: Challenges of the 1980s* (Phoenix: Arizona Academy, 1984), p. 2.

2. Herbert Sydney Duncombe, *County Government in America* (Washington, DC: National Association of Counties, 1966), p. 20.

3. *State of Maryland v. Baltimore and Ohio R.R.*, 44 U.S. 534, 550 (1845) cited in Ibid., p. 23.

4. Duncombe, p. 28.

5. John C. Bollens, *American County Government* (Beverly Hills, California: Sage, 1969), p. 41.

6. Tanis J. Salant, *County Home Rule: Perspectives for Decision Making* (Tucson: University of Arizona, 1988), Chapter II.

7. Ibid.

8. Blake Jeffery, Tanis J. Salant, and Alan L. Boroshok, *County Government Structure: A State-by-State Report* (Washington, DC: National Association of Counties, 1989), pp. 8–14.

9. Tanis J. Salant, *Arizona County Government: A Study of Contemporary Issues* (Tucson: University of Arizona, 1989), pp. 160–162.

10. Ibid., p. 152.

CHAPTER 13

ORGANIZATION OF COUNTY GOVERNMENTS

Herbert Sydney Duncombe

"County governmental organization is characterized by diversity, not only from state to state but even within states…. As has been aptly observed, if any 'principle' could be distinguished in American county government, it is the principle of confusion."[1]

"On the average, counties have not been viewed by political scientists as particularly flexible and modern instruments of grass roots democracy. The two most common criticisms are that county governments have archaic organizational structures and that these units have only limited, if any, capacity to perform nonroutine and nonrural functions, being ill-equipped in most instances to handle the most pressing demands of a rapidly growing urban society."[2]

"During most of the 330-year history of counties in the United States the traditional plural executive, or commission, plan has been maintained for administering the county government. Over the past 15 years, however, widespread reform of county government structure has occurred."[3]

County government organization is undoubtedly the most criticized feature of county government. The first two quotations, cited above, are from excellent state and local government textbooks and give the impression that county government organization is confusing and archaic. The third quotation is from *The County Year Book of 1975* and emphasizes the reform that has occurred in county government in the 1960s and early 1970s.

Before describing the forms of county government today, it is important to describe the nature of the criticism of county organization. In 1917, H.S. Gilbertson focused his attack on the many elective officials which he felt misled the average voter and splintered executive responsibility within the county.[4] Lane Lancaster has contended that the county is too small in population and too weak financially to support an efficient administrative organization.[5] More recently, Maddox and Fuquay stated that:

> One outstanding weakness of county government in general is the absence of a chief executive. There are far too many independent "executives" and department heads whose activities are subject to no effective supervision and coordination.[6]

The criticisms of county government organization are primarily criticisms of the traditional commission (or plural executive) form of county government. Gilbertson, Maddox and Fuquay, and others favored alternative forms of county government featuring an elective or appointive county executive.

Were past criticisms of county organization valid or did the critics of county government

---

Originally published as "County Government Organization," Chapter 3 of *Modern County Government,* 1977. Published by the National Association of Counties, Washington, D.C. Reprinted with permission of the publisher.

misunderstand the strengths of the collegial decision-making process which occurred in county boards of commissioners? If these criticisms were accurate at the time Gilbertson wrote in 1917, are they still valid or have they become outdated as county government organization has changed in the past two decades? Have counties, in fact, actually changed or are their new organizational structures a facade covering inherent weaknesses? The strengths and weaknesses of the current forms of county government organization will be examined in this chapter.

Alternative Forms of County Government

The form of local government determines the major organizational features such as the relationship between the voters, the legislative body, and the major elective and appointive officials. For example, one major form of city government is the mayor-council form in which voters elect separately a mayor (as chief executive) and council (as legislative body).

There are three basic forms of county government and several important variations of each. The commission form of county government accounts for about 77 percent of all counties but governs only about 49 percent of the people of the United States having county-type government. More populous counties tend to use the council-administrator or council-elected executive forms.

COMMISSION FORM

Florence Zeller estimates that more than 2,500 counties, of a total of 3,101 county-type governments, operate under the traditional commission form of government.[7] In Idaho, Iowa, Massachusetts, Oklahoma, Texas, Vermont, West Virginia, and Wyoming, it is the only form of county government permitted. Frequently called a board of county commissioners or a board of supervisors, the governing body has legislative functions such as enacting ordinances, adopting a budget, and setting county tax rates. The county board also has numerous executive and administrative functions such as appointing certain county employees, reviewing applications for licenses, and supervising county road work. A characteristic of the commission form of organization is that the county commissioners share administrative responsibility with a number of independently elected "row" officers who frequently include: a county clerk, auditor and recorder, assessor, treasurer, prosecuting attorney, sheriff, and coroner.

The pros and cons. A 1975 study of county organization summarizes the frequently cited advantages and disadvantages of the commission form of government as follows[8]:

Advantages of Commission Form

Longevity: The commission form of government is the traditional structure in county governments.

The commission plan brings government administration close to the people through the independent election of government department heads: therefore, it is the most democratic form of government.

A broadened system of checks and balances is provided by the individual election of officials: there is less chance of a totally corrupt government.

It promotes a unified administration and policy-making government because, with legislative and executive functions combined in one branch, conflicts are avoided.

Disadvantages of Commission Form

The commission plan is antiquated: a form of government that predates the American Revolution cannot answer the complex needs of the twentieth century.

Lack of a chief executive officer is one of the most glaring deficiencies of most local governments, and results in a lack of efficiency in delivering governmental services to citizens.

Technology and increased citizen dependence on government service and government regulation make administration by the citizen legislator no longer feasible. The commission plan lacks professionalism.

It is often nearly impossible for voters to know the myriad functional officials they are electing. Quite frequently clerks, recorders, engineers, auditors, treasurers, coroners, and sheriffs are elected term after term without opposition. This concentrates the power for selection of county officials in political parties and special interest groups.

The commission plan lacks accountability because responsibility for legislative and executive functions is so diffused.

The first three advantages cited are largely the traditional, Jacksonian arguments which are extremely difficult to prove or disprove. The fourth advantage (that the commission form results in unified administration and policy-making) is particularly debatable. Unified administration and policy-making can occur if there is strong party leadership in the county and the commissioners and other elected county officials are of the same party and follow agreements worked out with party leaders. Unified administration can also occur if commissioners and other elected officials are in basic agreement on county programs. However, in the absence of these conditions, there may be major divisions of opinion among the commissioners or sharp differences between the commissioners and one or more of the independently elected officials. The resulting conflicts can be severe.

Variations in practice. There are important differences in how the commission form of government operates. In some counties, the chairman of the county board of commissioners, as a result of seniority, greater ability, more experience, (or a longer work week) may make most of the administrative decisions leaving the other commissioners to share in the legislative and policy-making functions. The author observed one county in Idaho in which the chairman of the board for years made the administrative decisions, and the other two commissioners always voted to support him. A second example of the strong board chairman was observed in Baker County (Oregon) which has a full-time elected county judge with no judicial duties but considerable executive responsibilities for supervision of most county departments. Baker County also has two part-time commissioners who meet with the county judge about five or six days a month primarily on legislative and policy matters.

A second variation in the commission plan occurs when the county clerk is an experienced, full-time county official with many fiscal and administrative duties, and the county commissioners are part-time officials with time consuming non-governmental responsibilities. An able, experienced county clerk (with the approval of the commissioners) can make many of the day-to-day administrative decisions that the board of county commissioners would otherwise have to make.

A third version is found when there is an appointed county clerk or administrative assistant who aids the county commissioners in preparing the budget, developing agendas for board meetings, following-up on board decisions, and advising the commissioners on emergencies that require their attention. In Franklin County (Ohio), this administrative assistant is called a "county administrator" and functions almost as a county administrator in a council-administrator form of government.

Still another variety can be observed in some Texas, Tennessee, and Alabama counties where a county judge is elected at large and is the presiding officer of the county board. The judge (who has judicial functions) also has important financial and administrative powers. In many cases, the county judge has most of the strengths of a county executive.

The strongest criticism of the commission form is that it lacks a chief executive officer to unify administration and be accountable to the people. This is a valid argument in those counties in which the county commissioners and other independently elected officials have nearly equal power. However, as previously described, in a number of commission counties, a county judge, county clerk, or the chairman of the board of county commissioners can help unify administration by assuming a strong leadership role. In this instance, defenders of the commission form may claim this as evidence that it does provide executive leadership. Detractors, however, may state that the emergence of a very able, experienced official should be viewed as an opportunity to change the form of government and elect this able leader as county executive.

The effectiveness of the commission form of government may also depend on the cohesiveness of party leadership in the county. A strong, cohesive party leadership can unify county administration if the county commissioners and other elected county officials are of the same party. Advocates of the commission form of county government may claim that this circumstance provides the necessary unified leadership. Those in opposition may point out that cooperation might break down if the strong party leader does not control all county elective offices. Furthermore, there is concern about unifying the government under a party boss who may not be an elected county official. Some would say it is far better for the party boss to unify county administration from an elective position within county government where his power would be subject to check by the public at the polls.

COUNCIL-ADMINISTRATOR FORMS

It was estimated that 500 counties, serving more than 60 million people, operated under the council-administrator forms of county government in 1975, and this number probably reached 580 by 1977.[9] By title, the county administrator is called a county manager, chief administrative officer, administrative assistant, assistant to the county board chairman, or even executive or executive director. The major difference in the forms of council-administrator government is whether the administrative officer has the basic authority of a county manager, a chief administrative officer, or an assistant to the chairman of the county board.

Council-manager plan. The county manager has the most extensive powers of the three types of county administrator. The manager is appointed by the county board as principal administrative officer of the county and serves at the pleasure of the county board. The board retains its legislative functions such as enacting ordinances, appropriating funds, setting tax rates, and exercising general oversight of administration. It also determines broad program policies and reviews program operations with the manager. The county manager appoints all or most of the department heads and is responsible to the board for the administration of county programs. Both the manager and the department heads make the day-to-day policy decisions on programs. The manager is also responsible for preparing an annual budget for submission to the board, drafting reports and ordinances requested by the board, and serving as staff arm to the county board. The council-manager plan was first adopted by Iredell County (North Carolina) in 1927, and by 1965 there were 35 counties

using this form of government. Currently, manager counties vary in size from Dade County (Florida), with a population of more than 1.2 million, to Petroleum County (Montana), with a population of less than one thousand.

In practice, the voters generally elect some officials such as a clerk or county judge, and the county council (rather than the county manager) may appoint other county officials.

Chief administrative officer plan. The chief administrative officer (CAO) has some, but not all, of the powers of the county manager. He or she is appointed by the county board and is generally responsible for preparing the budget for submission to the county board. Serving the board as chief of staff, the CAO drafts ordinances, prepares reports, and coordinates county programs under the board's direction. The CAO directly supervises administrative and staff services such as budgeting, purchasing, personnel, management analysis, data processing, and capital improvements.

Unlike the county manager, the chief administrative officer does not directly supervise most county departments and does not appoint most department directors. The county board retains the appointment of line department directors but gives the chief administrative officer power to coordinate county departments. The chief administrative officer plan is the most widely used form of county government in California and is the form used in the nation's most populous county, Los Angeles.

County administrative assistant plan. The administrative assistant is also appointed by the county board and, having many of the powers of the chief administrative officer, serves the county board by preparing drafts of ordinances and reports and following up on administrative action for the board. The administrative assistant usually does not appoint or directly supervise department directors, but may be responsible for budget preparation.

The administrative assistant may be given a number of different titles including that of county administrator.

There are a number of important advantages of the council-administrator forms of county government including:

- "The council-administrator plan separates policy making and administration, thus removing administration from political influence.
- The appointed administrator, who is often recruited on a nationwide basis (unlike elected officials who must be county residents), can provide highly professional administrative leadership.
- The council-administrator plan is a less dramatic departure from the traditional commission plan and makes for easier transition from the commission form.
- The appointed administrator usually serves at the pleasure of the county board and can be replaced immediately should he or she fail to fulfill the duties of the position.
- The county legislature (board) under the council-administrator plan is free to spend time on policy development while the administrator handles the day-to-day business of the county government.
- Greater control over performances and expenditures is possible under the supervision of the appointed administrator than with the commission form."[10]

There are three particularly significant disadvantages. The appointed administrator is dependent upon the strength and cooperative spirit of the county board, and may find it difficult to take effective action when the county board is split. The appointed administrator may also find it difficult to provide policy leadership on important issues facing the county. On the one hand, with a passive role, inaction may result. On the other hand, if the administrator becomes an agent to crystallize public opinion behind a particular issue, he or she may become vulnerable if the board takes a different stand. Nevertheless, for many counties the disadvantages of the plan are far outweighed by the advantages of unified and more effective provision of county services.

THE COUNCIL-ELECTED EXECUTIVE FORM

In 1977, there were 142 counties, city/counties, and independent cities, with over 43 million inhabitants, which employed the elected executive form of government.[11] The county executive is elected by the voters and heads the executive branch of government. The county board is the legislative branch of government enacting ordinances, adopting a budget, and exercising the usual oversight of administration. It has the same roles as the council in the strong mayor-council form of city government and the state legislature in state government. The county executive has the power to veto legislation passed by the county board, and the board usually has the power to override the county executive's veto with a two-thirds or greater majority.

The county executive takes general responsibility for county administration, prepares the county budget, suggests policy to the county board, acts as spokesman for the county on ceremonial and other occasions, and sees that the acts and resolutions of the county board are executed. The county executive appoints and may dismiss department heads, usually with the consent of the county board. Under the county executive form, the voters may elect some "row" officers but not as many as in the traditional commission form of government.

Supporters of the council-elected executive form frequently cite the following advantages:

- "The elected executive plan provides the most visible policy-making for the community through providing the public an opportunity to hear the pros and cons of each issue.
- The executive (particularly in urban areas) provides the needed strong political leadership for relating to diverse segments of the community. An executive elected at large is considered more dependable and less likely to resign during a crisis or crucial period of change for the county than an administrator who serves at the pleasure of the county board.
- The elected executive is responsive to the public will; he or she must answer to the county electorate in the next election.
- Greater visibility and prestige is achieved for the county with the council-elected

plan. State legislators, governors, the United States Congress, and the President can focus on one individual who clearly represents the entire county.

- The best system of checks and balances is provided by this complete separation of powers. Through the veto, which can be overridden by the county board, both branches can express their commitment to their positions on various issues."[12]

One of the arguments against the council-elected executive form is that it may lead to bossism. In counties like Westchester and Nassau in New York which have used the system for nearly 40 years, however, bossism has not developed. A more serious criticism is that it is difficult to find an elected executive who is both a skillful political leader and an expert administrator. Elected executive counties remedy this deficiency by providing professional administrative staff assistance for the elected executive. Under one variation of the elected executive form, the county executive appoints a professional chief administrative officer to assist him.

Critics of the form contend that conflict between the executive and the legislative body may impede county progress, but there is no evidence that this is more of a problem than conflict among the members of a county board in the commission form of government. The executive form is not the best plan for every county, but it does provide more unified administration and a better coordinated service delivery system than the commission system.

STATE ACTION TO ALLOW MORE OPTIONS

One past criticism of county government organization was that the form of government was inflexible because it was established by state constitution and law. This criticism is becoming less valid as more states allow optional forms of county government organization. By 1965, 18 states had granted counties the right to choose from optional forms of organization. By 1975, 40 states permitted at least one alternative to the commission form.

Counties in nine of these states gained the needed legislation between 1972 and 1974.

County Governing Boards

The county board is usually called the board of county commissioners but may also be called the board of supervisors, commissioners court, county court, fiscal court or one of several other titles. The size of the county board is often set by state law or constitutional provision and follows one of five patterns.

SMALL GOVERNING BOARDS

The predominant type of small governing board is the county commissioner board which originated in Pennsylvania in the 1720s. The typical county commissioner board has:

- three or five members elected for two to four year terms;
- a board chairman who does not have much more legal authority than the other commissioners; and,
- commissioners who have administrative as well as legislative responsibilities and who do not hold a judicial or township office.

Idaho boards of county commissioners are typical of many small boards. The three county commissioners in each Idaho county are elected by the voters of the entire county, but each must be a resident of a specific election district.[13] Elected by the board at its first regular meeting each biennium, the chairman presides over its meetings but does not have significantly greater legal powers than the other commissioners. The county commissioners in Idaho have many legislative functions, such as enacting ordinances and adopting a budget, but they also have many executive and administrative duties such as directly supervising county employees.

The judge and commissioner board. This second type of small county board is found in many counties in Alabama and Texas and a few counties in Oregon. A typical Alabama county has a five member board composed of four commissioners and a judge of probate.[14] The judge is elected at large from the entire county and the commissioners are generally elected by district. The probate judge presides over the county board, has fiscal responsibilities such as maintaining financial records and preparing the county budget, and performs judicial functions such as the probating of wills and administration of estates. With financial and judicial responsibilities, the county judge has significantly more power than the county commissioners, but the commissioners still retain some administrative responsibilities.

The small legislative board. This board is generally similar to the county commissioner board in structure, except that an elected or appointed executive handles all or most executive and administrative functions. Marion County (Indiana), for example, has a three-member commissioner type board as do other Indiana counties, but the mayor of the city-county government, not the county board, appoints and supervises the appointed county department directors.

There are many advantages to a small board. It is usually less costly than a large board, and the members of a small board tend to spend at least half-time on county work and become more knowledgeable of county operations. However, familiarity with county operations may lead to "meddling" in administrative detail, according to one writer.[15] Moreover, in a populous county the small county commissioner type board, without the services of a county manager, administrative officer, or administrative assistant, may find itself overwhelmed with supervisory and administrative responsibilities.

In larger urban counties, the best type of small board is one which can leave administration to an elected or appointed executive and concentrate mainly on legislative functions. Montgomery County (Ohio) and Alameda County (California) are among the many large urban counties with small county boards which have delegated much administrative responsibility to appointed county administrators.

LARGE GOVERNING BOARDS

Large governing boards are the rule in all four of the states (New York, Michigan, Illinois, and Wisconsin) which extensively use the township supervisory board. As originally constituted, the township supervisory board was composed of township supervisors having the dual role of executive head of their townships and members of the county board and was a unique way of linking township and county government. By 1960, however, many populous counties with township supervisory boards were giving representation on the county board not only to a supervisor from each township but additional representation to each city in the county on a population basis.

The "one man, one vote" principle posed serious problems for county supervisory boards because although each township had one representative, there were often great population differences between the largest and smallest. In case after case, state and federal courts held invalid state laws and county practices requiring each township to have one representative on the county board.[16] As a result of court action, the Wisconsin Legislature enacted a statute requiring county boards to establish supervisory districts as nearly equal in population as practicable. Michigan now has an apportionment system in which county commissioners are elected from single member districts approximately equal in population.[17] Each Michigan county must have at least 5 commissioners, with the maximum varying from 7 (for a county of 5,000 people or less) to 35 (for the state's largest counties).

The net effect of the changes is that the county boards in the more populous counties of New York, Michigan, Wisconsin, and Illinois are similar in some ways to a small state senate. Michigan counties, for example, make extensive use of the committee system, with a number of them reporting 20 or more standing committees. Formal rules and parliamentary procedures are more widely used by these larger boards. Moreover, individual members of these large county governing boards are more likely to view themselves as county legislators rather than commissioners with administrative powers.

The judge and justice of the peace system has also evolved into a large governing board (often called the Fiscal Court) in Tennessee.

The judge, elected by the people, has administrative, fiscal and judicial powers with the justices of the peace having minor judicial functions. The county judge has a powerful position in Tennessee counties. It is significant that when Davidson County (1970 population 447,877) reorganized its judge and justice of the peace system to establish a Metropolitan mayor-council form of government, the able county judge of Davidson County was elected mayor of the new Metropolitan Government of Nashville and Davidson County.

On the one hand, large governing boards which are elected by district have the advantage of better representing most geographic areas and racial, ethnic, and interest groups in the county. With fewer citizens to represent, the member of a large board is likely to find it easier to have face-to-face contacts with a greater proportion of his constituents. The committee system can give the members of large boards the opportunity to specialize in various types of legislative and policy matters.

On the other hand, large boards tend to be too unwieldy for administration, leaving this responsibility to elected and appointed executives. Another disadvantage is that members elected from small constituencies may have a parochial rather than a county-wide perspective. Still another weakness is that a large board with a staff can be expensive. One writer stated that large governing boards tend "to create power blocks and special interest groups which effectively control segments of county functions."[18]

POWERS OF COUNTY BOARDS

County boards differ from state to state in the powers granted them by state constitutions and laws. There are important differences between commission counties, council-administrator counties, and council-elected executive counties in the powers exercised by county boards. All county boards have three types of powers commonly exercised by legislative bodies:

- the power to enact ordinances similar in many respects to the ordinances enacted by city councils;
- the power to review budget requests, appropriate funds, establish county tax

levies (up to state tax limits), and incur debt (however, the incurrence of debt usually takes approval of the voters after action by the county board); and,

- the power to hear reports from county officers and exercise oversight of administration.

In addition, county boards may have one or more of the following powers depending on state constitutions, state laws, and the form of government used. These include the power to:

- appoint administrators, department directors, and members of boards and commissions;
- provide day-to-day supervision of administrative officials not under the supervision of elected or appointed executives;
- issue licenses and regulate business;
- adopt (and change) by resolution a comprehensive plan and adopt (and make changes in) a zoning ordinance, subdivision regulations, and housing, building, and other codes;
- take actions to create and finance dependent special districts;
- let contracts, authorize purchases, maintain buildings, pay bills, and take other actions needed to maintain county offices;
- equalize property tax assessments; and,
- adopt policies and regulations for a variety of county functions.

Do county boards have adequate legal powers to meet the needs of their citizens for the many programs which county governments administer? There is no easy answer since conditions vary from program to program and state to state. Even within a state, a home rule county may have adequate powers to carry out a particular function and a non-home rule county may not. In addition to the presence or absence of a home rule charter, the adequacy of a county board's authority depends on a variety of factors.

The provisions of state constitutions. For example, a constitutional provision requiring an elected coroner may block the attempts of the county board to replace an unqualified coroner with an appointed professional medical examiner.

The provisions of state law. Very specific provisions of state law may unnecessarily hamper county boards. For example, reforms in the procedures for recording and microfilming legal documents supported by the county board, county clerk, auditor, and recorder may be blocked by specific laws requiring certain indexes and records.

The flexibility to start new programs. Counties are best served by laws which provide great flexibility in establishing new programs. Particularly helpful is a state law which allows counties to establish new programs not specifically prohibited by state law.

The form of county government. County boards have more adequate powers to establish and make changes in programs in counties in which the administration is not split with many important programs under independently elected officials.

The impact of the political party system of the county. A strong, unified party system under the leadership of the chairman of the county board, for example, could enhance the power of the county board.

Elected Executives and "Row" Officers

In commission counties, administrative responsibilities are divided between the county governing board and a number of independently elected officials. The term "row" officers is sometimes used to describe these officials because their titles appear in a long row on the organization chart of the county. There are independently elected "row" officers in council-administrator and council-elected executive counties as well, although there are often fewer of these officials and some of their powers may be diminished.

In the council-elected executive form of county government, another type of elective official is found—a county executive whose powers to supervise and administer extend generally to all county agencies not under the supervision of "row" officers. This section will describe the powers of elected officers and discuss the effect of their offices on the coordination of county programs.

ELECTED EXECUTIVES

It is not farfetched to say that an elected county executive is comparable to a governor, or even to the President of the United States, in the many demanding roles which must be filled simultaneously. The executive is the county's chief policy-maker who incorporates in a proposed budget the direction and priorities the legislative body ought to pursue.

As chief administrator, the executive is responsible for seeing that ordinances and other examples of legislative intent are actually carried out. The appointment power covers most, but not all, department heads, and there are important departments under the direction of other independently elected officials, as at the state level.

Although there may be legislators elected on an at-large basis, the county executive is not only considered a notch or two higher for the above stated reasons, but also because this official is the top elected party official on the county level.

In sum, the county executive regardless of personal preference, is likely to be the most visible elected county official. Like a governor or the president, the executive sometimes receives blame from citizens for the actions of officials he or she does not appoint. Rightly or wrongly, it is the executive who will ultimately be responsible for public satisfaction or dissatisfaction.

The Westchester County Charter states that "the county executive shall be the chief executive and administrative officer of the county and the official head of county government."[19] Among the duties of the county executive specified by the Westchester County Charter are:

- to supervise, direct and control the administrative services and departments of the county in accordance with the county charter and local laws;
- to present an annual budget to the county board and to provide the county board, at least once a year, a general statement of the finances, government and affairs of the county;
- to present to the county board, from time to time, such other information that he may deem necessary or the board

may request. To recommend measures he deems expedient;

- to see that county officers, boards, agencies, commissions and departments faithfully perform their duties;
- to make studies and investigations in the best interests of the county, to compel the attendance of witnesses, and (if necessary) to examine the books, records, or papers of county agencies to ascertain facts in connection with any study or investigation;
- to veto acts of the county board in a manner prescribed by the county charter;
- to appoint the head or acting head of county departments, offices, boards, and commissions subject to confirmation by the county board; and,
- to perform other duties as may be prescribed to the county executive by the county charter or acts of the county board.[20]

CLERK, COURT CLERK, AUDITOR AND RECORDER

The county offices of clerk, court clerk, auditor, and recorder may be separate elective offices, or two or more of the offices may be combined. In Idaho, all four offices are combined into a single elective position. Nebraska has separate offices of county clerk, clerk of the district court, and register of deeds. Utah counties have clerks, auditors, and recorders. Although the functions may be combined or separated in different ways, the offices of county clerk, auditor, and recorder usually have the following responsibilities.

Assistance to the county board. An important duty of the county clerk in commission counties is often serving as secretary to the county board. In this capacity, the county clerk compiles the agenda for the board, records the action of the board, and follows up on board actions by writing letters and memoranda requested by the board. The county clerk may also help the board prepare a county budget.

Election responsibilities. The county clerk (or similar county officer) may be responsible for registering voters, supervising precinct election officials, publishing election notices, and handling much of the detailed work in election administration.

Serving the court system. The court clerk (or a deputy county clerk where the functions are combined with the county clerk) serves as an important staff officer to the main trial court having jurisdiction in the county. The court clerk is usually responsible for collecting and recording fines, forfeitures, penalties, and costs in criminal cases. Personnel in the court clerk's office keep records of court proceedings, handle judicial correspondence, type court documents, and may prepare the formal writs and process papers issued by the court.

Recording legal documents. The county recorder or registrar of deeds (or a deputy clerk where the functions are combined with the county clerk) plays an important role in the orderly transfer of title to property. By recording each deed, mortgage, and lease, the recorder or registrar of deeds is providing a record needed for a thorough title search. The county recorder may also record, index, and microfilm other important legal documents such as marriage licenses, mining claims, wills, liens, and official bonds.

Accounting and auditing. A common function of the elected county auditor (or a deputy clerk or auditor) is to audit bills or other claims against the county and prepare warrants in payment of these bills. In making the audit, the county auditor will make sure that the goods or services have been actually received, that there is no error in calculating the amount of the charge, and that the agency receiving the goods or services has sufficient funds and the authority to make the expenditure. To insure that county agencies are not over-spending their appropriations, it is common for the county auditor to maintain accounting records on all appropriations. The county auditor may also have responsibilities in computing and collecting property taxes.

COUNTY TREASURER

In Michigan, as in many other states, the county treasurer is charged with the responsibility of receiving county moneys from all sources.[21] The treasurer deposits county funds in banks and keeps records of revenues and bank balances. The treasurer may also keep records of the expenditures, revenues, and balances of county funds. In some states, the treasurer participates in the property tax collection process by sending out delinquency notices and following up on delinquent taxes.

The county treasurer generally invests funds not immediately needed for county expenses and may earn substantial amounts of interest for the county through skillful investment of these idle funds in government securities. In some states, the county treasurer also acts as public administrator of the estates of persons who die without a will. If the county treasurer has discretion in designating which banks are to receive county deposits, the treasurer's position can be politically sensitive.

COUNTY ASSESSOR

The county assessor has the responsibility for appraising or setting the value of all property subject to county property taxes. The assessor has extensive maps of all parcels of property in the county and records the physical characteristics and value of all buildings. When a new building is constructed, the assessor and his staff will usually know of this from the issuance of the building permit and will make an inspection to determine the assessed valuation. The determination of assessed valuation of a home is based on a number of factors, such as the number of square feet of floor space, specific features (such as a finished basement), the location of the home, and the sales price of similar homes in the same neighborhood.

The assessor frequently is responsible for sending out notices of assessment to property owners so they may have the opportunity to challenge the assessment if they think it is excessive. This official may also send out tax notices and collect property taxes. In some counties, the assessor has non-property tax functions such as issuing automobile license plates and collecting a number of taxes and fees. Minimum qualifications for the position of assessor have been established in only a few states, but elected assessors and their deputies gain skill in assessing through experience and attending training conferences and courses.[22] Assessors are in a politically sensitive position

and may be under pressure from taxpayers to under-assess their property.

PROSECUTING ATTORNEY

The county prosecuting attorney has two major roles. His first is to act as attorney to the county board and county officials by providing legal advice on a variety of matters and giving informal opinions on the legality of proposed action. He also represents the county in many types of cases in which the county is a plaintiff or defendant. The county attorney may, for example, represent the county in a suit in which a citizen claims injury because of the negligence of a county employee, a case relating to the bankruptcy of a creditor, or a dispute between an employee and the county involving compensation.[23]

A second role of the county prosecuting attorney is to prosecute, in the name of the state, persons suspected of crimes. In this role, the prosecuting attorney is a vital part of the criminal justice system. With an important responsibility in the preferral of charges either by grand jury or by the information system, the county attorney normally appears at the arraignment and presents the state's case at the trial.

In some counties, the roles are separated, with a county counsel serving as legal advisor to county officials and a district or state's attorney having criminal justice responsibilities.

SHERIFF[24]

The county sheriff and his deputies serve as the county law enforcement agency patrolling streets and highways, checking the speed of motor vehicles, investigating crimes, and arresting suspected criminals. The sheriff's office also helps to enforce laws on the closing hours of taverns, illegal possession of narcotics, arson, burglary, assault, and many other crimes against persons and property. In many counties, the sheriff's office provides the largest police force in the unincorporated areas and in the small communities of the county.

As a county law enforcement officer, the sheriff is usually responsible for the county jail, the custody and feeding of prisoners, and courthouse security. In many small counties, the county sheriff maintains the only jail in the entire county. County administration of jails occurs even in the northeastern states in which towns and townships provide the primary law enforcement for the unincorporated area of the county.

The sheriff and his deputies generally serve process papers on a variety of court matters such as divorces, damage suits, and bankruptcy proceedings. Under the authority of a court, they may have the task of securing, storing, advertising, and selling property to satisfy a debt. The county sheriff often acts as a court officer, attending sessions of the court and serving subpoenas, summonses, and arrest warrants. The sheriff and his deputies are often called upon to give assistance in accidents and to lead search parties in rural areas to find wrecked planes or lost hunters.

CORONER

Coroners were elected county officials in 26 states in 1973.[25] When a person has died by violence, under suspicious circumstances, or when a physician is not in attendance, the coroner is called upon to determine the cause of death. Before preparing an official report on his findings, the coroner usually examines the body, may have an autopsy performed, and may assemble a jury to conduct an official inquest. Many coroners lack medical training, and the election of county coroners has been severely criticized by some writers.

An alternative to the elected county coroner is the appointment of a physician as a medical examiner. An examiner with medical training is much better able to determine the cause of death than an elected coroner without medical training. A 1973 report states that in 15 states the office of coroner has been abolished, and in other states the county is given the option to replace the coroner with a medical examiner.[26]

OTHER COUNTY ELECTIVE "ROW" OFFICERS

Elected county superintendents of schools have been abolished in most states but continue to provide specialized financial and program services in some states. The county surveyor's office has been abolished or stripped of most of its former land surveying duties. There are a few other elective "row" officers such as drain commissioners in Michigan. With a few exceptions, these other "row" officials play a minor role in county government.[27]

FRAGMENTATION OF THE COUNTY EXECUTIVE FUNCTIONS

There is little doubt that the existence of many independently elected "row" officers fragments the executive functions of county government and makes more difficult the problem of coordinating county services. The problem may be particularly serious in many of the approximately 1,500 counties of 25,000 people or less, governed under a commission form of government. In these counties, all or nearly all full-time county employees may be under the direction of independently elected "row" officers.[28] If these officials refuse to cooperate on county problems, such as streamlining the property tax assessment and collection system, there is no means of forcing cooperation except the limited budget pressure at the disposal of the county commissioners. Part-time county commissioners have a difficult task in coordinating the work of full-time "row" officers. In some counties, political party leaders are able to provide an important coordinating role particularly when all county officials are of the same party.

Appointed County Administrators

The term "county administrator" has generally been used to describe the appointed administrator in the council-administrator form of government. This official is appointed by the county legislative body and may be given the title "county manager," "administrative officer," "county administrative assistant," or a similar designation. He or she may be appointed by the county executive in the council-elected executive form of county government. The various county administrators have one common characteristic — they hold the highest administrative post in their respective counties, and they are in a key position to bring professional expertise and coordination to county government. Their skills, training, and responsibilities are of importance to a study of the operation of county government.

BACKGROUND OF
COUNTY ADMINISTRATORS

An extensive study of county administrators in 202 counties, conducted by the International City Management Association, revealed these factors about those responding to the survey:

- the median age of administrators was 43;
- nearly all (99 percent) were men and nearly all were Caucasian;
- 44 percent were registered as Democrats, 17 percent were independents, and 21 percent were registered as Republicans;
- the administrators were highly educated (97 percent had some education beyond high school, 83 percent had a college degree and some work toward a masters, and 35 percent had a masters degree);
- county administrators with college degrees tended to specialize in public administration (31 percent), political science (25 percent), or business administration (23 percent);
- about 62 percent of the respondents had participated in at least one professional institute or training program in the last three years; and,
- more than 95 percent belonged to at least one religious, fraternal, service, or community organization with 48 percent belonging to a service organization, 44 percent to a fraternal organization, and 44 percent to the International City Management Association.[29]

This profile of county administrators gives the picture of a highly trained, professional group with membership in community organizations — a group similar in many respects to city managers and school superintendents.

CAREERS

The study of county administrators revealed that most of the respondents had spent an average of nearly six years in their present positions.[30] The typical county administrator had worked most of his professional life in government with only 16 percent having previously been in private industry. About half of the administrators reported their most recent previous job was in municipal or county government, with many holding the position of chief administrative officer, assistant manager, or department director.

From the survey results, Larry Brown suggested that the county administrators "tend to have had substantive experience in top governmental positions and to have come to their present management position with a solid exposure to the management of local government operations."[31] Most county administrators left their previous post for career advancement, a salary increase, or a desire for a new type of experience.

In listing their career objectives, 45 percent of the administrators reported that they hoped to seek an administrator's position in a larger county, 16 percent hoped to move into private enterprise, and 14 percent wanted to seek a position in a county of about the same size. County administrators are an upwardly mobile group who usually advance by accepting better paying jobs in larger counties. County administrators in counties of 250,000 or more people are paid salaries comparable to higher level state civil servants.

RESPONSIBILITIES

According to the poll, county administrators do not want to exercise political leadership. Larry Brown points out that an appointed administrator "cannot become the political representative of the county without destroying the employee-employer relationship and without destroying the basis for electing the governing board."[32]

Most administrators want general supervision from the governing board, but do not want the governing board to spend its time on administrative details. They see themselves as more frequently participating in policy formulation than in initiating policies. They nearly always consult with the county council before drafting budget proposals or appointing or removing department heads. They generally orient new council members on major issues and advise the council on a variety of matters, but they feel that their most frequent role is exercising administrative leadership.

The profile gives the impression of an able group of generalists working primarily in supervision, budgeting, and day-to-day administration.[33]

The specific responsibilities of county administrators vary depending on whether the county has a council-manager, chief administrative officer, or some other council-administrator plan of government. The exact duties of the administrator are often described by the county charter (if one exists) or by an ordinance passed by the county board. The Dade County (Florida) Charter, for example, states that "The Board of County Commissioners shall appoint a County Manager who shall be the chief executive officer and head of the administrative branch of county government."[34] The Charter gives many specific responsibilities to the county manager, such as appointing certain department executives and recommending a county budget to the Board. In addition, it states:

> The Manager shall be responsible to the Board of County Commissioners for the administration of all units of the county government under his jurisdiction, and for carrying out policies adopted by the Board.
>
> The Manager shall have the power to issue and place into effect administrative orders, rules, and regulations. The organization and operating procedure of departments shall be set forth in administrative regulations which the Manager shall develop, place into effect by administrative orders, and submit to the Board. The Board may, by resolution, modify such orders, rules or regulations providing, however, no such orders, rules or regulations creating, merging, or combining departments, shall become effective until approved by resolution of the Board.[35]

In Alameda County (California), the basic duties of the county administrator are described, not by a county charter but by an ordinance passed by the Board of Supervisors. The Alameda County Administrator does not have the appointment powers of the Dade County Manager but has a number of important administrative functions, including

- advising, assisting, and acting as agent

for the Board of Supervisors and carrying out orders or regulations as directed by the Board;
- studying the proper organization of departments and recommending systems and procedures;
- conducting continuous research in administrative practices;
- reviewing the functions of departments to eliminate duplication and recommending to the Board policies for coordination and orderly conduct of departmental business;
- directing and performing central administrative services such as central statistical, office appliance, and clerical pools;
- establishing the enforcement of proper personnel policies and practices;
- exercising continuous control of expenditures under the supervision of the Board of Supervisors and reviewing, examining, recommending and controlling financial procedures;
- recommending a long-term plan of capital improvements when requested by the Board of Supervisors; and,
- analyzing budget requests and preparing a budget for the County Board of Supervisors.[36]

Appointed administrators, such as the Dade County Manager and Alameda County Administrator, are able to bring unified supervision and coordination to county government thus blunting criticism that most counties lack a single chief executive.

County Politics and Organizational Structure

There are three main forms of county government (commission, council-administrator, and council-elected executive) and many variations of these forms. The home rule movement has accelerated the trend toward optional forms of county government and toward voter selection of the form of government they consider best. For example, the 1971–72 Montana home rule constitutional amendment requires each county and municipality "to review its structure and submit one alternative form of government to the qualified electors…"[37]

A 1975 Montana law permits 4 main forms of county government and 12 structural sub-options.[38] Furthermore, the Montana law allows six types of cooperative arrangements such as county-municipality consolidation, county-municipality confederation, consolidation of two counties, and consolidation of services between cities and counties. Thus, Montana voters can choose among more than 100 variations of organizational forms, structural sub-options, and cooperative arrangements to shape a form of government that best fits their individual needs. This trend towards more organizational options is also evident in Utah, Pennsylvania, and other states.

The organizational structure of a county is only one of a number of factors which influence how county government operates in practice. The political system of a county can bring policy coordination to a commission form of county government if all county officials are of the same party, or it can bring deeper division between officials if there is bitter strife between parties or party factions. Wearing the mantle of majority party leader in the county, a county judge, strong board chairman, or experienced county clerk may achieve nearly the powers of a county executive. Further research is badly needed to show the manner in which the party system and interest groups influence county government policies.

The political system within a county not only affects how county government operates in practice but the strength of county government in securing more adequate funding for county services and a greater measure of county home rule.

References

1. Russell W. Maddox and Robert F. Fuquay, *State and Local Government*, 3rd ed. (New York: D. Van Nostrand Company, 1975), p. 439. The authors use the quotation as an introduction to the diversity of county organizational structure.

2. Hugh L. LeBlanc and D. Trudeau Allensworth, *The Politics of States and Urban Communities* (New York: Harper and Row, 1971), p. 194.

3. Florence Zeller, "Forms of County Government," National Association of Counties and International City Management Association, *The County Year Book* (Washington: National Association of Counties and International City Management Association, 1975), p. 27.

4. Henry S. Gilbertson, *The County, The "Dark Continent" of American Politics* (New York: The National Short Ballot Association, 1917), pp. 34, 49, 50.

5. Lane W. Lancaster, *Government in Rural America*, 2nd ed. (New York: D. Van Nostrand Company, Inc., 1952), p. 54.

6. Russell W. Maddox and Robert F. Fuquay, p. 452.

7. Florence Zeller, p. 27. For further information on the plural executive and other forms of county government, see the previously cited article by Florence Zeller; also Clyde S. Snider, *Local Government in Rural America* (New York: Appleton-Century-Crofts, Inc., 1957), pp. 119–194; and Herbert Sydney Duncombe, *County Government in America* (Washington: National Association of Counties Research Foundation, 1966), pp. 9–12 and 55–59.

8. Florence Zeller, pp. 27, 28.

9. The 1975 estimate was made by Florence Zeller of the National Association of Counties staff. Ibid., p. 28. It is difficult to determine the number of counties which are operating under the council-administrator form of government because the titles of council administrator positions vary widely. Using criteria established by the National Association of County Administrators, a National Association of Counties staff member counted 587 county administrators as of January 1977.

10. Ibid., pp. 29, 30.

11. The National Association of Counties, *NACo Fact Sheet—Elected Executives* (Washington: National Association of Counties, 1977).

12. Ibid., p. 31.

13. Michael S. Vollmer, Herbert Sydney Duncombe and Katherine D. Pell, *Handbook for County Officials in Idaho* (Moscow: Bureau of Public Affairs Research, University of Idaho, 1974), pp. 3, 9. Informally, a county board chairman of ability and long experience can greatly influence other board members.

14. James E. Thomas, *A Manual for Alabama County Commissioners* (University: Bureau of Public Administration, University of Alabama, 1975), p. 10. There are also county boards in Alabama with three, four, six, and seven members.

15. S.B. Chadman, "Organization of the County Governing Body," National Association of Counties, *Guide to County Organization and Management* (Washington: National Association of Counties, 1968), p. 120.

16. For a description of cases in New York, Wisconsin, and Michigan on this issue, see Herbert Sydney Duncombe and Clifford Dobler, "Local Legislative Apportionment," *Guide to County Organization and Management* (Washington: National Association of Counties, 1968), pp. 125, 126.

17. Kenneth VerBurg, *Guide to Michigan County Government* (East Lansing: The Institute for Community Development and Services, Michigan State University, 1972), p. II-5.

18. S.B. Chadman, p. 119.

19. Westchester County Government, *Westchester County Charter*, Article III, Section 16.

20. Ibid.

21. An excellent description of the county treasurer in Michigan may be found in Kenneth VerBurg, pp. III-3 and III-4.

22. In 1968, only California, New Jersey, Oregon, and Tennessee had statewide qualifications for assessors. For a description of the qualifications and work of assessors, see International Association of Assessing Officers, "Assessing," *Guide to County Organization and Management* (Washington: National Association of Counties, 1968), pp. 252–255.

23. For a thorough description of the types of cases which a county attorney may handle and the work of a county counsel, see Harold W. Kennedy, "Legal Functions," *Guide to County Organization and Management* (Washington: National Association of Counties, 1968), pp. 273–289.

24. For an excellent description of the work of the sheriff in Georgia counties, see Claude Abercrombie, "Sheriffs" (Washington: National Association of Counties, 1968), *Guide to County Organization and Management*, pp. 258–266.

25. Statistical information on the offices of coroner and medical examiner are from the National Association of Counties, 1975), p. 45.

26. Ibid.

27. One exception is the drain commissioner in Michigan counties who administers almost all aspects of the establishment and maintenance of drainage facilities in the county. Kenneth VerBurg, pp. IV-47 through IV-54.

28. In 1966, in one Idaho county, the county commissioners appointed only two full-time county employees — the courthouse janitor and the weed supervisor. In 1976, the commissioners of the same county of about 25,000 people appointed seven full-time employees out of a total of seventy. As new functions, such as civil defense, planning, parks, and solid waste, were undertaken by the county, the number of employees appointed by the county commissioners grew.

29. The study was reported in Larry J. Brown, "County Administrators: Characteristics and Managerial Styles," *The County Year Book* (Washington: National Association of Counties and International City Management Association, 1975), pp. 34–43.

30. Ibid., p. 36.

31. Ibid.

32. Ibid., p. 38.

33. Ibid., p. 41. County administrators were asked to rank their managerial style on a scale from one (always) to five (never). Participation in policy formulation ranked lower on the scale (1.6) than initiating policies (2.4).

34. Metropolitan Dade County, *County Charter*, Section 3.01.

35. Ibid., Sections 3.04 and 4.02.

36. Alameda County, *Ordinance*, Article 5-6, and letters from County Administrator Loren W. Enoch to Sydney Duncombe, dated January 20, 1977, and February 18, 1977.

37. Montana, *Constitution*, Article XI, Section 9.

38. The four main options are the commission-executive, commission-manager, commission and commission chairman forms. For an excellent description of the many structural sub-options and cooperative arrangements, see James J. Lopach and Lauren S. McKinsey, *Handbook of Montana Forms of Local Government* (Missoula: University of Montana, 1975), pp. 122–163.

CHAPTER 14

THE SUBURBAN COUNTY

R. Scott Fosler

Over the past century, America's population center has shifted from farm to city to suburb. In the process, the reality behind these concepts of place had been transformed to the extent that they mislead more than they inform. Urban regions are far more diverse than the conventional model of a nuclear central city surrounded by suburban bedroom communities. And suburban areas have long since been transformed from the homogeneous track housing of popular imagery into diverse economic and residential geo-complexes that defy common description.

Counties, meanwhile, have become the frontline agents of governance in the new urban regions. Suburban counties confront the challenge of governing their own affairs as well as growing leadership responsibility for determining how America's urban regions will be governed.

The New Mainstream

The concept of a metropolitan area reflected in such statistical definitions as "Metropolitan Statistical Area" (MSA) is based on an outdated demographic and economic model, one in which a metropolitan area is comprised of concentric circles around a dominant core. The core includes a central business district (CBD), interspersed with generally high-density housing. Adjacent to the CBD is an industrial zone of factories and lower density working-class neighborhoods. Beyond lie the suburbs, a fringe of single-family residential neighborhoods on ample lots, generally occupied by middle- to upper-income families whose husband commutes to work in the CBD and whose wife stays at home. Surrounding the metropolitan area is a rural, predominantly agricultural, countryside.

This model is at odds with reality.

The suburban zone — whose very name implies that it is subordinate to the central city — now contains the dominant share of the metro population. In 1988, about 76 percent of the American population (or 185 million people) lived in the nation's 282 MSAs. Of the total MSA population, about 60 percent lived outside central cities in the zone defined as "suburban."

If one includes counties adjacent to MSAs as de facto extensions of the metropolitan area, the "suburban" population is even larger. In 1980, about 10 percent of the total national population resided in counties of 20,000 or more that were adjacent to MSAs. The 1990 census is likely to show that metropolitan areas account for close to 90 percent of the total national population and that the "suburban" proportion is home to about one-half of all Americans.

Equally important, economic power also has shifted from the central city to the once dependent suburbs. In 1989, the non-central city parts of metro areas had 58.1 million jobs, or 63 percent of all metropolitan jobs. During 1980–89, the number of jobs in central cities increased by 8 million or 23 percent, while the number of metro jobs outside of

Originally published as "The Suburban County: Governing Mainstream Diversity," *Intergovernmental Perspective*, Vol. 17, No. 1, Winter 1991. Published by the U.S. Advisory Commission on Intergovernmental Relations, Washington, D.C.

central cities jumped 17.5 million or 30 percent.[1] By 1980, fewer than one in five of the nation's workers were making the stereotypical commute from the suburbs to downtown; in contrast, twice as many were commuting from suburb to suburb.[2]

The CBD is only one of many employment centers scattered throughout most metropolitan areas. It may still be the biggest and most centrally located, but in few places does the downtown comprise even a majority of office space, employment, or retail sales. Nor is "downtown" necessarily the economic engine of growth for the metropolitan economy. During the 1980s, suburban employment growth was determined relatively independently of central city growth, while central city growth was influenced in part by suburban growth.[3]

Assertive Diversity

If the vast zone of the metropolis outside the central city no longer conforms to the suburban stereotype, neither has it evolved into one new pattern.

Its prime characteristic is its very diversity. In sharp contrast to the popular perception of boring sameness or monotonous homogeneity, the organizing concept of this new suburban pattern, to the extent there is one, is the drive to meet the specialized needs, desires, and choices of individuals. The result is wide variation in housing types, specialized shopping, customized workplaces, and personalized automobile transportation.

Another element of diversity is that parts of the suburban zone vary greatly from one another. For example, Daniel Garnick has divided the metropolitan area into four county types: the core county, which contains the "central city" and parts of the metropolitan area outside of the central city; core-contiguous counties next to the central city (or near suburbs); non–core-contiguous counties with population of at least 250,000 (or far suburbs); and non–core-contiguous counties with population of less than 250,000 (or exurbs).[4]

The inner tier of near suburbs may have many of the problems plaguing the central cities: a population with a high proportion of the aging and very young that is poorer and losing its middle class, deteriorating housing stock and physical infrastructure, loss of higher paying jobs, high rates of crime, and the mounting pressures of AIDS, drugs, and homelessness.

The middle-tier far suburbs are likely to be more stable, with ample middle-class homeowners and relatively strong employment centers, although even many of these areas are feeling economic stress.

The outer-tier exurbs are the expanding edge of the metropolis, with new housing, increasingly crowded schools and roads, and young adults forming new families or establishing themselves in single-person households. The outer tier must contend with such issues as farmland preservation and the location of LULUs ("locally unwanted land uses"), including landfills, incinerators, and prisons. At the edge of the outer tier is the twilight of "penturbia" and beyond—the new sweep of low-density residential, industrial, commercial, and agricultural land uses that fades imperceptibly into rural areas, which themselves show an increasing diversity of economic and residential patterns.

Even the notion of suburban "tiers" pays more homage to the conventional metropolitan model of concentric circles than is warranted, because development in most urban regions rarely conforms to such neat patterns.

A third element of diversity results from important differences among urban regions. Some of these differences are due to varying stages of development. For example, since the 1960s, according to Garnick's data, the core counties on average in all metropolitan areas have experienced sluggish population growth, while the central cities have declined in population. Beyond the core counties, the growth pattern varies. In the older metropolitan areas of New England and the Middle Atlantic, the far suburbs and exurbs have been growing more rapidly than the near suburbs. In the newer metro areas of the Southeast, Southwest, and Rocky Mountain, the near suburbs have been growing more rapidly than the far suburbs and exurbs. During the 1970s, the near suburbs had the highest relative employment growth rates in every region except New England, where the exurbs grew faster.

The wide differences in form and function among urban regions also suggest the evolution of quite different types of urban regions. For example, the size, geographical reach, economic dynamics, transportation patterns, and social structure of the Greater Los Angeles area of 13 million people suggest a regional form that is significantly different from the Minneapolis–St. Paul metropolitan area of 2.5 million. The Northeast megalopolis stretching from Maine to Virginia is comprised of a series of converging metropolitan areas that constitute an urban region different in important respects from either Southern California or the Twin Cities. The Southeast Florida, Puget Sound, Chicago, and Phoenix metropolitan areas all have still other unique characteristics.

The Challenge to Governance

Suburban counties are likely to become the centers of action in addressing the fundamental challenges to governance in the 1990s.

The nature of the challenges will depend, first, on their location within the urban region. There are 738 counties in MSAs, or 24 percent of the nation's more than 3,100 counties. Nearly all of these cover some portion of the MSA outside of the central city, including those that cover all or parts of the central city.

County governments that serve the inner tier may have more in common with central city governments, and those that serve the outer tier may have more in common with rural governments, than either has with the other. Some suburban counties, meanwhile, serve areas in all three tiers. They may also reach into traditional rural and agricultural areas, and thus are likely to face urban poverty and population outmigration, along with rapid growth, demands for new schools and roads, and the issue of farmland preservation. Consolidated city-county governments may cover all three suburban tiers as well as the central city.

In some suburbs, the overbuilding of office and retail space (and, in some cases, middle- and upper-income housing) combined with recession will provide a respite from the pressures of growth even as they create new problems. For other suburbs, growth will persist or resume after a hiatus, so that counties will continue to face the dilemma of accommodating economic and residential expansion even as they seek to protect the quality of life of existing residents. One key question is whether counties will use a hiatus in growth to catch up with the backlog of infrastructure problems and plan for future expansion.

Whatever part of the urban region they cover, nearly all suburban counties will confront problems across a range of functions common to most local governments, such as deficiencies in education, inadequate affordable housing, traffic congestion, weak mass transit, pollution, and a burden of waste, crime and drugs, and inadequate social services. Of 423 MSA counties responding to a National Association of Counties (NACo) survey in 1985, at least 95 percent provided services for police protection and corrections, legal assistance and prosecution, public health, social services, transportation, public utilities, natural resources, land use, community and economic development, parks, and education.

The challenge of meeting service needs can be expected to increase due to pressures from changing demographics (e.g., as increasing numbers of elderly people and educationally disadvantaged children), fiscal tightening, and economic distress. This pressure will be all the greater as federal and state governments confront growing fiscal pressures and squeeze local governments by reducing grants and imposing unfunded mandates on them.

Consequently, the capacity of suburban counties to provide services will depend increasingly on their ability to improve the productivity of public services systems, to find new sources of revenue, and to strengthen the local and regional economy. To do so will require more innovative managements and more creative interaction with the private sector and citizens. It will also mean moving beyond "privatization" and "partnership" to redefine public needs, rethink government responsibilities, and redesign public systems that involve government, business, nonprofits, civic groups, and individual citizens.

This will require more than a technical adjustment, but rather a wholesale conceptual, organizational, and political restructuring of the relationship between government and citizens. Indeed, one consequence of a society tailored to the desires and choices of individuals is that the pursuit of personalized desires can easily conflict with the interests of the general public. For example, the spread of single-family housing reduces open space and increases automobile congestion. Central to the governance challenge, therefore, will be to define narrow and overlapping communities of interest more precisely, and to find more creative and efficient ways to serve them.

A related challenge is to link land use management more closely to the provision of public services. This will require, at minimum, an adjustment in the traditional planning function. Planning in most suburbs has been equated with "land use planning" — master plans, zoning, subdivision regulation, and the like. In the future, planning will need a broader concept of foresight, including economic, programmatic, and strategic planning.

The Leadership Imperative

Suburban counties will not only confront new issues of governance in their own jurisdictions but will also be pushed to take a stronger leadership role in regional governance.

Effective and efficient governance will require increasing interaction across the political boundaries of the entire urban region. Most metropolitan areas in the United States are governed by many local jurisdictions. There are, to be sure, benefits that derive to smaller units of government by permitting residents choice in the level and quality of services they desire, and by permitting governments to take advantage of economies of small scale.[5] Most metropolitan areas, therefore, are likely to rely principally on interlocal agreements to deal with broader service needs and problems.

There also will be a need for regionwide institutions to deal not only with such familiar areas of regional cooperation as transportation, water supply, and waste management, but also areas such as human resource

development.[6] Consequently, the potential for city-county consolidation or other more comprehensive regionwide institutions may be reconsidered as local governments confront new challenges.

Urban regions are also prime units of economic geography in the new global economy, and their competitiveness will depend in part on the actions of local government. As global integration and competition increase, the importance of national boundaries and economic policies is diminishing relative to the power of international economic forces and the capacity of regions to shape their own economic destiny.[7]

The principal determinants of local economic competitiveness cannot be disassociated from those of the region as a whole. They include:

- Human investment to assure a competitive work force;[8]
- Technology, knowledge, and information services, which are central elements in the economic "infrastructure" of the future;
- Industrial clusters of small, medium, and large producers, suppliers, and related services that work through networks in specific industries concentrated in the region;
- Physical infrastructure, such as telecommunications networks, transportation systems (including cross-county rather than suburb-to-downtown links), water supply, and waste disposal facilities;
- Protection of the natural environment — including air, water, parks and forests, watersheds, stream valleys, and farmland — to enhance the quality of life and to attract and retain a quality work force and job base.

The economic vitality of any one jurisdiction will depend increasingly on the strength of these factors for the region as a whole.

Suburban counties will also be pushed into a stronger leadership role to deal with both metropolitan governance and economic development because they will have the comparative political influence, institutional capacity, and resources to do so. In the past, the central city government was seen as the natural leader of the metropolitan area. Today, however, many central cities confront stresses that make it difficult for them to meet their own needs, let alone assume primary leadership duties for their region. To be sure, other types of local government — municipalities, towns, villages, and special districts — play important roles. But counties are more likely to have the population and economic weight, geographical coverage, and range of governmental powers that give them the stake and the capacity to take a more active leadership role. Some 164 counties, or nearly 40 percent of all MSA counties responding to the 1985 NACo survey, reported that they had home rule. The point here is not that leadership will shift completely from the central city to the suburban counties, but rather that local governments throughout the region will need to find a collaborative style of relationships suitable to regions that no longer have one dominant jurisdiction.

Failure of urban regions to deal with their own needs will lead to stronger state involvement in regional affairs. The question then will be whether growing suburban political clout is exercised to strengthen the entire region, or to serve the interests of suburban jurisdictions alone. In some instances, city-suburb tensions may be heightened as suburbs seek to enhance their power in state government by building coalitions with other suburban jurisdictions throughout the state.

Part of the metropolitan political battle also will be played out in the national arena. The national political strength of the suburbs is increasing, especially in the U.S. House of Representatives. However, because the federal deficit will limit new federal spending for local programs, both central city and suburban jurisdictions may well find it in their mutual interest to reconcile their differences and find common cause within their state and region rather than the federal arena.

Notes

1. *Employment and Earnings*, January 1981 and January 1990.

2. Robert Fishman, "America's New City: Megalopolis Unbound," *The Wilson Quarterly* 14 (Winter 1990): 27.

3. Anita A. Summers and Peter D. Linneman, "Patterns and Processes of Urban Employment Decentralization in the U.S. 1976–1986," prepared for the Conference on Comparisons of Urban Economic Development in the U.S. and Western Europe (Bellagio, Italy, July 9–13, 1990).

4. Daniel Garnick, "Local Area Economic Growth Patterns," in M. McGeary and L. Flynn, eds., *Urban Change and Poverty* (Washington, DC: National Academy Press, 1988).

5. U.S. Advisory Commission on Intergovernmental Relations, *The Organization of Local Public Economies* (Washington, DC, 1987).

6. See, for example, Robert Agranoff, "Managing Federalism through Metropolitan Human Service Intergovernmental Bodies," *Publius: The Journal of Federalism* 20 (Winter 1990): 1–22.

7. "International Economic Competitiveness," *Intergovernmental Perspective* 16 (Winter 1990): entire issue; and "State and Local Governments in International Affairs," *Intergovernmental Perspective* 16 (Spring 1990): entire issue.

8. Committee for Economic Development, *An America That Works: The Life-Cycle Approach to a Competitive Work Force* (New York, 1990) lays out a comprehensive strategy for human investment, with strong reliance on state, local, and regional roles.

CHAPTER 15

THE RURAL COUNTY

Kaye Braaten

The 1990s will present rural communities with great challenges. The principal challenge will be the ability of counties to forge brave leadership for citizens to help themselves. Responses to coming changes will either be carefully thought out by county leaders or forced by circumstances. Counties and their incorporated cities must be poised to create a workable atmosphere for the action of the 1990s.

Counties are one of the oldest forms of government, dating back to sixth century England. Counties were formed in America as a means of establishing local order prior to 1776. There are more than 3,000 counties in the U.S. today, and of those, 2,670 or 88 percent have populations of less than 100,000.

Many counties have fulfilled their responsibilities in law enforcement, judicial services, tax collection, and other areas in the same unobtrusive manner for generations. County organizational structure, in most cases, has not changed since the counties were incorporated. Although the stability of government entities is to be applauded, often that same stability has led to stagnation and a failure to adapt to the changing needs of society.

Falling Population and Rising Problems

Major shifts in population from rural to urban areas in the last two decades have forced many counties to evaluate the way they do business. While counties with growing populations struggle to provide services for more people, rural counties face the problem of continuing services to a declining population, with an eroding tax base and less support from state and other local governments. Rural counties face growing problems in declining economic opportunity, education, transportation, and care of the aging.

Problems in many rural and nonmetropolitan counties are made more acute by the fact that the number of rural jobs is growing more slowly and that nonmetropolitan unemployment has been higher than in urban areas.

Between 1969 and 1988, nonmetropolitan poverty rates remained consistently higher than metropolitan rates, and the gap widened in the 1980s, when the rural economy went through major adjustments. Since 1973, per capita income in nonmetropolitan areas has fallen in relation to metropolitan income. The nonmetropolitan poverty rate has risen, and now stands 35 percent higher than the metro rate.

Between 1980 and 1988, the nonmetropolitan population grew only 4.7 percent, less than half the metro area growth rate. Between 1982 and 1987, almost half of the nonmetropolitan counties lost population. This decline occurred primarily in counties that are considered rural because of low population and because they are not in close proximity to metropolitan areas. These rural counties experienced outmigration due to slow economic expansion and better economic opportunity in urban areas.

Originally published as "Rural Counties: The Challenges Ahead," *Intergovernmental Perspective,* Vol. 17, No. 1, Winter 1991. Published by the U.S. Advisory Commission on Intergovernmental Relations, Washington, D.C.

Revenue Losses
and Human Impacts

The immediate effect on rural counties has been a loss of tax revenue to support the services they provide as mandated by the state and federal governments. Information on fiscal problems facing counties was gathered in a 1989 survey by the National Small Government Research Network (NSGRN). In North Dakota, where 19 of the 21 county auditors contacted responded, none reported population growth. Eighty-four percent said taxes had been raised in the last two years to maintain services. At the same time, 79 percent reported a decrease in state aid, and 84 percent reported cutbacks in federal revenue sharing.

The report said counties were especially hard hit by federal program cutbacks. In addition, few officials thought the situation with federal mandates would improve. To cope with their fiscal problems, taxes were raised, administrative changes made, levels of service reduced, and more services were shared with other political subdivisions.[1]

By far, the people expected to be most affected by the reduction of state and federal funding were low-income people, the elderly, children, farmers, and the unemployed.

The conclusion was that local governments in North Dakota, like local governments throughout the nation, are experiencing demands for increased services in the face of cutbacks in federal government assistance. However, it was also reported that the picture was not entirely gloomy because many communities were responding in creative and innovative ways.

Transportation

Key issues, like transportation, affect every facet of society. County roads are the lifeline between farms and towns, the field and the marketplace. Rural roads constitute 98 percent of North Dakota's 106,000-mile road system, with county and township rural roads accounting for 90 percent of the total. Counties are also responsible for over 4,000 bridges, 60 percent of which are classified as deficient.

The problem is compounded by railroad abandonment. Since 1936, over 850 miles of North Dakota rural branch lines have been abandoned, most in the past 15 years. These branch-line abandonments changed the pattern for getting agricultural products to market. County roads that are now used to transport commodities were not built to handle either the weight or the number of vehicles they must now bear.

The impact of federal highway funding on society as a whole cannot be underestimated. If fewer dollars are earmarked for rural states, problems of getting commodities to market will increase, chances of rural economic development will decrease, and more people will be forced to move to cities, compounding urban transportation problems.

Solutions to some transportation problems are emerging. In-depth planning is taking place locally in North Dakota and in other states to determine the best way to spend scarce funding. Replacement of obsolete bridges with lower cost structures, like culverts, can reduce costs without severely detracting from road service levels. Some paved roads are now being converted back to gravel for less expensive maintenance.

The Aging

A specific group of people affected by mounting rural problems is the aging. In 1900, only about 4 percent of the population was over age 65. By 2000, that number is projected to hit 13 percent. This trend will have varying impacts on rural counties. As younger people move away from rural areas in search of economic opportunity, there are fewer support systems for older people. Medical care is often not available in rural communities, and transportation services are often inadequate.

Some medical schools, such as those at the University of North Dakota and the University of Minnesota, were developed to help train physicians for family practice in rural areas. These programs, along with the National Health Corps, help place physicians in rural and urban areas. These programs provide some relief, although it is not always permanent or adequate.

Cooperative Service Arrangements

As population declines in rural counties, there is a greater need to overcome turf protection and find ways to coordinate, cooperate, and consolidate services within the county structure and with cities within counties.

City-county consolidations, sharing of service among political subdivisions, cluster communities, and changes in government forms are some ways that rural counties are responding to the dilemma of providing services with fewer tax dollars.

Although no two counties have yet combined, there are about 22 city-county consolidations. Among the better known urban consolidations are Davidson County and Nashville, Tennessee, and Marion County and Indianapolis, Indiana. Often in urban areas, the motivation to consolidate comes from the migration of taxpayers from the city to suburbs and unincorporated areas, which creates a need for more services by the county in outlying areas, as well as a need for sharing the costs.

In rural areas, however, consolidation is often a forced necessity in order to survive. It can be augmented by the willingness of the state to open the way, as in the case of Montana, where a new constitution in 1972 gave local governments the opportunity to consolidate. Two cities and counties, Anaconda and Deer Lodge County, and Butte and Silver Bow County, dependent economically on a floundering mining industry, chose consolidation in order to conserve resources and manage services more efficiently. The constitution provides Montana cities and counties the opportunity every 10 years to review their form of government and make needed revisions.

Combining of services between cities, counties, and other political subdivisions takes place more frequently than consolidation of governments. In the NSGRN survey, 37 percent of the North Dakota counties reported joint service provision with other governments. A National Association of Counties survey of 800 counties resulted in 600 responses identifying 1,500 to 2,000 contacts in counties for various local intergovernmental agreements covering fire and police protection, park maintenance, solid waste disposal, and road repair.

Some examples are relatively simple and practical. For instance, road grading and snow removal is done by Weld County, Colorado, for the city of Windsor on a county road inside the city limits.

More complex negotiations took place in Washington State when a bridge in Pierce County, Washington, which was owned jointly by the county and the city of Puyallup, needed repairs. An agreement was reached in which the county, city, and the city of Sumner shared the expenses for the repairs. Once they were complete, ownership and responsibility for the bridge was turned over to the two cities.

Adams County, North Dakota, provides an example of full integration of services. The county has assumed much of the responsibility for services in its four municipalities, including the county seat, either by combining services or through contracts. These services include law enforcement, street repair, snow removal, and water and sewer system maintenance. City utility billing is provided through the central county computer, and landfill service is provided for the entire county, the county seat, and portions of the next state. The result is that the county seat no longer has any employees, although the two political subdivisions have not formally consolidated.

Consolidation of services between counties is another trend, involving county-to-county intergovernmental agreements in which counties agree to cooperate on road maintenance, airport authority, social services, and other areas that overlap boundaries.

Clustering of communities is another new idea in rural development. A cluster is an expanded community formed when people from several communities combine services and cooperate rather than compete with one another. A number of clusters are in operation in Iowa. In North Dakota, the state economic development commission, university extension service, and rural county-commissions are working to develop community and county clustering.

Another innovation in North Dakota is a contract that five counties have with Washington, DC, to house prisoners. The counties thus have a new way to finance their county jails, meeting both the need for more financing in rural areas and the need to provide housing for urban prisoners.

Governance and Outreach

Changing forms of county government can help counties meet changing needs. Richland County, North Dakota, undertook a project called "Spirit of the 90s" in 1989 to help citizens determine their own destiny. This was an ambitious undertaking for a county with less than 20,000 citizens. Almost 150 volunteers participated in the process. As a result, in the November 1990 election, voters approved a home rule charter that will make numerous changes in the way the county is governed.

County commissioners, both rural and urban, are becoming more cognizant of their role in education and other policy areas. The connection between county board, school board, and corporate board, for example, is no longer a straight line, but rather a smaller and smaller circle that is drawing these separate entities closer together.

Technology and education will be crucial to meeting the challenges faced by counties in the 1990s. More sophisticated technological capabilities are needed, not only to improve efficiency, but to tell the county story. Although the same pressing needs exist in rural America that are found in urban and suburban America, rural counties do not have the data necessary to tell their stories to the state legislatures or the Congress. The National Association of Counties is working to overcome this problem by linking urban, suburban, and rural counties with state-of-the-art technological information.

The circles we live in can overpower and dominate us, or they can serve as sources of cooperation and unity that bring strength and economic well-being to county government. The challenge to meet and solve the problems facing counties belongs to county leaders, other local governments, and citizens alike as they work together.

Note

1. Small Local Government Fiscal Trends in North Dakota, (Grand Forks: University of North Dakota, Bureau of Governmental Affairs, August 1990).

CHAPTER 16

COUNTY LEADERSHIP MODELS

Ann Klinger

One of the greatest challenges in the federal system is for state and federal officials to create "the policy structures that allow local governments to solve problems." This observation by Robert B. Hawkins, chairman of the U.S. Advisory Commission on Intergovernmental Relations (ACIR), sums up the reality for counties in the last decade, and the future for counties in the 1990s.[1]

When treated as intergovernmental partners in the federal system, and not just another special interest group, county governments have generally met the challenge of change with innovation and creativity. Counties have been forced to become more creative and innovative in order to deliver services more efficiently in the face of state and federal cutbacks and voter tax revolts.

The most successful counties exhibit the spirit of entrepreneurism. They have the willingness to risk, to discard what does not work, and to build on what does work — public enterprise using the same strategies as private enterprise. Delivering services in a different way is the norm in many counties. This has occurred despite federal and state mandates and the propensity of federal and state governments to micromanage by rule and regulations with little consideration for county size or diversity.

The diversity of our 3,041 county governments can be demonstrated by three facts[2]:

1. Over half of the nation's population resides in the 167 counties with populations over 250,000.

2. Almost three-fourths of all counties

(more than 2,200) have populations of under 50,000.

3. The largest, Los Angeles County, California, has more than 8 million residents (larger than 42 states[3]) and the smallest, Loving County, Texas, has about 150.[4]

There is one major, common thread. In 1985–86, with analysis and editorial assistance by Barbara P. Greene, the National Association of Counties conducted a survey of county governments. The survey showed "the overwhelming concern from all population ranges is with state and federal requirements without appropriate funding and federal fiscal cutback."[5]

Regardless of size, counties are on the front line of service delivery, which is sometimes not well understood or considered by federal and state governments. One good example is the federal war on drugs. There was a general clamor for more resources in law enforcement, especially more cops on the street in urban areas.

Once an arrest is made, whether on a city street corner or in a rural area, it is the county criminal justice and social service systems that take the biggest impact. When the largest city in one urban county in California added 116 patrol officers to the city police force, the county's increased cost was determined to be $7.4 million. Except for trial appearances, the responsibility of city police ends at booking. "The responsibility of the county only starts at booking. The county must then house, feed, clothe, medicate, adjudicate, prosecute, defend, and supervise most offenders returned

Originally printed as "County Leadership and Models for Change," *Intergovernmental Perspective*, Vol. 17, No. 1, Winter 1991. Published by the U.S. Advisory Commission on Intergovernmental Relations, Washington, D.C.

to the community."[6] Intergovernmental issues, such as the need for new jails, more courtrooms, judges, etc., are easily overlooked as we respond to the need for more law enforcement on the street.

Let's follow the process through. Those arrested are taken to the county jail for booking and detention by the county sheriff's office or county corrections. They are prosecuted by the county district attorney and appear before a county judge, with a report and recommendations written by a county probation officer. If the defendants have no personal funds, they will be represented by the county public defender or a court-appointed attorney at county expense. If defendants are a high risk from IV drug use or other behavior, they probably will be tested for HIV/AIDS by the county health department. They also may receive treatment, education, and prevention services by the county health department or county hospital, with counseling and treatment of their addiction by county substance abuse or county mental health programs. Of course, if the defendant has a family, the county welfare department and county family support office may be involved.

In another urban county "as a result of the federal 'War on Drugs,' drug felon filings have doubled in three years."[7] Eighty-five to 90 percent of the inmates in this county's jail system test positive for drugs. "For the district attorney, criminal caseloads have quadrupled since Proposition 13."[8] The sheriff/corrections budget has more than tripled in six years.

Following the problem of addiction and drug abuse through to successful resolution would call for a proportionate increase in treatment and prevention funding as more drug addicts go through the justice system — through a revolving door without intervention. Further, some drug busts in rural areas with huge amounts of illegal drugs involved suggest that "wholesale" operations are taking place in sparsely populated areas where there is scant law enforcement personnel. Solving the drug crisis will require a strong federal-state-local partnership. Balance in the intergovernmental process is not an easy outcome.

Just as the drug war requires county leadership, county officials must be clear about those areas where the state and federal governments help or hinder innovations.

Waive the Rules vs. Wave the Rules

Regardless of the unit of government, we all know bureaucrats who have "waved the rules" in the face of an innovator seeking a model for change. Convincing these individuals to "waive the rules" instead can be quite a challenge. Perseverance pays, especially in open-ended, caseload-driven programs such as welfare.

Three major waivers in my own county over a period of years have saved millions in federal-state-county dollars, and have the potential to save much, much more. All required federal and state waivers or sign-offs to accomplish — a difficult process at best, with much "waving" of the rules.

Hard hit by the economic downturn of the early 1980s, simultaneous with an unprecedented secondary migration of Southeast Asian refugees, the county experienced a dramatic increase in welfare costs and workload. A look at the ethnicity of school children in the county's largest elementary school district tells the story. This year, schools in that district average 7 percent black, 25 percent Asian, 32 percent Hispanic, and 35 percent other white students.[9] As welfare costs continued to skyrocket, the county's share of cost was negatively affecting other essential services.

Housed in the county's least efficient building where you couldn't plug in another adding machine much less computerize for efficiency and economy, county human services management and line staff were determined to find a solution. It was the toughest financial time in county history. The board of supervisors and county administrative officer gave their word: be innovative and we'll support you, but you must do it within the budget allocation.

The employees, after 10 months of negotiation and with a sound business plan of savings, won waivers of capital expenditure rules and reached agreement with both state and federal agencies to be equity partners in a new building. Instead of the building being amortized at 2 percent a year for 50 years, the new plan called for a public-private venture with lease-purchase and full public ownership in 12 years by the county (25 percent), state (25 percent), and federal (50 percent) equity partnership. This was a first for the public welfare system. A day-care center on site was built under a similar arrangement.

With no up-front cash available for preliminary design work, the county project team determined what would be required to deliver efficient services and proceeded to design a "smart" building with future technology in mind. An architect was hired for basic schematic plans, which were used for the bid process. The outcome was a turn-key, state-of-the-art, 65,000-square-foot facility built at a comparatively low cost. Federal, state, and county governments realize a total cost savings of more than $.5 million annually. New systems enabled a decrease in personnel through attrition. This staff savings "pays for" 75 percent of the monthly lease-purchase payments.

The county could not afford new furniture, but was able to acquire used "interior landscaping" from a failed financial institution at greatly reduced cost. Old county files and desks were refurbished to match for a coordinated, new look. Estimated savings on furnishings was $575,000. The county had now demonstrated its ability to innovate and deliver. Our flexible county employees moved from 1960 technology to 1985 technology literally overnight with voice mail, central dictation, security access by magnetic card, and a centralized information services center.

Energized by their success and poised for the future, county staff members focused on bringing new technology and innovation to state public assistance administration, whose Statewide Public Assistance Networks (SPAN) System for welfare automation had failed to be implemented several years before. As an incentive, California and the federal government were willing to cover the costs of automation development for pilot counties. County plans for automation were presented to federal and state agencies and, as partners, a common understanding was reached on how California should approach public assistance automation. Bottom line, the county made a business case for a successful automation project that can be transferred to other counties and states.

Demonstrating a willingness to risk for big gain, the county encouraged vendors to propose alternative solutions to main-frame processing, suggesting that cooperative processing combined with expert system technology would reduce main-frame and other resources required in more traditional automated welfare systems. This approach pushes processing power via PC work stations into the hands of users. This technology has been projected to save 60 percent of data center costs, which would otherwise have been incurred, and to position the county to take advantage of the technological advances of this decade. Without the original waiver for capital expenditure, none of this would have been possible.

With twice the state and national unemployment rates and with high welfare costs (more than 24 percent of the county population qualifies for Medicaid, food stamps, or public assistance), the county is especially dedicated to leading-edge technology and aggressive cost savings over the long term. The goal is efficient, effective, and equitable service delivery.

For immediate benefit, the county sought state and federal waivers in eligibility determination to encourage rather than discourage people to work part time if they can not find full-time employment. Experience gained in part-time work has given participants the possibility of moving off public assistance and into self-sufficiency while saving federal, state, and county tax dollars.

Obtaining waivers has been a lengthy, time consuming, and costly process, with numerous control studies and independent evaluations required along the way. The most needy counties in the direst of straits have no choice but to run this gamut. How nice it would be to have simple problem solving and assurance for the taxpayer that rules, regulations, and policy will not get in the way of common sense approaches to saving tax dollars.

Sometimes common sense goes into hiding when the status quo is challenged. Given the choice between risk taking and laissez faire, the former is the responsible approach. Perhaps the day will come, as we become more used to rapid change in government, when two questions will be asked: "What is the common sense factor?" and "Does it meet the common sense test?" Problem solving in a pluralistic society requires many approaches. Given national complexity and diversity, there is not necessarily one "right" approach. Tough times require creative solutions and maybe a little conflict resolution along the way, if necessary. The county charge is clear: Officials must create environments where responsible, innovative change is encouraged.

Leadership Innovation

The Innovation Group of the Rensselaerville Institute says that innovation comes not from bright ideas but from individual efforts. "The key is individual 'sparkplugs' who will lead change by example. Innovation often rests on an entrepreneurial act." Further, "organizations and institutions which empower and enable their members will outperform those who seek to control and direct."[10] Again, balance and empowerment for counties in the federal system could lend a big assistance to county entrepreneurism. As former U.S. House speaker Tip O'Neil liked to say, "All politics is local." Well, most program implementation in the federal system is local, too.

Counties are fortunate that a number of foundations are allied in promoting models for change. The W.W. Kellogg Foundation gives both project and leadership grants. Its commitment is "for the application of knowledge to the problems of people" using pragmatic problem-solving in projects for positive change.[11]

The Health Policy Project at the National Association of Counties, funded by Kellogg through Brandeis University, promotes dissemination of creative programs and helps counties solve problems through university expertise and bootstrap efforts. This exchange of ideas and these connections are especially important because universities and their institutes provide information to the Congress and the Administration for public policymaking.

Counties are working "smart" by sharing data and cooperating in university studies that actually will reflect reality in county government. This kind of "third party" review and validation of facts can facilitate change in the federal system and can help build confidence and trust among the intergovernmental partners — a role ACIR plays so well.

Counties are inviting researchers for a firsthand look at front-line service delivery, helping them gain a practical and broader perspective of county issues. The Kellogg Foundation funds leadership training "to help develop leaders with broad perspectives about national and international issues; and to improve their skills and abilities to find creative solutions to social problems."[12]

Leadership training is serious business in counties today. Georgia counties sponsored legislation last year to require leadership training of all newly elected commissioners with training to be provided by the school of government of a major university. Such training helps create the climate for innovation.

A look at the 1990 Innovations in State and Local Government Awards Program is a study in the "can do" attitude of county government. Funded by the Ford Foundation in collaboration with the John F. Kennedy School of Government at Harvard University, ten $100,000 awards are granted annually; this year, half of the recipients were county governments.[13]

The five winners included a landfill reclamation project in Collier County, Florida, which used mining technology; two health programs; a mental health program; and a welfare program that uses a magnetic card for distributing of public assistance. All demonstrated high value in meeting community needs and potential for replication in other counties. The two health programs were public-private partnerships that work. Fairfax County, Virginia, provides health access and care for children of the working poor. Community physicians charge a fraction of their usual fee, and local businesses raise funds to match the county's annual allocation. Montgomery County, Maryland, solved a problem of access to obstetrical care by extending the county's liability insurance program to private obstetricians and making them part-time employees for the purpose of delivering poor women's babies.

Ramsey County, Minnesota, set up an electronic benefits systems using automated teller machines (ATMs) in cooperation with area banks so that welfare clients can withdraw their monthly benefit as needed with safe, convenient access.

Merced County, California, set up a specialized treatment service for sexually abused boys, who tend to be more reluctant than girls to admit abuse. A cooperative venture, the Human Services Agency makes referrals of suspected sexually abused boys and their families to the Mental Health Department for evaluation and possible treatment. Both mental health and welfare have federal and state mandates on confidentiality. Interagency agreements guarantee client protection while providing needed services.

Competitiveness and Productivity

Other county innovations show a renewed commitment to collaboration and cooperation. More than a decade ago, the National Association of Counties, the National League of Cities, and the International City Management Association formed Public Technology, Inc. (PTI), a non-profit research, development, and commercialization organization, to use the power of public enterprise to create revenue. With the focus, "Vision for the future ... solutions for today," PTI uses technology as a platform for innovation.

Counties across the country have become very innovative in assisting local business and agribusiness to tap into foreign markets.[14] International competitiveness is and has been a "Main Street" issue of great concern to policymakers at county courthouses. Seeking to strengthen and diversify their economies, county officials have made their own connections with foreign trade possibilities and established programs for in-county capacity. Coping with international competitiveness in the global marketplace has become as much a

county issue as a federal and state issue. Counties are, of course, political subdivisions of the state, and have only those powers allowed by the state. Certainly, counties are not at the table negotiating world trade agreements. Counties can and are doing something about the balance of trade. A recent research report adopted by ACIR in January 1990 indicated that, "Strengthening the competitive position of American businesses in the global economy has become a pervasive challenge for all governments in our federal system. As such, competitiveness has become a prominent motivator of innovations in state and local economic development programs."[15]

There is much discussion today that this will be the first generation that cannot look forward to a higher standard of living for their children. At the Education Summit, President George Bush and the nation's governors agreed on new goals for education that will move the country toward higher productivity. The action, however, must be in every county and community in America if we are to succeed. County officials know this and are working to bring together business, educators, and community leaders to implement programs locally to reduce the high school dropout rate and improve the education level of those entering the workforce.

National model programs, such as Jobs for America's Graduates, are being implemented in states and counties for successful transition from school to work or from "classroom to careers."[16] Such programs are being implemented in many counties in collaboration with those funded by the federal Job Training Partnership Act (JTPA), with the key to success being local flexibility and control. To quote one business leader, "We need that local flexibility and the emphasis on the private sector to keep JTPA grounded in reality, not in regulation."[17] This focus on "intellectual infrastructure" or "human capital" must be a major effort of all players in the intergovernmental system if we are to succeed.

Summary

A climate for innovation must be created in all our governments without unnecessary rules and restrictions just for the sake of control. Federal, state, and local governments must work together to build trust, facilitate change, and recognize that reasonable risk taking is a component of business success and government success. Leadership is key, and models for change must be disseminated widely, especially in technology. Adequate public investment in human capital as well as physical infrastructure must be priorities if counties, cities, states, and the nation are to maintain and improve our standard of living and our standing as a world power.

Notes

1. Robert B. Hawkins, "ACIR Roundtable on International Economic Competitiveness," *Intergovernmental Perspective* 16 (Winter 1990): 23.

2. "1990 Fact Sheet, County Statistics & Financing" (Washington, DC: National Association of Counties).

3. *1990 World Almanac*, Los Angeles County is larger than all states except California, New York, Texas, Florida, Pennsylvania, Illinois, Ohio, and Michigan.

4. These figures exclude the 27 city-county consolidations, such as San Francisco, New York City, New Orleans, and Denver, and the 44 independent local governments that deliver both city services and those usually performed by counties.

5. Barbara P. Greene, "Counties and the Fiscal Challenges of the 1980s," *Intergovernmental Perspective* 13 (Winter 1987): 14.

6. Richard P. Simpson and Gary S. Jung, "Summary of Findings," *California Counties on the Fiscal Fault Line* (November 1990).

7. Ibid. p. 25.

8. Ibid.

9. *Merced Sun-Star,* November 26, 1990.

10. *The Rensselaerville Institute News* (Spring-Summer 1989).

11. Robert A. DeVries, Unpublished Speech, National Association of Counties Board of Directors, July 1990.

12. Ibid.

13. Beverly A. Schlotterbeck, "Counties Win Big in Ford Foundation Competition," *County News*, October 8, 1990.

14. See also "State and Local Governments in International Affairs," *Intergovernmental Perspective* 16 (Spring 1990).

15. Bruce D. McDowell, "State and Local Initiatives on Productivity, Technology and Innovation," *Intergovernmental Perspective*, 16 (Winter 1990): 29. See also U.S. Advisory Commission on Intergovernmental Relations, *State and Local Initiatives on Productivity, Technology, and Innovation* (Washington, DC: ACIR, 1990).

16. *Crossroads*, Jobs for America's Graduates, Fall 1990.

17. Hugh Miller, *Quarterly Report*, Merced County Private Industry Council, October 1990, p. 3.

PART IV
Regions

CHAPTER 17

REGIONAL GOVERNANCE AND THE POST-INDUSTRIAL ECONOMY

Allan D. Wallis

In 1991 Denver lost out to Indianapolis in a competition to win construction of a $250 million United Airlines maintenance facility. After a speech in Denver a year later, former Indianapolis mayor Bill Hudnut was asked why Indianapolis had been successful even though Denver's incentive package was more generous. His answer was that in his city when negotiations took place with a major corporation, only three people had to be in the room: the corporate executive, the mayor, and someone from the governor's office. Because of Unigov — the consolidated city-county government — the mayor could speak for the region.[1]

A story with similar implications is told by Clarke County (Georgia) commissioner Tal DuVall. Several times the county and its core city of Athens attempted to win voter approval of a consolidation plan. The primary rationale presented to the voters had always been economical service delivery and infrastructure development. Although analysis demonstrated that consolidation would achieve significant savings, the voters weren't buying.

But in 1992, a consolidation referendum passed. Success resulted from a change in strategy. Rather than using an argument based on service and infrastructure cost savings, commissioners justified consolidation this time as a way of improving economic competitiveness. DuVall said,

When you have a corporation that wants to locate, they want to know that you can provide the necessary permits and deliver the services they need. If you can't give them an answer quickly, then they start to look elsewhere. It's easier to provide a timely response when you're speaking as one government.[2]

Across the country communities are beginning to realize that economic competitiveness requires a regional approach. The real competition is not among communities of the same region, but among regions here and abroad. Even regions long divided by bitter rivalries among local governments are finding common cause in the threats of job and population loss. This shift in attitude is evident in places like the Mon Valley that previously comprised the heart of Pennsylvania's steel-producing region. The mills are now closed, and the 37 local governments in the valley are having to learn to cooperate regionally in efforts to restore their economy (Ehrenhalt 1995).

The desire to achieve economic competitiveness has always been one of the basic reasons for strengthening regional government (Wallis 1994a). In the nineteenth century city, size was equated with economic strength. The rapid expansion of central cities to encompass their populated suburbs was justified as making the city more competitive. Size assured an adequate labor supply, as well as the capacity to deliver the services and infrastructure necessary to support industrial growth.

From *The Regionalist,* Vol. 1, No. 3, Fall 1995. Published by the National Association of Regional Councils, Washington, D.C. and the University of Baltimore, Baltimore, MD. Reprinted with permission of the publishers.

In today's economy, size does not necessarily result in strength. Instead, competitiveness comes from the ability to mobilize regional resources in response to rapidly changing demands. Most regions in the United States have not figured this out yet. Communities within the same region continue to compete with one another for economic base, and in cases where metropolitan communities do unite, it is often against the central city, which is seen as a common enemy. This internal competitiveness assumes that the United States maintains economic hegemony among nations. By contrast, regions in other advanced industrialized nations are reorganizing to become effective competitors in a global economy. They realize that in such an economy national policy may be less important than effective regional governance.

Characteristics of the Global Economy

In a mass-production economy, wealth is made by transforming raw materials into consumer products — for example, coke and iron into steel, and steel into automobiles. The process is labor- and resource-intensive. In a post-industrial economy, wealth is generated by the exchange of information and the transformation of ideas (Reich 1991). Microsoft has become one of the wealthiest corporations in the world by manufacturing information-organizing products for a market that did not exist 20 years ago. U.S. communities may compete for a Japanese automobile assembly plant, but the real wealth of the parent corporation is generated by its design, engineering, and marketing side, which it is not likely to ship overseas.

A post-industrial *global* economy is characterized by three interrelated trends (Accordino 1992):

- **Globalization of Production.** In a mass-production economy, manufacturing is concentrated in metropolitan regions, especially in central cities. But in a post-industrial economy, routine production activities are transferred to rural areas and or less developed coun-

tries. Such relocation is motivated by the search for lower labor and land costs in a politically stable environment. It is made possible by such technological changes as wide-body cargo jets, which reduce transportation costs, especially for valuable electronic goods, and by electronic communications, which allow a high level of production control from remote headquarters.

- **Globalization of Consumption.** In a mass-production economy, efficiency requires a market that demands large quantities of a standard product. If the market can be controlled by a few major manufacturers, they can regulate the product obsolescence cycle to assure profits. In a post-industrial economy, the product obsolescence cycle is accelerated as consumers in advanced industrial nations seek newer products from an ever broadening range of suppliers. Shorter product obsolescence cycles place pressure on manufacturing to become more flexible and market responsive, while remaining cost competitive. Lowering or eliminating tariff barriers also served to promote a global flow of products.

- **Globalization of Investment.** In today's economy, capital is increasingly free to move around the world, seeking the highest return. This mobility has significantly increased with the free-floating exchange rate system that was initiated in the early 1970s. Moreover, participation in global capital markets is no longer restricted to large-scale investors. Today, anyone with an interest can become involved.

Globalization of the economy has been occurring for several decades, but the end of the Cold War, combined with a lowering of international trade barriers, has accelerated the pace. A recent study sponsored by the German Marshall Fund of the United States (1992, 6) concludes, "As national trade barriers are lowered ... 'city-regions' in the European Community and the North American Free Trade Area are [becoming] the real arenas of global economic competition...." Similarly, urbanologists Richard Knight and Gary Gappert (1989, 11–12), writing about city-regions, observe,

> With the advent of the global economy, nation building is becoming more and more synonymous with city building. Cities serve as the nexus of the global society. As the global society expands, a nation's welfare will be determined increasingly by the roles its cities play in the global society.

Effects on the Structure of Regions

The global shifts just described have produced a significant restructuring of what economic geographers refer to as the "system of cities" that consists of the patterns of production and labor dependencies among metropolitan centers (Bourne and Simmons 1978). A mass-production economy results in a system characterized by dominant central cities and, in later phases, polycentric regions. By contrast, because a post-industrial economy depends more on the flow of information than on the movement of material goods, the system of cities it produces is less dependent on spatial proximity (Castells 1984). Consequently, the vitality of suburban and "edge-city" employment centers has become less dependent on the health of the central city, or cities, in their region. Instead, they may depend on the vitality of corporations located in wholly different regions.

One manifestation of changing employment locations is that incomes for central-city residents, which historically have been higher than those of suburban households, today are significantly lower and declining (Rusk 1993; Barnes and Ledebur 1994). Another manifestation is that an increase in vehicle miles traveled in urban areas is now primarily generated by intra-suburban trips rather than in commutes between central cities and suburbs (Federal Highway Administration 1990).

The transformation of the system of cities is also evident in the restructuring of labor markets within regions. In the mass-production era, metropolitan regions with an economic base of heavy industry supported a high proportion of blue-collar employment. Workers in this segment — often benefiting from organized-labor negotiated wage agreements — could expect to achieve relatively high salaries that outpace inflation. By contrast, the service-based economy of a post-industrial era consists of significantly fewer blue-collar workers on one end and a growing number of highly skilled service professionals and semi-professionals at the other. This labor market reflects a dual economy in which employees in the low-skilled segment have little opportunity to earn wages comparable to those in the skilled segment (Noyelle and Stanback 1981).

The loss of middle-income jobs in both manufacturing and services has produced a widening gulf between classes, with fewer bridges of opportunity. It has also produced a socially isolated "underclass" with extremely poor access to new job markets (Kasarda 1989). Again, in socio-spatial terms, this earnings gap manifests itself in the form of suburban alienation from the central city.

These changes often are used to question the central city's significance in the region's economy. But that debate draws attention away from a more fundamental point — the importance of the interdependency of all of a region's communities for its economic competitiveness. The implication of the foregoing analysis is not that a post-industrial economy allows all communities to function as free agents, independent and indifferent to their neighbors. Rather, it suggests that the communities of a region are now bound up in a far more complex set of interdependencies, and the relationship between central cities and their suburbs is only one aspect (Savitch 1992).

Pathways through the Post-Industrial Economy

Over the last 20 years, regions across the country have been struggling to keep pace with the trends associated with globalization of the economy. Some regions, faced with factory closings, offer extremely attractive incentives to keep existing manufacturing plants and lure new ones. Others have abandoned efforts to maintain their old industrial base and seek either to attract or incubate firms capable of competing in the new high-tech service sector (Miller and Cotes 1987). Some approaches clearly are predicated on a desire to restore the old economic order, while others attempt to comprehend emerging trends and apply them in their plans. Major corporations similarly are engaged in prognostications on how best to restructure.

How a region chooses to respond to the changing economic realities reshaping it depends very much on how current trends are interpreted and future directions are perceived. At this point in its evolution, the post-industrial economy appears to have at least two distinct pathways through it. Each has very different implications for the competitive mobilization of regions and, in turn, for their governance.

THE NEO-FORDIST PATH

Many of the largest corporations in the United States continue to adhere to mass-production, or "Fordist," principles. These corporations are attempting to extrapolate those principles on a global scale by promoting an international division of labor on one hand and an international organization of markets on the other. This is especially evident among automobile manufacturers (Barnet and Cavanagh 1994). Such corporations continue to be structured hierarchically, with a strong division between upper-management decision makers and line production workers. Neither trust nor power flows downward through their organizational structure.

Variants of the neo–Fordist approach, however, accept a degree of decentralization. In some cases, individual factories or firms are encouraged to diversify. More power is given to the worker on the line, especially where total quality management principles have been adopted.

Large firms also create smaller subsidiaries focusing on specialized production and innovation. For example, major steel manufacturers have created or acquired subsidiaries that produce relatively small batches of special allow steels. These mills often are built in new locations, rather than replacing older mills that have been closed due to technological ob-

solescence and changing demands. Likewise, chemical companies have subsidiaries specializing in products ranging from new fibers to insecticides (Sabel 1982; Bianchi 1992).

Some analysts suggest that the neo–Fordist approach contains inherent contradictions. Its attempts to achieve greater flexibility to respond to rapidly changing consumer demands require a redistribution of power and responsibilities that is antithetical to the corporate hierarchies that continue to concentrate control (Sabel 1982; Lorenz 1992).

THE REGIONAL
INDUSTRIAL-DISTRICTS PATH

In the early phases of the industrial revolution, efficient production occurred in districts where skilled artisans learned to employ machines to increase their output of traditional goods. Some shops produced only components of a finished good — fabric but not cloth, cloth but not clothing — but the district as a whole created market-competitive products. Such districts maintained a high level of craft, but they also provided an environment conducive to continuous, if relatively modest, innovation. In addition to a shared ethic for quality craftsmanship, such districts cultivated strong social solidarity. Indeed, analysts of such districts emphasize the importance of trust and reciprocity in structuring social relations (Sabel 1982; Lorenz 1992).

The manufacturing districts of early industrialization were largely displaced by mass-production techniques that sought to reduce reliance on craftsmanship by dividing production tasks into small steps that could be reproduced, without variation, by machines. But the idea of industrial districts never wholly disappeared. The production of highly specialized goods, especially those sufficiently high priced to cover rising labor costs (e.g., musical instruments), continues in a district form of organization. In some cases, districts have developed a symbiotic relationship with mass producers. The fashion industry, for example, still relies on highly specialized districts to create new designs that subsequently provide the basis for mass-produced imitations.

In addition to traditional industrial districts such as those associated with the garment industry, new high-tech districts have grown in prominence since the end of World War II. The Draper Labs of MIT helped provide the knowledge base for many of the firms that now dot Route 208 west of Boston. Similarly, Stanford University helped give rise to Silicon Valley. These high-tech districts have several characteristics of their traditional counterparts. They, too, rely on shared craft knowledge that can best, and perhaps only, be gained by being immersed in the environment of production — an environment that typically includes proximity to major research universities (Miller and Cotes 1987).

The vitality of both traditional and high-tech districts relies on orderly competition among local firms, but this internal competition limits itself to maintaining and enhancing competitive advantage over similar districts located elsewhere. Both types of districts develop strong reciprocal relationships among firms — relationships built on trust and mutual advantage.

Implications for the Governance of Regions

Each path through the post-industrial economy has significant implications for the definition and conduct of governance, especially at the regional and even at the neighborhood level.

GOVERNANCE SUPPORTING THE NEO-FORDIST PATH

Under a neo–Fordist regime, large firms become even larger through mergers and acquisitions and more global in their expanse. In effect, they operate in a "borderless world" (Ohmae 1990). As such, it might be expected that they would want an end to all government regulation of trade. In fact, they lobby for streamlining and or eliminating certain forms of regulation that are costly to large corporations, such as those pertaining to environmental protection, workplace safety, and minimum wage and benefit levels. Nevertheless, such firms continue to support national policies offering specific market protections, production subsidies, funding for research and development, and advantageous tax policies.

Since neo–Fordist firms benefit from the flexibility to relocate where labor-market conditions are most favorable, they presumably support federal policies that are non–place specific — for example, policies that favor accelerated obsolescence of capital investment in factories. Conversely, they oppose funding that is directed toward the problems of declining cities or regions.

At the state, regional, and local levels, governments respond to conditions of neo–Fordist competition by offering generous incentives to attract new industry. Regional cooperation often is required to put together an adequate package of incentives, and the communities of a region often must lobby collectively to secure sufficient state support. The resulting bidding wars among regions is advantageous to locating corporations but not always advantageous to the regions.

In many cases, winning a bid for a new industry can result in downstream losses. The public sector may be left with debts from upfront incentives if companies move out within the payback period (Faux 1987). States have tried to protect themselves by implementing "clawback" provisions, requiring corporations to pay back incentives if they relocate before a specified period (Ledebur and Woodward 1990). But if such policies have real talons, they can act as disincentives to locating in those states. Alternatively, some neighboring regions and states have agreements not to compete to avoid bidding wars, but these agreements have proven to be conspicuously nonbinding when a large relocation prospect is highly prized. In short, although competition for jobs can result in increased inter-governmental cooperation, especially at the regional level, it is just as likely to result in predatory competition.

Even when public-sector cooperation is achieved, the private sector may maintain a tenant-at-will mentality, failing to commit itself to the region's long-range future. If firms are not committed to being regional citizens, neither are their executives. Local nonprofit institutions have long been dependent on the involvement of such executives to raise funds and lend expertise. But executives in neo–Fordist corporations are more likely to identify with their firm's worldwide network, rather than the local social networks of the communities in which they are located. When the Rockefellers left Cleveland they still felt a strong civic obligation to the community, leaving it with a significant endowment. Will British Petroleum feel a similar obligation?

All this is not to suggest that corporations are totally footloose. Many have significant plant investments, as well as concentrations of skilled employees, at specific locations. Consequently, they continue to have a strong vested interest in the ability of local and regional governments to deliver essential public services and infrastructure in an efficient and timely manner. One potential implication for governance growing out of this demand is increased use of single-purpose regional authorities, for example, port and or airport authorities, water districts, sewage districts, and the like. Such authorities overcome local fragmentation, and corporations can work with them easily.

However, many corporate requirements are not amenable to such an approach. For example, providing an adequate supply of affordable housing so that skilled employees can be attracted to and retained in an area often involves working with local governments on reform of their land-use policies. In this case, corporate interests may promote regional governance designed to override local controls that limit the supply of needed goods and services (Association of Bay Area Governments et al. 1990; Danielson and Doig 1982).

Similarly, corporations may find it necessary to become involved in issues of public education to assure an adequately trained workforce. Again, promoting regional governance to address the problem may be more attractive to corporate interests since it provides an organized forum through which to influence performance. By contrast, social equity issues, such as concentrated poverty and fiscal disparities among communities of a region, are not likely to be issues of central concern to neo–Fordist corporations (Mollenkopf and Castells 1991). The collective implication for regions is a somewhat strengthened form of governance, but in areas of narrow and strategic corporate interest.

GOVERNANCE SUPPORTING THE INDUSTRIAL-DISTRICTS PATH

In contrast to the neo–Fordist path, which focuses attention on federal policies that can promote mobility, the industrial-districts path is much more concerned with developing effective regional and local policies. Likewise, whereas the neo–Fordist path prefers policies that are not place-specific, the industrial-districts path is firmly rooted to place and emphasizes building local capacity.

Nevertheless, advocates of an industrial-districts path see a strong role for federal policy if it is structured to support and enhance local and regional efforts at strengthening the industrial-districts approach (Accordino 1992). Developing a national industrial policy could have this effect, depending on how it is crafted. Likewise, a federal enterprise zone program could be structured to support industrial districts. Unfortunately, the current empowerment zone/enterprise community program, although emphasizing the importance of community capacity building, does not embrace an industrial-districts philosophy.

Since the industrial-districts approach emphasizes development of local production networks, advocates of this position see benefit in creating a regional government capable of providing a wide variety of public goods ranging from training and education to support for research and development, medical care, and housing (Lorenz 1992; Clavel 1986).

Economists Piore and Sabel (1984, 301) conclude,

> Successful industrial reorganization in the United States will require reinvigoration of local and regional government — not necessarily its supersession in favor of an expansion of corporate autonomy. Industrial policy will have to be regional policy; to be effective, the coordination of training programs, industrial research, transportation networks, credit, marketing information, environmental protection, and other elements of infrastructure will have to be done at the regional level.

In addition to suggesting a strong role for regional governments, the industrial-district paradigm also suggests a restructuring of *governance*, defined as participation in the processes of public decision making. In this conception, governance involves considerable interaction between the public, private, and nonprofit sectors. This restructuring goes beyond the creation of partnerships, focusing more broadly on achieving genuine collaborations in which all sectors — public, private, and nonprofit — provide distinct services and capacities in pursuit of a common regional vision (Wallis 1994b).

The type of governance advocated to support industrial districts also emphasizes neighborhood/community participation in decision-making processes (Peirce et al. 1993). Interest in neighborhood-level governance is indicative of the place-based orientation of an industrial-district approach, as distinct from the "borderless world" of the neo–Fordist alternative.

Emphasis on cross-sectorial governance also recognizes the importance of strengthening local civic infrastructure as an integral aspect of economic development. Robert Putnam (1993a, 106), drawing from his research on regions in Italy, observes,

> Of two equally poor Italian regions a century ago, both very backward, but one with more civic engagement, and the other with a hierarchical structure, the one with more choral societies and soccer clubs has grown steadily wealthier. The more civic region has prospered because trust and reciprocity were woven into its social fabric ages ago.

Part of the effort to strengthen civic infrastructure involves reengaging the poor living in isolated neighborhoods, as well as tapping into the talents available from new immigrants. The justification for placing resources in these populations of a region is that they represent human capital, which if abandoned creates inertia to competitive development.

Comparing the Paths

The two paths through a post-industrial economy, which are briefly described here, are ideal types. Most U.S. regions are of a scale and complexity that elements of both types are evident, but neither exists in a pure form. Nevertheless, distinguishing between these two paths may help regions in thinking about their current economic structure, how it is changing, and where it might be heading.

Each path through the post-industrial economy has very different implications for regional government and governance. The neo–Fordist alternative, based on the growing dominance of large multinational corporations, requires regions with the capacity to deliver necessary infrastructure and services. This demand could be met by developing and or strengthening special regional authorities or by enhancing the capacity of existing organizations, such as metropolitan planning organizations and councils of government.

In many regions, a neo–Fordist alternative also would benefit from strengthening regional capacity to override local government opposition to siting various supportive land uses, ranging from power plants to landfills to affordable housing. None of these requirements necessitate a radical reinvention of regional government or governance, but all involve a degree of state and interlocal commitment that to date has been very difficult to achieve.

By contrast, the industrial-districts scenario implies a substantial restructuring of regional government and governance. Few if any U.S. regions have developed an effective means to analyze adequately the linkages of industries comprising their current or nascent industrial districts, and few have the ability to connect such analysis to the formulation of a complementary, strategic policy agenda.

If the emerging global economy favors industrial districts, then U.S. economic competitiveness will be substantially disadvantaged by its lack of governance capacity to support such development. European and non-western regions appear to be ahead of the game in this respect, not simply due to recent efforts at "harmonization," a term for reducing local government fragmentation (van den Berg et al. 1993), but because of well established political cultures in many regions that already support the types of governance conducive to industrial districts (Lorenz 1992; Putnam 1993b; Sabel 1982; Piore and Sabel 1984).

Which Path?

Global restructuring of the economy is no longer an esoteric phenomenon confined to specialized conferences and journals. It has become material for the evening news. Increased awareness of change can motivate desire for shared dialogue and eventually for collective action.

Asking the question "Which path?" assumes a deliberative process by which interest groups in a region get together and think about what is happening to their economic structure and what they need to do to change it. In some cases this does occur, but only rarely. There are many efforts at visioning, but few engage in the kind of rigorous economic analysis necessary to generate informed conclusions. Several regions have developed coalitions of corporate interests dedicated to developing strategies to enhance regional economic competitiveness.[3] Some of these coalitions even include public agency members, but more often community dialogue occurs in an environment of crisis defined by the threat of a factory or military base closing.

If the question "Which path?" is to be asked, several things have to happen:

- **Identity.** If interests from different sectors within a region are to enter into dialogue, they must first identify themselves as active participants in the life of their region.
- **Citizenship.** People not only need to see themselves as part of a region, they need to develop a sense of citizenship for its well being (Cisneros 1995).
- **Dialogue.** Once identity is established, opportunities must be provided for genuine dialogue. Coming together in dialogue helps reinforce identity with the region.
- **Vision.** Beyond dialogue, visioning involves a structured attempt to think about the future. It works best when it is strategic (about specific, pressing issues) rather than general (Dodge 1992).
- **Mobilization.** If visioning is effective, it should lead to mobilization to implement elements of the vision.

Realistically, regions do not have the capacity to control global economic forces, but they can actively decide how they want to respond to them. In formulating their responses, alternative forms of regional governance should be a central consideration.

Notes

1. William Hudnut, keynote speech at Town Meeting West (Denver, Colorado), April 3, 1992.
2. Personal interview with Commissioner DuVall, April 21, 1993.
3. Examples of such coalitions include Cleveland Tomorrow, Greater Philadelphia First, and the Greater Seattle Trade and Development Alliance.

References

Accordino, John. 1992. *The United States in the Global Economy.* Chicago: American Library Association.

Association of Bay Area Governments et al. 1990. *Bay Area Housing.* The Local Housing Element Assistance Project.

Barnes, William, and Larry Ledebur. 1990. *Toward a New Political Economy of Metropolitan Regions.* Washington, DC: National League of Cities.

_____. 1994. *Local Economies: The U.S. Common Market of Local Economic Regions.* Washington, DC: National League of Cities.

Barnet, Richard, and John Cavanagh. 1994. *Global Dreams: Imperial Corporations and the New World Order.* New York: Simon and Schuster.

Bianchi, Patrizio. 1992. "Levels of Policy and the Nature of Post-Fordist Competition." In *Pathways to Industrial and Regional Development,* edited by Michael Stroper and Allen J. Scott. New York: Routledge.

Bourne, Larry S., and James W. Simmons, eds. 1978. *System of Cities.* New York: Oxford University Press.

Castells, Manuel. 1984. "Space and Society." In *Cities in Transformation: Class, Capital and the State,* edited by Michael Smith, Vol. 28, Urban Affairs Annual Reviews.

Cisneros, Henry. 1995. *Regionalism: The New Geography of Opportunity.* Washington, DC: U.S. Department of Housing and Urban Development.

Clavel, Pierre. 1986. *The Progressive City.* New Brunswick, NJ: Rutgers University Press.

Danielson, Michael N., and Jameson W. Doig. 1982. *New York: The Politics of Urban Regional Development.* Berkeley: University of California Press.

Dodge, William R. 1992. "Strategic Intercommunity Governance Networks." *National Civic Review* (Fall-Winter).

Ehrenhalt, Alan. 1995. "Cooperate or Die." *Governing* (September): 28–32.

Faux, Jeff. 1987. Industrial Policy and Democratic Institutions. In *The State and Local Industrial Policy Question*, edited by Harvey Goldstein. Chicago: American Planning Association.

Federal Highway Administration. 1990. *Personal Travel in the United States*. Washington, DC: U.S. Department of Transportation.

German Marshall Fund of the United States. 1992. "Divided Cities in the Global Economy" (November).

Hanson, Royce, ed. 1983. *Rethinking Urban Policy: Urban Development in an Advanced Economy*. Washington, DC: National Academy Press.

Kanter, Rosabeth Moss. 1994. Collaborative Advantage. *Harvard Business Review* (July-August): 96–108.

Kasarda, John. 1989. Urban Industrial Transition and the Underclass, in *The Annals of the American Academy of Political and Social Sciences*, v. 501.

Knight, Richard V., and Gary Gappert. 1989. *Cities in the Global Society*. Newbury Park, CA: Sage.

Ledebur, Larry, and Douglas Woodward. 1990. "Adding a Stick to the Carrot: Location Incentives with Clawbacks, Rescissions and Calibrations." *Economic Development Quarterly* 4(3): 221–237.

Lorenz, Edward H. 1992. "Trust, Community and Cooperation: Toward a Theory of Industrial Districts." In *Pathways to Industrial and Regional Development*, edited by Michael Stroper and Allen J. Scott. New York: Routledge.

Miller, Roger, and Marcel Cotes. 1987. *Growing the Next Silicon Valley: A Guide for Successful Regional Planning*. Lexington, MA: Heath and Company.

Mollenkopf, John, and Manuel Castells. 1991. *Dual City: Restructuring New York*. New York: Russell Sage.

Noyelle, Thierry J. 1983. "The Implications of Industry Restructuring for Spatial Organization in the United States." In *Regional Analysis and the New International Division of Labor*, edited by Frank Moulaert and Patricia W. Salinas. Boston: Kluwer/Nijkoff Publishing.

_____ and Thomas Stanback, Jr. 1981. *The Economic Transformation of American Cities*. New York: Conservation of Human Resources, Columbia University.

Ohmae, Kenichi. 1990. *Borderless World: Power and Strategy in the Interlinked Economy*. New York: HarperCollins.

Peirce, Neal, Curtis Johnson, and John Stuart Hall. 1993. *Citistates: How Urban America Can Prosper in a Competitive World*. Washington, DC: Seven Locks Press.

Piore, Michael J., and Charles F. Sabel. 1984. *The Second Industrial Divide*. New York: Basic Books.

Putnam, Robert D. 1993a. "What Makes Democracy Work." *National Civic Review* (Spring): 101–107.

_____. 1993b. *Making Democracy Work: Civic Traditions in Modern Italy*. Princeton, NJ: Princeton University Press.

Reich, Robert. 1991. *The Work of Nations*. New York: Random House.

Rusk, David. 1993. *Cities Without Suburbs*. Baltimore: Johns Hopkins.

Sabel, Charles. 1982. *Work and Politics: The Division of Labor in Industry*. New York: Cambridge University Press.

Savitch, Hank. 1992. "Ties That Bind." *National Civic Review* (Summer-Fall).

van den Berg, Leo, H. Van Klink, and J. Van Der Meer. 1993. *Governing Metropolitan Regions*. Brookfield, VT: Avebury.

Wallis, Allan. 1994a. "Regionalism: The First Two Waves." *National Civic Review* (Spring).

_____. 1994b. "Inventing Regionalism: A Two-Phase Approach." *National Civic Review* (Fall-Winter).

CHAPTER 18

REGIONAL COOPERATION: GLOBAL COMPETITVENESS AND URBAN REFORM

Theodore Hershberg

When historians render their judgments on the last quarter of the twentieth century, they will conclude that its defining phenomenon was the emergence of a global economy. Driven by free trade, international capital markets, and extraordinary changes in communications and information technologies, this new economy will make the future very different from the past. In every field of endeavor, strategic thinkers are now asking how best to adapt to these changes, how to position their businesses, institutions, and organizations to take advantage of the new world marketplace. What should those of us interested in the future of America's cities learn from the remarkable transformations underway?

The first lesson of the global economy is that regions — not cities nor the suburban counties that surround them — will be the units of economic competition. As Neal Peirce, Kenichi Ohmae, and many others have argued, only regions have the necessary scale and diversity to compete in the global marketplace.[1] Only regions have an asset profile capable of projecting overall strength to compensate for the clearly less attractive profiles of individual counties or cities which lack either essential infrastructure or a sufficiently skilled pool of labor.

Regions, moreover, are the geographic units in which our goods and services are created. We hire from a regional labor force. We count on a regional transportation system to move the people and the materials involved in their production. We rely on a regional infrastructure to keep the bridges and roads intact and our sewers and pipelines functioning. We live in a regional environment where water and air do not recognize political boundaries.

If regions are the units of economic competition, *the second lesson of the global economy is that cities and their neighboring suburban counties must embrace strategies of regional cooperation.* To compete effectively, regions have to be cohesive. That is, they have to be capable of solving problems and seizing opportunities in a timely fashion. In a nation with precious few examples of regional government, this means that cities and suburbs have to find ways to work together for their mutual benefit.

The Global Economy Poses Three Regional Challenges

The good news in the global economy is that markets are enormously larger. There will be six billion people in the world in 2000 —

Originally published as "Regional Cooperation: Strategies and Incentives for Global Competitiveness and Urban Reform," *National Civic Review,* Vol. 85, No. 2, Spring-Summer 1996. Published by the National Civic League, Denver Colorado. Reprinted with permission of the publisher.

more than twenty times the size of America's population. The bad news is that the competition will be fierce as our firms vie for profits and market share with their counterparts across the globe.

To succeed, regions must respond to three major challenges posed by the global economy. *First, regions must develop their human resources because human capital will be the source of comparative advantage in the future.* Between 1973 and 1992, while per capita GDP grew 25 percent (adjusted for inflation), only the top 20 percent of American male workers saw their real wages rise; the next 20 percent were stagnant, and the bottom 60 percent actually experienced a decline. Our standard of living did not fall at the same time largely because women entered the labor force in record numbers. But since 1989, even median household income has fallen despite the fact that Americans now work longer hours and a greater proportion now hold at least two jobs more than in the last half century.

Inequality in the distribution of income and wealth, according to Lester Thurow, is also growing.[2] Among men working full time, the earnings gap between the top and bottom quintiles doubled in the last 25 years. Between 1979 and 1994, while the bottom three-fifths of American families lost ground in terms of real income, the second fifth gained 6 percent, the top fifth gained 25 percent, and the top 5 percent gained 44 percent. The share of wealth held today by the top 1 percent of the population now exceeds 40 percent, a proportion last observed in the late 1920s.

Why the sharply diverging trends in inequality? An informal poll of 18 prominent economists, conducted at the Federal Reserve Bank in New York at the end of 1994, concluded that 10 to 20 percent of the growing wage disparity was due to international trade; 10 percent came from declining union memberships and 9 percent from the erosion of the minimum wage. But almost half of the increases in income inequality resulted from technological changes that benefit the better educated.[3]

To counter these trends, regions should adopt rigorous, internationally benchmarked, academic standards and assessments for their students, expand greatly post-secondary training, make admission to their colleges and universities far more demanding, and increase the availability of advanced on-the-job training in the work place. Regions that respond to the human capital challenges brought by the global economy and rapid technological change will close the wage gap, ensure social stability, and improve the quality-of-life for all their inhabitants.

Second, regions must lower the cost of their goods and services to be competitive. The inefficiencies embedded in the configuration of local, state, county, and federal governments — duplicated personnel, facilities, and services, limited management incentives, and tax structures that distort the most efficient location for economic activities — lead to increased business costs. In a domestic economy, these higher costs did not matter very much because businesses passed them on to their customers in the form of higher prices, leaving their profit margins unaffected. Since all domestic producers did the same thing, no one derived competitive advantage.

But when the competition grows increasingly international — and, for whatever reasons, prices for foreign goods and services come in lower than our own — inefficiencies that spring from domestic practices undercut our competitiveness. In *World Class: Thriving Locally in the Global Economy*, Harvard Business School professor Rosabeth Moss Kantor illustrates the nature of global competition through the experience of a small American envelope manufacturer.[4] The company learns that the contract it has long held with a large local corporation has just been won by a Taiwanese competitor who provided a quality product at a lower price. After streamlining its internal operations, the local company reviews further options to stay competitive: it can reduce its profits; it can lower the wages of its workers; or it can look outside the firm to find ways to lower its costs.

When voters — workers and their families — understand that the choice they will increasingly face to maintain the competitiveness of American goods and services in a global economy is either to lower their wages or to find other ways of reducing costs, they will not surprisingly choose the latter. Government practices considered sacrosanct today will change far more rapidly than most people now appreciate because politicians will quickly grasp that Americans are more committed to their pocket books than to traditional governance structures.

Regions should be asking what size "service shed" is appropriate for individual services and, for that matter, whether government should produce the service or contract it out to the private sector. The issue is not structural — requiring the consolidation of governments into larger units, but functional — offering services at the most efficient geographic scale. Efforts to tackle this politically sensitive subject are underway in several regions, including promising starts catalyzed by SUNY Buffalo and the Rockefeller Institute of Government at SUNY Albany.[5]

Third, regions must use scarce investment capital more productively. When crime, drugs, homelessness, and other social problems spill over into adjacent suburban communities, the response of those who can afford it has been to move even farther away to more pristine areas at the peripheries of our regions. This process is embedded in the concentric rings of growth that emanate outward from our central cities.

Very troubling signs in the older, inner-ring suburbs suggest that the pace of out-migration and other indicators of deterioration — job loss, housing depreciation, drugs, crime and related social problems — are accelerating faster than in the central cities they surround. The reason is that these small communities lack the basic resources big cities rely on to slow down and mediate the process of decline. These inner-ring communities do not have large central business districts generating substantial tax revenues to underwrite essential services in the neighborhoods; they do not have large police forces to maintain safety and a sense of social order as the crime rate climbs; and they do not have the sizable public and not-for-profit social service agencies to address the needs of the poor and disadvantaged.

This out-migration from the cities and the inner-ring suburbs leads to new development in the exurbs, requiring new roads and highways, water mains and sewer lines, schools and libraries, homes and shopping centers, offices and sports complexes. When this happens, our scarce investment dollars are spent redundantly because we are essentially duplicating an infrastructure that already exists in older suburbs and central cities. Such growth also often represents a highly inefficient use of our land. In Southeastern Pennsylvania between 1970 and 1995, for example, while population declined by 140,000, one-quarter of the region's prime farmland was lost to development.

This redundant spending imposes heavy opportunity costs because these dollars are not available for vital investments in productivity. While we build shopping centers, the Japanese are investing in R&D. To improve our competitive position in the global economy, America's regions would be far wiser to undertake more cost-effective development by adopting metropolitan growth rings, increasing residential and job densities in existing suburbs and cities, and investing the savings in research and development, plant and equipment and human capital. America should not behave in the 2000s as it did in the 1960s. The current practice of redundant spending is akin to eating our seed corn. The nation can ill afford public policy that leads to throw-away cities, throw-away suburbs, and throw-away people.

The Search for Solutions

Regions whose cities and suburbs succeed in finding ways to work together will fare better than those whose constituent governments choose to go-it-alone. Whatever the direction of causality, cities and suburbs are linked together through the integration of their regional economies. Whether they like it or not, or even whether they are aware of it or not, cities and suburbs are their region's primary stakeholders.

Unfortunately, one of the partners is not doing well. Most of America's cities are on greased skids, and what distinguishes one from the other is the angle of descent. Our political leaders act as if America will be a stronger nation and our regions will be more competitive in the future if we lose our cities and are left not simply with our current social problems, but ones far worse because they will have festered unattended. They behave much like the proverbial ostrich that sticks its head in the sand rather than contend with the dangers at hand. The presidential campaigns treat cities like tar babies — mention them and you're bound to get stuck in unpopular or costly solutions.

Yet there are credible responses to the urban question that involve neither significant outlays of cash nor failed policies. My colleagues at University of Pennsylvania's Wharton Real Estate Center are now engaged in an important study quantifying the costs to suburbanites of decline in the central cities they surround. Last year, for example, they calculated a conservative estimate for the value of taxable and exempt real estate in ten of the nation's largest cities: $1.6 trillion.[6] A 10 percent decline in value would represent a loss of $160 billion — roughly what the savings and loan scandal cost Americans. Who are the big losers? Not city residents. Since the value of urban real estate is dominated by the large concentration of commercial office buildings in the downtowns, and these are owned by banks, insurance companies and pension funds, the losers turn out to be shareholders in these institutions, who not surprisingly live largely outside cities (along with 75 percent of the nation's population and a disproportionate share of our better-off citizens).

I look forward to the results of this research and the publication of more such examples of how urban decline affects the fortunes of suburban residents. These empirical findings are welcome weapons in the fight against the folly of disregarding the plight of our cities and their residents. But while these new data are necessary, they will not prove sufficient. To explain why the continued deterioration of our cities and the serious long-term consequences they pose for the nation are ignored, we have to look elsewhere.

Greater Philadelphia First, an organization of over 30 chief executive officers of the area's largest corporations, recently undertook an annual tracking survey to gauge public attitudes in a scientific sample of the region's population. In 1994 and 1995, roughly three-quarters "of suburban residents acknowledged a symbiosis between the city and the suburbs."[7] They appear to understand the economic consequences and the spillover of social problems into the adjacent inner-ring suburbs that inevitably follow the decline of the central city. These attitudes resemble those found by my graduate students in two dozen informal focus groups held in the last several years.

The reason suburbanites have not supported further efforts to aid urban centers, I suspect, is not the absence of empirical evidence documenting the negative effects on the suburbs, but widespread distrust and cynicism about what can be done to save our cities. There is an all-pervasive sense that taxpayers have been generous in the past. Just about everything has been tried with at best limited success, and there is no sense throwing good money after bad.

The work of a research team led by my Wharton School colleagues, Anita Summers and Joseph Gyourko, addresses these concerns. Their conclusion is that cities are beset by three major structural problems: the loss of jobs and population that undermined their tax base; a mismatch between the limited resources they possessed and the much larger set of social problems from which their residents suffered disproportionately; and the misuse of the available resources to address these problems.

Their *New Urban Strategy* argues that the federal government should accept responsibility for the costs of national problems — poverty and immigration — that are now borne disproportionately by cities. While there would be no net change in aggregate intergovernmental aid, they propose an "Urban Audit" that would first determine the extent of unfunded burdens that cities are bearing for the nation and then divide the pool of intergovernmental funds so that those bearing the largest burdens would receive the most aid.

The second component of the "Urban Audit" is intriguing and pregnant with potential for catalyzing urban reform: the federal government would adopt a rational incentive system that would define the road to "good government" and then reward cities which engage in reform and punish those which do not.[8]

Consider the experience of Philadelphia. In 1992, at the brink of bankruptcy, the city faced an accumulated deficit of $250 million. Working together, Mayor Ed Rendell, who is white, and City Council President John Street, who is African-American, produced a labor agreement that did not give away the store, consolidated health and related benefits that saved megabucks, and won back significant management prerogatives bargained away by previous administrations more interested in union support for the next election than in the day of fiscal reckoning another mayor would inevitably face. By 1996, the pursuit of reform policies produced an $80 million surplus. Under a rational incentive policy, cities like Philadelphia would receive more funding from the federal (and state) government, while cities which refused to make the tough political decisions would receive less.

Which cities would get rewarded and which cities would get punished would be determined not by politics, but by the empirically derived "Urban Audit" noted above. At this stage, the mechanism is incomplete and certain to be controversial. To be sure, the "devil is in the details," but the concept of a rational incentive system for the nation's cities is the right direction in which to move.

Cities *cannot* save themselves with their own resources and most *will not* save themselves given a deeply entrenched political culture which makes sustaining reform over the long term impossible. Cities lack sufficient funds to deal with the vast array of problems now concentrated within their borders, and scores of studies chronicling efforts over the last century prove that reform is at best temporary. As the energy of the reformers diminishes, the returning bureaucrats restore business as usual.

A rational incentive system — in crude terms, money for reform — could leverage and sustain good government. While there is no guarantee that suburban support will follow, there is also no doubt that suburban residents will refuse to provide further urban aid as long as the evening news remains filled with stories of mismanagement and corruption. Putting aside posturing and partisanship will not be easy for either urban or suburban politicians. The former, especially minorities, will fear a loss of power, and the latter will fear the strident opposition of suburban residents who dislike central cities, which in metropolitan Philadelphia is estimated in the 25 to 33 percent range.[9] But the large majority of urban and suburban residents understand the economic and social stakes of continued urban decline, and they can be mobilized by effective political leadership under a banner of rational incentives.

It is time for suburban Republicans to sit down with urban Democrats. Both sides would come to the table aware of shared interests. City politicians would recognize that the dollars they need depend upon political support from the suburbs. Suburban politicians would acknowledge their economic stake in the city, knowing that its decline will not destroy them as if by atomic blast, but realizing that they would suffer from the fallout.

What is the basis for a new quid pro quo? Under what circumstances are the suburbs prepared to help the cities? What behaviors are expected from cities to demonstrate that they are in fact sustaining reform? If the cities live up to their part of the bargain, what are the suburbs prepared to provide in return? We need concrete answers to these questions. Advocates of regional cooperation need to help specify the "Urban Audit" and define the "road to reform."

The other missing ingredient — effective political leadership — will be more likely to emerge if the signposts on the road to reform are spelled out in terms of coherent public policy. Ed Rendell, "America's Mayor," could articulate this agenda as well as anyone in public life today if he put his mind to it. So could Indianapolis' Steven Goldsmith. Finding suburban counterparts is always difficult. The sheer number of municipalities precludes productive collaboration among local governments and complicates even county-level partnerships. Republican governors could play these roles effectively.

To get the job done, of course, would require what most of us would associate with statesmanship. Politicians would have to want to solve the problems of the cities rather than position themselves for the next election. They would have to believe that partisanship is a luxury America can ill afford in the fiercely competitive global economy.

States have a pivotal role to play. The "devolution revolution" Richard Nathan has written about affords an opportunity to help cities as well as improve the competitiveness of regions in the global economy. States may soon receive large amounts of money in the form of block grants. Instead of disbursing these funds entirely to each county according to formulas hammered out in state capitols, governors and state legislatures could set aside a pot of dollars, perhaps 20 percent of the total. While each county would get its share of the 80 percent, the reserved portion of block grants funds would be available only to contiguous counties which come forward as regions with strategic plans demonstrating how resources could be better deployed on a regional, rather than a purely county basis. Duplicated facilities, personnel, and services abound within regions, and these regional proposals could identify new "service sheds" and rational allocations that would minimize costs and maximize service delivery. The plans submitted would have to contain real cost-benefit analysis so counties would not come together as regions simply to win the funds and then divvy them up among themselves.

The public policy that undergirded the Intermodal Surface Transportation Efficiency Act suggests how this might work. Funds were earmarked for highways and mass transit, but metropolitan planning organizations were given authority to spend an additional pot of "flex" dollars according to the unique circumstances of the region. "Regional allocation agencies," as Tony Downs refers to them, would similarly determine the best configuration of funds and delivery systems for health care, welfare, job training, education, environment, and the like.[10] These decision-making groups could be popularly elected as in Portland, Oregon, or appointed by the governor and the state legislature as in the Min-

neapolis–St. Paul area, or chosen by local governments.

In sum, success in the global economy requires cohesive and competitive regions. The future of the nation's cities is tied to the health of their regions, and the success of regions in the global economy depends in large part on the health of their central cities. Cities and the suburban counties that surround them should be working together to develop their human resources, lower the costs of their goods and services, and invest their scarce capital productively. A rational incentive system agreed to by city and suburban politicians and embedded in national and state policies can provide aid to cities and sustain them on the road to reform. The devolution of power from the federal to state governments and the wise allocation of new block grant funds can stimulate regional strategic planning and result in more cost effective service delivery and more cohesive and competitive regions. The growth of regional thinking over the last decade is succeeding in clarifying the policy directions in which the nation must move to save its cities and ensure the competitiveness of its regions in the global economy. The critical next phase depends upon recruiting a generation of political leadership capable of recognizing the trends, the real policy options, and the possibilities.

Notes

1. Neal R. Peirce with Curtis Johnson and John Stuart Hall, *Citistates: How Urban America Can Prosper in a Competitive World* (Washington, D.C.: Seven Locks Press, 1993); Kenichi Ohmae, *The End of the Nation State: The Rise of Regional Economies* (New York: Free Press, 1995); Theodore Hershberg, "The Case for Regional Cooperation," *The Regionalist* (September 1995).

2. Lester Thurow, "How Much Inequality Can a Democracy Take?" *The New York Times Magazine* (November 19, 1995).

3. Jason DeParle, "Class Is No Longer a Four-Letter Word," *The New York Times Magazine* (March 17, 1996).

4. Rosabeth Moss Kantor, *World Class: Thriving Locally in the Global Economy* (New York: Simon and Schuster, 1995).

5. "Assessing Regionalism in Erie County," from *Governance in Erie County: A Foundation for Understanding and Action*, The Governance Project: State University of New York at Buffalo (January 1996);

"Growing Together within the Capital Region," from *The Draft Report of the State Commission on the Capital Region* (February 1996).

6. Joseph Gyourko and Anita Summers, "Wharton Research Impact Conference Summary: A New Urban Strategy," *Real Estate Research Bulletin*, The Wharton School (Spring, 1995).

7. *The Attitudes and Opinions of Residents of the Greater Philadelphia Region*, conducted for Greater Philadelphia First by Response Analysis of Princeton, N.J., in 1994 and 1995.

8. Anita Summers, "A New Urban Strategy for America's Large Cities," Association for Public Policy and Management (Chicago, 1994).

9. This estimate is based on the proportion of suburban residents who would not "be willing to see a greater share of current state tax dollars directed to the region's urban problems" (see note 7 above); and a proprietary marketing survey done for a regional newspaper several years ago that concluded that "33 percent of those sampled had anti–Philadelphia attitudes."

10. Anthony Downs, *New Visions for Metropolitan America* (Washington, D.C. and Cambridge, Mass.: The Brookings Institution and the Lincoln Institute of Land Policy, 1994).

CHAPTER 19

FROM METROPOLITAN COOPERATION TO GOVERNANCE

David B. Walker

Snow White nearly lost her heart. But she overcame the hostility of her stepmother and was kept alive in the forest by a family of dwarfs.

Metro America is Snow White. Migration to suburban areas nearly took the heart out of her. Federal hostility toward taking a role in metro governance has driven metro America into a temporary disappearance from public view. The good news is that she is being kept alive by 17 distinct types of interlocal approaches, on a spectrum from intergovernmental cooperation to full regional governance.

Some view this spectrum as a path out of a dark forest of problems, toward a regional Camelot.

Increasing Need for Metro Approaches

The nation's metro areas are growing, and their problems along with them. Substate regionalism seeks to address problems that spill over the artificial boundaries of central city limits. As metro America expands, the substate regional drama is being played out in more arenas. Note these seven current trends:

1. More Metro Areas. More metro areas exist today (1982 data) than ever before, with a more than two-thirds increase since 1962.

2. More People in Metro Areas. Three-quarters of our total population is located there, compared to 63 percent in 1962. More

people also live in suburban jurisdictions than previously — some 45 percent of total population compared to 30 percent two decades earlier.

3. Continued Metro Government Fragmentation. Growth in metro areas hasn't meant consolidation. More of the nation's local governments are located in metro areas now: over 36 percent of the 82,000 total as against 27 percent in 1972. The average metro area still encompasses about 100 governmental units, despite the slight increase in the percentage (48 percent of the total) of single county and presumably jurisdictionally simpler metro areas.

4. Increased Metro Diversity. Compared to their situation in the 1960s, metro areas are now more diverse in (a) population and territorial size, (b) the mix of private economic functions and the range of public services offered, (c) the respective position of central cities vis-à-vis outside central city jurisdictions, and (d) the kinds of jurisdictional complexity.

5. Advisory Disharmony. For officials seeking guidance from governmental gurus, theoretically harmony is more elusive than ever. More theories are in vogue as to how metro areas should be run. No wonder actual practice is more eclectic than ever before.

6. Reduced Federal Aid. Direct federal aid to localities, from day care funds to revenue sharing, has been cut back year by year without

From *National Civic Review,* Vol. 76, No. 1, January-February 1987. Published by the National Civic League, Denver, Colorado. Reprinted with permission of the publisher.

a concomitant reduction in federal regulations.

7. Reduced State Aid. Because non-educational state aid has been reduced without changes in state mandates and conditions, metro (and, though not the focus of this article, rural) communities' budgets have suffered a double whammy.

These metro area trends point to regionalism as a solution because it can (a) handle certain functions (usually of a capital-intensive or regulatory nature) on a multi-jurisdictional basis, (b) achieve economies of scale in providing various services by broadening the basis of fiscal support and the demand for certain services, (c) handle "spillover" servicing problems caused by rapid urban population growth and sometimes decline, and (d) confront the necessity for retrenchment by seeking more effective ways of rendering public services.

The 17 Approaches to Regionalism

Regionalism is a gold mine for officials seeking to solve local problems, and 17 different miners may be put to work to extract the gold. These 17 approaches to regional service problems can be arrayed on a spectrum from the easiest to the hardest — from the most politically feasible, least controversial, and sometimes least effective to the politically least feasible, most threatening to local officials, and sometimes most effective, at least in the opinion of many in jurisdictions that have made these fairly radical reforms (see box, page 153).

Easiest Eight

The first eight approaches are the easiest:

1. **Informal Cooperation.** For many up against the wall, this is the easiest of them all. This approach is clearly the least formal, and the most pragmatic of the 17. It generally involves collaborative and reciprocal actions between two local jurisdictions, does not usually require fiscal actions, and only rarely involves matters of regional or even subregional significance. Although reliable information on the extent of its use is generally absent, anecdotal evidence suggests that informal cooperation is the most widely practiced approach to regionalism.

2. **Interlocal Service Contracts.** Voluntary but formal agreements between two or more local governments are widely used. Some 45 states now sanction them broadly. Survey data suggest a slight decline (4 percent) between 1972 and 1983 in their use, but well over half the cities and counties polled in 1983 had used such contracts to handle at least one of their servicing responsibilities. Metro central cities, suburbs, and counties generally rely on them to a greater extent than non-metro municipal and county jurisdictions.

3. **Joint Powers Agreements.** These agreements between two or more local governments provide for the joint planning, financing, and delivery of a service for the citizens of all the jurisdictions involved. All states authorize joint service agreements, but 20 still require that each participating unit be empowered to provide the service in question. Surveys indicate that the number of cities and counties relying on joint services agreements for at least one service rose from 33 percent in 1972 to 55 percent in 1983, making them slightly more popular than interlocal contracting, although usage closely parallels interlocal servicing contracts.

4. **Extraterritorial Powers.** Sanctioned in 35 states, extraterritorial powers permit all or at least some, cities to exercise some of their regulatory authority outside their boundaries in rapidly developing unincorporated areas. Less than half the authorizing states permit extraterritorial planning, zoning, and subdivision regulation, however, which makes effective control of fringe growth difficult. Because a number of states do not authorize extraterritorial powers, and because this approach does not apply to cities surrounded by other incorporated jurisdictions, this approach is less used than other techniques.

5. **Regional Councils/Councils of Governments.** In the 1960s, no more than 20 or 25 jurisdictions had created wholly voluntaristic regional councils. That figure had soared to over 660 by 1980, thanks largely to federal aid and especially to federal requirements (notably Section 204 of the Model Cities legislation) that required a regional review and comment

Regional Approaches to Service Delivery

Easiest

1. Informal Cooperation
2. Interlocal Service Contracts
3. Joint Powers Agreements
4. Extraterritorial Powers
5. Regional Councils/Councils of Governments
6. Federally Encouraged Single-Purpose Regional Bodies
7. State Planning and Development Districts
8. Contracting (Private)

Middling

9. Local Special Districts
10. Transfer of Functions
11. Annexation
12. Regional Special Districts and Authorities
13. Metro Multipurpose District
14. Reformed Urban County

Hardest

15. One-Tier Consolidations
16. Two-Tier Restructuring
17. Three-Tier Reforms

process in all metro areas for certain local grant applications. Title IV of the Intergovernmental Cooperation Act of 1968 built on the Section 204 base to create a "clearinghouse" structure at the rural and urban regional as well as state levels. Local participation in regional councils still remained primarily voluntary, however, with jurisdictions resisting any efforts at coercion.

Regional councils, also known as Councils of Government (COGs) which rely so heavily on interlocal cooperation, assumed far more than a clearinghouse role in the late 1960s and 1970s. Thirty-nine federal grants programs with a regional thrust sometimes utilized COGs for their own integral parts of a strong state-established substate districting system, as well. Rural COGs tended to take on certain direct assistance and servicing roles for their constituents, while the more heavily

urban ones usually served a role as regional agenda-definer and conflict-resolver.

With the advent of Reagan federalism a reduction in the federal role in substate regionalism occurred. Reagan's Executive Order 12372 put the prime responsibility for the A-95 clearinghouse role with the states, while providing a back-up federal role (48 states picked up the challenge). Twelve of the 39 federal regional programs were scrapped, 11 were cut heavily, 9 lost their regional component, and 6 were revised substantially; only 1 was left fully intact.

To survive, COGs had to adapt and the overwhelming majority did so; less than one-fifth (125) of the 660 regional councils shut their doors. Some got greater state support both in funding and in power. Many others sought more local fiscal contributions and became a regional servicing agency for constituent local units. A majority of regional councils now serve as a chief source of technical services and provide certain direct services under contract to their localities. Some state functions have been transferred to regional council and many serve as field administrator of certain state-planned and fund services. All still perform some type of clearinghouse function and some assume specialized regional planning and other related functions under at least 11 federal single-purpose grants and loan programs as of FY 1983.

Most COGs, then, reflect a greater "nativism," "pragmatism," and service activism than their predecessors of a decade ago.

6. Federally Encouraged Single-Purpose Regional Bodies. Single-purpose regional bodies came into being when institutional strings were attached to some 20 federal aid programs (as of 1980). According to the 1977 Census of Local Governments, these federally encouraged special-purpose regional units numbered between 1,400 and 1,700 depending on definitions and classifications. A less rigorous, private, and meagerly funded survey identified more than 990 such bodies in 1983. Although the actual number as of 1983 was probably higher, by 1986 the total was probably a lot less, given the number of regional program revisions, budget cuts, and eliminations during the 1983–86 period. Single-purpose regional bodies now exist only in a few federal aid programs (notably economic development, Appalachia, Area Agencies on Aging, Job Training, and metro transportation). Continued federal fundings make them easy to establish and they play a helpful, non-threatening planning role.

7. **State Planning and Development Districts (SPDDs).** These districts were established by the states during the late 1960s and early 1970s to bring order to the chaotic proliferation of federal special purpose regional programs. A state's own substate regional goals were a prominent part of the authorizing legislation (19 states) or gubernatorial executive orders (24 states) that established SPDDs. By 1979 18 states had conferred a "review and comment" role on their SPDDs for certain non-federally aided local and state projects. Sixteen conferred such authority for special district projects and 11 authorized SPDDs to assume a direct servicing role, if it was sanctioned by member governments or the regional electorate.

As a matter of practice, practically all SPDDs adhere to the confederate style of regional councils/COGs. Many regional councils have been folded into the SPDD system, although boundaries have sometimes changed. Approximately the same number of SPDD systems (43) exist today as in the late 1970s, although in the hard-pressed midwest funding problems have rendered some moribund. All of these states took on the devolved responsibilities under Reagan's Executive Order 12372 for the "clearinghouse function," as did five others. Over half fund their SPDDs but only five in a respectable fashion.

Although feasible, SPDDs are somewhat difficult because special authorizing legislation is required, state purposes and goals are involved, and the establishment of a new statewide districting system can at least initially appear threatening, especially to counties.

8. **Contracting (Private).** Contracting with the private sector is the only form of public-private collaboration analyzed here and is the most popular of all such forms. Service contracts with private providers are now authorized in 26 states — far fewer than their intergovernmental counterparts and usually with far more detailed procedural requirements. Their use has clearly increased from the early 1970s to the present with scores of different local services sometimes provided under contracts with various private sector providers. Joint powers agreements and inter-local service agreements, however, are both more popular than contracting with private firms.

This approach rounds out the cluster of interlocal approaches that we term easiest. Contracting with private organizations has been placed last because authorizing legislation, especially non-restrictive statutes, may be difficult to obtain. Moreover, the fears of public sector unions as well as certain public employees are aroused when local officials seek to contract services privately.

Middling Six

The middle cluster in the spectrum includes four institutional and two tough procedural approaches for new and usually broader territorial service delivery systems. These approaches present somewhat greater hurdles than those in the prior group but each is a more stable way to effectively align governmental and service delivery boundaries.

9. **Local Special Districts.** These districts are a very popular way to provide a single service or multiple related services on a multi-jurisdictional basis. Three-quarters of all local special districts serve areas whose boundaries are not coterminous with those of a city or county, a situation that has prevailed for at least two decades. Forty-one percent of all special districts were found within metro areas, making special districts the most numerous of the five basic categories of local government in metro America.

10. **Transfer of Functions.** This procedural way to change permanently the provider of a specific service jumped by 40 percent in a decade, according to a 1983 survey of counties and cities. The larger urban jurisdictions were much more likely to transfer functions than the smaller ones. Over three-fifths of the central cities reported such transfers compared to 37 percent of the suburban cities and 35

percent of the non-metro municipalities. Among counties, 47 percent of the metro-type counties transferred functions compared to only 29 percent in the non-metro group. Cities were likely to shift services, first to counties, then to COGs and special districts.

Despite its increased popularity, the difficulties involved in transfer of functions should not be overlooked. Only 18 states authorize such shifts (8 more than in 1974) and in half these cases voter approval is mandated. In addition, the language of some of the authorizing statutes does not always clearly distinguish between a transfer and an interlocal servicing contract.

11. **Annexation.** The dominant 19th century device for bringing local jurisdictional servicing boundaries and expanding settlement patterns into proper alignment remains popular. The 61,356 annexations in the 1970s involved 9,000 square miles and 3 million people. The 23,828 annexations in the first half of the 1980s affected 1 million citizens and 3 million square miles. Although the vast majority of these annexations involved very few square miles, they are an incremental solution to closing the gap between governmental servicing boundaries and the boundaries of the center city.

A look at the larger-scale annexations of the past four decades highlights a dozen municipalities that serve almost as de facto regional governments: Phoenix, Houston, Dallas, San Antonio, Memphis, San Jose, El Paso, Huntsville, Concord (Cal.), Ft. Worth, Omaha, and Shreveport. Most large-scale annexations have occurred in the southwest and west, thanks to the large amount of unincorporated land on municipal peripheries and to pro-city annexation statutes. Students of public finance point out that central cities that were able to annex substantial land are usually in good fiscal shape since they have escaped the "hole in the doughnut" problems of central cities in the older metro areas of the east and midwest.

Annexation is limited by the nature of state authorizing laws (most do not favor the annexing locality); its irrelevance in most northeastern states, given the absence of unincorporated turf in their urban areas; and a

reluctance to use the process as a long-range solution to eliminating local jurisdictional, fiscal, and servicing fragmentation. Annexation, then, has limited geographic application and is usually used incrementally; but when it is assigned a key role in a city's development, it can transform a municipality from a local to a regional institution.

12. **Regional Special Districts and Authorities.** These big areawide institutions comprise the greatest number of regional governments in our 304 metro areas. Unlike their local urban counterparts, these Olympian organizations are established to cope on a fully areawide basis with a major urban surviving challenge such as mass transit, sewage disposal, water supply, hospitals, airports, and pollution control. Census data show there were approximately 132 regional and 983 major subregional special districts and authorities in 304 metro areas in 1982, compared to 230 and 2,232, respectively, in non-metro areas.

Relatively few large, regional units have been established because they (a) require specific state enactment and may involve functional transfers from local units; (b) are independent, expensive, professional, and fully governmental; and (c) are frequently as accountable to bond buyers as to the localities and the citizen consumers.

13. **Metro Multipurpose Districts.** These districts differ from the other regional models in that they involve establishing a regional authority to perform diverse, not just related regional, functions. At least four states have enacted legislation authorizing such district, but they permit a comparatively narrow range of functions.

This option clearly ranks among the most difficult to implement, with metro Seattle the only basic case study. While multipurpose districts have a number of theoretical advantages (greater popular control, better planning and coordination of a limited number of areawide functions, and a more accountable regional government), political and statutory difficulties have barred their widespread use.

14. **The Reformed Urban County.** Because it transforms a unit of local government, a move frequently opposed by the elected

officials of the jurisdiction in question, new urban counties are difficult to form. As a result, though 29 states have enacted permissive county home rule statutes, only 76 charter counties (generally urban) have been created.

In metro areas, however, three-quarters of the 683 metro counties have either an elected chief executive or an appointed chief administrative officer. The servicing role of these jurisdictions has expanded rapidly over the past ten decades or so. Since 1967, outlays for what used to be traditional county functions (corrections, welfare, roads, and health and hospitals) have declined, with expenditures for various municipal-type, regional and new federally encouraged services have risen commensurately. Overall, the range of state-mandated and county-initiated services have risen rapidly in metro counties, during the past two decades, which has necessitated a better approach to fiscal and program management.

In the 146 single-county metro areas this reform county option is excellent. However, since county mergers and modification of county boundaries are almost impossible, in the 159 multi-county metro areas the option is less valuable. It can only provide a subregional solution to certain service delivery problems, not a fully regional approach.

The Tough Trio

The hardest approaches to metro regionalism are the three general governmental options: one-tier or unitary, two-tier or federative, and three-tier or super-federative.

All three involve the creation of a new areawide level of government, a reallocation of local government powers and functions, and, as a result a disruption of the political and institutional status quo. All three options involve very rare and remarkable forms of interlocal cooperation.

15. **One-Tier consolidations.** This method of expanding municipal boundaries has had a lean, but long history. From 1804 to 1907, four city-county mergers occurred, all by state mandate. Then municipalities proliferated but city-county mergers virtually stopped for 40

years. From Baton Rouge's partial merger in 1947 to the present there have been some 17 city-county consolidations, most endorsed by popular referendum. Among the hurdles to surmount in achieving such reorganizations are state authorization, the frequent opposition of local elected officials, racial anxieties (where large minorities exist), an equitable representational system, concerns about the size of government, and technical issues relating to such matters as debt assumption. Only one out of every five consolidation efforts has succeeded in the past 25 years.

Most consolidations have been partial, not total, with small suburban municipalities, school districts and special districts sometimes left out but the new county government generally exercises some authority over their activities. In addition, the metro settlement pattern in some cases has long since exceeded the county limits, so that the reorganized government may be the prime service provider and key player, but not the only one. This, of course, is another result of rigid county boundaries.

To sum up, one-tier consolidations have generally been most suitable in smaller nonmetro urban areas and in smaller and medium (ideally uni-county) metro areas.

16. **Two-Tier Restructurings.** These seek a division between local and regional functions with two levels of government to render such services. These and other features, notably a reorganized county government, are spelled out in a new county charter that is adopted in a countywide referendum. The Committee for Economic Development advanced one of the most persuasive arguments for this approach in the 1970s. Metro Toronto, which created a strongly empowered regional federative government to handle areawide functions and ultimately led to some local reorganization by the merger of some municipalities, is a model for this approach.

The prime American example of this federative approach is Metro Dade County (Miami-Dade). Unlike the incremental reform approach of the modernized or urban county, a drastically redesigned county structure and role emerged from a head-on confrontation over the restructuring issue. Narrowly approved in a countywide referendum in 1957, the new Metro government's cluster of strong charter powers and its authority to perform a range of areawide functions were steadily opposed until the mid–1960s. Since then, its powers have grown and it is widely considered a success. Witness the extraordinary responsibilities Metro Dade assumed during the various waves of immigration since the early 1960s. The level of metro-municipal collaboration is better now than it was a generation ago, but tensions and confrontations are still part of the relationship — as they are in most federative systems. In my opinion, however, its survival is assured.

17. **The Three-Tier Reforms.** This is a rarely used approach, with just two U.S. examples. However, it deals with the special problems of multi-county metro areas.

The first example is the Twin Cities (Minneapolis–St. Paul) Metropolitan Council. Launched as a metro initiative and enacted by the state legislature in 1967, the Council is the authoritative regional coordinator, planner, and controller of large-scale development for its region which includes seven counties and a dozen localities.

It is empowered by the state to review, approve, or suspend projects and plans of the area's various multi-jurisdictional special districts and authorities; it is the regional designee under all federally sponsored substate regional programs for which the area is eligible, and has the right to review and delay projects having an adverse areawide impact. Direct operational responsibilities do not fall within its purview but it directly molds the region's future development. Like any body that possesses significant power over other public agencies and indirectly over private regional actors, the Council has become somewhat politicized in recent years but its rightful place in the governance of the Twin Cities is not questioned.

The other three-tier experiment is the Greater Portland (Oregon) Metropolitan Service District (MSD), a regional planning and coordinating agency that serves the urbanized portion of three counties. Approved by popular referendum in 1978, the MSD supplanted the previous COG, and assumed the waste disposal and Portland Zoo responsibilities of the previous regional authority. The enabling legislation also authorized the MSD to run the regional transportation agency and to assume responsibility for a range of the functions, subject to voter approval, but these options have not been utilized. A 1986 referendum on a new convention center did pass and this task was assigned to the MSD. Unlike the Twin Cities' Council, the MSD has an elected mayor, an appointed manager, and an elected council of 12 commissioners, which provides a popular accountability that the Met Council has yet to achieve.

Both three-tier examples suggest how other multi-county metro areas might approach areawide service delivery and other metro challenges but they are arduous to achieve and not easy to sustain.

This probe of metro Snow White's current status suggests that she is alive and well, and is being looked after by her 17 regionable dwarfs:

1. Overall Growth in Regionalism. Virtually all of the various approaches have been on the increase. Since the early 1970s, the use of the eight easiest approaches has seen a net increase despite a reduction in the number of regional councils and federally supported substate districts. Meanwhile five of the six middling approaches grew markedly (the exception was the metro multi-purpose authority). Even the three hardest approaches have grown in use.

2. Multiple Approach Use. Very few metro areas rely on only one or two forms of substate regionalism.

3. The easier procedural and unifunctional institutional types of service shifts tend to be found more in larger metro areas while the harder restructurings usually take place successfully within the medium-sized and especially the small metro areas.

4. The expanded use of at least 10 of the 14 easiest and middling approaches is largely a product of local needs and initiatives, as well as of a growing awareness of their increasingly interdependent condition.

5. Jurisdictional fragmentation has not been reduced as a result of restructuring successes, but even incomplete forms of cooperation are

useful. Such approaches are used extensively; in a majority of metro areas they are the only feasible forms of regional and subregional collaboration.

6. Like much else in the American system of metro governance, the overwhelming majority of interlocal and regional actions taken to resolve servicing and other problems reflect an ad hoc, generally issue-by-issue, incremental pattern of evolution. However, most of the major reorganizations were triggered, at least in part, by a visible crisis of some sort.

7. The intergovernmental bases of substate regional activities remain as significant as ever. The states, which always have played a significant part in the evolution of their metro areas, must move into a new primary role if the federal role in this arena continues to erode.

Our Snow White would be ever so happy if her Prince Charming would gallop up soon, wake her from the slumber induced by her stepmother, take her out of the forest and — please — make room in the palace for 17 hardworking dwarfs!

Bibliography

Advisory Commission on Intergovernmental Regulations, *Intergovernmental Service Arrangements for Delivering Local Public Service: Update 1983 (A-103)*. Washington, D.C., October 1985.

_____, *Pragmatic Federalism: The Reassignment of Functional Responsibility (M-105)*. Washington, D.C., July 1976.

_____, *Regional Decision Making: New Strategies for Substate Districts (A-43)*. Washington, D.C., October 1973.

_____, *State and Local Roles in the Federal System (A-88)*. Washington, D.C., April 1982.

Bollens, John C. and Schmandt, Henry J., *The Metropolis*, Fourth Edition, New York, N.Y., 1982.

Florestano, Patricia and Gordon, Stephen, "County and Municipal Use of Private Contracting for Public Service Delivery," *Urban Interest*, April 1984.

Hatry, Harry P. and Valente, Carl F., "Alternative Service Delivery Approaches Involving Increased Use of the Private Sector," *The Municipal Year Book*. International City Management Association, Washington, D.C. 1983, pp. 199–207.

Henderson, Lori, "Intergovernmental Service Arrangements and the Transfers of Functions," *Municipal Year Book*. International City Management Association, Washington, D.C. 1985, pp. 194–202.

Jones, Victor, "Regional Councils and Regional Governments in the United States," paper presented at the Annual Meeting of the American Society for Public Administration, Detroit, 1981.

Marlin, John Tepper, ed., *Contracting Municipal Services: A Guide for Purchase from the Private Sector*, Ronald Press, John Wiley & Sons, New York, 1984, pp. 1–13.

McDowell, Bruce D., "Moving Toward Excellence in Regional Councils," based on a paper presented at the New England Regional Council Conference in Portland, Maine on October 26, 1984.

_____, "Regional Councils in an Era of Do-It-Yourself Federalism," a paper presented to the Regional Council Executive Directors of the Southeastern States," March 20, 1986.

_____, "Regions Under Reagan," a paper presented at the National Planning Conference, American Planning Association, Minneapolis–St. Paul, Minnesota, May 8, 1984.

National Association of Regional Councils, *Directory of Regional Councils, 85–86*, Washington, D.C.

_____, *Matrix of Regional Council Programs, 1985–86*, Washington, D.C.

_____, *Special Report— No. 91*. Washington, D.C., January 1984.

U.S. Bureau of the Census, *Local Governments in Metropolitan Areas* (1982 Census of Governments, Vol. 5-GC82 [5]). Washington, D.C.

U.S. Senate, Committee on Governmental Affairs, Subcommittee on Intergovernmental Relations, *Metropolitan Regional Governance*, Hearing, February 6, 1984. Washington, D.C.

Wikstrom, Nelson, "Epitaph for a Monument to Another Successful Protest: Regionalism in Metropolitan Areas," *Virginia Social Science Journal*, Vol. 19, Winter 1984, pp. 1–10.

Wirt, Frederick M., "The Dependent City: External Influences Upon Local Autonomy," paper delivered at the 1983 Annual Meeting of the American Political Science Association, September 1–4, 1983.

CHAPTER 20

THE EVOLUTION OF REGIONAL PLANNING

American Planning Association

Regional planning is planning for a geographic area that transcends the boundaries of individual governmental units but that shares common social, economic, political, natural resource, and transportation characteristics.[1] A regional planning agency prepares plans that serve as a framework for planning by local governments and special districts.

Throughout the United States, there are regional planning agencies that are either voluntary associations of local government or mandated or authorized by state legislation (e.g., the Metropolitan Council in the Twin Cities or the Metropolitan Services District in Portland, Oregon). These exist for purposes of: undertaking plans that are typically advisory in nature, providing information, technical assistance, and training; coordinating efforts among member governments, especially efforts that involve federal funding; and providing a two-way conduit between member governments and the state and federal agencies. Regional planning agencies may also serve as a forum to discuss complex and sometimes sensitive issues among member local governments and to try to find solutions to problems that affect more than one jurisdiction. Sometimes these organizations have direct regulatory authority in that they not only prepare plans, but also administer land-use controls through subdivision review and zoning recommendations, review proposals for major developments whose impacts may cross jurisdictional borders, and review and certify local plans.

States authorize the establishment of these regional planning agencies in different ways. In some parts of the country, the regional agencies take their structure from general enabling legislation (e.g., for regional planning commissions or councils of government). In other places, they are the product of intergovernmental or joint powers agreements, as in California, or interstate compacts, as with the Delaware Regional Planning Commission in the Philadelphia, Pennsylvania/Camden, New Jersey, area, or the Tahoe Regional Planning Agency in Nevada and California. In some states, regional agencies are created by special state legislation that applies only to one particular agency (e.g., the Northeastern Illinois Planning Commission in the Chicago area, or the Cape Cod Commission in Massachusetts). In still others, they may exist as private, voluntary organizations that seek to provide a regional perspective through independently prepared plans and studies. Examples of such agencies are the Regional Plan Association in New York City and Bluegrass Tomorrow in the Lexington, Kentucky, area.

Originally published as Chapter 6 of *Growing Smart Legislative Guidebook: Model Statutes for Planning and the Management of Change,* Phase I Interim Edition, 1996. Published by the American Planning Association, Chicago, Illinois. Reprinted with permission of the publisher.

Reasons for
Regional Planning

- Provision of technical assistance to local governments.
- Maintenance of forum for exploring and resolving intergovernmental issues.
- Development of regional plans to guide, direct, and or coordinate local planning.
- Articulation of local interests and perspectives to other levels of government.
- Establishment of two-way conduit between local governments and other agencies.

The Origins of Regional Planning Agencies

The first regional planning agency with planning powers was the Boston Metropolitan Improvement Commission created by the Massachusetts legislature in 1902. Seven years later, in 1909, the Commercial Club of Chicago, a private organization, financed the preparation of the Plan of Chicago, which was completed by a team headed by Chicago architects Daniel H. Burnham and Edward H. Bennett. The plan placed the city of Chicago in a regional context and contained regional proposals for parks and transportation.[2]

From 1913 to 1915, when the state legislature repealed the statute creating it, Pennsylvania authorized the establishment of a Suburban Metropolitan Planning Commission. Within a 25-mile radius of Philadelphia, the commission could levy assessments and prepare comprehensive plans for highways, parks and parkways, sewerage and sewage disposal, housing, sanitation and health, civic centers, and other functional areas.[3] The commission had the authority to make recommendations to governmental units on a wide variety of issues, including "the distribution and relative location of all public buildings, public grounds, and open spaces devoted to public use, and the planning, subdivision and laying out for urban

uses of private grounds brought into the market from time to time."[4]

The major regional planning effort of the 1920s — and for many years afterwards — was the *Regional Plan for New York and Environs*, financed by the Russell Sage Foundation and prepared by an advisory committee. Work began on the plan in 1921 and was completed in 1929. The eight-volume document covered a 5,528–square mile area with 500 incorporated bodies. Even by today's standards, the Regional Plan is an impressive work. It contained regionwide proposals for transportation, land use, and public facilities, as well as specific design proposals for New York City. After its publication, the advisory committee issued periodic reports on its implementation.

In 1922, the first metropolitan area planning commission was established in Los Angeles to advise the County Board of Supervisors on planning for the county and on approving subdivisions. In 1923, the Ohio General Assembly enacted the first enabling legislation for regional planning commissions. That legislation, which was drafted by Cincinnati attorney Alfred Bettman, was to provide the model for the regional planning provisions of the Standard City Planning Enabling Act (see below), on whose advisory committee Bettman would become a member. The same year, the Chicago Regional Planning Association, a quasi-public organization, and the Allegheny County Planning Commission (Pittsburgh) were created.

The SCPEA: Model Legislation for Regional Planning

The Standard City Planning Enabling Act (SCPEA), drafted by an advisory committee to the U.S. Department of Commerce and published in 1928, contained model legislation for regional planning. The SCPEA authorized the planning commission of any municipality or the county commissioners of any county to petition the governor to establish a planning region and create a planning commission for that region. The governor was to hold at least one public hearing before making a determination to grant the application, define the region, and appoint the regional planning commission.[5]

Under the SCPEA model, the regional planning commission was composed of nine members, all of whom would be appointed and removed by the governor. The commission had the authority to prepare, adopt, and amend a "master regional plan for the physical development of the region."[6] After adopting the plan, the regional planning commission was required to certify it to the governor, to the planning commission of each municipality in the region, to the council of each municipality that did not have a planning commission, to the county commissioners of each county located wholly or partially in the region, and to other organized taxing districts or political subdivisions wholly or partially included in the region.

Adoption of the regional plan by the municipal planning commission was optional; however, once the regional planning commission adopted it, the plan would have the same force and effect as a plan made and adopted locally. In addition, the municipal planning commission, "[b]efore adopting any amendment of the municipal plan which would constitute a violation of or departure from the regional plan certified to the municipal planning commission," was required to submit the amendment to the regional commission. The regional commission would then "certify to the municipal commission its approval, disapproval or other opinion concerning the proposed amendment."[7]

Once the regional plan was adopted by the regional planning commission, no street, park, or other public way, ground, or open space; no public building or other public structure; and no public utility, whether publicly or privately owned or operated, could be constructed or authorized in unincorporated territory until the project was submitted to and approved by the regional planning commission. However, the planning commission's disapproval could be overruled by the body or officer having authority to determine the location, character, or extent of the improvement, provided that, in the case of a board, commission, or body, not less than two-thirds of its membership voted to do so and provided a statement of reasons for such overruling in the minutes of records of the body or officer.[8]

One analyst of this period observed that:

> By the end of the 1920s, metropolitan and county planning was a major topic of concern among professional planners. Many city planning commissions found that central city development plans ignored the surrounding local governments and that regional planning and cooperative political solutions were required. Some saw the need for an agency empowered to take an overall view of serious problems besetting the entire metropolitan area.[9]

Regional Planning During the Depression and War Years

The federal government, through the National Planning Board (later the National Resources Committee) in the Department of the Interior, provided the major push for metropolitan, regional, state, and interstate planning. The federal government supported the creation of the Pacific Northwest Regional Planning Commission, a four-state body covering Idaho, Montana, Oregon, and Washington, and the New England Regional Planning Commission, which included Massachusetts, Vermont, Rhode Island, Connecticut, and Maine.[10] It backed a bi-state St. Louis Regional Planning Commission, which it hoped would provide a model for similar efforts elsewhere in the U.S. It also supported the use of interstate compacts, in the words of a report by one federal agency, "as a means of solving regional problems wherever this procedure is found to be feasible."[11]

By the end of the 1930s, according to a report of the U.S. Advisory Commission on Intergovernmental Regulations, federal support had greatly expanded metropolitan and regional planning:

> In 1934, there were only 85 metropolitan and county planning bodies and 23 regional planning agencies in existence. By January 1937, there were 506 metropolitan multicounty and county planning agencies, of which at least 316 were official public bodies. Two years later, metropolitan planning agencies or regional planning boards, commissions, or associations were operating in at least 30 major cities. In

addition to these metropolitan developments, by the close of the decade areawide planning had also been extended to a number of small urban areas and several nonmetropolitan regions.[12]

Of note during World War II was the formation of privately financed regional planning councils in San Francisco, St. Louis, Boston, Cincinnati, and Kansas City. In Pittsburgh, the Allegheny Conference on Community Development was established in 1945. Its membership drew from leaders in business, labor, and government, and it emerged as a prime mover in the transformation of Pittsburgh in the postwar era.[13]

Regional Planning in the Postwar Period

In the 1950s, federal aid for comprehensive planning became available with the enactment of Section 701 of the Housing Act of 1954. This statute provided monies for local planning and planning for metropolitan areas by official regional or metropolitan planning agencies.

According to a study by the U.S. Advisory Commission on Intergovernmental Relations, at least 13 states passed regional planning enabling acts in the 3 years following the enactment of the 1954 Housing Act. This set the stage for a tremendous increase in the number of multijurisdictional planning organizations. During this period, according to the ACIR, the legislatures of at least nine of these states enacted legislation requiring or permitting the establishment of planning agencies for entire urbanized areas. The statutes usually authorized the agencies to apply for and receive federal grants. Some states adopted specific statutes that created planning commissions for certain metropolitan areas. By the beginning of the 1960s, some two-thirds of the nation's metropolitan areas were engaged in some type of areawide planning.[14]

Complementing the "701" program was the Federal-Aid Highway Act of 1962. This statute required a "cooperative, comprehensive, and continuous" planning process as a prerequisite for federal financial assistance for interstate highway development in metropolitan areas. The act required regional transportation plans in urban areas with populations more than 50,000 as a condition to construction funds. In contrast to the "701" grants, which split costs evenly with local governments, the Highway Act provided matching grants of 70 percent of the cost of preparing the necessary studies.

In some parts of the U.S., metropolitan transportation planning was assigned to a special commission or entity. This was the case, and still is, in Boston, San Francisco, and Chicago. In others, the transportation planning function was assumed by a regional planning commission or metropolitan councils of government (COG), which were voluntary alliances of local governments formed to undertake planning or any type of joint governmental activity that its members could agree upon.

One of the earliest studies of COGs was conducted in 1962 by the American Society of Planning Officials (ASPO), one of APA's predecessor organizations. The study examined eight councils. It observed that the agencies were operating without an overall metropolitan government that would carry out any plans they might propose. As a consequence, the agencies

> must rely on persuasion to convince numerous local governments that joint area-wide action is necessary — a method not notable for its past successes....
>
> Probably the most important advantage of the voluntary governmental council is its acceptability to local political leaders. No change in government structure is necessary and there is no transfer of power from local units to a larger agency. The council is easily set up and established by the local governments themselves. Membership is voluntary and the organization is flexible and adaptable to many situations.[15]

During the 1960s and 1970s, the nation was almost completely covered by multistate river basin and economic development commissions and by metropolitan and nonmetropolitan regional councils. The expansion of COGs, prompted by the availability of federal funding, was dramatic. In 1961, for example, there were only 36 COGs, including 25 among the 212 metropolitan areas. By 1966, this number included 119 councils, of which 71 were metropolitan. By 1971, there were 247 metropolitan areas, and all of them had official regional planning, mostly under elected COGs. By 1978, there were 649 councils in the U.S. Of these, 292 were in metropolitan areas.[16]

Four federal laws were responsible for this expansion, and they were all enacted in a watershed year of 1965. The Housing and Community Development Act of 1965 made regional councils eligible for planning funds. The Public Works and Economic Development Act of 1965 provided funding for multicounty economic development districts and authorized the establishment of federal multistate economic development commissions. The Appalachian Regional Development Act established the multistate Appalachian Regional Commission, which accomplished its work through multicounty development districts. Finally, the Water Resources Planning Act of 1965 authorized the establishment of federal multistate river basin commissions.[17] Under Circular A-95, promulgated by the U.S. Office of Management and Budget, regional agencies received authority to review applications for federal assistance for compliance with regional and local plans. In addition, regional agencies began to prepare regional water-quality management plans under Section 208 of the Federal Clean Water Act of 1972.

Bruce McDowell of the U.S. Advisory Commission on Intergovernmental Relations observed:

> This explosion of "areawide" regional councils and the multistate river basin and economic development regions occurred because of very intentional and systematic federal action which drew in the states as well as local governments. In the cases of the areawide councils, the federal actions included establishing 39 grant programs designed to require and fund regional planning, and direct appeal to the governors of all 50 states to establish statewide systems of substate districts to systematize the administration of the federal programs supporting regional councils. And many of the states did so.[18]

New Roles for Regional Agencies

Between 1960 and 1980, there were a number of studies that proposed new roles and authority for regional planning entities. These studies also called for changes in state statutes. Their chief recommendations are summarized below.

1. **ASPO Connecticut Report.** In 1966, ASPO, assisted by the Chicago law firm of Ross, Hardies, O'Keefe, Babcock, McDugald & Parsons, produced a report entitled *New Directions in Connecticut Planning Legislation*. The report, prepared for the Connecticut Development Commission, recommended major changes in the Connecticut planning statutes. Its major recommendation regarding regional planning agencies was an extension of their jurisdiction to review matters that may have regional significance, such as decisions involving property within specified distances from state highways, and development affecting the region, such as water, sewerage, and utility projects. The regional agency would still not be given veto power over local decisions. If a local or state agency took action contrary to a regional planning agency's recommendation pursuant to a referral, that agency would be required to state in writing the reasons that had led it to a different conclusion. But if the regional agency chose not to comment on a proposal, such an action would be neutral, rather than constitute a project endorsement.

The ASPO report also recommended amending the state statutes to define a regional plan as distinct from a local plan. "The statute should direct the *regional* plan to cover *regional* facilities," noted its authors, "and, especially, to give attention to regional resource and conservation problems."[19]

2. **National Commission on Urban Problems (Douglas Commission).** In 1968, the National Commission on Urban Problems, also known as the Douglas Commission, after its Chair, Senator Paul Douglas, issued its report, *Building the American City*. The Commission's charge, among other things, was to examine "state and local zoning and land use laws, codes, and regulations to find ways by which States and localities may improve and

utilize them in order to obtain further growth and development."[20] To date, the study, with its wide-ranging scope, is one of the most comprehensive and thorough in terms of examining authority of governments to plan and regulate development.

Two Commission proposals to broaden choice in the location of housing called for regional approaches:

> (1) Enactment of state legislation requiring multi-county or regional planning agencies to prepare and maintain housing plans. These plans would ensure that sites are available for development of new housing of all kinds and at all price levels. In the absence of a regional planning body — given the broader-than-local nature of the plan and the importance of political approval of such plans — the state government should assume responsibility for the necessary political endorsement of the plan.

> (2) Amendment of state planning and zoning acts to include, as one of the purposes of the zoning power, the provision of adequate sites for housing persons of all income levels. The amendments would also require that governments exercising the zoning power prepare plans showing how the community proposes to carry out such objectives in accordance with county or regional housing plans. This would ensure that, within the region as a whole, adequate provision is made for sites for all income levels.[21]

3. ACIR Report on Substate Districting.

In 1973, the U.S. Advisory Commission on Intergovernmental Relations published *Regional Decision Making: New Strategies for Substate Districts*. This report assessed the effectiveness of regional councils of local elected officials and substate planning and development districts. The report contained a number of recommendations for the federal, state, and local levels of government. The recommendations for state governments are especially relevant to the Growing Smart[SM] legislation. The ACIR recommended that states establish a formal procedure for the delineation and revision of the boundaries of substate districts. It called for a process involving the governor and units of general local government in a substate region, which would result in the governor's designation of a single "umbrella multi-jurisdictional organization" or UMJO in each region, with such designation

conferring the legal status of an agency of local governments.[22]

The UMJO's membership should be at least 60 percent local elected officials. The ACIR proposed that such organizations have a voting formula that involved the application of the one-government, one-vote principle in most voting matters, but permitted certain larger local jurisdictions to overrule this procedure on certain issues — such as actions that would affect the finances and operations of constituent local governments — and employ a proportionate, population-weighted rule. The UMJO would be responsible for the adoption and publication of regional policies or plans and of a program for their implementation.[23]

The ACIR called for the UMJO to review and approve, in the context of adopted regional plans and policies, all proposed major capital facility projects of state departments and agencies scheduled for location in the UMJO's region. Similarly, the UMJO would have the authority to review and comment on major capital projects proposed by local governmental units. The ACIR proposed conferring on the UMJO "a policy controlling role" over multijurisdictional special districts operating within the UMJO's region. "The emphasis on a single functional purpose," wrote the ACIR, "often results in decisions which have side effects on other areawide policies, programs, and jurisdictions. *For this reason, a generalist-oriented and dominated multipurpose regional agency must have authority not only to plan, but also to set basic policy for special districts that transcend city and county boundaries*"[24] (emphasis supplied). Means for securing policy control over the special district, according to the ACIR, included: appointment of the special district's policy board by the regional council; review and approval of the district's budgets and basic policies; assignment to the council of the power to halt temporarily or permanently any proposed district project; and empowering the council to serve as the special district's fiscal agent for bonding.[25]

The UMJO could provide member governments with technical assistance and promote interlocal problem solving and contracting. Financing of the regional agency's operations was to come from member governments under a mechanism authorized in enabling legislation and from state funds.[26]

The ACIR recommendations were later translated into model legislation. A portion of this legislation has been adapted for Sections 6-601 to 6-604, which deal with designation of substate districts and substate district agencies.[27]

4. **ALI Model Land Development Code.** The American Law Institute's (ALI) *A Model Land Development Code* (1976) specifically rejected the establishment or designation of regional planning agencies as having a role in a statewide land development planning and regulation system. Instead, the Code proposed the creation of regional planning divisions of a state land planning agency with regional advisory committees to advise the director of the state agency.

The drafters of the ALI Code were highly skeptical of the potential for regional planning under voluntary associations of elected officials and questioned whether they could provide an independent perspective. "The more that metropolitan agencies have been asked to review functions that bring them into potential conflict with local governments, the more the structural weaknesses of such organizations become apparent," they wrote.[28] The drafters quoted one critic of the system's effectiveness:

> [The COG] receives its legitimacy from its member governments — but those governments do not seem to want the COG to emerge as a force different and distinct from the sum of its governmental parts. Member governments do not generally see the COG as an independent source of regional influence, but rather as a service giver, a coordinator, a communications forum, and an insurance device for the continued flow of federal funds to local governments.[29]

Because of these and other political factors, COGs, wrote the Code's drafters, "engage in passive, consensus planning, giving each local government whatever it wants, regardless of the effect on the region," resulting in the "absence of regional planning that really faces tough issues."[30]

As a consequence of this skepticism, the Code required that the basic land planning power "remain at the state level to be delegated by the State Land Planning Agency to the regional divisions or withdrawn therefrom as the state agency sees fit."[31] The ALI Code saw this as "essential to enable the coordination of regional land planning with other state activities and to ensure that regional land planning carries the weight and authority of the state government."[32] The Code noted that this would eliminate a "key defect" in most metropolitan planning agencies, which was "the absence of close ties to a governing body and 'a strong chief executive who is able to override the contenders and force resolution of disagreements.'"[33]

Regional Planning in the 1980s and Beyond

In the 1980s, the federal government withdrew almost entirely from its support of regional planning. "Of the 39 programs designed and enacted during the preceding two decades to promote regional organization," wrote Bruce McDowell, "only one — metropolitan transportation planning — remained relatively unscathed by this sudden reversal of federal policy."[34] In the multistate programs, which had created most river basin and economic development regions, the federal government withdrew funding and the organizations died. Only multistate agencies created by federal law or interstate compact survived. The federal economic development programs, through the Economic Development Administration, and the Appalachian programs managed to continue, but in greatly abbreviated form.

A number of states — Connecticut, Florida, Georgia, Kentucky, and Virginia, among them — provided state support for regional planning agencies that replaced the lost federal funds. Florida, in 1972 with the enactment of the Environmental Land and Water Management Act, and Georgia, in 1989 with the Georgia Planning Act, strengthened the authority and responsibility for the agencies in statewide growth management systems. Florida's regional planning councils were required to prepare regional policy plans, review developments of regional impact, and establish mediation and arbitration processes to resolve regional disputes. Under the new Georgia act, the regional planning agencies were recast as "regional development centers" and were given powers similar to the regional councils in Florida. Massachusetts enacted one of the most progressive special purpose regional planning statutes in the nation when it passed, in 1989, special legislation establishing the Cape Cod Commission with broad powers to plan and regulate development in an area of statewide significance.

Regional planning agencies responded to the federal cutback, in some cases, by becoming more entrepreneurial. They undertook joint purchasing programs, forecasting, data collection and dissemination, arranged training, operated programs such as regional ambulance services, or provided consultant planning services to member governments.[35]

Where are regional planning agencies headed? The ACIR's Bruce McDowell suggests that one role of such agencies is the development of "negotiated policies and programs." Regional planning agencies, he observed, are "negotiating bodies" and provide "forums for mediating disputes, finding solutions to tough problems, and working out agreements, and developing cooperative action."[36] A British planning professor, Urlan A. Wannop, predicts that giving regional planning agencies "real duties in planning and implementation" in a statewide growth management system of the type enacted in Florida and elsewhere will make them effective, offering a promise of reinvigorating them.[37] Allan Wallis, an assistant professor of public policy at the University of Colorado at Denver, suggests that, in the current fluid environment, solutions to regional problems will evolve from an identification of "strategic interests over which coalitions already have formed." Thus, there will be no single solution or approach that will work in every region, even if the problems are, in Wallis' words, "fairly generic and common to most other large metropolitan areas." Developing out of the perception of the regional problems and the legitimacy of the coalitions that defined them, the particularized governance structures that result to address those problems "will be highly idiosyncratic, reflecting, as they should, such unique circumstances as local political culture."[38]

ORGANIZATIONAL STRUCTURE

Contemporary Regional Planning Agencies

Regional councils or some type of regional planning organization representing local governments operate in all states except Hawaii, Alaska, and Rhode Island, according to the National Association of Regional Councils (NARC). Regional planning in the U.S. is made institutionally complex by the federal requirement that a metropolitan planning organization (MPO) oversee transportation planning. The MPO may be separate from the established regional planning agencies — the situation in several metropolitan areas including Boston, Chicago, and San Francisco — or governed by a special policy committee inside the agency.

Twenty-five states have "wall-to-wall" regional councils. Regional councils in at least 10 other states serve from 75 to 90 percent of all local governments. For the remainder, except for four, reports NARC, councils cover from 60 to 74 percent of all local governments. New Jersey does not have state-designated regional councils. Three councils, two of them MPOs and one a regional planning agency headquartered in Princeton, serve areas of the state. Alaska has divided the state into regions for economic development purposes, but no formal regional agencies exist. In Montana, there are no state-designated regional planning councils, but there are a number of regional planning commissions.[39]

There are at least five possible structures for regional planning agencies:

1. **Regional Planning Commission.** Regional planning commissions may be single county, multicounty, or composed of multiple jurisdictions. Typically, their governing board is composed of citizens who are appointed by local governments, although elected officials may also serve. They are primarily established to prepare plans, provide technical assistance to member governments, and, in some cases, administer development regulations (such as reviewing and approving subdivision plats). Interstate regional planning commissions cover portions of multistate areas, most typically metropolitan areas. In Ohio, such regional planning commissions are the result of special enabling legislation.[40] In Philadelphia, the Delaware Valley Regional Planning Commission, whose jurisdiction covers portions of New Jersey and Pennsylvania, was created by a special interstate compact approved by Congress.[41]

2. **Council of Governments.** While they may undertake planning, councils of governments (COGs) are somewhat different than regional planning commissions in that they can carry out virtually any service delivery activity that a member government can undertake, provided the membership agrees that the COG should do so. For example, a council could operate a regional wastewater treatment plant or a regional ambulance service if the members permit. The governing structure of a COG typically involves appointed representatives from member governments but may include others, such as representatives of economic development organizations in the region. A variation includes a COG whose representatives are from local governments and from the state.

In Florida, for example, regional planning councils include representatives of member counties and other local general purpose governments in the geographic area covered by the regional planning council as well as representatives appointed by the governor from the geographic area covered by the council. The governor also appoints, as ex officio nonvoting members, representatives of several state departments.[42] The Metropolitan Washington Council of Governments includes one member of the Maryland General Assembly and one member of the Virginia General Assembly, representing portions of the Washington, D.C., metropolitan area. Both are selected every two years by separate caucuses of the members of the council from those legislative bodies.[43]

In some states, like Michigan, Ohio, and North Carolina, COGs are creatures of special enabling legislation.[44] In others, like California, they are established through a joint powers agreement.

3. **Regional Advisory Committee.** The American Law Institute's *Model Land Development Code* rejected the creation of independent regional planning agencies. Instead, it proposed the optional establishment of regional planning divisions for portions of the state. The divisions could be delegated all or a portion of the authority of the state planning agency and would exercise that authority subject to the planning agency's oversight. The governor could also create regional advisory committees and could delegate all or a portion of the powers of the regional planning division to the committees. The committees were also charged with advising the state planning director.[45] The ALI model of regional advisory committees to a state planning agency has not been adopted anywhere in the country.

4. **Regional Allocation Agency.** Economist Anthony Downs, in his 1994 book, *New Visions for Metropolitan America*, proposed the creation of regional allocation agencies.[46] The regional allocation agency would be responsible for allocating federal funds within various program areas either to local governments or to households, service delivery agencies, or other recipients. At the outset, Downs wrote, the agency would be responsible for allocating federal funding for transportation, environmental control, housing, urban planning, education, welfare, and health care. Within each categorical program, the regional agency would have to develop an allocation plan that addresses the needs and capacities of all potential recipients on an areawide basis and show how it was meeting those needs for persons living in all parts of the metropolitan area.

Examples of such agencies — although they might not reflect all of Downs' criteria —

would include the Metropolitan Service District or "Metro" in Portland, Oregon, and the Metropolitan Council in the Twin Cities in Minnesota.[47]

According to Downs, governing members of the agency could be elected by the residents of the entire metropolitan area (as in Portland), appointed by the governor (as in the Twin Cities), or appointed by the local governments in the region. Once chosen, the members of this agency may delegate some of their powers to existing organizations, appoint subagencies to handle funds within each program category, or use any other administrative methods they selected.

With respect to growth management activities, Downs proposed that a single government agency — either at the state level or regional (including county) level — be empowered to review all local land-use plans. The agency would check the plans' consistency with state planning goals — adopted by the state legislature and applicable to all communities in the state — and their consistency with each other, and suggest revisions where inconsistencies of either type are found. Downs contended that the agency must have the power to withhold its approval of local plans and that withholding it should carry significant penalties in the form of ineligibility for various types of state financial assistance.

"In some cases," he wrote, "the agency should have the power to override local government decisions, such as zoning decisions that prevent the creation of low-cost housing. Most often, however, the agency would simply request the local government to revise its plans and repeat the process until final approval is obtained."[48] In order to ensure consistency of state functional plans with local government plans and with each other, the same agency that performed the local plan review would also coordinate activities of state transportation departments, utility regulation departments, environmental protection departments, and other agencies.

5. **Special Purpose Regional Agencies.** Several states have special purpose regional agencies with the authority to plan and control development in environmentally sensitive areas or areas having statewide resource significance. Examples of such long-standing organizations include the Pinelands Commission in New Jersey, the Cape Cod and Martha's Vineyard Commissions in Massachusetts, the San Francisco Bay Conservation and Development Commission in California, the Adirondack Park Agency in New York, and the bi-state Tahoe Regional Planning Agency in California and Nevada.[49]

The last two alternatives, the regional allocation agency and the special purpose regional agency, require specialized drafting that takes into account regional and local political traditions and the issues that brought about the need for the agency. In the case of the regional allocation agency, the legislation must go beyond regional planning and into the area of restructuring metropolitan governance.

Under model legislation, a regional planning agency can have the planning responsibilities of a regional planning commission and the service provision responsibilities of a council of governments. Various organizational options are also provided including: (a) a voluntary regional agency versus a regional agency mandated by state statute for each substate district; and (b) a structure to be determined by agreement of member governments versus a mandated structure composed of local elected officials, appointees of the governor, and state agency representatives serving in an ex officio, nonvoting capacity.

A related issue is whether membership by local governments will be mandated; model legislation provides alternative language for this, based on the Florida and Georgia legislation. In Florida, membership by counties in regional councils is mandated by statute, but municipal government membership is not required.[50] By contrast, in Georgia all local governments must be members of a regional development center (RDC), the state's term for a regional planning agency. Georgia, through its department of community affairs, also provides funding support for the RDC.[51] This suggests that where state law mandates local participation in the regional agency (and hence local costs), the state must be prepared to assume a portion of the burden of financing its operation. The model legislation also contains provisions for partial state funding of regional planning agencies.

There is no ideal form for a regional planning agency. The approach taken here, therefore, resists endorsing one, leaving that option up to local officials in the region and the state legislature.[52] For that reason, model legislation does not propose metropolitan or regional "super-agencies" or new forms of regional governance, although this may always be an alternative.[53] Economist Anthony Downs has commented that regional growth management policies do not have to be administered "through a single agency acting as a regional policy czar." Instead, he wrote, it might be desirable to have different growth management policies run by different local and regional agencies that are organized in ways best suited to their individual tasks, "as long as they are linked through formal and informal coordination."[54]

As a practical matter, the formal organizational structure of a regional planning agency is less important than the powers and duties that it has, the clarity with which those powers and duties are described, how effectively those powers and duties are actually carried out, and its actual — as opposed to theoretical — relationships with implementing local governments and special districts. Conceivably, a regional planning commission whose representatives are lay citizens appointed by their local governments and who are their region's leaders could have just as much informal independence, influence, and authority as the Twin Cities Metropolitan Council, whose board members are appointed by the governor, or the Portland, Oregon, Metropolitan Service District, whose board members are elected. *In adapting these models to local conditions, public officials must look at the desired outcomes of planning and consider modifying the authority of existing agencies before deciding to create new ones.*

Notes

1. See, e.g., Alfred Bettman, "How to Lay Out Regions for Planning," in *Planning Problems of Town, City, and Region: Papers and Discussion* (Baltimore, Md.: Norman, Remington, 1925), 287–301; John Friedmann, "The Concept of a Planning Region — The Evolution of an Idea in the United States," in John Friedmann and William Alonso, eds., *Regional Development and Planning: A Reader* (Cambridge, Mass.: MIT Press, 1964), 497–518.

2. Daniel H. Burnham and Edward H. Bennett, *Plan of Chicago* (reprint of 1909 edition) (New York, N.Y.: DaCapo Press, 1970), esp. Chs. III, IV, and V.

3. This statute appears in Frank B. Williams, *The Law of City Planning and Zoning* (New York, N.Y.: MacMillan, 1922), 594–597.

4. Ibid., 596.

5. Advisory Committee on City Planning and Zoning, *A Standard City Planning Enabling Act* (Washington, D.C.: U.S. GPO, 1928), §26.

6. Ibid., §28.

7. Ibid., §29.

8. Ibid., §30.

9. U.S. Advisory Commission on Intergovernmental Relations (ACIR), *Regional Decision Making: New Strategies for Substate Districts; Substate Regionalism and the Federal System, Vol. 1* (Washington, D.C.: U.S. GPO, October 1973), 54.

10. National Resources Committee, *Regional Factors in National Planning* (Washington, D.C.: U.S. GPO, December 1935), 117–135.

11. Ibid., x.

12. ACIR, *Regional Decision Making*, 55.

13. Judith Getzels, Peter Elliott, and Frank Beal, *Private Planning for the Public Interest: A Study of Approaches to Urban Problem Solving by Nonprofit Organizations* (Chicago, Ill.: American Society of Planning Officials, October 1975), 10–19. See also Jeanne R. Lowe, *Cities in a Race with Time* (New York, N.Y.: Random House, 1967), 110–163.

14. ACIR, *Regional Decision Making*, 57–58.

15. James G. Schrader, *Voluntary Metropolitan Governmental Councils*, Information Report No. 161 (Chicago: American Society of Planning Officials, August 1962), 13.

16. Urlan A. Wannop, *The Regional Imperative: Regional Planning and Governance in Britain, Europe, and the United States* (London, England: Jessica Kingsley Publishers, 1995), 385.

17. Bruce D. McDowell, "The Evolution of American Planning," in *The Practice of State and Regional Planning*, Frank So, Irving Hand, and Bruce D. McDowell, eds. (Washington, D.C.: American Planning Association in cooperation with the International City Management Association, 1986), 56.

18. Bruce D. McDowell, "Regionalism: What It Is, Where We Are, and Where It May Be Headed," a speech given to the 1995 Annual Conference of the Virginia and National Capital Area Chapters of the American Planning Association, Falls Church, Va. (December 4, 1995), 2.

19. American Society of Planning Officials (ASPO), *New Directions in Connecticut Planning Legislation: A Study of Connecticut Planning, Zoning and Related Statutes* (Chicago, Ill.: ASPO, February 1966), 166. The ASPO report recommended that the definition of a regional plan be amended to include the following: (1) conservation and management of water

resources, including ground and surface supply, pollution abatement, flood control, and watershed protection; (2) abatement of air pollution; (3) conservation of land resources, including forest, wetlands, wildlife refuges, and seashore; (4) population and general housing types in the several parts of the region; (5) regional facilities, such as major commercial centers, regional parks, transportation, industrial parks, sewerage, and other facilities that would serve the region rather than a single municipality; and (6) a statement of objectives, policies and standards on which recommendations are based. Requiring the factual basis on which policies and standards were derived, wrote ASPO, "will facilitate review of plans by interested public or private group[s] and help them gauge the reasonableness of regional planning proposals. In addition, this requirement will focus attention on development policies underlying specific development proposals such as those for regional land use."

20. National Commission on Urban Problems, *Building the American City: Report of the National Commission on Urban Problems to Congress and to the President* (Washington, D.C.: U.S. GPO, 1968), vii.

21. Ibid., 242.

22. ACIR, *Regional Decision Making*, 354.

23. Ibid.

24. Ibid.

25. Ibid., 360.

26. Ibid.

27. U.S. Advisory Commission on Intergovernmental Relations, "An Act Providing for Designation of Uniform Substate Districts and Coordination Thereof," in *ACIR State Legislative Program: Local Government Modernization* (Washington, D.C.: U.S. GPO, November 1975), 119–132.

28. American Law Institute (ALI), *A Model Land Development Code: Complete Text and Commentary* (Philadelphia, Pa.: ALI, 1976), Note to §8-102, 312.

29. ALI, *A Model Land Development Code*, 311–312, quoting Melvin Mogulof, "Regional Planning, Clearance, and Evaluation: A Look at the A-95 Process," in *Journal of the American Institute of Planners* 37 (1971): 419.

30. ALI, *A Model Land Development Code*, 312.

31. Ibid., 316.

32. Ibid.

33. ALI, *A Model Land Development Code*, 316–317, quoting Melvin Levin, "Planners and Metropolitan Planning," in *Journal of the American Institute of Planners* 33 (1967): 80. See also Richard F. Babcock, "Let's Stop Romancing Regionalism," in *Billboards, Glass Houses and the Law and Other Land Use Fables* (Colorado Springs, Colo.: Shepard's, 1977), 11–23. The late Chicago land-use attorney Richard F. Babcock saw regional planning agencies as "political bastards, the offspring of a loveless dalliance between cynics and dreamers, with no general government willing to acknowledge more than a foster parent relationship." Babcock, who chaired the ALI committee that oversaw the development of the Code and served as the governor's appointee on the Northeastern Illinois

Planning Commission, believed that only the state had sufficient independence and power to require the resolution of metropolitan planning conflicts: "The governor can — if anyone can — compel operating agencies such as the highway department and the state housing authority to recognize in their programs the inescapable interdependence of each with the other. The governor has a broad constituency that permits him to take greater political risks than would be ventured by any mayor or other local representative on a regional commission. If any agency can act as broker between central city and suburb — and perhaps none can — it will be the state. If any negotiation of our bitter metropolitan conflicts is foreseeable, it can occur in our reapportioned and increasingly responsible state legislatures, not in some politically irresponsible regional institution." Babcock's views, of course, colored the approach taken in the ALI Code.

34. McDowell, "Regionalism, What It Is," 3.

35. Wannop, *The Regional Imperative*, 288.

36. Bruce D. McDowell, "Regional Councils Then, Now, and in the Future," a speech to the Board of Directors Retreat, Economic Development Council of Northeastern Pennsylvania (October 7, 1993), in *Regionalism: Shared Decision Making: A Background Reader* (Richmond, Va.: Commission on Population Growth and Development, July 1994), 4.

37. Wannop, *The Regional Imperative*, 292, citing John M. DeGrove, "Regional Agencies as Partners in State Growth Management Systems," *Proceedings of the Joint ACSP and AESOP International Congress*, Oxford, UK (July 1991).

38. Allan D. Wallis, "Investing Regionalism: A Two-Phase Approach," *National Civic Review* 83, no. 4 (Fall-Winter 1994): 447, 450; see also William R. Dodge, "Regional Problem Solving in the 1990s: Experimentation with Local Governance for the 21st Century," *National Civic Review* 79, no. 4 (July-August 1990): 354–366; Patricia S. Atkins and Laura Wilson-Gentry, "An Etiquette for the 1990s Regional Council," *National Civic Review* 81, no. 4 (Fall-Winter 1992): 446–487; Symposium issue on the future of regional governance, Janis Purdy, ed., *National Civic Review* 85, no. 2 (Spring-Summer 1996).

39. National Association of Regional Councils (NARC), *Directory of Regional Councils in the United States* (Washington, D.C.: NARC, April 1995), 3.

40. Oh. Rev. Code §§713.30–713.34 (1994). The Ohio law permits creation by agreement of a board of county commissioners and the legislative authority of a municipality with such boards and authorities of adjoining states. An interstate regional planning commission may also be created by compact which must be reviewed by the attorneys general of the states included in the region and approved and signed by the governors of such states. §713.30.

41. Delaware Valley Urban Area Compact, P.L. 1974, c. 193.

42. Fla. Stat. Ann. §186.504 (West 1987 and Supp. 1995).

43. By-Laws of the Metropolitan Washington

Council of Governments, §5.02(e) (December 14, 1988).

44. Mich. Comp. Laws Ann. §124.651 *et seq.* (1991); Oh. Rev. Code, Ch. 167 (1994); N.C.G.S. §160A–470 *et seq.* (1989).

45. American Law Institute, *A Model Land Development Code*, Note to §8-102, 306–319.

46. Anthony Downs, *New Visions for Metropolitan America* (Washington, D.C.: Brookings Institution and Lincoln Institute of Land Policy, 1994), 176–179.

47. Ore. Rev. Stat. Ch. 368 (1993); 1992 Metro Charter; Mn. Stat. Ann., Ch. 186 (1994 and Supp. 1995).

48. Downs, *New Visions for Metropolitan America*, 180.

49. See N.J.S.A. §13.18A-1 *et seq.* (Pinelands Commission); Commonwealth of Massachusetts, Ch. 716 of the Acts of 1989 and Ch. 2 of the Acts of 1990 (Cape Cod Commission Act); Commonwealth of Massachusetts, Ch. 637 of the Acts of 1974 (Martha's Vineyard Commission); Cal. Gov't. Code, §65500 *et seq.* (San Francisco Bay Conservation and Development Commission); N.Y. Executive Law, Art. 27 (Adirondack Park Agency Act, 1990); Nev. Rev. Stat. §278.870 (Nevada Tahoe Regional Planning Agency).

50. Fla. Stat. Ann. §186.504 (4) (West 1987 and Supp. 1995).

51. Ga. Code. Ann. §50-8-33 (1989).

52. For a discussion of the question of support for strong planning roles by regional government, see Mark Baldassare, et al., "Possible Planning Roles for Regional Government: A Survey of City Planning Directors in California," *Journal of the American Planning Association* 62, no. 1 (Winter 1996): 17–28.

53. For an argument favoring metropolitan government or reorganization under a variety of structures, see David Rusk, *Cities Without Suburbs* (Washington, D.C.: Woodrow Wilson Center Press), 91–119.

54. Downs, *New Visions for Metropolitan America*, 182.

CHAPTER 21

MODELS OF
REGIONAL GOVERNANCE

Richard Sybert

This chapter reviews four models and examples of regional government: (1) one-level; (2) two-level; (3) cooperative: and (4) metropolitan council.[1]

Nashville-Davidson County provides an example of the first model, where the city and county governments are consolidated into one. In this case, the new government was able to save its taxpayers an estimated $18 million in the first ten years by providing a more efficient government and cutting duplication of services. The one government could represent both local and regional interests through a combination of district and at-large representation. However, this model has never been successful in metropolitan areas that extend over more than one county or have populations of over one million people, limiting its usefulness in California.

Miami-Dade County's two-level comprehensive government has successfully integrated and coordinated the county's previously disorganized departments and agencies. "Metro" was successful in financing water and sewer treatment, transit, a seaport, traffic, and law enforcement projects in its first two decades. It also established a South Dade Governmental Center to make services such as public works, pollution control, traffic and transportation, water and sewer, and housing and urban development, more accessible. Metro's main problem is that the growth of the region is extending beyond the Dade County line. With no governing power outside the county, Metro is facing difficulties dealing with the region's problems. This is possibly a problem for California as well, with its urban regions often crossing multiple county lines.

Another two-level model is federation. Through government reorganization, Toronto's Metro, like Miami-Dade County, has been successful in finding solutions considered unachievable in the previous government system. Metro has successfully stabilized the region's governmental finances and resolved specific service crises. Its accomplishments include: water and sewer facilities, a regional highway network, a coordinated public transportation system, a traffic control system, and the establishment of a large parks system. One problem facing Toronto's Metro is factionalism. The Metro Council is often divided by local interests, limiting its ability to deal with regional problems.

The Lakewood–Los Angeles cooperative approach is an efficient and effective form of government whereby the county provides needed services — generally fire, sanitation, and police services — to the city of Lakewood and others in the Los Angeles County without unnecessarily duplicating government agencies. Opponents say the plan limits a city's powers to land use decisions. Further, Lakewood was a new, small city with no previous

Originally published as *Models of Regional Government,* October 1991. Published by the Governor's Office of Planning and Research and the Governor's Interagency Council on Growth Management, Office of the Governor, State of California, Sacramento, California. Reprinted with permission of the publisher.

service capabilities; the approach may not be applicable to California's existing, large urban regions.

Finally, there is the model of metropolitan councils. Two examples are the Twin Cities Metropolitan Council in Minneapolis–St. Paul and the Portland, Oregon Tri-County Metropolitan Council. Both these plans are examples of regional governments in multi-county areas. Through legislation passed in the Minnesota Legislature, the Twin Cities Metropolitan Council was formed in 1967. Although it possesses rather weak powers, the Council was originally successful in developing regional approaches for sewers, transportation, airports, housing, parks, and open space. However, the Council later encountered difficulties in its effectiveness as a governing body. Portland's Tri-County Council was an evolution of regional agencies. Although it too has weak powers, it has increased its effectiveness through popular support.

One-Level Alternative

Since the beginning of the 20th century, many urban reformers have contended that the entire metropolitan area or "sphere of influence" of the modern city should be brought within its actual legal boundaries. These reformers believe that the creation of a single or "one level" governments for an entire urban region would be more efficient, effective, and economical than multi-level governments. However, opponents of this model maintain that it results in the loss of local control, decreased citizen access to public officials, and reduced attention to local services. This is because one-level urban government in a metropolitan area necessarily is on a larger scale than traditional local government.

The one-level alternative can be accomplished by three basic techniques: (1) annexation (the absorption of nearby unincorporated territory); (2) municipal consolidation (the merger of two or more incorporated units); and (3) city-county consolidation (the union of one or more municipalities with the county government).

This chapter focuses on city-county consolidation because it is the most dramatic or strongest of these techniques. To achieve city-county consolidation, two legal battles normally must be won. First, a state constitutional amendment or legislative enabling act must be passed to permit the metropolitan areas to pursue the consolidation. Second, the consolidation must win the approval of the local voters, usually by separate majorities of the city or cities and the unincorporated part of the county.

An example of the one-level alternative through city-county consolidation is Nashville-Davidson County in Tennessee.

NASHVILLE-DAVIDSON COUNTY
Background. The metropolitan government of Nashville-Davidson County is located in the north central area of the State of Tennessee. Prior to consolidation, Davidson County had 12 governments within its boundaries: the county, the city of Nashville, six incorporated suburbs, and four special utility districts.

The Nashville region faced problems similar to those of many other medium or small metropolitan areas in the country. There existed a single urban area with overlapping governments — one, the city, with substantial authority but little area; and the other, the county, with substantial territory but little power. This situation created constant attempts between local governments to "pass the buck" and avoid responsibility, with each government trying to keep its own taxes low by taking advantage of the other's services.

The Nashville region also provided an example of a tax dispute often seen between the city government and its "daytime citizens" — i.e., commuters — from the suburbs. Most citizens in the region paid taxes only in their resident communities, despite the fact that their jobs were located in and arguably depended upon the city of Nashville. Suburban commuters also used many city-supported services. While county residents argued that they contributed to the city's wealth, the city believed that its own citizens were effectively subsidizing services to county residents in this manner. The city tried to correct this perceived inequity by overcharging county residents for city-supplied water and electricity. In addition, the city levied a "wheel tax" on all motor vehicles using the streets of Nashville for 30 days or more. However, the strict enforcement of these taxes created considerable resentment on the part of county residents. As an example of conflict, city and county police withheld information from each other. Also, the two school systems fought over how to split state education funds. Additionally on some roads where the city-county line went down the middle, the speed limit was 35 mph in one direction and 45 mph in the other.

These conflicts made it increasingly evident that the needs of the residents in the Nashville-Davidson County area were not being efficiently and effectively met by the existing multi-level government arrangement. Accordingly, in 1957 the Tennessee State General Assembly enacted enabling legislation permitting city-county consolidation.

A first attempt to approve a county-city consolidation failed in 1958. It was supported by the mayor of Nashville, the Nashville Chamber of Commerce, the Tennessee Taxpayers' Association, labor, and a variety of other groups. Opponents, including suburban private fire and police companies, some suburban businessmen, and members of the county legislature (analogous to a California board of supervisors), argued that the consolidation would mean bigger government, higher taxes, and city control over the suburbs. In 1962, a new "Metro" charter election was called for in the Nashville-Davidson County region. This time, with a greater grass roots effort (telephoning, doorbell ringing, and neighborhood coffees), the charter won approval both in the city and the county, by margins of 57–40 percent and 55–44 percent respectively.

The System. The metropolitan government of Nashville-Davidson County merged the functions previously held separately by the city of Nashville and Davidson County. The six suburbs were frozen at their existing boundaries, and given the opportunity to use Metro's services, which most did.

The Metro government has a strong mayor-council system. The chief executive is the "metropolitan mayor," who is elected by the area's voters to a four-year term. His tenure in office is limited to three consecutive terms. The mayor is responsible for the supervision, administration, and control of the executive departments, agencies, boards, and commissions. The mayor is authorized to approve or disapprove council ordinances, subject to an override by two-thirds of the council. The mayor may also veto line-item budget expenditures, again subject to a two-thirds override by the council.

The legislative branch consists of two parts: the metropolitan council and the urban council. The metropolitan county council is comprised of 40 councilmembers and the vice mayor. Thirty-five of these councilmembers are elected from single-member districts of approximately equal population, and five councilmembers are elected at large. The charter provides for a high number of councilmembers to ensure that local concerns [are] represented. The five at large members were included to make sure that regional problems were addressed.

The charter designates two separate service-tax districts with[in] the metropolitan government's geographic limits: the general services district (GSD) and the urban services district (USD). The GSD comprises the total area of Davidson County and provides such services as general administration, police, courts, jails, health, welfare, schools, transit, and parks and recreation. The USD provides additional services, such as urban level fire protection, trash collection, street lights, storm drainage, and additional police protection. Separate taxes are levied in each district to support the level of services within the respective district.

The USD may be expanded whenever areas in the GSD need additional urban services, and when the metropolitan government is capable of providing such additional services within one year after the additional USD tax rate is imposed. While there is no formula to determine when additional services are needed, expansion usually occurs when enough local support is gathered to join the USD and pay the additional taxes. If the USD is not capable of providing the services within the one-year deadline, Metro can delay the application until the services are ready to be provided.

Two-Level Alternative

The two-level alternative of regional reorganization is based on the theory of federalism. With this technique, area-wide functions are delegated to area-wide governments, while purely local functions remain with the local units, creating a two-tier system.

The two-tier system can take three basic forms:

1. Metropolitan district: A governmental unit that usually encompasses all or a substantial part of the entire geographic metropolitan area, but is normally authorized to perform only one function or a few closely related activities of an area-wide nature. California examples would be school districts, water districts, air quality and transit districts and the like. The existing city-county structure is retained.

2. Comprehensive urban county plan: The simultaneous transfer of selected functions from municipalities and other local units to the county governments. The existing city-county structure is retained, with the county performing a number of municipal functions county-wide.

3. Federation: The establishment of a new area-wide government that is assigned new responsibilities and customarily replaces the existing county government. Again, the upper tier performs a number of municipal functions region-wide.

Because metropolitan districts are single-interest entities, with no general jurisdictions to address metropolitan-wide problems, this chapter will focus on the other two systems.

All of these forms are structural variations and may accomplish the same functional result.

COMPREHENSIVE URBAN COUNTY PLAN

Under a comprehensive urban county plan, a county assumes those functions that are determined to be area-wide in nature, while the municipalities continue to administer those functions considered to be of purely local concern. Thus, the county is transformed into a metropolitan government, with the simultaneous reallocation of a variety of functions from all municipalities to the county.

Politically, such a plan can have considerable appeal if the county is viewed by the public as an acceptable unit of local government. Unlike other techniques of reform, the urban county plan does not require the creation of still another unit of government. Instead, it merely strengthens the county to serve as a second tier. The success of this type of regional government in California is questionable because most major metropolitan areas often cross county lines.

An example of a comprehensive urban county plan is Miami-Dade County in Florida.

Miami-Dade County

Background. Dade County, located in the southeast corner of Florida, covers approximately 2,300 square miles. It encompasses all of the Miami area and stretches westward to the Everglades. Population growth in Dade County over the last few decades has been high, increasing six-fold in the 45 years after World War II to over 1.9 million people. Historically, the county had experienced a series of municipal incorporations by the core city, Miami, and its surrounding suburbs.

Metropolitan government, or "Metro," was created in 1957. Prior to this, there was no effective countywide agency responsible for long-range regional planning in such areas as economic development, welfare, recreation, and the environment. Local planning boards did exist, but were ineffective because of relatively poorly trained technical staffs, inadequate financial support, and what some believed to be lack of appreciation by local officials and the general public of the need for adequate planning.

The needs of the unincorporated areas of Dade County, home to one-third of the total county population, constituted a particularly serious problem. These unincorporated areas frequently entered into informal agreements with incorporated municipalities for provision of essential services, such as fire protection and police communication and training, to rapidly growing populations. The major problem with these agreements was that larger cities were burdened with the expenses of providing the services to the smaller areas.

A number of proposals to consolidate Dade County with the city of Miami and a varying number of smaller communities failed in the late 1940s and early 1950s. However, the closeness of a referendum in 1953 led to the formation of the Metropolitan Miami Municipal Board (3M Board) to study the feasibility of governmental reorganization.

In November 1956, the citizens of the State of Florida by a two to one margin, passed a home rule constitutional amendment, thus freeing Dade County and its cities from dependence on the state legislature for the enactment of local laws. The home rule amendment also permitted the county's voters to create a metropolitan government. Following this approval, the 3M board developed a proposal for a metropolitan system.

The principal recommendation of the 3M Board was creation of a two-tiered form of government for the Dade County region. The city level would be responsible for local functions, such as zoning and police and fire protection, the minimum standards for which would be set by the county. The second level would be a reorganized and enlarged county government, responsible for such regional functions as water, sewage, solid waste disposal, all public transportation construction and operation, traffic control, and overall metropolitan planning.

Prior to the referendum election, a Dade County League of Municipalities committee established to study the proposal returned a negative report. In spite of the League's opposition, Dade County voters narrowly approved (51–49 percent with only a 26 percent turnout) a charter based on the 3M recommendations in May 1957.

The System. The powers of the county government under the terms of the charter are separated into four distinct categories: (1) municipal-type functions, (2) responsibilities in unincorporated areas, (3) responsibilities for setting minimum standards, and (4) elastic powers.

The municipal-type functions include transportation systems, traffic control, police and fire protection, county development plans, health and welfare programs, parks and recreation, housing, water supply, waste disposal, and taxing. County government's responsibilities in unincorporated areas include the same municipal-type functions, such as police and fire protection and waste disposal, plus other functions performed by municipalities, such as licensing and regulation of the limousines and taxis, and establishing and enforcing regulations for the sale of alcoholic beverages.

To provide local control of municipal services, the county government is empowered to set minimum performance standards for services provided by all local governmental units. If a municipality does not comply with such standards, the county government is empowered to take over and perform or contract out to other organizations to operate the service. Finally, under the so-called "elastic" provisions of the charter, the county government is authorized "to exercise all powers and privileges granted" to municipalities and counties under the Florida Constitution to "adopt such ordinances and resolutions as may be required in the exercise of its powers" and to "perform any other acts consistent with laws which are required or which are in the common interest of the people of the county."

Although the division of powers under this scheme is strongly weighted on the county government's side, the individual municipalities are given certain protections and prerogatives. The county cannot abolish an incorporated municipality without the express permission of the municipality's voters, nor can the county rearrange municipal boundaries. Municipalities retain the right to change their respective charters, provided the provisions do not conflict with the county charter. Each city can exceed county minimum standards for zoning, and, subject to county standards, regulate taxis and other rental vehicles, determine hours for sale of alcoholic beverages, and provide for fire and police protection.

A board of county commissioners is designated under the terms of the charter to serve as the legislative and governing body of the county and to oversee the entire metropolitan system. The board consists of nine commissioners, with eight elected by the voters of the county at large, subject to the requirement that each commissioner must reside in a different county commission district. The ninth member, who serves as the mayor and chairman of the board, also is elected by a countywide vote. All commissioners serve four-year terms.

FEDERATION

Another variation of the two-level alternative is a federation. This approach involves the creation of an entirely new area-wide government with either multi-county or one-county territorial limits. The newly created unit is usually designated as the metropolitan government and is charged with carrying out numerous area-wide functions. The original municipal units continue to operate and perform local functions that are not performed by the new metropolitan government.

Most of the federation plans proposed in the United States have called for the metropolitan legislative body to be made up of local representatives from the municipalities. Thus, federation, as a metropolitan concept, requires replacing the existing county government with a new metropolitan unit, while the previous urban county plan involves retaining the county unit as the area-wide tier.

Toronto

Background. An example of federation is Toronto, Ontario. Metropolitan Toronto is situated on the northern shore of Lake Ontario in the Canadian province of Ontario. Prior to governmental reorganization in 1953, the 240–square mile metropolitan area contained 13 municipal jurisdictions.

Between 1945 and 1953, there was an exodus of business firms and middle-class citizens from central Toronto to the outlying districts and a steady in-migration of lower-income families. At the same time, new industries were locating in the suburbs rather than the central city. This population shift generated rising concerns over the city's ability to finance and provide water, sewage disposal, housing, and other municipal functions to its residents. To finance these increasing needs, the city was forced to increase its tax rate. However, the smaller, established suburbs, located between the city and the growing industrialized suburbs, benefitted from using Toronto's hospitals, libraries, and parks without taxation, and felt no pressure to expand their facilities or raise their low tax rates. Needless to say, this scenario is strikingly similar to situations faced by the older U.S. central cities in the wake of post-war suburbanization.

The Ontario Municipal Board (OMB), a provincial board, was requested by the province to create an area for joint administration of municipal services in order to redress this situation. In January 1953, the chairman of the board, Lorne Cumming, submitted a report calling for the creation of a metropolitan federation. Although the proposal was controversial, the premier of Ontario's support ensured that the report's recommendations would be adopted by the Ontario provincial legislature.

The System. Under the terms of the 1953 Act for the Toronto Region, a Metropolitan Council was created to serve as both the executive body of metropolitan Toronto ("Metro"), and the legislative body for the 13 represented municipalities. The Metropolitan Council was comprised of 25 members, 12 from the city of Toronto, the mayors from each of the 12 suburbs, with an independent chairman to be elected by the council. Toronto's delegation consisted of its mayor, two controllers, and an alderman from each of the nine city wards.

The chairmanship of the Metro Council was assigned little formal power under the Act, being limited to such functions as presiding over meetings, interpreting the rules of procedure, and casting a vote only in the case of a tie. However, unlike the members of the council, the chairman was a full-time official who could devote his total time and energy to Metro matters, and thereby acquire considerable influence with other council members.

Frederick Gardiner, the council's first

chairman, used these limited powers to successfully influence the decision process. Gardiner succeeded in convincing the council that it could work more effectively through a smaller group. A seven-member executive committee was chosen by the entire council and possessed all of the powers of boards of control in municipal governments — preparing budgets, nominating department heads, awarding contracts, etc. Some believe that Gardiner knew that the smaller committee could also be more easily controlled by him.

For the most part, the metropolitan government dealt with the more critical regional problems, particularly finances to build schools, transportation, and water facilities, while such matters as police, fire, public health, and public welfare were left primarily in the preserve of the 13 municipalities. A system of shared responsibilities was set up among the municipalities under Metro in such areas as street construction, road maintenance, traffic control, public assistance, zoning and planning. Only public transportation became a fully Metro function.

While the local communities retained the right to assess taxes, Metro was given the power to cope with regional problems through exclusive borrowing authority for all of the municipalities and independent boards of the region, thereby obtaining very favorable interest rates. It also secured the power to apportion revenue it raised through assessment among the 13 communities, utilizing a formula whereby each municipality's share was based upon a total assessment area.

Cooperative Alternative

The "cooperative" alternative model of regional government, also referred to as "interlocal agreements," calls for greater cooperation between existing governments without the creation of new ones. This approach represents a voluntary technique to address regional problems while maintaining local control.

Supporters of the cooperative alternative view themselves as political realists, because cooperative proposals appear and probably are less radical than other proposed metropolitan structures. Proponents also favor dispersed local government and argue for the right of public choice between competing community locations, services, and tax bases. Proponents argue that the cooperative alternative, although maintaining existing structures, still contributes to greater governmental efficiency and lower costs, since through the possibility of interjurisdictional agreement, it can eliminate the necessity of each local government's hiring its own personnel or constructing new facilities for particular services.

Interjurisdictional cooperation is a broad concept with numerous variations. These range from verbal agreements which may consist merely of the exchange of information, to formal agreements that relate to specific functions or services. Agreements can take the following basic forms:

1. A single government performs a service or provides a facility for one or more other local units.

2. Two or more local governments administer a function or operate a facility on a joint basis.

3. Two or more local governments assist or supply mutual aid to one another in emergency situations.

The cooperative approach has been the subject of considerable criticism. First, critics argue that it is a piecemeal approach since each service agreement normally involves only two governments and one service or facility, resulting in a patchwork of agreements that usually relate to noncontroversial matters. Second, and perhaps the most serious criticism, is financial inadequacy. Cooperative agreements are not devices that equalize public resources among localities within a metropolitan area. Although most interjurisdictional agreements call for provision of services by one local unit in exchange for payment by another, some local governments do not have sufficient financial resources to pay for needed services.

The county of Los Angeles provides an excellent example of the cooperative approach to metropolitan government.

LOS ANGELES COUNTY–
LAKEWOOD PLAN

Background. Millions of Americans migrated to Southern California to work in aircraft plants and shipyards after World War II. The population of the Los Angeles–Long Beach metropolitan area expanded rapidly during this period.

California state law gives counties control over services vital to all governments, and cities in particular. These include relief for the poor, public hospital care, property tax assessments, registration of voters, the administration of elections and support of the trial court system including jails, prosecution, probation administration, courtroom facilities and staffs. California counties also provide unincorporated areas with many municipal services, including water, sewage, roads, street lighting, and fire [and police] protection.

County provision of such services helped moderate the trend of incorporation of suburban areas within Los Angeles County, which is California's largest county (indeed the nation's) by far in population. Since the county provided services, pressure to incorporate was reduced. However, city-county relations were not always amicable. There had been charges that the county had effectively subsidized unincorporated areas with dollars raised through the county's general fund, which was funded in part by taxes on city residents. In 1950, a study by a League of California Cities committee found that a large part of city residents' county tax dollars were going to provide services to the unincorporated areas of the county. As a result, the county reduced the number of its services available to the unincorporated areas.

The System. Lakewood began as an unincorporated planned housing development within Los Angeles County in 1950. The development was built on land that the city of Long Beach planned to annex to help provide services and increase its tax base. In 1953, Long Beach began a series of annexation proceedings and successfully annexed a part of Lakewood Village with a population of 24,000.

Residents of the remaining unincorporated area of the Lakewood area began a drive to incorporate in order to save it from annexation. An election was set that would have allowed a choice between incorporation and annexation to Long Beach. Pro-incorporation forces argued that incorporation would ensure local control at low costs. On March 9, 1954, the voters approved the incorporation petition.

A new state law, permitting a newly incorporated city in California to contract with its county for all essential services, enabled Lakewood to have a wide variety of services available immediately through Los Angeles County. These services included the county-administered special districts (fire, library, sewer, and lighting), self-governing special districts (sanitation, recreation, and mosquito abatement), and county contracts for general services (animal regulation, assessment and collection of taxes, health services, industrial waste regulation, jails, law enforcement, planning and zoning staff services, street maintenance and construction, and treasury and auditor services).

By contracting with the county for needed services, the new city of Lakewood was able to function with only ten employees and a very reasonable tax rate. While the county lost some tax revenues as a result of incorporation, by contracting with Lakewood it was able to maintain its departments, such as law enforcement and sanitation, at strength.

The Lakewood plan was so successful that it spurred new incorporations within Los Angeles County. Most of the new cities entered into similar agreements with the county for provision of services. However, ultimate control over service levels remained with each city, because each city purchased only specific services that it believed were both needed and affordable. Effectively, this arrangement allowed smaller cities to pool their needs for services and purchase them on a "volume discount" basis from a single, cost-effective provider, the county.

The Lakewood plan eliminated the need for additional municipal service departments and duplication of services. However, it did not attempt to address other pressing regional concerns of planning, water supply, sewage, and education. Further, as the county is the actual producer of the services, the county tends to dominate any bargaining process with the cities over the quality of services and their costs.

Metropolitan Council Alternative

A fourth category of regional or metropolitan government is the metropolitan council. Metropolitan councils are permanent associations of governments that meet on a regular basis to discuss and seek agreement on various issues. While metropolitan councils can be classified as variations of the cooperative approach, there are some key differences. A metropolitan council can be defined as a voluntary association of governments designed to be an area-wide forum for key officials to research and discuss issues and eventually determine how best to address common problems. However, because of its lack of authority, the council mechanism cannot be classified as a true metropolitan government.

Examples of a metropolitan councils are Minneapolis–St. Paul in Minnesota and the Tri-County/Portland area in Oregon.

MINNEAPOLIS–ST. PAUL

Background. The Twin Cities Metropolitan Council in the Minneapolis–St. Paul area of Minnesota was created in 1967. It is comprised of 7 counties, 25 cities, 105 villages, 68 townships, 77 school districts, and 20 special service districts.

The problems leading to creation of the Twin Cities Metropolitan Council arose from the usual causes: an expanding population, changing population patterns, scattered and uncontrolled growth, and the accompanying need for services such as sewers, waste disposal, housing, and transportation.

There were three main reasons why existing local governments seemed unable to handle all issues. First, some problems, such as pollution, tended to spill over into other jurisdictions. Second, some of the proposed solutions to these problems were potentially very costly and beyond the means of a single local jurisdiction. Finally, no single existing jurisdiction, including any of the involved counties, possessed the authority to make decisions for the entire metropolitan area. Minnesota counties have been traditionally weak, and in this case the metropolitan region crossed county lines.

Unlike many other metropolitan areas, when Twin Cities area leaders recognized that the problems needed to be dealt with from a metropolitan perspective, there was an almost even balance between the central cities and the suburban areas both in population and property value. This prevented either area from dominating the other and made it politically easier to proceed.

The System. Between 1965 and 1967, a consensus was built among metropolitan leaders that an area-wide government body should be created to handle such issues as sewer works, open space, transit, airports, and a zoo. These functions had previously been provided by special purpose districts, not individual municipalities, so that this consensus implied consolidation of various single-purpose agencies or districts.

A group of civic leaders was formed to study regional government in the Twin Cities. By 1967, the group presented its proposal to the Minnesota Legislature. The legislature considered two alternative pieces of legislation, one calling for an elected council with planning and operating control of regional functions, and one creating a council appointed at large by the governor and responsible for planning and coordinating the operation of regional agencies. The latter proposal was passed to establish the Twin Cities Metropolitan Council.

The Council is composed of 16 members appointed by the governor for staggered six-year terms. Each member represents two state senate districts of equal population size. The chairman is selected at large and serves at the governor's pleasure.

The Council's powers are mostly of a coordinating nature. Specifically, the Council is directed to perform three functions. First, it must review all regional plans and projects affecting the Council's metropolitan systems plans for airports, parks, transportation, and sewers, against development guidelines developed by the Council. Within 60 days of submission of such plans, the Council may indefinitely suspend, in total or part, any project that it finds to be inconsistent with the guidelines. While the Council has the power to delay a project, it uses its powers mainly to leverage changes in projects, not to prevent their development.

Second, the Council reviews and comments on long-term municipal comprehensive plans and any other matters that the Council determines may have a "metropolitan effect," such as a project that would have an effect on the entire Twin Cities region. These local plans must be consistent with metropolitan systems plans developed by the Council for airports, parks, transportation, and sewers, and which together function as the regional comprehensive plan.

Local plans do not have to be updated at any specific time interval, but rather when they affect the regional systems plan, as determined by the Metropolitan Council. The plans are required to include current and future land use; community facilities, such as transportation, airports, sewers, and parks; and implementation — how the plan will be carried out. Local plans are not subject to council veto, although as a practical matter the existence of the Council with its powers generally leads local governments to be consistent with the regional plans. If one local unit objects to the plans of another unit, the Council may hold hearings and mediate any differences.

Finally, the Council performs an advisory evaluation of applications for federal grants emanating from local governments, boards, and agencies.

The Twin Cities Council can be classified as a metropolitan government because it is comprised solely of local representatives, and it is concerned only with regional interests, decisions, services, and needs. Moreover, the Council is empowered to levy an area property tax to finance its operations. It can be viewed in one sense as a state agency, since the governor appoints the representatives who comprise the Council. In addition, it is the legislature that assigns the Council its powers, controls its finances, determines its structure, and requires it to submit reports.

At the forefront of regional governance in the late 1960s, the Metro council has more recently become less relevant in many regional issues. In its early years, the Council succeeded in creating a regionwide sewer system, founding the Minnesota Zoo, and blocking the construction of an unneeded airport. However, with an ambitious legislature, which did not want to provide the Council with substantial power, and an uninterested governor, the Council's powers dwindled. In recent years, the Council has been left out of the site selection and project definition of the Metrodome, the site selection of a horse racing track in the suburbs, and the consideration of a light-rail system between the two cities. In addition, it was unable to determine a site for a new landfill.

Most of the blame for the Metro Council's recent failures center on its lack of public support: because the Council is appointed by the governor, not elected by the people, citizens and public officials do not believe it has the clout to make necessary changes. In 1985, the Citizens League, a Minneapolis non-partisan research group, concluded that the Council was "in danger of sliding into irrelevance" because it was considered by state and local officials as just another level of bureaucracy. Recognizing the troubles facing the Council, Governor Arne Carlson recently instructed his nine new appointees to revitalize the agency.

PORTLAND

Background. Regional government in the Portland, Oregon, area has evolved over the past six decades. In 1926, in response to rapid and unplanned suburbanization of the area caused by the invention of the automobile, the state established a committee to examine the problems facing the various local governments in the Portland area. The 1944 conference of the League of Oregon Cities passed a resolution that "sporadic, scattered, and unregulated growth of municipalities and urban fringes has caused tremendous waste in money and resources" and requested legislative action at the state level to permit "the creation of metropolitan or regional planning districts and the establishment of metropolitan or regional planning commissions." The state legislature responded by enacting legislation authorizing county planning commissions and county zoning to complement municipal planning programs.

The Metropolitan Planning Commission (MPC) was created in 1957. The Commission had a four-member board representing the city of Portland and the three surrounding counties (Multnomah, Washington, and Clackamas) and was funded by federal grant money. Although it was created to provide planning, the Commission actually provided information and reports on population and industrial sites and assisted local planning departments rather than prepare long-range plans for the region.

In the early 1960s, activists contended that the studies and work produced in the 1950s had done nothing to address the problems of public services in the region. In the 1940s and 50s, the number of special districts in the three counties increased from 28 to 218. In a 1960 study, *A Tale of Three Counties*, the League of Women Voters reported that the local agencies were inefficient and unaccountable, which resulted in poor services. Civic leaders joined together to request that regional options for government services be examined. In response, the state legislature created the Interim Committee on Local Government Problems, whose primary recommendation was the creation of a "metropolitan study commission," later called the Portland Metropolitan Study Commission (PMSC).

The PMSC's *Interim Report* of December 1966 made ten recommendations for more efficient service, including:

- Special district consolidations where possible.
- Legislation authorizing the creation of metropolitan service districts.
- Formation of a regional council of governments with memberships from counties, cities, and port districts.
- Organization of an area-wide air quality control program.
- Development of intergovernmental cooperative agreements among cities and counties for health, planning, law enforcement and engineering services.

The PMSC's work toward a more regional approach to government services helped produce the Columbia Region Association of Governments (CRAG) in 1966. Structured similar to the MPC, CRAG was a council of governments representing the region's cities and counties. All of the participating city and county governments were represented in CRAG's General Assembly, but its Executive Board was comprised of three county representatives, a Portland representative, and three representatives from other cities in the three counties. CRAG was charged with studying, recommending, rendering technical assistance, and adopting comprehensive metropolitan plans. Although it carried out its duties regarding studies and reports, intergovernmental rivalries slowed its work to develop a comprehensive land use plan. After failing to pass plans in 1970 and 1974, CRAG adopted a general set of goals and objects as a plan.

Another proposal of PMSC was the creation of the multi-purpose Metropolitan Service District (MSD). The MSD governing board was made up of seven elected officials, one from Portland, one from each of the three counties, and one representing the other cities in each of the three counties. While the voters approved the District in May of 1970 (54–46 percent), they overwhelmingly rejected a district-wide tax in November of 1970. Thus the new agency was presented with a wide range of problems, with few resources to address them.

In 1975, several regional government supporters applied to the National Academy for Public Administration for an 18-month grant to study the possibilities of multi-level government in metropolitan areas. In November and December of 1975, the "Ad Hoc Two-Tiered Planning Committee," the official recipient of the grant, transformed itself into the Tri-County Local Government Commission. The Tri-County Commission set out to design "an upper tier system of government that will attend to the common needs of the entire Tri-County community." The Commission established a goal of drafting specific legislation for the 1977 Legislative Session.

In 1976, the Commission decided to propose a reorganization of the MSD. Some of the key components to provide a strong and responsive regional government were:

1. Combining the planning functions of CRAG and the regional services of MSD.

2. Direct election of the regional policy makers.

3. A relatively large number of councilors (15) to be elected from relatively small districts.

4. Direct election of the executive director.

The legislature made a number of changes to the proposal, reducing the size of the Council to 12 and deleting a proposed veto for the executive director, before passing it in June 1977. In May 1978, the proposal, Measure 6, passed by 20,000 votes in the three-county area. The new Metropolitan Service District (Metro) was officially established on January 1, 1979.

The System. The enacting legislation did not stipulate any formal relationship between the Council and executive, instead leaving it to them to decide. At the outset, the executive acted more like a city manager, supplying information, setting agendas, and offering recommendations, with the Council being similar to a large city council. However, the relationship gradually changed to one where the Council acts as a miniature legislature, establishing its own policies and programs, with the executive director much like an executive branch, carrying out the Council's policies and programs.

As with most newly established programs, Metro made a number of mistakes in its early years. Its overambitious plan, for example, to address flooding in the Johnson Creek watershed produced one of its first defeats. In 1981, Metro proposed establishing a basin-wide Local Improvement District to fund flood control measures. Although the proposal was technically sound and fiscally creative, it was politically unachievable. Residents on higher lands in the basin were upset that they were, for all intents and purposes, paying assessments to help property owners on the valley floor. Metro's arguments that their paved streets, driveways, and parking lots increased runoff and directly contributed to the flooding in the basin were scientifically correct but politically unacceptable. Metro later withdrew its proposal.

Metro has seen its share of successes as well, both major and minor. In 1979, the Oregon Land Conservation and Development Commission accepted the Portland area's Urban Growth Boundary as designed by Metro. Under Metro's control, the Washington Park Zoo has grown in visitors and national reputation. Metro was able to solve a dispute over the selection of a new landfill site by identifying an alternative site. Metro was also successful in the siting, construction, and operation of the Oregon Convention Center in Portland.

Except for siting regional facilities and accepting or denying the region's Urban Growth Boundary, Metro has not infringed on local jurisdictions' land use powers. Cities and counties also continue to provide municipal services, except for solid waste disposal which is overseen by Metro.

In response to its success, Metro has gained expanded powers. In 1987, the legislature restored the executive veto power that had originally been part of the Tri-County Commission proposal. The Council has also set up a committee structure, hired a legislative staff, and produced independent policy initiatives. The legislature also passed a measure that now permits Metro to collect an excise tax on its operations to fund its central administration and planning.

Conclusions

This chapter analyzed several different forms of regional structure and consolidated government. All of the models have been valuable in varying degrees in their respective jurisdictions and regions. The variety of options reaffirms the need for flexible state policy in California, allowing maximum local choice to address local needs, priorities, and state goals.

None of the examples in this chapter dealt with regions as large, complex, or diverse as California's. However, there are regions in the state which reflect comparable situations to each of the noted examples. City/county consolidation has been considered and rejected in Sacramento, and is being discussed in Stanislaus County. Models proposed by cities and the county under the auspices of San Diego Area Association of Governments (SANDAG) resemble the structure in Miami/Dade County. Coordinated planning between multiple counties, similar to the Twin Cities approach, can be anticipated as one option in the nine Bay Area counties, as per the recommendations of Bay Vision 2020.

However, the similarities and differences between these examples also raise a number of considerations in dealing with regional problems. First, a common element in all models is recognition that there are regional problems that need to be addressed. Regional entities were created to deal with specific problems that existing local governments could not or did not appropriately address.

Second, each model was implemented with assistance from the state (or provincial) legislature. There were different levels of involvement, ranging from legislation forming or authorizing the government (Twin Cities), to requesting that a board review regional problems and governments (Miami-Dade County and Toronto), to removing possible roadblocks (Nashville-Davidson County and Lakewood).

Beyond recognition of a problem and the need for some form of regional solution, the models go in separate directions. One key difference is in the varying selection methods for representatives selected to the regional body. While Nashville-Davidson County had districts and at-large representatives to ensure local and regional responsiveness, the Twin Cities had gubernatorial-appointed representatives to ensure regional responsiveness. Toronto had city representatives, while Portland's Tri-County Council members were elected directly by the people, in both cases to ensure local responsiveness. It appears that directly elected officials, such as in the Portland area, have proven to be more successful than appointed officials, such as the Twin Cities.

Another notable difference between the models is the scope and powers of the regional body. These were often dependent on the pre-existing government structures and the size of the region. Nashville-Davidson County was able to consolidate all the powers and responsibilities into one government; Toronto and

Miami-Dade County had strong powers to deal with regional problems, leaving other "local" matters to the cities; Lakewood decided to temporarily contract out some of its powers to Los Angeles County; the Twin Cities Council had only advisory powers on limited regional issues; and the Tri-County Council assumed the planning and service responsibilities of existing agencies.

Finally, each body's finances were determined by the problems that each specific region faced and the form of the government it decided to pursue. While most of the governments received tax funds directly from the taxpayers, regional governments can also be financed by the state or by participating cities or cities and counties.

As one model was not appropriate for all the cited examples, so too one model may not be right for all or any of California's regions. While many of the state's urban areas face similar problems, such as traffic, air pollution, and housing, their differences, including population and geographic size, could lead to solutions using different or variable models.

Although it is possible for the state to determine whether a regional government is needed, and the appropriate structure, choosing whether or which approach is best for a given region may also be left to the individual areas. California has a long history of home rule, and the state can continue to respect this concept by giving local jurisdictions the opportunity to solve regional problems on their own. Under this approach, only after giving local governments in a region a reasonable opportunity to deal with problems should the state intervene and impose some form of regional approach on specific issues.

This need not mean the state necessarily must take a hands-off approach. General goals can be set for the entire state. Each region would then be responsible for establishing its own more specific goals consistent with the state's, and a specific plan, including means of meeting stated goals and the structure of regional governance if any; goals might also be met through local cooperation. The state would be responsible for certifying that each region's goals were consistent with the general state goals, and that the regional plan [was] feasible. Alternatively, a regional plan could be self-certified against state goals. If not consistent or not achievable, the plan would be returned by the state for adjustment. Plans would also be reviewed and updated periodically.

The strengths of this proposal are that it provides regions with local control to deal with regional problems, while the state oversees the process. It emphasizes that the state has a role in determining the regional problems that need to be addressed, but provides local jurisdictions the opportunity to develop their own solutions. This is, of course, a general notion. Other details, such as financing, state oversight agency, region composition, and default regional governments, would still have to be addressed.

Ultimately, the effectiveness of any regional structure will be up to the credibility and effectiveness of the leadership in each region.

The "local heroes" who can convene a political constituency for change, and bring together the interests which must cooperate for solutions, will provide the leadership and direct the structure of the region. Even now, within the cities and counties of California, there are many local differences in program administration and structure. Nothing in the state's growth management policy should restrict the ability of strong local leaders to work within their own agencies and organizations to form whatever planning or service delivery system meets the needs of the local area best, so long as state goals are reasonably met.

Note

1. These models were developed in *Experiments in Metropolitan Government*, James F. Horan and G. Thomas Taylor, Jr., Westport, Conn.: Praeger Publications, 1977.

CHAPTER 22

REGIONAL GOVERNANCE AND REGIONAL COUNCILS

J. Eugene Grigsby III

Data from the 1990 census indicate that the United States had 39 metropolitan areas of at least one million people. The combined population of these areas was 124.8 million, or approximately half of the nation's total population. In 1950, there were only 14 metropolitan areas of this size, and their total population was about 45 million, which was less than 30 percent of the nation's total. Thus, in a span of 40 short years, a significant proportion of the country's population steadily migrated from small towns and rural settings to more densely populated urban centers.

During this same 40-year period, two significant shifts were also occurring within these metropolitan areas. The first involved middle- and upper-income whites migrating away from central city areas to suburban locations. This resulted in an increasing number of low-income minorities, particularly African Americans, being confined to central cities. The second shift taking place during this period was the deindustrialization of the economies in many of these areas, resulting in an exodus of jobs from central cities to suburban locations.

The rapid population growth followed by population redistribution and economic restructuring have given rise to what is often referred to as "urban problems": traffic congestion, smog, polluted water, urban development encroaching on open space, crime, poorly funded school systems, and increasingly low income minority populations trapped in decaying inner-city locations.

It is within this context — rapid metropolitan growth and metropolitan restructuring — that planners and elected officials have sought to develop and implement strategies designed to: 1) induce growth and manage it simultaneously by focusing on infrastructure capacity, 2) respond more effectively to growing social service demands through coordinated delivery systems, and 3) seek ways to be competitive in a rapidly changing economic climate while not exacerbating inequalities between the poor and those with means.

Regional councils have emerged as one of the mechanisms thought capable of meeting challenges posed by these changing conditions. While the success of regional organizations in effectively meeting these challenges has been mixed, there is little doubt that the changing dynamics which metropolitan areas will continue to face will demand more regional approaches to problem solving. In the past, the federal government has been the primary driver behind formulating regional strategies. In the future, it will be states prompted by the private sector and community-based groups who forge the types of partnerships required for regional organizations to become more effective.

From *National Civic Review*, Vol. 85, No. 2, Spring-Summer 1996. Published by the National Civic League, Denver, Colorado. Reprinted with permission of the publisher.

The Role of the Federal Government

In the 1950s, few people ever heard of regional councils because there were fewer than 50 nationwide. The number of regional councils reached a peak high of 669 in 1976.[1] The primary factor accounting for this rapid growth in the number of regional councils was the federal government.

During the 1960s, the federal government offered many incentives to local jurisdictions to create and or enhance the position of regional councils. This was achieved by making additional funding available through categorical grant programs and giving preferential treatment in legislation or regulations to regional councils as eligible recipients. The federal government also required the preparation of a regional plan, or formation of a regional planning agency as a pre-condition for receipt of certain types of funds. The objective of coordination was first introduced in 1959 under Section 701 of the Housing Act as amended. Greater emphasis was added in Section 204 of the Demonstration Cities and Metropolitan Development Act, which established a regional review requirement for projects proposed under 30 different federal grant and loan programs. The Intergovernmental Cooperation Act of 1968 and OMB's associated A-95 grant-review procedures extended coordination requirements to 50 federal programs, and in 1971 it was further expanded to cover almost 100 federal programs.[2]

By the mid–1960s, federal government promotion of regional planning rapidly accelerated. In addition to the extension of Section 701, new legislation authorized regional conservation and development districts. In 1962, Metropolitan Planning Organizations (MPOs) for comprehensive transportation planning were initiated and required, where feasible, to plan for entire urban areas on an inter-jurisdictional basis. In 1965, economic development districts were authorized, and local development district legislation followed in 1966. The number of federal grant programs supporting state and local planning efforts increased from 9 in 1964 to 160 by 1977.[3]

In a 1992 article in the *National Civic Review*, Patricia S. Atkins and Laura Wilson-Gentry suggest that the cumulative effect of these 1960s era federal programs was the widespread use of regional councils for comprehensive land-use and economic development planning.[4]

It should be noted, however, that not all councils during this era were initially formed to function as coordinating agencies, a number of them were first created as single-purpose organizations and later emerged into a broader coordinating entity. The Metropolitan Council of the Twin Cities, for example, was established in 1967 to address a water-pollution crisis, and the catalytic agent in creating Seattle's Metro was pollution in Lake Washington.[5] Over time these single-purpose agencies have evolved into multi-service agencies which combine planning and operating responsibilities, often by absorbing existing single-purpose organizations.[6]

In the 1970s, the focus of regional organizations broadened to include efforts at coordinating fragmented human services delivery systems. Amendments to existing legislation created criminal justice coordination councils (CJCCs) to administer comprehensive regional law enforcement and criminal justice programs. In 1973, legislation was passed allowing "prime sponsor" designations for regional councils and other entities to provide job training and employment improvement for the unemployed and underemployed. Areawide agencies on aging (AAAs) were also authorized by legislation in 1973 to provide comprehensive, coordinated social service networks for the elderly. Legislation passed in 1975 created health systems agencies (HSAs) designed to enhance economies of scale and quality in regional health services delivery systems, and authorized social service agencies to extend a wide selection of social services to the eligible poor.[7]

Even though much emphasis was focused on coordinating human services programs during the 1970s, physical and economic planning programs, initiated in the 1960s were also augmented by federal legislation during this period. New pollution-mitigation initiatives in coastal zone management, resources planning, and noise pollution control legislation were enacted in 1972, and legislation related to disaster assistance planning passed in 1974. In 1976, solid waste management planning was created. In 1977 came water pollution control legislation, followed by air pollution control with air quality control regions (AQCRs), and airport systems planning was authorized.[8]

By the end of the 1970s, there were nearly 48 federal programs which required a regional plan or regional planning organization as a condition of funding, or which gave preference to regional councils within any pool of eligible recipients. Thus, the very essence of regional councils was derived from the strong push of federal policy decisions. But there were signs that things were beginning to change. The U.S. Advisory Commission on Intergovernmental Relations turned from being a champion of strong regional governance to an advocate of public choice with its tacit acceptance that fragmentation is good.[9]

Too much reliance on federal funding, however, ultimately proved to be the Achilles' heel of regional councils. The dependence of most regional councils on the federal government was significant by the close of the 1970s. According to a 1989 report by Richard Hartman, three-fourths of their budgets came from federal programs.[10]

Turning Off the Federal Spigot

As a part of his campaign strategy, Ronald Reagan promised that if elected, his administration would place more control and authority in the hands of states and reduce the size of the federal budget. Once elected, Reagan moved with all deliberate speed to implement his earlier promises. Reduction in federal spending was felt almost immediately by the nation's regional councils. The number of regional councils declined from a high of 669 in 1976 to 529 in 1991. Staff sizes dropped from an average of 21 in 1977 to 17 in 1988. The number of federal programs administered by regional councils averaged around 4 from 1977 to 1983, but decreased to 2.5 by 1988. The federal contribution to the regional council budget, as a share of the total budget,

plummeted from 75 percent in 1977 to 45 percent in 1988.[11]

The federal government shifted the locus of regionalism to the state — through block grants and changed categorical grants — permitting much discretion as to how regional councils should be used. The transfer of the A-95 review-and-comment responsibilities to the states was accomplished through Executive Order 12372. This shift enabled states to accomplish intergovernmental review of federal project applications, with the option of deferring participation or, if maintained, doing so without the regional council as the mechanism. By 1992, ten states, Alaska, Idaho, Kansas, Louisiana, Minnesota, Montana, Nebraska, Oregon, Pennsylvania, and Virginia conducted reviews without the benefit of a regional process.[12] The federal government was rapidly distancing itself from sub-state regional agencies by establishing the state as the preeminent connection. By 1991, only 13 of the 48 federal programs promoting sub-state regionalism that were founded in the 1970s were still funded. The only new federally sponsored legislation which still promotes a strong role for metropolitan planning councils has been the Intermodal Surface Transportation Efficiency Act (ISTEA) which was enacted into law in late 1991.

Because of the reduction of federal monies during the 1980s, regional councils found that they had to diversify their activities, shift from federally mandated comprehensive planning to membership and contract services, become more attuned to customer preferences, enhance their coordination with state policy and administrative cost concerns, establish active advocacy agendas in the state capitals, do more with less funding, and learn how to compete with an expanded pool of recipients of federal funds.[13]

While it is true that much of this shift resulted from direct reduction in federal expenditures, other forces were also in play, influencing this change in strategy. The strongest was the growth of suburban areas as the new locus of power. This shift increasingly called into question the necessity for having a suburban-urban linkage. The majority of metropolitan growth which occurred during the decade of the 1980s occurred in non-central city locations. At the same time, industrial restructuring meant a greater decentralization of the work place, with more new jobs being created outside of central city areas. In a sense, one could argue that the initial strength of the federal government's support for regional councils emanated from the strength of central city elected officials. By the same token, the rapid disengagement of the federal government during the 1980s reflects the shifting of power from central city constituents to the emerging suburban constituent base. Ironically, constrained resources at the metropolitan level resulting from both a nationwide recession and global competition may once again focus more attention on regional councils as viable entities for addressing urban problems. Only this time, the federal government will not be the dominant player.

Emerging New Directions

Some scholars have suggested that regional councils as we know them today are not inevitable beyond the 1990s. From their perspective, what is more likely to emerge are increasingly effective integrated networks of intercommunity problem-solving and service delivery mechanisms.[14] There seems to be growing evidence that this view may prevail.

Allan Wallis, for example, identifies two strategic arenas in which these new networks, or alliances as he calls them, will occur. The first arena is economic development. Competition in the global economy is forcing these regional alliances to take place. Examples include Seattle, Detroit, Hartford, Cleveland, Houston, Orlando, Philadelphia, and Pittsburgh.[15] Capitalizing on the work initiated by RLA, a public/private/nonprofit partnership created in 1992, the city of Los Angeles is currently engaged in creating alliances to focus on what the city has identified as major regional growth sectors. Common to these efforts is an agenda requiring public sector participation but with a focus which is primarily business oriented. Typical of these efforts is the attempt to engage in strategic planning explicitly designed to capitalize on growing market opportunities.

The second strategic arena identified by Wallis is social equity and fiscal disparity. Here the questions are what constitutes fair share, whether or not a focus of the planning process should be on redistribution, and of course who pays and who benefits. For Wallis, it is nonprofits who must play a major role in resolving these dilemmas. According to him, providing solutions to these problems cannot fall solely on the shoulders of the public sector. A number of different efforts such as the Atlanta Project, the Federation of Community Planning in Cleveland, the Regional Fair Housing Compact Pilot Program in Connecticut, the East Suburban Council for Open Communities in Ohio, and the Scientific and Cultural Facilities District in Denver are identified as examples of how the non-profit sector and business together can help to develop a regional response to these problems.[16]

Much of the strategy being designed to foster economic development and social equity hinges on the question of whether or not prosperity can exist within suburban locations independent of healthy central cities. Few doubt that major inequities continue to exist between these two geographic locations. What to do about these disparities has been a continuing dilemma since the early days of regional councils. On the one hand, there are the regional economic growth proponents who argue that if you grow the region, then you will lessen the inequalities. Advocates of this position seem to agree that less centralization and less federal involvement will enable this regional economic growth to take place. There is growing empirical evidence that this may not necessarily be the case.

David Rusk, for example, described cities as either elastic or inelastic.[17] He finds that elastic cities "capture" suburban growth and inelastic cities "contribute" to suburban growth. Furthermore, elastic cities tend to expand their city limits, while inelastic cities do not. Not a new finding but one which should be uppermost in our thinking, is that racial prejudice continues to shape city growth patterns. Based upon Rusk's criteria, inelastic areas are more segregated. He also found that city-suburban income gaps were more critical a problem than overall income levels in metropolitan areas (a finding similar to that of Myron Orfeld),[18] and that poverty is more concentrated in inelastic cities than in elastic cities. Most important is his finding that the smaller the income gap between city and suburb, the greater the economic progress for the entire metropolitan community.

Rusk's findings are also interesting relative to their implications for future regional problem solving efforts. For example, he found that fragmented local government fosters segregation, and unified local government promotes integration. Dispersed and fragmented public education is more segregated than centralized and unified public education.

Rusk's findings, as well as those of Neal Peirce[19] and Oliver Byrum[20], suggest regional decision making is critical, and more of it, not less, is better. Furthermore, his findings suggest that no matter how regional councils evolve, two critical issues will have to be addressed: 1) How to assure that future suburban growth does not occur at the expense of central city areas; and 2) How to facilitate growth and development while simultaneously narrowing the gap between the poor and the non-poor.

Strategies for the Future

It should be fairly evident at this point that the role that regional councils play has changed significantly over the past 30 years. In the coming years, they undoubtedly will undergo even more changes. John Kirlin[21] and Allan Wallis[22] both seem to agree that one of the central thrusts of the new change will be a shift from the concept of metropolitan government as a separate entity to a focus on governance. This belief is supported by a number of recent surveys which indicate that while there is some general support for regional government, most respondents question the ability of regional government to solve problems or respond effectively to local issues. Indeed, the extent to which regional governments are perceived to interfere with local self-interest appears to be directly correlated with the degree of opposition to such entities.[23] Attempts to strengthen regional structures by giving

them more authority or by changing the selection process of governing board members to make them more representative have not been successful. And there is little likelihood that stronger regional government structures will emerge in the foreseeable future.

On the other hand, there is growing support for organized entities that promote a return to a collective sense of civic mindedness. The extent to which the influential business leaders effectively promote this vision of the future will be the degree to which the general public believes that it has some chance of succeeding. Earlier indications in cities like Atlanta, Philadelphia, and Denver suggest that there may be a great deal of merit to this new form of regional problem solving.

But what seems more likely to occur is that a clearer distinction will be drawn between regional agencies that continue to function as governmental entities because their mission is to plan and implement regional infrastructure requiring massive capital investment (or because they are carrying out a federal mandate such as pollution control) and the emerging entities which function as loose affiliations. Local interest will reluctantly continue to support the more structured government entities because in the long run it is more cost effective. But successful as many of these agencies have been in influencing the infrastructure development process, they simply have not been capable of addressing issues of social equity, and thus the need to explore alternative structures to address these problems will become even stronger.

Regional entities which are emerging as partnerships between the business sector and non-profit institutions have the potential to address social equity concerns more directly. In no small part, this is because influential business people supporting these partnerships see that growing income and class inequalities within a region simply do not bode well for the future economic health of that region, let alone for promoting a more civil society.

Regional government is here to stay. As long as its primary function is to provide infrastructure capacity and implement federal or state regulatory mandates, it will receive tacit support from local municipalities and contribute little to the growing problem of regional inequalities. Regional organizations working both in concert with and independent of regional governments have a much higher probability of tackling the more politically volatile social equity issues facing every metropolitan area in the country. In the final analysis, however, dedicated leadership resolved to address these difficult social equity issues will be the factor which makes the difference.

Notes

1. Atkins, Patricia S. and Wilson-Gentry, Laura, 1992: "An Etiquette for the 1990s Regional Council" *National Civic Review*, Volume 81, Number 4, Fall-Winter, p. 466.

2. Wallis, Allan D., 1994: "Inventing Regionalism: The First Two Waves" *National Civic Review: Realizing Human Potential*, Volume 83, Number 2. Spring-Summer, pp. 168–169.

3. Wallis, op. cit., p. 170.

4. Atkins and Wilson-Gentry, op. cit., p. 469.

5. Wallis, op. cit., p. 170.

6. ACIR, 1973–74: *Substate Regionalism and the Federal System*, Washington, D.C., U.S. Government Printing Office.

7. Atkins and Wilson-Gentry, op. cit., p. 469.

8. Ibid., p. 470.

9. McDowell, Bruce as cited in *Substate Regional Governance: Evolution and Manifestation Throughout the United States and Florida* (Tallahassee, Fla.: Florida Advisory Commission on Intergovernmental Relations, November 1991), p. 28.

10. Hartman, Richard, 1989: *A Report to the Membership*, Washington, D.C., National Association of Regional Councils, p. 1.

11. Ibid., p. 4.

12. Symonds, Richard N., Jr., 1992: "Montana Discontinues Process," SPOC-NET, Vol. 7, No. 7, 19, February 1992, p. 1.

13. Atkins and Wilson-Gentry, op. cit., p. 468.

14. Dodge, William R., 1992: "Strategic Intercommunity Governance Networks" (Signets of Economic Competitiveness in the 1990s), *National Civic Review: Partnerships for Regional Cooperation*, Volume 81, Number 4, Fall-Winter, p. 412.

15. Wallis, Allan D., 1994: "The Third Wave: Current Trends in Regional Governance" *National Civic Review: Renewing America*, Volume 83, Number 3, Summer-Fall, p. 294.

16. Ibid., p. 303.

17. Rusk, David, 1995: *Cities Without Suburbs*, Second Edition, The Woodrow Wilson Center Press, Washington, D.C.

18. Lecture presented to the Graduate School of Architecture and Urban Planning, Spring 1995.

19. Peirce, Neal R. with Curtis W. Johnson and John Stuart Hall, 1993: *Citistates: How Urban America Can Prospect in a Competitive World*, Seven Locks Press, Washington, D.C.

20. Byrum, Oliver E., 1992: *Old Problem in New Times: Urban Strategies for the 1990s*, American Planning Associates, Chicago, Illinois.

21. Kirlin, John J., 1993: "Citistates and Regional Governance" *National Civic Review: Tales of Turnaround*, Volume 82, Number 4, Fall 1993.

22. Wallis, op. cit., 1994.

23. Baldassure, Mark, Joshua Hassol, William Hoffman, and Abby Kanarek, 1996: "Possible Planning Roles for Regional Government: A Survey of City Planning Directors in California" *Journal of the American Planning Association*, Volume 62, Number 1, Winter, pp. 179–183.

PART V
City Studies and Trends

CHAPTER 23

CONTEMPORARY TRENDS IN MUNICIPAL GOVERNMENT STRUCTURES

Tari Renner and Victor S. DeSantis

Public policy making within American city governments is an incredibly complex process. The local context (or political environment) and types of public officials necessarily differ among the country's nearly 20,000 municipalities. In addition, there is tremendous variation from community to community in the rules that define how public officials interact with each other; that is, who has what authority within the policy-making process? There are generally considered to be five basic forms of city government that structure these relationships in different ways.[1]

The two most widely used forms are, of course, the mayor-council and council-manager systems. The former is the only form of city government with an element of separation of powers that is typical in American federal and state governments. The chief executive is elected separately from the city council and exercises some distinctive executive authority (although the precise contours of that authority vary from jurisdiction to jurisdiction). Alternatively, the council-manager plan vests all authority in a popularly elected council, which, in turn, hires an appointed executive.

Powers are also unified in the commission form of government. The voters elect a legislature (the commission) in which each legislator also serves as an executive department head. The commission form is distinguished

from both the mayor-council and the council-manager structures in that it has no provision for singular executive leadership. This has become an important point of criticism of the commission form and is one reason why that form has consistently declined in usage over the last several decades.

Town meeting and representative town meeting governments, often cited as the last remaining examples of direct democracy, are almost exclusively found in New England communities. Under the town meeting form, the annual mass public meeting in which all adult voters may participate is considered to be the local legislative body with the authority to pass bylaws and to raise and appropriate funds. State statutes typically mandate that each community have at least one town meeting each year but may hold as many additional (special) town meetings as deemed necessary. During the remainder of the year, the elected board of selectmen, with usually three or five members, is charged with running the daily operations of the town. Under the representative town meeting form, however, the voters elect a limited number of citizens to represent them at town meetings. All citizens may attend and participate in the debates, but only the duly elected representatives may actually vote. This structure, which is a more recent variation of the town meeting form, is an

Originally published as "Municipal Forms of Government: Issues and Trends," *Municipal Year Book* 1998. Published by the International City/County Management Association, Washington, D.C. Reprinted with permission of the publisher.

attempt by increasingly urban New England communities to keep many of the elements of direct popular democracy but, simultaneously, to promote greater efficiency in the policy process.[2]

There is considerable controversy among academics, practitioners, and community activists over the consequences of different city government structures. In the first systematic examination of the fiscal impact of different municipal forms of government, published in 1967, Robert Lineberry and Edmund Fowler found that reformed systems (council-manager or commission plans with at-large and nonpartisan elections) tend to tax and spend at lower levels than so-called unreformed systems (mayor-council governments with district and partisan elections).[3] However, they also found that political structure is a significant intervening variable affecting the relationship between a municipality's socioeconomic characteristics and its public policy outputs. Specifically, unreformed jurisdictions tend to be more responsive to the demographic characteristics of their communities than reformed jurisdictions. The authors concluded that "reformed governments make public policy less responsive to the demands arising out of social conflicts in the population."[4]

Not all subsequent research, however, has supported these findings. In 1968, for example, Terry Clark used a somewhat different research design and found that the correlations between structure and spending were in the opposite direction.[5] And in the early seventies, Roland Leibert found that if the number of functions that cities perform is controlled, the relationship between structure and policy outputs disappears altogether.[6]

Although the above researchers used different sampling frames and statistical techniques, their studies were all cross-sectional in scope. More recent projects that have attempted to examine this controversy with longitudinal research designs have also produced contradictory results. William Lyons, for instance, found that as citizen demands and resource opportunities increase over time, unreformed jurisdictions tend to increase expenditures more rapidly than do reformed jurisdictions.[7] However, David Morgan and

John Pelissero studied 11 cities that changed to reformed structures, matched them with a group of 11 cities that retained their unreformed structures, and found no significant differences in spending patterns between the two groups.[8] These are the most widely cited academic articles examining the consequences of city government structures in America. They not only illustrate the lack of consensus among scholars but also underscore the reality that structural change is absolutely no guarantee of public policy change.

One important limitation of the existing body of empirical research is that it tends to focus on the general form-of-government categories that have been found to be grossly oversimplified. Since "cities have adopted a myriad of structural arrangements that cannot easily be considered part of one model or the other, researchers must reflect this situation in order to be more useful from both a theoretical and practical standpoint."[9]

Methodology

This research does not attempt to sort out the controversies over the consequences of different forms of city government. Rather, its more modest goal is to examine the characteristics of these forms. Specifically, this work analyzes some of the cross-sectional patterns and longitudinal trends in ICMA's *Municipal Form of Government* survey. This landmark survey is conducted systematically every five years. The 1996 survey instrument was mailed to city clerks in all jurisdictions with populations of 2,500 or more and in 643 jurisdictions with fewer than 2,500 people that ICMA recognizes as providing for a position of professional management. In all, 7,331 jurisdictions were given two opportunities to respond.

Questionnaires were received from 4,555 jurisdictions for an overall response rate of 62.1 percent. The response patterns are similar across the population groups except that the rates are somewhat lower for the smallest and largest groups. Regionally, the highest response rates come from the West North Central and Pacific Coast divisions while the lowest are found in the Mid-Atlantic and East South Central divisions. There is less variation in response rates by metropolitan status. The rates for central, suburban, and independent municipalities are 54 percent, 62.4 percent, and 63.5 percent, respectively. However, the most substantial decline in responses from the 1991 to the 1996 surveys is found in central cities, which were the most likely to respond in the former year (74.8 percent) and the least likely to respond in the latter (54 percent).

Policy-Making Structures and Procedures

The responses for the five general municipal forms of government are also examined. Overall, there is a plurality of council-manager systems. A total of 48.5 percent of the respondents report this form, compared with 35.2 percent reporting the mayor-council form. The other three forms are each found in fewer than 5 percent of the responding communities. As discussed above, the commission system is the only minor form found in substantial numbers outside New England. In the 1996 survey, for the first time, ICMA gave city clerks the option of designating "not sure" when asked about their current form of government; 11 (0.2 percent) chose this category. A total of 429 (9.4 percent) did not report a form of government.

The cross-sectional patterns of municipal forms of government in the current survey are similar to those in previous years. Jurisdictions with the largest populations are the most likely to have mayor-council systems, with council-manager systems most prevalent in midsize communities. The decrease in the percentages reporting mayor-council structures is most precipitous between the 500,000–1,000,000 (71.4 percent) and the 250,000–499,999 (32 percent) categories. However, the highest proportions of council-manager governments are found among cities in the 100,000–249,999 (68.3 percent) and 50,000–99,999 (67.3 percent) categories. This form then consistently declines with population through the 2,500–4,999 category and then appears to increase in the smallest population

category (under 2,500). However, it is important to remember that the jurisdictions with fewer than 2,500 people are unrepresentative of all jurisdictions in this population category because, to be included in the survey, they must provide for a position of professional management. In addition, there are thousands of cities with a population under 2,500. Consequently, the reported figures understate the proportion of mayor-council and other structures in this population category.

Predictably, there are substantial differences in city government structures by geographic division. In New England, a plurality of jurisdictions have the town meeting form of government (43.8 percent), followed by the council-manager (30.8 percent), mayor-council (10.5 percent), and representative town meeting (3.9 percent) forms. Mayor-council systems are found in a majority of East South Central communities (65 percent), as well as in pluralities of Mid-Atlantic (44.08 percent), East North Central (47.9 percent), and West North Central (47.5 percent) communities. Alternatively, the council-manager form is reported by majorities of South Atlantic (67.9 percent), West South Central (58.7 percent), Mountain (54.5 percent), and Pacific Coast (78.5 percent) communities. Commission governments are reported by 3.5 percent or less of the respondents in each of the nine geographic divisions.

The variations by metropolitan status are small compared with those by geographic division. There are proportionally more council-manager than mayor-council systems reported for each of the three categories. Central jurisdictions split 56.7 percent to 36.9 percent for council-manager over mayor-council systems. The comparable percentages among suburban jurisdictions are 50.5 percent to 32.8 percent, respectively, and those among independent jurisdictions are 44.3 percent to 38.2 percent, respectively.

Structural Change at the Aggregate Level

To obtain an accurate aggregate estimate of the ratio of council-manager to mayor-council forms of government among all American municipalities, two statistical adjustments were made in the data. First, since the unadjusted survey totals include an unrepresentative sample of jurisdictions with fewer than 2,500 people, these communities were removed. Second, those respondents who were not sure about their jurisdiction's form of government were removed to ensure comparability of results with previous surveys. However, these changes made very little difference in the percentage gap between the two major types of structures. The aggregate unadjusted survey results indicate a 48.5 percent to 35.2 percent split for council-manager over mayor-council jurisdictions. With the cities under 2,500 and unsure respondents eliminated, this split becomes 52.7 percent to 40.1 percent, respectively. The adjusted figures also indicate that commission, town meeting, and representative town meeting systems are found in 1.7 percent, 4.9 percent, and 0.6 percent of jurisdictions, respectively.

This study presents some longitudinal data to examine the changes in municipal government structures over time. It includes data from the last four ICMA *Municipal Form of Government* surveys (1981, 1986, 1991, and 1996) for jurisdictions with 2,500 people or more that reported having one of the three *national* forms (council-manager, mayor-council, or commission). (Recall that the town meeting and representative town meeting systems are almost exclusively found in New England communities.) Among jurisdictions with one of the three national forms, mayor-council municipalities declined from a slight majority in 1981 (51.7 percent) to minorities in 1986 (43.8 percent), 1991 (47.4 percent), and 1996 (42.4 percent). Council-manager governments increased from a minority in 1981 (45.5 percent) to majorities in the next three surveys, reaching a new peak (55.8 percent) in 1996. Alternatively, commission cities have consistently declined during this period. They were found in approximately 3 percent of the communities in 1981 and 1986, but fell to 2.1 percent in 1991 and to 1.8 percent in 1996.

However, the changes in aggregate responses in these surveys only indirectly indicate that there were corresponding changes among individual jurisdictions. Differences in response patterns from one survey to the next could produce some of the observed differences. It is also possible that some of the aggregate change is a result of a tendency among newly incorporated municipalities to adopt the council-manager plan. A large number of new municipal incorporations are occurring in southeastern and western states, where council-manager government is more prevalent. The ICMA survey instrument does, however, have several questions that directly address proposed and successful structural changes within the cities.

Proposed and Adopted Structural Changes

Respondents to the 1996 survey were asked whether there were attempts to change their city government structures since the previous ICMA survey in 1991. Overall, the proportion of municipalities reporting an attempt at structural change in the current survey is 14.6 percent. This represents a slight increase over the 12.7 percent reported in the 1991 survey. In 1991, however, city clerks were reporting on attempts at structural change since the 1986 survey. Consequently, the data indicate a slight increase in attempts at structural change from the 1987–1991 period to the 1992–1996 period.

There appear to be few differences in attempted changes by population group, geographic division, or metropolitan status. The variations by general form of city government, however, indicate that changes were most likely to be proposed in town meeting (22.1 percent) and representative town meeting (33.3 percent) systems.

This study reviewed the types of changes that were proposed and those that were actually approved, as reported in 1996 compared with both 1991 and 1986. In the most recent survey, the structural changes that were most likely to be proposed were changing the basic form of city government and adding the position of a chief administrative office (CAO); in both cases there are noticeable increases over the figures reported in 1991 and 1986. There are corresponding increases in the changes that were actually approved for both the form of city government and the addition of a CAO. The absolute numbers of cities reporting either a proposal or an approval to change forms of government in 1996 are approximately twice as large as those in 1991 or 1986. These data are consistent with the overall movement toward the council-manager form of government indicated earlier. Alternatively, there is also a very slight increase in the number of proposals and approvals to eliminate the position of CAO.

The data indicate that attempts to change election systems from at-large to ward or district during the same time period have been reduced. They also suggest that there has been a small decrease in proposals to increase the number of members serving on city councils.

Chief Administrative Officers

Respondents were asked whether their municipalities have the position of a CAO. This person may be called a city manager, city or town administrator, village administrator, or something similar. This position of professional management can be found in all forms of city government. These survey results are based on the relevant data from the 1996 survey. Overall, 77.5 percent of the jurisdictions report having a CAO position. The cross-sectional patterns predictably vary by population, geographic division, metropolitan status, and form of government.

There is an important longitudinal shift between the 1991 and 1996 surveys: the substantial increase in the overall proportion of communities that report having a CAO. The change from 67.1 percent to 77.5 percent between 1991 and 1996 represents an increase of 10.4 percentage points over the five-year period. Although some of this shift may be a result of differing response patterns between the two surveys, the near uniform increases by population group, geographic division, metropolitan status, and form of government strongly suggest that this trend is not primarily a product of sampling variation. The most

substantial increases from 1991 to 1996 appear to have occurred among suburban cities (68.9 percent to 80.9 percent), mayor-council cities (36.9 percent to 50.8 percent), commission cities (33.7 percent to 48.5 percent), and communities with representative town meetings (45.0 percent to 70.8 percent). The trend among mayor-council cities is particularly interesting since the data indicate that a majority now report having a CAO. In these jurisdictions, however, the role of the CAO might be limited to assisting the elected mayor with budget preparation and personnel management or conducting policy research and making recommendations; and the mayor alone, without a majority vote of council, may be able to fire the CAO. The authority and responsibility of the CAO in non–council-manager cities are usually not as substantial as those of a city manager under the council-manager plan.

This study reviews the method of establishing the position. A plurality of municipalities with CAOs established the position by charter (44.6 percent). Those positions established by ordinance or state statute constituted 40.6 percent and 10.6 percent of the total, respectively. The proportion created by charter varies with population. The largest municipalities are the most likely and the smallest are the least likely to establish by charter. The reverse is apparent for ordinances. State statute establishment does not appear to vary substantially by population, except that no jurisdictions of 500,000 and over indicate this source for the position of CAO. Charters are most likely to be the source in South Atlantic and West South Central cities. Ordinances are most often used in Mid-Atlantic and West North Central cities. State statute establishment is reported most frequently in New England. The overwhelming majority of central communities (77.7 percent) establish by charter, as do modest majorities of council-manager (54.6 percent) and representative town meeting (62.5 percent) communities.

The authority of appointed CAOs and elected mayors is compared in two critical areas: responsibility for budget preparation and appointment of department heads. Budget authority is much more likely to be solely vested in a CAO (64.2 percent) than in a mayor (12.9 percent). The two share this responsibility in 6 percent of jurisdictions, finance departments have it in 4.2 percent, and other procedures are used in 12.6 percent.

The proportion of jurisdictions in which the mayor has responsibility for developing the budget decreases with population size. This is consistent with the conventional wisdom that although mayor-council systems are most likely in the largest cities and those with a population from 2,500 to 4,999, the former group tends to have strong mayor versions of the plan whereas the latter tends to have weak mayor versions in which the executive has few formal powers.

Mayors appear to have somewhat more power in appointing municipal department heads than they do in developing the budget. CAOs are more likely to appoint department heads than are mayors, but the percentage gap is not as substantial as that for budgetary authority. CAOs have appointment power in 39.3 percent of responding jurisdictions compared with 20.2 percent for mayors. The mayor and CAO share the authority in 16.6 percent of jurisdictions, with other procedures used in 23.9 percent. The differences by population group indicate that mayoral appointment power is the greatest among cities with 500,000 or more people. Predictably, the CAO patterns are similar to those for the form-of-government data. CAOs are most likely to have the power to appoint department heads in midsize municipalities. The highest percentages are found among the 25,000–49,999 (59.2 percent), 50,000–99,999 (62.4 percent), and 100,000–249,999 (58.4 percent) categories. Except for one case in the 500,000-and-over group, the highest percentages of shared authority between the mayor and CAO are apparent in the smallest municipalities.

The form-of-government patterns indicate that mayors have the power to appoint department heads in a narrow majority of mayor-council municipalities (50.3 percent) and CAOs have the power in a solid majority of council-manager municipalities (65.7 percent). These somewhat predictable figures are substantially higher than the percentage of mayors with budget authority in mayor-council municipalities (30.3 percent) and substantially lower than the percentage of CAOs with budget authority in council-manager municipalities (92.6 percent).

This study also examines the changes in mayor and CAO powers from 1991 to 1996. The data suggest that CAOs have fared well compared with elected executives in terms of increased appointment and budgetary authority. The percentage of jurisdictions reporting that the CAOs have appointment authority increased from 31.4 percent to 39.3 percent over the time period. Even more striking, the percentage of jurisdictions reporting that the CAOs have budget authority increased from 46.8 percent to 64.2 percent over the same period. A large portion of this shift is from the "other" category to the CAO category, although the mayors' power has diminished slightly also.

Mayors

The role of the mayor in American municipalities changes depending on the structural relationship between the mayor and council, on whether the mayor's position is full or part time, and on formal authority.

SEPARATION OF POWERS

One of the most important structural variations distinguishing the different forms of city government is the degree of separation of powers among the key actor and institutions. Although distinctive branches of government are traditional in American state and national governments, they are comparatively rare at the local level. For example, the data revealed that 65 percent of the jurisdictions responding to the survey report that their mayor (or chief elected executive) is also a member of the legislative body. Mayors are somewhat less likely to be members of council in the largest communities and in those responding from the West North Central and East South Central geographic divisions. There are surprisingly few differences among suburban, independent, and central jurisdictions: the first group is only slightly more likely to report that the mayor is a member of council (69.6 percent) than either independent (59.5 percent) or central (61.4 percent) jurisdictions. While the response patterns by form of government are predictable, it is important to note that mayors are members of the legislative body in more than one-third of mayor-council jurisdictions (34.5 percent). This underscores the conclusion of previous research that the traditional models of American city and county forms of government are over-simplified.

Similar patterns are evident from the data, which indicate whether mayors are full or part time. Overall, the distribution of full- and part-time mayors (15.1 percent and 85 percent, respectively) is similar to that in previous surveys. In 1991, for example, the comparable figures were 15.5 percent and 84.5 percent, respectively. There are, however, clear cross-sectional patterns, the most dramatic of which is the consistent decline in the percentage of full-time mayors by population of the responding jurisdiction. Among the geographic divisions, full-time mayors are most likely to be reported in East South Central communities (34.4 percent) and least likely to be found in Mid-Atlantic communities (7 percent). The differences by metropolitan status suggest that central city mayors (38.8 percent) are much more likely to serve full time than either suburban (11.5 percent) or independent (15.7 percent) city mayors. The response patterns by form of government are predictable. Council-manager communities report the lowest percentage of full-time mayors (5 percent). However, it is noteworthy that only 27.8 percent of mayors are full time in mayor-council communities.

Regarding the methods of mayoral selection used in American communities across the 1991–1996 time period, almost three-fourths of mayors are elected directly by the voters (73.7 percent), slightly lower than the percentage reported in the 1991 survey (77.1 percent). Although far fewer mayors are selected from among the council membership (23.3 percent), this percentage did increase by 2.2 percent over the five-year time frame. Only a very small number of jurisdictions rely on other methods of mayoral selection.

MAYORAL VOTING AND VETO POWER

In the traditional American separation-of-powers model, the elected executive is autonomous from the legislature. The executive's power typically includes a veto over legislative enactments as part of the checks and balances inherent in the system. These critical elements are absent from the policy-making process in most American municipalities, however.

This study reviewed the circumstances in which mayors are permitted to vote *within* the legislature. Overall, a majority of communities (54.6 percent) indicate that their mayors can vote on all issues before the city council. Another 35.9 percent allow the mayor to vote only when a tie must be broken. The remaining jurisdictions either do not allow the mayor to vote in council meetings (7.4 percent) or have some other procedure (2.1 percent). There are few patterns in the responses by population except that the largest cities are the least likely to have mayors voting on the council. Pacific Coast communities are the most likely to report having mayors with voting power on all council issues (80.4 percent) while West North Central communities are the least likely (40 percent). There is surprisingly little variation in the data by metropolitan status, but the form-of-government patterns are comparatively strong and predictable. However, the complexities of American municipal structures are illustrated by the fact that more than one-fifth (22.1 percent) of mayor-council cities report that their executive votes on all issues before the legislature.

An important source of executive power may come from the authority to veto legislation passed by the legislative body. This power often comes not only from an executive's actual ability to veto but also from the perceived threat that the executive may use his or her formal authority. Both the actual and potential use of the veto can significantly enhance a mayor's ability to influence council actions in a particular way. The survey data indicate that, overall, only 28.1 percent of jurisdictions give their mayor a veto, whether it be over entire ordinances, resolutions, or appropriations, or only over specific sections or line items of each. The total percentage of jurisdictions reporting mayoral vetoes has consistently declined from 34.6 percent in the 1986 survey to 31.2 percent in 1991 and to 28.1 percent in 1996. These changes are consistent with the apparent movement toward council-manager governments discussed earlier.

The cross-sectional patterns demonstrate that the presence of mayoral veto powers decreases with the population size of jurisdictions. By geographic division, it is most likely to be found in West North Central communities (47.4 percent) and least likely in New England communities (12.5 percent). There are comparatively few differences, however, by metropolitan status. The form-of-government patterns, although generally predictable, provide further evidence of the complexities in American city government structures. While mayor-council jurisdictions are the most likely to report having an executive veto power (55.9 percent), nearly half of these systems (44.1 percent) do not. Alternatively, more than one out of ten (11.1 percent) of council-manager jurisdictions give their mayor a veto. These data illustrate that many American cities do not necessarily conform to one of the traditional form-of-government models.

City Councils

Next, we turn our focus to the legislative institutions that make public policy in American communities. While these institutions can vary in size, procedures, responsibilities, and traditions, the individual members of these bodies share a fundamental principle: all are directly elected and reelected by voters. Local legislative bodies are most commonly referred to as councils; however, a small number of communities may use the title of board, selectmen, or trustees. The most common size for local legislative bodies across the nation is 6, although this ranges from a low of 2 to a high of 50 council members. Generally, the average size of the council is positively related to population size.

FREQUENCY OF COUNCIL MEETINGS

How often the council meets in formal session may be one indication of the council's workload. Just over two-thirds of the responding communities reported that their councils meet twice each month (69.1 percent). Just over 10 percent reported that their councils meet more frequently than twice a month, with 7 percent meeting once a week or more and 3.4 percent meeting three times a month. Just over 20 percent of respondents reported monthly or fewer than monthly council meetings.

The frequency of council meetings is positively related to population size. Weekly council meetings are held in 71.4 percent of the 500,000–1,000,000 population jurisdictions and in 56 percent of the 250,000–499,999 population jurisdictions. Conversely, weekly council meetings fall below the 5 percent rate in the three population groups below 10,000. In these smaller communities, bimonthly or monthly council meetings are much more common. Similarly, weekly council meetings are more likely in central communities (21.1 percent) than in either suburban (6.5 percent) or independent (3.9 percent) ones.

Although few noteworthy patterns emerge when the council meetings data are presented by geographic division, New England communities are again the outliers. Almost one-fifth (19 percent) of the respondents from this division report weekly council sessions. The next highest rate is among the jurisdictions of the Pacific Coast at 9.3 percent. Not surprisingly, 29.4 percent of town meeting communities and 25 percent of representative town meeting communities rely on weekly council meetings. This may again be an indication of political values and the desire to provide constant access and information to community residents.

COUNCIL STANDING COMMITTEES

In addition to the frequency with which the council meets in formal session, the need for standing committees to handle legislative matters may be another indication of council workload. Standing committees are the most common type of committees used by legislative bodies. Overall, 53.1 percent of all responding jurisdictions use standing committees in the policy-making process. This is a small increase over the percentage reported in the 1991 survey (52 percent) but is still below that reported in 1986 (54 percent).

The use of standing committees appears to be positively correlated with population size. All of the largest jurisdictions (500,000 and over) use them, as do 92 percent of the 250,000–499,999 population jurisdictions and 63 percent of the 100,000–249,999 population jurisdictions. Only the smallest population group (under 2,500) falls below the 50 percent mark of communities with standing committees. Similarly, the use of standing committees varies by metropolitan status. Nearly two-thirds (65.9 percent) of central jurisdictions report using standing committees. This drops to 54 percent for suburban and 49.8 percent for independent jurisdictions.

Local traditions are often important determinants of local government institutions and processes. Accordingly, geographic patterns often emerge in studies of how people relate to local government and how they design local charters. The data reveals there are substantial geographic differences in the use of standing committees by local councils. The greatest usage is seen among the East North Central (69.7 percent) and Mid-Atlantic (62.3 percent) jurisdictions, while the lowest usage is seen among the New England (37 percent) and West South Central (39.3 percent) jurisdictions.

FILLING VACANT COUNCIL SEATS

Although council members are normally elected through direct election by citizens, alternative systems are often used when a council seat is vacated before a term ends. A majority of responding jurisdictions allow a vacant council seat to be filled by council appointment (52.4 percent). Fewer jurisdictions use appointment by chief elected official (11.2 percent), special election (9.8 percent), or other methods (9.3 percent). Another 17.3 percent of communities reported that the method of filling a vacant council seat depends on the length of term remaining.

When data are presented by population size, no consistent pattern for council appointment of vacant seats emerges, although

this method is somewhat more likely in smaller rather than larger communities. While the highest rate of council appointment is for communities under 2,500 (59.7 percent), the lowest usage can be seen among the 100,000–249,999 population group (42.5 percent). The highest rate for special elections can be seen in the 250,000–499,999 population group (24 percent), and the highest rate for appointment by chief elected official can be seen in the 2,500–4,999 population group (16.5 percent).

All the geographic divisions except New England report a majority (or close to a majority) of communities using council appointment to fill vacant council seats. New England communities rely less on council appointment than do other areas (34.7 percent) but also report a greater use of special elections (30.8 percent). Similarly, almost half of the town meeting and representative town meeting systems use the special election feature (40.5 percent and 34.8 percent, respectively). The form-of-government differences demonstrate that, as expected, council-manager jurisdictions, which tend to vest more power with their councils, rely more on council appointment (61.5 percent) than do any other form of government.

Term Limits

In recent years, term limitation for elected officials has garnered a great deal of attention among American voters. Feeling that many elected leaders have become too entrenched in their positions and that elected offices at all levels could use an infusion of new ideas, reform-minded citizens in many parts of the county have called for term limits. This movement has taken on great visibility during the 1990s with many state and local ballot items being placed before voters and winning passage.[10] Over the 1991–1996 time period, the use of mayoral term limits among responding jurisdictions almost doubled from 5.3 percent to 9.7 percent, and the use of council term limits more than doubled from 4.2 percent to 8.7 percent. Although term limits remain infrequently used at the local level, they have received much more widespread attention in the past five years and their use at the local level has certainly increased.

When mayoral term limits are distributed across population groups, the data show that their usage is positively related to population size. The larger cities tend to use this legal mechanism at higher rates, from 55.6 percent in the 500,000-and-over group, to 44 percent in the 250,000–499,999 group, to 28 percent in the 100,000–249,999 group. Related to population size, central communities (20.2 percent) use such mechanisms more often than suburban (9.2 percent) or independent (8.6 percent) communities.

Geographically, the highest frequency of use can be seen among the communities in the Mountain (30.4 percent) and West South Central (17.1 percent) divisions. This should not be surprising since some Mountain states (Colorado in particular) have seen public support for, and a host of ballot referenda on, term limits for many elected government offices in recent years. Also, term limits seem to be used more often in the reform-minded council-manager communities than in communities with the mayor-council form of government.

The data on council term limits reveal very similar patterns to those on the mayoral term limits. Council term limits are also positively correlated with population size. Among those jurisdictions with populations of 500,000 and above, 55.6 percent have this mechanism, compared with fewer than 10 percent of communities with populations of less than 25,000. As expected, central communities use council term limits at the highest rate (16.1 percent) among the metro status categories.

Geographically, council term limits appear to be most popular in the Mountain (28.3 percent) and West South Central (15.7 percent) areas. Of course, these were the two geographic divisions where the mayoral term limit was also the most popular. The council term limit is used least often by communities of the East South Central area (2.7 percent).

Election Systems

Although the last decade has seen a substantial legal battle surrounding the use of at-large elections in local governments around the country, this type of election method remains entrenched at the local level. This study revealed that 60.9 percent of responding jurisdictions rely on at-large systems to elect their local leaders. Previous analysis of the ICMA survey results showed an aggregate decline in the percentage of jurisdictions reporting the use of at-large elections, from 66.5 percent in 1981 to 60.4 percent in 1986 to 59 percent in 1991.[11] While this slight increase back over 60 percent might be due to specific respondent variations from survey to survey, the data suggest that the shift away from at-large elections has leveled off over the 1990s. Historically, the largest shift was apparently toward mixed or combination plans, in which some members of the city council are elected by district and some are chosen at-large. However, mixed systems, which increased from 26.8 percent in 1986 to 29.3 percent in 1991, decreased to 22.3 percent in 1996. The 1991–1996 time frame showed a noticeable increase in the use of district systems, from 11.7 percent to 16.8 percent.

When analyzed in the context of population size, the proportion using at-large elections decreases as population size increases. The reverse is true for mixed systems. The presence of district elections does not appear to vary substantially by population levels. The one clear outlying group is the under-2,500 population category: the distribution of election system types among these smallest communities is 80.7 percent at-large, 8.8 percent district, and 10.6 percent mixed.

The differences by geographic division and metro status are generally consistent with the conventional wisdom regarding the types of cities in which the municipal reform movement was the strongest. At-large elections are most prevalent in Pacific Coast (85.5 percent) and suburban (69.7 percent) jurisdictions. Mixed systems are most likely to be found in West South Central (32.5 percent) and central (44.6 percent) jurisdictions. District elections are most prevalent in West North Central (29 percent) and central (23.2 percent) jurisdictions.

Partisan and Nonpartisan Elections

Just as at-large elections were an important component of the municipal reform movement of the Progressive Era, so too were nonpartisan elections. The data from the 1996 survey confirm that nonpartisan election has been one of the most successful reforms. Overall, 76 percent of the responding cities report having nonpartisan elections compared with only 24 percent for partisan elections. This distribution is similar to the 74.5 percent to 25.5 percent and 70.2 percent to 29.8 percent splits reported in the 1991 and 1986 surveys, respectively. The 1996 and 1991 data are slightly higher because they include valid responses from the entire sample, whereas the earlier survey figures exclude the jurisdictions with under 2,500 people and those with either town meeting or representative town meeting forms of government — groups that are overwhelmingly nonpartisan in their election procedures. Therefore, the slight differences between the data presented here and those in previous ICMA publications should not be construed as representing a recent trend toward nonpartisan systems. In fact, given the changes in election systems over the past decade, the nonpartisan election data have been remarkably stable over time.

The distribution patterns of partisan versus nonpartisan elections are predictable. As with at-large elections, the patterns generally reflect the types of jurisdictions in which the reform movement was strongest and weakest. There are few consistent differences by population size, but the variations by geographic division are rather dramatic. Virtually all jurisdictions in the Pacific Coast (98.1 percent), West North Central (94.8 percent), and Mountain (94.8 percent) divisions have nonpartisan systems. On the other hand, 89.2 percent of Mid-Atlantic jurisdictions use partisan elections. The differences by metropolitan status are small but mildly surprising. Suburban communities are the most likely to

have partisan elections (28.8 percent), followed by central (21 percent) and independent (18.1 percent) communities.

Provisions for Direct Democracy

A variety of provisions for direct democracy, in which voters can influence public policy through their vote, exist across the country. Among these mechanisms are the initiative, the binding and nonbinding referenda, and recall and petition procedures. Splitting the referendum category between binding and nonbinding was new to the 1996 *Municipal Form of Government* survey; the difference between these two provisions is that the binding referendum enacts a ballot measure while the nonbinding referendum may be more advisory in nature and does not specifically change policy or force governmental action. A petition is sometimes called a protest referendum as it allows voters to delay enactment of a local ordinance or by-law until a referendum is held.

As this study revealed, the initiative is reported in 58.1 percent, binding referendum procedures in 41.6 percent, nonbinding referendum procedures in 39.8 percent, recall elections in 68.5 percent, and petitions in 35.7 percent of jurisdictions. When analyzed within the context of population size, the presence of initiative, recall, binding referendum, and petition elections declines with population; however, the nonbinding referendum pattern is relatively consistent. When broken down by metro status, it appears that central jurisdictions are more likely than either suburban or independent ones to have these direct democracy provisions in place (with the exception of the nonbinding referendum).

The geographic division differences are also more dramatic for initiatives and recall elections than for either referendum elections or petitions. The presence of initiatives ranges from 83.3 percent in the Pacific Coast to 25.3 percent in the East South Central division. Recall elections range from 95.8 percent in the Pacific Coast to 40.2 percent in East South Central division. The amount of variation among geographic divisions is much smaller for the other three types of direct democracy methods.

Conclusion

This research examined the cross-sectional patterns for the 1996 *Municipal Form of Government* survey and analyzed several longitudinal shifts from previous surveys. It appears that there has been a modest, but consistent, movement over the last 15 years toward council-manager and away from mayor-council and commission forms of government. The 1996 survey reports the largest gap to date between the two main systems. This is supported by the trends of increasing structural changes toward council-manager governments, increasing percentages of communities with CAOs, increasing budgetary and appointment powers of the CAO relative to the elected mayor, and decreasing percentages of jurisdictions that report giving their mayor a veto power over council actions. However, the 1996 data also suggest that local election systems, one of most volatile features of municipal government in recent decades, have begun to stabilize over the past five years.

While this research attempts to shed some additional light on the characteristics of policy making and electoral structures in American municipalities, there are substantial controversies that are not addressed regarding the consequences of alternative systems. Future research in the field should seek to make substantive contributions by examining the impact of separate structural elements (such as the location of budgetary authority or the presence of a mayoral veto) rather than just the broad form of government categories, which this study has found to be oversimplified. A more accurate understanding of the linkage between political structures and public policies is still illusive but nonetheless very important to practitioners and reformers as well as to academics.

Notes

1. The term *city* refers also to towns, townships, villages, and boroughs.
2. For an analysis of recent trends in town meeting and representative town meeting forms of government, see Victor S. DeSantis and Tari Renner, "Democratic Traditions in New England Town Meetings: Myths and Realities" (paper presented at the 1997 Midwest Political Science Association annual meeting, Chicago, Ill., 10 April 1997).
3. Robert Lineberry and Edmund Fowler, "Reformism and Public Policy in American Cities," *American Political Science Review* 61 (September 1967): 701–16.
4. Lineberry and Fowler, "Reformism and Public Policy," 714.
5. Terry Clark, "Community Structure: Decision-Making, Budget Expenditures, and Urban Renewal in 51 Cities," *American Sociological Review* 3 (August 1968): 576–93.
6. Roland Leibert, "Functions, Structure and Expenditures: A Re-analysis of Recent Research," *Social Science Quarterly* 54 (March 1974): 765–83.
7. William Lyons, "Reform and Response in American Cities: Structure and Policy Reconsidered," *Social Science Quarterly* 58 (June 1978): 118–32.
8. David Morgan and John Pelissero, "Urban Policy and City Government Structure: Testing the Mediating Effects of Reform," *American Political Science Review* 74 (December 1980): 999–1006.
9. Tari Renner, "Elected Executives: Authority and Responsibility," *Baseline Data Report* 20 (Washington, D.C.: International City Management Association, May/June 1988): 8.
10. Victor S. DeSantis and Tari Renner, "Term Limits and Turnover among Local Officials," in *The Municipal Year Book* (Washington, D.C.: International City/County Management Association, 1994), 36–42.
11. Tari Renner, "Municipal Election Processes: The Impact on Minority Representation," in *The Municipal Year Book* (Washington, D.C.: International City Management Association, 1988), 13–22.

CHAPTER 24

FORM AND ADAPTATION OF MUNICIPAL GOVERNMENT STRUCTURES

Robert P. Boynton and Victor S. DeSantis

Local governments must develop organizational structures in order to function effectively and efficiently. While some local governments may be more or less successful in accomplishing these two performance objectives, how the organization is set up to accomplish its tasks plays a vital role in determining its achievements. Indeed a long-standing municipal research topic has been the effects of different organizational structures in governments. With the introduction and subsequent success of the council-manager plan since the turn of the century, the debate over form and structure in local government has continued.

This chapter is an attempt to uncover the extent to which the dominant forms of local government, mayor-council and council-manager, adapt their values and practices to meet the changing needs of their internal and external environments. Variations in legal basis and geographic region as well as political and economic factors may prompt local governments to make certain adaptations. This phenomenon will be examined through an analysis of how executive authority is distributed in municipalities between the office of the mayor and the office of the city manager or chief administrative office (CAO). While the respective roles of the chief elected and the chief appointed officials may have been more clearly defined in earlier decades, the complexity of municipal administration has caused the two roles to become more ambiguous.

This is not to suggest that some municipalities don't adhere to the basic tenets and traditional structures of the council-manager or mayor-council models. More precisely, the spectrum of local government forms has broadened, and the use of a hybrid model transcending the two dominant forms has increased. Local governments have begun to consider and accept some of the core values of each form in adapting their local government structures to the pressing needs in their jurisdictions.

Long-time local government scholar Charles Adrian suggested that there may be a "converging" of government forms.[1] He pointed to the fact that managers in council-manager and CAOs in non–council-manager cities have taken on expanded roles in their own jurisdictions and in the intergovernmental arena. Adrian optimistically looks to the future and the further interchange between the dominant forms.

Originally published as "Form and Adaptation: A Study of the Formal and Informal Functions of Mayors, City Managers, and Chief Administatrative Officers," *Baseline Data Report*, Vol. 22, No. 1, January-February 1990. Published by the International City/County Management Association, Washington, D.C. Reprinted with permission of the publisher.

Structure in Form of Government

The two primary forms of government have some fundamental theoretical differences.

MAYOR-COUNCIL FORM OF GOVERNMENT

The mayor-council form of government, which is used in a majority of the larger cities over 250,000 in population and in smaller cities under 10,000 in population, is characterized by a separation of executive and legislative duties between two elected branches — the mayor and the council. This practice is based on the American ideal of constitutional separation of powers, designed to give neither branch a plurality of power. Two versions of the mayor-council form exist in practice today: the strong-mayor form and the weak-mayor form. While the formal role of the council may change slightly in the two forms, the primary differences are found in the role and authority of the mayor.

In the strong-mayor system, the mayor is elected separately from the council and may have substantial power to check the legislative branch, including a veto power. The mayor has administrative authority over city departments and over the preparation and administration of the budget. The high degree of coordination and centralization in the office of the mayor and an independent electoral base allow strong leadership in the government. In the weak-mayor version, the mayor may be a member of the council selected either by rotation or from among the council membership. In this situation the mayor may be one among equals, with the same voting privileges of other council members and no authority to veto legislation. The mayor may preside at council sessions and perform only ceremonial functions. This form may operate better in small cities where governing is less complex and the need for strong centralized leadership is not as great.

The legislative body in mayor-council systems may be elected by an at-large or district system or by some combination of both. Studies have shown that the district election plan, much more prevalent under the mayor-council model, allows more equitable representation, especially for minority groups. Renner noticed the movement away from the at-large systems in a study that examined changes in election systems between 1981 and 1986.[2] Adrian also commented on this shift in election systems. Other research has pointed out, however, that officials from more narrowly defined constituencies tend to take a focus that is less jurisdiction-wide and to concentrate more on programs and policies that affect their particular districts' needs. While the legislature sets policy under each type of mayor-council government, it occupies a more central role in systems that call for a less prominent leadership position for the mayor.

COUNCIL-MANAGER FORM OF GOVERNMENT

It has been suggested that the council-manager plan is a positive alternative to the separation of powers doctrine embodied in mayor-council government. This idea, put forth recently by Chester Newland, stresses that the council-manager plan affords better management in three important respects:

1. Ultimate authority is placed in the popularly elected council in a parliamentary-like, shared-powers system.

2. Greater civic, political, and career expertise and professionalism are encouraged and practiced.

3. A more coordinated, systems-oriented responsiveness occurs.[3]

While this argument may be somewhat optimistic, Newland was reacting to what he saw in the 1980s as a condition of amateurism and spoils that increasingly characterized many of the fragmented, unreformed governments — similar to the period preceding the reform movement.

Since the beginning of the reform movement, a dominant thrust of public administration has been to support enhanced executive power as a means of overcoming governmental inefficiency. Newland claims that the council-manager governments are consistent with this force in that final authority has been concentrated in the popularly elected legislative body, with the executive directly responsible to the council. Through this organizational arrangement, the enhanced executive power of the manager serves the public interest under close supervision by the elected representatives. It is this supervision by the elected council that ensures that the administrative bureaucracy remains ultimately accountable to the people.

In theory, the council-manager form, which is used in a majority of medium- to large-size jurisdictions between 10,000 and 250,000 in population, departs from the mayor-council model by placing executive and legislative authority with the council. The council is generally smaller and elected through nonpartisan, at-large elections. The executive or city manager, is an appointed official who serves at the pleasure of the council. The manager is expected to provide policy advice, direct the daily operations of the government, handle personnel functions, and prepare the budget. The mayoral function is similar to that of the weak mayor in that this official is generally recognized as the political head of the municipality but is a member of the council and has no veto powers. In theory, the mayor and council, acting as a collegial body, decide policy, approve the budget, and rely on the manager to faithfully implement their decisions.

The council-manager plan was formed while the progressive spirit was sweeping through the United States during the early 1900s. In the area of management and public administration, the Progressive Movement heartily embraced the scientific approach. Along with this spirit arose the penchant in business and public administration for efficiency and expertise. Richard Childs, the founder of the council-manager movement, believed that if the difficult task of finding the most highly qualified city manager was carried out, an efficient and economical administration would be virtually assured. At that point in history however, the "economic and efficient administration" ideal was someone with a technical background, usually an engineer or city planner.

The council-manager model is structured on two basic principles — choose qualified administrators, appoint; find representative policymakers, elect. This model is consistent with

the prevailing wisdom at the turn of the century embodied in the writing of many theorists.[4] Their writings are most representative of the paradigm known as the "politics-administration" dichotomy. The job of city manager, the professional appointed administrator, was outside the scope of the political environment. As its founders claimed, the council-manager plan represented a perfected goal and all political efforts should be directed towards its universal installation.

A review of the early council-manager plan and its progress was prepared by Childs in 1937. For Childs, the value of the council-manager plan was that through the administrative leadership of the city manager, policy could be separated from implementation. This separation would allow passionate policy debate to be confined to the council, while leaving the administrative staff on the sidelines to grow in strength and public esteem. During the early years under the council-manager plan, the debt and taxes diminished, the death rate decreased, and the frequency of garbage collection increased. In summation, the founder of the movement claimed that the city management profession proved that it could manage the nation's cities with democracy and efficiency, while remaining sensitive to local attitudes and scientific in method.

The ideal of apolitical management has withered over time, partly due to its basic prescription that it be a closed system. The managerial complexity of the modern world has forced changes, and the pure Childs model has been modified in many instances. This can readily be seen by looking at the changes in the *Model City Charter* of the National Civic League. Over time, the original reform model has been altered due to changing societal forces and conditions that have craved goals beyond efficiency in the operation of government.

Debates on the Council-Manager Plan

Nonetheless, many arguments have centered on the merits of the council-manager plan and the universal application of its principles. Many have argued that manager cities are not fiscally responsible, not responsive to the city council, and not responsive to citizen needs. One of the greatest battles has been over the politics-administration dichotomy and whether it is possible to keep the manager out of the policy-making process. Over time there has been increased recognition of managers' involvement in the political aspects of local government, even in cases where managers can limit their roles solely to implementation. Fundamentally, the argument can be made that implementation itself is a political process. Choosing among competing implementation strategies can be highly political. Managers must often choose a strategy and follow it though within a political and economic environment in which many groups want a particular outcome. Deciding on how to distribute limited resources among these groups is at the heart of political decision making.

While the early council-manager model revered the separation of politics and administration, by mid-century theorists were questioning the wisdom of such thinking. Luther Gulick asked, "(s)hould the administrator be a dynamic and aggressive community leader, or should he stick narrowly to administration and let the council make the policies?"[5] The argument put forth by Gulick and others suggested that politics and administration could not be separated into mutually exclusive categories and that many policy decisions intensely involve administration.

More recently, scholars studying the role of managers have recognized a more active role for these professions. James Svara, in a 1988 article, concluded that the manager can have a high level of involvement in all dimensions of the governmental process without diminishing the role of the council.[6] He asserts that the council-manager plan is a system under which the council determines the purpose and goals of the government with advice from the manager, and the council and the manager share in making and implementing policies.

Another argument advanced by Svara is that the manager should conduct comprehensive administrative planning in order to identify emerging trends and problems and to frame issues for the council. It is in the interest of the manager to promote appraisal of the whole organization and to encourage the oversight and review function of the council, which could support improved management and strengthen the prerogatives of the manager. These prescriptions add up to a strong policy role for the manager, not as innovator, but as a facilitator interested only in the effective and efficient role of the government.

Though the merits of separating politics and administration came under attack many years ago, some of the arguments surface periodically for a more narrow role for managers. While theorists and practitioners continue to discuss the proper role for city managers, the movement continues toward professional leadership in cities. While the data on council-manager governments show steady gains for the plan, the number of professional administrators (CAOs) in non–council-manager governments also continues to rise. A professional has been hired to help run city affairs in some highly political environments (San Diego, California; Washington, D.C.; Newark, New Jersey; and others). As early as 1955, Thomas Reed pointed out that the trend of pairing professional public administrators with mayors indicates the need for professional guidance in the office of the chief executive.[7]

While CAOs in mayor-council systems illustrate particular instances of transferring the managerial component of government, the cities under study in this analysis point to a wide acceptance of governing principles between the two forms. Although previous research is in virtual agreement that managers and CAOs are not apolitical administrators, few studies have examined in any comprehensive manner the managers' level of authority vis-à-vis the power of the mayor. Specifically, the hypothesis is that managers and appointed administrators have come to occupy more of a political role in both council-manager and mayor-council governments.

The idea of adaptation and transfer of function is not new. In an earlier article, Boynton provided a historical perspective on the council-manager plan and claimed that it had been the most significant organizational invention for local governance during the twentieth century. The manager plan, as he referred to it, has become a symbol of professional management of urban affairs, and the impact of the plan has extended to all forms of local government.[8]

Boynton notes that the primary intention behind the council-manager movement was not only to break the power of the party but to establish a municipal government service career by removing administrative personnel from the electoral process. He contends that the plan has survived because it allows adaptability and professionalism on the part of the city manager.

The form has survived and flourished through some of the most turbulent periods of this century for local governments — the urbanization of the 1920s, the depression and wars of the 1930s and 1940s, and the social upheaval of the 1960s. This proven record of adaptability to meet changing societal forces suggests that the council-manager form should have the capability of meeting challenges on the horizon.

Some evidence suggests that the council-manager form is not responsive to the needs and opinions of the citizenry. Research has pointed to managers' alleged lack of interest in citizen participation.[9] One study by Huntley and MacDonald found that the activity city managers prefer least is discussing controversial issues with civic groups. While this may be the case, it may be that few officials would relish such a task.

Stillman supports Huntley and MacDonald, showing that participation in the more political aspects of city affairs was one of the activities least favored by city managers.[10] Managers found that a great deal of their time was spent resisting attempts by the mayor and council to intrude in administrative affairs. Stillman points out that the future roles for city managers must balance the fundamentalist pure-management approach and the forward-looking facilitator of innovations approach.

There is great variation in city managers' perceptions of their roles, given the personality and jurisdictional differences that each brings to the job. Possibly, the roles that managers envision themselves to be occupying are more important than the actual roles they take (if the two are not congruent). For it is their role perceptions that dictate managers' approaches to their responsibilities.

In a recent article, City Manager Eric Anderson addressed the issue of role perception of city managers in his study of the different forms of government.[11] He found that the most important role for managers in recognized[12] council-manager cities was that of "facilitator," followed by the roles of "policy director" and "financial administrator." In non–council-manager cities, the highest ranking was given to the role of "coordinator," with "facilitator" and "financial administrator" following closely behind. These data suggest that managers and CAOs in both forms of government view their roles as encompassing both the political (policy director, coordinator, facilitator) and the administrative (financial administrator) areas of government.

Methodology

The data for this research were collected through a mail survey, *Organizational Structure and Decision Making in Local Government.* The survey was sent in October 1987 to all municipalities over 2,500 population and to a small group of municipalities under 2,500 that are recognized by ICMA. Those cities not responding to the initial mailing were sent follow-up surveys in December 1987. In all, 3,332 cities (47.1 percent) responded to the questionnaire.

To test the hypothesis posited earlier, which was that managers and appointed administrators have come to occupy more political roles in both the council-manager and mayor-council forms of government, the results are analyzed of several survey questions that dealt with powers of the mayor, manager, and CAO. The responses to these questions are cross-tabulated by several important independent variables, including the size of the jurisdiction, the geographic location, its urban characteristics, and the general form of government. By cross-tabulating the data in this way, it is possible to identify any significant relationships between variables. Because respondents did not answer all of the individual questions, total responses to individual questions may vary.

Formal Roles of Mayors, Managers, and CAOs

Four of the formal roles that may be part of the mayors' or appointed administrators' responsibilities are examined in this section: preparing the budget, setting the legislative agenda, administering municipal services, and supervising department heads.

PREPARING THE BUDGET

One of the most important duties in government policy making is preparation of the budget. This task is paramount, and its placement may indicate where authority exists in the government. This survey identifies by form of government which local official or group has the overall responsibility for budget preparation. Of those responding, 73.6 percent identified managers and CAOs as responsible for budget preparation. Among the respondents, mayors had substantially less authority in budget preparation with only 11.5 percent reporting that they took the lead in budget preparation. The data indicates several important trends:

1. In council-manager cities, managers almost invariably have responsibility for budget preparation (97 percent). There is little variation in this phenomenon when examined by population size, geographic region, or metro status. Further, in the small percentage of cases in which the manager does not take the lead on budget preparation, the task is usually left up to another official or group, but rarely is this task a mayoral responsibility.

2. While mayors rarely participate in budget preparation in council-manager cities, a different pattern emerges in mayor-council jurisdictions. A positive relationship exists between city size and mayoral involvement. In cities over 100,000 in population, 54 percent report that the mayor is charged with budget preparation, while in the smallest mayor-council cities (under 5,000 in population)

only 18 percent rely on the mayor for this function. Indeed, jurisdictions in the two smallest population groups rely more heavily on the appointed administrator to submit the budget (53 percent and 47 percent, respectively).

There seems to be a relatively modest number of mayor-council jurisdictions across all of the population groups that use personnel other than the manager or mayor for budget submission (ranging from a high of 36 percent to a low of 21 percent).

3. The variation in which position is responsible for budget preparation is not pronounced among geographic regions. But it becomes noticeable again when broken down by metro status, which is correlated with population to some degree. CAOs have less budgetary authority than mayors have in mayor-council central cities. Mayors are in charge of budget development in 60 percent of the jurisdictions, while CAOs have this authority in only 18 percent.

This trend reverses itself in suburban and independent cities however. In suburban jurisdictions, managers are responsible for the budget in 52 percent of the responding jurisdictions, compared with only 21 percent reporting mayoral responsibility for the budget. Similar proportions appear in the data on independent mayor-council jurisdictions.

Overall, while managers have almost complete budgetary authority in council-manager cities, CAOs also have substantial authority in the smaller or non-central city jurisdictions with the mayor-council form. The mayor is more likely to lead the budget process in only the larger and more urbanized central cities.

SETTING THE LEGISLATIVE AGENDA

Another important policy-making duty is the establishment of the legislative agenda. Controlling which issues are brought before the council is an important policy task that both appointed and elected officials may have. This survey identifies which local official has responsibility for setting the agenda for the regular council meetings. A substantial portion of the respondents indicated that someone other than the manager or the mayor was responsible. In most of these cases, the city clerk, usually an elected officer with overall responsibilities for assisting the legislative staff and the chief elected officials, set the council agenda.

In 83 percent of the responding council-manager jurisdictions, the manager prepares the council meeting agenda. Mayors have this responsibility in a small percentage (2 percent) of these jurisdictions. In the responding mayor-council local governments, the appointed administrator sets the council agenda less frequently (45 percent), but this proportion is nonetheless almost half. While mayors set the agenda in 16 percent of the mayor-council jurisdictions, they remain behind the CAO and the "other" categories. This points out that the positions of city manager and CAO in council-manager and mayor-council cities have considerable influence in defining the issues and setting the legislative agenda, both of which are highly political roles.

Few differences in the overall trends come about when looking at council-manager cities' data distributed by population, region, or metro status. A slightly greater percentage of jurisdictions in the small population groups report that the manager sets the agenda. Regionally, only the Northeast jurisdictions report any notable difference, with a somewhat smaller percentage reporting that the manager prepares the agenda for council meetings. Suburban and rural jurisdictions report more frequently than central cities that managers set the agenda.

In mayor-council jurisdictions, CAOs set the agenda much more frequently in smaller jurisdictions, with someone other than either the mayor or the manager responsible in a majority of jurisdictions over 25,000 in population. While the mayors' roles are not especially strong in any of the population groups, they fare best in the cities under 100,000 in population. Regionally, the power of the mayor to set the legislative agenda is strongest in the South and weakest in the Northeast and West. The CAOs, on the other hand, have the most authority in the West. Mayors have responsibility for agenda preparation more frequently in central cities and rural jurisdictions than in suburban areas, where the manager seems to perform this task more often.

ADMINISTERING MUNICIPAL SERVICES

Another formal role for mayors and managers is that of administering services or functions. Respondents were asked to identify who was directly responsible for the administration of eight separate functions ranging from economic development to public relations.[13]

In mayor-council jurisdictions, CAOs were responsible for an average of 3.5 of these services, and mayors were responsible for 1.6 services. This gap is even wider for council-manager jurisdictions, with managers taking on responsibility for about five services, while mayors have almost nonexistent responsibility for the services in this study.

When the data are presented by population size, several important trends appear. While mayoral authority remains relatively constant across all sizes of jurisdictions, managers and CAOs tend to have much greater direct responsibility in small cities. This substantiates what David Booth found in examining the roles of managers in small cities. His research revealed that these managers were often understaffed, required to hold multiple positions, and clearly overworked. Additionally, Booth found that the popular election of the mayor did not reduce the operational effectiveness of the council-manager system in small communities. His findings show that mayors of small local governments are not in conflict with managers and do not infringe on their prerogatives. Indeed, how government forms are altered to meet the special needs of small communities remains an important and understudied issue in local government research.

The data show that managers in council-manager cities over 100,000 in population are responsible for an average of 2.5 services, while managers in cities with populations under 5,000 are in charge of an average of 6.6 areas. Similarly, while CAOs in the largest mayor-council jurisdictions average less than 1.0 service area, managers in the smallest cities average 3.7.

The amount of administrative responsibility also varies across regions and with metro status. While managers in the western council-manager jurisdictions report direct responsibility for the fewest services (4.4), their counterparts in the Northeast have considerably more direct responsibility (5.8 services). In mayor-council jurisdictions, CAOs in both the West and Northeast have charge of 3.9 services, an amount that is lower than the reported low for council-manager cities. Managers of central cities with both forms of government have considerably less administrative authority than either suburban or rural managers retain.

DEPARTMENT HEAD SUPERVISION

Another dimension of administrative responsibility is supervision. In council-manager cities, the average number of department heads that report to the manager (7.3) is much greater than the number that report to the mayor (2.1). This trend remains across all population groups, geographic regions, and types of metro status. Not surprisingly, however, there is a positive correlation between the number of department heads reporting to the manager and jurisdiction size. Managers in council-manager cities over 100,000 in population have an average of 12 department heads reporting to them, while their colleagues in jurisdictions under 5,000 in population supervise an average of 5 department heads.

In mayor-council jurisdictions, administrators generally have fewer department heads reporting directly to them than report to managers in the council-manager cities. In fact, in medium-size jurisdictions and central cities, the average number of department heads reporting to the mayor is greater than those reporting to the manager.

APPOINTMENT AND DISMISSAL AUTHORITY

Still another aspect of administrative responsibility and an important personnel function is the appointment and dismissal of department heads. While this authority is usually accompanied by the overall responsibility for the department, it may not always be.

Appointment. It can be assumed that if a manager may unilaterally hire department heads, that manager has more authority than one who needs consent of the council or who makes hiring recommendations to the council. Requiring consent of the council and recommending a candidate to the council constitute manager input, not authority. This also applies to the mayor who must have council consent or who makes recommendations for hiring department heads. This survey identifies the extent of authority to appoint department heads that is found in the positions of mayor, manager, and CAO.

In council-manager cities, the data show that in large jurisdictions the manager has more unilateral authority. In the smallest population group, the power of the manager is checked to a much greater extent, with 42 percent needing the consent of the council. Thus, authority over the departments may be a more shared, or at least a more restrained, power in small council-manager jurisdictions. The mayor has sole authority over department heads in only a small percentage of council-manager cities (0.1 percent). When the data are broken down by region and metro status, managers seem to have greater unilateral authority in southern and central city jurisdictions.

In mayor-council jurisdictions, mayors have far greater authority over department head appointments, with either unilateral or restrained authority in slightly over 60 percent of the responding jurisdictions. The authority of the CAOs in mayor-council jurisdictions is far less (7 percent unilateral, 23 percent with consent) than that of managers in council-manager forms of government. The percentage of jurisdictions in which the mayor alone appoints department heads decreases as population decreases. CAOs, on the other hand, more frequently play a role in appointing department heads in the small and medium-size jurisdictions.

When the data are distributed by region and metro status, several important trends emerge. Mayors have more unilateral authority in the North Central mayor-council jurisdictions, while CAOs exercise greater unilateral authority in mayor-council cities of the South and West. In central cities with mayor-council governments, mayors have more authority than CAOs do. The authority of the CAOs is greatest in suburban mayor-council jurisdictions.

Dismissal. Equally important may be the authority to dismiss department heads in the local government. Not surprisingly this responsibility reflects many of the same trends seen in authority to appoint department heads, since the responsibilities are usually given in conjunction with one another. However, there is greater unilateral authority to dismiss department heads in both forms of government for managers, CAOs, and mayors than there is authority to appoint.

Managers may unilaterally dismiss in 75 percent of the council-manager cities, while they may unilaterally appoint in only 66 percent. Likewise, mayors can unilaterally dismiss in 16 percent of the jurisdictions, while unilaterally appointing in only 9 percent. Again, while mayors have extensive dismissal authority in the mayor-council cities, their role is almost nonexistent in council-manager jurisdictions.

According to the data, managers have extensive authority to dismiss department heads in council-manager cities, but in mayor-council jurisdictions, CAOs have marginal dismissal power.

The examination of formal roles provides some evidence supporting the research hypothesis. Clearly, managers in council-manager cities and CAOs in mayor-council jurisdictions have substantial authority. While there is more variation in the form and scope of this authority in the mayor-council jurisdictions, it still remains substantial, especially for the CAOs in the smaller mayor-council jurisdictions. Such findings may lend support to the "converging forms" phenomenon put forth here and offered by Charles Adrian.

Informal Roles of Mayors, Managers, and CAOs

City managers and CAOs, in addition to having formal tasks, perform many less formal functions in their municipalities. One of these informal activities is that of conferring with various other local leaders and community groups. Some scholars have pointed out that this task of linking the government to the

community may be an increasingly important role for the manager to play.[14] In addition, David Booth would suggest that this role extends far beyond the boundaries of the city. He claims that there is a need to reappraise the management profession because the position of manager as ambassador will become crucial in dealing with federal, state, and other local governments, as well as with the metropolitan area councils of governments (COGs).

The ICMA survey included questions on the role of the manager as a liaison to the community, mass media, and other governments.

CONTACT WITH COMMUNITY LEADERS AND GROUPS

This survey reveals the frequency with which managers confer with mayors, councils, community groups, and citizen leaders about local business. The respondents were asked to indicate on a five-point scale their levels of contact. The scale ranged from one (very infrequent) to five (very frequent). The data show that managers in council-manager cities have slightly greater levels of contact with councils, citizen leaders, and community groups than their counterparts have in mayor-council cities. In contrast, however, the CAOs in mayor-council cities have slightly more contact with the mayor than the managers in council-manager cities have with the mayor. This latter finding is consistent with the organizational structure that exists in the mayor-council jurisdictions where the CAO is usually the appointed professional administrator working under the mayor.

When the data are distributed by population size, it is apparent that the frequency of contact with other officials or groups decreases as the city size decreases. In council-manager and mayor-council jurisdictions, the highest frequency of contact with these groups takes place in cities over 100,000 in population. Regionally, it appears that the managers in western jurisdictions, regardless of government form, are slightly more active with individuals or groups. The only exception is in the Northeast, where managers in both forms confer more frequently with the council. In the larger cities, managers and CAOs in central cities are usually most frequently viewed as the liaisons to the community, media, and other governments.

These findings suggest that managers and CAOs are quite involved in conferring with groups inside and outside of the government on matters of municipal business. While there have been occasional arguments about the extent of managers' involvement with citizen groups, the fact remains that they engage in this type of activity.

The manager often takes the lead role as ambassador for the government. In mayor-council jurisdictions, the mayor usually takes this visible role in the community. It may be that managers are hired to assist the mayor in mayor-council forms of government to enable the mayor to have a more visible leadership role in the community.

CONTACT WITH THE MEDIA

Another area in which municipal officials may act as ambassadors for municipalities is in dealing with the media. In both council-manager and mayor-council jurisdictions, the aggregate data show that managers represent the municipality more often than mayors do. This difference is more pronounced in the council-manager cities.

Overall, managers play a more substantial role with the media than mayors do, but differences appear when the data are examined by population size, geographic region, and metro status. In cities over 100,000 in population, regardless of government form, mayors more often than managers or CAOs are in the visible leadership role with the media. In addition, mayors more frequently perform this role in medium-size mayor-council cities. It is in the small to medium-size cities where managers and CAOs more frequently deal with the media.

Across all the regions, managers in council-manager cities play the role of ambassador more frequently than mayors do in these jurisdictions. Mayor-council cities show a similar trend in all but the southern region where the mayor and the CAO have the same level of contact with the media. When distributed by metro status, the data show that mayors take the lead with the media in central jurisdictions of both government forms.

APPOINTMENT OF COMMITTEES AND ADVISORY BOARDS

Another important informal role that officials are often charged with is the appointment of government commissions and advisory boards. These boards can play an important role by helping to generate public policy decisions and by providing a necessary link between the government and the citizenry. Regardless of government form, the average number of boards appointed by CAOs or managers is lower than the average number of boards appointed by the mayor. This disparity is much greater between mayors and CAOs in mayor-council cities, where mayors appoint an average of 2.5 boards, and CAOs appoint approximately 0.1 boards.

When the data are distributed by population size, region, and metro status, some variation is apparent in the average number of boards appointed by the mayor. In mayor-council cities, the mayor has substantial appointment authority in the largest cities (5.3 boards) and in the medium-size cities (3.9 boards). The average number of mayor-appointed boards drops off somewhat in the population groups below 25,000. Similarly, mayors appoint more boards in central cities than in either suburban or rural jurisdictions. CAOs in mayor-council governments have little authority to appoint boards, regardless of community characteristic variables.

This may suggest that appointing boards and commissions remains a political patronage device, one that the elected officials retain solely. In mayor-council jurisdictions, mayors have extensive authority to appoint boards, while in council-manager cities, it may be the council that retains both the power to appoint both the manager and the community commissions and boards.

Institutionalization of the Chief Appointed Officer

Two factors that indicate the extent to which the position of manager of CAO has been institutionalized were included in the survey: staff resources and employment contracts.

STAFF RESOURCES

Given the large number of tasks that must be performed by city managers in some communities, the staff resources allocated to managers are important to managers' effective performance. The survey respondents indicated the number of professional staff (other than department heads) that report directly to the manager or CAO. The average size of the managers' staffs is almost identical in council-manager and mayor-council jurisdictions (3.0 and 3.2, respectively). However, some noticeable variation exists when the data are distributed by population size and metro status.

Within population groups, it becomes apparent that staff size correlates positively with jurisdiction size, regardless of form of government. In cities over 100,000 in population, CAOs had average staffs of 6.2 in mayor-council cities and 4.3 in council-manager cities. While suburban and rural jurisdictions reported staffs of similar sizes, central cities reported greater staff resources for CAOs in mayor-council cities (4.8) than for managers in council-manager cities (3.3).

Regionally, CAOs in the mayor-council jurisdictions of the South and West have staffs slightly larger than those of managers in council-manager cities. The Northeast is the only region where the manager has more staff in council-manager cities than in mayor-council cities.

EMPLOYMENT CONTRACT

While the legal framework for the position of city manager or CAO is found in the city charter or in legislation passed by the council, an employment contract can be a positive force in formalizing the relationship. An employment contract is one way to ensure that both the manager and the council understand and accept their respective roles. The contract may protect managers from unwanted or unnecessary political intrusions by the council, and it may help the council appraise the performance of the manager.

Employment contracts are more prevalent in council-manager jurisdictions (46 percent) than in mayor-council jurisdictions (35 percent). The medium-size jurisdictions in both government forms are those that use contracts with the highest frequency. Regionally, western council-manager cities use contracts more frequently, as do the North Central mayor-council jurisdictions. Marginal differences in the use of contracts exist when the data are reviewed by metro status, except that in council-manager jurisdictions, central cities are those most likely to bind the relationship with a contract.

Managers' and Chief Administrative Officers' Perceptions of Their Roles

The survey instrument asked the responding managers and CAOs to identify what they felt were their most important roles. Four roles emerged. The largest percentage of respondents (24 percent) reported that their most important role is that of *financial administrator*. This is probably the most traditional role for city managers and would fit well into what the founders of the movement had envisioned for the position. The next highest percentage (22.9 percent) of respondents reported that their most important role is that of *facilitator* of actions and policies in the municipality. This role is much more politically oriented than the financial administrator role, in that it portrays someone who helps guide and drive decision making for the local government.

The third and fourth most important roles identified by the respondents were those of *coordinator* (22 percent) and *policy director* (19.6 percent). The first is defined in the survey instrument as "coordinator of activities and information," while the latter is defined as someone "who identifies policy advantages and disadvantages, makes recommendations, and advocates policy to the council." As with the financial administrator model, the coordinator role seems to be more in line with the efficient, apolitical manager model. In contrast, the policy director role is probably the most political role that a manager could have. It portrays an activist manager who is involved in deciding which policies are to be pursued. The facilitator and policy director managers are most likely to play an active part in council activities.

Several important trends emerged in the data. In mayor-council cities, the respondents split evenly between the coordinator model and the financial administrator model (28.5 percent), with the facilitator model and policy director model selected by 20.3 percent and 12.8 percent, respectively. This suggests that administrators in cities with mayor-council systems more frequently occupy the less overtly political roles. However, the fact remains that a substantial proportion of those administrators in mayor-council governments still occupy important positions in guiding, shaping, and recommending policy actions.

In contrast, managers in council-manager jurisdictions take on a more overtly political role. The respondents in these cities identified the roles of facilitator (25.3 percent) and policy director (23.6 percent) as the most apropos.

The basic findings show that CAOs and managers in both mayor-council and council-manager cities occupy prominent positions as policy makers. While the actual percentages vary across the groups, it is obvious that few managers are not in some way connected to the core of the political process.

Conclusion

The power of the manager in council-manager cities is strong in both administrative and policy-making roles. This has been cited in some of the literature previously discussed in this chapter. However, this conclusion is not particularly important or surprising. Surprising is the finding that extensive policy-making and administrative authority exist in mayor-council jurisdictions. The data suggest a strong role for the CAO and managers in preparing and implementing the budget, setting the legislative agenda, and serving in an administratively responsible role in both council-manager and mayor-council cities. Further, managers are increasingly asked to serve as the government's ambassador to various individuals and groups.

The authority of the appointed manager or CAO is more important and meaningful than many people might expect. Managers collab-

orate on and guide policy determination in addition to their work as financial and technical administrators. The continuing complexity of modern society may provide more avenues for managerial authority to develop as local governments are asked to take on more roles and tasks.

While this research is fairly simplistic and uses limited variables to describe and measure the amount of authority of the manager, the CAO, and the mayor, it points out that strong managerial leadership can exist within mayor-council jurisdictions. While we cannot estimate whether professional management is making a difference in these municipalities, we have pointed out that CAOs in these cities take on a wide array of responsibilities with differing levels of authority. Importantly, however, the large number of cities that have adopted such hybrid forms of government signifies the growing acceptance of this organizational relationship and the enhanced role of professional management in council-manager and mayor-council cities.

Notes

1. Charles Adrian, "Forms of Government in American History," in *The Municipal Year Book* (Washington, D.C.: International City Management Association, 1988), 3–11.

2. Tari Renner, "Municipal Election Processes: The Impact of Minority Representation," *Baseline Data Report*, vol. 19 no. 6 (Washington, D.C.: International City Management Association, November/December 1987), 1–2.

3. Chester Newland, "Council-Manager Government: Positive Alternative to Separation of Powers," *Public Management* (July 1985), 7–9.

4. For more information on the school of thought known as the politics-administration dichotomy see the turn-of-the-century writings of Woodrow Wilson, "The Study of Administration," *Political Science Quarterly*, vol. 2, no. 1 (June 1987); and Frank Goodnow, *Politics and Administration*, (New York: Russell and Russell, 1900).

5. Luther Gulick, "Political and Administrative Leadership," *Public Management* (November 1963), 243–247.

6. See research projects by James Svara including "Dichotomy and Duality: Reconceptualizing the Relationship between Policy and Administration in Council-Manager Cities," *Public Administration Review* 45 (January/February 1985), 221–232; and "The Complementary Roles of Officials in Council-

Manager Government," *The Municipal Year Book*, (Washington, D.C.: International City Management Association, 1988), 23–32.

7. Dr. Thomas Reed had a long and distinguished career in municipal government, serving as the first city manager in San Jose, California, and as a writer and professor of government. See Thomas Reed, "Trends in City Management," *Public Management*, (December 1955), 266–271; and "Manager versus Mayor," *National Municipal Review*, (July 1958), 325–334.

8. Robert P. Boynton, "The Council-Manager Plan: A Historic Perspective," *Public Management* (January 1983), 7–10.

9. For an overview of the council-manager plan see Richard Stillman, *The Rise of the City Manager*, (Albuquerque: University of New Mexico Press, 1974); R.J. Huntley and R.J. McDonald "Urban Managers: Organizational Preferences, Managerial Styles, and Social Policy Roles," *The Municipal Year Book* (Washington, D.C.: International City Management Association, 1975), 149–155; Harold A. Stone, Don K. Price, and Kathryn H. Stone, *City Manager Government in the United States* (Chicago: Public Administration Service, 1940).

10. See Richard Stillman, "City Manager — Professional Helping Hand or Political Hired Hand?" *Political Administration Review* 37 (November/December 1977), 659–670.

11. Eric Anderson, "Two Major Forms of Government: Two Types of Professional Management," *The Municipal Year Book*, Washington, D.C.: International City Management Association, 1989), 25–32.

12. The term *recognition* refers to a procedure that ICMA uses to formally identify those local governments that provide for a position of city manager or that provide for a position of overall general management according to criteria established by ICMA.

For additional information, see ICMA's *Who's Who in Local Government Management, 1989–1990*, (Washington, D.C.: International City Management Association, 1989), 322.

13. Service areas chosen for this analysis include economic development, public relations, budgeting and research, purchasing, personnel, risk management, planning, and contract administration.

14. See David Booth, *Council-Manager Government in Small Cities* (Washington, D.C.: International City Management Association, 1968) for elaboration on managing small communities.

CHAPTER 25

FRACTURED CITIES: WHEN POWER BECOMES FRAGMENTED

Rob Gurwitt

In the end, Larry Brown had little choice but to resign as city manager of Kansas City, Missouri. By late June, when he finally agreed to give up his office atop the city's oddly graceful, Depression-era skyscraper of a city hall, Brown was a man beset, openly mistrusted by the council and sniped at by employees. His imminent departure was a universal assumption within local political circles.

There are those in Kansas City who, in hindsight, trace Brown's downfall to his 1994 arrest for drunken driving, which they contend cost him the respect of city staff. Others point to his decisions last year to give his top aides large pay raises and to send them to California's Napa Valley for taxpayer-supported training sessions — steps that turned into public-relations nightmares. By April, when a city council majority lambasted his proposed budget and yanked funding from his efforts to transform city government, it was just a matter of time.

But the truth is that the seeds of Brown's departure were sown at the beginning, at the very moment he was hired. Never short on ambition, Brown wanted nothing less than to assert the authority of the city manager to run Kansas City government as he saw fit. Instead, encountering more and more resistance the harder he tried, Brown learned a painful and expensive lesson: Nobody runs Kansas City. And a complex array of political forces is organized to keep it that way.

Power rests everywhere within the community — in the corporate boardrooms, with neighborhood developers and community organizations, within city agencies, on appointed boards, with the city council, in the hands of the mayor and in the office of the city manager. Building consensus on any issue is a time-consuming, frustrating process, and it is made harder by a structure that deliberately impedes the clear-eyed exertion of political will. Yet, as Brown discovered, so many people have a vested interest in the status quo that — for a city manager, at least — trying to change this state of affairs may be impossible.

This is a schizophrenic moment in the political history of America's big cities. For many of them, even some that were once branded ungovernable, the 1990s have brought a restoration of managerial competence, symbolized by New York's attack on crime, Cleveland's downtown revival, Chicago's school reform crusade and Philadelphia's return from the brink of bankruptcy.

All of the surging cities of this decade have had leaders with the ability to articulate and then enforce their priorities. These may be, as in New York, Chicago and Philadelphia, strong mayors in both the structural and political sense. Or they may be, as in Phoenix, a dynamic and widely admired city manager working with an elected council. But, in every case, there is a palpable sense that someone is in charge, setting an agenda about what is

From *Governing*, Vol. 10, No. 12, September 1997. Published by Congressional Quarterly, Inc., Washington, D.C. Reprinted by permission of the author.

needed to make them attractive places to live and work.

Meanwhile, however, another set of cities, symbolized by Kansas City, Cincinnati, Miami and Dallas, among others, is stuck at the opposite end of the scale — mired in bickering, divided responsibility and long-standing political confusion. Nobody is in charge in these places. And it seems to take forever for anything to get done.

For the most part, these cities never fell quite as far as the Philadelphias and Clevelands of America. As a result, they have not been forced to look as hard at remaking local government. But, in the end, they will have no alternative. In the coming years, the struggle for urban viability will be hard enough, even under the best of circumstances. The fragmented cities will be at a profound disadvantage.

And they may finally be realizing it. In Kansas City, in the wake of Brown's resignation, popular but constitutionally weak Mayor Emanual Cleaver has begun talking about the need to give more authority to his successors. In Cincinnati, there have been nine attempts during the past decade to give the mayor more control, and another — with the quiet backing of the current mayor, Roxanne Qualls, and the city's business leadership — is in the works. Dallas, shocked by a decade of political incivility following generations of close-knit cooperation, is openly debating where it went wrong, and what sort of governmental structure it might need to set things right. The forces backing change in all of these cities seem to agree that, although there may be no one formula for success in urban government, there is a recipe for failure, and it is the absence of leadership.

At first glance, it might seem odd to include Kansas City anywhere near the top of the list of troubled American cities. The regional economy is doing just fine, with unemployment in the metropolitan area below 4 percent. The city itself has seen new employers — Gateway 2000 and Harley-Davidson among them — set up plants in town. According to U.S. Census Bureau estimates, Kansas City actually has grown in population since 1990 — although pretty much all of that

growth has been in the long-annexed rural and suburb-like reaches north of the Missouri River.

Mayor Cleaver has embarked on a revitalization effort that includes creating a jazz hall of fame and a Negro Leagues baseball museum. Several of the city's leading businessmen are hoping to launch a huge hotel and entertainment complex on a dormant parcel of downtown land. And a committee that draws from both sides of the Missouri-Kansas state line is overseeing the resurrection of Kansas City's famous beaux arts Union Station as a hands-on science center.

Still, beneath the glowing press releases, there is trouble. Kansas City faces the same disquieting trends as other depressed central cities. "Projections show an increase in the number of jobs in the core, but as a share of the region's jobs, Kansas City's will either not increase or will decline," says David Warm, of the Mid-America regional council. "Most of the jobs, wealth and people are locating at the edges of the region. So there is the same clear and continuing pattern of decline in the center, disinvestment in the inner-tier suburbs and rapid growth on the edges that you see elsewhere." In the competition with its suburbs, in other words, Kansas City is, at the moment, losing.

On the day he announced Larry Brown's resignation, Emanual Cleaver made it clear that there is another competition that weighs on him as well. Pressed by reporters about what he thought of a governmental structure that, in essence, makes him merely the most prominent member of the city council, Cleaver could not hold back his frustration. "Kansas City is now a big-league city," he said, "and when the mayor of the city sits around with the president and CEO of a major corporation trying to get them to relocate here, the mayor is at a disadvantage, because other mayors can cut the deal at the table. We are at a disadvantage in many instances when we are out competing."

The fact is, running Kansas City is mostly a matter of indirection. Mayors and city managers have to deal not only with a set of department heads who historically have had great room to pursue their own priorities, but also with circumstances that couldn't be better designed to water down their authority. The police are funded by the city but controlled by a state board. Libraries are under a separate board. Economic development, which is much of what Cleaver has been about in recent years, is under the control of the Economic Development Corp., which has become a sort of independent deal-maker for the city. The schools have been answerable to a federal court for 20 years, foster care services are in court hands as well, and the housing authority is in receivership. No one who wants to get things done in Kansas City, in other words, can do it directly.

As you might expect, many Kansas Citians have grown to like this state of affairs — it leaves each player within city government, along with those who try to affect it, with a fair degree of autonomy. It also means, though, that when their agendas differ, the city looks rudderless. "When communities have well-organized voices or a broad community ethic that's widely shared," says the head of one organization in Kansas City, "when there's a strong leader with clear ideas and directions, when there are well-organized plans and a well-organized and directed civic leadership that pursues those plans, that's when you get a healthy politics of ideas. Kansas City is not there at the moment.... The city is up for grabs."

In the year or so leading up to Brown's forced resignation, there were at least three distinct sets of priorities being laid out in city hall. Cleaver's had to do with bringing in new economic development, redeveloping Kansas City's historically black neighborhoods and tackling the issue of race relations head-on. The city council was focusing on how to pay for the city's infrastructure needs and shoring up basic services to residents. With all this going on, Brown was maneuvering to redesign the entire process by which Kansas City government worked. In retrospect, there was no way he could have succeeded.

In his defense, Brown was doing pretty much what the council had said it wanted when it hired him, back in 1993. Its members had asked for someone to bring Kansas City government in line with the movement to-

ward cost containment and quality service that other cities had been pursuing. "We wanted someone to take charge and run the city wisely and economically and efficiently," says George Blackwood, the council's mayor pro tem. "We said, 'We're out of control. Get good people, get the job done, let's create a lean, mean fighting machine.'"

Brown's response was a process he called "transformation." Part of his goal was to introduce the notions of customer service and efficient, responsive bureaucracy that have taken hold elsewhere. But he also set out to break down the barriers that, over the decades, had grown up among departments that had become accustomed to being treated as sovereign entities. Most important, Brown wanted to reestablish the city manager's authority over the day-to-day running of the organization. Over the years, not only had department heads grown accustomed to following their own lead but city council members also had grown accustomed to making requests directly of department heads and even mid-level managers. The result was a city organization in which the right and left hands often didn't keep track of each other.

Brown made every effort to deal with this problem. As it turned out, though, few of his efforts sat well with others in city hall. Although some departments and lower-level managers responded to the service-oriented freedom Brown offered them — the city's fire department being, perhaps, the leading example — others resisted; they found sympathetic ears on a council that already saw Brown cutting off its direct pipeline to city departments.

The council was especially vulnerable on this point because there was no real leadership pushing it to embrace the principles that "transformation" was supposed to instill; indeed, there was no particular leadership pushing it in any direction at all. A set of scandals during the past few years — 4 council members have been indicted on corruption charges — has created an ominous level of mistrust, turning the council into a set of 12 independent players who may come together around specific priorities — fixing the city's decaying infrastructure or backing neighborhood services — but otherwise prefer to be seen as individuals, not as a collective municipal leadership. "It is not an individual responsibility of each member to be responsible for the next," says Ken Bacchus, whose six-year tenure makes him one of the council's senior members.

Given those circumstances, council members' political legitimacy has rested, in large part, on their day-to-day involvement in city government; it was Brown's difficulty grasping the importance they placed on this that, more than anything else, undermined him. The budget he submitted to the city council this spring is a good example: It was essentially all text, a budget designed to get the council to think about policy without worrying about particular line-items. As a matter of theory, this should be all a council needs from a city manager in order to pass judgment on the general direction city government is headed. But as Cleaver points out, "Politics 101 is, Don't call the politicians stupid. His statement, as I interpreted it, was, 'You guys set policy, I'll worry about the rest.' Well, in 1997, politicians don't fade into the woodwork. That ain't going to happen anymore." When it became clear that Brown had no intention of setting aside his priorities in favor of the council's and the mayor's — that, indeed, there was no way to reconcile them — he left.

There are those in Cincinnati, too, who have become increasingly impatient with a political process that treats issues crucial to the city as though they were mice let loose among a swarm of cats. "I think that the city of Cincinnati is an essentially scandal-free, well-managed city with a work force of good, dedicated people," says Nick Vehr, a recently retired Republican councilman. "But ... things get mired down in endless political debate and a kind of bureaucratic morass that pounds them to a pulp before they can be implemented."

Cincinnati, too, is a council-manager city. Unlike Kansas City, however, its mayor isn't even elected separately. Instead, he or she is simply the council member who gets the most votes in the general election. Because no one actually runs for mayor, and because the mayor is no more powerful than any other member of the city council, there is very little political accountability in Cincinnati. The result, says Zane Miller, a political scientist at the University of Cincinnati, is an "absence of coherent leadership."

The city bounces from problem to problem," agrees John Fox, editor of *City Beat*, Cincinnati's local alternative weekly newspaper. "The bottom line is city government becomes a reactionary body rather than a proactive body that says, 'Here's our vision for where we're going in the next 10 years.'"

This is not necessarily for lack of trying. For two years, in fact, administrative staff worked with the council to develop a strategic planning process that was to produce a clear set of priorities on which the city manager could focus. In a series of sessions with the council, however, city hall's vision of the future became muddier, not clearer. Rather than establish a handful of priorities with a few "action steps" attached to each, council members decided they had dozens of priorities. The "strategic plan" sank under its own weight.

Visiting Cincinnati, one does not get a sense of a city at loose ends. Its long-neglected riverfront is about to become a new focus for city life as two sports stadiums — one for the football Bengals, the other for the baseball Reds — are built there. Main Street, which was pretty much derelict 10 years ago, now has become a restaurant- and bar-filled entertainment zone at night. Parts of the neighborhood known as Over-the-Rhine, which was essentially a ghetto sitting on downtown's heels, are rapidly being gentrified. A new department store is going up on a prime downtown parking lot that many had despaired would never be replaced. "If you look ahead 10 years," says Al Tuchfarber, director of the Institute for Policy Research at the University of Cincinnati, "you're going to see a very revitalized downtown and riverfront."

Yet, the good things that are taking place in Cincinnati are taking place more in spite of city government than because of it. The revitalization of Over-the-Rhine might have materialized years ago had the city not set up barriers to redevelopment there. The new department store on Fountain Square West took a decade to materialize because the council spent most of that decade squabbling over just how the land ought to be used.

Perhaps the most troubling example of the city's problems, though, is the stadium deal. Given a deadline by the Bengals to come up with a plan that would keep the team in town, the city — after much hair-tearing — essentially punted. The financing deal was finally put together by surrounding Hamilton County, which, with three county board members, can move much more quickly. In exchange, the county will own the stadiums. "It wasn't until we shifted authority to the county," Nick Vehr says, "that the sports franchises seriously began negotiating to stay in this town.... I think there's a general perception in this community that the ability to manage the future no longer resides, as it did in the past, in city hall."

There are, to be sure, plenty of people in both Kansas City and Cincinnati who believe that their cities are better off precisely because power is so fragmented. "The successful person negotiates coalitions and puts them together on a given issue," says one former Kansas City government staffer, "and that's not a bad thing. With coalition-building, there's some kind of consensus reached. Maybe it takes longer and demands more skill, but maybe the stuff that results is more durable."

It can also, of course, be argued that forceful leadership is hardly a panacea for American cities. If it were, neither Detroit under Coleman Young nor Washington, D.C., under Marion Barry would have fallen into the disrepair both cities now struggle against.

But for a much larger number of cities these days, it is fractured leadership — not abused personal power — that constitutes the main political problem. In Miami, for instance, the fiscal insolvency and corrupt practices of its former city manager and finance director flourished in no small part because each major player in city government was content to go his own way — the manager pursued his own political goals, each city commissioner was wrapped up in his own pursuits, the finance director was given a free hand, and the business community and many onlookers were

convinced that the city itself did not matter. There was, simply put, no one in charge who cared about Miami as a whole.

Dallas, meanwhile, has been an exhibit of fragmentation for the entire decade of the 1990s. Once, it was a prime example of the opposite: a place where decisive mayors and city managers worked quietly and efficiently with a single-minded business establishment to set clear community priorities. Thirty years ago, when Mayor Erik Jonsson felt he needed a blueprint for long-term urban planning, he simply rounded up 80 civic leaders, spirited them off to a county club for a weekend and returned with a short list of major goals for the 1970s — most of which were implemented.

But that Dallas power structure eventually succumbed to its own weaknesses. It was so tightly controlled, so exclusive and so overwhelmingly affluent, male and white that it bred long-standing resentments among the groups in town that felt left out of its processes. When the establishment expired, it set in motion a long period of chaos during which the newly enfranchised elements jostled for power without paying much attention to the interests of the community as a whole.

In 1991, under court pressure, Dallas switched from a council whose members were elected at-large to a district-by-district system. Ever since then, the council's deliberations have been one long bout of factionalism — ethnic, ideological and geographic. Presided over by a mayor with little formal power, the council has drifted from one crisis to another.

Recently, some of the tumult on the council has quieted down amid Mayor Ron Kirk's efforts to build a consensus around long-term plans for the city. At the same time, however, the school board threatens to explode under the pressure of racial feuding — for the most part between African-Americans and Hispanics — and much of the rest of the city's political leadership is finding it difficult to avoid being dragged into that battle.

It may be too much to say that all fragmented cities are alike these days, but all of them seem to be a little like Dallas, Cincinnati and Kansas City: so enmeshed in rivalries and personal politics that they are having trouble living up to their potential — or even seeing clearly just what that potential might be. If they are to remain competitive when it comes to attracting businesses, rebuilding the public schools and drawing middle-class residents back to their neighborhoods, they somehow need to rely upon leaders who can help them coalesce around coherent visions of where they're going. Such people clearly exist in all of these cities; the only question is whether they will be allowed to emerge.

"Leaders shackled by unreasonable restrictions are forced to engage in compromises and deal-making that slows forward movement and inhibits development of wide-ranging vision," the editor of the *Kansas City Star*'s editorial page wrote not long ago, in a commentary that just as easily could have been applied to Cincinnati and any number of other places casting about for direction these days. "The way Kansas City's government now works," Rich Hood wrote, "there are so many safeguards built in to prevent dramatic leadership (or risky gambles that might not pay off) that we too frequently witness government by paralysis."

CHAPTER 26

WHAT TO DO WHEN REFORMED GOVERNMENT DOESN'T WORK

Gerald E. Newfarmer

Cincinnati, Ohio: a city routinely associated with quality local government, and an early leader in the Progressive reform movement. How could it be that its political workings had become so dysfunctional as to inspire a serious proposal to switch back to pre-reform conditions by reinstituting a mayor-council structure? On August 30, 1995, the citizens of Cincinnati voted on a proposal to change the structure of their city government from the council-manager plan to the strong mayor plan. That such a proposal would even make it to the ballot in a city with Cincinnati's history of good government was cause for grave concern among those who favor the council-manager plan as the epitome of progressive, reformed local government.

The Background

Cincinnati enjoys a long tradition of good government. In 1926, after decades of political bossism, a citizens group known as the Charter Committee decided enough was enough. They drafted a new city charter adopting the council-manager form of local government to rid the city of its strong mayor form of government. Its adoption marked the beginning of a 70-year period during which Cincinnati was widely recognized as having clean, good government.

Under the city charter, the nine-member city council appoints and supervises the professional city manager, who serves as the chief executive of the municipal corporation. The entire council is elected every two years in a single election, at-large and without primaries, ostensibly on a non-partisan basis. Anyone interested in serving on the council can run; the nine candidates receiving the most votes are elected and the top vote-getter among them is elected mayor. While the mayor is the presiding officer of the council — and is regarded as the political leader of the city — the mayor has no more power on the council than any of the other eight members.

Although the ballot is non-partisan, elections in Cincinnati are thoroughly "partisan." Both the Democrats and the Republicans run slates of candidates for city council, as does the Charter Committee.[1] For years the council has had representatives of all three groups, although in recent years the representation of the Charter Committee has declined to a single member. In recent years, council seats are held by full-time politicians — persons whose primary occupation is elective office.

The Cincinnati political scene has some other important features. Since the mayor and members of the council are elected in a field race, it is not possible to run directly for the office of mayor or against any individual member of council. Thus, there is no individual electoral accountability. If an incumbent mayor or council member performs

From *National Civic Review,* Vol. 84, No. 4, Fall-Winter 1995. Published by the National Civic League, Denver, Colorado. Reprinted with permission of the publisher.

poorly, it is not possible to challenge that person directly. One can only run for the council at-large.

Unlike many cities in America without enthusiastic leadership from the business community, Cincinnati has always enjoyed the active engagement of private sector leaders in civic affairs. The Cincinnati Business Committee provided the impetus for reform of the city's maintenance of its public works infrastructure (led by John Smale, then CEO of Procter and Gamble) and of the public schools (led by Clem Buenger, then CEO of Fifth Third Bank), two major areas of concern regarding the quality of government services. But in spite of its effectiveness in providing leadership to achieve these reforms, the business community does not have meaningful representation on the city council.

Another significant political feature is that Cincinnati is located within a media market of 1.7 million people. Given its size, politicians must become known to the public through media attention (wholesale politics), rather than through the one-on-one contact that is characteristic of a small community (retail politics). Under normal circumstances, this means politicians must vie for media attention by providing leadership in resolving issues; when every member of council must compete in a field race with every other member of council for election every two years, the competition for media attention is severe.

When this competition is coupled with an intensely partisan framework, the result is council meetings that have, as their primary defining characteristic, competition among members for the political edge and public notice. The city council is charitably described as "fractious"; council meetings may be uncharitably — but accurately — described as political food fights.

Stewarding Reform

In recent years, recognition that the city council needed reform became so widespread as to constitute a community consensus. A Charter Review Committee was launched by the heads of the three political parties in July

of 1994, chaired by Dr. Henry Winkler, President-Emeritus of the University of Cincinnati. The Charter Review Committee met frequently over the ensuing ten months, but had difficulty agreeing on proposals to report out, since it was just as divided as the partisan environment that had created it.

On April 28, while the Charter Review Committee was still trying to develop a consensus, the two leading CEOs of Cincinnati's largest businesses held a press conference. Reflecting the leadership of the 26 top Cincinnati-area companies, the Cincinnati Business Committee (CBC), they announced the business community's intention to circulate initiative petitions to place a proposed charter change on the ballot.

The ballot proposal provided for significant changes to the existing structure. The mayor and all council members would be elected for four-year, rather than two-year terms, with the mayor directly elected and the nine-member council elected at-large. The mayor, rather than the city manager, would be the chief executive, but would appoint a city manager who would serve at his pleasure. The mayor would no longer sit as a member of council, and would have veto power over the council's legislative acts subject to a six-vote override. Except for its power to appoint and oversee the city manager, the council retained all of its legislative authority. In short, what was proposed was the classic mayor-council form of government.

The Charter Review Committee finally submitted its package of proposals to the council for consideration on May 9. It called for the mayor to be assigned limited additional power to lead the city council, and for the direct election of the mayor by majority vote (the CBC proposal required only a plurality). The Committee's proposal agreed with the CBC proposal that the council members should serve four-year, staggered terms, but differed in that it proposed repeal of the recently adopted concept of term limits.

As the campaign battle lines were forming, Mayor Roxanne Qualls announced another proposal to circulate petitions and place an alternative plan on the ballot.[2] The Qualls proposal retained the council-manager form, but strengthened the ability of the mayor to lead the city council by giving the mayor the power to designate the vice mayor and the chairs of council committees. Her proposal, like the CBC initiative, lengthened council terms to four years and retained the concept of term limits, a reform adopted by the voters in 1991. But unlike both the CBC and Charter Committee proposals, Qualls's plan curiously would not stagger the terms of council members. The Cincinnati *Post* quickly announced its editorial support for the mayor's approach, excepting the failure to stagger council terms, of which, the *Post* said interestingly, "This, we fear, would perpetuate the backbiting and non-stop search for media attention."[3]

The Campaign

On June 7, after having been presented with the successful initiative petition, the city council called a special election (as required by law), which it scheduled for August 30, 1995.[4]

Though the city's many political factions could not agree on an alternative to the existing system — or even the CBC's strong mayor proposal — they could agree that the latter, designated by the Board of Elections as Issue One, was not the solution. The coalition opposed to the proposal included the Democratic Party, the Charter Committee, the AFL-CIO, League of Women Voters, and the city's African-American and women's organizations. Only the Republican Party and the Chamber of Commerce took positions in support of the CBC proposal.

The proponents argued that it was time to end the fractiousness at city hall by reorganizing to give administrative and executive powers to a strong, directly elected — and presumably more accountable — mayor. As the Cincinnati *Enquirer* editorialized in support of the proposal:

> The system is broken. City council is a dysfunctional regional joke, in deep denial. The best argument for change is council itself: Given two years to come up with its own Charter reforms ... city council dumped the issue on a committee [and] failed to agree on any proposals.... It has been a sorry spectacle.[5]

Proponents reasoned that the current system lacks the accountability that a directly elected mayor affords. The "Executive Mayor" would be able to function unfettered by council interference. Council's role would be further limited by the mayor's power to veto council acts. Again, from the *Enquirer* editorial:

> Take a look at what we have: Chronic bickering has crippled the mayor; nine council members act like pretender presidents; there is no single voice of leadership. A veto will let the mayor set the agenda that the voters have chosen. There will be one leader who is clearly accountable....[6]

Opponents, on the other hand, argued that the Issue One cure was worse than the disease. It would remove the mayor from the city council and the professional city manager from the chief executive role. Since the problem with the current system was a fractious, ineffective city council, removal of the mayor from membership on the council, they argued, would weaken rather than strengthen the legislative body. Opponents also warned that shifting the executive responsibility from a professional manager to a political leader would be sure to result in a politicized city work force.

The defining moment of the campaign came on August 19, less than two weeks before the election, when the Cincinnati *Post* reported the campaign contribution filings on record with the Hamilton County Board of Elections. The *Post* revealed that $254,682 (later to be increased to $270,000) had been donated to finance the Issue One campaign, all from Cincinnati corporations in the CBC.

Shortly thereafter, with the sponsorship of the International City/County Management Association (ICMA), several current and former city managers visited Cincinnati to participate in a League of Women Voters seminar about the structure of local government. They pointed out that the city manager in the Issue One proposal was one in title only and no longer retained the characteristics of a recognized council-manager government. As former Dallas City Manager Jan Hart noted, Issue One "...fixes the executive branch which is not broken, but does not fix the legislative branch, which is."[7]

In their election eve recommendations to voters, the city's two newspapers voiced different opinions, with the Cincinnati *Enquirer* editorializing in favor of Issue One, and the Cincinnati *Post* against. On Wednesday, August 30, as Cincinnatians went to the polls, the County Board of Elections was predicting a low, 20 percent voter turnout for the single-issue special election. When the polls had closed, however, an unexpected 26 percent of the city's registered voters had voted to resoundingly defeat Issue One, with a 64 percent vote against the proposal.

Analysis and Implications for Good Government

Issue One failed primarily for two reasons, as acknowledged editorially by the *Enquirer* a few days after the election.[8] It was perceived as a power grab by big-money business interests and it went too far by eliminating the council-manager form of government, a system that Cincinnatians hold in high regard. The extreme, over-reaching character of Issue One had managed to turn a two-to-one margin in favor of direct election of the mayor into a two-to-one defeat in four short months.[9]

The success of the campaign against the proposal was due to the ability of the opponents to coalesce in opposition, in spite of their inability to agree on an alternative to the CBC proposal. In the "retail politics" of a special election, with its limited turnout, only those who really care about an issue will make the effort to go to the polls. Since the majority of the Cincinnati electorate, those in the middle, would not turn out to vote, the expensive media campaign approach, or "wholesale politics," was largely wasted. The one-on-one, get-out-the-vote effort was predictably decisive.

There were other factors that led to the failure of the business community's effort to reform Cincinnati city government. The poorly crafted proposal reflected a serious misunderstanding of the role of the legislature in local government structure and gave opponents numerous opportunities to criticize Issue One.

Indeed, perhaps one of the more unfortunate results of the election is that it has been widely interpreted as a rejection of the business community's involvement in the politics of the city. Cincinnati has benefited in a way that most cities would envy from an active, involved business community, as noted above. It is too bad that this attempt at reform was undertaken without more advance consultation about the probable consequences.

The council-manager form of government does have an Achilles' heel that this Cincinnati experience demonstrates: the dysfunctional city council. City councils work together poorly when the partisan or personal self-interests of individual politicians become the principal determinants of behavior. The usual early symptoms of this malady are council members engaging in staff-bashing (being critical of their own employees), or routinely denigrating each other in their desperate attempts to secure a political advantage.

As in Cincinnati, the election system itself can contribute to the problem, where every council member is pitted against every other member of council in political competition. The "9-X,"[10] at-large, election system, with its absence of individual accountability for elected officials, guarantees political bickering and fractiousness. As noted by the Cincinnati *Post*, this circumstance is exacerbated in a media-driven political environment, where politicians must scramble for media attention.

When the council is successful in enacting policy for the municipal corporation and supporting its professional staff in executing that policy, the council-manager form of government works well. As in everything, success starts at the top, in this case, the council. But if the legislative body becomes dysfunctional, the solution must be to introduce a source of discipline within the legislative body, and that can only be done by empowering the mayor to provide leadership for the council. That is the point that was misunderstood by this most recent effort by the business community to provide reform leadership in Cincinnati.

Conclusion

The structure of local government and the power assigned to its leaders is important, but it is also important that it be operated well by people of ability and goodwill. In addressing the needs for structural change, the part that is broken should be the part that gets fixed. Without detracting from professional management, a source of strength in the council-manager plan, it is possible to empower the mayor to provide leadership to the city council. Then, together, city leaders can work to make city government successful, on behalf of the citizens they serve.

Notes

1. The Charter Committee disdains being referred to as a "party," but within the partisan context of Cincinnati politics is generally regarded as the third party, in addition to the Democrats and Republicans.

2. This move appeared to be taken with the knowledge that six votes could not be obtained on a divided council to submit the Charter Review Committee's recommendations to the voters.

3. Cincinnati *Post*, "Sensible Reform at City Hall," 9 June 1995.

4. Given the basic nature of the political battle being waged, it was not surprising that a second front of the battle was in the courts. There were a number of suits filed, but the most significant were over the date of the election, the council's ministerial responsibility to submit the proposal for a vote, and the number of signatures required for a valid initiative petition. Those battles went up and down the Ohio judicial system during the months preceding the election, with no net effect on the political process or outcome.

5. Cincinnati *Enquirer*, "Issue 1: Yes," 29 August 1995 (editorial).

6. Ibid.

7. Cincinnati *Post*, "Managers: Issue 1 fixes what isn't broke," 24 August 1995.

8. Cincinnati *Enquirer*, "Try again," 3 September 1995 (editorial).

9. Cincinnati *Enquirer*, "CEOs start drive for direct vote on mayor," 29 April 1995. The news story stated: "Announcement ... comes on the heels of an independent *Enquirer* poll that reflects strong dissatisfaction among Cincinnati residents about the system of electing mayors and council, in general. Sixty-eight percent said the city should switch to direct election of the mayor."

Issue One was defeated, of course, with 64 percent of the vote.

10. Cincinnati's at-large election system is dubbed "9-X" because voters mark their ballots with an X next to the nine individuals they wish to serve on the council. Under the current plan, the council member receiving the most votes in the at-large field is declared mayor.

CHAPTER 27

WRITING HOME-RULE
CHARTERS

Susan B. Hannah

Increased charter revision activity in Michigan presents a timely opportunity to study the process of local constitution-making or "writing your own government" as one commissioner put it. Michigan was the seventh state in the Union to adopt the principle of home rule. Under provisions of the 1908 Constitution and the Home Rule Cities and Villages Acts of 1909, the citizens of every Michigan city and village enjoy broad "power and authority to frame, adopt, and amend its charter."[1] The 1963 Constitution further declared the meaning of home rule "shall be liberally construed" in the citizens' favor.[2]

As a result of these generous provisions, all but one of Michigan's 266 municipalities and 48 villages have adopted home-rule charters. Every year some 20 to 30 communities are engaged in studying, developing, rewriting, revising, or amending their charters to fit changes in state law and judicial opinions and to respond to shifts in social, economic and political circumstances.[3]

To learn more about the process of "writing your own government," the Michigan Municipal League (MML) and the Michigan Association of Municipal Attorneys (MAMA) sponsored a study of all elected charter commissions and appointed charter-study committees active in 1992. Resulting information about who serves on commissions, how commissions operate, and what issues they address were summarized in *Charter Revision Activity*

in Michigan, published by the Michigan Municipal League Foundation in 1993.[4]

The present study expands on the 1992 survey by focusing on the issue of success: Which of the charter commissions went on to see their proposals adopted by the voters and which did not? What are the differences in successful and unsuccessful charter-revision efforts? Does the nature of the community matter? The characteristics of the commissions? The way the commissions go about their work? The issues they consider? Answers to these questions will contribute to an improved understanding of the dynamics of local constitution writing and its relationship to the political life of the community.

A growing collection of case studies on municipal charter reform suggests that the unique political history of the city, the goals of revision, timing, and the community's "mood about change" affect the process and content of charter revision.[5] These studies confirm conventional wisdom that a city's size, political history, culture, and socio-economic characteristics are closely related to its governmental structure.[6]

Mediated by culture and leadership, changes in environment have often meant changes in governmental structure. In a study of charter amendments in Michigan cities which had experienced significant population growth and decline, this author previously found that the greater the shift in population,

Originally published as "Writing Home-Rule Charters in Michigan," *National Civic Review*, Vol. 84, No. 2, Spring 1995. Published by the National Civic League, Denver, Colorado. Reprinted with permission of the publisher.

the greater the change in government structure.[7] More precisely, Maser's national study of charter-revision–tied structural reforms intended to enhance representation to increases in the proportion of the non-white population.[8] Benjamin and Mauro conclude that in contrast to classical reform, these contemporary initiatives aim for greater democracy rather than greater efficiency.[9]

Research on the consequences of charter reform shows that changes in the structure of local government has altered who gets elected to city councils and how government operates, but has not necessarily influenced municipal policy outcomes.[10] There is also evidence that the new wave of charter writing is blurring the clear distinctions between the mayor-council and council-manager forms under concurrent demands for political leadership, professional management and representative governance. City managers make room for directly elected mayors in reformed cities under pressure for political leadership; strong mayors appoint CAO's to provide professional management expertise; councils increase their supervision of professional managers to assure accountability; and citizens adopt single-member districts and partisan elections or institute residence requirements to enhance representation.[11]

The Charter-Writing Process in Michigan

Michigan's Home Rule Cities Act specifies the process for developing and amending a charter and establishes mandatory, permissive and prohibited municipal powers and functions. The Act requires that each home-rule city be a body corporate, have a legislative body, a mayor, a clerk, a treasurer, and an assessor. Citizens may decide how to elect the legislative body, whether by wards, at-large, or a combination. They may choose to select the mayor or any other officer by election or by appointment. Elections may be partisan or non-partisan and nominations may be by primary election, petition, affidavit, or convention. The charter establishes the administrative structure of the city and the qualifications,

duties and compensation of its officers. Other required provisions address tax rates, taxing procedures, ordinance adoption, accounting systems, and public records.

The Act also includes an extensive list of permissive provisions concerning city powers, administrative structure and council rules, and establishes the rules for incorporation, consolidation and annexation. Final provisions of the Act spell out the procedure for charter commission selection and operation and for the adoption and amendment of charters.[12]

To initiate the process, the electors of a city or village must first vote upon whether or not to revise or, following state law regarding incorporation, write an initial charter. If the vote is positive, citizens then elect nine (five for a village) charter commissioners (often the resolution vote and the election occur simultaneously), who have three years to propose a charter. The proposed charter must be reviewed by the attorney general, acting for the governor, and submitted to the voters for approval. Cities sometimes begin with a charter study committee, appointed by the mayor or city council, to explore the need for charter adoption or revision. The committee's recommendation then becomes the basis for the initial ballot resolution on revision.

1991 Charter Commission Survey Results

The large majority of the charter commission members who responded to the 1992 MML-MAMA survey were white, middle-aged, well educated males. They earned middle- to upper-middle class incomes as professionals or managers and were long-time community activists and home owners. Retirees made up a significant portion of commission membership in many cities. Commissioners were less diverse, better educated and more highly paid than the citizens they represented.

In general, commission members were satisfied that legal requirements regarding commission size and time allotment were adequate for the task. Most commissions adopted their own rules, met twice a month, worked as a committee of the whole, received no compensation, and had little or no funding to support their work. As a result, commissioners depended on themselves or city staff for research, drafting and clerical support. The primary research resources were surveys of other cities, the National Civic League's *Model City Charter* and state-specific materials provided by the Michigan Municipal League.

Commissioners expressed concern about the lack of public interest and involvement in charter development, although commissions varied in the degree of effort they made to solicit community participation. Few commissions actually campaigned during the charter referendum and the support of city officials and employees appeared to be important for adoption. Commissions varied significantly in the degree of conflict or controversy they experienced.

The most frequently discussed charter issues concerned the structure of local government, its officers and their powers. Selection issues — term length, residency requirements, council selection, advisory board appointment — were rated next. The third set of issues were related to city finances and administrative operations. "Newer" ideas, such as sunset provisions and ethics codes, were least discussed.

The great majority of charter-review commissioners felt positively about their charter-writing experiences and believed that it was educational and rewarding.

Comparison of Successful and Unsuccessful Commissions

Thirteen of the 20 study commissions (65 percent) were successful in seeing the charter they had written approved by voters in a special election as required by the Home Rule Cities Act.[13] Seven (35 percent) were unsuccessful — either their proposed charters were voted down or never reached the referendum stage. To compare their work, the responses were sorted by city and supplemented with demographic information from the 1990 census. This study examines the demographic

characteristics of the cities involved, the characteristics of the commissioners, the nature of commission operations, and the charter issues under discussion.

Community Characteristics. Interestingly, the demographic characteristics of the community do not appear to be related to charter-revision success. Neither the size of the city, its unemployment rate, percentage of minority residents, degree of population change, nor median education level appear to affect the failure or success of charter revision.

Commission Characteristics. Of the variables describing the characteristics of the charter commissioners themselves, only the self-reported evaluation of the experience appears to distinguish between successful and unsuccessful commissions. The median levels of commission members' education, income or political and community involvement were not related to a successful outcome. Commissioners whose work was eventually adopted by the voters, however, did offer much more positive evaluations of the entire charter-writing experience. These results are all the more striking since the survey was distributed before most charter referenda were completed.

Commission Operations. Commission success is also related to commission operations. Commissioners on successful commissions rated their staff support, leadership and internal operations much more positively than did commissioners whose proposals eventually failed. Successful commissions also experienced much less conflict. Members of both types of commissions rated the level of public input as unsatisfactory, although there was no difference in their efforts to solicit community participation.

Issues. Structural issues such as form of government or mayoral and council powers clearly distinguished successful from unsuccessful commissions. Commissions that took on these core structural and leadership issues were much more likely to be unsuccessful than those focusing on mere operational provisions. This study also compares the major topics discussed by successful commissions with those discussed by commissions that were not.

Content of charter reform. Of the 13 successful commissions, 4 had proposed significant reforms: 2 to a council-manager form from a strong mayor, 1 the reverse, and 1 from village to city status (which was only narrowly approved). Two others adopted term limits for their mayor and council positions and one changed from elected to appointed clerk and treasurer positions (also only narrowly approved). The remaining revisions consisted largely of updates to bring the charter into conformance with state law or improvements in administrative operations (increasing purchasing limits, spelling out administrative officers).

By comparison, all but one of the seven unsuccessful commissions had proposed major structural or financial change. One proposed changing to a council-manager form (only 200 out of 5,300 registered voters even voted); another proposed moving in the opposite direction to a strong mayor. One wanted to strengthen the manager's role over department head appointments, while another proposed to check the manager by changing to a directly elected mayor. Another proposed raising the tax limit. One commission did not finish its work within the three-year limit, and for another this was the second defeat in a row. Only one unsuccessful commission reported that its revisions consisted largely of updates.

Conclusion

Charter writing in Michigan is carried out by a familiar political elite and successful revisions are more incremental than radical. Successful commissions take on relatively minor revision issues, have smooth internal operations, and rate their experience very positively. Unsuccessful commissions address core issues of structure and power, endure greater conflict, rate staff support, leadership and internal operations less highly, and are less positive about their overall charter-writing experience.

Other studies have shown the relationship between significant structural revision and the socio-political environment: the greater the shift in these environmental and leadership factors, the greater the likelihood of structural reform. The results here help explain why.

Working in relative isolation and with little financial or staff support, the political elites who write new charters face significant obstacles if they propose radical change in the status quo. To be successful, charter commissioners must make sure there is a compelling and widely accepted reason for whatever changes they propose. Success is more likely if the changes are incremental, staff support strong, internal operations smooth, and conflict limited. The more radical the proposal, the weaker the internal operations, the less the staff support and the greater the conflict, the more likely the charter-revision effort will fail.

Notes

1. CL 1948 #117.4j, MSA 5.2083 (3).

2. *Michigan Constitution*, Article VII, Section 21 (1963).

3. W.L. Steude, General Counsel, Michigan Municipal League, "Home Rule in Michigan: Why Charters Are Important," a paper presented at the meeting of the Michigan Public Management Institute, Lansing, May 1993; updated in a report to the League's Charter Focus Group, Ann Arbor, January 1995.

4. S.B. Hannah, *Charter Revision Activity in Michigan* (Ann Arbor: Michigan Municipal League Foundation, 1993).

5. For example, for New York City, see E. Lane, "The Practical Lessons of Charter Reform," *Proceedings of the Academy of Political Science* 37 (1989), pp. 31–44; for Illinois, see J.M. Banovetz and T.W. Kelty, *Home Rule in Illinois* (Springfield: Illinois Issues, 1987); for Lafayette Parish, see M.W. Mallory, "Home Rule in Lafayette Parish: A New Beginning," *National Civic Review* 73 (1984), pp. 556–570, 574; for Maine, see R. Josephson and G. Herman, "Municipal Charters: A Comparative Analysis of 75 Maine Charters," *Maine Townsman*, August 1992, pp. 5–15; and for Syracuse, see J.M. Harkin, "Structural Change and Municipal Government: The Syracuse Case," *State and Local Government Review* 15 (1983), pp. 3–9.

6. C.R. Adrian, "Forms of City Government in American History," *Municipal Year Book* (Washington, D.C.: International City Management Association, 1988).

7. S.B. Hannah "Checks and Balances in Local Government: City Charter Amendments and Revisions in Michigan, 1960–1985," *Journal of Urban Affairs* 9 (1987), pp. 337–353.

8. S.M. Maser, "Demographic Factors Affecting Constitutional Decisions: The Case of Municipal Charters," *Public Choice* 47 (1985), pp. 121–162. See also Maser's more recent paper, "Analyzing Constitutions

as Relational Contracts or Why People Negotiate Procedural Safeguards in Municipal Charters," presented at the Midwest Political Science Association Meetings, Chicago, April 1994.

9. G. Benjamin and F.J. Mauro, "The Reemergence of Municipal Reform," *Proceedings of the Academy of Political Science* 37 (1989), pp. 1–15.

10. For the impact of structure on representation, see W. Welch and T. Bledsoe, *Urban Reform and Its Consequences* (Chicago: University of Chicago Press, 1988); for impact on operations see J.H. Svara, *Official Leadership in the City* (New York: Oxford University Press, 1990); for impact on outcomes see T.N. Clark, *City Money: Political Processes, Fiscal Strain, and Retrenchment* (New York: Columbia University Press, 1983), K. Hayes and S. Chang, "The Relative Efficiency of City Manager and Mayor Council Forms of Government," *Southern Economic Journal* 57 (1990), pp. 167–177, and T.R. Sass, "The Choice of Municipal Government Structure and Public Expenditures," *Public Choice* 71 (1991), pp. 71–87.

11. J.M. Banovetz, "City Managers: Will They Reject Policy Leadership?" *Public Productivity and Management Review* XVII (1994), pp. 313–324.

12. D. Morris, *The Nature and Purpose of a Home Rule City Charter* (Detroit: Citizens Research Council in Michigan, 1971). Updated by W.L. Steude and D.C. Matsen in *The Nature and Purpose of a Home Rule City Charter*, Report No. 311 (Ann Arbor: Michigan Municipal League and Detroit: Citizens Research Council of Michigan, 1993).

13. Note that 2 of the 13 won by narrow margins.

CHAPTER 28

THE BENEFITS OF THE COUNCIL-MANAGER PLAN

Betsy D. Sherman

Opponents of the council-manager plan argue that this system of government does not work in rapidly growing local governments like Toledo. The League asked managers from larger jurisdictions in the United States to participate in this press conference and to explain how the plan works successfully in their communities.[1] Copies of population data from several cities in the United States, with populations similar to Toledo and governed under the C-M plan, are available through ICMA.

The League has thoroughly studied alternative forms of local government, and it continues to strongly believe that the council-manager form works the best. It believes that the council-manager form ensures a competent and professionally managed local government, without the patronage and favors to special interests that can be found in the more political strong mayor or executive-mayor-council form of government.

Participants at this forum include Bill Hansell, executive director of the International City Management Association (ICMA); Louis Fox, city manager, San Antonio, Texas; Scott Johnson, city manager, Cincinnati, Ohio; Richard Knight, city manager, Dallas, Texas; and David Olson, city manager, Kansas City, Missouri.

Opening Statement from Bill Hansell

ICMA appreciates the invitation of the League and the opportunity to come to Toledo to discuss the merits of the council-manager plan.

The individuals participating in this press conference share the beliefs of the people who work for local government in this country and who make communities work. While professional management and competence can exist in other systems, we believe that the best system of local government organization in terms of efficiency, effectiveness, and political leadership is the council-manager form of government.

Alexander Pope, a quaint English satirist from many centuries ago, once penned an interesting and pertinent couplet. He said, "For forms of government, let fools contest; whatever is administered best is best." Under that test, the council-manager system wins hands down, because it is almost never challenged on the basis of competence in the delivery of services and excellence in the administration of government — the programs, the services, and the facilities that are required for the citizens. It is challenged on the issue of political leadership, and I have three points to make on this issue.

The council-manager system, which was designed at the turn of the century to fight

From *Responsive Local Government*, November 1988. Published by the International City/County Management Association, Washington, D.C. Reprinted with permission of the publisher.

corruption in local government, had as one of its basic tenets that it would open access to political power to all citizens, regardless of economic means, regardless of political affiliation. Any citizen would have the ability not only to run for positions of political power, but also to effectively participate as a member of an elected governing body, regardless of whether he or she was a friend of the mayor, was in the right political party, had a lot of money, or had particular influential supporters behind him or her.

The council-manager system — with political power concentrated in the council, and with each member of the council having an equal vote and equal opportunity to influence the direction of the community — is the system that gives and ensures open access. Not everybody could run for the position of an elected executive. Not everyone would feel qualified. Many professional people who might bring competent, excellent service to local government through a council would not be able to divert time from their own careers or professions to be elected executives. But all could participate equally and openly as members of a council.

The second point I would make is that really two systems of government are under discussion here. The first is the council-manager system, and the emphasis is deliberately on the first word *council*— the group chosen through representative democracy to govern the city in a collegial and cooperative way. The second is the mayor-council system. And the emphasis again should be on the first word *mayor*.

Under the mayor-council system, if in fact the pejorative adjective "strong" is to be used for the mayor, then you should use the word "weak" for the council, because political power is concentrated very heavily in one single individual. It is a system that does not have a commitment to a representative system of democracy, where a group of citizens is elected as a governing body and asked to work together to represent all segments of a community. Instead, political power is focused in the mayor. And that is done by taking much of that power from the elected council. A "strong" mayor's executive authority or power

is very different from that of a manager. Local government managers have virtually no power. They are hired by and responsible to a council and can be fired any time for any reason by a majority vote of that council. Unlike mayors, they are not in office for any set term. There is no political power.

The third point that I would make is in the area or question of leadership. Leadership in every community is clearly essential in terms of a sense of direction, a sense of prioritization. But I don't think leadership is exclusive to any particular structure of government. It has to do as much with the individuals who run for, compete for, and are elected to office as it does with any structure of government. Maybe one way of judging that leadership might be to ask or look at what peers of elected officials say of one another in regard to leadership. At this time, every officer of the National League of Cities, which is the organization representing city government and its elected officials in this country, is in a council-manager city. These include, for example, Terry Goddard, mayor of Phoenix, Arizona, and Pamela Plum, vice mayor of Portland, Maine.

Question: Would Mr. Fox and Mr. Johnson tell us why the city-manager form of government, in their opinion, is the best form of government over the strong mayor?

Fox: As Bill mentioned, it is the council-manager form of government, not the city manager form of government. In my community of San Antonio, a minority city that is 56 percent Hispanic, 8 percent black, and the balance Anglo, the council concluded that the council was strongest under the council-manager form of government. In other words, representative government worked best with the administrative responsibilities delegated by charter to the manager so that the manager treated each district and each representative equally.

Our mayor, who has been considered one of the best mayors in the country, is a strong advocate of this form of government. He knows, as a directly elected mayor, that he has incredible responsibilities for the political dynamics of the city. He is not bothered or bogged down by problems in the police department or garbage collection or street maintenance. That is my job. As Bill mentioned, I am instantaneously accountable for that. Somebody said, "Well, you never ran for office." I run every day. Every time the city council meets, they can fire me just like that.

Question: So without the district plan, would the form of government have been just as effective?

Fox: I think so, although I believe our community was moving toward a districting system at that time. The council-manager system has been in place since 1952 in San Antonio, and I think it has worked very effectively.

Question: In Toledo, we don't have a district plan.

Fox: I understand that. Many cities are not operated under a district form of government. People often misunderstand that issue and confuse it with the council-manager form of government. Frustrations in a community can seem to relate to the lack of district representation. If the community wants district representation, this issue should be addressed whether or not there is a manager.

Hansell: I might add that 57 percent of council-manager communities in the United States elect their councils either by district or by a combination of district and at-large. So as Lou points out, it is very compatible with the council-manager system of government.

Johnson: You asked for my response, too, and I would say that Cincinnati is a cosmopolitan city for its size. It contains high-income people; it contains low-income people. It has a large minority population. It has managed through use of the council-manager plan to provide representation for all of those groups. It has done so effectively, although, like Toledo, Cincinnati has at-large elections. We managed through that system to elect minority candidates very early in the city's history. Very early we had a woman mayor, very early we had black representatives.

This has also been a system that provided services to the public effectively and efficiently. That is its forte. It has also provided the kind of leadership the community has expected. Cincinnati, almost uniquely among cities in this part of the country, has been able to have steady, solid economic growth. This has been true even under circumstances like those last year in which two of our Fortune 500 companies were in play in the takeover game; one succumbed and one escaped. Even under that kind of economic circumstances, the number of jobs in our community has increased dramatically.

Cincinnati has, perhaps, the most successful downtown development in the state, and one of the more successful in the nation, as a result of the kind of leadership the council-manager plan provides. Cincinnati has been satisfied with this plan since it moved in the early part of this century to eliminate a system that caused it to be known nationally as the worst-governed city in the country. This transition moved Cincinnati out of a mayor-council government with a very strong individual as mayor.

Question: In any of your cities, has a similar threat to your current form of government, and to your jobs, arisen? Have strong mayor proposals appeared on the ballot?

Olson: I think most of us, at one time or another, have experienced some interest in changing the particular plan that is in place. In Kansas City, we have had some interest shown in charter amendments. We have not proceeded to put anything on the ballot, and I think that any well-intending citizen group needs to, from time to time, take a clear look at whether the government is working well for them.

One of the points I wanted to second, in terms of representation, is that many different modifications of council makeup can function very nicely under the council-manager form. Our particular city is organized with six at-large and six from districts. On any given issue, it would be very difficult to determine who are the district people and who are the at-large people. It works very nicely and is very representative of our total populace.

Question: Obviously you as an association feel that the status of the council-manager form of government is at a fairly critical point here in Toledo — the decision could go either way. As an association, have you been to other cities where a similar situation has occurred, where you thought it was as important for you to show up?

Hansell: No. This is a first, for many reasons. Up until about seven years ago, the profession felt that it should stay completely removed from any kind of election process, even regarding the plan. We have, as you probably know, a Code of Ethics that each of us as a member of ICMA subscribes to, that insists that we take no part in any partisan issue or any election regarding our councilmembers.

In fact, however, about 10 years ago, we began to hear from groups like the League of Women Voters, groups like the Chamber of Commerce, and some of the unions that have been active supporters of the council-manager system. They pondered that if city managers, the professionals who have now reached a maturity level, can't speak out and articulate in support, who will? And isn't it time that we were willing and able to say that this is the best system of government? Since that time, we have produced significant materials, great numbers of information pieces, and distributed them to every community that has had a referendum or an abandonment issue. We had one earlier visit, when the city manager of Cincinnati, Scott's predecessor, Sy Murray, was president of ICMA and was invited to go into Eau Claire, Wisconsin, in the middle of an abandonment campaign. But since the League invited us here, and we do believe that the system can work here very well, we decided to make this kind of commitment.

Your question before seemed to be probing whether there have been other abandonments or other attempts. We keep very careful statistics on that at ICMA. It might interest you to know that since 1975 there have been 150 attempted abandonments of the council-manager system. Only 32 of those, or 21 percent, have succeeded. In 79 percent of the communities, the voters have voted to retain the council-manager system and continue good government in those communities.

Question: Before you arrived, were you briefed on what has happened in the city from the standpoint of government interaction with residents over the past seven years? If you were briefed, why would you still say that there would be no need to consider or even change the present form of government in this city?

Johnson: As Cincinnati's manager, it would be hard for me to tell you that I was not aware of what was happening in Toledo. We do hear about Toledo news in Cincinnati. Furthermore, Phil Hawkey, the city manager in Toledo, was formerly a deputy in Cincinnati, and a friend from a period of time when he was the city manager in a smaller city and so was I, also in Ohio. So certainly, I am aware of what has transpired in Toledo over the past two or three years, and I would say that, to me, none of that represents anything that is wrong with the system. In fact, what I see is an effective professional manager attempting to deal with problems created for the system by people placed in it who were not professional managers. I think that Toledo probably owes him some great debt for attempting effectively to correct deficiencies that he found when he came here.

Hansell: I think, apart from Scott, that it is fair to say none of us are really prepped on your local situation. Our purpose here is to counter statements that the system cannot work in large, growing, dynamic, complex urban areas. Our answer is that it is working in these cities and working very well.

Question: So what you are saying is that if the feeling that government is breaking down persists, it is not because of the form of government but because of the individuals who have been assigned the responsibility to carry out government?

Knight: My city is a fairly large city. In fact, it is one of the largest cities in the country now making use of this form of government. I think Lou Fox said it well earlier: As city managers, we are accountable every day. You may think that if you go to an electoral system where the chief administrative officer is elected, that person will be more accountable to you because of being elected every two or every four years, depending on how you choose to modify the charter. But that means that if you in fact think you have problems, you won't be able to address those problems until the end of that term, if then.

I subscribe to the theory that the council-manager form of government is the best form of government for professional managers, and for managing cities professionally. If by chance the manager is not working out, that is not a function of the form but rather of the personality. You enjoy the opportunity to change that immediately. So I would suggest to you that you are well off here in Toledo with the council-manager form of government, with respect to professionalism and with respect to accountability.

Olson: You could say, "Well, you are very biased — your jobs are all dependent on the council-manager form." I want to assure you that everyone here has at least 20 years of experience as a student of local government. In those 20 years plus, we have looked at different forms of government. I am confident none of us would be in the business we are in today had we not very clearly in our own minds come to the conclusion that council-manager is the best form for our city.

Question: I would suspect that at some time during your positions you have encountered a situation where a council is divided or split evenly at odds with each other. How do you remain effective when you are getting mixed signals, or power-plays on one side or the other?

Hansell: I think we have the right group to answer that.

Fox: I count to six. I have a total of eleven on the council, and I count to six. If they can get six votes to do something, it represents action. And I think it is the manager's responsibility to try to make that happen.

Olson: I would like to say in that regard that as city councils have become more representative, consensus has been more difficult to reach. But that doesn't mean that the government is less effective, or less representative of the people. Councils are more representative,

but it just takes longer to get that consensus, to get those six or seven votes. And that is healthy as far as I am concerned. It makes it a tougher job today than it was 30 years ago, I'll tell you that. Thirty years ago in Kansas City, the council wore virtually the same suit, had the same ideas, perhaps were business leaders in the community. They came to consensus in no time at all, but to the exclusion of many groups of society. Not so any more. It's a tougher process, and sometimes it looks very disjointed and very, very difficult. But I am not so sure that's bad. I think people in this society need to be represented, and our councils are reflecting that representation.

Knight: I agree. I have often said that one of the challenges for managers in the 1980s and beyond will be that of understanding how to manage [diversity]. I will offer today an additional comment, which is that the manager must also understand how to manage ambiguity. That ambiguity is, I think, to a great extent a direct result of the diversity.

Communities are different. The values that people have from their respective areas of the city are different. As a result, as both Dave and Lou said, we have to work harder at building consensus.

But when we think long-range, and when our visions suggest to us that it is an integral part of the process, then the product is also much better, because it is an inclusive one as opposed to an exclusive one.

Question: Don't your systems ever suffer from paralysis by over analysis?

Johnson: No, no. Let me turn that question back on you and say how, under those circumstances, does a mayor deal with that situation when he or she is a member of one faction? I am reminded of a situation that occurred in Cincinnati (not during my tenure), when council was split three ways — three, three, and three. That is a situation that would create the kind of paralysis you foresee. Because the city manager was not a member of any of those three factions, he was able to deal with all three and continue to function. A mayor in that sort of situation could not have functioned, so this system can work under those circumstances. I submit to you that city councils more frequently are split than not. We seldom have city councils that are made up of all one party or the other party. They are almost always split. The city manager, because that position is nonpartisan, can work with those people, while a mayor frequently cannot.

Hansell: I would add to that that I spent eight years in my career working in a mayor-council system of government as the equivalent of a deputy mayor. The title was business administrator, in the city of Allentown, Pennsylvania, a city of about 110,000. The assumption behind your question is that moving to a mayor-council system will eliminate that fractiousness, or that the mayor will simply be able to do whatever he or she wants and ignore the council. Well, in point of fact, that is not true. That diversity, that ambiguity that Richard talked about, does not go away in a mayor-council system. In fact, the separation of power that happens causes far more finger-pointing than occurs in a council-manager system of government. If there is policy inertia, it is the council's responsibility. If there is ineffectiveness in the delivery of services or execution of policy, it is the manager's responsibility. It is very clear in a council-manager system.

During the last national political election we heard President Bush saying, "We didn't cause the federal deficit — Congress spends all the money." And Governor Dukakis was saying, "The Congress just authorizes — the President and the Executive Branch spend and it is their responsibility." Well, I think a lot of people are wondering whose responsibility it is, and that is endemic to the separation of powers that we have in this country. It is a very important concept, by the way, and I don't attack that at the federal level. I think it is a valid part of our system of government. But the basis for separation of powers was based on an entirely different set of reasons than to improve efficiency, economy, or accountability. It was based on limiting government — making government unable to in any way impinge on individual liberty or to impinge on economic freedom. These are very important values for a sovereign government.

In our country, local governments do not possess sovereignty. There is no action taken by local government that cannot be corrected overnight by a state legislature. The reformers who initiated the council-manager system recognized that and said separation of power is not significant and not important and not a value that we want to build into local government. That is why the council-manager system concentrates political power and political responsibility in the council.

Question: To get to the bottom line, what you have all been saying is, if there is some discontent with the delivery system, that the system itself, the form of government, shouldn't be changed. The individual, the manager, should be removed.

Hansell: I don't think you should overreact to that, because we can't comment on local situations. Other factors besides the manager could be involved. Our understanding is that you have a specific proposal to abandon the council-manager system of government and to move to a mayor-council system of government. That is a total change. There are many modifications to the council-manager system. Lou mentioned one, the district elections of councilmembers. I understand your term for the mayor is two years. In most council-manager systems, the term is four years, so the mayor has an opportunity to really become a more politically effective leader.

System changes are possible, modifications that can be made while still retaining the basic essentials of a council-manager system. That is what we are saying you should really consider.

Note

1. The League of Women Voters of Toledo, Ohio, held a press conference on November 6, 1988, to show its continued support for the council-manager form of government in Toledo. The press conference was held to offer Toledo citizens an opportunity to learn how the council-manager plan operates in larger cities. On November 7, 1988, the citizens of Toledo voted to retain the plan. This article is adapted from the press conference proceedings.

PART VI
County Studies and Trends

CHAPTER 29

COUNTY GOVERNMENT: A CENTURY OF CHANGE

Victor S. DeSantis

County government in the United States has undergone tremendous change during the last century. In one of the most well-known early studies of county governments, H.S. Gilbertson depicted them, unfortunately, as the "dark continent[s]" of American politics.[1] The characterization stemmed from the rampant corruption and incompetence that was associated with the political machines and boss rule at the turn of the century. By mid-century however, Clyde Snider, a prominent scholar of county government, reported optimistically about the modernization of county government organizations and the expansion of the county role in the federalist state.[2] By the mid–twentieth century, counties were asked to take on more functional responsibility and were better equipped to handle their new role. The period since the mid-century assessment of the state of the county can also be seen as a continuation of more-significant involvement from county government in the operation of American democracy. Indeed, many of the recommendations offered by Snider to enhance county government further, such as authority centralized in a chief administrative officer position and increased power to conduct county business, have been instituted.

Historically, one of the most remarkable features of county government has been its stability as an American institution. The number of county units reported in the 1987 Census of Governments stands at 3,042.[3] This number has changed little from the 1942 total of 3,051 and the 1962 figure of 3,043. When viewed beside the steady increase in the number of municipal and special district governments over the same time frame, the stability appears even more dramatic.

Roots of the American County System

The evolution of the American county can be traced back to its use in Britain as an administrative arm of the national government.[4] The tradition of county government was well ingrained in the lives of the British colonists as they began to settle in North America, though the role of the county differed slightly depending on the region of the country. Regardless of the different roles delegated to the county, it is not surprising that the county unit as a layer between town and state governments should become a permanent fixture in America from its inception.

During the early colonial days, towns and counties were the basic units of local government in New England. While the towns were at the heart of local decision making with the annual town meeting, counties were established to carry out a variety of functions not performed by the smaller towns. Counties were responsible for such functions as judicial, military, and fiscal administration.

From *Municipal Year Book* 1989. Published by the International City/County Management Association, Washington, D.C. Reprinted with permission of the publisher.

However, even in the early days of the nation, the county operated in the background of the town government and failed to achieve the same level of importance. This tradition has remained throughout the history of New England. In fact, Connecticut and Rhode Island function without the existence of counties as organized units of government. Thus, the impression of the county as the "lost child" of local government was visible quite early.

The counties of the middle colonies held a position somewhat more important than those in New England and grew to be more instrumental in the delivery of public services. While performing the same duties as their New England counterparts, the counties of the middle colonies also became involved in law enforcement, with the county sheriff a principal focal point. The more important status of these counties allowed them to further their functional responsibilities to include road construction and maintenance and many welfare programs for the poor. In New York and New Jersey, one supervisor with taxation duties was elected from each town or township. In addition this taxation supervisor served on the county board of supervisors (or board of chosen freeholders as they became known in New Jersey). This county board had control over many of the county administrative functions. This arrangement of county government became the most traditional form of county government and later evolved into what is now known as the commission form. As the population spread westward, this pattern of county government became widely adopted by Midwestern areas.

Quite different from the system of local government adopted in either New England or the Middle Atlantic states was the system established in Virginia by the early settlers of the Tidewater region. Since the county covers a much larger geographic area, it performed better as the basic unit of local government in this region. This was primarily a reflection of the predominantly agricultural society with its widely dispersed rural population. This made it necessary to establish the county government as the primary unit of local government in the delivery of public services with much more importance than the smaller units of municipal government.

The early models of county government that developed in the different regions of the original colonies set forth the basic patterns of county government still in existence. Many of the foundations set out in these early forms continue to affect the ongoing administration of American counties.

Evolution of Modern County Government

Like other units of local government, counties are essentially creatures of the state government and have only derivative powers. As such, they have often been limited in the amount of freedom to conduct their internal affairs. The ability of a county or municipality to bring about more autonomy or self-government is acquired through home-rule provisions. The primary argument behind such provisions stems from the feeling that the local government has a better understanding of local needs and traditions and is better suited to handle such requests.

Historically, the movement toward greater autonomy and home-rule authority has come much slower for counties than for cities in many states. This is not to suggest, however, that all states have moved at a constant pace. Today, the National Association of Counties (NACo) reports that 36 of the 48 states with county governments grant those units some form of home-rule authority, either in the form of home-rule charters or optional forms of government.[5] Of those 36 states, 23 offer counties the ability to adopt a home-rule charter, while the remaining 13 offer counties limited autonomy through limited home-rule provisions or optional forms of government.

Regardless of the form of government, the trend toward such legal grants of authority from the states reached a peak during the period between 1972 and 1974, when nine of these provisions were passed.[6] However, autonomy is a much more recent phenomenon in most counties. As recently as 1965, only 18 states granted counties the right to choose from among optional forms or charter government.

While the scope of authority granted under these provisions varies widely, the powers can be divided into the general areas of structure, functional responsibility, and fiscal administration.[7] In the structural area, home-rule authority gives counties the authority to have a position of appointed manager, or the position of elected executive, or both. It gives counties the ability to change the method of electing commissioners and the size of the legislative board. Additionally, it enables counties to move away from the tradition of electing many of the other county administrative officials and to fill these positions by appointment instead.

The ability to change the basic structural arrangements in counties is based on the idea that there is not one best way to organize the governmental machinery. The newer demands placed on counties require that there be some flexibility in their operation. As Florence Zeller points out, movement away from the traditional structure allows for greater professionalism and more centralization and accountability through the addition of a county manager or county executive.[8] The charges of lack of professionalism and accountability are those most often leveled against the commission form of county government still mandated in some states. Giving counties the authority to institute changes through home-rule charters or optional forms have greatly enhanced their ability to deal with the growing complexity of local government.

In the area of functional responsibility, granting home authority can allow counties to increase their level of efficiency in public service provision. The ability to exercise independence in choosing alternative approaches for delivering public services has enabled some counties to better manage their resources. In addition to outright city-county consolidation, the use of intergovernmental service arrangements has allowed counties and their cities to avoid the duplicated and uncoordinated efforts that confront many neighboring jurisdictions. As Joseph Zimmerman points out, in 1974 only ten states had the constitutional or legislative authority to transfer voluntarily functional responsibility among units of government.[9]

Several types of functional arrangements can be used in the delivery of public services. The first involves a complete transfer of functional responsibility from one governmental unit to another. This has become more popular as many cities, under circumstances of fiscal stress, began realizing that the larger county unit may be better prepared to handle certain services. The other alternatives are to provide for an intergovernmental service contract or a joint service agreement. Under a service contract one or more cities can enter into a voluntary contract with the county to provide any number of services. A joint agreement may be entered into by a city and county for the joint financing and implementation of a service. A 1983 study by ICMA and ACIR showed that a substantial number of counties were using all three of these approaches, and the trend has increased over the previous decade.[10] Regardless of the approach used, counties are now handling the provision of more services than ever before. Clearly, this new responsibility indicates the growing role of the county in the intergovernmental framework.

The last area of powers granted under home-rule authority relates to fiscal administration. The ability of counties to control their own finances and promote budgetary stability is greatly enhanced when the rules governing county debt and revenue raising are loosened by the state government. Historically, counties were not free to issue bonds and raise debt limits on their own authority. Counties were also limited in their ability to raise revenue through taxation. Although there are wide differences, grants of fiscal control that accompany home-rule provisions allow counties greater financial flexibility to operate in the changing society. The current revenue data for counties point out the increased use of approaches that were not available to many counties until the last 20 years.

The trend toward greater autonomy suggests that counties have improved their position vis-à-vis the states over the past several decades. Interestingly, however, the rush toward adoption of home-rule charters has not proceeded quickly. Few counties in states that allow full home-rule charter provisions have attempted to institute such new forms. While this may suggest that many counties have made better use of the states optional forms without going the full route toward self-determination that a home-rule charter would bring, it may also indicate other obstacles faced by counties in establishing home rule. One of the major obstacles involves the nature of charters themselves, which call for local approval. Many counties in the pursuit of local self-governance have tried and failed to establish home-rule charters. As Tanis Salant notes, "It appears an easier task for states to pass relevant proposals than it is for individual counties to adopt charters."[11]

Legally, the home-rule movement for counties has come far in affording counties a more-substantial degree of self-governance. This may be the most-important ingredient in promoting county modernization. According to Alastair McArthur, the ability of counties to move beyond the constitutional requirements mandated by the states is an important provision if counties are to confront the many demographic and economic changes that continue to occur.[12]

The City-County Consolidation Movement

One of the areas of change in intergovernmental relations has been the use of city-county consolidations. While this approach received popular support during the 1960s and early 1970s, the practice dates back to 1805 with the consolidation of New Orleans and Orleans County. A number of other large city and county areas also took this step by the turn of the century. Among them were New York, Boston, Philadelphia, and San Francisco.

A city-county consolidation involves the merger of one or more municipalities with a county to form a metropolitan government performing the functions of both cities and counties. Such consolidations can be established through voter referendum or state legislative action. Along with the governmental unification comes a merger of the geographic boundaries of the consolidated area. The current number of city-county consolidations stands at 21.

While the first half of the twentieth century saw few consolidations, the move toward this approach began to pick up again in the early 1960s. Unfortunately, while interest in this alternative had picked up, political and social realities confronting many areas trying to consolidate made success hard to come by. Some states have made consolidation difficult through restrictive provisions in the state constitution and statutes.

The benefits of consolidating an area come mainly in the provision and delivery of public services and the advantages that accrue from the consolidation of functional responsibility. Specifically, some of the frequent arguments in favor of consolidation are that it promotes efficiency and coordination in the provision of services, reduces the amount of governmental fragmentation, provides for greater resources by combining those of both areas, and reduces the need to establish special district governments.[13]

An independent city is one that performs the functions of both the city and the county but operates independently of any county unit. Though this phenomenon is found primarily in Virginia, in which there are 41 independent cities, several others also exist: St. Louis, Missouri; Baltimore, Maryland; and Washington, D.C.

Virginia is a special circumstance because it allows incorporated communities the ability to seek state legislative approval for designation as an independent city when the city reaches 5,000 in population and meets the requirements of the law to become a city. Such cities, if granted the designation, operate independently of any county governmental unit.

Form of Government

While a variety of different arrangements exist for the organization and administration of American counties, there remain three basic forms of county government: commission, council-administrator, and council-elected executive. Historically, the commission, or plural executive, form of government has served as the most extensively used form of county government. It has only been because of the more recent home-rule movements and optional form passages that county government has begun to use the alternative forms.

In order to gain precise information about the use of different forms of county government, ICMA conducted a "County Form of Government Survey" during the summer and fall of 1988. The survey included questions related to form of government, the county legislature, the chief elected officer, and the election process. The results of that survey form the database for this chapter.

The Commission Form. The commission or plural executive form of government in counties is the oldest and most traditional organizational structure. It is characterized by a central governing board with members usually elected by district. Though a variety of names exist for this board, among the favorite are the board of commissioners or supervisors and the county court (sometimes known as the levying court). Most often, the board selects one of its members as the presiding officer. Members of the governing board may act as department heads. The governing boards share administrative and, to an extent, legislative functions with independently elected officials: the clerk, the treasurer, the sheriff, the assessor, the coroner, the recorder, etc. No single administrator oversees the county's operations. In some counties with the commission form, the structure includes an official (generally full-time), such as the county judge, who is independently elected at-large to be the presiding officer of the governing board. As noted previously, many disadvantages associated with the commission form stem from the usual lack of a chief administrator to provide more professionalism, executive leadership, and accountability.

Among those counties that responded to the survey, the highest percentage use the commission form of government (39.7 percent). This is a relationship between form of county government and both population and metro status. The smaller and more rural counties are those that most frequently choose to remain under the traditional commission form. There would also appear to be substantial variation among the geographic divisions in the use of the commission form.

The Council-Administrator Form. Interestingly, the survey results point to increased usage of the council-administrator form and the council-elected executive form. While these findings may be partly a result of biases in the survey response group, the overall trend toward these two forms cannot be masked. In the past few years, counties have made dramatic leaps in moving toward these alternative structural arrangements.[14] Indeed, as noted previously, the overall trend toward professional management in counties can be seen by the ever-increasing number of counties recognized by ICMA as providing for the manager form of government.

The council-administrator form of government for counties is similar to the council-manager form for cities. But three distinct variations are identifiable. In its strongest variation, the council-administrator form provides for an elected county board or council and an appointed administrator. The county board adopts ordinances and resolutions, adopts the budget, and sets policy. The administrator, appointed by the board, has responsibility for budget development and implementation, the hiring and firing of department heads, and recommending policy to the board. In some counties, where a weaker version of the council-administrator plan is in place, the administrator usually has less direct responsibility for overall county operations and less authority in hiring and firing, and may consult with the board on policy issues.

There is more widespread use of the council-administrator plan among the more populated counties. This may be a result of the need for more professional management on a continual basis to accompany the complexity of governing large counties. While over half of the counties use this plan in each of the population groups above 50,000, none of the population groups below 50,000 use it with more than a 44.9 percent frequency. Counties with suburban status use this form most often, followed by counties with central status. The geographic breakdown reveals quite a high degree of variation also, with the South Atlantic counties having the highest percentage (75.6 percent) and the West South Central counties having the lowest rate (16.4 percent).

Admittedly there is some degree of correlation between these variables. For example, the counties of the West South Central region are also those in Texas and other states that have a larger percentage of smaller rural county governments. In addition, the 254 Texas counties are mandated by state law to operate under the traditional commission form of government.

Another variation of the council-administrator form used in some areas combines elements of the council-administrator plan and the commission form. Here, an assistant to the presiding officer may serve in the capacity of administrator. For example, in Michigan the auditor, or controller, appointed by the governing board to audit the county's finances, may serve as an administrator; in other states, the county clerk, who is by statute clerk to the governing board, may have some administrative responsibility.

The Council-Elected Executive Form. The third form of county government is the council-elected executive form. This system has two branches of government — legislative and executive — and more clearly resembles the strong mayor form of city government. Here the county council or board assumes responsibility for county policies, adopts the budget, and audits the financial performance of the county. The elected at-large executive is considered the chief elected official of the county and often has veto power, which can be overridden by the council. The executive prepares the budget, carries out the administration of the county operations, appoints department heads (usually with the consent of the council), and suggests policy to the governing board. In addition, this official carries out appropriations, ordinances, and resolutions passed by the board and generally acts as the chief spokesperson for the county. When the executive is considered the chief political spokesperson, the executive often delegates the administrative responsibility for the daily county operations to a chief administrator.

This form, along with the council-administrator form, has begun to receive more popular support over the past several decades. In 1977, only 142 counties or about 5 percent op-

erated under this form of county government, and those that did use it were often the larger more-populated counties.[15] A total of 269 (22.1 percent) of the responding counties reported operating under this form. Additionally, some noteworthy variations appear when this figure is broken down by population, region, and metro status. The counties in the population group between 500,000 and 1,000,000 put this form to use most frequently, with a percentage of 45.8 percent. None of the population groups below 250,000 reported using this form at a rate any higher than 24.9 percent. Regardless of such differences, the fact remains that this form has received much greater usage over recent years and has helped to push counties forward in their quest toward modernization.

Among the responding counties, 37.7 percent indicated that the county had established the position of chief administrative officer. When broken down by population group, it becomes clear that the larger counties are those that use the chief administrative officer most frequently. Not surprisingly, these results are similar to those for the council-administrator form of government. The majority of the counties report that the position was established through state statutes that allowed for the optional form. As noted previously, few counties have chosen to use the home-rule charter as a route to alter their form of government. Indeed only 7.3 percent claimed to have established the position through a charter adoption. Additionally, of those that did use the charter as a means of acquiring a CAO, the highest percentage (53.8 percent) came in the second largest population group.

The Elected Head of County Government

While the official title of the presiding officer in counties has long been a traditional title such as county judge, county supervisor, or county board president, this has begun to change. The movement toward independently elected executives has made the title of county executive much more prevalent. Though the terms of office for the top official vary somewhat, almost all serve terms of less than five years. The greatest percentage of terms (58 percent) are only one year in duration. This is mostly an artifact of the plural executive form of county government in which the county council selects the presiding officer from among its members. This selection process may be a council vote or some rotational scheme. The rise in the number of two- and four-year terms may be a result of the increased use of the council-executive form, which allows the popularly elected executive the pleasure of a longer term.

The most popular method of selecting the elected head of county government is from the commission or council membership. While 69.1 percent use this method, only 22.2 percent of presiding officers are elected directly by the voters for that position. Few counties use an alternative method such as the rotation of a commission member to select their presiding officer.

Though the powers of the elected head of the county government vary among jurisdictions, one indication is the ability of the elected head to veto measures passed by the county council. The data shows few (8.1 percent) of the elected heads of government can veto council-passed measures. The breakdown by population group indicates that larger counties grant this right with the greatest frequency indicating this may be a function of the form of government, particularly the elected executive.

The County Legislature

One of the traditional aspects of county commissions is the smaller size of most legislative boards. Close to three-quarters (63.6 percent) of the county boards have sizes that range from three to five members. Another 15.2 percent range in size from six to ten members. A small percentage of county boards (5.6 percent) have over 20 members. The ability to increase the size of the county board is one of the reforms associated with the home-rule movement. The tradition of small councils is one that was long mandated by state requirements.

As previously mentioned, the presiding officer or elected head of the county government is often a member of the county board or council. As the data reflects, 93 percent of the responding counties indicated that the elected head of the government is also a member of the county board. This high percentage suggests that even under the council-executive form, the elected head may serve on the council in some capacity.

The length of the term for commission members is broken down between those elected from at-large and ward systems. Under both methods of election, the majority of commission members are elected to serve four-year terms. For those elected from at-large systems, 82.9 percent of commission members have four years to serve, while 75.9 percent serve four-year terms under ward systems. While there are small percentages of two-, three-, and over six-year terms in the at-large systems, the only substantial percentage of respondents (21.5 percent) in the ward system are those using two-year terms.

Use of overlapping terms in legislative bodies is one way of providing stability and continuity in the legislative process. The data indicates 69.5 percent of the responding counties allow for the overlap of commission member terms. The breakdown by population group reveals little relationship between the size of the county and overlap of commission member terms. However, it is noticeable that the overlap mechanism is used most often in the smaller counties (those under 5,000 in population).

The results indicate that there is substantial variation in overlap between geographic divisions. While the Mid-Atlantic and East South Central divisions use overlapping terms the least frequently, the West North Central and Pacific Coast use overlap most frequently. Metro status does not seem to be relevant to the use of overlapping terms.

The type of election system used in counties was also examined. The highest percentage of counties (45.5 percent) that responded indicated the use of district elections. For many counties without home-rule authority, the district plan is required under state law. While 30.1 percent use a system that mixes the at-large and district plan, only 24.4 percent use the pure at-large system. The predominant use of district elections in counties may stem from the larger size and more diverse nature of counties. While some geographic variations exist, there seems to be little correlation between either population or metro status. Populations of under 2,500 report use of at-large systems at a rate of 51.2 percent, an amount that is 15.9 percentage points higher than the next highest frequency of 35.3 percent.

One of the political reforms instituted in an effort to break the control of party organizations in local government was the establishment of nonpartisan elections. But only 17.6 percent of the responding counties have opted to exclude party labels from the election ballot. Further analysis of the partisan election phenomenon reveals that for those counties that have partisan elections, over 60 percent allow for the presence of both national and local party labels on the ballot. These election trends are surprising in light of the more widespread use of both at-large and nonpartisan election systems at the city level. Possibly the political reform movement that occurred so profoundly at the city level has never been felt as great at the county level.

County Finances

While the effects of fiscal stress on local governments is now a well-known reality, the problem remains an important aspect of managerial decision making. The tough decisions that are made to keep expenditures in line with revenues while citizens beckon for increased service levels remain with city and county administrators. While most managers have discovered new tools for dealing with such macrobudgetary issues, the impact of eight years of "new federalism" has been quite dramatic. One of the most detrimental policy changes may have been the demise of general revenue-sharing funds. In addition, many local government administrators have found their options limited in the wake of citizen initiatives to curtail the use of property taxes. Such efforts to hold down property tax rates

have forced local governments around the country to look for alternative sources of revenue.

One of the most widely accepted alternatives has become current charges, or user fees as they are known. Current charges accounted for nearly one-quarter (24.8 percent) of the total county revenues in 1985–1986.[15] In contrast, current charges made up roughly 16 percent of the total county revenue as recently as 1976–1977. While the future promises continued growth in the use of current charges, increases in functional assignments to counties may spell even more widespread use of this mechanism. Current charges, though somewhat controversial, can work to offset the costs of both delivering the public service and determining the level of service demanded by the citizens. Without question, however, the popularity of current charges as a revenue mechanism should continue to increase in the future.

In spite of the policy shifts at the federal level, intergovernmental fiscal transfers remain the greatest single source of county revenues. In 1985–1986, such revenue accounted for slightly over 35 percent of the total revenue pool. The revenue data from 1976–1977 show that intergovernmental revenue accounted for roughly 44 percent of the total county revenue. These figures point to a much reduced role for the federal and state government in their fiscal assistance to county governments.

The 1988 presidential election may have bolstered the hope of many local governmental officials, however. Many of them are taking an aggressive role in determining their economic fate. Such groups as the National Association of Counties, the National League of Cities, and the U.S. Conference of Mayors joined forces to lobby many of the presidential and congressional candidates long before the election in the hopes of getting local government support higher on the list of priorities in the upcoming years.[16]

Another trend in county revenues is the decreased reliance on property taxes as a revenue source. Though property taxes accounted for 26.2 percent of total revenue in 1985–1986, this amount represents a decline since 1976–1977 when over 30 percent of total revenue was acquired through property taxes. Offsetting this decline, however, has been the increase in non-property tax revenue over the same time period. While such taxes accounted for a mere 7 percent of total revenue in 1976–1977, they made up 9 percent of total revenue by 1985–1986.

Examination of the data reveal that counties have responsibility for provision of a variety of public service functions. The top-three expenditure areas for county government in 1985–1986 are health and hospitals, public welfare, and education, in that order. This trend has remained consistent since 1979–1980.[17] The greatest percentage of county expenditures (15.9 percent) goes toward the maintenance and operation of hospitals and implementation of various health programs. This percentage has increased since 1979–1980 when the health and hospital expenditures accounted for 15.6 percent. While 14.3 percent of county expenditures was devoted to public welfare programs in 1985–1986, this represented a decrease on a percentage basis from the 1979–1980 figure of 15.3 percent. This decrease indicates the overall trend that has been seen as county spending in the area of public welfare decreases. During the early 1970s, the percentage of direct expenditures toward public welfare was roughly 25 percent.

The 1985–1986 expenditures in education account for 13.8 percent of total expenditures, down from 15 percent in 1979–1980. Importantly, these aggregates do not reveal the variations among the different states in county expenditure patterns. County educational expenditures for example are relatively high in those states in which counties are responsible for the direct administration of that function.

In the aggregate, county expenditures have increased dramatically during the 1980s. While counties spent over $56 billion in 1979–1980, the total expenditure increased to over $92 billion for 1985–1986. This represents an increase of 65.3 percent over the six-year period. However, revenues have increased at a slightly higher rate. While the total revenue amount in 1985–1986 was over $96 billion, in 1979–1980, the total revenue was just over $56 billion. The percentage-increase in revenues between those time periods was 72.6 percent.

The date for the start of new fiscal years and the settling of the various revenue and expenditure reports required in modern government also shows some variation. While the highest percentage of counties (45.9 percent) opts for 1 January as the start of the new fiscal year, a large percentage also relies on the mid-year date of 1 July as a start of the fiscal cycle. Interestingly, only a small percentage of counties (11.2 percent) coordinates its fiscal cycle with the federal government's.

Conclusion

If counties were in a period of flux at the time of Snider's mid-century review, the same can be said of today's county government. The county government has grown in importance and plays an increasingly integral role in the intergovernmental framework. This can be seen most emphatically in the amount of service responsibility that has been granted to the county. While providing more services, they have also found new approaches to enhance their revenue base to cover the costs of delivering these services. Additionally, and most importantly, counties have been given more discretion in the organization and structure of their government through grants of home-rule charters and optional forms. These factors add up to a county government that is more professional, more flexible, and better equipped to handle the complexities that confront local governments in today's political and social environment. While much more remains to be accomplished at the county level, they clearly are an integral part of American politics.

Methodology

The data used in this survey were collected through ICMA's 1988 County Form of Government survey. The survey was mailed to county clerks in 3,044 counties in the United States. Counties not responding to the first request were sent a second survey. A total of 1,295 counties (42.5 percent) responded to the survey.

Notes

1. H.S. Gilbertson, "The Dark Continent of American Politics," in *The County* (New York: The National Short Ballot Organization, 1917).

2. Clyde Snider, "American County Government: A Midcentury Review," *American Political Science Review* 46 (March 1952): 74.

3. 1987 Census of Governments (GC87–1CP), November 1987, 1.

4. Herbert S. Duncombe, *Modern County Government* (Washington, D.C.: National Association of Counties, 1977): 20.

5. National Association of Counties, (telephone interview with Research Department), 15 November 1988.

6. Duncombe, 51.

7. Tanis Salant, "County Home Rule: Perspectives for Decision Making in Arizona," in *County Issues* (University of Arizona, 1988), 10.

8. Florence Zeller, "Forms of County Government," in *County Year Book* (Washington, D.C.: International City Management Association, 1975), 28.

9. Joe Zimmerman, "Transfers of Functional Responsibilities," in *County Year Book* (Washington, D.C.: International City Management Association, 1976), 59.

10. Harry P. Hatry and Carl F. Valente, "Alternative Service Delivery Approaches Involving Increased Use of the Private Sector," in *The Municipal Year Book* (Washington, D.C.: International City Management Association, 1983), 201.

11. Salant, 41.

12. Alistair McArthur, "3,049 Labs for Local Government Testing," *Public Management* (April 1971): 3.

13. From *America's Counties Today 1973* (Washington, D.C.: National Association of Counties, 1973).

14. Zeller, 28.

15. *County Government Finances in 1985–1986*, U.S. Bureau of Census, 1988, 1.

16. Kim Beury, "Counties Hopeful for New Deal," *American City and County* (August 1988): 31.

17. *County Government Finances in 1979–1980*, U.S. Bureau of Census, 1981, 5.

CHAPTER 30

COUNTIES IN TRANSITION: ISSUES AND CHALLENGES

Robert D. Thomas

When confronted by changing socioeconomic, demographic, and governmental conditions, county officials often face critical problems without authority to legislate locally, raise sufficient revenues, or engage in area-wide or neighborhood planning and land use management. Such problems vary dramatically across the spectrum of counties, from the most urbanized (e.g., Los Angeles County, California, and Cook County, Illinois) to the most rural (e.g., Loving County, Texas, and Hillsdale County, Colorado). Many counties are confronting economic shifts, changing residential patterns, and more governments delivering public services and issuing regulations. These transitions intensify demand for traditional county services and also compel consideration of how county government should respond to the changing environment. The issue, of course, is framed partly by the county's legal powers, or lack thereof.

Five Counties in Transition

The five counties of the Houston Metropolitan Statistical Area (MSA) — Ft. Bend, Harris, Liberty, Montgomery, and Waller — provide an example of counties in transition. These counties serve 3,247,000 people (1986) within 5,345 square miles of the upper coastal plains of Texas. MSA employment increased from 300,000 in 1945 to 1.6 million in 1988.

Harris County has 85.8 percent of the MSA's population, with 60.8 percent of its population living inside the city of Houston. Thus, the city and Harris County form the core of the area's economy.

GROWTH TRENDS

From a metropolitan perspective, with population increasing 74.6 percent and personal per capita income rising 314 percent from 1970 through 1988, Houston's MSA counties underwent a massive face-lift. Growth varied among the counties, however, arraying them along an urban continuum: Harris County on the urbanized side; Ft. Bend and Montgomery moving in an urbanizing direction; and Waller and Liberty the least urbanized.

During the 1980s, the populations of Ft. Bend and Montgomery counties skyrocketed (72 percent and 42 percent, respectively), mainly because they became bedroom communities of Houston.[1] Comparatively, population growth in Harris, Liberty, and Waller counties was modest (17 percent or less).

Population growth also brought new residential, commercial, and industrial developments in each county. New single-family housing, building permits, capital expenditures, and value added by manufacturing — as well as other elements of urban growth — rose sharply in the 1970s and 1980s. As the area experienced an economic boom in the late

From *Intergovernmental Perspective*, Vol. 17, No. 1, Winter 1991. Published by the U.S. Advisory Commission on Intergovernmental Relations, Washington, D.C.

1970s and early 1980s, the landscape of each county began to change. While the total number of houses increased by an average of 107 percent (1972–1982), the size of farms decreased by an average of 25 percent. In Montgomery and Waller counties, urban conditions seemed to replace rural conditions. Ft. Bend County, however, became more bifurcated, experiencing the greatest increase in housing and substantial increases in manufacturing simultaneously with the smallest decrease in farm sizes and the greatest increase in the value of farm products.

CHANGES IN THE TAX BASE

How did these growth trends affect tax valuations? The data provides some insight. Given that growth has had an impact on the tax value of land, we might expect such changes to result, eventually, in a shift of county government's priorities from rural to urban concerns. However, the growth effects on tax values are not uniform. While Harris County's tax base in the 1980s was substantially urban (e.g., residential and commercial/industrial property valuations averaged about three-fourths of total valuations), the other counties presented a mixed picture. Waller and Liberty were consistently skewed toward farm, ranch, and acreage. Ft. Bend and Montgomery were more bifurcated, relying both on urban-type sources and on farm, ranch, and acreage sources.

GOVERNMENTAL RESPONSES

Governmental complexity seems to mirror urbanization and taxation trends. As counties change, more governments are created to provide an urban infrastructure for new residential, commercial, and industrial developments or for servicing these developments once they are in place. Municipal utility districts (MUDs) and, to some extent, independent school districts (ISDs), but counties only secondarily, are the vehicles used in the Houston MSA to support new developments in unincorporated areas. (Numerous MUDs exist in Harris County, and MUDs are especially important in rapidly developing Ft. Bend and Montgomery counties.)

THE STATE CONNECTION

Governmental complexity in the five counties is linked directly to the structure of state authority for local governments. Consider how the state forms the legal parameters for MUDs and ISDs.

The legal antecedent of MUDs is a 1917 Texas constitutional amendment. That amendment was the foundation for state statutes allowing landowner initiative in the creation of taxing entities to fund improvements on undeveloped land. Originally, farmers and ranchers used these authorities to finance land improvements to protect against hurricanes and floods and to have higher productivity.[2] State statutes subsequently expanded the constitutional concept, allowing such financing to be used for urban infrastructure improvements supporting residential, commercial, and industrial developments.[3]

Likewise, because the Texas Constitution provides authority for independent school districts and explicitly authorizes the legislature to form ISDs embracing "parts of two or more counties," education services can emerge around land development patterns rather than being corralled inside either cities or counties.[4] Thus, many school districts have overlapping boundaries, especially in the most urbanized and urbanizing counties.

WHO PAYS FOR URBAN DEVELOPMENT? THE DEBT PICTURE

The Texas Constitution makes counties first and last administrative arms of the state government.[5] A review of public indebtedness for the governments of the five counties shows how this role shapes not only county responses but also other governments' responses to change. The study revealed that MUDs have the largest share of debt in the most urban county (Harris) and in the most urbanizing counties (Ft. Bend and Montgomery). In these counties, as well as in the least urbanized counties, ISDs are also key entities in establishing an urban infrastructure through debt financing.

These data suggest that the county is generally a secondary player in debt financing, but there are interesting exceptions on each end of the urban continuum. One of the least urbanized counties, Liberty, bears relatively more indebtedness in relation to its other local governments than the more urbanized counties. On the other side, in Harris County, special purpose authorities, which are either quasi-county agencies (e.g., Toll Road Authority and the Flood Control District) or closely allied with the county (e.g., Port Authority), have 18 percent of the total indebtedness for all governments in Harris County, thus making them significant actors in area-wide developments.

Consequences and Challenges: Whence Counties?

What do these trends imply for county governments? Perhaps a football analogy illustrates the implications. In Texas, as in many other states, counties operate substantially as administrative arms of state government. As a result, counties are often placed in the position of being second or even third stringers in responding to changing patterns of growth and decline. If local circumstances warrant it, the state may allow the county to play an important skilled position, although not always one that is central to the challenges at hand.

Harris County is a case in point. The state has permitted the creation of quasi-county agencies and authorities closely allied with the county to respond to public needs where other local governments cannot or do not take action. Still, there are limits to the county's ability to respond to growth. Of course, county governments also carry out state administrative services that are an integral part of metropolitan governance (e.g., criminal justice administration). However, the state does not provide counties with sufficient statutory authority or legal latitude to be first-team players able to shape responses to permanent and transitional needs arising from urbanization.

Instead, statutory embellishments of selected provisions of the Texas Constitution have placed MUDs and ISDs at the forefront in providing counties with an urban infrastructure and delivering important services.

This differentiated structure of local service provision has given rise to a free-market atmosphere in which land use patterns are shaped largely by land ownership and by what the market will bear. Given that MUDs and ISDs are formed around or along with developments, the initial, if not always final, urban infrastructure created in counties is financed mainly on a neighborhood-specific basis, not by the county's entire population.

A recent ACIR report argues that a cluster of local governments inside and overlapping counties, such as that found in the Houston MSA, can be viewed as a "local public economy." This economy is created by local actors, public and private, within a "framework of rules ... supplied largely through state constitutions and laws, not by metropolitan or regional governments."[6] For the Houston MSA, the multiplicity of governments emerging with urbanization does seem to serve "a number of useful purposes: it increases the sensitivity of local government to diverse citizen preferences; it increases efficiency by matching the distribution of benefits more closely to the economic demand of communities; and it enables citizens to hold public officials accountable to a specific community of interest."[7]

In the Houston area and across the nation, however, the "rules" for local governments are not static, nor are they framed only by the state's constitution and statutes. Increasingly, the U.S. Constitution and statutes also have come to overlay local governance. Sometimes, perhaps often, what works at one time must later be altered to deal with new circumstances. The problem, though, is that the "rules" established by the state and federal governments do not always allow counties and other local governments to respond adequately to challenges in order to build a more functional local public economy where conditions are dysfunctional. In the Houston MSA, for example, a number of local governance challenges will have to be addressed in the near future.

For one, Texas faces major questions of equity in the financing of public education. With ISDs created to serve economic enclaves, as opposed to citywide or countywide jurisdictions, many differences in fiscal capacity exist among school districts, although with urbanization, the creation of more ISDs does give metropolitan residents more choices. Of course, such disparities are not confined to the Houston MSA; they exist statewide. Thus, how this issue is finally resolved will require changes in state "rules." The political challenge will be to equalize funding under state court orders largely within the present structure of ISDs. Two possibilities, each with consequences for local governance, are interjurisdictional transfers from rich to poor districts or statewide financing based on uniform assessments.

Several intergovernmental questions also need resolution. For example, many MUDs in the Houston MSA use groundwater and have small wastewater treatment plants that were built to meet population projections that were too low. Eventually, MUDs will have to be supplied by surface water because of depletion and subsidence problems, and their treatment plants will have to be upgraded or integrated regionally.[8] In resolving these issues, local government boundary questions will arise around the complex issues of incorporation and annexation.

Through incorporation, MUD costs and benefits can be absorbed by existing cities. Such incorporations are unlikely, however, because all Harris County MUDs and most MUDs in Ft. Bend, Montgomery, and Waller counties are inside the city of Houston's extraterritorial jurisdiction (ETJ), which extends five miles beyond the city's corporate limits.[9] State law prohibits new incorporation within a city's ETJ unless the city grants permission. Given that Houston is not likely to grant such permission, incorporations are out of the question. The surrounding counties, therefore, have little leverage under the existing rules to help fashion a more functional local public economy.

Ironically, the state's ETJ rules were intended, in part, to allow municipalities to respond to growth. Indeed, since World War II, Houston has dissolved many MUDs and taken over their liabilities and assets through large-scale annexations. (A home-rule city may annex by simple ordinance action within its ETJ.) This annexation power, however, has been complicated by two major factors. One is the *Voting Rights Act of 1965* and its later amendments. This act, which is applicable to Houston, prohibits boundary changes that dilute minority voting strength.[10] The second factor is the 1963 Municipal Annexation Act that requires cities to provide equivalent city services to annexed areas within three years of annexation — a hurdle that is sometimes difficult for cities. Thus, these federal and state statutes — which have laudable equity objectives — have some counter-equity consequences, while they also limit the ability of the city and its surrounding counties to respond to growth challenges.

How county governments can fit more effectively into the overall pattern of local governance in the future will require a thorough reshaping or at least fine tuning of existing state rules and, perhaps, some federal rules. On the educational equity question, for example, county governments are not even in the picture. On many intergovernmental questions, county governments can only react and adapt to the actions of other governments. At this time, moreover, county governments can only venture selectively from their traditional service responsibilities.

Hence, county empowerment needs to be addressed in Texas as well as in many other states, especially where the challenges to local governance posed by urbanization are stretching the limits of existing governments. Such empowerment, moreover, can be seen as a logical extension of the traditional service responsibilities of counties, an extension that does not require the county to take over and centralize all functions, but rather an extension that allows a county to serve its local communities by facilitating the development of a functional local public economy.

Notes

1. A 1989 Missouri City (Ft. Bend County) survey, for example, found that 61 percent of the city's residents worked in Houston.

2. The 1917 amendment gave landowners *unlimited and unrestricted* debt financing for flood control, drainage, irrigation, and power projects — financial latitude not available to cities and counties.

3. Under the 1917 amendment, the legislature

has authorized 13 different types of districts, but only 3 have been used to support urban developments. As forerunners of MUDs, Fresh Water Supply Districts and Water Control and Improvement Districts were used to finance urban improvements. The Municipal Utilities Act of 1971 applied the concept directly to urban developments, authorizing MUDs to provide all types of water supplies, waste disposal services, and drainage. MUDs were also authorized to alter land elevations, provide parks and recreation facilities, as well as other functions. Combined, these functional responsibilities made MUDs "small" towns. Cf. Lee Charles Schroer, "The Water Control and Improvement District: Concept, Creation and Critique," *Houston Law Review* 8 (March 1971): 712–738; and Texas Water Code, Chapter 54.201, p. 297.

4. The Texas Constitution (Art. VII, Sec. 3) also authorizes cities to constitute separate school districts; however, there are 1,064 ISDs in Texas and only a few city districts.

5. Art. XI of the Texas Constitution creates counties as legal subdivisions of the state (Sec. 1), and then controls their authorities through general laws (Sec. 2).

6. U.S. Advisory Commission on Intergovernmental Relations, *The Organization of Local Public Economies* (Washington, D.C., 1987), p. 35.

7. Ibid., p. 1. See also U.S. Advisory Commission on Intergovernmental Relations, *Metropolitan Organization: The St. Louis Case* (Washington, DC, 1988).

8. See also Virginia Lacy Perrenod, *Special Districts, Special Purposes: Fringe Governments and Urban Problems in the Houston Area* (College Station: Texas A&M University Press, 1984).

9. Home-rule cities in Texas have ETJs of one-half mile to five miles beyond their corporate limits, depending on their population, as follows: more than 100,000, five miles; 50,000 to 100,000, three and one-half miles; 25,000 to 50,000, two miles; 5,000 to 25,000, one mile. Municipal Annexation Act, General and Special Laws of the State of Texas, 57th Legislature (1963), Ch. 160, pp. 447–545.

10. See also Robert D. Thomas and Richard W. Murray, "Applying the Voting Rights Act in Houston: Federal Intervention or Local Political Determination?" *Publius: The Journal of Federalism* 16 (Fall 1986): 81–96.

CHAPTER 31

CITY-COUNTY CONSOLIDATION: A MATTER OF EFFICIENCY?

Julianne Duvall

City and county officials have been discussing issues of consolidation for years in hopes of increasing services, productivity, and savings by having one local government preside over both former jurisdictions. In fact, local officials have been attempting to streamline local government for greater efficiency and cost savings since 1805, when the city of New Orleans and Orleans Parish, Louisiana merged in the first city-county consolidation in the United States. Since that time, cities and counties have attempted complete consolidation more than 84 times, with a success rate of only approximately 29 percent. Currently, 25 consolidated cities and counties exist, with 18 of those having merged after World War II.

In recent years, cities and counties have pushed the issue of consolidation more frequently as a way of answering the growing problems of local government, such as revenue losses in terms of intergovernmental transfers and increased service demands. However, the influx of new consolidation proposals faces a declining success rate because citizens typically resist the idea. Many times, the mere prospect of consolidation explodes into a volatile issue among the citizens of both jurisdictions. The division among citizens over city-county consolidation stems from citizens' desire to have local government operate responsively and efficiently. In a democracy, however, this is difficult to achieve without some type of local government coordination.

The consolidation issue also relates to the roles cities and counties play in providing services. Counties, as administrative arms of the state, must provide services with state limitations on the amount and source of revenue.[1] Therefore, with restrictions on funds, counties and cities often view consolidation as an appropriate measure to meeting increasing citizen expectations as well as regional planning needs. Some form of consolidation can indeed help local governments fulfill their obligations.

Pressures to Consolidate

In these days of tighter purse strings for local governments, there are more incentives for cities and counties to attempt consolidation. City incorporations have been on the rise because of conflicts between unincorporated areas and counties over the organization of government services, limited sources of local revenue, regional planning efforts, and land-use control.[2] Unfortunately, as more cities incorporate, counties cannot meet service needs with the declining revenue base. Counties must then look for alternatives in providing services for lower cost. And, as the number of incorporations within a county increases, fragmented systems develop, ignoring areawide issues. Cities take over planning and zoning powers from the county while city land-use decisions can create problems regionally.[3]

Originally published as "City-County Consolidation: An Answer to Local Government Efficiency," *Issue Brief,* January 1989. Published by the National League of Cities, Washington, D.C. Reprinted with permission of the publisher.

The proliferation of fragmented local government systems has economic implications as well. Local governments have a difficult time attracting new business if the geographic area is divided into different tax structures, rules, and regulations. In fact, the prospect of new business often spurs the consolidation movement. York 2000, a governmental reorganization commission in York County, Pennsylvania, has been studying consolidation of its 72 political divisions in order to revitalize its economy and compete for business on a larger scale. Floyd Warner, chairman of York 2000, sees that "there is no coordination among municipalities. That is paramount to economic development."[4] County officials in St. Louis County, Missouri, want to dismantle its 90 jurisdictions and combine them into 21 as a way to continue prosperity and attract out-of-state companies to its growing business corridor. The city of Georgetown and Scott County, Kentucky, are also reviewing consolidation to keep a planned Toyota plant interested in the area. New business can revitalize an area's economic system and even change its image. When Indianapolis and Marion County, Indiana, merged most government functions in order to become the futuristic-sounding UNIGOV in 1978, Indianapolis' image and economy boomed. UNIGOV's success has brought in $850 million in private development and the highest Moody Bond Rating of AAA. Among the results of the new government operations, Indianapolis was named one of "America's Most Livable Cities" by Partners for Livable Places.

Revenue limits combined with the loss of federal funds that local governments previously enjoyed have reduced the service capabilities of both cities and counties, forcing them to search for new methods of delivering services. Duplication of services by the county and city governments has led to increased costs and inefficiency. Combining services and facilities seems to offer the cities and counties a way to balance area needs with area supply capabilities.

State laws, such as Proposition 13 in California and Proposition 24 in Alaska, which limit the amount of taxes that local governments can impose upon their citizens, also force local governments to search for new ways to save money. Proposition 13, which promoted city incorporations after it passed in 1978, is pushing some counties in 1988 to consider abolishing themselves because of the loss of revenue areas to incorporated cities; counties cannot provide the state-mandated services. Because of this problem, the chances for city-county consolidation in California are on the rise. Martin Nichols, Administrator of Butte County, California, says that his county is considering turning its functions over to specialized community service districts with more financial flexibility.[5] And in Alaska, the state assembly has cut municipal budgets by $7 million, forcing cities to consider the options of local cooperation.[6] Both Fairbanks and Ketchikan, Alaska, are reviewing unification commissions and proposals.

Finally, cities and counties consolidate to address the regional and metropolitan problems that affect the jurisdictions, such as air pollution, water pollution, and transportation needs. When jurisdictions deal with these issues in fragmented sections, they produce narrow solutions to larger problems. Officials sometimes choose consolidation as a method of dealing with environmental and area concerns.

Of course, not all the pressures to consolidate would warrant a full consolidation; many could be solved through partial consolidation of specific public services. So, when determining whether or not to consolidate fully or partially, there are many considerations having both advantages and disadvantages.

Full City-County Consolidation

Full consolidation has different meanings as defined by different state statutes. Generally, cities and counties consolidate fully by disincorporating the city and absorbing it into the county, or by passing a law to establish one body which governs over the city and county. Most states share this definition. Florida, however, lists full consolidation as a dissolution of all jurisdictions within a county. If some cities remain independent, the consolidation is not complete.

Because it requires dismantling one or more local governments in exchange for another, full consolidation becomes an emotional issue with the citizens of both city and county. Voters must approve the referendum to consolidate, and, as previously stated, these attempts rarely succeed. Counties surrounding urban areas tend to oppose consolidation because they fear cities are trying to rob revenue rich suburban areas. Minorities, also, tend to fight consolidation attempts because they feel the strength of their vote will be diluted in a larger election. Due to the controversy, local governments should take into account several issues before weighing the rewards and liabilities of consolidation.

Planning, zoning, levels of service, and facility logistics are important considerations, of course, but the political environment with regard to state regulations, political feelings, taxing and debt limits, and community emotions determines the feasibility of total consolidation.

Most state statutes dictate that a consolidated government charter cannot affect the status of nonparticipating entities, abolish courts, or repeal any general laws, while it must accept the debts and contracts of the former jurisdictions and put the proposal in front of the citizens of both entities for a majority vote. These requirements do not, in any way, limit the prospect of consolidation except in states where the requirements contradict each other or are not clear. Confusion over state regulations can make consolidation an impossible task from the beginning. For example, in Pennsylvania, the General Assembly may have the right to order mergers, yet the Pennsylvania constitution guarantees the voters a choice in the matter. Officials feel that the state must take the lead and provide a uniform law in order to make attempts legally possible.[7]

Proponents of consolidation should also consider the political situation and congruity of the areas. The Indianapolis-Marion County UNIGOV excludes three cities within Marion County — Speedway, Beechgrove, and Southport — because the political sentiment in those areas would have defeated the entire UNIGOV proposal.

Full consolidation requires the creation of special tax districts in order to match taxes with services received and debts incurred. In a consolidation proposal, especially those with more than two participants, it becomes difficult to assess tax rates so that citizens who received services in the previous government pay for the debt that jurisdiction suffered while it provided the services. The UNIGOV consolidation, although hailed as a great success, does not operate simply. It retains 56 tax districts and 101 tax bill combinations so that citizens will not be taxed for other entities' outstanding financial obligations. Most areas, as a way to appease citizens, cannot allow taxes to increase in a consolidated government, but must find other ways to increase the revenue base. Research Atlanta, a group which has been studying city-county consolidation measures, found that property taxes did actually fall in consolidated governments, while the tax base increased because of higher sales taxes, income taxes, and federal aid.[8]

The biggest and most divisive consideration is community feeling toward consolidation. In nine instances, six of which occurred in the 19th century, the state legislatures ordered consolidation; in all other cases, consolidation proposals live or die at the polls. Many times, the voter approval becomes a matter of public relations. The demise of the effort, according to Linda C. Strutt in her article "The Okeechobee Experience: Florida's First Rural City/County Consolidation Effort," is due in most part to opposition from officials, confusion over government roles, confusion over the taxing system, emotionalism and community identity, as well as lack of understanding of the problems of the existing government.[9] Two sides always emerge in consolidation proposals and the forceful arguments in favor and against consolidation reflect the community values of efficient government performance and responsive local officials. Notwithstanding the benefits of consolidation, voters have rejected proposals more than once. Voters in Fairbanks, Alaska, have defeated attempts two times, while officials in Athens and Clark County, Georgia, failed three separate times to convince the citizens of the merits of consolidation. Many other jurisdictions have given up on consolidation attempts after many unsuccessful tries.

Advantages and Disadvantages of Full Consolidation

For local governments interested in efficient streamlining in order to cut costs and gain greater revenues, proponents argue that total consolidation has many advantages. First, consolidation into a larger political body could allow the consolidated government greater political power in the state to control outcome and protect its interests. Secondly, municipalities can solve the problems within their own boundaries, but eventually cause problems outside their borders through uncoordinated regional planning. Small political subdivisions cannot effectively address such large scale issues as environmental protection and development. Finally, consolidation matches the entire area's needs with its resources, rather than having an excess of a needed resource in one jurisdiction and a lack of it in another; cities and counties can share their assets and lessen their liabilities.

Opponents of consolidation tend to have emotional arguments on their side. They argue that efficiency is not guaranteed in a consolidated government, while losing the responsiveness of a smaller local government inevitably occurs in a merged situation. Consolidations are supposed to cut costs when actually larger governments have greater per capita expenditures. Moreover, citizens lose the "local" aspect of local government; the opportunities for participation may decrease and the merger weakens community identification. Voters expect services to rise when, in fact, the larger governments often have more service delivery problems than before the consolidation. Also, political problems arise when one jurisdiction absorbs another, leaving power struggles in the new government. Consolidation may dilute the political strength and representation of minorities and create new majorities, while political leaders retain their ties to the area from which they came. And, most important, consolidations change the status quo for the unknown.

In an impartial study, Research Atlanta compiled some results on consolidated governments and concluded that the benefits actually outweighed the disadvantages.[10] They found that consolidated governments made more of an effort to provide services to previously underserved areas. In addition, an increase in black representation on the new council compensated for the expected decrease in black voting strength. Consolidation generated savings and costs, but due to inflation and expanded services, it did increase governmental expenditures.[11]

The volatility surrounding consolidation issues makes proposals political taboo; yet, local governments need to cooperate in some way to respond to fiscal and regional issues. Given the success rate of consolidation attempts, local government officials may wish to pursue alternative methods of cost savings and planning through cooperation.

Partial Consolidation

Partial consolidation involves agreement between local governments to consolidate one or more functions of government while participating entities retain their own identity. The extremes of partial or functional consolidation range from minimum to radical, from simple cooperation to incorporated counties. The authors of *An Analysis of State-Local Relations in Florida*, a 1987 report on governmental reorganization and intergovernmental interaction, concluded:

> In lieu of consolidation, governments have been engaged in less comprehensive reforms, such as functional consolidation and intergovernmental service agreements.... [T]hese incremental changes, rather than governmental consolidation, are more feasible now and probably will continue to predominate in the future.[12]

When two or more governments wish to consolidate certain functions, they need to consider several items. The proximity of the areas, the social distance of the communities, the political influence of the officials within the jurisdictions, and the structure of government can be important factors depending on the aspects the governments wish to consolidate. The different types of partial consolidation do not need voter approval and therefore are easier to implement.

Cooperation, the simplest "consolidation," revolves around a brief issue or a time of crisis during which entities commit their support to one another in order to solve an immediate problem. Formal cooperation can develop on long-range issues of interest to both parties. These interlocal agreements tend to address policy and service issues much more than administrative ones.

Contractual service agreements, in which one government provides a service for another, work effectively in 52 percent of all cities and counties.[13] Maintenance delivery, fire and police protection, solid waste services, utilities, and health services operate well under these agreements.

Functional transfers occur when cities and counties decide to reassign control over some services among themselves. Counties may opt to provide services other than state statutes require in exchange for city responsibility of other services county-wide. These transfers usually become permanent after they are included in the city and county charters. Fulton County and Atlanta, Georgia, reassigned functions between them and established urban service tax districts in unincorporated areas where additional service levels were in demand. A commission recommended various services and obligations which should be transferred in order to reduce duplication and improve service delivery.

County Study Commission

Fifty-five percent of all cities and counties, although primarily the more populous areas, enter into joint service agreements for planning or financing.[14] By contracting out to a third party or by jointly financing projects, smaller areas receive more service and larger areas pay less money for the same service. Public safety and health departments most frequently function under joint service agreements, although the controversy surrounding consolidated police and fire services mirrors the arguments supporting and opposing total consolidation. Proponents argue that consoli-

dation increases public safety officers' efficiency, specialization, resources, and training, while opponents insist that a larger force promotes a loss of community control and accountability.

The Sacramento Local Government Reorganization Committee, which is studying the possibilities of consolidation in Sacramento County and the city of Sacramento, recommends the metropolitan-federalism system of partial consolidation to best solve the local and regional problems.[15] The consolidation operates on two tier levels which handle regional or local interests. The first tier consists of a series of local governments which provide local services, planning and functions. One member from each local council represents the area on the second tier, which is a metropolitan or county-wide government with jurisdiction over regional issues. In addition to its recommendation, the Sacramento committee lists regional services or agencies which should function on the second tier, such as transportation systems, air pollution, drainage and flood control, regional sanitation, and parks and open space planning. The local entities retain control over their own local problems, while the regional board addresses the concerns of the entire area. Herbert H. Hughes and Charles Lee, in their article "The Evolutionary Consolidation Model: A Response to Revenue Limits in Growing Metropolitan Areas," argue that cities and counties "should consolidate … only under a federated approach, in which authority is shared between the central city and other areas in a consolidated jurisdiction."[16]

Miami and Dade County, Florida, function in a complicated system which some experts label a modified metropolitan-federal approach,[17] and which others describe as a comprehensive urban county.[18] The local governments within Dade County have autonomy on local issues, while an eight member at-large county commission presides over the county-wide issues. The incorporated cities function in the two-tier model, but the unincorporated areas are the responsibility of the county commission. The county provides many services to the cities in exchange for tax revenues, prompting the use of the title of comprehensive urban county.

The comprehensive urban county consolidation involves the county provision for an agreed upon number of services to the cities within the county or the county incorporation of all its unincorporated areas. St. Louis County proposals for consolidation include one in which the entire county would incorporate so the county would not lose revenue by providing services to the unincorporated areas. Some states, however, regulate the formation of a comprehensive urban county in their statutes on government reorganization, due to minimum population density requirements for incorporation. Virginia, for example, prohibits counties from incorporating and merging services with their cities. Kentucky, on the other hand, allows cities to abolish all existing governments within a county in order to develop an incorporated charter county.

The evolutionary model of consolidation, coined by Hughes and Lee, yet described by other experts, occurs when cities and counties cooperate on some issues and over time develop more formal relations. The model seems to work well for areas experiencing controversy over consolidation. Many researchers on consolidation believe that merger attempts that evolve from cooperation through the stages of partial consolidation stand a better chance of eventually succeeding.[19] Hughes and Lee say "Local governments should consolidate only when strong evidence shows that the collective government and community capacity will increase."[20] Many local governments feel comfortable using any one of these partial consolidations permanently or experimenting with different services without reorganizing the structure of the entities. The advantages and options of evolving into a partial consolidation stage attract local governments into considering cooperation. The effects of a partial consolidation are not irreversible, while officials can even experiment with service levels, department mergers, and joint contracts. At the same time, community identities of the participating areas remain intact while the voters do not offer roadblocks to the effort. Partial consolidations can function effectively between dissimilar governments, while standardizing service and costs between the areas. Finally, if the governments choose, partial consolidation can lead to a total merger.

Conclusion

Consolidation of city and county government will always remain a divisive issue as long as citizens expect both efficiency and responsiveness from local government. Local governments, however, are realizing the need for cost saving techniques and regional planning which consolidation may provide. Not all services in a full consolidation are better or even more economically delivered on an areawide basis, while citizens wish to retain local control over their government. At this point, due to the opposition involved in enacting a full consolidation proposal, varying degrees of partial consolidation seem to be the most politically and economically feasible solution to meeting areawide problems and revenue squeezes.

Notes

1. Barbara P. Greene, "Counties and the Fiscal Challenges of the 1980's," *Intergovernmental Perspective*, vol. 13, n. 1, Winter 1987, p. 15.

2. Robert Feinbaum, "Counties Lose: Climate Right for Creating New Cities," *California Journal*, vol. 18, n. 10, October 1987, p. 497.

3. Feinbaum, p. 499.

4. Michael Argento, "Weight of Numbers Intimidating," *York Daily Record*, 16 June 1987, sec. A, p. 1.

5. Rebecca LaVally, "Proposition 13, Ten Years Later," *California Journal*, vol. 19, n. 4, April 1988, p. 175.

6. "The Budget Crisis in the Years Ahead," *Anchorage Daily News*, opinion editorial, 24 June 1988.

7. Michael Argento, "Consolidation Too 'Hot' to Handle Politically," *York Daily Record*, 15 June 1988.

8. Kenneth Town and Carol Lambert, *The Urban Consolidation Experience in the U.S.* (Atlanta, Georgia: Research Atlanta, 1987), cited by Richard W. Campbell, "City-County Consolidation: Learning from Failure," *Urban Georgia*, April 1988.

9. Linda C. Strutt, "The Okeechobee Experience: Florida's First Rural City/County Consolidation Effort," cited by Florida House of Representatives Committee on Community Affairs, *Getting Together: The Forming and Reshaping of Local Government in Florida* (Tallahassee, Florida: Florida House of Representatives March 1988).

10. Town and Lambert, cited by Campbell, p. 28.

11. Town and Lambert, cited by Campbell, p. 28.

12. Wayne A. Clark, J. Edwin Benton, and Robert Kerstein, *An Analysis of State-Local Relations in Florida*

(Florida State University: 1987) p. 43, cited by Florida House of Representatives Committee on Community Affairs, *Getting Together: The Forming and Reshaping of Local Government in Florida* (Tallahassee, Florida: Florida House of Representatives March 1988) pp. 4–9.

13. Lori M. Henderson, "Intergovernmental Service Arrangements and the Transfer of Functions," *Baseline Data Report*, vol. 16, n. 6 (Washington, D.C.: International City Management Association, June 1984) p. 1.

14. Henderson, p. 3.

15. Joint Commission of the County of Sacramento and the City of Sacramento, Sacramento Committee Report, *City-County Local Government Reorganization Commission, Volume I: Observations and Recommendations* (Sacramento: Joint Commission, June 1988) p. 26.

16. Herbert H. Hughes and Charles Lee, "The Evolutionary Consolidation Model: A Response to Revenue Limits in Growing Metropolitan Areas," *Urban Resources*, vol. 4, n. 2, Winter 1987, p. 6.

17. Joseph F. Zimmerman, "Dade County Reviews Charter," *National Civic Review*, vol. 71, n. 5, May 1982, p. 265.

18. Glen Sparrow and Lauren McKinsey, "Metropolitan Reorganization: A Theory and Agenda for Research," *National Civic Review*, vol. 72, n. 9, October 1983, p. 493.

19. Hughes and Lee, p. 3.

20. Hughes and Lee, p. 6.

Bibliography

Argento, Michael. "Weight of Numbers Intimidating," *York Daily Record.* 16 June 1987, and "Consolidation Too 'Hot' to Handle Politically," *York Daily Record* 15 June 1987.

"The Budget Crisis in the Years Ahead." *Anchorage Daily News.* opinion editorial. 24 June 1988.

Clark, Wayne A., J. Edwin Benton, and Robert Kerstein. *An Analysis of State-Local Relations in Florida.* (Florida State University: 1987) cited by Florida House of Representatives Committee on Community Affairs. *Getting Together: The Forming and Reshaping of Local Government in Florida* (Tallahassee, Florida: Florida House of Representatives, March 1988).

Feinbaum, Robert. "Counties Lose: Climate Right for Creating New Cities." *California Journal,* 18, n. 10. October 1987.

Greene, Dr. Barbara P. "Counties and the Fiscal Challenges of the 1980's." *Intergovernmental Perspective,* 13, n. 1. Winter 1987.

Henderson, Lori M. "Intergovernmental Service Arrangements and the Transfer of Functions." *Baseline Data Report,* 16, n. 6 (Washington, D.C.: International City Management Association, June 1984).

Hughes, Herbert H. and Charles Lee. "The Evolutionary Consolidation Model: A Response to Revenue Limits in Growing Metropolitan Areas." *Urban Resources,* 4, n. 2. Winter 1987.

Joint Commission of the County of Sacramento and the City of Sacramento, Sacramento Committee Report. *City-County Local Government Reorganization Commission, Volume I: Observations and Recommendations* (Sacramento: Joint Commission, June 1988).

LaVally, Rebecca. "Proposition 13, Ten Years Later." *California Journal,* 19, n. 4. April 1988.

Sparrow, Glen and Lauren McKinsey. "Metropolitan Reorganization: A Theory and Agenda for Research." *National Civic Review,* 72, n. 9. October 1983.

Strutt, Linda C. "The Okeechobee Experience: Florida's First Rural City/County Consolidation Effort." Cited by Florida House of Representatives Committee on Community Affairs. *Getting Together: The Forming and Reshaping of local Government in Florida* (Tallahassee, Florida: Florida House of Representatives, March 1988).

Town, Kenneth and Carol Lambert. *The Urban Consolidation Experience in the U.S.* (Atlanta, Georgia: Research Atlanta, 1987) cited by Campbell, Richard W. "City-County Consolidation: Learning from Failure." *Urban Georgia.* April 1988.

Zimmerman, Joseph F. "Dade County Reviews Charter." *National Civic Review,* 71, n. 5. May 1982.

CHAPTER 32

CITY-COUNTY CONSOLIDATION: LEARNING FROM FAILURE

Richard W. Campbell

City-county consolidation is an important local government issue. Between 1959 and 1984, 37 cities and counties in the United States tried to consolidate and failed, 14 of them on more than one occasion.[1] During the past several years, consolidation of city and county governments has been unsuccessfully considered in a number of Georgia communities, including: Brunswick, Glynn County; Athens, Clarke County; Lakeland, Lanier County; Macon, Bibb County; and Tifton, Tift County. The purpose of this article is to summarize what is known about city-county consolidation based upon past experience nationally. Before doing this, however, it is necessary to explore the changing role of county government in Georgia and its implications for city-county consolidation and to discuss how performance ambiguity and the conflicting values of efficiency and democracy serve as obstacles to the successful merger of city and county governments.

The Changing Role of Counties

The issue of city-county consolidation is inherently tied to the respective roles played by cities and counties in the delivery of local government services. During the past 15 years, the role of county government has changed dramatically. Today, in Georgia, both cities and counties are full service local governments. They each provide the full range of local government services and they function in an environment where they compete with one another for customers and for resources to support those services.

Cities and counties are both creatures of the state. They are constitutionally recognized entities created by the General Assembly. Despite these common roots, there are basic historical differences between them. Cities are incorporations which are created "for the convenience of the locality." They are corporate entities with the authority to respond to local demand for services. Counties, on the other hand, are "created with a view to the policy of the state at large." For most of their existence, they have been viewed as administrative arms of state government. As such, they have historically provided services mandated by the state (e.g., roads, tax collection, sheriff). Thus, while cities have traditionally had the authority to provide the full range of services demanded by its citizens, county service delivery authority has been more limited, with counties providing services specifically authorized by the state rather than in response to local demand.

In the 1960s and 1970s, events seemed to challenge this simple distinction. Three events stand out: (1) the processes of urbanization, (2) the proliferation of federal grant programs, and (3) the expanded role of the state in the intergovernmental system. The processes of

From *Urban Georgia,* Vol. 38, No. 4, April 1988. Published by the Georgia Municipal Association, Atlanta, Georgia. Reprinted with permission of the publisher.

urbanization are complex and involve demographic changes and shifts in the location of economic activity. Specifically, the processes involve: (1) growth in the unincorporated areas of the counties, (2) suburbanization or the movement of people and economic activity out of the central cities and into the suburban areas outside central cities, and (3) dense settlement patterns in areas outside incorporated areas. As a result of these demographic and economic changes, greater demand for services has been directed at county government, especially from residents and businesses in the unincorporated areas.

Second, the 1960s and 1970s also witnessed a proliferation of federal categorical grants-in-aid. Since many of these grant programs were urban oriented, counties became more involved in urban-related services (e.g., public housing, construction of sewage treatment plants, and air and water pollution control). And, third as the state role in our intergovernmental system increased with such federal initiatives as "the New Federalism," the role of counties increased as well. Primarily because of their historic role as administrative arms of the state, counties were called upon to administer expanding state functions (e.g., highways, welfare, and criminal justice programs).

The county, then, has emerged as a hybrid form of local government in Georgia. It is not only viewed as an administrative sub-unit of the state but also as a corporate local governmental entity with the power to respond to local service needs. This power was specifically given to county governments in 1972 by a constitutional amendment (Amendment 19) which authorized counties to provide at their discretion a host of urban services, ranging from police and fire protection to sewage collection and disposal to air quality control. As counties attempt to respond to local service demands, they become increasingly involved in the delivery of non-mandated or optional service (e.g., water and sewer, police and tire protection, and planning and zoning). Clearly, the county in Georgia has emerged as a pivotal unit of local government service delivery, with the power to respond to increased demand for local government services generally associated with population growth and urbanization.

Performance Ambiguity

Efforts to consolidate city and county governments inevitably involve the question: Will the newly created consolidated government perform better than existing city and county governments? Unfortunately, this ostensibly simple and very appropriate question is in fact a very difficult question, for which there are no quick and simple answers. Part of the problem is methodological. When a consolidated government is created, the city and county are abolished. Since the city and county are no longer operating, in assessing the consolidated government's performance, there is nothing to compare it to. The principal difficulty, though, lies primarily in the problems associated with assessing or measuring performance of governmental organizations generally.

In the private sector, performance is measured with precision and automatically through market transactions. At any given point in time, corporations and firms know exactly how well they are doing, whether they are operating at a profit and how much of a profit, and what kind of return investors are getting on their investments. On the other hand, in the public sector, there is an absence of precise and automatic measurement of performance. There are no automatic yardsticks that indicate whether taxpayers are getting a good return on their investments. There are no prices attached to public services funded out of the general fund which provide an indication of how much people value those services. If a government wants to know how well it is doing, it needs to conduct an evaluation study or performance audit, and even then, it is hard to develop good measures of performance because of the nature of governmental activity and services.

Contributing to the difficulty, performance assessment will vary depending upon which of two basic governmental functions are examined. The two primary functions of cities and counties are: (1) to govern and (2) to deliver services. With regard to the governance function, cities and counties provide a forum for the identification of public needs and the articulation of demands for governmental response to these needs. Since cities and counties confront limited resources making it impossible to respond to every need and to every demand, they also serve as arenas within which inevitable conflicts can be resolved. City and county governments, then, serve as mechanisms for sifting through competing needs and determining which needs are responded to and which are not.

With regard to the governance function, the major evaluative or performance criterion is "responsiveness." Unfortunately, there are no readily available objective indicators of the extent to which a particular government is responsive. The problem is that whether a government is judged as responsive or not will vary significantly depending upon who you ask. If a particular citizen's needs have been met, they are likely to view the government as responsive. On the other hand, if you ask a citizen whose needs have not been met, he/she is likely to respond that the government is not responsive.

The second basic function performed by cities and counties is the delivery of local government services. Cities and counties deliver the full range of local public services. Concern for the service delivery function generally reflects a focus on governmental operations. Consequently, the two primary evaluative criteria are: "efficiency" (Is the service provided efficiently or is the city or county providing the most service for the least cost?) and "effectiveness" (To what extent are programs doing what the council or the commission intended?). Performance assessment related to the service-delivery function, then, involves examining the activities of government, relating the cost of those activities to the product produced (service delivered) as well as an assessment of the results or impact of those activities or programs, comparing actual results with expected or anticipated results.

Conflicting Values

The difficulty of assessing performance and making judgments about whether one type or form of government is better than others is complicated even further in that these judgments about governmental performance are made within the context of conflicting values. In our society, we as citizens share many values which are dichotomous, meaning that the more you have of one value the less you have of the other. Some examples of dichotomous values include: democracy and efficiency, liberty and equality, change and stability, rule by the people and rule by experts.

Let's examine one set of dichotomous values that is particularly relevant to the issue of city-county consolidation. Cities and counties function within the context of our commitment to democratic values. Emphasis is placed on the protection of individual rights and a belief in fundamental democratic principles, such as openness in governmental decision making and government which is responsive to the people. At the same time, we value that government conduct its operations in a business-like manner, that government operate efficiently. Emphasis is placed on management control and maximizing the specific service goals of the governmental unit. These two sets of values are in conflict. In the late 19th century, Woodrow Wilson, in an essay entitled "Democracy and Efficiency," claimed that democracies are intrinsically inefficient, suggesting that the most efficient organizations tend to be the least democratic and vice versa. The problem is that the citizenry values democracy and efficiency simultaneously. These competing values produce some irreconcilable tensions within our local governmental systems. Consequently, in making specific decisions, local government officials are forced to make critical trade-offs, they must function in an environment which requires a constant process of balancing conflicting values.

What does this abstract discussion of values imply for the issue of city-county consolidation? Students of government generally agree that local government is characterized by considerable fragmentation. In the United States, there are over 82,000 local governments, with many of these governments having different and overlapping boundaries. Students of government disagree over whether this fragmentation is good or bad. Those who see it as good (public choice theorists) believe that many local governments offer the potential for greater responsiveness. In their view, smaller governments are closer to the people and therefore more responsive. On the other hand, there are those who see this fragmentation at the local government level as dysfunctional (reform theorists). They see considerable service duplication and overlap and a lack of control and coordination in the delivery of local government services.

Like students of government, the citizenry will also have divergent views about the desirability of such governmental fragmentation. Their views will tend to relate to how they perceive the basic function of government as discussed above. Those citizens principally concerned with the governance function will tend to see a large number of local governments as positive while those principally concerned with the service delivery function will tend to see fragmentation as bad. While the former are fundamentally concerned that government be "closer to the people," the latter seek to minimize the dysfunctions and inefficiencies associated with duplication and overlap. At the risk of oversimplification, one might argue that those who see many governments as good and who judge governmental performance primarily in terms of responsiveness, tend to oppose consolidation while those who see fragmentation as bad and who judge governmental performance primarily in terms of efficiency tend to support consolidation.

Consolidation: What Do We Know?

In light of the difficulties confronted in assessing governmental performance and the conflicting values which tend to dominate debates over city-county consolidation, it is not surprising to conclude, after a search of the literature, that little is known about consolidation. Moreover, what is known tends to be descriptive of the existing consolidation experiences, with very little known about the effects or impacts of a consolidated government. The following generalizations are descriptive of the 18 successful consolidations which have occurred since World War II.

1. City-county consolidations are not a common experience in the United States. There have been 18 consolidations since World War II.

2. Consolidation is largely a southern phenomenon, with 12 of the 18 consolidations occurring in southern states.

3. Most consolidation proposals originate with upper and middle class groups and all but one were approved by voter referendum (Indianapolis).

4. Consolidated governments are split between mayor-council (9) and council-manager (8) forms of government. In most consolidated governments, the voters choose the mayor directly, while eight of these governments elected their council through at-large elections exclusively. Four governments used districts while five governments used a combination of at-large and districts.

5. Supporters of city-county consolidation generally claim that consolidation will increase government efficiency and reduce costs while opponents argue that it will decrease citizen control of government and increase taxes. A survey in one Georgia community, however, suggests that taxes is not always the critical issue. In Conyers-Rockdale County, it was found that those who supported consolidation would vote for it even if taxes went up and those who expressed opposition to consolidation would oppose it even if taxes went down.[2]

As suggested above, it is much more difficult to offer general statements about the impact of consolidation. Research Atlanta, though, recently completed a major study of city-county consolidation, including a survey of officials from the 18 consolidated governments in the United States. They concluded that "merger is not an automatic panacea for local government problems, but the 18 city-county consolidations examined here apparently yield more benefits than disadvantages." More specifically, they found that:

1. Much of the effort of the new government went into expanding service delivery in the underserved areas of both the municipality and the unincorporated area of the county.

2. Consolidation usually decreased black voting strength by adding large numbers of

suburban white voters to the new government. However, black council representation usually grew after consolidation, mainly because many of the charters included electoral systems where council members were elected by districts rather than at large.

3. Consolidation can generate both savings and additional costs, its net effect depending on each community's specific circumstances. However, other factors (e.g., inflation, expanded public services) typically contribute to an overall increase in government expenditures after consolidation.

4. The consolidated governments usually tied residents' taxes more closely to the services they received by increased use of user fees and special tax districts. Property tax rates often fell, but the tax base was generally expanded (e.g., greater use of sales tax, income tax, user fees, and federal aid).

5. While many consolidations do not allow a termination of city and county employees, among those consolidations that did allow termination there was a measurable reduction in the local government workforce.[3]

Conclusion

City-county consolidation is a complex and difficult issue which seems to surface in at least two or three Georgia communities every year. These efforts usually fail. In fact, Columbus-Muscogee, created 18 years ago, is the only consolidated government in Georgia. Given the competitive position of cities and counties, the fact that both types of local governments have the authority to provide the full range of local government services, city-county consolidation is an issue that will continue to surface in Georgia on a regular basis.

While there are many reasons offered for the failure of specific consolidation efforts, it is suggested here that the problem of drawing firm conclusions about governmental performance seems to be a pervasive factor. Unfortunately, students of government structure have not been able to demonstrate empirically that consolidated governments perform better than cities and counties operating separately. This should not imply that they don't perform better. It means simply that it is hard to compare the performance of public organizations generally, and it is particularly difficult to show that a consolidated government performs better than a city or a county.

Part of the problem lies in defining the term "better." How do we know that one government's performance is better than another? Does better mean more responsive or more efficient or both? Probably both. Clearly, the debates over city-county consolidation are complicated by citizen attachment to conflicting values, values which have implications for how individual citizens perceive the relative performance of cities, counties, and consolidated governments. It has been argued here that the citizenry values both "responsive" and "efficient" government, and that those who are fundamentally concerned with responsive government will tend to oppose consolidation proposals while those concerned with efficiency will tend to support such proposals. This suggests that if a city-county consolidation effort is to succeed, the challenge for proponents of consolidation is to demonstrate how a consolidated government is not only efficient but how it can be responsive to diverse interests as well.

Notes

1. Kenneth Town and Carol Lambert, *The Urban Consolidation Experience in the United States* (Atlanta, Georgia: Research Atlanta, 1987).

2. Governmental Research and Services Division, *Consolidation of the City of Conyers and Rockdale County Governments: An Assessment of Community Attitudes* (Athens, Georgia: Carl Vinson Institute of Government, September 1987).

3. Kenneth Town and Carol Lambert, *The Urban Consolidation Experience in the United States* (Atlanta, Georgia: Research Atlanta, 1987).

CHAPTER 33

THE EVOLUTIONARY
CONSOLIDATION MODEL

Herbert H. Hughes and Charles Lee

For growing metropolitan areas facing new and changing demands for complex urban services and infrastructure, federal, state, and local revenue limits pose a serious problem.[1] Management solutions, such as privatization and productivity improvement, abound,[2] but only local government consolidation directly confronts the issue of local interjurisdictional fragmentation, which many feel is a major contributor to the problem of revenue limits in metropolitan areas.[3] Full administrative and political consolidation has pitfalls and, judging from the low number of consolidations reported nationwide, is seldom seen as a realistic solution.[4] Nevertheless, consolidation can be an appropriate and practical solution if it is allowed to evolve from minor cooperative arrangements among local governments into consolidated administrative or policy efforts whenever these interjurisdictional solutions are called for. This notion of consolidation as an evolutionary process is entirely consistent with the general philosophy and practice of local government in our country and with the strong tendency for individual local governments to cut across local jurisdictional boundaries through cooperative policy or administrative arrangements.[5]

Conceptual Framework

The Evolutionary Consolidation Model has been conceived and developed chiefly from experience with efforts to cooperate and consolidate in the Albuquerque/Bernalillo County metropolitan area and from ideas on local government capacity set forth by Gargan.[6] Although possibly unique in its small number of local government units (six), the Albuquerque/Bernalillo County area resembles other metropolitan areas in two important ways. Through annexation the area has experienced the same rapid central city growth through annexation characteristic of metropolitan areas nationwide,[7] and it reflects many of the same patterns of local interjurisdictional service transfers and cooperative service provisions reported in the nationwide Advisory Commission on Intergovernmental Relations study.[8]

Metropolitan Capacity. Metropolitan capacity and metropolitan government capacity are the foundation of the Evolutionary Consolidation Model. Metropolitan capacity may be defined simply as "the ability of a metropolitan community to solve its problems." Metropolitan government capacity, a subset, may be defined as "the collective ability of local governments in a metropolitan community to solve their problems." Metropolitan capacity is a function of expectations and resources, both concepts of John Gargan,[9] and harmony. All three are appropriate to interlocal community situations, but "harmony" is the key ingredient necessary to address fully the complicated environment of a

From *Urban Resources,* Vol. 4, No. 2, Winter 1987. Published by the Division of Metropolitan Studies, University of Cincinnati, Cincinnati, Ohio. Reprinted with permission of the publisher.

metropolitan community and its governmental units. According to Gargan, *Expectations involve perceptions and attitudes on "adequate" levels of public services, appropriate styles of political leadership, and accepted ways of conducting public affairs. Expectations are based in local practices, traditions, and cultures.*[10] Expectations may be heavily influenced by resources available to adjacent local governments and communities in a metropolitan situation. *Resources involve those community elements that can be brought to bear on community problems. Resources include, but are not limited to, money, knowledge, administrative skills, private sector associations, neighborhood organizations, and political popularity.*[11] Limits on resources may create an imbalance in the metropolitan situation where expectations are high. *Harmony* involves the appropriate balance between community expectations and resources to solve problems in a metropolitan area. The timing of the mixture of resources and expectations is essential for appropriate balance. Harmony is critical to the effective marshalling of resources to cope with expectations in a metropolitan situation.

Evolutionary Consolidation. Evolutionary Consolidation may be defined as *the persistent tendency of local governments and communities to build metropolitan government capacity through progressively more centralized, cooperative arrangements as a metropolitan area urbanizes.* In this model, both revenue and jurisdictional limits have significant potential to create disharmony among the community expectations and government resources in metropolitan settings. Evolutionary Consolidation is the major solution precisely because it directly addresses the disharmony commonly found in a metropolitan situation.

The Evolutionary Consolidation Process. Table 1 on page 274 depicts the entire evolutionary consolidation process starting at Stage 1, Informal Discussion, with occasional cooperation among adjacent local governments, and ending at Stage 5 with consolidation of the governments in a metropolitan area. Maximum capacity is most attainable at Stage 1, before intense interdependence among communities in a metropolitan situation has occurred. Communities are sufficiently isolated

to minimize disharmony from divergent, interlocal expectations; and resources, expectations, and limits are simple to evaluate, thereby allowing expectations within a given community to adjust easily to the level of resources. During Stage 1, only an occasional, informal discussion with adjacent local governments is necessary because harmony is high, limits are not a critical concern, and no jurisdiction fears losing control of resources to adjacent governments. For the same reason, annexation is not perceived as a high priority unless some very specific problem forces the issue.

In Stage 2, growing populations of adjacent communities are creating new urban problems which sharpen awareness of revenue and jurisdictional limits and require consideration of local government resource control through aggressive annexation and possibly other means. Resources are not yet strained to the point that they are unable to meet the still moderate level of expectations in the area communities, but the clear emergence of a central city is beginning to draw attention to common, rising expectations for urban services despite apparent resource variations among the area's local governments. In such an environment, local governments begin to explore the possibilities of cooperation.

During Stage 3, most communities in developing metropolitan areas are struggling to meet converging and rising expectations for urban services. Limits on operational revenue and bonding capacity, compounded by jurisdictional fragmentation, are severely limiting the ability of local governments to keep pace with the support and infrastructure expected in these rapidly growing areas. General disharmony throughout the metropolitan government structure is common during this period. With metropolitan government capacity at a low point, adjacent local governments are forced to explore every avenue of interlocal cooperation in order to cope with the service expectations of their constituents.

Stage 4, "Trial Consolidation," begins a trial marriage period between the central city and one or more other major local governments in a metropolitan area. After considerable experience with earlier contractual

---

The Evolutionary Consolidation Model as a Process in the Metropolitan Situation

Stage 1 Informal Discussion

Informal Joint Policy Discussion
  limited period, one issue
  extended period, multiple issues

Stage 2 Formal Cooperation

Cooperative Joint Policy Body
  one or multiple minor issues
  one or multiple major issues
Formal Contractual Arrangements
  part-time services, equipment
Formal Policy Arrangements
  zoning or other authority

Stage 3 Contract Consolidation

Policy or Management Sharing
  Equipment Sharing
  Facility Sharing
  Policy Delegation
  Management Delegation

Stage 4 Trial Consolidation

Master Joint Powers Agreement
  some major policy
  some major administrative
  formal joint decision body

Stage 5 Consolidation

Partial, Full Consolidation
  federated
  centralized

---

for the cooperation to terminate without going to the voters.

Finally, in Stage 5, local governments in a metropolitan area join in the most permanent cooperative arrangement, partial or full consolidation. This final stage is not inevitable, nor is it always desirable; disharmony and significant decreases in metropolitan capacity may result from premature or inappropriate centralization. Local governments should consolidate only when strong evidence shows that the collective government and community capacity will increase. They should also consolidate only under a federated approach, in which authority is shared between the central city and other areas in a consolidated jurisdiction.

Evolutionary Consolidation in One Metropolitan Situation

Named as one of the nation's ten new cities of great opportunity,[12] Albuquerque and the Bernalillo County metropolitan area provide an excellent laboratory for the study of the evolutionary consolidation process. Since 1940, Albuquerque's population has shown a continual urbanizing trend, growing from 35,000 or 50 percent of Bernalillo County to about 341,000 or 78 percent of the 1982 Bernalillo County population of about 433,000.[13] During this time, the community has been transformed from a small town with moderate expectations to an urban community whose citizens expect the delivery of a variety of complex urban services by both city and county governments. Basic structural changes affecting revenue limits and jurisdictional powers in city government have also taken place at the state level, and aggressive annexation, extensive interlocal cooperation, and consolidation have each been prominent in attempts to solve local government problems. Further, revenue limits on local government are firmly embedded in the state constitution, and jurisdictional limits are now surfacing as a problem due to incorporation efforts on the fringe of the metropolitan area.

The following is an examination of the evolutionary consolidation process in the

arrangements, these governments have decided that the inconveniences of living together may be worth a try, particularly since severe revenue limits and jurisdictional fragmentation are making it very difficult to live alone. Annexation is fading as a realistic means for the central city to control resources, and the emphasis is shifting to building comprehensive policy and administrative cooperation which provide permanent solutions to metropolitan problems. Some rights are retained, however,

Albuquerque/Bernalillo County area since 1940. The *Albuquerque Data Book* (1985), *City of Albuquerque Budget* (1985), *Bernalillo County Official Budget* (1985), and *Albuquerque City Charter* (1983) are sources for the demographic and financial data.[14] Other data come from the junior author's staff research for the recent Albuquerque/Bernalillo County Unification Task Force[15] and the senior author's observations from participation in civic, governmental, and political affairs at both the state level and in Albuquerque.

Stage 1: Informal Discussion. In 1940, most of the population outside the Albuquerque city limits resided in the rural Rio Grande River Valley areas on the north and south edges of the city. Most of the annexation in the 1940s was in the East Mesa area between the city and the Sandia Mountains, where the major population growth was occurring, and in the populated area of the North Valley. Until the early 1950s, city and county governments felt little pressure to move beyond the information discussion stage of evolutionary consolidation. Possibly because of the relatively low expectations for complex urban services, the clear separation of roles between city and county government, and the abundance of vacant land within the metropolitan area, they found little need to cooperate in overcoming the revenue limits imposed by the state constitution and related statutes. Major annexation by the city was occurring, but primarily in previously uninhabited areas on the East Mesa or in the North Valley adjacent to downtown. Annexation may well have been perceived as a mutually beneficial decision for neighborhoods, developers, and city government rather than an aggressive encroachment of urban development on rural areas to gain revenue and to control life style.

Stage 2: Formal Cooperation. In 1949, the first signs of formal cooperation between the governments of the city of Albuquerque and Bernalillo County appeared. At that time, the county commission passed a formal resolution requiring that all proposed plats or subdivisions of land within five miles of the city limits be approved by the city planning board before the county commission acted on them. Although the city had approval authority

through a 1947 state statute, the 1949 county commission resolution was significant because its language was cooperative in tone and it was formulated in cooperation with the city planning board.

During the 1950s, annexation and development on less expensive land on the East Mesa toward the Sandia Mountains began creating urban sprawl, and the accelerated population growth, which would push the city's population to 200,000 in 1960, was rapidly urbanizing the entire area. A major indication that metropolitan government capacity was indeed becoming a serious concern came in 1953, when the city and county commissions appointed a joint citizen's committee to study consolidation of city and county governments under enabling legislation passed by the state legislature in 1952. The consolidation committee worked for six years, and in 1959 the question of consolidation and a proposed new charter were put before the electorate. The vote failed almost 2 to 1 in the city and over 20 to 1 in the unincorporated area. The major issues in that election illustrate the complex relationships between the cooperative efforts of interlocal governments and capacity building in the metropolitan situation. On the one hand, the central governing bodies of both the city of Albuquerque and Bernalillo County supported consolidation as a way to meet rising expectations for urban services under existing revenue limits. On the other hand, opponents (mostly unincorporated area residents and some full-time county elected officials) were convinced neither that a problem existed nor that centralization would solve it. Opponents were particularly incensed that consolidation would achieve increased revenue through a property tax increase for unincorporated area residents and would require participation in retiring the bonded debt of the city. Zoning authority in the unincorporated area was also an issue, as was control of the resource priorities in the proposed new government.

During the 1960s, the 107 percent growth rate in the city during the 1950s declined to about 21 percent. Combined with the major influx of federal aid during the 1960s, the slower growth rate provided a breathing spell for the metropolitan area. With the exception of joint agreements on airport zoning and parks and recreation, few major cooperative efforts between city and county governments occurred until the late 1960s. With the Council of Governments (COG) providing significant joint transportation planning capability and direct federal aid flowing to both city and county for a variety of services, there was less pressure to build capacity through interlocal cooperation. Both the airport zoning and parks and recreation agreements, however, may reflect some local government capacity concerns. The airport zoning agreement addressed an overall metropolitan area problem by assigning administrative responsibility to the city, while for the sake of efficiency the parks and recreation agreement consolidated all such services in the county under the city.

Stage 3: Contract Consolidation. In the mid–1960s, the city and county governments in Albuquerque were edging into the Contract Consolidation Stage. Then a 1969 contract for city government to provide all planning services for the county, followed by a flurry of joint agreements in the early 1970s, ushered in contract consolidation on a broad scale. Aggressive annexation was continuing but was limited by the boundaries of Indian jurisdictions on the north and populations already established in some unincorporated areas. City growth was accelerating to a rate of 35 percent in the 1970s and a 1980 population of 332,000—75 percent of the population of Bernalillo County. A 1969 effort to revise the state constitution, city charter revisions in 1971 and 1974, another consolidation attempt in 1973, a state-sponsored study of city financing in 1976, and the service priorities addressed in the many cooperative agreements all clearly reflect the struggle of citizens and officials in the metropolitan area to overcome limits on the ability to meet rising urban service expectations.

The results of the 1973 consolidation referendum were similar to those of 1959. In 1973, unincorporated area residents voted about nine to one against, and both the proposed new charter and consolidation passed with a slight majority in the city. A post-election study discloses some other similarities between the 1973 and 1959 efforts.[16] Much like 1959, the major issues in 1973 were tax increases, rural lifestyle (zoning authority), and control of the new government. Another finding in the post-election study, that expectations for better services from consolidation correlated highly with a positive consolidation vote, reinforces the significance of expectations. But why, in the midst of a period of thriving cooperative activity, does consolidation fail? From an evolutionary consolidation view, the answer is simple. Full consolidation puts the major emphasis on increasing metropolitan government capacity, sometimes to the detriment of overall metropolitan community capacity, which requires harmony among community expectations, resources, and governments.

An analysis of the formal cooperative agreements between the two governments since 1969 confirms that significant cooperation became a critical concern at that time. Of the approximately 70 formal joint agreements since 1949, 33 were signed in the 1969–1979 period. At least 10 of the 33 involve major sharing of policy and resource control:

1. City provides planning services for county government.

2. City and county governments jointly contract out ambulance services.

3. City government manages adult jail facilities throughout the county.

4. North Valley unincorporated area gains access to city water system.

5. South Valley unincorporated area gains access to city water system.

6. City government provides animal control facilities for the county.

7. City government establishes sanitary sewage disposal system for valley unincorporated areas.

8. City and county governments, through COG, jointly sponsor general aviation facility planning for the county.

9. City government is designated lead agency in wastewater treatment plan for the county.

10. County government issues General Obligation (GO) bonds for new adult jail facility.

An examination of these ten formal

agreements reveals that in Agreements 1, 3, 4, 5, 6, 7, and 9 county officials granted major administrative control to city government in exchange for constituent-expected services which revenue limits in county government would not readily permit. In the case of ambulance services (Agreement 2) and aviation facility planning (Agreement 8), which required relatively low expenditures, service expectations were more critical than revenue limits. The construction of the jail facility (Agreement 10) is an excellent example of using interlocal government agreements to cope with revenue limits. In Bernalillo County, city government has remained at or near the GO bonded debt limit and county government at or near the operational millage limit since the 1960s; city government has had access to major gross receipts and enterprise fee revenue for operational purposes while county government has seldom exceeded under 50 percent of its GO bonding capacity. Under the two major jail facility agreements, city government has assumed responsibility for 50 percent of the operational funding, and county government has floated the bond issue for construction of the new jail facility.

Frequent communication between city and county governments now occurs during the planning of bond projects, and, in particular, county bond issues have broadened to include major urban concerns such as roads and bridges related to industrial developments and a new criminal justice center in the downtown area. A trend in recent bond elections is to take pressure off the city bonding capacity limits by use of county GO bonding capability in exchange for joint ownership in physical facilities built by the bond issue proceeds, or shared administrative control of the service involved, or operational revenue and fee arrangements which reduce the pressure of operational revenue constraints. The advantages to the city of using county government bonding capability are obvious. The advantages to the county are also obvious where operation revenue relief is obtained. In the case where the county government receives only ownership rights in the tradeoff, the increase in political capacity resulting from the leverage of ownership can be substantial.

Stage 4. Trial Consolidation. Perhaps the single most important step along the path of evolutionary consolidation for the Albuquerque/Bernalillo County metropolitan area was the creation of the city-county Intergovernmental Committee (IGC) during the 1970s. Although the idea was a natural outcome of the growing cooperation between city and county government, it was recommended by a 1976 state-sponsored study on the financing of urban services in Albuquerque.[17] The IGC is a permanent body consisting of three county commission members, three city council members, and the mayor. Meetings are routinely covered by the press, and both the city and county governing bodies delegate considerable authority to the IGC. The IGC provides a forum for joint discussion of metropolitan area concerns and has been involved in most of the major cooperative arrangements between city and county governments since the late 1970s.

Most departments in city and county government are now involved in some type of cooperation with the other government, either formally or informally. About 36 formal agreements of cooperation between city and county government have been signed since 1980. At least seven of these agreements involve major sharing of policy and resource control:

1. County government designs and constructs key street expansion.

2. City government designs key street expansion.

3. County Sheriff Department leases space in City Police Building.

4. City and county governments jointly construct/occupy new building.

5. City and county governments jointly use city mainframe computer.

6. County government GO bonds fund City Police Building addition.

7. Regional Solid Waste Authority is formed by the city and county.

Together, these agreements illustrate the depth of the cooperation between the two governments. To be more specific, in Agreement 2 (key street expansion), administrative control is granted to the city government in exchange for constituent-expected services which revenue limits in county government would not readily permit. Agreement 3 exchanges some loss of control of the space in which the sheriff is housed for a very low lease fee; both governments stand to improve service through increased communications between their law enforcement officers and to gain political capacity from the perception that attempts are being made to eliminate duplication. Agreements 5 (joint computer use) and 7 (Regional Solid Waste Authority) were signed on the assumption that both parties would benefit financially due to economies of scale, but the gain in political capacity from elimination of duplication was strongly anticipated, especially in Agreement 5. Although severely criticized, both agreements continue in effect. Agreement 2 involves street improvements which had long been expected by many residents both in and outside the city limits, and Agreement 1 is a key street expansion critical to major new city and county industrial development and to the use of a bridge which has been a major issue in the metropolitan area for over ten years. Both city and county governments should gain political capacity and outside matching revenues from these joint efforts.

The joint construction of the new city/county building (Agreement 4), and the issue of county GO bonds for joint construction of a new addition to the city police building (Agreement 6), may well represent the most significant movement along the path of evolutionary consolidation since the formation of the IGC. The addition to the city police building enabled city government, which is near the limit of its bonding capacity, to use available county government bonding capacity to obtain additional space for both city and county law enforcement agencies. The county will obtain joint ownership of the building, thereby saving operational revenue previously required to lease space in it. Originated by the IGC, which had full responsibility for design and construction, the new city/county building was financed by county government GO bonds and city government revenue bonds. Thus, the county was able to trade use of available bonding capacity for savings in its severely limited operational revenue; similarly, the city government could thus conserve its limited bonding capacity by paying the major share of the revenue bond obligation with more readily available operational revenue. Ownership of the building is shared under this arrangement. Even deeper concern for revenue limits can be found in the events which led to the agreement to fund this building. The original idea for a joint city/county building was generated principally from earlier county-wide voter rejection of a bond issue for a new county government office building. Since city voters overwhelmingly voted against that proposal, a joint city/county building provided the means to gain support of city and unincorporated area voters for county and city government office space. In terms of metropolitan government capacity, this project provides another example of how interlocal cooperation can maximize harmony among community expectations, resources, and local governments.

One other major cooperative effort occurring in 1985 was the Albuquerque/Bernalillo County Unification Task Force, formed by the city and county governing bodies to investigate the feasibility of policy and administrative consolidation. The task force deliberations reinforced the premise in the Evolutionary Consolidation Model that revenue limits are significant in consolidation considerations. The task force suggested the "municipal," rather than "county," form of combined government because New Mexico municipalities have higher gross receipts tax limits and broader bonding, enterprise fee, and home rule options than do counties. The task force endorsed eventual consolidation and immediate expansion of the IGC concept into a sixteen-member Intergovernmental Council comprised of the mayor, all city councillors, and all county commissioners. It also recommended the adoption of a City/County Master Joint Powers Agreement to serve as a charter for the Intergovernmental Council. Each governing body received and discussed the recommendations in early 1986, but no further action has been taken since then. In the meantime, the IGC continues to function as the major organizational link between city and county governments.

Concluding Remarks

Evolutionary consolidation may well be the major solution to revenue limits in growing metropolitan areas because it directly addresses the appropriate balance between diverse community service expectations and resources necessary to increase capacity in complex metropolitan environments. The common emphasis nationwide on interlocal government cooperative arrangements, rather than full consolidation, suggests that the Albuquerque/Bernalillo County experience may have general application to many other metropolitan situations. Now the Evolutionary Consolidation Model needs to be tested in a variety of urban communities to determine its value in understanding and solving metropolitan problems.

Notes

1. Roy Bahl, *Financing State and Local Governments in the 1980s* (New York: Oxford University Press, 1984).

2. Charles H. Levin, "Citizenship and Service Delivery; The Promise of Co-production," *Public Administration Review*, 44 (March Special Issue, 1984), 178–89.

3. Herbert H. Hughes and Dan Weaks, et al., *Albuquerque Municipal Financing: Final Report* (Governor's Albuquerque Municipal Financing Task Force, 1976), 3–10; David B. Walker, "Localities under the New Intergovernmental System," in L. Kenneth Hubbell, ed., *Fiscal Crisis in American Cities: The Fed-*eral Response (Cambridge, MA: Ballinger Publishing Company, 1979), 25–57; Advisory Commission for Intergovernmental Relations, *State and Local Roles in the Federal System* (Washington, DC, 1981); Robert E. Firesline, Bernard I. Weinstein, and Shelley M. Hayden, "Inter-governmental Fiscal Cooperation in Growing Metropolitan Economies," in James H. Carr, ed., *Crisis and Constraint In Municipal Finance*, (New Brunswick, NJ: Center for Urban Policy Research, Rutgers, 1984), 221–29; Bahl, 1984.

4. Governmental Research Institute, *Reorganizing Our Counties* (Cleveland, OH: Cleveland Foundation, 1980).

5. Advisory Commission on Intergovernmental Relations, *Intergovernmental Service Arrangements for Delivering Local Public Services Update 1983* (Washington, DC, 1985).

6. John J. Gargan, "Consideration of Local Government Capacity," *Public Administration Review*, 41 (November/December 1981), 649–58.

7. Robert D. Thomas, "Metropolitan Structural Development: The Territorial Imperative," *Publius*, 14 (Spring 1984), 83–115.

8. Advisory Commission, 1985.

9. Gargan.

10. Gargan, 652.

11. Gargan, 652.

12. John Naisbitt, *Megatrends* (New York: Warner Books, 1982).

13. City of Albuquerque Municipal Development Department, *Albuquerque Data Book* (1985).

14. Bernalillo County Department of Finance, *Bernalillo County Official Budget* (1985); City of Albuquerque, *Albuquerque City Charter* (1983); City of Albuquerque Department of Finance and Management, *City of Albuquerque Budget* (1975).

15. Joint Albuquerque/Bernalillo County Unification Task Force, *Final Report*, (1985).

16. Dan Weaks, *An Analysis of the Consolidation Effort in Albuquerque/Bernalillo County*, (1974).

17. Hughes, Weaks, et al., 1976.

CHAPTER 34

A REPORT TO THE CHARTER REVIEW BOARD

Donald C. Menzel

Hillsborough County voters went to the polls in 1983 and adopted a new charter to produce "... a more responsible and effective government"—so states the Charter's Preamble. Toward this end, the Charter drafters attempted to define clearly and sharply who is responsible for making policy and who is responsible for its implementation. Simply stated, the Board of County Commissioners is to do only two things: (a) set overall policy and (b) appoint and remove the County Administrator and advise and consent on the selection of key personnel. Similarly, the County Administrator is the Chief Executive Officer and is also charged to do only two things: (1) to faithfully implement policy set by the Board of County Commissioners and (2) to recruit qualified people to assist him.

Whether or not this arrangement has or will result in a more responsible and effective government is an important question now before the Hillsborough County Charter Review Board (CRB). Some citizens have expressed confidence in the appointed professional administrator arrangement. Other citizens have asserted that strong political leadership must be mated with administrative leadership and are, therefore, in support of an elected county executive.

To examine these arguments more thoroughly, the Charter Review Board asked the USF Center for Public Affairs & Policy Management to collect relevant data and report the findings to the CRB. This report presents the findings. The report is organized in the following fashion: (1) the questions which the study seeks to answer are listed, (2) the research methodology is described, (3) experiences with elected and appointed executives in other jurisdictions are detailed, (4) the "pros and cons" of the elected and appointed executive governmental forms are presented, and (5) arguments for adopting or rejecting the elected or appointed executive form of government in Hillsborough County are developed.

Study Questions

A series of questions, some practical and some more speculative in nature, can be asked about the elected county executive form of government. The questions which guided the research reported in this paper include:

- What has been the experience of the elected county executive in other governmental jurisdictions? How many counties in Florida and other counties have elected executives?
- Is there any evidence that the governance/management process has worked "better" with an elected executive?
- Has this system produced higher quality public services? Are public services delivered in a more cost-effective manner?

From *Final Report to the Hillsborough County Charter Review Board*, July 15, 1986. Published by the Center for Public Affairs and Policy Management, University of South Florida, Tampa, Florida. Reprinted with permission of the publisher.

- What problems, difficulties, or conflicts might arise between the Constitutional officers (i.e., county clerk, tax collector, sheriff, supervisor of elections, property appraiser) and the general county government under an elected executive?
- Could an elected county executive be an effective office with little or no change made in the independence and authority now accorded the Constitutional officers? Or, would it be necessary to make significant adjustments in the roles and responsibilities of the Constitutional officers, perhaps placing them more fully or entirely under the authority of the elected county executive?

Research Methodology

The study team employed several methodologies to collect information and data. The first task was to conduct a thorough search of the scholarly and professional literature. This literature review was intended to find out what is known or not known about county executives, particularly elected county executives. Our efforts included a computerized library search of several thousand journals and books which have been published since 1970. Additionally, we conducted a manual search of the journals most likely to report findings of interest. These included *The National Civic Review, State and Local Government*, and *Public Management*. We also reviewed a dozen textbooks dealing with local and urban government.

Other sources from which information was secured included the Florida State Association of County Commissioners, the National Association of Counties, the New York State Association of County Commissioners, the Pennsylvania State Association of County Commissioners, the Citizens Forum on Self Government, and the International City Management Association. Representatives of these associations were contacted by mail, and, in several instances, by telephone. Relatedly, we contacted scholars who have published in this area to insure that we had not missed recently published materials or papers awaiting publication. (It is not uncommon for a scholarly paper to sit on an editor's desk for 12–24 months before it is reviewed, edited, and published.)

Two other components contribute to the study methodology: (1) a survey[1] conducted by telephone with 442 Hillsborough County residents, and (2) interviews[2] which were conducted with 21 elected and appointed county officials.

Experiences in Other Jurisdictions

Historically, county governments in the United States have had two purposes: to serve as the arm of state government such as recording deeds, wills, and marriages and to provide certain local services, such as maintaining roads and bridges. The first counties in Florida, which date from 1821, were administered by "county courts," consisting of five justices of the peace. Although these county courts were principally concerned with judicial matters, they were also responsible for legislation and administrative matters for the unincorporated areas of the county. This process was later changed to provide for four elected members, who together with the judge of probate, comprised of five-member boards of county commissioners, which is still the case for most Florida counties.

Since the adoption of the 1968 Florida Constitution, counties have been given additional authority to constitute themselves as "charter counties." If they choose to follow the process that is required, as Hillsborough County did in 1983, they are afforded "all powers of local self-government not inconsistent with general or with special law approved by a vote of the electors."

Under the Constitution, a charter county may change the number and means of selecting its governing body. Moreover, it can abolish or change the way of selecting the Constitutional officers, who are elected department heads.

An important change for charter counties, under the 1968 Constitution, is that any special act adopted by the Legislature relating to a charter county can become effective only after approval by the voters of the county. This provision reduces the authority of a legislative delegation to make changes in the operation of the affairs of charter counties.

While the framework is provided in law, the actual operation and performance of county governments in Florida and, for that matter, in other states is something we know very little about. Indeed, American counties have been described as "forgotten governments" and a "dark continent."[3] One need only peruse recently published texts on urban and local government to appreciate how dark the continent of county government really is. In *Managing Urban America*, a text published in 1984 by David R. Morgan, counties are essentially ignored.[4] In fairness to the author, however, Morgan provides a few examples of the roles that counties play in intergovernmental relations and interlocal agreements. William A. Schultz in *Urban Politics* (1985) also ignores counties while giving substantial attention to cities, ideologies, and power structures.[5]

In *Urban America* (1975), David A. Caputo is not as inattentive.[6] He notes that counties are formal participants in urban policy making. In one telling sentence he states: "Counties have not been the subject of much research in the past few years, even though recently counties in general have become more important in local decision-making...."[7] Other writers acknowledge the importance of counties in more unsavory ways. The authors of a newly published book, *Urban Policy and Politics in a Bureaucratic Age* (1986), limit their observations to the "county machine," with all the evils that this label connotes.[8]

The texts identified thus far not only ignore counties, they do not even acknowledge the existence of the elected county executive. Lest this point be overdrawn, one author, Gerald L. Houseman in *State* and *Local Government: The New Battleground* (1986), informs the reader that counties have grown increasingly active and vital in large urban areas.[9] Indeed, " ... county government is now occasionally headed by an elected county executive, whose powers resemble those of a mayor in a mayor-council system. County executives are found, for example, in the Long Island counties ad-jacent to New York City and in Baltimore County, Maryland."[10]

Another author, John J. Harrigan, writing in *Political Change in the Metropolis* (1985) observes that efforts at reforming county government have centered heavily on strengthening the role and authority of the executive officer.[11] This has taken three forms: the appointed county administrator, the appointed county manager, and the elected county executive. The appointed county administrator/manager forms have been the most widely adopted, with approximately 25 percent of America's 3,042 counties adopting them. The elected county executive plan has been adopted in a fewer number of counties. The statistics vary from 3 to 10 percent of the nation's counties. The *1986 Directory* of the National Council of Elected County Executives list 355 counties/cities with elected executives. This low adoption level, according to Harrigan, is due in part to the resistance of incumbent commissioners who would lose visibility under such an arrangement.[12]

This meager treatment of county governments in textbooks is indicative of how little is known about this important form of local government and whether citizens are served well or poorly. By way of further illustration, we were unable to locate a single systematically conducted study of the elected county executive. What we did uncover were various descriptive accounts and a survey conducted by the National Association of Counties in 1970.[13] Therefore, the information reported in the remainder of this section is more descriptive than analytical. We have, however, been able to locate some information concerning the organizational forms of county government in the United States.

THE COMMISSIONER FORM

In general, American counties are governed by what is called the commission plan, similar to that which prevailed in Hillsborough County before the adoption of the County Administrator Act of 1973. The commission plan provides, in effect, for a plural executive and spreads administrative responsibility among members of the governing body, which also serves as the local government's legislature.

Most American counties (70 percent) continue to be governed by the commission plan.

THE COMMISSIONER-ADMINISTRATOR FORM

This governmental structure is an application to counties of the municipal council-manager form found in many cities. This form of government provides for separation of legislative and executive powers, and for the appointment of the county administrator by the county commission at whose pleasure he/she serves.

Presented below are the criteria established by the International City Management Association (ICMA) to classify county administrators. For ease of reading, where the words "manager," "council," "city" and "municipal" appear in ICMA materials, we have substituted "administrator," "commission" and "county."[14]

A. Appointment: The administrator should be appointed by a majority of the commission for an indefinite term and removable only by a majority of the commission.

B. Policy formulation: The position should have direct responsibility for policy formulation on overall problems.

C. Budget: The administrator should be designated by legislation as having responsibility for preparation of the budget, presentation to the commission, and direct responsibility for the administration of the commission approved budget.

D. Appointing authority: The administrator should be delegated by legislation the full authority for the appointment and removal of at least most of the heads of the principal departments and functions of the county government.

E. Organizational relationships: Those department heads whom the administrator appoints should be designated by legislation as administratively responsible to the administrator.

F. External responsibilities: Responsibilities of the position should include extensive relationships involving the overall problems of county operations.

G. Qualifications required for position: The qualifications for the position should be based on the educational and administrative background of candidates.

The first recorded appointment of a county administrator occurred in 1927 in Iredell County, North Carolina. By 1941 more than 300 counties had taken similar steps to improve the administration of their governments. The 1984 *Municipal Yearbook* reveals that in counties with populations over 25,000 the council-administrator form (appointed administrator) is in place in 27 percent of those counties.[15] In Florida, 25 percent of the 39 counties with populations over 25,000 have retained a commission form while 75 percent have adopted a commission-administrator form.

THE COUNCIL-ELECTED EXECUTIVE FORM

The elected executive plan emerged in the 1930s. By 1975, there were 51 counties in the United States with elected executives, a majority having adopted this form between 1965 and 1975.[16] Several variations have evolved. Some counties have required elected executives to appoint a chief administrative officer to assist him/her carry out the day-to-day operations of county government. Other counties such as those in Montana, New Jersey, and Pennsylvania have vested formal administrative responsibilities with the chairman or president of the county commission. This person is elected at large and is a voting member of the legislative body. He/she does not have formal veto powers and participates as an equal in policy formulation. Except for being directly elected to this position, this position appears to be structurally equivalent to the situation found in Hillsborough County before the adoption of the County Administrator Act in 1973, when the five commissioners elected one of their peers to serve as commission chairman with administrative powers.

The states with the largest number of elected county executives are Arkansas (75 counties), Kentucky (120 counties), Maryland (7 counties), Wisconsin (8 counties), New York (18 counties), and Tennessee (95 counties).[17]

New York's counties are increasingly receptive to the elected executive plan, with 18 of the state's 58 counties having elected executives.[18]

The larger, more urbanized counties were the early adopters, with less populated counties adopting at a later date. Currently, the elected executive plan is in place in counties ranging in population from 77,000 (Putnam) to 1.3 million (Nassau County). The plan has become popular in New York because each county has considerable legal flexibility to tailor the plan to fit local needs and conditions.[19]

The elected executive occupies a highly visible and increasingly important political role in New York. Indeed, over the past decade two county executives were elected to statewide offices. In 1977, Erie County's elected executive, Edward V. Regan, was elected state comptroller. More recently (1982) Alfred B. DelBellow who served as the elected executive in Westchester County was elected lieutenant governor.[20] Mr. DelBellow's successor, Andrew P. O'Rourke, is a serious candidate (1986) for the Republican nomination for governor.[21] All executives in New York are elected on a partisan ballot.

This visibility is due to several factors, with perhaps the most important being that he/she is elected at large while members of the legislative body are elected from districts. It is worth noting that the legislative bodies are large, ranging in size from 7 members to 39 members. In short, the county "commission" behaves like a state legislature in conjunction with a governor (elected executive).

In Wisconsin eight counties operate with an elected executive — including Milwaukee County which is required by state law to have an elected executive. The Wisconsin experience is mixed. One presumed advantage of the elected executive is that it centralizes power and enables decisiveness in government. This has not happened in Wisconsin. For example, the county executive in most Wisconsin counties does not hire, evaluate, or fire the directors of the two largest agencies — social services and unified services. They are hired and fired by independent, statutorily mandated boards. The directors of several other agencies — parks, health, and library — are similarly appointed and unaccountable to the executive.[22] As a whole, according to one observer of the Wisconsin experience, the typ-

ical management structure is "held together through a fickle amalgam of elected and appointed bureaucrats whose individual sufferances of — not accountability to — the elected county executive determine the success or failure of the executive's management policies and initiatives."[23]

The state of Arkansas has 75 counties, all of which have elected county administrators (officially called county judges). Arkansas has always had elected county officials and a spokesperson for the Arkansas association of counties reports that it has been very successful. Presently, they are acquiring signatures in order to attempt to change the length of the term served from two years to four years.[24]

The spokesperson further indicated that they are cost effective and are providing quality services for the taxpayers because they have someone running for office about every 13 months. This affords the voters frequent opportunities to voice their opinions at the polls. No major conflicts have arisen between elected executives and the constitutional officers due to the fact that the state statutes clearly set forth all duties and responsibilities. All officials file for election by party — Democratic, Republican or Independent.

Arkansas added flexibility to their system in 1977 with an amendment that permits that the county legislative body (called a quorum court) to cause a governmental organization study to be undertaken. If the study finds it is more beneficial for offices to be combined or appointed, the quorum court can refer the issue to the voters in a general election. The citizenry is then able to decide if they want appointed officials or combined elective offices.

No county in Florida has an elected chief executive, unless one considers the Jacksonville-Duval consolidated government as a county. The *Municipal Yearbook* categorizes Jacksonville-Duval as a city.

Pros and Cons

The advantages and disadvantages of an elected county executive in contrast to an appointed county administrator can be stated in several ways. One way is to be general and abstract. Another way is to compare the elected county executive form with the appointed manager form. Let's look first at the more general features of each plan.

APPOINTED COUNTY EXECUTIVE

The 1975 *County Year Book* lists the following as frequently cited advantages of the commission-administrator form of county government[25]:

1. The council-administrator plan separates policy making and administration, thus removing administration from political influence.

2. The appointed administrator, who is often recruited on a nationwide basis (unlike elected officials who must be county residents), can provide highly professional administrative leadership.

3. The council-administrator plan is a less dramatic departure from the traditional commission plan and makes for easier transition from the commission form.

4. The county administrator serves at the pleasure of the county board and can be replaced immediately should he or she fail to fulfill the duties of the position.

5. The county legislature (board) under the council-administrator plan is free to spend time on policy development while the administrator handles the day-to-day business of the county government.

6. Greater control over performances and expenditures is possible under the supervision of the appointed administrator than with the commission form.

Supporters of the appointed county administrator maintain that a skilled management professional who is answerable to an elected board is the best arrangement for bringing about responsible and effective government. A professional in charge of the day-to-day management of county business will result in the best expenditures of taxes and will create a climate of professionalism that will deter corruption and minimize inequities in the provision of public services.

Disadvantages of the commission-administrator form are, according to the 1975 *County Year Book*, the following[26]:

1. An appointed administrator cannot provide policy leadership on important issues facing the county, crystalize public opinion, and be an effective advocate for critical county issues. The appointive nature of the position places the administrator in a less influential role than a directly elected executive.

2. The administrator is at the mercy of the whims of the county board, particularly when the county board is split politically.

3. Members of a part-time governing board are dependent on the full-time administrator for information needed to make policy decisions and, in many cases, for policy direction; an appointed administrator should not have such extensive control.

4. A "professional" administrator, recruited from outside the county, may not understand the community.

ELECTED COUNTY EXECUTIVE

Proponents of the elected executive seek to fuse political power and accountability with effective administration. The 1975 *County Year Book* lists the following as often cited advantages of the elected executive plan[27]:

1. The elected executive plan provides the most visible policy making for the community through providing the public an opportunity to hear the pros and cons of each issue.

2. The executive (particularly in urban areas) provides the needed strong political leadership for relating to diverse segments of the community. An executive at large is considered more dependable and less likely to resign during a crisis or crucial period of change for the county than an administrator who serves at the pleasure of the county board.

3. The elected executive is responsible to the public will; he or she must answer to the county electorate in the next election.

4. Greater visibility and prestige is achieved for the county with the council-elected executive plan. State legislators, governors, the United States Congress, and the President can focus on one individual who clearly represents the entire county.

5. The best system of checks and balances is provided by this complete separation of powers. Through the veto, which can be overridden by the entire county board, both branches can express their commitment to their positions on various issues.

Critics of the elected executive plan contend that this more "political" approach is not well suited for modern, complex government. Indeed, this approach may promote diseconomies in the provision of public services, inefficiencies and waste, and public policies that serve special interests. Moreover, it does not assure professional management of the day-to-day operations of local government.

A Question of Values

No one, including proponents of the elected executive, is an advocate of waste and inefficiency in government. The fundamental question is: "What arrangement is most likely to produce a government which is responsive, accessible, accountable, efficient, effective, and decisive?" Can an elected executive form of government realize these often competing sets of values? Or, is the appointed manager form of government more likely to achieve these values?

An answer to these questions can be gleaned in part from scholarly research on "reformed" local government.[28] The reform tradition has its roots in two movements — the waste, fraud, and abuse associated with big-city machine politics at the turn of this century and the view first articulated by Woodrow Wilson in 1887 that "government should be run like a business." Wilson believed that efficiency, economy, and effectiveness should permeate government, and they could best be realized by approaching government in the same way as one would approach business.

The council-manager form of government is a clear expression of the business approach to government. For example in 1930 when the council-manager plan was under consideration in Dallas, a newspaper asked: "Why not run Dallas itself on a business schedule by business methods under businessmen.... Dallas is the corporation. It is as simple as that."[29] By 1941, the council-manager plan had become so popular that 315 cities embraced it. By 1966, the number of cities had grown to 1,245. As of November 1984, there were 3,331 U.S. cities with council-appointed managers, and 803 commission-appointed county administrators.[30]

The council-manager plan has been adopted most widely by cities in the population range of 50,000 to 250,000 and least widely in small communities and cities over 500,000. Several explanations are typically offered for this adoption pattern. Small communities (especially those with less than 25,000) oftentimes cannot afford a full-time professional manager. At the other end of the continuum, it is argued that the diversity of interests which often characterizes large populations is more compatible with a mayor-council structure than with a council-manager structure. Nonetheless, several large American and European communities operate under the council-manager structure, including Dade County, Dallas, San Diego, Kansas City and London. Mid-sized cities, the argument continues, are more homogeneous and compatible with a more businesslike approach.

But have "reformed" local governments made a difference? Are they more economical, efficient, effective, accessible, and responsive? One response to this question is provided by a pioneering study of 200 cities of 50,000 or larger population which was completed in the late 1960s. This study found that reformed cities had lower taxing and spending levels than did unreformed cities.[31] It also found that the spending patterns of reformed cities tended to emphasize programs benefiting middle-income residents more than lower-income residents. Another study completed in 1975 reported that civil rights groups were more successful in having their demands met by unreformed cities than by reformed cities.[32] Muddling the picture some, a third study which matched 11 cities that changed political structures with 11 that did not found "... taxing and spending differences were largely unaffected by changes in city government structure."[33]

These studies present, then, a mixed picture of the benefits which result when a city changes its structure of government. Moreover, they tell us very little about the center of power. Nor do they speak directly to the experiences of county governments. There is, however, one research project underway which addresses these matters in part. The study is limited to five large, urbanized cities and counties in North Carolina.

The study's findings have been reported in a paper entitled, "Leadership Roles in City and County Government."[34] Dr. James H. Svara of the University of North Carolina at Greensboro surveyed more than 100 county commissioners, city council members, and city/county staffs representing five cities and counties to determine what differences in roles and behaviors might exist among and between these important officials. He began the investigation expecting to find significant differences between cities and counties but, after examining the data, concluded that more similarities than differences exist. More specifically, he noted that "the attitudes concerning the governing boards, role definitions for managers, and board-manager relations do not differ markedly."[35]

These findings provide some confidence that our knowledge of municipal government can be applied to county government. Still, there are limitations, one of which is that the counties which Svara studied are not elected-executive counties. They are commissioner-administrator counties. In fact, 80 of North Carolina's 100 counties have an appointed administrator. There are no elected county executives in North Carolina.

One other finding in Svara's study should be noted. It is the variation found to exist in the patterns of behavior shown by city council members and their staffs and county commissioners and their staffs. In particular, the study indicates that county commissioners and staff are more likely to share or jointly exercise policy/management responsibilities than are their counterparts in the cities. In other words, there is a more well-defined line drawn between policy and administration in council-manager cities than in commissioner-administrator counties. Viewed from one vantage point, one might conclude that this finding merely reaffirms the widely held view that county commissioners dabble much too frequently in administrative matters. Such dabbling, however, may be due to the greater blurring of roles and responsibilities which exist in county government in contrast to municipal government. If this is indeed the

case — that policy/management responsibilities are more intertwined in counties — then efforts to effect a successful form of council-manager government in counties may be difficult.

A caution should be sounded before turning to another subject. The studies described above and the findings are not definitive, but merely suggestive. To repeat a point made earlier, "despite the increasing importance of counties as units of local government, counties have been little studied."[36] We are just beginning to understand the behavior of those who make county government work, and we are not much better off in our understanding of how the structure of county government shapes those behaviors.

Should Hillsborough County Adopt an Elected Executive Form of Government?

A simple "yes" or "no" answer cannot be supplied. The preceding review of scholarly research does not allow us to predict that Hillsborough County government will be more or less "responsible and effective" by adopting an elected executive form of government. The reasons are:

1. "Research" dealing with the elected county executive has been entirely descriptive.
2. There have been no systematic, empirical studies of the elected county executive which inform us as to whether or not
   a) the governance/management process has worked effectively,
   b) high quality public services have been provided,
   c) public services have been delivered in a cost-effective fashion,
   d) the public has had greater access to policy makers.
3. Previous research has examined aggregate tendencies at the municipal level. Such studies tell us little about a localized experience. What may be workable in one jurisdiction may or

may not be workable in another jurisdiction.

Our knowledge, in short, is very limited. Still, this is not reason to fail to make reasonable arguments about the relationships between governmental structure and policy outcomes. Therefore, the next section of this report presents arguments for adopting or rejecting the elected county executive in Hillsborough County. In the final analysis, the persuasiveness and meaningfulness of the arguments must be determined by the reader.

Arguments for the Appointed Administrator

1. An argument in favor of the appointed county administrator is that competent professional management will be brought to bear on problems facing Hillsborough County citizens. Hillsborough County government is big government, having a 1985–86 budget of $750 million and employing more than 6,800 people. It is much too big and complex to be placed in the hands of individuals who are not skilled, experienced urban managers. One authority referred to the elected executive as putting a "transient amateur" in charge of the government.[37]

2. The present form of government is organized like a business corporation, with its board of directors being the Board of County Commissioners, who appoint the chief operating officer — the county administrator. The stockholders of no major corporations elect the general manager directly, which is what the elected county executive system proposes to do.

3. The commission-administrator form of county government will maximize representation and insure citizen access to elected decision makers. The present configuration insures representation for most groups and constituents. One commissioner put it this way, "the appointed administrator who serves at the pleasure of an elected board will allow the public greater access to elected policy makers and therefore make the Board a more representative body than would be the case under a single, elected administrator."

4. An appointed professional public manager will foster a climate of professionalism throughout county government. Such professionalism is reinforced by the administrator's involvement with national associations such as the International City Management Association, the American Society for Public Administration, and the National Association of County Administrators. A climate of professionalism is essential in light of the political corruption which has plagued the county for the past two decades.

5. The present commission-administrator arrangement preserves an important continuity. Hillsborough County has had an appointed administrator since 1973. A shift to an elected executive would disrupt the administration of the county and, in effect, be a destabilizing influence. Moreover, the existing fragmentation of governmental power between the Board of County Commissioners and the Constitutional officers would be exacerbated with an elected county executive. To be effective, an elected county executive would have to have more control over the sheriff, tax collector, clerk, and property appraiser. However, this would be difficult to effect.

6. An appointed administrator would be largely immune to "politics" and the dispensing of favors. One has only to reflect on the recent corruption cases in Hillsborough County to realize that the four county administrators

who have served since the adoption of the County Administrator system in 1973 and who have been governed by a strict professional code of ethics, have not been tainted by the scandals nor have their subordinates been tainted.

Arguments Supporting the Elected Executive

1. Hillsborough County is a rapidly urbanizing county and cannot escape the responsibilities of providing services which, historically, have been provided by municipal governments. At the same time, as a county government, it cannot escape the responsibilities accorded to it as a subdivision of state government. It is a hybrid which would make it, therefore, more compatible with a hybrid governance structure such as the elected county executive.

   County government is also at the core of a largely invisible (to the public) but powerful set of intergovernmental influences. An elected executive would be a more powerful actor in the intergovernmental arena, allowing him or her to exercise greater influence vis-à-vis administrative officers and elected officials at other levels — city, state, regional, and federal.

2. The 1983 Charter was preceded by a steady progression to centralize authority and decision-making in Hillsborough County government. Thus, an effort to further strengthen the role of the chief executive officer would be fully in line with what has already transpired. The 1979–80 Charter Study Committee recommended an elected executive, although it was not included in subsequent charter drafts in the 1980–83 period. Thus a charter was eventually adopted which would be acceptable to a sitting commission but

at the same time, provide for a "strong" county administrator. Therefore, one interpretation of the present charter is that it requires the administrator to assume both policy and management roles without providing him or her with the necessary authority to do so. The consequence is likely to be frustration and tension between the Board of County Commissioners and the administrator. This, in turn, could foster weak government.

3. The Elected County Executive form of government is based on a system of "checks and balances" and a separation of policy and administration. The elected executive is typically responsible for making key personnel appointments, subject to review and approval by the legislative body. He or she also has veto powers, subject to a legislative override. Finally in key budgetary/financial areas, auditing functions typically rest outside the executive's control — which is a valuable checking mechanism. The existing charter attempts to force a separation of policy and administration but does not provide "checks and balances." Moreover, the underlying premise of the charter is cooperation, not conflict. This premise may be suspect in a growing and increasingly diversifying population. A more appropriate model may be a conflict model or some variation of it. The elected executive plan is such a variation.

4. Hillsborough County is different, perhaps unique in its local conditions and circumstances. It is a large county which contains one major city, and the city and the county are often in conflict over important issues. These circumstances foster the need for a highly visible elected executive who can deal with the mayor of Tampa on an equal political footing and who can be held accountable

by the electorate. At the same time, an elected executive would be responsive to citizen and political demands for effective government.[38]

5. An elected county administrator is needed because the commission-administrator arrangement is not working satisfactorily. Since May 28, 1985, when the five new members of the Board of County Commissioners were sworn into office, there has been considerable tension between the administrator and some members of the commission. In one instance, some members of the commission gave serious consideration to seeking a legal remedy to the limitations which the administrator placed on the commissioners' access to staff.

Additionally, interviews conducted with incumbent commissioners indicate there is divided opinion on the effectiveness of the appointed administrator arrangement. One feels strongly about it, arguing that the "charter takes away the commission's power but not its accountability." Others are less critical of the charter and believe it can work if commissioners and the administrator want it to work. One commissioner explained, "the key to the Charter is having people in office who will implement it as intended — people, not the Charter, are the problem." Another commissioner believes that the charter's success hinges almost entirely on the attitude of the administrator. Still another feels "there's nothing in the charter which would prevent the ideal commissioner-administrator relationship from being realized — providing an almost rare Administrator can be recruited."

Viewpoints

The final section of this report draws on the interviews conducted with key elected and appointed county officials and the citizen survey to provide further perspective on whether or not Hillsborough County should adopt an elected executive form of government.[39]

COMMISSIONERS' VIEWS
Previously it was reported that the seven incumbent commissioners were divided in their opinions of an elected executive of Hillsborough County. One commissioner who had been a supporter of the elected executive several years ago feels that it is not a good idea at this time. Why? In this commissioner's opinion, such a move would add more instability to an already unstable situation. The county needs time to adjust to the 1983 Charter. The same commissioner when asked to cite the strongest arguments for and against an elected or appointed executive replied: "The strongest argument for an elected administrator is accountability whereas the strongest argument for an appointed administrator is professionalism."

Among other commissioners who favor an appointed administrator one commissioner feels that the present charter has not had enough time to work. Another commissioner supports an appointed administrator for a different reason. This commissioner feels an administrator who serves at the pleasure of BOCC (Board of County Commissioners) would allow greater public access to the center of power than would be the case with an elected executive. Finally, a fourth commissioner cites four specific reasons for staying with the present arrangement:

1. An election is a popularity contest which provides little assurance that a competent person will assume office.

2. If an incompetent administrator is elected, it would be very difficult to remove him/her. The public would have to wait four years until the next election to remedy the situation.

3. An elected administrator would find it necessary to hire a professional administrator.

4. An elected executive would be limited to Hillsborough County. The county would not be able to hire from a national pool of talented administrators.

The commissioners in support of an elected executive cite the following reasons:

1. Growth pressures require that explicit authority be placed in a single person so that timely decisions can be made. According to one commissioner, "we have not done a good job of running government by a committee."

2. An elected executive would emphasize

policy which is more well defined and consistent than is possible under the present arrangement.

3. An elected executive would be a more responsive public official. One commissioner put it this way, "elected people are more responsive and motivated ... Hillsborough County has suffered because there has never been a strong, central leader."

Regarding partisanship, four commissioners favor a non-partisan office. One feels that it does not matter one way or the other; another has no particular feelings on the subject. A seventh commissioner favors a partisan office for an elected executive.

Opinions are divided on whether or not an elected executive could be effective without having control over the constitutional officers. Two commissioners feel that an elected executive could be effective. The remaining five commissioners expressed degrees of misgiving about an elected county executive who cannot control all or most of the duties currently assigned to the five constitutional officers. One commissioner, for example, argued that the clerk and sheriff are very powerful political officeholders and an elected executive would have difficulty dealing with them.

CONSTITUTIONAL OFFICERS

Are these views shared by the constitutional officers? Could an elected executive function effectively without having control over the clerk, the sheriff, the tax collector, the property appraiser, and the supervisor of elections? The response is a unanimous "yes." All constitutional officers were interviewed, and all expressed the opinion that he/she could work with an elected executive. Several added that it would take cooperation, but there should not be insurmountable obstacles.

This is not, of course, to say that the constitutional officers prefer to work with an elected executive rather than an appointed executive. Indeed, when asked if they had a preference as to whether the county administrator should be appointed by the BOCC from among qualified professionals or should be directly elected by the public, the Consti-

tutional Officers expressed a preference for the appointed administrator. Said one of the constitutional officers: "the job requires administrative skills" and the appointed county administrator can serve as a "buffer" between county employees and the BOCC and the public. Another constitutional officer stated that he/she preferred an appointed county administrator because under the system the BOCC can draw from a nationwide pool of experienced administrators. "If the position is elected, you can't get that kind of assurance." Another predicted that "a power struggle would erupt between the elected executive and the BOCC."

The constitutional officers believe that the office of an elected executive should be non-partisan. Only one said it should be a partisan position—"if we would also have an elected full-time Board of County Commissioners."

How much formal education should the county administrator have? When asked this question, one constitutional officer said that the administrator, regardless of whether he/she is appointed or elected, should have at least a bachelor's degree in public administrator or political science. Two constitutional officers said that a master's degree would be desirable, although not necessary. Two others expressed the view that a master's degree should be a minimum requirement. Three constitutional officers added that experience was also very important.

COUNTY STAFF

County staffers expressed diverse views on the qualifications one should have to run Hillsborough County government. Two of the eight senior county administrators emphasized that experience is more important than formal education. As one put it, "it's desirable to have degrees but it's not essential; it's experience that matters." Another said, "it is the demonstrated ability to head an organization" that matters the most. Two other staffers said that the administrator should hold at least a bachelor's degree. Three emphasized the need for a graduate degree, especially in public administration. One staffer was "unsure" about how much formal education would be desirable.

With one exception, all senior staffers expressed a preference for an appointed rather than an elected administrator. Their reasoning is best stated in their own words:

> "It is difficult for me to understand how an elected executive would function with an elected board."

> "The appointed system is working. Let's give it a chance to work, especially in light of the political history and situation."

> "The appointed administrator is a part of their [BOCC] team. He may not be if he's elected."

> "The administrator's job should be outside politics entirely."

> "We risk the chance of electing a person who is not professional."

> "An appointed administrator will insure a more professional organization."

> "It would not be possible to set minimum qualifications. Anyone can be elected. How wise is the electorate?"

> "An elected executive would open County government up to special interest groups and constituencies."

The staff member who expressed a preference for an elected executive summed up his/her views in the following way: "This is such a volatile, unstable, undirected place ... a strong political executive is needed to clarify the focus and direction of the County."

County staffers feel very strongly that, should the county adopt an elected executive form of government, the office should be nonpartisan. However, as one person put it: "It's not going to make any difference whether it is or is not listed officially as non-partisan because it's still going to be partisan."

Finally, in regard to how well an elected executive would function without control over the constitutional officers, senior staffers are of a divided opinion. Four expressed the view that there should not be any more problems than exist under the current arrangement. Three staffers said that an elected executive would have a difficult task working with other independently elected officials. In one person's view, "the elected executive would have to compromise with the Constitutional Officers."

CITIZEN VIEWS

Citizen views of Hillsborough County government drawn from a survey conducted earlier this year have been detailed in three previous reports (April 15, 1986, June 16, 1986, and July 3, 1986). The June 16 report in particular analyzes citizen views toward the selection of the county administrator. Briefly stated, a majority of the citizenry (64 percent) favor an elected administrator. Further analysis indicates a relationship between citizen informedness and preference for an appointed rather than elected administrator. That is, the more informed and educated a citizen is, the more likely it is that he/she will state a preference for an appointed county administrator. At the same time, it should be noted that within categories of "informedness" or education levels, a majority prefer an elected administrator. For example, among those residents (N=104) who are college graduates, a majority (63.5 percent) favor an elected administrator whereas 36.5 percent favor an appointed administrator.

What, if anything, should be made of these findings? Certainly some caution is in order in interpreting the meaning of citizen feelings. The purpose of conducting the survey was and continues to be a vehicle for informing the deliberations of the Charter Review Board.

Throughout America's political history there has been a continuing debate on the relationship between governing and consenting to be governed. Woodrow Wilson, a constitutional scholar and practitioner, felt that "the springs of practical action are hopelessly confused with governing power."[40] People are mislead into thinking that they are actually the governors. Wilson denounced popular sovereignty as "dogma" that stands for nothing less than the proposition "that anything that the people willed was right."[41] Another well known publicist Walter Lippmann expressed similar misgivings. "Where mass opinion dominates the government," Lippmann writes, "there is a morbid derangement of the true functions of power."[42] The capacity to govern is enfeebled and paralysis can occur.

Underlying these concerns is a fundamental question of citizenship. Is a sense of citizenship an essential ingredient for government to work the way that we want it to work? This is a difficult question which faces all Americans in the 1980s. If, as some authors contend, a sense of citizenship must be brought into the operation of government itself, how should we bring it about? Consider the following suggestions:

> Such a spirit is not entirely lacking today, but it is severely weakened by suspicion of government and politics on the one hand and the idea of impersonal efficient administration on the other. In order to limit the danger of administrative despotism, we need to increase the prestige of government, not derogate it. That prestige should be based on substantive commitments, not formal efficiency. We need to discuss the positive purposes and ends of government, the kind of government appropriate for the citizens we would like to be.[43]

If the Charter Review Board, political, business, and community leaders, and professional public administrators are engaged in dialogue over the kind of government appropriate for the citizens we would like to be, then this county is on the path toward bringing a sense of citizenship into the operation of government itself. Finally, all engaged in this dialogue would do well to remember Wilson's admonition, although made many years ago in a different era, "it is getting harder to run a Constitution than to frame one."[44] Is it getting harder to run a county charter than it is to frame one?

Notes

1. In February–March 1986, the Center for Public Affairs & Policy Management conducted a survey of citizen views and attitudes toward Hillsborough County government. The survey, the most comprehensive in the County's history, canvassed 442 randomly selected residents. The results were reported to the Hillsborough County Charter Review Board in a document entitled *Citizen Views of Hillsborough County Government*, April 15, 1986.

2. The interviews were conducted in March–April 1986.

3. The major studies of county government include Herbert S. Duncombe, *County Government in America* (Washington: National Association of Coun-

ties Research Foundation, 1966), Herbert S. Duncombe, *Modern County Government* (Washington: National Association of Counties, 1977), Vincent L. Marando and Robert B. Thomas, *The Forgotten Governments* (Gainesville: University of Florida Press, 1977), and Susan W. Torrence, *Grass Roots Government* (Washington: Robert R. Luce, Inc., 1974). The Marando and Thomas book reports and analyzes empirical data collected on county commissioners in Georgia and Florida.

4. David R. Morgan, *Managing Urban America* (Monterey, California: Brooks/Cole Publishing Co., 2nd ed., 1984).

5. William A. Schultze, *Urban Politics* (Englewood Cliffs, N.J.: Prentice-Hall, Inc., 1985).

6. David A. Caputo, *Urban America: The Policy Alternatives* (San Francisco: W. H. Freeman and Co., 1976).

7. *Ibid.*, 93.

8. Clarence N. Stone, Robert K. Whelan, and William J. Murin, *Urban Policy and Politics in a Bureaucratic Age* (Englewood Cliffs, N.J.: Prentice-Hall, Inc., 2nd ed., 1986).

9. Gerald L. Houseman, *State and Local Government: The New Battleground* (Englewood Cliffs, N.J.: Prentice-Hall, Inc., 1986).

10. *Ibid.*, 226.

11. John J. Harrigan, *Political Change in the Metropolis* (Boston: Little, Brown and Co., 3rd ed., 1985).

12. *Ibid.*, 322.

13. National Association of Counties, "A National Survey of the County Executive and the County Administrator," *American County* 35 (August 1970): 10; John Herbers, "Counties Gain Power and Federal Influence Wanes," *New York Times* November 10, 1985, p. 17; Governmental Research Institute, *Reorganizing Our Counties* (Cleveland: Governmental Research Institute, 1980); "Twelve Wisconsin Counties Have Chief Officials," *National Civic Review* (July 1975): 361–362; "Chief Executive Plan Popular in Counties," *National Civic Review* (October 1979): 501–502; and John M. DeGrove, *Metropolitan Counties in Florida: Structure, Function, Finance*, an In-House Project completed by the FAU/FIU Joint Center for Environmental and Urban Problems, August 1977.

14. *Who's Who in Local Government Management* (Washington: International City Management Association, 1985): 305.

15. International City Management Association, *The Municipal Year Book* (Washington: International City Management Association, 1985).

16. National Association of Counties and the International City Management Association, *The County Year Book* (Washington: NACO, 1975): 31.

17. *National Council of Elected County Executives 1986 Directory*, National Association of Counties, Washington, D.C.

18. Edwin L. Crawford, Executive Director, New York State Association of Counties, 150 State Street, Albany, New York 12207.

19. *Local Government Handbook*, 3rd ed. State of New York, 1982, p. 74.

20. Edwin L. Crawford, Executive Director, New York State Association of Counties, 150 State Street, Albany, New York 12207.

21. William N. Cassella, Jr., Executive Director, Citizens Forum on Self Government, letter dated March 31, 1986.

22. Richard D. Bingham, *State and Local Government in an Urban Society* (New York: Random House, 1986), p. 261.

23. *Ibid.*

24. Jim Baker, Association of Arkansas Counties.

25. National Association of Counties, *The County Year Book 1975*, pp. 29–30.

26. *Ibid.*

27. *Ibid.*, 31–32.

28. A reformed government is typically defined by scholars as one in which structural and electoral changes have been made to remove politics from government and to maximize the application of expertise in the day-to-day management of government. Thus a fully reformed local government would be one which has adopted most or all of the following measures: at-large, non-partisan elections, part-time elected officials whose terms of office are short and nonrenewable, and a full-time professional manager to "run" the government.

29. Schultze, *op. cit.*, 162.

30. International City Management Association Urban Data Service, telephone request.

31. Robert Lineberry and Edmund Fowler, "Reformism and Public Policies in American Cities," *American Political Science Review* 75 (June 1981): 352.

32. Albert Kernig, "Private Regarding Policy, Civil Rights Groups, and the Mediating Impact of Munic-

ipal Reforms," *American Journal of Political Science* 19 (February 1975): 91–106.

33. David Morgan and John Pelissero, "Urban Policy: Does Political Structure Matter?" *American Political Science Review* 75 (December 1980): 999–1006.

34. James H. Svara, "Leadership Roles in City and County Government," paper presented at the Annual Meeting of the Southern Political Science Association, Nashville, Tennessee, November 1985.

35. *Ibid.*, 22–23.

36. *Ibid.*, 1.

37. Richard S. Childs, *The First 50 Years of the Council-Manager Plan of Municipal Government* (New York: National Municipal League, 1965).

38. John Thomas, formerly Executive Director of the Florida Association of County Commissioners and currently Executive Director of the National Association of Counties in remarks before the Hillsborough County Charter Review Board noted that Hillsborough County may be uniquely configured for an elected county executive. See Charter Review Board minutes, January 6, 1986.

39. The interviews were conducted in March–April 1986.

40. Quoted in John A. Rohr, *To Run a Constitution* (Lawrence, Kansas: University Press of Kansas, 1986), p. 84.

41. *Ibid.*, p. 70.

42. Walter Lippmann, *The Public Philosophy* (New American Library, 1956), p. 19.

43. Robert N. Bellah, et al., *Habits of the Heart* (New York: Perenial Library–Harper & Row, 1985), p. 21.

44. Quoted in John A. Rohr, *To Run a Constitution* (Lawrence, Kansas: University Press of Kansas, 1986), p. 59.

PART VII
Regional Studies and Trends

CHAPTER 35

THE CASE FOR REGIONAL COOPERATION

Theodore Hershberg

Will metropolitan Philadelphia be better off in the global economy if the city at the core of the region collapses? If you live in the suburbs, do you believe that what happens to Philadelphia is without significant consequence for you and the community in which you reside?

Let us be clear about the argument. It is not that the suburban communities surrounding a failed Philadelphia will be wiped out by virtue of their proximity to ground zero in an atomic blast. They won't. But suburban residents are wrong if they think they won't suffer any fallout. The fact is they have a compelling economic interest in Philadelphia's viability.

Ample evidence documents that suburbs surrounding healthy central cities are better off than those surrounding unhealthy ones, and proof is mounting that regions — not cities or counties — will be the preeminent competitive units of the global economy. The issue is not whether the city and suburbs are tied together in a regional economy — they are — but how to ensure that the region will prosper in the future.

The fear and frustration felt by so many suburbanites about the problems of big cities is understandable, but their economic interests are not well served by turning their backs and ignoring the troubles next door. Such a course guarantees that problems will grow, opportunities will be lost, and, in the long run, everyone will be worse off. The time has come to recognize the mutual interests across the region and to begin a rational dialogue about what is required to work with each other to shape a prosperous future.

Regional cooperation spins on two axes, not one. Although the focus of this article is on the more familiar and difficult *city-to-suburb* relationships, *suburb-to-suburb* cooperation remains an important part of the larger challenge facing the region. Southeastern Pennsylvania has 239 municipalities and 63 school districts. These units of government offer citizens highly valued local control, but they also give rise to a cloud of parochialism that obscures the necessity for change that is demanded by the competitiveness of the new global economy.

New Global Economic Realities

There is an apocryphal story about an American in the 1930s who grew weary with the world rushing off to war. To get away from the madness, he sold all his possessions in the states and bought a piece of land on a remote South Pacific isle known for its beauty and tranquillity. Unfortunately, he settled on Guadalcanal, the site, as World War II buffs know, of the fiercest fighting in the Pacific theater. The moral of the story is that the past is not always a useful guide for the future.

The global economy ensures the future will

From *The Regionalist*, Vol. 1, No. 3, Fall 1995. Published by the National Association of Regional Councils, Washington, D.C. and the University of Baltimore, Baltimore, Md. Reprinted with permission of the publishers.

differ from the past. International trade, which equaled only 11 percent of America's gross national product (GNP) in 1960, reached 25 percent in 1990 and is growing rapidly. Already 25 percent of agricultural produce is exported, 30 percent of autos sold in America are produced by foreign manufacturers, 40 percent of corporate profits among Fortune 500 companies and 20 percent overall are derived from international activities, and 40 percent of all commercial loans in the United States are made by foreign banks. Ten percent of American pension funds, $500 billion, are invested in Asian companies alone.

Many Americans, particularly those in leadership positions who came of age between 1945 and 1970, still do not fully understand the nature of this change. The subconscious assumptions they hold about America's place in the world order were formed when we were the world's undisputed leader after World War II decimated the economies of our friends and enemies alike. In the late 1940s, America's GNP was half of the world's; in 1950, American per capita GNP was 4 times that of West Germany and 15 times that of Japan.

But world dominance was temporary, and it gave way rapidly in the years following 1970. By the late 1980s, America accounted for only 23 percent of the world's GNP, and by 1990, Japan's per capital GNP slightly exceeded America's. Since 1970, dominance has been lost in industries that were once synonymous with America — steel, machine tools, chemicals and autos — while consumer electronics has been virtually wiped out.

As the rest of the developed world caught up with us in these difficult decades, the lives of working men and women were affected. Real wages have been flat since 1970; only the top 20 percent of American male workers have improved their standing, 20 percent were stagnant, and 60 percent actually experienced a decline. Our standard of living did not fall at the same time, largely because women entered the labor force in record numbers, but absent polygamy there will be no third spouse to send into the labor force to bail us out in the future. Moreover, since 1989, even median *household* income has fallen despite the

fact that Americans now work longer hours and a greater proportion now hold at least two jobs than in the last half century. According to Lester Thurow (1995), income inequality also is growing — among men working full time the earnings gap between the top and bottom quintiles doubled in the last 25 years — and the distribution of wealth is worsening, with the share of wealth held today by the top 1 percent of the population — more than 40 percent — rising to what it was in the late 1920s. Although these troubling statistics result from many factors, including new labor-saving technologies and the decline of unions, it is clear that America must adapt to the competitive challenges of the global economy.

The global economy has already affected the lives of all Americans in powerful ways, and its impact will increase as barriers to free trade continue to fall, global capital markets become more fluid, and telecommunication technologies accelerate the flow of information. If we understand the future, we greatly increase our chances of successfully adapting to the changes it will bring.

The Regional Implications of the Global Economy

The starting point is to recognize that the competitive unit of the global economy is the *region* — not the city, suburb, or county. Victor Petrella, director of science and technology forecasting for the European Union, believes:

> Within fifty years, such nation states as Germany, Italy, the United States, and Japan will no longer be the most relevant socioeconomic entities and the ultimate political configuration. Instead, areas like Orange County, California; Osaka, Japan; the Lyon region of France; or Germany's Ruhrgebeit will acquire predominant socioeconomic status. The real decision-making power of the future ... will be transnational companies in alliance with city-regional governments [quoted in Toffler and Toffler 1993].

Kenichi Ohmae (1995), former senior partner at McKinsey & Company and leader of a Japanese reform movement, put it this way in his new study, *The End of the Nation State*:

The noise you hear rumbling in the distance is the sound of the later twentieth century's primary engine of economic prosperity — the region-state — stirring to life. No longer will managers organize the international activities of their companies on the basis of national borders. Region-states have become the primary units of economic activity. It is through these region-states that participation in the global economy actually takes place.

Neal Peirce, nationally syndicated columnist and, with Curtis Johnson and John Stuart Hall (1993), coauthor of *Citi-states: How Urban America Can Prosper in a Competitive World*, contends, "Only when the central city and its surrounding counties work together will they be able to compete effectively. It won't be America versus Japan or Germany, but Greater Philadelphia versus metropolitan Tokyo or Stuttgart."

It is not difficult to understand why this is true. Only regions have the necessary scale and diversity to compete in the global marketplace. Only regions have an asset profile capable of projecting overall strength, in sharp contrast to the much less attractive profiles of individual counties or cities that lack either key infrastructure or a sufficiently skilled labor force.

Regions, moreover, are the geographic units in which we create our goods and services. We hire from a regional *labor force*. We count on a regional *transportation system* to move the people and the materials involved in their production. We rely on a regional *infrastructure* to keep the bridges and roads intact and our sewers and pipelines functioning. We live in a regional *environment* whose water and air do not recognize political boundaries.

Finally, although most people don't realize it, regions have always been the geographic units of economic competition. The national economy is a set of summary statistics drawn from the performance of distinct regional economies.

The global economy has important implications for regions. Let us consider three: develop human resources, lower the costs of goods and services, and use scarce investment capital wisely.

DEVELOP HUMAN RESOURCES

The source of comparative advantage in the future will be human capital. Future competition, argues Lester Thurow (1992) in *Head to Head: The Coming Economic Battle Among Japan, Europe, and America*, will be characterized by competition over seven "brain intensive" industries — computers and software, robotics and machine tools, civilian aviation, microelectronics, material sciences, biotechnology, and telecommunications — that offer high paying jobs to their workers and bring prosperity and world prestige to their countries. But even jobs requiring lower skills will be far more demanding than in the past. While only 30 percent of the jobs in the year 2000 will require college degrees, fully 89 percent will require post-secondary training.

Employers may recruit their top managers from a national labor pool, but they must rely on the regional labor force for the lion's share of their workers. If the region's schools and training institutes are not producing workers with adequate skills, the premium that employers will have to pay to attract qualified labor from outside the region will erode their competitiveness. Even though big corporations have the resources to compensate by retraining their workers, such a strategy unavoidably adds to their costs. Small businesses, utterly dependent on the quality of local institutions, lack even this option.

The central argument of *America's Choice: High Skills or Low Wages*, the report of the Commission on the Skills of the American Workforce (1990), was summarized by William Brock, a commission co-chair and former U.S. labor secretary. If companies in every country in the world can now buy "idiot-proof machinery" to compensate for workers with terribly deficient skills, and if there are people elsewhere in the world who will work for $5 per day with the same equipment as Americans who want $10 or $15 per hour, then we cannot compete on the basis of wage. We can compete only on the basis of skill.

Suburban schools generally have lower dropout rates, better achievement scores, and higher college enrollment rates than city schools, but there should be no comfort in this comparison. Nor does it matter if our schools are somewhat better than they were 20 years ago. The appropriate comparisons are first to schools in the rest of the developed world, and the results are sobering.

On average, American students are measurably far behind students in other nations — their future competitors — in math, science, and critical thinking skills. Only the top 10 to 20 percent of our children can be considered truly competitive.

The second comparison — how does the human capital of our children match up with the skill requirements of twenty-first century jobs — is equally troubling. Of new entrants to the nation's labor force between 1985 and 2000, roughly 80 percent have the skills for only the bottom 40 percent of the jobs, and only 5 percent have the skills for the top 40 percent of the jobs.

As corporate leaders well understand, America cannot succeed in the global economy unless every able-bodied citizen has the skills required by the demanding jobs of the new economy. The results of the recent *National Adult Literacy Survey* (Kirsch et al. 1993) are shocking: half the adult population in the United States is ill-equipped for the job requirements of the twenty-first century global economy. Although this makes clear that the challenge is national rather than solely urban, the fact remains that great efforts to improve human capital must be made in our cities. Here is where a disproportionate number of the fastest growing segment of new labor-force entrants — immigrants and minorities — reside, which means they are attending some of the nation's worst schools and living in some of our worst environments.

The cost of supporting people who are unable to contribute to the economy — those without skills, on welfare, or in prison — will hold us down just as surely as a weight tied to a kite's tail. The suburbs cannot be sealed off from the city or the world. The future standard of living of the children of the *haves* will be determined to a significant extent by the productivity of the children of the *have-nots*.

The region — city and suburbs together — must work to adopt rigorous academic performance standards for its students and schools, benchmarked against the toughest in the developed world; greatly expand training for high school graduates not going to college; make admission to its colleges and universities far more demanding; and increase the availability of advanced on-the-job training in the workplace.

LOWER THE COSTS OF GOODS AND SERVICES

The good news is that the global economy means vast new markets; with 5.5 billion people, the world has more than 20 times the population of the United States. The bad news is that our goods and services must now compete with those from firms around the world. As the latest round of corporate downsizing suggests, the competition is fierce, in part because of a dramatic shift that is making commodities out of what used to be specialized products. A decade ago an IBM personal computer was unique. Today many manufacturers produce high quality clones, making computers a commodity, like so much rice, wheat, and potatoes. The result in industry after industry is rapidly falling prices, and the message is clear: firms that can keep costs down will remain competitive; others will fade away.

Grasping how global competition differs from domestic competition is absolutely essential. For 30 years, critics have pointed out the inefficiency of duplicated services, facilities, and personnel that result from too many local governments. Others have lamented the inadequate management of regional resources such as labor force, transportation, infrastructure, and environment. But despite the higher costs resulting from inefficiencies found outside the firm and beyond the direct control of company managers, reformers found few supporters.

These inefficiencies did not matter very much when the competition was *domestic* for two reasons. First, the inefficiencies noted above did not cut into profit margins because producers passed their costs to their customers as higher prices. Second, since all domestic producers did the same thing, no one derived competitive advantage.

But when the competition is *international* — and for whatever reasons the prices of foreign goods and services are lower than our own — inefficiencies that spring from domestic practices undercut our competitiveness. Thirty years ago, 20 percent of General Motors' assembly line workers were illiterate, but it didn't matter, as David Osborne and Ted Gaebler (1992) remind us, because 20 percent of Ford's and Chrysler's workers were illiterate as well. Today, when 100 percent of Toyota's workers are literate, it matters a great deal. When voters understand that to maintain the competitiveness of American goods and services in a global economy, the choice is either to lower their wages or to find ways outside their firms of more efficiently reducing costs and managing resources, they will, not surprisingly, choose the latter. Behaviors and governance structures considered sacrosanct today, I contend, will change far more rapidly than most people currently think.

The time has come to scrutinize a host of current behaviors. In metropolitan Philadelphia, for example, fiscal policy, land use, growth management, and zoning decisions are being made by municipalities — 239 in Southeastern Pennsylvania and 100 in southern New Jersey — rather than at the level of multiple municipalities, the county, or the region. But the response should not assume that the regional scale is automatically best. Rather, the political smog that obscures our choices should be blown away by an objective cost-benefit analysis to determine what size "service shed" — on a geographic scale — is appropriate for what service and, for that matter, whether government should produce the service or contract it out to the private sector. The issue before us, as Richard Nathan (1994) has argued, is not *structural* — requiring the consolidation of local governments into larger units, but *functional* — offering services at the most efficient geographic scale.

USE SCARCE INVESTMENT CAPITAL MORE PRODUCTIVELY

When crime, drugs, homelessness, and other social problems spill over into adjacent suburban communities, the response of those who can afford it has been to move even farther away to more pristine areas at the peripheries of our regions. This process is em-bedded in the concentric rings of growth that emanate outward from our central cities.

Very troubling signs in the older, inner-ring suburbs suggest that the pace of out-migration and other indicators of deterioration — job loss, housing depreciation, drugs, crime, and related social problems — are accelerating faster than in the central cities they surround. The reason is that these small communities lack the basic resources the big cities use to slow down and mediate the process of decline. These inner-ring communities do not have large central business districts generating substantial tax revenues to underwrite essential services in the neighborhoods; they do not have large police forces to maintain safety and a sense of social order as the crime rate climbs; and they do not have the sizable public and not-for-profit human and social service agencies to address the needs of the poor and disadvantaged.

This out-migration from the cities and the inner-ring suburbs leads to new development in the exurbs requiring new roads and highways, water mains and sewer lines, schools and libraries, homes and shopping centers, and offices and sports complexes. When this happens, we end up spending our scarce investment dollars redundantly because we are essentially duplicating an infrastructure that already exists in older suburbs and central cities. Such growth also often represents a highly inefficient use of land. In Southeastern Pennsylvania between 1970 and 1995, for example, while population declined by 140,000, one-quarter of the region's prime farmland was lost to development.

This redundant spending imposes heavy opportunity costs because these dollars are not available for vital investments in productivity. To improve our competitive position in the global economy, America's regions would be far wiser to undertake more cost-effective development by adopting metropolitan growth rings, increasing residential and job densities in existing suburbs and cities, and investing the savings in research and development, plant and equipment, and human capital. The current practice of redundant spending is akin to eating our seed corn. America can ill afford public policy that leads to throw-away cities, throw-away suburbs, and throw-away people.

"It's the economy, stupid" read the now famous sign on James Carville's wall, announcing the central message for the 1992 Clinton presidential campaign. For those of us who want to see our metropolitan areas prosper in the twenty-first century, the sign should be amended to read "It's the *global* economy, stupid!" In sum, the global economy has forever changed the rules of competition. Either we adapt intelligently, or we face a significant deterioration in our standard of living and an increasingly worrisome unequal distribution of wealth within our regions that threaten the stability of our democracy.

Economic Linkages Between the City and the Suburbs

The nation's economy is an aggregation of metropolitan economies in which the fortunes of the cities and suburbs are intertwined. Here are just a few examples of the economic linkages that bind them together. We'll first consider relationships between cities and suburbs in general and then review some of the specific linkages between Philadelphia and the surrounding suburban counties.

DETROIT AND ITS SUBURBS
Skeptics about regional cooperation often pose the "Detroit question": if cities and suburbs are so interdependent, then why are Detroit's suburbs doing well while the city is an economic wasteland? While the Detroit suburbs are doing well relative to the city, it turns out this is a misleading comparison. According to a Philadelphia Federal Reserve Bank study (Voith 1992) of 28 metropolitan areas in the Northeast and Midwest, the better off the central city is, the better off its suburbs are. The Detroit suburbs have experienced considerably slower job, population, and income growth than the suburbs surrounding healthier central cities. For example, although the population of the Detroit suburbs grew 2 percent between 1980 and 1990, the average for the northeastern suburbs studied for that period was almost 7 percent.

NATIONAL LEAGUE OF CITIES
In its recent study, *All in It Together: Cities, Suburbs, and Local Economic Regions* (Ledebur and Barnes 1993), the National League of Cities documents that in each of the 25 metropolitan areas with the most rapidly growing suburbs, central city incomes also increased from 1979 to 1989. "No suburb in this high growth set experienced income growth without corresponding growth in their central city.... For every $1.00 increase in central city household incomes, suburban household incomes increase by $1.12." Cities and suburbs are not two distinct economies, the report concludes, "but a single highly interdependent economy.... Their fortunes [are] inextricably intertwined. Cities and suburbs grow or decline together."

CITIES WITHOUT SUBURBS
In *Cities Without Suburbs*, David Rusk (1993), former mayor of Albuquerque, New Mexico, describes a fascinating set of differences between *elastic* cities (those that have been able to annex or merge with their suburbs so they are "without" suburbs) and *inelastic* cities (those whose growth stopped at their historic political boundaries and therefore are surrounded by suburbs). In elastic cities, income distributions are more equal, poverty is less concentrated, crime rates are lower, residential segregation is lower, and schools are less segregated. By contrast, Rusk argues, inelastic cities like Philadelphia "are programmed to fail." He does not write off the Philadelphias of the world, however, because he believes public policies promoting regional responses can produce greater social and economic equity.

CITISTATES
In *Citistates: How Urban America Can Prosper in a Competitive World*, Peirce, Johnson, and Hall (1993) argue that the true economic units of the global economy are *citistates*, a new name for metropolitan areas. With the end of the Cold War, the battleground of the future will be economic, not military, a shift that will diminish the role of nations and enhance the importance of regions. Based on case studies of metropolitan areas that included

Baltimore, Dallas, Phoenix, and Seattle, Peirce contends that only when the central city and the surrounding suburban communities work together will they be in a position to compete effectively against the metropolitan economies of Frankfurt, Milan, and Osaka. Peirce urges metropolitan residents to recognize the indivisibility of the citistate, find a niche for the region in the global economy, focus on workforce preparedness, plan for a multicultural future, fight for fiscal equity, and build a sense of regional citizenship.

The consequences of continued urban decline will be felt well beyond city borders. A 10 percent decline in the value of real estate in just 9 of America's largest cities would mean losses of $160 billion, reports Joseph Gyourko (Gyourko and Summers 1994), real estate professor at the University of Pennsylvania's Wharton School. This amount roughly equals the cost of the entire savings and loan bailout. A great many suburbanites — shareholders in the banks, insurance companies, and pension funds that own these properties — would be among the losers.

The evidence from around the nation, then, is compelling, but does it hold true for Southeastern Pennsylvania? Despite the striking growth of the suburbs in past decades, research done here strongly suggests that many economic ties bind Bucks, Chester, Delaware, Montgomery, and Philadelphia counties together.

COMMUTING PATTERNS IN METROPOLITAN PHILADELPHIA

Although most people live and work in a single county and suburb-to-suburb commuting is on the rise, a great many people cross Philadelphia's borders as part of the journey to work. Each day 395,000 commuters are on the move in and out of the city. Fifteen percent of suburban residents come into the city (down from 20 percent in 1980), and altogether, Philadelphia imports almost one-third of its labor force. Meanwhile, 20 percent of city residents commute to jobs in the suburban counties (up from 15 percent in 1980). These commuting patterns are important linkages between the city and surrounding counties that are experienced by real people in very real ways.

PURCHASES OF GOODS AND SERVICES

A 1991 survey of more than 1,000 area firms conducted by the Center for Greater Philadelphia revealed that despite considerable suburban economic growth, the region's economy remains tightly integrated. For example, nearly 20 percent of all goods and services purchased by firms in Bucks, Chester, and Delaware counties are acquired from Philadelphia firms. Overall, when direct and indirect purchases are considered together, roughly one-quarter of Southeastern Pennsylvania's $110 billion gross metropolitan product in 1991 was a function of city-county business transactions.

BEST-CASE AND WORST-CASE SCENARIOS FOR THE YEAR 2000

When Philadelphia was at the brink of bankruptcy in 1991, leaders of the Pennsylvania General Assembly asked the Center for Greater Philadelphia to consider the question "what would happen to the suburbs if the city went down the tubes?"

Two regional job scenarios were constructed for the Sixth Southeastern Pennsylvania State Legislators' Conference (Hershberg 1991). The *worst case* was based on the 1970s when the city lost 40 percent of its manufacturing jobs, 18 percent of its total jobs, and 13 percent of its population. The *best case* was based on the 1980s when the city ended the decade with roughly the same number of jobs it had at its start and population loss slowed to less than half the prior decade's rate.

The difference between these two scenarios in the year 2000 is 268,000 fewer jobs in Bucks, Chester, Delaware, and Montgomery counties and 178,000 fewer jobs in Philadelphia. This would represent a loss to the region of $11.6 billion in wages and a loss to the state treasury of $585 million in personal income, corporate net income, and sales taxes (in 1990 dollars).

IT WON'T BE A ZERO-SUM GAME

Nor would Philadelphia's deterioration be a zero-sum game for Pennsylvania in which city jobs move to the suburbs and the state treasury breaks even because only the location of economic activity changes. Although many city firms would move to the suburbs, some would close rather than relocate, others would downsize, and still others would leave the region entirely. One study of manufacturing firms in the 1970s estimated that at least 30 percent of jobs eliminated in the city did not relocate. Such losses are shared by everyone.

SUBURBAN HOUSING VALUES ARE AFFECTED BY PHILADELPHIA'S ECONOMY AND ACCESS TO COMMUTER RAIL

Another glimpse into the integrated regional economy comes from the work of Richard Voith (1993), senior economist at the Federal Reserve Bank of Philadelphia. Voith set out to learn whether access to commuter rail service in the suburban counties boosts home values. In a careful study that controlled for access to highways and the quality of homes, Voith found that residences in neighborhoods with rail service — about 258,500 owner-occupied houses — enjoy a premium of 6.4 percent in housing values over those areas without service. This amounts to $1.45 billion in the value of residential real estate over the five-county region. In examining the value of homes in Montgomery County located near commuter rail lines, Voith found that prices fell in the 1970s as the city's manufacturing economy collapsed and rose sharply in the mid–1980s when the Philadelphia economy, especially downtown jobs, rebounded.

Good Things Happen When the City and Suburbs Cooperate

The case for regional cooperation is solid. Intense new competition in the global economy makes regions the strategic units of future economic competition. Moreover, economic linkages between the city and the suburbs make cooperative strategies in everyone's self-interest. But there is a third basis for this approach, and that is, simply put, good things happen when the city and the suburbs cooperate. Let's consider three of the leading achievements of regional cooperation in Southeastern Pennsylvania in the last decade.

REGIONAL SUCCESS STORIES

Pennsylvania Convention Center: The new center, the most important economic development project in Philadelphia's modern history, functions as the cornerstone of an ambitious, multi-pronged effort to make Philadelphia a "Destination City" in the burgeoning global hospitality industry. The suburban counties are now working with the city to develop a regional tourism strategy. The $525 million facility was made possible with a contribution of $185 million from the Commonwealth of Pennsylvania, an investment that required cooperation between political leaders from both parties across the region.

Philadelphia Regional Port Authority (PRPA): In 1990, the General Assembly created the PRPA, a partnership between the state and Bucks, Delaware, and Philadelphia counties. PRPA has been a "win-win" proposition: the city was freed from a multi-million drain on its annual budget; $60 million was made available for port capital and marketing projects, including Philadelphia's first intermodal facility; and PRPA was instrumental in attracting a new rail line to the region. The port's competitive position will be greatly improved by the recent affiliation of PRPA and the South Jersey Port Corporation under the auspices of Delaware River Port Authority.

SEPTA Capital Funding: In a historic breakthrough in 1991, the Pennsylvania General Assembly provided a source of predictable capital funding for all 37 of the commonwealth's mass transit agencies. Numerous studies have documented the significant impact the Southeastern Pennsylvania Transportation Authority (SEPTA) has on the region's economy, and the guarantee of a reliable funding stream allows SEPTA to continue its rebuilding process. Once the region's leaders reached consensus on ensuring SEPTA's future capital needs, the debate between city and suburbs gave way to the search for a politically viable funding formula.

SOUTHEASTERN PENNSYLVANIA COMMANDS CONSIDERABLE STATE POWER

The reason good things like these can happen when city and suburban state leaders cooperate is that Southeastern Pennsylvania is the most powerful region in the state. John Stauffer, the former majority leader of the Pennsylvania State Senate from Chester County, recognized this at the first regionwide conference of elected officials in 1985 when he said, "If we in Southeastern Pennsylvania ever flexed our political muscle on *both* sides of the aisle, we'd be a formidable force to be reckoned with in Harrisburg."

While Bucks, Chester, Delaware, Montgomery, and Philadelphia counties are only 5 of the state's 67 counties, they account for 31 percent of the state's population, 33 percent of its jobs, and 36 percent of its income. The 5 counties, moreover, are home to many leaders of the General Assembly. As of November 1995, these include House Speaker Matthew Ryan (R–Delaware County); House Majority Leader John Perzel (R–Philadelphia); Senate Majority Leader Joseph Loeper (R–Delaware County); and all four appropriations committee chairmen — Rep. Dwight Evans (D–Philadelphia), Sen. Vincent Fumo (D–Philadelphia), Rep. Joseph Pitts (R–Chester County), and Sen. Richard Tilghman (R–Montgomery County).

Philadelphia Rebounds

The 1990s are critical years for Philadelphia and the region. The decade began with a national recession, which in conjunction with an accumulated deficit of $250 million, brought the city of Philadelphia to the brink of bankruptcy. But in November 1991, Edward G. Rendell won election as the city's new mayor and has led Philadelphia in a remarkable comeback.

Central to his success was a political alliance with John Street, president of the Philadelphia City Council. This partnership has meant that for the first time since 1980, the city's mayor and city council have worked in tandem to promote Philadelphia's best interests. Since Rendell is white and Street is African-American, it has also meant that highly divisive racial politics have been avoided in a city where whites and non-whites share political power.

Working together, Rendell and Street produced a five-year fiscal plan that won approval from the Pennsylvania Inter-governmental Cooperation Authority, the fiscal oversight committee created by the state with the power to issue bonds on Philadelphia's behalf. Bankruptcy was avoided, budgets were balanced, and new labor contracts containing remarkable wage, health benefits, and work rule concessions were signed with all four of the city's municipal labor unions. The public financial markets have responded by buying Philadelphia's bonds at low, prevailing market rates of interest. In 1995, the city reported an $80 million surplus, and Rendell was reelected by a 77 percent margin.

The restoration of Philadelphia's fiscal image has been paralleled by other events with high national visibility:

- metropolitan Philadelphia was ranked third in overall livability by the 1993 *Places Rated Almanac,*
- *Fortune* magazine rated Philadelphia among the ten "Best Cities for Knowledge Workers" (November 15, 1993), and
- FBI statistics documented that the Philadelphia region is the safest of the twelve largest U.S. metropolitan areas.

The city's long-term economic prospects hold real promise. The city and region have considerable strength in higher education, with 80 institutions granting degrees in higher learning and 50,000 college graduates annually. The region has enormous strengths in health care, medical education and research, biotechnology, and pharmaceuticals. Organized venture capital companies can now be found throughout the region, and they support synergies among universities, entrepreneurs, and the growing base of companies in what promoters call "Medical Valley" and "America's High-Tech Mainstreet."

The $525 million Pennsylvania Convention center opened in downtown Philadelphia in 1993, and by all measures is living up to its advance billing as the anchor institution for the city's growing hospitality industry that promises to become a major sector of its economy. Efforts valued at several hundred million dollars are now underway to develop the

Avenue of the Arts on South and North Broad Street as lively settings for the performing arts, and entertainment-based development is proceeding smartly on the Delaware River waterfront. Along with the city's unique comparative advantage as the birthplace of American democracy, these multiple developments are helping transform Philadelphia into an exciting "Destination City" in a global economy marked by extensive travel, tourism, and trade.

SERIOUS SOCIAL PROBLEMS REMAIN

Despite these strengths and the mayor's *Economic Stimulus Plan*, Philadelphia's prospects are not without serious threats. The city's tax base has eroded precipitously, as Philadelphia lost 10 percent of its jobs between 1990 and 1993. Although the city added jobs in 1994, other significant weaknesses endure. One family in five is mired in poverty, and unemployment, particularly for non-whites, remains high. The 1980s saw the rise of new and costly social problems, including AIDS, homelessness, and the crack epidemic. The condition of public housing is disgraceful, and the past performance of public schools has been dismal (although it is gratifying to see the efforts of the new school superintendent, David Hornbeck, to implement fundamental reform through his "Children Achieving" agenda).

So it can be argued that despite all the positive trends described above, Philadelphia and America's other big cities are on greased skids. What distinguishes one from the other is the angle of descent. Aid is needed at least to help level the fiscal playing field so that cities can stabilize their revenues by holding on to their job and population base. But without intervention from federal and state governments, America in the long run may well lose all its big cities, Philadelphia included. The time has come to get the suburbs involved.

Toward a Dialogue Between the City and the Suburbs

If I've convinced you that the region's best chance for success in the global economy requires city-suburb cooperation, it should also be clear that the counties' and state's best interests are to help Philadelphia survive in the face of declining federal aid, an eroding local tax base, and mounting social problems. Philadelphia's neighboring suburban counties can help in three important ways.

First, modest county funds are needed for varied *regional* projects. Bucks, Chester, Delaware, Montgomery, and Philadelphia counties should undertake joint strategic planning, expand regional marketing strategies, embrace tax base sharing for *new* economic development, promote regional tourism, dedicate funds for the region's arts and cultural institutions, protect open space, and create a regional airport authority. While the details and the politics behind each initiative differ, they share the common notion that regional opportunities require regional responses.

This agenda was advanced by the 2,000 business, civic, and political leaders, as well as concerned citizens, who gathered at the Call to Action Conference on May 25, 1995, which was organized by the University of Pennsylvania's Center for Greater Philadelphia, the Greater Philadelphia Chamber of Commerce, and Greater Philadelphia First. They heard addresses by Pennsylvania Governor Tom Ridge, Philadelphia Mayor Ed Rendell, and Neal R. Peirce and considered 89 regional initiatives collected in the *Greater Philadelphia Investment Portfolio*.

Second, Philadelphia will need political support from suburban legislators in the General Assembly to provide additional state funding for the social costs associated with the support of the disadvantaged. Fairness dictates that these costs should be shared more equitably by citizens across the Commonwealth. These disadvantaged people are Pennsylvanians, not just Philadelphians, and their problems are not of the city's making. To overcome the perception that "giving additional funding to Philadelphia is like throwing the money down a hole," most Philadelphians would likely accept some form of state control over social programs in return for adequate state aid to meet needs. Neither economic nor moral ends are served by balancing the city's budget on the backs of the poor or by driving Philadelphia into bankruptcy in a futile attempt to meet social needs beyond its fiscal capacity. Cities cannot solve social problems because they cannot redistribute income without driving out businesses and middle-income taxpayers.

The devolution of federal authority to the states in the form of block grants also presents an excellent opportunity for the states to stimulate regional approaches. Instead of distributing all block-grant funds directly to individual counties, states would reserve portions only for counties that joined together as regions and submitted strategic plans defining how they would allocate funds for health care, welfare, job training, education, environment, and the like. In *New Visions for Metropolitan America*, Anthony Downs (1994) calls for the creation of "regional allocation agencies" to decide how such funds would be spent. Their members could be popularly elected as in Portland, Oregon, or appointed by the governor and the state legislature as in the Minneapolis–St. Paul area, or designated by local governments.

Third, and perhaps most importantly, political leverage from the suburban counties is needed to help the city continue government reform and to use more effectively the large sums of money it already spends on education and government operations.

I am not suggesting that the suburbs should come to the table with a blank check — that would be both counterproductive and politically impossible. But the time has come to begin a candid dialogue about what can be done to keep central cities like Philadelphia fiscally stable and economically viable. Voters in the city and suburbs must ask Republicans and Democrats to stop the histrionics and get on with the difficult task of finding solutions because partisan politics is now a luxury neither the region nor the nation can afford.

If suburban residents believe state funds have been put to poor use in Philadelphia, this is the moment to sit down and agree on the changes that need to be made to use these funds more effectively. If further aid is required in the city, suburban political support could be conditioned on the adoption of fundamental reforms. A possible model is the Wharton Real Estate Center's "New Urban Strategy," which proposes no new net funding for urban America. However, Joseph Gyourko and Anita Summers (1994) argue that cities that undertake serious reform should be rewarded with additional dollars, while those that refuse to make the tough political choices should receive fewer dollars. In short, many desired changes in cities may prove impossible without this new politics of leverage from the suburbs.

Although there is no line item in the federal budget for "cities," as HUD secretary Henry Cisneros (1995) has pointed out, the aggregate impact of the cuts proposed by Congress for Medicaid, food stamps, welfare, Head Start, education, job training, mass transit, and the earned income tax credit will have a devastating impact on urban America because this is where those in poverty and with low incomes disproportionately reside. Suburban leaders need to understand that these cuts will further destabilize the cities they surround, with serious consequences for their communities as well.

We also must not become captives of our own language. Words such as *city* and *suburbs* suggest monoliths where none exist; they give rise to false but powerful images of we/they and us/them. The images are reinforced with census data, and the political numbers favor the suburbs; nationwide one-quarter of Americans live in cities and one-half live in suburbs.

Yet many older, inner-ring suburban communities more closely resemble the cities than they do the affluent suburbs where the wealthiest 20 percent of Americans live. During the 1980s, these older, inner-ring suburbs generally lost population, had little or no job growth, saw housing values stagnate or decline, and watched urban social problems such as homelessness, crime, and drugs spill over into their communities. The city-suburb duality distorts reality, buttresses partisan approaches, and complicates the cooperative arrangements that should follow economic self-interest.

Not too long ago *regional cooperation* was an oxymoron, but efforts by a great many people and organizations in the last decade have made it a strategy taken seriously by business, civic, and political leaders. Although substantial progress has been made, much of what remains to be done will be more controversial. When asked to move in these more difficult directions, elected officials in the city and suburbs first look over their shoulders to see if their constituents are behind them. For those of us who believe in regional cooperation, it is time to build a host of parades.

Of course the barriers of race, class, and politics that divide the city and suburbs are formidable. But we must accept the fact the global economy is putting Americans on the same team. The economic realities of the 1990s make clear that we are in this together and that cities and suburbs must work cooperatively. In our region people must recognize that Philadelphia bashing is *old* politics. The failure to respond to the fiscal factors that undermine the city's competitiveness is *old* economics. It is time to change. It is time for city dwellers and suburbanites to develop a quid pro quo — to ask what they expect from each other and to explore what they will do if each fulfills the respective commitments.

Although a compelling argument based on morality and social justice can be made to bring the city and suburbs together, the case presented here is based on economic self-interest. This is not an exercise in what we *should* be doing but in what we *have* to do to be competitive in the global economy.

Lest this task seem overwhelming, it is good to recall in closing that truly radical changes can occur; the Soviet Union has collapsed, the Berlin Wall has come down and the Germanys have united, Arabs and Israelis are making peace, and black and white South Africans are peacefully building a new nation together. Surely we can have regional cooperation in metropolitan Philadelphia.

References

Cisneros, Henry G. 1995. "Aid to the Cities Is Being Chopped into Little Pieces by Republicans." *Philadelphia Inquirer*, 4 October, Op-Ed.

Commission on the Skills of the American Workforce. 1990. *America's Choice: High Skills or Low Wages.* Rochester, NY: National Center on Education and the Economy.

Downs, Anthony. 1994. *New Visions for Metropolitan America.* Washington, DC and Cambridge, MA: The Brookings Institution and the Lincoln Institute of Land Policy.

Gyourko, Joseph, and Anita A. Summers. 1994. *Working Towards a New Urban Strategy for America's Larger Cities: The Role of an Urban Audit.* Wharton Real Estate Center, University of Pennsylvania.

Hershberg, Theodore. 1991. At the Crossroads: The Consequences for the City, Region and Commonwealth of Economic Stability or Decline in Philadelphia. Pre-conference report for the Sixth Annual Southeastern Pennsylvania State Legislators' Conference, Center for Greater Philadelphia.

Kirsch, Irwin S., Ann Jungeblut, Lynn Jenkins, and Andrew Kolstad. 1993. *Adult Literacy in America: A First Look at the Results of the National Adult Literacy Survey.* Washington, DC: National Center for Education Statistics.

Ledebur, Larry C., and William R. Barnes. 1993. *All in It Together: Cities, Suburbs and Local Economic Regions*, National League of Cities.

Nathan, Richard P. 1994. Reinventing Regionalism, Keynote Address for the Regional Plan Association Meeting, 26 April, New York.

Ohmae, Kenichi. 1995. *The End of the Nation State: The Rise of Regional Economies.* New York: Free Press.

Osborne, David, and Ted Gaebler. 1992. *Reinventing Government: How the Entrepreneurial Spirit Is Transforming the Public Sector.* New York: Addison-Wesley Publishing Company, Inc.

Peirce, Neal R., with Curtis Johnson and John Stuart Hall. 1993. *Citistates: How Urban America Can Prosper in a Competitive World.* Washington, DC: Seven Locks Press.

Rusk, David. 1993. *Cities Without Suburbs.* Baltimore: Johns Hopkins University Press.

Thurow, Lester. 1992. *Head to Head: The Coming Economic Battle Among Japan, Europe, and America.* New York: Morrow.

_____. 1995. "How Much Inequality Can a Democracy Take?" *The New York Times Magazine* 19 November.

Toffler, Alvin, and Heidi Toffler. 1993. "Societies at Hyper-Speed." *The New York Times*, 31 October, Op-Ed.

Voith, Richard. 1992. "City and Suburban Growth: Substitutes or Complements?" *Business Review*, September-October.

_____. 1993. "Changing Capitalization of CBD-Oriented Transportation Systems." *Journal of Urban Economics* 33.

CHAPTER 36

REGIONS IN ACTION: REGIONAL GOVERNANCE AND GLOBAL COMPETITIVENESS

Allan D. Wallis

Before there were nation-states there were city-states, functioning as the primary units of economic competitiveness. In their book *Citistates* (1993), Neal Peirce, Curtis W. Johnson and John Stuart Hall argue that the era of city-states has been reborn. They suggest that "the reasons for this reemergence lie in a remarkable confluence of events. Telecommunications has become global and instant. With access to an international airport, goods can be moved between any two continents in a single day. Trade barriers are crumbling, opening distant markets, forcing inefficient manufacturing out of business" (p.1). In the wake of these and other changes, "it has become increasingly clear that preoccupation with macroeconomics at the nation-state level may not be particularly productive, that national economies are, in fact, constellations of regional economies, each with a major city at its core, each requiring specific and customized strategies" (p.2). Other analysts, such as Kenichi Ohmae in *Borderless World* (1990), and Rosabeth Moss Kanter in *World Class* (1995), draw similar conclusions.

There are three trends which together characterize the emerging economy.

Globalization of Production. This development is well illustrated by current practices in automobile manufacturing. Today different components of the same car may be made on several continents depending on where the best economies of labor and materials can be found.

Globalization of Consumption. Consumers have a wide range of products from which to choose and, with the lowering of trade barriers, less restrictions in choosing their preferences. For example, the elimination of tariff barriers in Europe makes it reasonable for an individual purchasing an automobile to consider whether prices for the same model are better in Spain, France, or Germany.

Globalization of Capital. Just as consumers are increasingly free to purchase products wherever they find the best prices, those with capital to invest are increasingly free to make their investments where they yield the best returns.

Arguably, the economy has been transforming since the end of the period of post–World War reconstruction and recovery. But developments associated with this transformation have been masked by attention to national economies, especially in the US. Going off the gold standard was an important signal of fundamental restructuring, but the events which most conspicuously opened eyes were the end of the Cold War and the signing of international trade agreements eliminating

---

Originally published as "Regions in Action: Crafting Regional Governance Under the Challenge of Global Competitiveness," *National Civic Review,* Vol. 85, No. 2, Spring-Summer 1996. Published by the National Civic League, Denver, Colorado. Reprinted with permission of the publisher.

many tariff and associated barriers. As in a gestalt switch, in which a *vase* is suddenly seen as *two profiles looking at each other*, elements of global economic transformation have suddenly moved from background to foreground.

There is a good deal of consensus regarding the basic characteristics of the global transformation just described, but beyond that point, opinions rapidly diverge (see Wallis 1996). Some analysts interpreted globalization as producing an increasingly footloose form of production, particularly in knowledge-based industries. To the extent that workers as well as corporations are willing to move, regions become interchangeable commodities, and they must work hard to attract and hold firms. Other analysts see globalization in terms of flexible manufacturing operating in industrial districts. In this interpretation, the social structure of regions is inextricably tied to their economic structure, and their place-based characteristics become a central aspect of competitiveness. Each interpretation has profoundly different implications for how regions should mobilize to improve their competitiveness and, consequently, very different implications for governance. It should also be acknowledged that some observers feel that the potential significance of global competitiveness for fostering regional solidarity is exaggerated, or as one wag expressed: "It's a lot of Globaloney."

The Challenge of Governance in Achieving Regional Competitiveness

The rise of city-states in an environment of global competitiveness poses a major challenge to institutions of government and processes of governance. Competitiveness requires a degree of regional cohesiveness that can be thwarted by governmental fragmentation and parochial governance. In the American system of federalism, cities only have those powers granted to them by their states. When states have seen their own destiny in terms of their cities, they often grant them new powers or create institutions necessary to help them succeed. But expanding the power of metropolitan regions runs counter to a cultural prefer-

ence for keeping government as small as possible with powers exercised closest to the people affected. The inherent conflict between ends and means has made achieving effective regional government or regional governance extremely difficult. Whether the forces of global competitiveness can foster development of more effective US metropolitan regions is an open question. What is clear is that an increasing number of regions are pursuing strategies toward this end.

Two brief illustrations serve to make the point. Gary R. Severson, Area President of First Interstate Bank of Washington, in a commentary published by the *Seattle Times*, writes that:

> Metropolitan regions are the building blocks of our nation's economy. The problem is that our regions generally lack the governance mechanisms to make the important investment decisions for our scarce public capital. Old parochialism's among cities and their suburbs only hinder the important efforts needed to ensure that our metropolitan regions compete effectively in the global economy.
>
> My point is that global competition and the growing importance of the metropolitan economy are rendering the old adversarial styles ineffective and obsolete. In the United States, we have had the luxury of adversarial relations — labor vs. business, city vs. county, and so on. But this luxury is becoming more expensive in the face of global competition. We need to create an atmosphere of partnership and cooperation in all of our myriad economies. New mechanisms must be developed to allow local governments to work together to ensure the continuing economic competitiveness of the region [1993].

Another illustration is offered in a report entitled "An Economic Development Strategy for Greater Philadelphia," issued by the organization Greater Philadelphia First:

> The economic regions of the world compete with one another to provide jobs and income for their residents by attracting businesses and supporting their growth. At present Greater Philadelphia is falling behind in that competition.

The region faces a choice: it can take decisive action to gain the lead in the global economy, or it can drift and decline, allowing other regions to pass it by. This challenge is as broad as the image the region portrays to the rest of the world, and it is as concrete as the paychecks in local workers' hands (May 1995, p.1).

Philadelphia began to recognize itself as a region in the middle of the 19th century when the city and county consolidated, in part, to improve their competitive advantage over other regions of the northeast. Philadelphia's chief rival then was New York City, which ultimately consolidated its boroughs to form Greater New York. Although New York today is clearly a world city and Philadelphia is not, there is no irony in the challenge enunciated by Greater Philadelphia First, which looks past New York as it talks about making Philadelphia competitive in the global economy.

Matching Governance Capacity to the Challenge of Global Competitiveness

In September 1995, the Lincoln Institute for Land Policy of Cambridge, Massachusetts, convened a conference on "Global City Regions: Searching for Common Ground." The conference looked at a dozen regions around the world, including San Diego as its sole US case. A conference summary concludes that "most participants ... accepted and heartily embraced the new dynamic of globalization. Their governments are actively working to reposition their regions to attract foreign enterprises and real estate developments that promise modernization. They hope to convert their cities into beacons, leading their nations in the worldwide process of integration" (1996, p.2).

Having embraced the new reality of global competitiveness, conference participants acknowledged that "there is an inherent *mismatch between the global economy and government*, not only in the spatial sense of local or fragmented governments struggling to master regional or global economic forces, but in the contrasting operating modes of markets and government" (italics added, p.4). Following this line of reasoning, response to growing competitive pressures should be evident in

government reinvention and governance reform at the regional level. These pressures combine with continuing demands for achieving efficiency in delivery of public services and provision of infrastructure as justifications for regionalism. Regionalism is also fueled by concern about social and fiscal inequities, especially where there are declining central cities surrounded by affluent suburbs. In short, revitalization of interest in regionalism is justified as a way of meeting multiple demands, but even in combination these pressures may be insufficient to overcome resistance to formalizing regionalism in the US.

The challenge identified at the Lincoln Institute Conference is expressed as a mismatch between new competitive economic demands and government capacity. If this mismatch is correctly hypothesized, it suggests that regions with strong appropriate government capacity and effective governance will be more competitive, whereas those laboring with continued fragmentation of their capacity to formulate and execute policies affecting competitiveness, will be losers.

Types of Capacity Needed to Match the Global Challenge

Assuming that regions are in fact challenged to address the mismatch of competitiveness demands and government/governance capacity, what types of capacity must they develop? To begin, regions need the capacity to *identify opportunity*. This may involve sophisticated analysis of competitive advantage or a more limited evaluation of the benefits of marketing the region as a region. In any effort to identify opportunities, there are benefits to a region genuinely perceiving itself as an economic entity as opposed to an aggregation of independent and mutually competitive communities. To be sure, there will be some enterprises in which internal competition is healthy, but there must at least be some pursuits that are perceived as demanding solidarity, such as coordinated support for improving public education at all levels.

A fundamental part of developing a capacity for opportunity identification is developing a shared sense of regional identity. This does not mean that everyone shares a single image, but there must be sufficient consensus about what constitutes a core region to provide a basis for analysis.

Following on a capacity to identify opportunity is the ability to *formulate strategies* in response to those opportunities. Again, when formulating competitiveness strategies there is an advantage to communities perceiving themselves as jointly comprising a region. More specifically, there are benefits in having a strong regional civic infrastructure; that is, a network of organizations drawing from the public, private and nonprofit sectors.

Implementing strategies once formulated requires a capacity to *mobilize resources*. Sometimes this mobilization involves bringing together coalitions of organizations and interests cutting across public, private and nonprofit sectors in the region. Each sector can contribute based on its own unique strengths, compensating for potential limits in the others. Strategies may also involve regional efforts to secure resources from their states, as well as successfully competing for federal grants. Regardless of the specifics, mobilization involves finding new resources and combining them with existing ones.

Bringing this set of activities from opportunity identification to mobilization requires the capacity to *evaluate the effectiveness of actions* taken and reflect on what is learned. This is difficult, since parsing out effects requires distinguishing their contribution from other factors operating in the region. Nevertheless, a capacity for assessment and reflection is essential for reinforcing perceptions that communities of a region share a common destiny and benefit from common actions, as well as improving the strategies and action plans in the next cycle.

Developing these capacities often requires the structured engagement of organizations from the private and nonprofit, as well as the public sector. Such collaborations are difficult to establish and sustain. Harvard's Rosabeth Moss Kanter (1995) observes that in some highly competitive regions business acts as a shadow government. But efforts to give such arrangements sufficient power to be effective can easily provoke demands for accountability which can perversely undermine their capabilities. Furthermore, governance suggests the active participation of citizens, but processes that are too open may undermine the type of flexibility necessary to move quickly on opportunities.

Four Types of Governance Capacity for Global Competitiveness

- **Opportunity Identification.** The ability to analyze the competitive advantage based on a shared image of the region.
- **Strategy Formulation.** Development of strategies capable of strengthening areas of economic activity where regional competitive advantage has been identified.
- **Mobilization of Resources.** Bringing together a coalition of interests with sufficient resources to be able to implement identified strategies.
- **Evaluation of Action.** The ability to reflect on the effectiveness of actions taken to promote competitiveness and to refine them further based on that reflection.

Distinguishing Between Governance and Government

In achieving the types of capacity required for competitiveness, it is useful to distinguish between regional *governance* and *government*. At a time when the public expresses low confidence in government and a desire to see government budgets and activities reduced, the idea of introducing anything that hints of a new layer of government is difficult to win approval for even with convincing arguments for improved competitiveness. In part then, the distinction between governance and government is intended to alleviate concerns that what is being proposed is necessarily more government. But the distinction is not just rhetorical, as Professor John Kirlin of the University of Southern California suggests:

Governance is more than government. Government involves defined institutions and associated processes. Cities are governments, seen in their formal structures, elections, hearings and so on. Governance involves a system by which societies make collective choices and act upon those choices. Governance systems include governments, but also constitutions, policies with significant effects upon collective choices, and institutions with no formal public authority which influence collective choices and action. [Governance is not simply actions of the public sector.] The press and broadcast media and major civic associations provide examples of non-public institutions with significant impacts on governance.

Every region has a form of governance, even if it has no formal regional governments. The goal of contemporary reformers is to improve this system of governance so that it may more adequately address needs of the region. In some cases, new or revised regional governments will be needed, but in many cases, an important strategy will be to improve the other factors of governance [1995, p.16].

The distinction between government and governance is also suggested in *Making Democracy Work* (1993a), Robert Putnam's study of the introduction of regional government in Italy. In 1970 the Italian Parliament enacted legislation decentralizing many government responsibilities to newly created regional governments. Putnam and his colleagues tracked the performance of these regions over a 20-year period, including analysis of their economic performance. Over this period some regions excelled in global competitiveness while others fell ever further behind. Reflecting on the differences in performance of two contrasting regions, Putnam concludes:

> Of two equally poor Italian regions a century ago, both very backward, but one with more civic engagement, and the other with hierarchical structure, the one with more choral societies and soccer clubs has grown steadily wealthier. The more civic region has prospered because trust and reciprocity were woven into its social fabric ages ago. None of this would appear in standard economic textbooks, of course, but our evidence suggests that wealth is the consequence, not the cause, of a healthy civics [1993b. p.106].

Putnam's work offers some refinement to the competitiveness/governance mismatch hypothesis. It suggests that simply providing increased formal government capacity operating regionally does not necessarily improve competitiveness. Rather, what is of equal if not greater significance is governance capacity consisting of the ability of interests across sectors to develop a shared set of values, formulate a common vision, and mobilize resources to achieve it.

U.S. Regions Responding to the Challenge

The way US regions have responded to the perceived challenges of global competitiveness strongly reflects the existing organizational strengths of their public, private and nonprofit sectors (see Grell and Gappert 1993). Ironically, Rustbelt regions may have had a headstart in focusing resources on addressing this challenge, because they were so intensely experiencing export of their economic base to regions with cheaper labor. Today, it is increasingly Sunbelt regions that are looking for the meaning of this change for them, as they adjust to demilitarization of their economies.

CLEVELAND: PARALLEL BUT COMPLEMENTARY INITIATIVES

Cleveland is a classic Rustbelt city which has been actively engaged in transforming its economy for almost three decades. An important organization leading this transformation is Cleveland Tomorrow, an association of over 50 corporations with annual earnings in excess of $300 million. After conducting a careful economic analysis of the region, Cleveland Tomorrow began pursuing strategic projects that it felt would enhance the region's image and hence its economic competitiveness; for example, construction of a new baseball stadium. The association has also identified specific industrial clusters, and worked to secure state support for improving university capacity for conducting research in these areas. Cleveland Tomorrow has intentionally steered clear of broad public policy issues, such as entering into the Cleveland public schools debate. Indeed, it performs rather like a traditional coalition of competitively minded business interests, but with a regional perspective.

Cleveland benefits on the civic side by the presence of one of the nation's oldest citizen organizations, the Citizens League of Greater Cleveland. The League is in its fourth year of an initiative called "Rating the Region," which benchmarks regional performance as a measure of competitiveness. Utilizing corporate benchmarking methodology, 89 indicators are employed ranging from economy to education, and from government to open space. The same set of indicators is used to compare Cleveland's performance with 13 other regions.

Both Cleveland Tomorrow and the Citizens League are beneficiaries of major foundations headquartered in the city. The Cleveland Foundation and the Gund Foundations have provided strong support for many initiatives. For example, they sponsored the original economic competitiveness analysis which provided the baseline for work now conducted by Cleveland Tomorrow. In general, northeastern cities and those in the industrial midwest have benefited from early establishment of well endowed foundations. These organizations provide critical funds necessary to support regional analysis and organization building activities.

PHILADELPHIA: MULTIPLE ORGANIZATIONS COOPERATING ON SPECIAL PROJECTS

Closely paralleling activities evident in Cleveland are those in Philadelphia. As previously mentioned, Greater Philadelphia First (GPF)—which is an association of corporate chief executives—has actively pursued a variety of competitiveness strategies. In formulating economic development strategies, GPF has identified five industry clusters which it foresees as being critical to the competitiveness of the region's export economy: health care services and products; finance, insurance, and other information-intensive services; professional services; hospitality; and precision manufacturing. Having identified competitive clusters, GPF proceeded to establish cluster-level teams, responsible for defining goals as well as measures of how each cluster should

develop. In 1994, it organized the Greater Philadelphia Economic Development Coalition, which was given responsibility for developing regional action plans to make the targeted industrial clusters more competitive.

Conspicuously absent from GPF's list of clusters is the seaport, which for more than two centuries has been the very heart of the region's economy. Expanding the airport, however, is now viewed as critical to economic development. Interest in expanding airport capacity and service is just one example of GPF involvement in government policies and activities.

Unlike Cleveland Tomorrow, GPF has defined government and public policy as a basic area of interest. In relation to this interest, GPF has promoted the sale of city assets and establishment of an association to provide the city with financial oversight. GPF is also very active in promoting public education with access to opportunity. A project combining GPF's interest in economic competitiveness and education is a recently initiated benchmarking effort, "The Prosperity Index." The index focuses more narrowly on economic competitiveness than the Cleveland rating project. It is interested in employability as measured in terms of work force preparedness to meet the region's present and future labor force demands.

GPF also actively partners with other organizations. With the Pennsylvania Economy League—an independent nonprofit public policy research and development organization, with a mission to promote better government for a more competitive region—GPF has completed several projects, including "Building a Technically Proficient Workforce for Greater Philadelphia." GPF has engaged in strategic partnerships with the Greater Philadelphia Development Coalition and the Greater Philadelphia International Network to further economic development by strengthening the region's image. Like Cleveland Tomorrow, it associates image building with development of major tourism projects, specifically the new $522 million Pennsylvania Convention Center.

Like Cleveland, Philadelphia benefits from an organized university-based center providing capacity to help identify regional opportunities and act as a forum for incubating action programs. The Center for Greater Philadelphia operates out of the University of Pennsylvania, a private institution. Director Theodore Hershberg makes the case that cities and suburbs must cooperate in order to enhance regional competitiveness in a global economy. Through its "Regional Network Directory," the Center promotes development of policy networks that can be mobilized around development of specific strategic initiatives. As a mechanism for developing regional initiatives, the Center convenes Regional Network Roundtables covering a wide range of issues; for example, the Center initiated a project with local chambers of commerce to support establishing rigorous academic standards in public schools.

SAN FRANCISCO: PUBLIC/PRIVATE PARTNERSHIPS AND INDUSTRIAL NETWORKS

San Francisco provides another example of a corporate membership association working to promote regional competitiveness. The Bay Area Council was formed in 1944 for the purpose of bringing private interests to bear on coordination of the region's growth as it effects efficient corporate development. BAC's membership includes some of the nation's largest firms.

In *The Transformation of San Francisco*, Chester Hartman observes that "BAC is vitally interested in nourishing the growth of San Francisco as the brains and heart of this regional economic unit" (1984, p.6). Toward this end, BAC concentrates on influencing transportation development and industrial location. For example, it was extremely influential in winning passage of the bond issue supporting construction of the Bay Area Rapid Transit system (BART).

In 1988, in partnership with the Association of Bay Area Governments, BAC created the Bay Area Economic Forum. The Forum provides a catalyst for collaborative action to ensure and enhance the economic vitality of the economy of the San Francisco Bay region. Forum membership is comprised of leaders from business, government, labor, academia and community organizations in the region.

Similar to Cleveland Tomorrow and GPF, a primary objective of the Forum is to identify and promote development of competitive industrial clusters. In particular, the Forum has been active in promoting exports, through BAYTRADE, a program to promote international trade opportunities for the region. Associated with the Forum is the Bay Area Regional Technology Alliance (BARTA), a nonprofit consortium of organizations devoted to encouraging technology-based economic development in the bay region.

The Bay Area Council has long been active in politics, typically acting behind the scenes to support candidates for elective office who favored Council policies. Over the past decade the Council has become increasingly concerned about the fragmented public management of growth. Bay area housing costs are among the highest in the nation and traffic congestion is imposing significant delays on daily business activities. In 1990, the Council joined with a moderate environmental group, the Greenbelt Alliance, to sponsor a university-based visioning process called "Bay Vision 2020." The objective of 2020 was to propose regional governance measures capable of addressing the region's growth problems. By combining the planning authority of several existing regional bodies, the 2020 proposal hoped to create a more powerful and effective planning agency. The proposal made its way to the state legislature where it died in committee along with several other growth management bills. Even though unsuccessful, Bay Vision 2020 illustrates the desire of an organized regional corporate coalition to achieve sufficient governance as well as government capacity to address fundamental conditions of competitiveness, such as affordable housing, uncongested roads, adequate airport capacity and a trained workforce.

Although regional in scope, BAC's concerns focus strongly on the City of San Francisco. It has had relatively little involvement with developments in the San Jose portion of the region, known as "Silicon Valley" (see Saxenian 1994). The Valley has its own rich history of economic development since the end of the Second World War, building a world class electronics industry with expertise emanating from Stanford University. Today, San Jose is the most rapidly growing portion of the region. Vision 2020 includes San Jose, but in other respects each portion of the region seems to be pursuing relatively independent agendas.

SEATTLE: MOVING TO DEFINE AN INTERNATIONAL ROLE

For decades, Seattle's economy has been dominated by the Boeing Corporation. As that firm's sales have become increasingly international, Seattle has found itself ever more part of the global economy. When Boeing partners with a Japanese firm to sell aircraft, and the deal requires outsourcing components to Japanese manufacturers, Seattle's economy feels the effects. The Puget Sound region's other industrial giant is Microsoft, dominating an industry that barely existed 20 years ago.

Unlike San Francisco, which benefits from foresighted formation of the Bay Area Council, the Puget Sound region has only recently begun to organize a competitiveness strategy. The Trade Development Alliance of Greater Seattle is a collaboration of the Port of Seattle, King and Snohomish County governments, the city of Seattle, the Greater Seattle Chamber of Commerce, and labor union leadership. The Alliance was formed out of recognition that new local partnerships are necessary to retain the region's future competitiveness in a rapidly changing global economy. To this end, the Alliance has developed a strategic promotion plan to enhance the identity of Greater Seattle in targeted world markets.

Designed to foster a sense of regional identity and an educated regional leadership, several Seattle organizations co-sponsor annual inter-regional visits. A cross-sectoral group of regional leaders travel to selected regions, both to gather "best practices" from elsewhere, but also to scope out what their potential competitors are doing. Starting in 1983, tours have been conducted to regions like Baltimore and the Silicon Valley, as well as Europe and Japan.

The University of Washington is a partic- ipant in the Alliance. The University also houses the Northwest Policy Center. Established in 1987, the Center provides analysis of trends in the Pacific Northwest, and develops strategies promoting the economic and environmental vitality of the region. The Center defines the region as covering six US states, northern California, and two Canadian Provinces. The region as defined by the Center is dramatically different from the region of the Trade Alliance. Such contrasts are not unlike differences found in other regions. In Cleveland, for example, some associations define the region as the city and county, others see it in terms of a Cleveland/Akron axis, and still others include all of Northeastern Ohio. In San Diego, regionalism is defined by many as coordinated activities, such as growth management, taking place within the county. But for the university-based San Diego Dialogue, the region includes Tijuana and the northern portion of Mexico's Baja Peninsula. Such territorial differences suggest a basic difficulty in achieving regional strategizing and mobilization: If the region is so different for different interests, how can collaborative actions be developed?

NORTH CAROLINA'S RESEARCH TRIANGLE: A STATE/REGIONAL PARTNERSHIP

The examples discussed thus far represent initiatives emanating from regions, but often resulting in requests for state support of specific strategies. In other cases, the state takes the lead in fostering regional collaborations. One of the earliest and now fully matured examples comes from North Carolina.

In 1955, North Carolina Governor Luther Hodges set up a committee with the charge of attracting to the state companies with requirements that could be accommodated by one of the three research universities defining what is now called the "Research Triangle." In a recent essay, US Secretary for Housing and Urban Development, Henry Cisneros reports that "by 1958, an institutional structure supporting this initiative was developed consisting of three elements: a foundation (owned by the universities with profits reverting to them); the research park, acting as a profit-making land development subsidiary; and a new nonprofit research institute. By the early 1980s, the Research Triangle Institute (RTI) had become one of the major nonprofit research organizations in the country, with 1,100 direct employees and 20,000 indirect employees" (p.7–8). It is important to emphasize that this is a state initiative with significant joint support by both the governor and legislature, as well as strong private sector involvement.

Farsighted as the development of RTI was, it cannot be claimed as a response to global competitiveness. Rather, the state's concern was to diversify its economic base. Nevertheless, that early planning and the collaborative structure it established, provided a strong foundation from which to address current transformations in the global economy.

Other states have been following the North Carolina approach. In neighboring South Carolina, former Governor Richard Riley, now US Secretary for Education, also developed a strategy that built on educational institutions. Instead of trying to court new industries with low wages and tax incentives, Riley promoted the state's ability to deliver a prepared work force. As Rosabeth Moss Kanter describes it, "South Carolina's principal incentive was … its innovative job training program [that] guaranteed a custom trained work force at no expense to employer and employee" (1995, p.247). To deliver on this promise, the state established the South Carolina Board for Technical Training and Comprehensive Education and the Quality Institute for Enterprise Development.

In achieving transformation of its economy, private sector leadership was also essential. In this case, it came from such individuals as Roger Milliken, a transplant from New England to Spartanburg, South Carolina. Milliken moved his textiles firm to the state in 1954. As he saw that industry changing, Milliken worked to get ahead of the curve by instituting an internal quality improvement program. Kanter observes that Milliken brought a new cosmopolitanism to Spartanburg. Ultimately people like Milliken and Riley provided the foundation for changing the business climate of South Carolina.

How Well Are U.S. Regions Doing?

Although the examples of regions in action described here are very brief, they serve to illustrate some of the basic challenges involved in addressing the mismatch between the requirements for global competitiveness and governance/government capacity. A number of specific observations can be made about the state of current developments.

- A good deal of current competitiveness-oriented activities in regions operates in the first stages of capacity development; that is, opportunity identification and strategy formulation. By contrast, there are fewer illustrations of mobilization of resources. Moreover, many examples of mobilization take the fairly traditional form of regional coalitions lobbying their states for support of specific projects, such as sports stadiums, convention centers, and airports. It is harder to find comprehensive, multiple-strategy approaches working at the stage of mobilizing resources. Nevertheless, they are there and appear to have more profound rewards.

- Consistent with the observation that efforts at capacity building are at an early stage is evidence of relatively few effective cross-sectoral coalitions. By far, the most common type of coalition working to achieve economic competitiveness is comprised of private sector interests. This is hardly surprising since the private sector is most aware of changes in economic competitiveness. Nevertheless, cross-sectoral efforts are ultimately required to provide the level of capacity needed for effective and sustained mobilization of resources. In the new environment of competitiveness it may no longer be sufficient for private sector interests to play the role of shadow government. Rather, all sectors must be full participants in genuine governance.

- Leadership is essential, if for no other purpose than to convene and hold a diverse coalition of interests together and focused on action. Yet strong regional leaders are difficult to find. In the public sector, there are few benefits to an elected official acting as a champion of regional issues. The chair or director of a regional association of governments (COGs and regional planning councils) might play this role, but their members are often not interested in having them so engaged. The heads of special purpose authorities, especially those operating port facilities, can play a leadership role — as August Tobin did for the Port Authority of New York and New Jersey — but most executives are cautious about appearing to exceed their authority. Similarly, if a private sector leader is too aggressive in assuming the role of leadership, there may be suspicion that the role is being played in order to curry benefits for a particular firm.

- There is a paucity of governance solutions. Although there is considerable emphasis on such processes as visioning, strategic analysis and benchmarking, there is distinctly less activity with regard to inventing new structures that can more permanently house and sustain those processes. The ability to invent new alternatives is distinctly limited by the concern that they will give rise to new layers of government, and no amount of assurance that this will not occur seems to allay fears.

In conclusion, there are promising examples of regions in action responding to the challenge of global competitiveness, but these efforts are still a long way from resolving the mismatch between the demands of competitiveness and capacities of governance.

References

Henry G. Cisneros, "Urban Entrepreneurialism and National Economic Growth," (Washington, DC: US Department of Housing and Urban Development, 1995).

Greater Philadelphia First, "An Economic Development Strategy for the Greater Philadelphia Region" (May 1995).

Jan Grell and Gary Gappert, "The New Civic Infrastructure: Intersectoral Collaboration and the Decision Making Process," *National Civic Review* 82:2 (Spring 1993).

Chester Hartman, *The Transformation of San Francisco* (Totowa, NJ: Rowman and Allanheld, 1984).

Rosabeth Moss Kanter, *World Class: Thriving Locally in the Global Economy* (New York: Simon and Schuster, 1995).

John J. Kirlin, "Emerging Regional Organizations and Institutional Forms: Strategies and Prospects for Transcending Localism," NIRA-NAPA Conference, March 28, 1995.

Lincoln Institute for Land Policy, "Global City Regions: Searching for Common Ground." *Land Lines* 8:1 (January 1996).

Kenichi Ohmae, *Borderless World: Power and Strategy in the Interlined Economy* (New York: HarperCollins, 1990).

Neal Peirce, Curtis W. Johnson and John Stuart Hall, *Citistates: How Urban America Can Prosper in a Competitive World* (Washington, DC: Seven Locks Press, 1993).

Robert D. Putnam, *Making Democracy Work: Civic Traditions in Modern Italy* (Princeton, NJ: Princeton University Press, 1993).

_____, "What Makes Democracy Work," *National Civic Review* 82:2 (Spring 1993).

Ann Saxenian, *Regional Advantage: Culture and Competition in Silicon Valley and Route 128* (Cambridge, MA: Harvard University Press, 1994).

Gary R. Severson, "It's Time to Restart the Global Engines," *The Seattle Times* (September 5, 1993).

Allan D. Wallis, "Regional Governance in the Post-Industrial Economy," *The Regionalist* 3:1 (Winter 1996).

CHAPTER 37

REGIONALISM: THE NEW GEOGRAPHY OF OPPORTUNITY

Henry G. Cisneros

All of my life my home has been San Antonio, Texas, and always within a mile of the house where I grew up in Prospect Hill, a modest, working class neighborhood just two miles from the Alamo. I have watched my neighborhood and the city that surrounds it change dramatically over several decades, a transformation that mirrors in many ways what has happened in urban neighborhoods across America for the past half-century.

Built in the 1920s, many of Prospect Hill's original residents were railroad workers of German descent. By the time I lived there though, Prospect Hill had become almost entirely Hispanic. Nearly every man on our block worked as an aircraft mechanic at nearby Kelly Air Force Base. Our neighborhood battle cry was "Viva Kelly!" At the height of the Vietnam War, 35,000 local workers were employed there, and when my high school class graduated it seemed as if the base would open the door to stable middle-class prosperity forever.

When my friends and I weren't playing ball or going to dances at Central Catholic High School, we were in downtown San Antonio shopping at Joske's and Frost Brothers department stores, watching movies at the Aztec, Empire, and Texas theaters, or just hanging around street corners with friends whose families had "moved up" to new tract-home subdivisions springing up on the north side inside Loop 410. Outside Loop 410 was wilderness,

the beginning of the rolling Hill County. My Cub Scout pack hiked and camped out all through those Bexar County hills.

To the eyes of a young boy, San Antonio seemed big, but in the 1950s it was a small, compact world with downtown as its center. At that time only half-a-million people lived in the entire area — 80 percent within the city's 70 square miles.[1]

Today my family resides in Washington, D.C., but on trips home to San Antonio my son and I often visit the area where I used to hike. But my son doesn't really know that because those hills are now the site of one of the largest regional shopping malls in southwest Texas. Loop 410 — the edge of my childhood's civilized world — has been engulfed by endless subdivisions, malls and shopping strips, offices, and industrial parks. In fact, Loop 410 is now the "inner loop." The "outer loop," Route 1604, circles the area seven miles farther out, and new developments spring up every day far beyond that boundary. The three-county region's population has nearly tripled to 1.3 million, and the region's so-called "urbanized area" covers 438 square miles.

My parents still live in the same house in Prospect Hill, but the neighborhood has changed. Few young families live there; they're out in new subdivisions that are closer to their jobs. Kelly AFB has shrunk to about 15,000 workers and faces an uncertain, post–Cold War future. The neighborhood's average

From *National Civic Review,* Vol. 85, No. 2, Spring-Summer 1996. Published by the National Civic League, Denver, Colorado. Reprinted with permission of the publisher.

income is dropping, and many once-familiar neighborhood stores closed their doors years ago.

San Antonio's downtown area has changed dramatically too. There are soaring new office towers and the Alamo and the Riverwalk are the biggest tourist attractions in Texas. But downtown San Antonio is no longer the region's retail center: the River Center Mall is only the fifth largest shopping mall in the area and San Antonio's great old department stores and movie palaces have closed.

Suburban Growth/City Decline

The extraordinary growth that has transformed San Antonio's metropolitan area occurred throughout America's urban areas in the decades after World War II. Urban America has not grown upward but sprawled outward across the countryside. Since 1950 the metropolitan population of the United States has almost doubled, but the population density of the country's 522 central cities has been halved.

What happened to the *city* of San Antonio, however, stands in sharp contrast to the fate of many other American cities, including Detroit, Cleveland, and Hartford. Liberal annexation laws in Texas allowed San Antonio to expand and follow its sprawling suburban development. San Antonio is what David Rusk, former mayor of Albuquerque, New Mexico, has called an "elastic" city.[2] Through post-war annexations, San Antonio has increased its municipal territory nearly fivefold, adding over 260 square miles.

Like other elastic cities — for example, Charlotte, Columbus, Indianapolis, and Nashville — San Antonio incorporated new middle-class subdivisions, shopping centers, offices, and industrial parks within its expanding boundaries. Through expansion the city remains home to over 70 percent of the metropolitan area's population and has maintained a strong middle class, a broad tax base, and a high municipal bond rating despite the independent, upper middle-class suburban towns in its vicinity.

Yet with many aging, poorer neighborhoods in its older core area, today San Antonio would be one of the country's poorest cities if it had not annexed new development. That kind of stagnation occurred in older, "inelastic" cities like Detroit, Cleveland, and Hartford. Trapped within existing boundaries by incorporated suburbs and bad annexation laws, these cities were bled to support new suburbs. Middle-class families, stores and shops, factories, and offices relocated outside city limits. New office towers rose downtown but older city neighborhoods became dramatically poorer.

American Dream/ American Nightmare

The suburbanization of America was underwritten by a well-intentioned federal government. Federally insured, low-cost mortgages helped millions of veterans and working class families buy suburban homes. Federal highway funds built freeways that made it practical for Americans to travel great distances to work, shop, and play. Low federal gasoline taxes, which gave Americans the world's cheapest gasoline, helped fuel the cars needed for suburban living.

The American public has enjoyed enormous social advances during the post–World War II decades. Nearly two-thirds of American families own their own homes — 60 percent above the pre-war level and one of the world's highest rates of homeownership. Some 262 million Americans own 190 million motor vehicles, providing a level of individual freedom of movement unmatched in history. In 1950, only one-third of all Americans had graduated from high school and just 6 percent were college graduates; today over 80 percent are high school graduates and 22 percent have college degrees.

Others doors have opened as well. I was San Antonio's first Hispanic mayor — unthinkable only 30 years before the election. As late as 1970 there were only 1,500 African-American and 1,300 Hispanic elected officials in the country. Now there are 8,000 African-Americans and 4,600 Hispanics holding local, state, and federal offices.[3]

Pursuing the American dream, however, has also created an American nightmare — high concentrations of poor minorities in poverty-impacted, revenue-strapped, physically decaying inner cities and older suburbs who are isolated from the opportunities generated in wealthier, vigorously growing outer communities of metropolitan areas.

My grandfather moved from Mexico to San Antonio 70 years ago. He came seeking a better job, better schools for his children, better health care — in short, a better life. America's cities were meccas of opportunity for millions streaming in from farms and foreign lands. For those seeking opportunity today, the mecca must be the entire metropolitan area — the central city and especially its suburbs.[4] Achieving the American Dream for everyone requires opening up all of a metropolitan area's resources and opportunities to all of its residents. Only with diversity, balance, and stability everywhere can the decline of inner cities and aging suburbs be reversed.

Cities Without Walls

Annexation was San Antonio's strategy for sustaining growth. In the Suburban Era, annexation has been an effective countermeasure to suburbanization for about two-thirds of America's central cities. Over the past four decades central cities have annexed over 12,000 square miles and more than doubled in area. Annexation, however, has been a tool used primarily by cities in the south and west and more than 80 percent of all annexations have occurred in the Sunbelt. Annexations are increasingly rare around many midwestern cities, and in New England and the Middle Atlantic States annexations are all but impossible because of those areas' rigid political map.

A handful of cities have engaged in a form of "superannexation" — city-county consolidation. In the 1960s and 1970s, Nashville-Davidson County, Jacksonville-Duval County, Indianapolis-Marion County, Lexington-Fayette County, and Anchorage-Anchorage Borough were created through consolidation. All have fiscally sound, unified governments with strong credit ratings, and all are successful communities with rates of economic growth well above their competitors. Though none of these examples is without its flaws, in each case governmental unity seems to have fostered greater social mobility. Schools and neighborhoods are more integrated, public services and facilities are more equitably provided, and public officials serve a common constituency.

City-county consolidations are rare, however, and have often been rejected by Americans at the polls. Since World War II only 20 consolidations have been approved, and over 100 proposals have been voted down.[5] Though further consolidation movements are under way, it is likely that formal city-county unification will continue to be rare. Even in many southern and western states, annexation itself faces more and more political and administrative hurdles.

Things-Regionalism and People-Regionalism

How can the common problems of metropolitan regions be addressed when local governance is so fragmented? In recent decades the most common path to meeting regional needs has been the creation of "special districts." There are currently more than 33,000 special districts in the United States,[6] and they are now the most common form of local government in the country. More than 90 percent perform a single function: 36 percent provide water and sewer services; 16 percent are fire districts; 6 percent provide postsecondary technical and vocational education and library services; 4 percent are health and hospital districts; and 4 percent perform transportation-related functions. About 11 percent are either state-chartered housing finance agencies or local public housing authorities whose activities are often limited to a single sponsoring jurisdiction.

Although special districts come into being for many reasons, including limitations on the taxing and service powers of local general governments, many are created because the territorial scope of existing city and county governments is too limited to effectively address major regional problems. Air pollution control and watershed protection are common examples. Another is transportation planning: the Federal Intermodal Surface Transportation Efficiency Act of 1991 requires regional transportation planning to be carried out by multijurisdictional agencies.

Most special districts are examples of what may be called *things-regionalism*. For the regional community, special districts build and operate larger public works such as water and sewer facilities, flood control and irrigation systems, regional airports, major roads and highways, and mass transit systems. Some special districts' boards are directly elected by the districts' voters, although the majority of boards are appointed by the state or local governments that set them up.

Local officials often find it very difficult to make things-regionalism work, which requires negotiating initial agreements and continually balancing interests among many local communities. But what so many metropolitan areas desperately need —*people-regionalism*— is even tougher to accomplish.

People-regionalism must address the heart of America's "urban problem" — the new face of poverty. Forty years ago rural workers and the elderly constituted the greatest number of poor people in this country. Today, tremendous improvements in Social Security, Medicare, and federal pension laws have largely eliminated poverty among senior citizens, and the constant industrialization of American agriculture and migration to urban areas have reduced the numbers of rural poor. The most extreme poverty in America is now found in geographically isolated, economically depressed, and racially segregated inner cities and older, declining suburbs. Inner cities have become warehouses of America's poorest citizens.

But our inner cities are not warehouses of *all* groups of urban Americans living in poverty. In the country's 320 metropolitan areas there are 10.8 million poor whites, 6.9 million poor African Americans, and 4.8 million poor Hispanics. But in a typical metropolitan area three out of every four poor whites live in middle-class, mostly suburban neighborhoods. By contrast, three out of four poor African Americans and two out of three poor Hispanics live in inner-city "poverty neighborhoods" where at least 20 percent of the residents are poor. And many poor minorities live in neighborhoods were the poverty rate exceeds a shocking 40 percent. Highly concentrated minority poverty is urban America's toughest challenge.

We're All in It Together

Why should suburban residents care about the decline of distressed central cities? Why must all communities, as I argue, assume a common responsibility for "inner-city problems?" Haven't many suburban residents fled rundown city neighborhoods with their growing violence and crime, failing schools, rising tax rates, and declining city services? Why should suburbanites get involved?

THE REASONS ARE SIMPLE BUT COMPELLING
Together we can solve the problem. Many Americans are dismayed by the seeming magnitude of urban poverty, but the problem's size is an illusion created by its concentration. Hartford, the capital of Connecticut, for example, has become one of America's most distressed cities. Between 1950 and 1990 the city's population dropped 21 percent to 139,000. In 1989 city residents' average income was 53 percent of suburbanites' income, and over 27 percent of city residents were poor. Crime rates have soared and school failure rates were so high that last year the Hartford school board brought in a private management company to run the city's school system. Seen solely as "the city's problem," Hartford's social agony seems unsolvable.

Yet when viewed from a regional perspective, problems in the 1-million Hartford metropolitan area are not so insurmountable: out of every 100 residents only 3 are poor and white, 2 are poor and Hispanic, and less than 2 are poor and African American. Poor whites are scattered throughout the metropolitan area: only 12 percent live in Hartford, and only 13 percent live in poor neighborhoods. By contrast, 76 percent of poor Hispanics and 80 percent of poor African Americans live in city neighborhoods and nearly 9 out of 10 poor minorities live in neighborhoods of concentrated poverty.

The problem is not the region's overall level of poverty — only 7 out of every 100 area residents are poor — but the high concentration of minority poor in inner-city areas. Viewed in that light, greater Hartford is capable of absorbing poor minorities into the region's prosperous, middle-class society just as it already integrates poor whites into that society. And, indeed, the state of Connecticut and public and private organizations in metropolitan Hartford have begun to make a broader range of housing available to poor minority households (see case studies, pages 327–328).

With minor variations, Hartford's poverty ratios apply to all U.S. metropolitan areas. In elastic cities' metropolitan areas, poor minorities are somewhat less concentrated in poor neighborhoods, but in inelastic urban areas where suburban zoning practices often exclude low-income households they are much more concentrated in poverty-impacted, inner-city neighborhoods.

For both types of metropolitan areas, however, the overall weight of poverty is much the same. America is not a Third World country where the poor are many and the middle class are few. In America the middle class are many and the poor are few. *What this country lacks is not the capacity to end the isolation of the minority poor; it lacks the will.*

EVERYBODY WINS AS REGIONS BECOME GLOBAL COMPETITORS

Economic civil war has racked many American metropolitan areas. Sears abandoned its magnificent skyscraper in downtown Chicago for suburban Hoffman Estates. The city of Detroit paid $230 million to subsidize General Motors' new Poletown plant, but then watched General Motors' top executives leave the GM "World Center" in Detroit for suburban Macomb County. Detroit's real competition, however, is not its suburbs but the regions of Baden-Wurttemburg in Germany and Kyushu in Japan. In the emerging global economy, communities must compete as whole economic regions or what journalist-author Neal Peirce has called "citistates":

> The inescapable oneness of each citistate covers a breathtaking range. Environmental protection, economic promotion, work force preparedness, health care, social services, advanced scientific research and development, philanthropy — success or failure on any one of these fronts ricochets among all the communities of a metropolitan region. No man, woman, family, or neighborhood is an island.[7]

Peirce argued that a citistate divided against itself "will prove weak and ineffectual," and that "political boundaries do *not* seal off problems of pollution, solid waste disposal, transportation, schools, inadequate infrastructure."

More importantly, political borders do not seal off the problem of concentrated poverty. A growing number of economists and sociologists assert that cities and suburbs are highly interdependent parts of integrated regional economies that depend upon the health of each jurisdiction to be competitive.[8] The higher a region's internal disparities by jurisdiction, by race, and by income group, the less its economy can be competitive. A recent national news magazine's cover story, "Inequality — How the Growing Gap between Rich and Poor in America Is Hurting the Economy," noted:

> Most economists agree ... that education and skills are key to economic growth. And there's a lot of evidence that skills suffer when the wealthy go it alone. For example, school districts that mix rich kids and poor kids have higher reading and math scores than those where each group attends different schools, according to a 1989 study of 475 California districts. Rich kids do score higher when they're all in one school. But with mixing "low-achieving kids are pulled up more than the high end is dragged down, so the average is higher ..."

The article concluded that

> Ever since slavery ended, the United States has at least partly lived up to the ideal that everyone should have an equal opportunity to prosper. Now, heightened inequality is undermining this concept. The United States will continue to suffer socially if the trend continues. And it's likely to suffer economically, too.[9]

DOING THE RIGHT THING COSTS LESS THAN CONTINUED NEGLECT

Treating only the symptoms of poverty is costly, and trying to eliminate poverty by isolating the poor sacrifices the approach proven to be most effective: integration into mainstream society. Housing mobility programs that allow poor, minority households to resettle in middle-class, suburban areas result in higher employment rates, higher wages, and higher school attendance and graduation rates.[10] By contrast, high-poverty, inner-city ghettos are destructive environments that generate high crime rates.[11]

The most effective antipoverty programs help move people to opportunity: most poor families succeed in more opportunity-rich environments. And taken together such programs are actually cheaper for society than current attempts to concentrate antipoverty programs in isolated areas. In Rochester, New York, for example, buying a home in a middle-class neighborhood typically costs $80,000 and renting an apartment in the same area costs about $5,000 a year. By contrast, a new jail costs $125,000 per cell to build and about $30,000 a year per prisoner to run. Prisons close doors, not open them. Saving lives is cheaper than wasting lives.

SPRAWL HAS ITS PRICE

For three centuries America grew as if there were no end to this continent's vast supply of land, water, and forests. By the 1970s we had begun to deal with the polluted air and water that resulted, but urban sprawl continues to accelerate. In the Minneapolis–St. Paul area, for example, urban land has expanded 25 percent for every 10 percent increase in population.[12] From 1970 to 1990, Chicago's metropolitan population grew only 4 percent, but land used for housing increased 46 percent and land used for commercial development increased an extraordinary 74 percent.[13]

Such exaggerated sprawl is driven not only by the lure of greener pastures, it is also driven by abandonment of older, poverty-impacted neighborhoods. In many of Minneapolis' distressed neighborhoods the housing vacancy rate has reached between 10 and 20 percent.[14] To restore their desirability as places to live, inner cities and older suburbs need balance and stability.

SUBURBS CAN BECOME "INNER CITIES" TOO

During the past decade social distress — poverty, crime, school dropouts — has increased more in many old, inner suburbs than in many long-poor city neighborhoods. Inner-suburban social disintegration generally has not reached inner-city levels, but the downward trend in these neighborhoods is clear. Inner suburbs and inner cities both have a vital interest that every community in their region, including the most prosperous, do its "fair share." People-regionalism means diversity, balance, and stability in every area of a region.

Forging Regional Bonds

For several centuries the world has been divided into nations, provinces and states, and local governmental jurisdictions. As we enter the 21st century, a new model is emerging, driven by global trends in technology, investment, and human skills. Our most vital relationships are increasingly shaped at the global, regional, and neighborhood levels.

To overcome concentrated urban poverty in this emerging world, access to social and economic opportunity must be opened at each level. For many regions an important framework through which access can be achieved is unified governance — central cities that annex potential suburbs, consolidated city-county governments, fully empowered urban counties, and unified school districts. For other large, complex regions, formal local government unification is no longer possible. The challenge is not to foster regional *government* but rather regional *governance* in these key areas:

"FAIR SHARE" LOW- AND MODERATE-INCOME HOUSING

Land use planning and zoning have been the exclusive responsibility of local governments and many suburban areas have adopted *exclusionary zoning* to discourage construction of low- and moderate-income housing. This problem is aggravated by private-sector developers who typically build for narrowly defined income groups. The result has been greater geographic segregation by income class. Some state legislatures, such as those in Connecticut or Massachusetts, have enacted laws requiring local municipalities to accept a "fair share" of affordable housing. Progressive communities such as Tallahassee and Tampa, Florida, have adopted similar policies. The nation's oldest and most comprehensive example of local *inclusionary zoning* policies is Montgomery County, Maryland (see case study, page 329).

METROWIDE HOUSING CHOICES FOR HOUSEHOLDS WAREHOUSED IN INNER-CITY PROJECTS.

Begun with the best intentions as temporary housing for wartime workers, the nation's public housing programs now simply do not work for people or communities. Our cities' poorest neighborhoods nearly always contain large, HUD-assisted public housing projects that provide shelter for many, but opportunity for few. Over the past two decades, HUD's housing assistance programs have become more flexible and private housing-oriented, but HUD is now seeking congressional approval to completely transform these programs. Our goal is to give all public housing residents a *genuine market choice* to stay where they are or to move to private rental apartments throughout the region. To promote more economically diverse neighborhoods, HUD will no longer support housing that is exclusively occupied by the very poor. This approach will make federal housing assistance a platform of opportunity for both poor households and communities. For maximum success, HUD must establish partnerships with local governments in metropolitan regions to assure diversity, balance, and stability everywhere.

EQUAL EDUCATIONAL OPPORTUNITIES

American public education traditionally has been based on locally controlled school districts and neighborhood schools. Segregated housing patterns and great disparities in local tax bases, however, have created unequal educational opportunities for our nation's children. In response, state legislatures have moved to equalize school funding, the federal government has allocated special funds to help the poorest schools, and state and federal courts have promoted racial and economic integration. Racially integrated, mixed-income housing markets are the foundation of successful, racially and economically mixed classrooms.

AREAWIDE GROWTH MANAGEMENT

To be global competitors, America's urban areas cannot afford the burden of either abandoned communities or abandoned people. Our current patterns of suburban growth have created both. As urban areas continue to develop, policies are needed to encourage both new "greenfields" development and older "brownfields" revitalization. In the past 20 years, nearly a dozen states have enacted growth management laws. One of the most effective, the Oregon Growth Management Act, gives the country's only directly elected regional government, the Portland Metro, the key local role in regional planning and growth management (see case study, page 330).

AREAWIDE REVENUE SHARING ARRANGEMENTS

To achieve the goals of people-regionalism, moving money is much less important than moving people. It is true, however, as one neighborhood leader once told me, that "money isn't everything, but it's a nice piece of everything." Many state governments provide aid to local governments, which helps equalize their tax revenues. County governments have also had some service-equalizing impact on local communities through their support of public health and social services. The special districts discussed previously play a similar role.

Despite this history of cooperation across levels of government, few formal regional revenue sharing arrangements exist. The state legislature enacted Twin Cities Fiscal Disparities Plan for the 7-county, 189-municipality Minneapolis–St. Paul region is perhaps the most far-reaching. Elsewhere, Louisville-

Jefferson County in Kentucky has created an income tax-sharing "Compact," Rochester-Monroe County in New York has implemented the sales tax-sharing Morin-Ryan plan, and the Denver and Pittsburgh areas have created "regional asset districts"— all models that other regions could follow (see case studies, pages 330–331).

Building Communities

Although people travel significant distances to jobs, shopping centers, concert halls, movie houses, or ballparks, they are still part of a "community." More than anywhere else, our poorest inner-city neighborhoods need community strengthening. What does "community" mean? We know what community is not. It is not streets darkened by the shadows of vacant buildings, deserted by people who fear sudden and vicious attack and who know no one will help. It is not giant public housing projects where children die in the crossfire of rival gangs and security guards crouch around staircases to avoid Uzi-wielding drug sentries. Community is not a public housing project where decisions are not made by residents but by everyone else— planners, architects, city officials, federal bureaucrats, housing authority managers.

So, what is "community?" A community first needs housing that is functional, sturdy, dignified, and attractive. But housing must be more than just shelter. It must be a stable place from which we can create opportunities for people: opportunities to go from homelessness to rental housing to homeownership; opportunities to go from joblessness, without education and training, to acquiring skills and self-sufficiency. Building community means helping neighborhood residents organize and develop partnerships with local government, nonprofit agencies, and businesses.

For a quarter of a century the federal government has helped build communities through community action programs, model cities, community development block grants, and enterprise and empowerment zones. Government has helped build the capacity of neighborhood organizations, insisted that the preferences of neighborhood residents be considered in important programs, and rewarded those residents who work together.

Our efforts have had many successes. Neighborhood leaders have become school board members, city council members, mayors, legislators, and members of Congress. Neighborhood residents have found jobs as community aides and risen through their competence and effort to professional roles. Homes have been renovated and new low-cost housing built. Streets have been paved, sewers laid, sidewalks installed, and parks planted.

Yet many inner-city neighborhoods and their residents are worse off today than they were decades ago, and it is clear that government's concept of "community development" has been too narrow. The forces of metropolitan development — and abandonment — have overwhelmed the achievements of many good community-based programs. If, as the old African adage says, it takes a whole village to raise a child, then it also takes a whole region to make a good community.

Civic Life and Civility: The Key to People-Regionalism

People-regionalism cannot be mandated by Washington. It must evolve from direct, constant, honest, and communitywide conversation and hard work in each metropolitan region. In his persuasive essay, "Bowling Alone," Harvard sociologist Robert D. Putnam commented on the decline of communal participation in America.[15] He points out that though more Americans now go bowling than ever before, participation in bowling leagues has dropped 40 percent. Labor unions, parent-teacher associations, women's clubs, and fraternal organizations have all seen membership decline. Nonprofits find it harder to recruit volunteers. People find fewer friendships among neighbors. Fewer Americans take time to vote. This decline in "public capital," Putnam argued, has been accompanied by a decline in trust in our public institutions and in each other.

Pleading for a restoration of "the tolerant

democratic spirit that can help us solve our problems," Vernon Jordan, former National Urban League president, recently said that "such civility is all the more important at a time when we are sailing in uncharted waters, when the world is changing faster than our ability to control change, when a confused and anxious people seek policies that take us forward without punishing those left behind."

Commenting on Putnam and Jordan's insights in a column earlier this year, Washington Post columnist David Broder called for "a strengthening of civic life and return of civility in our public discourse."

No problem in American life demands strengthened civic life and greater civility more than repairing the tattered social and political fabric of many of America's metropolitan areas. To compete and succeed, America's urban regions must act like true communities.

Charlotte, Hartford, Minneapolis–St. Paul, Portland, Denver, and Pittsburgh are all urban areas where business leaders, state and local officials, and citizen activists are forging new mechanisms to strengthen regional bonds. These pioneers of people-regionalism are new coalitions trying to heal old wounds and build new bridges. Their approaches may differ — city-county consolidation, metro housing strategies, empowered regional councils, tax sharing — but the goal is the same: a greater, more competitive regional community with greater opportunity for all.

Case Studies

CONSOLIDATION OF CHARLOTTE-MECKLENBURG COUNTY, NORTH CAROLINA

The regional development of Charlotte, North Carolina, has combined strong economic growth and steady racial progress. In the 1980s the gap between African American and white family incomes narrowed in the Charlotte area while increasing nationally. Charlotte ranks third in housing integration among all major U.S. metropolitan areas with a large African American population.[16]

The critical factors in the Charlotte area's success have been North Carolina's annexation laws (the most liberal in the nation since 1959), the court-ordered merger of the Charlotte-Mecklenburg County public schools in 1972, and the emergence of Charlotte as the nation's third-largest banking center, which was due, in part, to the North Carolina legislature's early permission for statewide branch banking.

Through annexation Charlotte has grown from 30 square miles to 204 square miles, tripled its population, and maintained average city incomes 22 percent *above* suburban levels. Within 10 to 15 years, however, Charlotte's annexations could end when the city's boundaries approach the agreed-upon spheres of influence of 5 smaller municipalities and the Mecklenburg County line.

To accelerate the unification process, Charlotte Mayor Richard Vinroot, the Charlotte City Council, and the Mecklenburg County Commission have initiated a formal process to consolidate the city and county. A citizens commission appointed by both bodies is currently drafting a consolidation charter.

The city and county governments have already achieved a high degree of functional unification. They share a new government center and have a common planning commission and planning staff. Law enforcement agencies have been combined under city jurisdiction with the exception of sheriff's court-support functions. Parks and recreation activities have been merged under the county. Both governments are continuing to pursue other functional mergers.

The vote on formal consolidation will probably come in November. The five smaller, independent municipalities can vote to opt out, which, given the precedents in Indianapolis, Jacksonville, and Nashville, they will likely do. In effect, the city-county consolidation represents Charlotte's final annexation and avoids a piecemeal takeover of Mecklenburg County in 10 to 15 years. A merged Charlotte-Mecklenburg County will then be able to turn its energies to forging better compacts with neighboring counties.

INTEGRATING THE
HARTFORD, CONNECTICUT,
REGIONAL HOUSING MARKET

Among all states Connecticut ranks ninth in housing segregation and first in average city/suburb income gap. For decades before the state's economic slump in the 1990s, Connecticut also had the highest housing costs east of California. To address these structural housing problems, the Connecticut General Assembly approved in the late 1980s a variety of state laws to promote more affordable housing.

Most notable is the Affordable Housing Appeals Act of 1989, which states that promoting affordable housing is Connecticut's highest priority and requires any of the 169 municipalities in the state with less than 10 percent assisted housing to change their zoning practices to permit a more diverse housing supply.[17]

A developer whose plans to build affordable housing are rejected by a town council can appeal to a special state court in Hartford. In court the burden of proof is on the town council, which must convince a special state judge that the town's reasons for rejecting the proposal should be deemed a higher priority than the state's requirement that communities take affirmative steps to make housing more affordable.

Other legislative action in 1988 spurred creation of the Hartford area's Capitol Region Fair Housing Compact on Affordable Housing.[18] The compact, endorsed by the region's 26 towns, projected the creation of 5,000 to 6,400 units of affordable housing in the region over 5 years. A slump in housing construction, however, caused projections to fall short.

A soft suburban housing market has greatly benefited Hartford's Special Mobility and Section 8 programs.[19] Administered directly by the city's Department of Housing rather than the public housing authority, the programs contract directly with suburban landlords. By mid-1994, 400 former Hartford households — about 15 percent of the city's total Section 8 certificate and voucher holders — had moved to suburban locations. Those who moved were 52 percent African American, 38 percent Hispanic, and 8 percent non–Hispanic white. The suburban neighborhoods they relocated to were over 80 percent white and had an average poverty level of 7 percent. By contrast, the city neighborhoods in which other Section 8 tenants continued to live were 75 percent minority and had a poverty rate 4 times that of suburban neighborhoods.

AN INNER CITY–INNER SUBURB
COALITION IN THE
MINNESOTA LEGISLATURE

"Well, the Twin Cities are different," skeptics often scoff when I cite the area as a model of regional reform. And they're right, the Twin Cities area is different — a high level of civic culture, a 27-year-old Metropolitan Council (the Met Council), and a 7-county, 189-municipality Fiscal Disparities Plan, the Nation's most far-reaching regional revenue sharing mechanism.

But what really distinguishes the Twin Cities area is that older, inner-ring, blue-collar suburbs are making common cause with the central cities. Primarily through the efforts of State Representative Myron Orfield of Minneapolis, legislators from communities such as Columbia Heights and Brooklyn Park now recognize that "inner-city" problems — poverty, crime, declining schools — are growing rapidly in their communities. Both older suburbs and central cities have been hurt economically by disparity in regional growth, three-fourths of which has occurred in wealthy "Fertile Crescent" suburbs like Bloomington, Edina, and Eden Prairie.

As a result legislators from the central cities, older suburbs, and Democrat-represented rural areas formed a powerful legislative coalition. In each of the past two sessions the coalition passed a metrowide "fair share" housing bill twice vetoed by the state's Independent-Republican governor, restricted the use of tax increment financing to only depressed communities, changed state tax laws to remove incentives to subdivide farmland, and placed three regional agencies controlling transportation planning, transit services, and sewer services under the Met Council. The coalition failed by a narrow margin to add high-end residential property to the 23-year-old tax sharing plan, and its attempt to convert the Met Council from gubernatorial appointment to direct election was defeated by a single vote.

The movement toward regional cooperation in the Twin Cities area continues to broaden its base: over 350 suburban churches have become members of a metropolitan alliance committed to "fair share" housing in the suburbs; two dozen older suburbs have embraced the proposal for a metrowide, unified tax base; and support from the press, civic and business groups, and religious leadership continues to grow.

In regional reform the Twin Cities area is the school of America. The successful political coalitions built between central cities and older suburbs there are a model for metropolitan areas across the county. What is missing in America's declining metropolitan areas is political leadership championing the common cause.

INCLUSIONARY HOUSING IN MONTGOMERY COUNTY, MARYLAND

Montgomery County, Maryland, may have the nation's most comprehensive and balanced local housing program.[20] A wealthy suburban county outside Washington, D.C., Montgomery County had 757,027 residents in 1990 and, standing alone, would be the nation's 54th largest metropolitan area.

Under a state law passed in 1927, the Montgomery County government exercises almost total planning and zoning control throughout the county. Using these legislatively endowed powers over the decades, Montgomery County officials have implemented one of the nation's most comprehensive local growth management systems. The system addresses a wide range of local planning and zoning issues and includes a long-range "wedges and corridors" plan, an annual growth policy, an ordinance that links subdivision approval to the orderly construction of public facilities, and a program to preserve one-third of the county's land for agricultural purposes.

In 1972, the Montgomery County Council adopted the Moderately Priced Dwelling Unit (MPDU) policy, then the nation's only mandatory inclusionary zoning ordinance. The MPDU policy requires new develop-

ments with 50 or more residential units to set aside 15 percent for low- and moderate-income tenants or buyers. To compensate developers for making units available below market price, the county gives them an "MPDU bonus," which permits the development of 22 percent more housing units than is normally allowed in each zone.

MPDUs are sold or rented to individuals. By county ordinance, however, up to 40 percent of MPDU units in any development may be purchased as "deep subsidy" rentals by the county's Housing Opportunities Commission (HOC) and nonprofit organizations.

By 1994, 8,842 moderate- and low-income housing units had been created through the MPDU policy. About two-thirds were sale units and one-third were rental units. Between 1988 and 1991 the average price for sale units was $69,979 — a bargain in a county where the median housing value was $208,000 in 1990. Sixty percent of these units' buyers were minorities with an average household income of $26,497. The county's median family income at that time was $62,000.

An important facet of the MPDU policy is the role HOC plays as the county's housing finance agency. Despite some limitations on funds, HOC has helped MPDU buyers with low-cost loans and has purchased 1,099 scattered site units throughout the county, making it the largest source of rental units for public housing families. HOC also manages 555 elderly apartments in 4 complexes and 328 family or mixed family/elderly apartments in 7 complexes, and administers the county's federally funded Section 8 rental subsidy program, which helps over 3,100 local families find low-cost housing each year.

HOC programs are particularly important because they spread low- and moderate-income housing around the county. HOC-assisted housing total 3.4 percent of the county's total housing stock and in 16 of the county's 18 planning districts, HOC-assisted units represent 2 to 7 percent of all housing.

The MPDU policy and HOC's programs have helped Montgomery County accommodate — even encourage — a remarkable social transformation. In 1970 the county looked like a classic American suburb: wealthy and 92 percent white. By 1990, however, Montgomery County looked much more like a "rainbow": 12 percent African American, 7 percent Hispanic, 8 percent Asian. Montgomery County has gained a rich diversity of income groups while maintaining its preeminence as one of the country's 10 richest urban counties.

PORTLAND METRO, A DIRECTLY ELECTED REGIONAL GOVERNMENT

We, the people of the Portland area metropolitan services district, in order to establish an elected, visible and accountable regional government that is responsive to the citizens of the region and works cooperatively with our local governments; that undertakes, as its most important services, planning and policy making to preserve and enhance the quality of life and the environment for ourselves and future generations; and that provides regional services needed and desired by the citizens in an efficient and effective manner, do ordain this charter for the Portland area metropolitan services district, to be known as "Metro."

With that preamble, Portland area voters adopted on November 3, 1992, a "home-rule" charter for the Portland Metropolitan Services District.[21] After nearly 70 years of experimentation, the charter was perhaps the boldest and most important step taken toward regional governance by voters in the Portland area, which now includes 3 counties and 24 municipalities.

In 1970, the Oregon State legislature authorized the creation of a Metropolitan Services District (MSD)—a flexible governmental "box" that could be assigned as many service responsibilities as voters or legislators in the Portland area wanted. Activated by local referendum, MSD's first project, planning a regional solid waste disposal system, was financed by a small regional tax on used auto tires. MSD added a second regional function, operating the Washington Park Zoo, with the city of Portland's agreement and approval by area voters of an earmarked tax levy in 1976. In 1986 regional voters approved a $65 million bond issue for the Oregon Convention Center, to be planned, constructed, and operated by MSD.

For its first eight years MSD was governed by a seven-member, federated board of local elected officials — one each from Portland and the three counties and three representing other cities in each county. In 1977, the state legislature changed MSD's governance, authorizing direct election of a 12-member board and a chief executive, local taxing powers by referendum, and regional planning responsibilities. Finally, in 1990, the legislature amended Oregon's constitution to allow MSD to have its own home-rule charter.

Most critical for the Portland area's future is the responsibility given Metro in regional land use planning and growth management; the area's citizenry affirmed in the new charter that regional planning is Metro's "primary function."

The charter charges Metro with developing a 50-year "Future Vision" and a "Regional Framework Plan" by December 1997, including revising the state-required Urban Growth Boundary. The charter also empowers Metro to adopt ordinances to require local comprehensive plans and zoning regulations to comply with the Regional Framework Plan, to adjudicate inconsistencies between regional and local plans, and to change inconsistent local land use standards and procedures.

After decades of patient development, the Portland Metro represents a powerful but flexible structure for addressing many of the region's most critical problems.

REVENUE SHARING THROUGH REGIONAL ASSET DISTRICTS

Who is the greatest patron of the Denver Zoo, the Denver Botanic Gardens, the Denver Museum of Natural History, the Denver Museum of Art, and the Denver Performing Arts Center? It's an organization with the jaw-breaking title of the Scientific and Cultural Facilities District (SCFD).[22]

The end of state subsidies in 1982 and drastically reduced support from the city of Denver created a financial crisis for Denver's civic facilities. Admission fees were rising, attendance was falling, and support from city residents was flagging because most patrons of the struggling institutions were residents of Denver's suburbs and other areas of Colorado.

In 1988, voters in metropolitan Denver's

six counties approved a referendum to create a special district — SCFD — that would levy a one-tenth-of-one-percent sales tax to support these facilities. The tax currently produces $14 million a year and funds are distributed by a formula that had to be hammered out by institutions and local government bodies with little experience in working together.

Such has been SCFD's success that the model was used again recently to set up a regional tax district to build and operate a new stadium for the Colorado Rockies professional baseball team. Suburban fans saw the Denver-based ballpark as a regional asset and supported the tax district overwhelmingly at the polls.

Across the continent in Allegheny County, Pennsylvania, 130 fiercely independent suburban cities surround Pittsburgh, the area's central city — a seemingly inhospitable environment for regionalism. Yet, with the success of Denver's regional model before them, the Pennsylvania General Assembly overwhelmingly supported a proposal to create a regional asset district in Allegheny County.[23] The District, approved by the Pennsylvania state legislature in December 1993, was subsequently activated by vote of the Allegheny County Commissioners.

Administered by an independent, seven-member board, half of the revenue from the District's 1 percent, countywide sales tax supports regional parks and libraries, as well as the Pittsburgh Zoo, Three Rivers Stadium, and other regional cultural facilities. The other half is divided among county and municipal governments, with at least two-thirds of that amount, the legislature specified, earmarked to reduce local taxes such as property taxes.

The region's major business organization, the Allegheny Conference on Community Development, called the creation of the District "a truly historic achievement for southwestern Pennsylvania" that represents "the most significant improvement in the structure of our government in 40 years."

Notes

1. Unless otherwise indicated, all data are from decennial census reports.

2. David Rusk, *Cities Without Suburbs* (Washington, DC: Woodrow Wilson Center Press, 1993).

3. Annual counts of minority elected officials are made by the Joint Center for Political and Economic Studies and the National Association of Latino Elected Officials, both in Washington, DC.

4. See Henry Cisneros, ed., *Interwoven Destinies: Cities and the Nation* (New York & London: W.W. Norton & Company, 1993).

5. U.S. Advisory Commission on Intergovernmental Relations, *State and Local Roles in the Federal System* (Washington, DC: U.S. Government Printing Office, April 1987).

6. U.S. Advisory Commission on Intergovernmental Relations, *State Laws Governing Local Government Structure and Administration* (Washington, DC: U.S. Government Printing Office, March 1993).

7. Neal R. Peirce, with Curtis W. Johnson and John Stuart Hall, *Citistates: How Urban American Can Prosper in a Competitive World* (Washington, DC: Seven Locks Press, 1993).

8. See H. V. Savitch, "Ties That Bind: Central Cities, Suburbs, and the New Metropolitan Region," *Economic Development Quarterly*, November 1993; Richard Voith, "City and Suburban Growth: Substitutes or Complements?" *Business Review*, September/October 1992; and William R. Barnes and Larry C. Ledebur, *Local Economies: The U.S. Common Market of Local Economic Regions* (Washington, DC: National League of Cities, August 1994).

9. Aaron Bernstein, "Inequality — How the Gap Between Rich and Poor Hurts the Economy," *Business Week*, August 15, 1994.

10. See James E. Rosenbaum, "Black Pioneers — Do Their Moves to the Suburbs Increase Economic Opportunity for Mothers and Children?" in Federal National Mortgage Association (Fannie Mae) *Housing Policy Debate* 2 (4); and Florence Wagman Roisman and Hilary Botein, "Housing Mobility and Life Opportunities," *Clearinghouse Review* 27.

11. Among many studies, see John P. Kasarda, "Inner-City Concentrated Poverty and Neighborhood Distress," *Housing Policy Debate* 4; and William Julius Wilson, *The Truly Disadvantaged: The Inner City, the Under Class, and Public Policy* (Chicago: University of Chicago Press, 1987).

12. Myron Orfield, *Metropolitics: A Regional Agenda for Community and Stability* (Minneapolis, MN, 1994). Unpublished manuscript.

13. "Cities: Onwards and Outwards," *The Economist*, October 15, 1994.

14. Orfield, op. cit.

15. National Endowment for Democracy, *The Journal of Democracy* (Washington, DC: National Endowment for Democracy, January 1995). Characterizations and quotations, including quotations from Vernon Jordan, are drawn from David S. Broder's column, "Civic Life and Civility," *Washington Post*, January 1, 1995.

16. For residential segregation indexes for all U.S. metropolitan areas, see Roderick J. Harrison and

H. Weinberg. "Racial and Ethnic Segregation in 1990," (Washington, DC: U.S. Bureau of the Census, April 1992).

17. Melinda Westbrook, "Connecticut's New Affordable Housing Appeals Procedure Assaulting the Presumptive Validity of Land Use Decisions," *Connecticut Bar Journal*, June 1992.

18. Allan D. Wallis, "The Third Wave: Current Trends in Regional Governance," *National Civic Review*, Summer-Fall 1994.

19. George E. Peterson, and Kale Williams, *Housing Mobility: What Has It Accomplished and What Is Its Promise?* (Washington, DC: The Urban Institute). Forthcoming.

20. See Rusk, op. cit.

21. Ibid.

22. See Wallis, op. cit.

23. See *Regional Directions* (Pittsburgh, PA: Allegheny Conference on Community Development, March 1994).

CHAPTER 38

THE METROPOLITAN COUNCIL: INTEGRATING PLANNING AND OPERATIONS

The Metropolitan Council

The Twin Cities metropolitan area of Minnesota enjoys a high quality of life and healthy rate of growth: the result of a beautiful natural setting, good planning, and a long-standing tradition of civic involvement and public initiative. From this public spirit was born the Metropolitan Council of the Twin Cities. Now popularly known as "the Council," it was created in 1967 as a regional planning agency charged with overseeing growth and development in a seven-county area that includes Minneapolis, St. Paul, and 187 cities and townships, and a population today that totals nearly 2.4 million.

For nearly 30 years, the organization served as a researcher and planner of the region's transportation, aviation, sewer, and park systems. Guided by policy decisions of a governor-appointed board, the Council was a problem solver, shaping solutions to issues confronting all metro-area communities. For example, the Council created a centralized sewer system in the 1970s, managed by the Metropolitan Waste Control Commission, to fend off water pollution problems stemming from inadequate septic systems. The Council was also a partner with local units of government, with authority to ensure consistency between city and regional development plans.

The "New" Metropolitan Council

In 1994, however, came sweeping change, when the Minnesota legislature passed the "Metropolitan Reorganization Act," merging the Council with the Metropolitan Transit Commission, the Metropolitan Waste Control Commission, and the Regional Transit Board. The goal was to increase regional government efficiency and accountability. As a result, the Council virtually overnight on July 1, 1994, became not only the planner and policy maker but also responsible for operating the region's wastewater treatment and transit systems. The Council work force jumped from 150 to more than 3,700, and the annual operating budget climbed from $13 million to $275 million.

Prior to the merger, the structure of regional government was extremely complex with varying appointment and reporting relationships. The governor-appointed Council, for example, appointed the Waste Control Commission and the Regional Transit Board, which in turn appointed the Metropolitan Transit Commission. By eliminating the three governing boards and consolidating the regional agencies, the legislation did away with an appointment process that diluted accountability.

Originally published as "The Metropolitan Council of the Twin Cities: Integrating Planning and Operations," *Government Finance Review*, Vol. 12, No. 3, June 1996. Reprinted with permission of the Government Finance Officers Association, publisher of Government Finance Review, 180 N. Michigan Ave., Suite 800, Chicago, IL USA 60601 (312/977-9700; fax: 312/977-4806; e-mail: GFR@gfoa.org). Annual subscriptions: $30.

Proponents of the change, including the Council, are hopeful it will improve regional government accountability to the governor, legislature, and the public. A second goal is better integration of planning and operations for more coordinated decision making and less bureaucracy.

The Reorganization Act also changed Council administration and the role of Council members, who each represent one of 16 districts, with the chair appointed at-large. Though there was a legislative initiative to make the Council elected, the proposal was defeated, and Council members continue to be appointed by the governor. Members, however, now serve at the will of the governor rather than staggered four-year terms.

Another significant change was creation of the regional administrator position to manage the Council's day-to-day operations, a responsibility previously relegated to the chair. The role of the chair in the new organization is to provide policy direction and leadership, engage the public, and serve as the agency's chief spokesperson at the legislature and among local units of government.

The Reorganization Act also defined the Council's basic organizational structure. The Council is organized into four divisions, including administration, community development, environmental services, and transportation. Most of the planning functions of the former Council, as well as the activities of the Council's Housing and Redevelopment Authority (HRA), are now housed in the community development division. Planning for water quality and supply, wastewater treatment, transportation, and transit are done within the environmental services and transportation divisions.

At the same time the legislature was revamping Council organization and structure, however, the Council was making some changes of its own. In September 1994, the Council adopted the *Regional Blueprint*, a policy document that outlines strategies for shaping growth and development in the Twin Cities and creating a strong and vital region. The *Blueprint* is part of the Metropolitan Development Guide and will be used as a tool in providing direction for future policy decisions and developing local government comprehensive plans.

Environmental Services

The Metropolitan Council's environmental services division (MCES) plays a broad and diverse role in preserving the Twin Cities' natural environment but is primarily responsible for protecting the region's vast network of lakes, rivers, and streams by collecting and treating wastewater. Nine plants take advantage of economies of scale and have replaced the 33 plants operating independently in the region in 1970.

The plants combined process 250 million to 300 million gallons of wastewater per day and operate at better than 99 percent compliance with state and federal operating permits. The Metropolitan Wastewater Treatment Plant in St. Paul, one of the largest in the country, treats about 225 million gallons per day, which is about half the wastewater in Minnesota and 80 percent of the wastewater generated in the Twin Cities.

Six-hundred-fifty miles of MCES interceptor pipe carry the wastewater from 104 communities to the regional plants — at a reasonable cost to residents. The average household in the Twin Cities generates about 80,000 gallons of wastewater per year at an annual rate of about $143. By comparison, the rate per household in Duluth, Minnesota, is $207; $274 in Milwaukee, Wisconsin; $205 in St. Louis, Missouri; and $269 in Seattle, Washington.

To meet future wastewater treatment demands with less staff and fewer resources, MCES initiated a program management project, looking at almost every aspect of work at the St. Paul plant. This joint labor-management effort is tapping people closest to the actual work to improve the way work is done. In addition to expected savings from restructuring the work force, the division will realize savings in 1996 from changes in labor agreements and attrition.

At the same time, findings of a sewer rate task force are prompting changes in the current rate structure. Made up of local government officials and industry representatives, the task force was appointed in 1994 to determine whether metro area cities pay a fair price for sewer service. The task force reviewed the current rate structure and other related matters, and its recommended changes will simplify the rate structure and ensure continued equity in the system.

Transportation

Transit and transportation funding pose some of the most difficult challenges facing the Council. To accommodate cuts in federal transit dollars, increasing operating costs, and a three-week transit strike in October 1995 which reduced ridership, the Council launched the "Transit Redesign Project," an effort to devise a more effective and efficient regional transit system. Although some long-term reform was accomplished by negotiating transit workers' labor contract in the fall of 1995, efforts to increase productivity and cut costs are ongoing.

Metropolitan Council Transit Operations (MCTO), formerly the Metropolitan Transit Commission, is the largest provider of regular-route transit service in the Twin Cities area. MCTO provides nearly a quarter of a million rides each weekday with a fleet of 800 buses. To meet passenger needs, the region's transit system provides several types of transit service in addition to MCTO regular-route service:

- other regular route service but with private providers;
- Metro Mobility, a paratransit service providing a door-to-door public transportation system for people of the region with disabilities;
- opt-out service, which allows some suburban communities to use most of their transit property tax levy to provide their own service;
- county dial-a-ride programs for seniors and others who do not have other transportation alternatives;
- community-based dial-a-ride programs for people with special needs in low density areas where regular route service is not cost effective; and

- Minnesota Rideshare, pairing drivers and passengers for car/van pooling.

These are hard times for public transit. Insufficient funding to accommodate the growing demand for Metro Mobility service is forcing the Council to cut paratransit service and increase fares to riders. In addition, reductions in federal dollars and limited state funding have forced staff layoffs at MCTO, along with service cuts and fare increases.

Community Development

The primary mission of the community development division is to help communities throughout the region make choices that will ensure their prosperity. The division has embarked on two major initiatives to strengthen communities through growth management and community development efforts.

Council planners forecast substantial growth in the region over the next 25 years, including 650,000 more people, 330,000 additional households, and 380,000 more jobs. To plan for that growth, the Council is evaluating the possible impacts of future growth on the region and examining development options. With public and community input, the Council is scheduled to decide in the summer of 1996 on a preferred growth option for the region that will help guide regional decision making about infrastructure investments and regional services in the future. Planners have identified three options as a basis for discussion: 1) continue the current development trend, most likely forming a new concentric ring of suburban growth; 2) concentrate development in the existing urban service area and hold the line on outward expansion of regional infrastructure and services; 3) focus on development, expansion, or redevelopment of mixed-use growth centers in the urban area, shaping the market by promoting jobs and housing in a few select mixed-use centers.

Another ambitious initiative comes in the form of the Metropolitan Livable Communities Act, passed by the Minnesota legislature in 1995. Hailed as landmark legislation, the new law provides funds to invest in local economic revitalization and community development initiatives. Participation in the program is voluntary, and participating cities are eligible to compete for dollars to provide affordable housing, clean up polluted sites, and encourage compact and transit-oriented development projects. To date, nearly 100 metro-area communities are signed up to participate in the program in 1996. Among targeted developing communities, where job growth is highest and the need for affordable and life-cycle housing is most apparent, 80 percent are participating.

Funding for the program totals about $12 million in 1996 and is divided into three separate accounts. Funds available for affordable housing total about $1 million; however, monies from the Minnesota Housing Finance Agency and the Minneapolis–St. Paul Family Housing Fund will increase resources to more than $5 million. Funds available for polluted site cleanup total an estimated $6.5 million, and $4.6 million is available to provide loans and grants to encourage local models of compact, creative, and efficient development.

The Council's Metro Housing and Redevelopment Authority also is housed in the community development division and operates a variety of housing programs that help implement the Council's regional housing policies. Metro HRA serves 135 cities in the Twin Cities area by providing Section 8 assistance to thousands of households with low incomes. In addition to the federal program, the HRA works in partnership with other agencies to help families move from poverty to self-sufficiency. These programs direct housing support to families where the head of the household is enrolled in education or training programs, homeless individuals and families, families where housing issues threaten its ability to stay together, and people with mental illness and disabilities. The HRA also developed a housing bond credit enhancement program that uses the Council's general obligation authority to back city and county housing development bonds.

Overall, the new structure expands the Council's ability to link decisions about future growth, infrastructure investments, and affordable housing. For example, the developing Minneapolis suburb of Maple Grove recently sought Council approval on a request to expand the city's urban service area, making more land available for future development. The request prompted discussion about the impact new growth would have on transportation services, sewer capacity, and affordable housing in that part of the region. In ensuing discussions, the city of Maple Grove and the Council agreed new development would result in the need for increased sewer capacity and more affordable housing for workers attracted to the city's job growth. As a result, Council and local officials negotiated housing goals calling for more affordable rental and owner-occupied housing in the city during the next 15 years. With the housing agreement in place, the Council has more of the information it needs to make a decision about a major sewer interceptor in the northwestern part of the region, including Maple Grove.

Financial Challenges and Initiatives

One of the most exciting challenges for the new Council is achieving greater efficiencies as it works to integrate planning and operations. Staff from throughout the organization joined together to determine how to improve services in the most cost-effective way. As a result, an evaluation of Council financing and accounting practices, and subsequent procedural and structural revisions, have been Council priorities.

Given its new structure, the Council has a number of diverse funding sources. Most are dedicated to specific areas of operations. The transportation division, for example, is funded with fares, federal funds, state appropriations, and property taxes. The environmental services division, providing the collection and treatment of wastewater, is funded primarily with user fees. The administration and community development divisions are funded through a number of sources including federal funds, state appropriations and grants, and property tax dollars.

Following the merger, there was considerable discussion among Council and local government officials, as well as other constituent groups, about financing policies and whether funds collected from one operating area, sewer fees for example, could be applied to another, such as transit, to alleviate budget shortfalls. As a result of a number of concerns about mingling funds in this manner, the Council in June 1995 adopted a policy restricting the use of financial resources to the purposes for which they were raised. The Council adopted the policy to retain funding integrity and ensure accountability for each operating unit.

Efforts to restructure administrative units began soon after the 1994 merger. The information systems, internal audit, general counsel, and intergovernmental relations units are now fully centralized. Human resources, communications, and budget and evaluation units are primarily centralized with support units in the operating areas.

Because the organization has three financial and payroll systems, an interim structure was established which created a centralized treasury function but left the remainder of the finance functions decentralized. The finance management team, composed of the top financial managers from each of the divisions and the chief financial officer, currently is working to develop the final organization structure for finance functions. The primary focus of the restructuring will be to meet the needs of managers in the operating units as well as to reduce the cost for transaction processing.

Work on a replacement financial system began in late 1995, with a decision on the new system expected in May 1996. Implementation is scheduled for 1996, and the administration and community development divisions are expected to be live on the system January 1, 1997. Implementation at the two operating units will follow. Key work processes will be evaluated and revised as part of the implementation of the new system to ensure the processes are as efficient as possible. Goals of the system implementation include improved accountability for managers, enhanced access to data through effective interfaces, support for activity-based costing, efficiency of data entry and report writing, flexibility, and centralization of financial data to provide greater consistency.

Privatization. Increasing competition in the delivery of regional services and providing opportunities for more privately operated service are other Council priorities in 1996. The Metropolitan Council would like to let the marketplace determine the most cost-competitive manner in which to deliver some of its services. The Council also is interested in giving employees the support needed to successfully compete with the private sector. Council staff is dealing with a number of issues related to the competitive process: Who should own the assets? Who should finance the capital investment? How should opportunities for competition be selected? How will private- and public-sector bids, both services and costs, be evaluated to ensure the playing field is level? The organization is studying experiences of other public-sector organizations around the country and developing a methodology to be used for the entire organization. Work on several pilot projects has begun and will help test the chosen methodology.

One of the projects the Council is looking at is to redesign the region's transit system to make it more cost-effective and competitive with the automobile. In January 1996, the Council adopted six strategies: offer more diverse service options and a combination of public and private providers, inject competition among transit providers, compete with cars, involve local governments in transit decisions, encourage urban development strategies friendly to transit, and shift transit away from dependence on property taxes. In addition, the Council is in the process of using competitive bidding to select a technology for solids stabilization and approach to produce marketing and distribution for two of its smaller wastewater treatment plants. As part of the project, use of competition in evaluating options for the designing, building, operating, and maintaining the facilities is being evaluated.

Debt Management. Even before the reorganization and consolidation in 1994, the Council issued long-term debt for regional agencies. During the last five years, the Council issued an average of $60 million per year in long-term debt to finance capital improvements for wastewater services, transit, and parks. The Council issues general obligation bonds for these purposes and receives loans from the Minnesota Public Facility Authority to finance wastewater services capital improvements.

Because of its public financing role, the Council adopted debt management policies in 1994 to ensure all transactions are completed in a cost-efficient and professional manner, in accordance with the highest standards of the industry, laws, and governmental practices. The goal is to provide regional services and capital facilities at the least cost to taxpayers and users and at the lowest risk. The debt management policies provide guidelines for issuing and refunding debt and selecting professional services.

Unified Budget. The Council's 1996 operating budget was the first to include all the operating and planning units of the organization in a single budget document, as directed by the Metropolitan Reorganization Act. The Council also adopted a unified 1996–2000 capital improvement program and 1996 capital budget.

The unified operating budget was developed under the leadership of the regional administrator's office, which provide fiscal and policy guidance to the operating areas. This centralized approach ensures the 1996 budgets of operating areas reflect short- and long-term financial resources, Council fiscal policies, and the development of centralized administrative units. Operating budgets in the future will continue to integrate Council operations and ensure their work programs reflect Council policies and legislative mandates.

The regional administrator's office also developed a unified capital budget for environmental services, parks, and transit as well as a five-year capital improvement program. It ensures the capital plans of functional areas and budget policies and procedures all reflect regional priorities. In addition, the unified capital budget, for the first time, provides comprehensive information on the fiscal impacts of the Council's capital plans. The Council also is developing a process for evaluating and establishing priorities for capital funding requests from transit providers that will lead to a more detailed capital improvement program for transit for 1996–2001.

The last year and a half has been exciting for the Metropolitan Council and its staff. While the merger has been difficult at times and required rethinking of policies at every level of the organization, the achievements to date have laid the groundwork for moving the organization and the region into the next century.

CHAPTER 39

REVENUE SHARING AND URBAN GROWTH

Richard M. Sheehan

Colorado has been experiencing enormous growth throughout the state and particularly in the Denver-metro area. In 1994, the governor started his "Smart Growth Initiative"; this program included organizing a summit of more than 1,000 people who discussed the creation of local councils to develop regional plans to deal with this growth. The group assigned to the Denver-metro region joined with the Denver Regional Council of Governments (DRCOG) plan, which was already in progress. DRCOG, consisting of 8 counties and 41 municipalities, was developing a plan to face the anticipated population growth of nearly 700,000 over the next 2 decades. DRCOG's *Metro Visions 2020* is a 25-year comprehensive plan designed to guide the development in these jurisdictions and examine issues such as transportation, air quality, water quality, and urban sprawl.[1] It was in this environment that the issues of urban planning crossed paths with the existence of local government competition for retail sales revenues.

In Colorado, urban sprawl has financially impacted local governments. To meet growth-financing needs and infrastructure demands, municipalities and counties often "face off" against one another to get more revenue into their own operating budgets. Local government revenues are collected at the local level

in Colorado to allow for more autonomous decisions regarding the use of these resources. In contrast, in some state systems, the state government acts as a central collection source that distributes revenues based upon a formula or population base.

Colorado's revenue collection structure does not automatically encourage cooperation among jurisdictions and often results in a struggle to gain revenue share. For the Denver-metro area, this struggle can produce inconsistent "flagpole" annexation (an attempt by municipal government to annex around residential development in the shape of a flagpole in order to gain property having retail sales) and undesirable urban planning as cities fight for a piece of the revenue pie. Inspired by "Smart Growth" and *Metro Vision 2020* planning, the Metro Mayors' Caucus initiated a task force to seek and study alternative solutions. The task force's goal is to identify tools that have been successfully employed in the past and to create models for voluntary agreements that reduce competition and increase cooperation between local governments around retail development. One common tool used by governments in the Denver-metro area has been a number of revenue-sharing agreements; other tools include county planning restrictions, comprehensive planning agreements including "development phasing,"

Originally published as "Revenue Sharing and Urban Growth Agreements," *Government Finance Review,* Vol. 14, No. 2, April 1998. Reprinted with permission of the Government Finance Officers Association, publisher of Government Finance Review, 180 N. Michigan Ave., Suite 800, Chicago, IL USA 60601 (312/977-9700; fax: 312/977-4806; e-mail: GFR@gfoa.org). Annual subscriptions: $30.

and creative alternatives such as transferring development rights.

Metro Mayors' Task Force

In an effort to seek our methods used to discourage competition between cities, the task force examined several regional revenue-sharing efforts as well as other methods used to increase cooperation and control the type of development in growing surrounding areas. Among these were:

- The Boulder Chamber of Commerce was encouraging the city of Boulder to consider an intergovernmental agreement (IGA) with its outlying cities. This agreement, although unsuccessful, would turn revenues over to adjacent cities in hopes of encouraging growth outside of Boulder's boundary. It was also the goal of Boulder to control development along its central access road of US 36 and to slow the growth of inner-city traffic congestion.
- Two cities outside Boulder, Superior and Louisville, recently achieved success in creating an IGA to share revenues and avoid a legal entanglement. The goal of the IGA is to discuss the determination of 80 acres based upon land-use and service-ability issues rather than solely on revenue sharing.
- To control unincorporated development, Adams County, just northeast of Denver, is negotiating intergovernmental agreements to encourage development within municipal boundaries. The county hopes that by having an IGA it will not be forced into providing expensive infrastructure before its time.
- Thornton and Westminster, cities on the northern border of Denver, in 1986 developed an IGA designed to define a "sphere of influence" related to revenues generated on the Interstate 25 corridor.
- During what was called the "annexation wars" of the 1980s, officials of Brighton and Commerce City developed an IGA, which defined the boundaries of two cities along a major access road that the

cities believe will one day be a thriving commercial district generated by development around Denver International Airport.

These models represent the Denver-metro area's effort to meet urban growth financing needs and attempts at minimizing urban sprawl before the infrastructure and municipal government are there to support it.

The Metro Mayors' Caucus Task Force, while exploring these projects, has stirred up a debate centered on sales tax collection policy and its impact on development: Is the current sales tax collection policy of Colorado creating uneven urban sprawl and encouraging unincorporated municipal-like communities, or would such haphazard development occur anyway? Should revenue-sharing agreements be used to curb the cost to local governments as they attempt to meet financing and infrastructure needs or should a more comprehensive approach be initiated to limit urban area growth in counties altogether?

The following sections of this chapter summarize five studies by the Metro Mayors' Revenue Sharing Task Force, providing examples of attempts by local government leaders to avoid a centralized state collection system with the use of revenue-sharing agreements and comprehensive land-use planning. These models have proven effective in developing co-operative approaches to what might otherwise be a divisive situation between local government entities. It is in these trenches that the battle will be won or lost to preserve autonomy and keep local sales tax control.

Boulder Regional Tax-sharing Plan

In 1995, the Boulder Chamber of Commerce recommended a regional sharing effort. After determining a base-year level of revenues, each city would share in the incremental growth of sales tax revenues based upon an allocation formula of population or existing retail share. Large cities might receive less sales tax than previously but still increase revenues based on their population. Smaller cities would have substantial gains, which would allow them time to develop income from market sources other than retail, such as manufacturing, tourism, service firms, or construction.

In theory, by equalizing sales tax revenue distribution, policy decisions would shift towards planning that focuses on neighborhood characteristics, land-use decisions, and environmental concerns rather than on the struggle to gain retail market share to meet short-term budgetary needs.[2] This attempt to create a revenue-sharing agreement was abandoned in 1997, as it became too difficult to gain a consensus in the political climate of the time. As growth continued, outlying cities around Boulder saw enough development in their jurisdictions to discourage continued dialogue of the IGA.

Tax Sharing for Two Cities

As a result of territorial battles around Boulder, the cities of Superior and Louisville entered into a revenue-sharing agreement. This agreement, ratified by citizens in the November 1997 election, concentrated more on land-use issues and serviceability than on urban growth. Superior and Louisville are separated by US 36, which forms a natural boundary; however, because 80 acres on the south (Superior) side of US 36 were included in the Louisville city limit, property owners of this region made two attempts to file with the court to disconnect from the city of Louisville. Rather than battle it out in court, the two communities entered into a revenue-sharing agreement through which the property would become a part of Superior, and Superior would collect any retail taxes generated from any development. In return, the city of Louisville would receive 50 percent of the retail sales tax revenues, and Superior allowed Louisville to include an additional parcel in its natural boundary north of US 36. Superior experienced some complication in implementing the agreement, as it had to accommodate three special districts inside its borders that also were counting on future revenues generated from any retail development. The agreement was careful to include specific provisions dealing

with utility sales tax, tax rate changes, and how the collection process would work within statewide law. Although forced by legal concerns, this model emphasizes the need to take a proactive posture when competitive issues arise.

Adams County: Growth Policies

The Adams County approach to revenue equalization is tied to its comprehensive planning process. Adams County and its constituent cities — Arvada, Aurora, Bennett, Brighton, Broomfield, Commerce City, Federal Heights, Northglenn, Thornton, and Westminster — are developing growth-related policies within a countywide comprehensive plan which uses a tiered system designed to phase in urban-level development in three tiers: the next five years, by the year 2020, and post-2020. The goal for these local governments is to promote contiguity, infrastructure compatibility, and formal integration of their comprehensive plan. This effort is supported by government officials in the area who generally believe that urban-level growth belongs in municipalities where services can be provided in a more cost-effective manner. Adams County officials hope to achieve this goal by a series of intergovernmental agreements.

If the comprehensive plan is adopted in Adams County, urban development during the next five years that occurs in unincorporated areas would be required to meet city development standards and be subject to city review. This is designed to discourage development efforts that historically have played cities and counties off against one another. With this policy, cities must annex development within their individual urban growth boundaries. By the year 2020, comprehensive planning will be done in concert with urban centers and the county to insure consistency between individual plans. These are lofty goals, but if the spirit to cooperate remains, Adams County might have a model other local area governments can adapt rather than "duking it out" over limited resources.

Westminster-Thornton IGA

Another case in point is the "sphere of influence" revenue-sharing agreement between Thornton and Westminster, two cities just north of Denver. For Thornton and Westminster the issue was boundaries.[3] The city of Thornton was considering the annexation of land west of I-25. The city of Westminster, however, viewed that same territory as "sacred ground" and it expected to annex one day. The two city managers met to discuss the development of an agreement that would outline boundaries and set the stage for future development in the area. The discussion evolved into a 10-page IGA that included a requirement for a cooperative master plan, outlined consistency in building codes, and suggested the kinds of public services to be provided. Most importantly, a revenue-sharing formula was agreed upon. This agreement, believed by some to have curtailed development in the I-25 corridor, has yet to reach fruition, as build-out has not occurred. The city manager stated that the reason development has not occurred is not the existence of the intergovernmental agreement, but rather because there is "a lack of roof tops" in the area — once there is more housing, retail development will follow. Both mayors felt that this agreement allowed the governments to retain control over development in the area, and they believe that it removed the pressure from the two cities to compete for sales revenues. As a model to potentially follow, other cities — Commerce City and Brighton, for example — were influenced by the Thornton/Westminster agreement.

Boundary Line Agreement

In February of 1989, Brighton and Commerce City both wanted to stake claim to certain potential annexation areas. Some property owners were petitioning one city to be included in its boundary while the other city was concerned that if it did not act quickly, it might miss out on an opportunity to expand its borders and achieve potential sales tax revenue from what looked to be an area of future retail development as an outgrowth of Denver International Airport.

A good line of communication existed between the two municipalities, and avenues existed for increased cooperation — the Adams County Council of Governments (ADCOG), for example. With a cooperative environment in place, and a willingness of both parties to seek a "win-win" scenario, Brighton and Commerce City developed a revenue-sharing agreement that included land-use issues and boundary specifications. This agreement carefully described the use of debt for infrastructure and the pledging of revenues.

With the state legislature closely watching these "annexation wars," the two cities developed a model that other municipalities could follow. One of the terms of the agreement required that a joint plan be prepared as a guide for the development of land and the provision of public services and that it include design standards and land-use criteria. A truly cooperative venture now gives both cities the ability to control development and insure a steady proportionate revenue stream. In addition, their government officials do not have to concern themselves with developers trying to pit one city against the other to gain tax advantages.

Future of Revenue Sharing

The next areas of study for the Revenue Sharing Task Force include investigating a regional agreement to limit urban-level development to municipalities and promoting a dialogue between cities and counties. Cooperative agreements of this type are being explored by Boulder, Adams, and Larimer counties.

Other alternatives to development phasing include encouraging developers to build in a city. To encourage density in the city rather than in potentially agricultural or unincorporated areas, in Boulder County a property owner can sell his/her right to build at a certain density level and grant that right to an owner of a parcel of land inside the city. The opportunity to sell this right (like a mineral right) encourages the owner not to sell to developers and to keep the land rural in nature; yet the owner may "profit" by not selling. In turn, property owners inside the city boundary, who cannot build high-density property due to historical zoning restrictions, now can purchase this right and increase their profit margin by developing more units and therefore selling more units.[4]

Jefferson County, also concerned about this urban sprawl into unincorporated areas, recently put together a task force to address this issue. This task force will examine the need for a tax increase or new taxes, cutbacks in services, and incorporation or annexation of incorporated areas. The commissioners have seen financial forecasts that suggest the county's tax base cannot support what are essentially municipal services that are incurred by the unincorporated areas and to which the rest of the county is contributing financially. Whether statewide law changes are necessary or a spirit of brotherhood among local governments must continue, solutions to this issue are not easily found.

Whether these models work or lead to statewide policy changes, the issue behind these cooperative plans and revenue-sharing models is clear: Philosophically, economic development in a community needs to be based on desired characteristics and local community needs, rather than on short-term revenue gains; in practice, however, sales tax policy in Colorado is one of the driving forces that often prevents this type of development from happening. The communities in the Denver-metro area have seen the result of this retail competition and redistribution of wealth in the financial misfortunes of two major shopping malls in the region.

Local communities like Adams County, nevertheless, have found ways and created models to benefit the citizens through comprehensive land-use planning. Local governments have kept their autonomy and avoided a centralized state collection system with the use of revenue-sharing agreements, in the cases of Louisville/Superior and Westminster/Thornton. Competition, although healthy to an economy, can be crippling to a community government that relies on retail sales taxes. Cooperation between communities continues to hold the key; if answers cannot be found at the local level, statewide solutions may become the only alternative.

Notes

1. Metro Vision 2020 Implementation Strategy: Economic Development/Regional Tax Policy, DRCOG, May 1996.

2. Clark, Tom, *Colorado Real Estate Journal*, "Regional Tax Sharing," July 1995.

3. Intergovernmental Agreement between the City of Thornton and the City of Westminster, January 1996.

4. Boulder County Transferred Development Rights, April 1995.

PART VIII
The Future

CHAPTER 40

THE LURE OF THE STRONG MAYOR

Rob Gurwitt

Sometime during the next few years, there is a good chance that Dallas will do the unthinkable: discard its city manager form of government. For the field of local administration, that would be a bit like England deciding to scrap Parliament. And it would be something more: a sign that the age of municipal reform, as it has been practiced in America for the better part of this century, is coming to an end. For Dallas is an emblem of sorts.

For years — until San Diego passed it in size — Dallas was the largest city in the country with a so-called "council-manager" form of government, in which an elected council sets broad policy guidelines but an appointed manager actually runs the city day-to-day. For decades, Dallas has been a thumb in the eye to those doubters who argued that the manager system might be fine for medium-sized, uncomplicated cities, but that large cities need the firm hand of a mayor with power. Dallas has routinely ranked among the best-run cities in the country, zealously guarding its triple-A bond rating and setting a national example for the businesslike way it has managed its affairs.

So why, all of a sudden, is there talk of change? For exactly the reason you'd expect: politics.

Dallas has changed radically since it first adopted the city manager plan in 1931. For years, the city was essentially run by its business community, the political leadership drawn exclusively from the prosperous white neighborhoods of north Dallas. The manager was essentially the instrument of that leadership.

These days, though, power has splintered. Many of the city's top business executives now work for out-of-town corporations or have moved themselves to the suburbs; meanwhile, the city's Hispanic and African American communities are starting to come into their own at City Hall and are finding they don't always like the established ways of conducting business. The present mayor — who is elected at-large but has little administrative authority — has been unable to develop a steady working relationship with either the council or the manager. As the entire community struggles to deal with a limping economy and a rising tide of the usual urban troubles, there is a growing feeling that Dallas is adrift without strong leadership.

So the city's hallowed institution of manager government is getting hit from all sides: from business leaders who mourn the loss of the old Chamber-of-Commerce consensus, and from newly elected black and Hispanic politicians who think their constituents are not getting enough attention. The result is that there is public talk of junking the whole system — quite possibly in favor of a strong-mayor plan.

"There are some who are beginning to appreciate that the great problem in Dallas is no

From *Governing*, Vol. 6, No. 10, July 1993. Published by Congressional Quarterly, Inc., Washington, D.C. Reprinted by permission of the author.

longer how to do those things on which the city leadership has a consensus, but instead is to figure out what to do in the first place," says Royce Hanson, dean of the School of Social Sciences at the University of Texas at Dallas.

It may be that in the end, Dallas will opt to keep its structure intact. If it does, though, it will be for reasons quite different from the good-government reform sentiments that have maintained the city manager system all these years. For what the city's situation makes clear is that the demands of the moment are not for less politics — they are for more.

"The era of municipal reform is clearly over," public administration scholar George Frederickson writes in a recent paper on the subject. The battle over reform, he points out, was fought on such issues as efficiency, economy and ending corruption. "Today," Frederickson argues, "issues of political responsiveness are as important as efficiency and economy."

That is because even in once-homogeneous communities the claimants to power — neighborhoods, minority groups, citizens' associations — are multiplying. It is no longer just the Chicagos and New Yorks of the country that must forge consensus from a cacophony of voices before they can move forward; that is now the task for Dallas and a host of other cities that used to pride themselves on being far less complicated.

So it shouldn't be startling that some communities are looking to reshape how they are governed, and in particular are considering boosting the powers of the mayor. It may not be possible to end poverty, house the homeless, disband gangs, repave corroding streets, find the money to revive a withering economy or put an end to civic squabbling. But one thing citizens clearly can do is refashion local government with the hope that someone — a mayor, an elected county executive — someone — can assemble the political authority to grapple better with those problems.

Which is why Dallas isn't alone in considering change. Dade County, Florida, which includes Miami and has a population of more than two million, is hearing a new round of demands for a strong elected executive. On the other side of the same state, St. Petersburg has just decided to jettison 60 years of city manager government in favor of a strong mayor. And in the West, where so-called "reform government" is considered as much a birthright as unlimited access to water, Sacramento is gingerly looking at change. A good 80 years after Dayton, Ohio, became the first major American city to put a manager system in place, the argument over which form of government is best appears ready to heat up again.

To some extent, of course, it never died down. Ever since the reform movement got rolling in the 'teens and '20s, cities have been turning to manager government in an effort to become more businesslike or to rid themselves of corruption.

The strong-mayor system, usually accompanied by intense partisan warfare, was seen by the original reform generation as fiscally wasteful and too susceptible to patronage abuses. The main alternative existing at that time — commission government, in which a small number of commissioners serve both as legislators and as the heads of city departments — seemed a poor substitute: It diffused leadership and often produced incompetent administrators. The idea of a professional, non-partisan city manager, administering government while avoiding politics, neatly matched the taste of reformers for reconstituting local government on a professional basis.

As a public policy idea and as a national movement, the city manager system probably reached the peak of its popularity by the 1950s. But cities continued to switch to it long after that. It was only in 1986 that the International City/County Management Association, in its quinquennial "Forms of Municipal Government" survey, found for the first time that manager government had passed the strong mayor form in popularity, holding sway in 53 percent of the cities that responded. That figure dropped to 51 percent in 1991, although the slight shift may have been due to changes in the sample, not to abandonments of the plan.

And over the years, the values that the reform movement advanced have become a permanent part of the civic landscape. The 1991 ICMA survey, in fact, found that the most likely structural change being made by cities — even those with strong mayors and partisan politics — was the addition of a chief administrative officer, a professional appointee who could coordinate the running of the city. Indeed, more than one-third of the strong-mayor cities have hired an administrator. The administrator in a strong-mayor city is sometimes in a rather tenuous position; the mayor can fire him or her virtually at will. Nevertheless the clear trend is for cities without managers to aim for some of the professionalism that cities using the manager system have achieved.

At the same time, though, manager government has itself been evolving. In fact, it is difficult these days to find places that still adhere to the orthodox reform structure. As laid out by Richard Childs, the generally acknowledged father of the city manager movement, a reformed city should have a small (generally five-seat) council whose members are elected at-large; the mayor comes from the council, and is little more than a presiding officer and ceremonial presence. The operations of government are the responsibility of the appointed manager.

In city after city, the result of those reforms was a government devoid of the patronage-mongering and political selfishness that had afflicted cities with strong mayors; it was also, however, a city government whose leaders were relatively insulated from the electorate and who, in many communities, were all drawn from the Chamber of Commerce and from a single upper-crust part of town. Those are difficult features to justify in an era when neighborhoods are trying to reassert themselves in the councils of power and Hispanics and African Americans are taking a place at the table.

And so the manager system has itself adjusted. Either by vote of the people or by judicial fiat, city councils have been expanding in size and abandoning at-large elections for district elections; only one-third of the councils in cities above 100,000 are now elected at-large. Just as important, a full 61 percent of the manager-run cities now have directly elected

mayors, a shift designed to give the system a greater measure of political accountability and leadership. These mayors still lack administrative clout — the manager continues to wield that — but they do serve as figures of political accountability to the community at-large. The council-manager plan has been greatly modified, and that has made it more responsive," says George Frederickson. "Like a willow, it has bent with the times." One political scientist, the University of Alaska's Greg Protasel, has in fact suggested that were it not for the council-manager plan's ability to become more politically sensitive, it might have been abandoned in greater numbers.

But there are times when "reforming reformism," as some onlookers have dubbed the process, is simply not enough. Take, as an example, St. Petersburg, a manager city that long ago modified its system by adding both district council elections and a directly elected, although administratively weak, mayor. This spring St. Petersburg decided to go much further — it threw out city manager government altogether.

On the surface, the city's decision to go to a strong mayor seemed mostly to be about personalities. The city manager system had become an issue after an acting manager fired Police Chief Ernest Curtsinger, whom many blacks considered racially insensitive but who was enormously popular with many white retirees. Curtsinger's firing led a group of outraged supporters to push for changing the city's council-manager charter to create a strong-mayor structure; that proposal wound up on the March election ballot, along with the regularly scheduled election for mayor — which, not coincidentally, featured both Curtsinger and the sitting mayor, David Fischer.

The contrast between the two candidates was striking. Fischer, a longtime consultant on municipal finance with an intellectual, somewhat remote style, drew the bulk of his support from the city's black and affluent white communities: Curtsinger, a smooth politician with a populist bent, took the white middle class. To a remarkable degree, voters' opinions on the charter change paralleled their opinions of the candidates: Where Curtsinger was strong, so was the proposal for a strong mayor; where Fischer drew support, so did opposition to charter change. And yet an odd thing happened on election day: The charter change passed while Curtsinger lost, and Fischer, who had supported keeping his position formally weak, suddenly found himself with new powers.

Even in an election so firmly rooted in the politics of the moment, though, the city's abandonment of the manager system had its origin in a far more basic question than whether Ernest Curtsinger should run the city or not. Over the past decade and more, the city's leaders have been trying to reshape St. Petersburg, to redevelop its downtown and change its image as a sleepy haven for senior citizens. After a major downtown redevelopment project was rejected by voters a decade or so ago, the city council — with the active support of the city manager and much of the downtown business establishment — went ahead on its own and pushed through both a new office/retail development and construction of a new baseball stadium. Both were approved and built without much input from the average citizen.

That might have been all right if the city's neighborhoods felt they had gotten something in return, but they haven't; both major projects, in fact, still sit unoccupied. So by this year's elections, the neighborhoods had grown restless.

"They feel all their tax dollars have gone downtown to this economic revitalization, their tax rates have gone up because of shortfalls in the projects and money has been reallocated from service areas to pay the debt," says Darryl Paulson, a political scientist at the University of South Florida. "So there's great dissatisfaction, particularly because they were not allowed to publicly participate in whether or not these projects should go ahead." The neighborhoods' vote for a strong mayor was, as a result, not only a vote against particular officials but a protest against the whole idea of a government system that seemed so unaccountable to citizens' desires.

Whether that same participatory impulse ultimately produces a similar result in Dallas remains very much in doubt. It is only in the last couple of years — since the 1991 court-ordered switch from an at-large council to 14 members chosen by district — that the Hispanic and African American neighborhoods of south Dallas have had real representation at City Hall. Some of the current calls for change come from newly elected black and Hispanic council members, who argue that their communities have been given the short end of the stick by the city's professional managers. "We can't prioritize based on community needs," says one of the city's new African American council members, Don Hicks. "The system is just not responding."

But other blacks and Hispanics, and liberal whites who are allied with them, believe something very different: that it would be foolish to change the system just as the disadvantaged begin to accumulate power within it. Indeed, for some of those who fought to make city government more pluralistic, the talk of moving to a strong mayor looks a lot like a ploy by the Old Guard to shift power away from the newly diverse council.

"Now that minorities are finally at the table, and we have all geographic areas of the city equally represented," asks Lori Palmer, a white council member from south Dallas, "why would there be a suggestion that we transfer power from the council to the mayor? In this city, voting strength is still in north Dallas, with Anglo voters, so for some time I would predict our mayors will be elected by the northern and Anglo side of city. It is suspicious that there would be interest in consolidating power in a mayor's position."

The argument that the city needs the steadying leadership of a strong mayor draws little sympathy from this camp. "We've just gotten into the loop," says Al Lipscomb, who as deputy mayor is the city's highest-ranking black official. "Are you saying that self-determination is cumbersome compared with one ruler?" His answer is straightforward. "Hell no. That's what makes this city thriving, refreshing and full of effervescence."

In fact, there is a strain of thought in Dallas that holds that, like an Eastern European country, the city is adjusting to the realities of democracy brought on by the *perestroika* of district elections. If all the city's politicians learn their roles under the current system, the reasoning goes, the city will get back on track. "What needs to happen is the city manager needs to exercise greater demand for policy decisions to come out of council, and less day-to-day micromanaging," says Jim Buerger, a former council member and one-time mayoral candidate. "And the council needs to establish its role in relation to establishing policy." In the meantime, Buerger and others argue, the mayor, Steve Bartlett, has been trying to act like a strong mayor despite the fact that he is a constitutionally weak one. In a system that demands consultation with the manager and the council, that cannot help but create bruised feelings and political squabbling.

If Dallas ultimately decides to stick with its council-manager form, then, it will be as much an effort to safeguard political diversity as it is to ensure administrative efficiency. The question is whether that sort of decision will produce the leadership the city needs.

That is because "effervescence," as Lipscomb puts it, exacts a price: The more hands there are on the tiller, the harder it is to steer. Diversity places a huge burden on the one person elected to perform the task of bringing people together: the mayor. But in a manager-run city, the mayor has very few tools he can use to accomplish that task.

The best that such a city can hope for is that its mayor will prove adept at what some experts like to call "facilitative" skills. James Svara, who teaches political science at North Carolina State University, argues that the pressures of civic diversity will, in fact, produce just such people. "The facilitative mayor," Svara wrote recently, "leads by empowering others — in particular the council and the manager — rather than seeking power for himself or herself." In this view, the mayor is a kind of information broker, promoting communication among politicians and trying to manage conflict and settle differences.

Interestingly enough, one of the more adept facilitators in office at the moment is the mayor of perhaps the preeminent strong-mayor city in the country — Ed Rendell of Philadelphia. Rendell has put an end to years of discord by carefully sharing both the spotlight and his thinking with other politicians,

especially City Council President John Street and members of the city's state legislative delegation. "He recognizes," says Frederick Voight, who directs a reform-era civic watchdog group known as the Committee of 70, "that while he possesses tremendous power, he has to share it; he has to deal in consensus politics."

At the same time, though, Rendell has been unabashed about using the powers of his office to face down public employee unions and make steep cuts in the city's budget. It has been an extraordinarily difficult task, in large measure because the city's disparate communities take pride in a sort of prickly independence. "It is a city of Balkan states," says Voight, "and that makes it politically, racially and ethnically combustible. They have had to distribute the pain equally, and that could not be done without the centrality of power. If you fragmented it, there would be too many discordant voices without anyone in charge."

A similar calculus lies behind the push in Dade County, Florida, to look seriously at moving to an elected chief executive. "It would be very difficult for a weak mayor in Dade County to call upon support from all the diverse elements of the community during a time when some of the decisions are bound to be unpopular," says Tom Fiedler, political editor of the *Miami Herald*. "It's too easy for the rest of the community to disown that person and say, 'Well, that's what Hispanics do,' or 'You can't trust the blacks,' or 'It's just the Anglo good-old-boy system.' There's got to be leadership in which every element of the community is invested in some way."

None of this is to say that it is impossible for manager-run cities to produce leadership of that sort. Several of the more highly respected mayors this country has produced in recent years gained their stature precisely because they were able to implement their visions in communities with appointed managers — among them Henry Cisneros of San Antonio, Pete Wilson of San Diego and, among current mayors, Emanuel Cleaver II of Kansas City, Missouri.

Nor, for that matter, do strong-mayor cities produce winners all the time. "Strong political leadership is a very rare commodity," says Bob Kipp, a former city manager of Kansas City. "It doesn't correlate with one structure or another: It's just difficult to find these little diamonds in the rough who turn out to be effective and courageous political leaders. People say you don't find many strong elective mayors in council-manager cities; the fact is, you don't find many of them anywhere."

That is probably so. Which makes it all the more sobering that in these days of shrinking municipal budgets, economic uncertainty and social decay, mustering the civic will to make gut-wrenching choices requires the deft touch of talented politicians. The most important challenge isn't to write charters for them; it is to nurture them in the first place.

CHAPTER 41

BEWARE OF THE LURE
OF THE STRONG MAYOR

Terrell Blodgett

Americans love the quick fix. We want to take a pill and lose 20 pounds. We would like to buy one lottery ticket and become millionaires overnight. And we would like to change city hall into an organization that instantly can reduce crime, create jobs, and enable us to live happily ever after.

Unfortunately, life is not that simple. No magic diet pill can take off 20 pounds. Only one lottery ticket in 16 zillion ever wins. And switching to the strong mayor system of government will not solve all of our local governments' problems. In fact, it may make things worse.

Form-of-Government Debate

Rob Gurwitt's article in the July 1993 issue of *Governing* magazine, entitled "The Lure of the Strong Mayor," examines some of the discussions taking place on the subject of U.S. local government structure. Gurwitt suggests that "boosting the powers of the mayor" through a change to the strong mayor system can help larger communities to deal more effectively with their complex problems. He writes:

"It may not be possible to end poverty, house the homeless, disband gangs, replace corroding streets, find the money to revive a withering economy, or put an end to civic squabbling. But one thing citizens clearly can do is refashion local government with the hope that someone — a mayor, an elected county executive — someone — can assemble the political authority to grapple better with those problems."

What is the "strong mayor" form of government that proponents feel gives a local government the political leadership necessary to make things happen? Under this type of charter, the mayor has the authority to hire and fire department heads, prepare the budget for council consideration, administer it after adoption, and veto acts of the council, which can override that veto only by an extraordinary majority. That is concentrating a tremendous amount of power in one person! And it can go even further. In the consolidated city/county of Denver, Colorado, the mayor can:

- Award any contract up to $500,000 without reference to the city council.
- Remit any fines or penalties levied under any ordinance passed by the city council. The only requirement is that the mayor must notify the council of the remittance and the rationale behind it.
- Submit an annual budget to the city council, in which not one line item can be changed without a two-thirds vote of the council.
- Appoint the heads of all administrative departments (some 50 in number), the county judges, and all boards and

From *Public Management*, Vol. 76, No. 1, January 1994. Published by the International City/County Management Association, Washington, D.C. Reprinted with permission of the publisher.

commissions under his or her jurisdiction. No city council advice or confirmation is provided for any of these appointments.

Gurwitt argues that to exercise political leadership, a mayor has to have administrative authority similar to that described above. In contrast to the council-manager form of government, the strong mayor form relies on a single, powerful leader who often forges coalitions by exchanging benefits for support and uses his or her power to gain leverage over opponents.

This approach has built-in limitations. There are too many actors whom a mayor can not control and too little power and too few resources to compel or buy support predictably. Leadership that uses power to forge coalitions is not necessarily responsive, particularly to those outside the ruling coalition.

On the contrary, a number of highly regarded American mayors have demonstrated that mayors can achieve political clout *without* being granted administrative responsibility. Two outstanding examples from large council-manager communities come immediately to mind: former San Antonio Mayor Henry Cisneros, who possessed the strong leadership skills necessary to become Secretary of the U.S. Department of Housing and Urban Development; and former Charlotte mayor Harvey Gantt, who continues to reside in that city and runs his own architectural firm.

Two Case Histories

When Cisneros took office as mayor of San Antonio in 1981, he inherited a sleepy, lower-income city with major problems in its educational system. Cisneros envisioned San Antonio as an international economic and tourist attraction, however, and he worked tirelessly to achieve that dream.

Although he had no responsibility over the city's public or higher educational system (in Texas, school boards are elected separately and are responsible for their own budgets), Cisneros recognized that education was the key to the realization of his vision. He unceasingly lobbied the University of Texas System and the State College Coordinating Board to locate an engineering school at the University of Texas at San Antonio, and he pushed the Texas legislature for more money for public education. He then went on the road to sell San Antonio as a biomedical headquarters.

His efforts to attract tourism also succeeded: San Antonio became only the fourth site in the country to boast a Sea World. His mayorship culminated in a drive to build the domed sports stadium that opened this summer [1994] to capacity crowds for the U.S. Summer Olympic Festival.

Cisneros also possess the leadership skills to build consensus among highly divergent city factions. He used a series of bond elections and other strategies to bring together the city's business community and Hispanic neighborhoods.

Strong leaders such as Henry Cisneros realize that they are most effective when they are supported by an effective professional manager. Cisneros has said that San Antonio's greatest successes "can be attributed directly to our council-manager form of government, characterized by top-flight professionals with a corruption-free, fiscally sound administration."

Harvey Gantt's record in Charlotte as the city's mayor from 1983 to 1987 is no less impressive. He was instrumental in the construction of the 24,000-seat Charlotte Coliseum and helped the team owner win an NBA franchise for the new facility. He also spearheaded the construction of a performing arts center in downtown Charlotte in partnership with Nations Bank's construction of its new 60-story corporate headquarters.

Through the city's neighborhood, small area, and district land planning processes, Gantt provided citizens with a voice; he also led the creation of a public-private housing partnership that leveraged private-sector funds to increase Charlotte's supply of affordable housing and promote home ownership.

Gantt is clear about his views on the different forms of government:

The council-manager form of government is absolutely the best form ... particularly because it leaves the mayor and council free to focus on the big policy issues. The day-to-day operations of the city do not distract the mayor from this focus; they are left to a professional city manager and professional staff. Therefore, the council-manager form is a better and cleaner form because roles are clearly defined.

Other Erroneous Assumptions

Rob Gurwitt makes a second assumption, namely, that the council-manager form of government is outdated because it can not respond to the new demands of highly diverse communities. In speaking with citizens in Dallas, Texas, however, a different story emerges — that what ethnic minorities really want is more participation in the process, *not* politics as usual. Gurwitt assumes that political clout and responsiveness can and should come from only one individual, rather than from the entire city council or county commission.

Reformers always intended that the council-manager form would strengthen the quality and responsiveness of service delivery and would address basic citizen needs. The council-manager form is not less responsive; indeed, the strongest examples of citizen participation can be found in council-manager communities. The city of Dayton, for example, was the first large city to adopt the council-manager form, and it remains a strong advocate of professional local government management. For years, Dayton's neighborhood boards have been cited as models of citizen involvement. Similarly, the city of Cincinnati has a long, distinguished history of neighborhood activism.

And remember the David and Goliath story about how the city of Alexandria, Virginia, went up against Virginia Governor Doug Wilder and Washington Redskins owner Jack Kent Cooke? The city had other plans for the land that Cooke and the governor wanted to use for a football stadium. Mayor Pat Ticer successfully worked with the city staff and citizens to fight the plan to move the stadium to Alexandria.

Gurwitt goes on to suggest that the council-manager form means "leaderless" government, that "the more hands on the tiller, the harder it is to steer." He discusses the perceived lack of tools that a mayor in a council-manager community possesses to bring people together toward a common purpose — particularly people of widely diverse racial and ethnic backgrounds. Gurwitt argues that council-manager mayors have only "facilitative" leadership to fall back on, and that this type of leadership is insufficient to deal with today's heterogeneous communities.

But do we really want a mayor's leadership tools to comprise trading votes for services? Political leadership should not be confused with reactive, demand-responsive leadership. Too often, the political leadership in strong mayor governments encourages conflict among elected officials, which, in turn, produces political gridlock and a reliance on short-term coalition building. As a result, officials in mayor-council cities are more likely to avoid making hard choices. An article recently published in the *Toledo Blade*, for example, assesses the current condition of Rochester, New York:

[S]ince Rochester adopted the strong mayor form of government in the mid–1980s, council allocated to itself a growing amount of resources to place a check on the power of the mayor. That figure has loomed as high as $500,000, or about .002 percent of its annual budget.

The council-manager form, on the other hand, uniquely blends political and professional leadership. Although political supremacy of the mayor and council are assured, the elected officials empower the manager with the independence needed to make sound recommendations to council, and to manage the local government organization using the highest professional standards.

In closing, Gurwitt implies that communities can switch to a strong mayor form of government and still retain the level of professional management that citizens have come to expect in council-manager cities. One of the big differences in the two forms, however, is the fact that in council-manager communities, the manager is appointed by and responsible to the entire government body. Under the strong mayor form, any chief administrative officer who may be appointed responds solely to the mayor. The council has little input in that individual's selection or supervision. Although some CAOs may have served previously as managers in council-manager communities, the average tenure of a CAO in a strong mayor city is much shorter in comparison and may undermine the city's continuity.

To be sure, council-manager communities also experience turnover. But in most cases, these communities hire experienced managers to replace experienced managers. Marvin Andrews, for example, retired from Phoenix, Arizona, after serving as the city's manager for 14 years. Rich Helwig recently finished his ninth year as Dayton's city manager. And in Charlotte, North Carolina, Wendell White has served an even dozen years in that capacity. This kind of continuity is less likely to occur in strong mayor-council communities, where a single individual frequently chooses a CAO based on political loyalties rather than professional management abilities.

Professional managers not only have the capacity to serve different types of governments; they also attract other top executives to administer their governments' functions and activities. Today, the complexity of service delivery calls for individuals with superb organizational skills, a good sense of strategic management, and the ability to communicate effectively with disparate city factions — not inexperienced political loyalists.

In a 1992 issue of *Public Administration Review*, author Irene Rubin examined the adoption of new and innovative budget techniques in six major U.S. cities over the past 20 years. Of the six cities — Dayton, Phoenix, Rochester, Tampa, Boston, and St. Louis — the more politically reformed were likelier to adopt budget reforms quickly and were more receptive to trying new approaches. The less reformed cities, on the other hand, incorporated budget reforms that "enhanced central control over departmental operations." For the purpose of her article, Rubin defined politically reformed communities as those that operated under the council-manager form, held at-large council elections, and had a weak history of employee patronage.

It is no accident that for the past two years, most winners of the National Civic League's All-America Cities competition have been council-manager communities. This year, 7 of the 10 honorees were council-manager communities. It also is worth noting that of *Financial World*'s nine best-managed communities, 3 of the top 5, including Dallas at No. 1 and Phoenix at No. 2, operate under the council-manager form.

A Closer Look at Dallas

Because Gurwitt showcased Dallas as a long-time council-manager city that has considered a change in its form of government, it seems appropriate to take a closer look at that city's political situation. Lori Palmer, a former Dallas councilmember who represented an inner-city district, describes the impact such change would have on the city:

If a strong mayor form of government were instituted, the real loser would be all 14 of Dallas's council-members. First, councilmembers necessarily would lose their power and see it transferred to the mayor. Second, councilmembers would lose their access to the city administrators and department heads, who would be responsible and beholden only to the mayor, who would have the sole authority to hire and fire them.

The bottom line [would be] that Dallas's councilmembers, by having to give up both power and staff access, would become less rather than more effective in representing and serving their diverse constituencies. In the end, the citizens would be the final losers.

In many council-manager communities, Hispanic and African American activists have realized that for the first time they are being represented on the council in numbers that reflect their communities' diversity. As Gurwitt reported in his article, "The talk of moving to a strong mayor looks a lot like a ploy by the Old Guard to shift power away from the newly diverse council."

Al Lipscomb is an African American businessman and long-time civil rights leader who also was, until June 1993, mayor pro-tem of the Dallas city council. Both he and Lori

Palmer "retired" from the Dallas council this spring after serving the maximum number of consecutive terms allowed by the city charter. Lipscomb opposes changing the Dallas form of government and observed that "every time minorities get into the loop, the rules are changed under some pretext or through some slick scheme."

At one time, Dallas's current mayor pro-tem, Domingo Garcia, thought he could support a move toward a strong-mayor government. Today, however, he states that "North Dallas has the economic and political clout to continue to elect a mayor, and under a strong mayor system, we would be left out. We finally are getting on the city council, and I want to increase the power and authority of the council, not decrease it as [a move to] a strong-mayor system would do."

Some Concluding Thoughts

To summarize, then, the stressful challenges facing today's urban communities definitely call for strong political leadership. As National Civic League President John Parr says, however, "Looking for political leadership does not need to mean getting rid of the council-manager plan or decreasing the role of the professional manager. This is not only a time of new partnerships across old political and geographical boundaries, but a time of new partnerships within local governments as well."

But what of the challenge of providing leadership within a metropolitan or regional framework in which units of government may number in the hundreds and special districts also abound? In such situations as these, is it not true that communities need a really strong mayor, who not only has a vision and can build consensus but who also has the authority to fix things, to make and enforce decisions, and to "twist tails" if necessary?

In his new book *Citistates*, Neal Peirce notes that "in some cities, there's still a nostalgia for the brand of decisive leadership exerted by a few exalted power brokers." He cites the work of banker Richard King Mellon and Mayor David Lawrence in Pittsburgh, who to-gether spearheaded a renaissance in that city in the 1940s. Peirce notes that:

Today, the Mellon-Lawrence Act can be seen as heavily elitist, a relic of the time when small power cliques controlled each American city and brooked little opposition. The old titans, the small bunch of senior white males that met in exclusive clubs to make decisions that swayed cities' whole futures, are a virtually extinct species. Power in American communities seems to have been atomized by the rise of fresh power groups: upstart industries and businesses, powerful developers, ethnic alliances, organized blacks and Hispanics and Asians, environmental and women's and social service groups, and many more.

Today's city or citistate leadership can not be one of power but rather one of consensus building and facilitation. Gurwitt fittingly quotes Dr. James Svara of North Carolina State University, who has studied the roles of mayors in both forms of government extensively over the past decade. Svara argues that the pressures of civic diversity will produce facilitative mayors who "lead by empowering others — in particular the council and the manager — rather than seeing power for himself or herself."

Under the council-manager form, the effective mayor is a leader who not only contributes to the smooth functioning of government but also provides a general sense of direction. These individuals enhance the influence of elected officials by unifying the council, filling the policy vacuum that can exist on the council, and guiding policy toward goals that meet the needs of the community.

They are actively involved in monitoring and adjusting relations within local government to maintain balance, cooperation, and high standards. Contrary to the view of some that strong mayors are harmful to the manager, effective mayors enhance the performance both of the manager and of the council.

In the final analysis, what really is needed in today's urban communities are strong mayors, strong councils, and strong managers. No two of the three concepts are mutually exclusive; they can and do work together today in many of the country's successful council-manager local governments.

CHAPTER 42

GOOD GOVERNMENT, BAD GOVERNMENT

Alan Ehrenhalt

These are heady days at City Hall in Phoenix. Ever since the fall of 1993, when Phoenix won the international Bertelsmann competition, certifying it as one of the two best-governed cities in the whole world, reporters have been checking into town on assignment from newspapers all over the county, asking the city manager for his secrets of success. Staff members have grown accustomed to looking up from their desks to find delegations of Japanese mayors besieging them with questions. Highway signs welcome visitors to "America's best-run city."

Local government in Phoenix is no longer merely an object of civic pride. It has become a tourist attraction.

In December, Phoenix held a seminar on state-of-the-art management and charged 800 visitors from all over the world $450 a ticket. Those who came heard all the stories of innovation for which the city has become famous: the privatization initiative under which city agencies compete for contracts with private providers; the labor relations deal in which unions tie their pay increases to city revenue growth; the solid-waste processing facility that doubles as an environmental education center. The audience seemed to love it.

Just across Jefferson Street from City Hall, however, is a government that the visitors did not see. It is the government of Maricopa County, population 2,292,200, the seventh-largest county in America, comprising most

of the people in Arizona and more people than 17 entire states. If Phoenix represents the best in local government, Maricopa comes very close to being the worst. It is the embarrassing family member that nobody in town wants to talk about — the big, clumsy oaf that never learned to do anything right. For years, its management has been as chaotic, hidebound and wasteful as the management of the city is orderly, innovative and efficient.

In the summer of 1993, while the city was demonstrating its managerial virtuosity to the visiting Bertelsmann judges, the county across the street was busy spending itself to the brink of bankruptcy. Nobody knows just how close it was to being broke that summer — the financial management system was so primitive that the budget shortfall was impossible to calculate precisely. There were no comparisons of budget against year-to-date spending; the quarterly financials normally didn't arrive on managers' desks until four months after the quarter ended.

The supervisors had approved a budget of $1.2 billion for that fiscal year, but as happens every year, the individual county agencies felt free to overspend it. During the flush times of the 1980s, this had not caused any disasters. In the 1990s, however, the combination of recession, exploding health care costs and reckless spending had taken its toll. Maricopa County was badly short of cash by mid–1993; that July, it issued $25 billion in general

From *Governing,* Vol. 8, No. 7, April 1995. Published by Congressional Quarterly, Inc., Washington, D.C. Reprinted with permission of the publisher.

obligation bonds in an offering whose pur-
chasers had no idea just what a sinking ship
they were investing in.

Meanwhile, the county was losing millions
in badly needed revenue through management
inefficiency. The assessor's office was 125,000
properties behind in its appraisal process, giving some homeowners a property tax vacation
of up to two years while they waited for the
appraisal to be made. There were estimates
that the county had lost as much as $100 mil-
lion over many years as a result of the backlog.

The irony was hard to miss. The city of
Phoenix had developed a financial management system that was being studied and imi-
tated by governments all around the world.
The only government that didn't seem to
know about it was the one a hundred yards
away.

In truth, though, the city and county have
never had a great deal to say to each other.
"There was always a sense that they were a
poor country cousin," say Terry Goddard,
who was mayor of Phoenix from 1983 to 1990.
"If you worked in the city, you didn't want to
cross the street."

City Hall wasn't the only institution in
town that frequently preferred not to know
what was going on at the county courthouse.
"The business community has never cared
much about the county," says Walter Meek, a
longtime political reporter and consultant.
"The papers have looked at it sporadically, but
it comes and goes. It's very hard to get a handle on what goes on down there."

But now, more and more people are starting to ask the obvious question: How did the
same community manage to produce a government this good and another one this bad?
"Phoenix is praised internationally as a successful, well-run city," columnist Paul Schott
wrote in the *Arizona Republic* a few months
ago, "and Maricopa County is looked upon as
a rotten pit, and is essentially bankrupt to
boot. Why?"

It is a very good question, and it offers a
lesson in government that applies far beyond
the borders of Phoenix. What you learn very
quickly is that the innovations of Phoenix, and
the frustrations of Maricopa County, are more

than anything else a product of structure.
Phoenix is structured to succeed. Maricopa
County is structured to fail.

The question of how to structure local government is one that scholars and practitioners
have been debating for most of the century. It
has been 80 years now since Richard Childs
shook up the entire field by launching his crusade for non-political city managers and
broad-brush legislative bodies that stayed
away from administrative detail. There continue to be passionate advocates of the view
that cities and counties work better when they
are run by professional managers, and equally
passionate advocates who insist that what local
governments need today are strong, tough
politicians with a mandate from the voters to
get things done.

On one point, though, there has never been
much difference of opinion: *Somebody* has to
be in charge, and whoever he or she is must
have the authority to hold the agencies of government accountable for their performance.
In Maricopa County, no one is in charge. It is
a riderless horse. "I don't care who the players
are," says former Supervisor Jim Bruner. "As
long as you have the structure you have, it's re-
arranging the deck chairs on the *Titanic*."

Five years ago, at Bruner's invitation, Roy
Pederson moved in as administrator of Maricopa County from a similar job in nearby
Scottsdale, where he had earned a national
reputation among his peers. Pederson soon
discovered something he now realizes he
should have seen earlier: He was not taking
over a government. He was joining a collection of fiefdoms.

Like all the other counties in Arizona,
Maricopa has endured the 83 years since state-
hood with a government consisting of five supervisors, who rotate the chairmanship among
them each year, and seven separate elected
officials: the assessor, recorder, sheriff, county
attorney, county treasurer, clerk of courts and
superintendent of schools.

This is a system that was designed for tiny
rural counties in the first decade of the century, and it still works reasonably well in some
of them. But it has fallen apart amid the pressures of running a $2 billion governmental en-
terprise, as Maricopa County has come to be.

Although there has been a "county administrator" since 1961, the administrator has no authority over the elected officials, who control half the county budget and half the staff, and who routinely insist that they have a mandate to spend money as they see fit.

Separately elected county officials are not unique to Arizona by any means. The majority of counties in the United States still elect a sheriff and a prosecutor, and many elect several others as well. In most of these counties, however, the legislative body or chief executive has managed to establish some informal mechanism of control over what these elected officials do. The problem in Maricopa County is not the fact that it elects some of its department heads; it is that nobody has ever succeeded in convincing them they were part of a team.

The Maricopa County sheriff, Joe Arpaio, sued the county in state court last year, challenging its legal right to restrict his budget and declaring that he planned to overspend his allotment by some $6 million. The way Arpaio sees it, the county's deficit is not his concern. "That's their problem," he says. "They did it. I don't report to the Board of Supervisors. I serve the people only." And the way Maricopa County government is structured, you have to admit he has a point. Maricopa County officials have every incentive to act for themselves, or their departments, and virtually no incentive, professional or political, to act for the larger good.

In the 1980s, when the agencies finally computerized, years behind most other county governments in America of comparable size, just about every agency bought a different system. Between 1988 and 1993, as the recession took hold in Arizona and an official county hiring freeze was in effect, the agencies hired so freely that the number of county employees grew 45 percent, from 8,700 to 16,600. At a time when the county's deepening revenue problems were well known and when the city of Phoenix was invoking an austerity program in order to stay solvent, the county was essentially doing what it had done in the prosperous years of the previous decade.

Barbra Cooper joined the government of Maricopa County in 1992, an American Express vice president recruited to modernize the information system. Like nearly all newcomers, she was astonished at what she saw. "There wasn't any consciousness of people working with a restricted amount of funds. There was no consequence of being several million dollars over your budget. If you ran over budget, it was just taken care of. There was no single bottom line. There were individual pots of money." When one office ran out of cash, the county financial officer simply shifted money out of another account to make up the difference. "It looked like we had a financial system," says Roy Pederson. "In reality, I don't think we did."

The fact is, it wouldn't have done much good for the city of Phoenix, at that stage, to offer the county a course in state-of-the-art financial management. The county didn't want one. It had in place exactly the system it preferred — which is to say, scarcely any at all.

"We became a feeding trough for localities, individuals, programs," says Tom Rawles, who became a supervisor in 1992 and is now chairman. "There was always enough money for whatever you wanted to do. Each manager had his supervisor who was his guardian angel. But when things went bad, no one was willing to say, 'We can't do this anymore.'"

Maricopa County's structural problem — the centrifugal forces that send all the different governmental components flying in different directions — has been obvious to virtually every county administrator who has served there in the past 20 years. But nobody has been able to solve it. The reason is not simply inertia. It is a second structural flaw that lies beneath the first one. The county is a constitutionally powerless creature of the state of Arizona.

Like all the other Arizona counties, Maricopa exists by grace of the 1912 state constitution. Any power that cannot be found or plausibly inferred from that document, county officials cannot exercise without legislative approval. "You can't just do what makes sense," says supervisor Betsy Bayless. "We can't make a move without asking the legislature for permission. I had to testify before the legislature to get authority over barking dogs in unincorporated areas."

If Maricopa County does not have home rule when it comes to barking dogs, it goes without saying that any set of reforms that might actually end its structural paralysis — creating a county manager with real power, or electing a county executive, or abolishing the seven elected fiefdoms — cannot be accomplished by the county on its own, no matter how much support there might be. The state has to go along.

And that presents a whole new set of problems. A bill to give Arizona counties the right to restructure their governments was introduced in the state Senate in 1971 by Sandra Day O'Connor, then one of the county's senators. The bill languished in committee for 20 years, bitterly opposed by the most powerful figures in county government in most of the state: the sheriffs and county attorneys. They did not want to risk local reform movements that might, if successful, eliminate their jobs. It was simpler not to let the issue come up at all.

The Maricopa County officials venture to explain how their government reached such a stage of crisis, they nearly always point first to the restrictions imposed by the state. Then they make another equally valid point: The county is stuck with the worst possible roster of governmental responsibilities.

In this it is not alone. While the city/county division of labor varies considerably from one part of the nation to another, and has changed some in recent years, it is fair to say that counties continue to perform most of the services that ordinary citizens do not use, rarely think about and are not eager to support.

Altogether, criminal justice and health care comprise nearly three-quarters of Maricopa County's general fund spending. Costs at the county Medical Center nearly tripled between 1984 and 1993. Half the patients who walk into the emergency room are uninsured. They are a crushing expense, but not one that the county taxpayers have shown any willingness to increase taxes to pay for.

"Most people," says Supervisor Bayless, "don't commit murders. They don't use the public hospital. They don't see the flood control system. They care about garbage pickup, streets, police — city functions. After the person is arrested, they don't care so much how he is treated — but that's the county's responsibility."

And that is the way life appears these days from the Maricopa County office building, whether one is a career manager or an elected official. The county, crippled by an impossibly fragmented political structure, hamstrung by restrictions from the state, saddled with the costliest and least popular jobs in government, loses control of its budget and becomes a laughingstock. Meanwhile, the city, faced with none of these problems, wins awards and covers itself with glory.

It is difficult to argue, however, that the city's laurels are undeserved. Phoenix does a great many things extremely well. Its successes represent what may be the greatest modern triumph of city manager government in America.

During the past few years, the city manager system in various parts of the country has been under increasing attack from critics who say it does not generate the political leadership necessary to solve the divisive problems of the 1990s. Cities with long histories of city manager government, such as Rochester, New York, and St. Petersburg, Florida, have abandoned it in favor of "strong mayor" government, with an elected mayor replacing the manager as chief administrative official. Even Dallas, long regarded as the flagship city of the movement, has debated making such a change.

Phoenix stands as the best argument against those efforts. Over the past decade, it has been innovative and efficient, fiscally sound and politically orderly, and it has managed substantial change without a great deal of obvious disruption either inside the government or outside it. The mayor and city council debate the issues, set policy goals and listen to constituent opinion. But the manager and his staff hire and fire, handle the money and essentially run the city. Last year, as a result of a resignation and special elections, there were four different mayors in City Hall. But city government scarcely seemed to be affected at all.

Any one of several areas of accomplishment

might serve to illustrate the way Phoenix does things, but one simple one may be the most important: the management of statistics.

On the first day of every month, or soon after, the city manager distributes a thick package of tables, graphs and charts tracing virtually every dollar, number and percentage in city government that can be quantified, and what happened to it during the preceding 30 days. It is possible, reading the city manager's report for November of 1994, to learn that the percentage of city ambulance calls answered in less than 10 minutes was 91; that the total number of nights spent in city homeless shelters was 27,994; that 28,654 rounds of golf were played on city courses during the month, at an average cost of $10.96 per participant; that 3,479 miles of city streets were swept, nearly twice as many as in November of the previous year.

In short, the government of Phoenix knows nearly everything about what it is doing, and it knows it very quickly. But the most important thing it knows is how it is spending its money. "Financial controls, financial controls, financial controls," says the current mayor, Skip Rimsza. "They make all sorts of things possible." Rimsza thinks the city's financial management gives it a better deal in negotiation with private contractors, who are willing to bid higher because they trust city numbers. He thinks the system helps Phoenix invest in new technology, because it encourages bond houses to lend the money to buy it.

Rimsza is engaging in some not-very-subtle civic boasting. But less biased observers think he may be right. "The city has spent much of the last 20 years implementing a very sophisticated budget system," says Louis Weschler, a public administration scholar at Arizona State who has studied it. "Very few big cities have anything like that. The president of the United States would like to have something that sophisticated."

All in all, the government of Phoenix in the 1990s is just the sort of government Richard Childs might have envisioned eight decades down the road when he began promoting the city manager system in the years before World War I. But the way Phoenix got there would probably surprise Childs a great

deal — and offers some lessons to any city looking to modernize the way it does business.

Phoenix actually has had city manager government since 1914, the virtual dawn of the system in America. For the first 35 years, however, it was undistinguished government, wasteful and frequently corrupt. During World War II, the city had to be declared off-limits to military personnel stationed nearby, because prostitution was rampant and venereal disease was raging out of control. The manager in those days was a puppet of the city council, powerless to prevent pay-offs to city workers or the larding of patronage employees onto city payrolls for political reasons. Only in 1950, with the passage of a city charter giving the manager full administrative control, did the system begin to approach the non-partisan quality of the Childs blueprint.

Even then, government in Phoenix for the next 30 years was respectable, conservative, generally unimaginative government — not the sort that wins international awards for innovation. The era of special accomplishment really began in 1980, with the arrival as city manager of Marvin Andrews, and took off at the end of the decade under Frank Fairbanks, who succeeded Andrews in 1990.

Andrews and Fairbanks, two soft-spoken, self-effacing bureaucrats with a distaste for press coverage, turned out to be a pair of determined and successful experimentalists. They also happened to break the normal city management pattern in an interesting way. Neither was a hot-shot from outside brought in to shake up the system; both were home-grown Phoenix civil servants, career employees who had spent years working their way up through the system. Andrews went to work for the city in 1958; Fairbanks started in 1972 answering complaints from citizens on the telephone.

Nearly everybody thinks that one secret of Phoenix's aptitude for change has been its continuity of leadership, and that the source of that continuity has been the city's willingness to stick with its own people as top managers — something most cities have been reluctant to do. Fairbanks thinks so too. "A piece of this is tradition," he says. "We are more trusted here, and we are trusted to do more."

As the 1980s began, however, it was far from obvious that Phoenix would become the global success story it has turned out to be. The city manager government had developed a reputation, as it had in many other cities, for being autocratic, insular and frequently contemptuous of the elected officials who were supposed to be its board of directors. The city council members complained that the manager's office felt like a foreign country to them; the manager, John Wentz, referred to the council as "temporary help." The council members had no input at all into top hiring decisions.

In 1983, Terry Goddard took over as mayor on a platform that included replacing city manager government with a "strong mayor system. "I had reservations about nearly everything they were doing," Goddard says.

It was at that point that Andrews launched the barrage of reform and innovation that not only killed Goddard's plan but set in motion all the subsequent successes. Under Andrews, the manager's office generated mission statements, productivity committees, pay for performance. He raised the reward for employees who came up with new ideas from $150 to $2,000. He transferred senior officials out of what had been a virtual "secretariat" of centralized power and into line departments such as Public Works, Finance and Human Services.

Equally important, he set about the political cultivation of the council members who had been on the verge of wanting to junk the system. In doing that, he broke one of the cardinal rules of orthodox city management: the separation of political and management jobs. He sent one of his senior assistants into the mayor's office as a liaison. For the past decade, there has been an assistant or deputy city manager of Phoenix working full-time for the mayor, often as chief of staff. The original theorists of city management, and some of the current ones, would consider this a form of treason. Nevertheless, it did the job. By the late 1980s, none of the elected officials were talking about junking the system any more. Goddard had decided that city manager government wasn't so bad after all. Whenever the manager wanted to set off in an innovative

new direction, the mayor and council were on board.

"It is unusual," admits Sheryl Sculley, who at the moment is both deputy city manager and Mayor Rimsza's chief of staff. "There are people who think I'm a traitor to the city management profession." But in her view, it was the willingness to break rules that got Phoenix where it is today. "Marvin Andrews saved the system," she says, "by doing unconventional things."

To a great extent, they are still being done. Last year, when the city built a new government center, it confronted the question of just how much to honor the tradition of politics/management separation that had been breached for nearly a decade by the liaison arrangement. Fairbanks, Andrews' protégé and successor, came up with an Andrews-like solution. He placed the manager's office and the mayor's office on separate floors. Then he designed an open staircase to connect them.

The two most interesting questions about public administration in Phoenix right now are these: Can the county government stay this bad? And can the city manage to stay this good?

For perhaps the first time in modern memory, there is reason to be hopeful about the county. In the view of many who work there, Maricopa County government hit bottom in mid–1994, when its managers had to roll over tax anticipation notes just to stay solvent for the rest of the year. During a visit to New York, county officials were told by Standard & Poor's that theirs was the worst financial management system the company had seen since New York City in 1975. Barbra Cooper, then the acting county manager, didn't really disagree. "I was selling smoke," she admits. "I was smiling a sweet little smile and saying, 'Trust Me.'"

Since then, however, the county has taken some surprisingly decisive steps. Later in 1994, at Cooper's direction, it drafted a business plan that called for the restructuring of $26 million of its $67 million debt, the elimination of more than 1,000 jobs, and $16 million in budget cuts for the 1994-95 fiscal year. More than $2 million in assets has been sold, nearly 300 employees laid off, job training programs eliminated and county parks closed for portions of the year. At the beginning of January, a new county administrator, David Smith, was hired amid promises from the five supervisors to grant him the authority to do the job.

In the long run, however, Maricopa County will not be able to solve its most serious problems until it finds a way to address its structural flaws. At some point in the next year, with the express permission of the legislature, the Board of Supervisors will probably ask county voters to establish a commission that would draft a new "home rule" charter, most likely creating either an elected county executive or a professional manager with genuine clout, à la Marvin Andrews or Frank Fairbanks in Phoenix.

On the one hand, the timing seems good. Nobody needs to be convinced that county government is in need of dramatic improvement. "It's an attempt to fix a dysfunctional machine," says Supervisor Tom Rawles. "Our selling point is that things are so bad, they need to fundamentally change." On the other hand, it will be easy for critics to argue that a county whose performance has been as inept as Maricopa's should not be given new home rule powers as a reward. Among those making this argument will be several of the current elected officials whose jobs would almost certainly be eliminated under a reform charter. The sheriff has already declared his opposition. "I will never go for an appointed sheriff," Arpaio vows.

Whether the charter will happen soon is very much in doubt. It may be the beginning of the next century before any charter decisions have real effect on the structure of county government. Still, there is growing agreement that it will happen eventually. "The best thing that will come out of this is an identity," say Barbra Cooper. "We have to have one. But it will take us a long time to get there."

Meanwhile, across the street, Phoenix city government faces the much simpler task of merely maintaining the momentum and creativity it has already established. There are many reasons why it might be expected to do that, not least of them the pool of talent that has been attracted to careers in government there during the past 15 years. In the early 1980s, Marvin Andrews instituted an internship program that brings bright young public administration students to Phoenix for work-study programs; a remarkable number of the early graduates of this program settled in town, and today, 15 years later, form the nucleus of a whole new generation of managers. At a time when other city governments are strapped for talent, Phoenix is amply stocked.

Equally important, the Bertelsmann prize and the ensuing publicity make it seem all but unthinkable that any mayor in the near future will do what Goddard thought about doing in the early 1980s — dismantle the structure that produced all the good fortune. The managers have managed to convince the politicians in Phoenix that tampering with the structure would amount to killing off a golden goose. And the politicians accept it. "The council here understands that they are policy makers," says Mayor Rimsza. "The managers run day-to-day business." At this point, "the system," as some like to call it, comes close to being an article of faith in Phoenix.

But structures of government are a lot more fragile than people tend to realize, especially when they are working well. A combination of bad choices in Phoenix — a manager who took the politicians and the voters for granted, or a mayor who insisted on being a micro-manager — and the prize-winning system might turn out to be in more jeopardy than seems possible at the moment. When it comes to building a government, no structure is quite as impregnable as it may look. That is the one sobering thought at City Hall in Phoenix these days — and it may be the one glimmer of hope at the county building across the street.

CHAPTER 43

COUNTY GOVERNMENT IN THE 21ST CENTURY

Donald C. Menzel

Governing the American county in the 21st century will be more challenging than ever before in the nearly 400-year history of this often maligned unit of local government. Why? Consider the following. First as federal and state governments shift, indeed mandate duties and responsibilities to local governments, counties have taken on greater importance as service providers and participants in the American federal system. Second, the pace of change (often referred to as modernization) of the American county has increased significantly in recent decades and shows little sign of slowing. Many counties have been transformed in both form and function. A growing number have shed their "boss and patronage" ridden images and have sought to place merit and performance high on their day-to-day work agenda. Others have changed from keepers of vital statistics to governments that compete, cooperate with, and, at times, resemble full-service American cities. Third, although historically little more than "arms of the state," many counties are "new wave" governments in that they resemble neither municipalities, state agencies, or regional governments. Instead, they are a unique, hybrid blend of each.

It is somewhat misleading to speak of the American county as if it were a monolithic social, political and governmental entity. Diversity rather than homogeneity characterizes America's 3,043 counties. Still, there are certain issues and challenges that are likely to face nearly all who govern these often "forgotten governments" as a new century approaches. This article outlines five issues and suggests what might be done to foster effective county governance in the 21st century.

Issues and Challenges Facing County Governments

A number of issues have surfaced or are likely to surface in the near future. These include the structure of county governments, their leadership capacity, fiscal conditions and management, intergovernmental roles and responsibilities, and their ability to affect local economic development.

STRUCTURE AND ORGANIZATION OF COUNTY GOVERNMENT IN THE U.S.

The debate with regard to how the structure of county government makes a difference in the ability of counties to provide efficient, effective and economical services continues, especially in urban America where city-county-regional jurisdictional boundaries disappear when problems such as crime, homelessness, pollution and poverty are present. The traditional commission form of county government, where three to five elected

Originally published as "Governing the American County in the 21st Century," from *Spectrum: The Journal of State Government*, Vol. 69, No. 3, Summer 1996. Published by the Council of State Governments, Lexington, Kentucky. Reprinted with permission of the publisher.

commissioners exercise day-to-day hands-on administration, is often regarded as inadequate to deal with these problems. "The infirmities of the commission system," notes Frank J. Thompson (1993, 19) executive director of the National Commission on the State and Local Public Service, "and the growing awareness of the vital tasks that county governments perform have spurred movement to strengthen the hand of either an appointed or elected executive." Currently, more than one of every four counties appoints a chief executive or manager and or elects a chief executive.

Strengthening the power and authority of chief executives to get the job done — to integrate, coordinate and empower their work-force — is an important step toward making counties more viable governmental entities. Still, in many states, there remain many constraints, notably the fragmentation and sharing of administrative authority with constitutional officers, also known as "row" officers. These independently elected executives (and they are just that) — county sheriffs, clerks, tax collectors, property appraisers, coroners and others — are often powerful political figures who can frustrate the ability of chief executives and county legislative bodies to make their governments high-performing units. In its 1990 *Model County Charter*, the National Civic League asserts that the really big break with tradition will occur "when a reorganized county government brings under council control (and administration by the appointed manager) functions previously performed by independently elected officers or substantially independent boards and commissions."

County home rule is another structural development that has grown in popularity in the 20th century. Many counties, like their municipal counterparts, have sought to free themselves from state legislative dominance by seeking authority to rule or enact ordinances on their own, i.e., without a legislative grant of authority. Such "home rule" was first secured by California's counties in 1911. Since then, 37 additional states have passed legislation enabling counties to practice home rule. In principle, counties that enjoy home rule are able to exercise greater freedom and flexibility when confronting local issues.

Principle and practice, however, do not always go hand-in-hand. Indeed, home-rule powers and practices vary widely across and within states. In Florida, for example, 14 charter counties exercise home-rule powers but some are not always able to fend off unwanted advances by zealous legislative delegations who feel they know what is best for their county. County home rule does not necessarily "free" counties from their historic state master.

So, does the structure and organization of county governments matter or not? Does having an integrated executive make a difference? Are counties with home-rule powers more effective governments than those counties without home-rule powers? These important questions are difficult to answer in a definitive manner. One might say that structure matters if it is defined in terms of the dynamics of authority, leadership, and decision making but does not seem to matter if defined only in terms of forms of government. While there is some evidence that the structure of county government — commission, commission-manager, elected executive — influences how much counties spend, there is little evidence that it makes much difference in the kinds of policies or programs enacted or the efficiencies produced. Park (1996), for example, reports that counties with an appointed chief administrator or elected executive spend more than those with a commission form of government but this finding is tempered by the fact that other variables such as state fiscal aid and region of country have a greater influence on spending levels.

LEADERSHIP CAPACITY OF COUNTIES

The linkage between structure and performance will be debated well into the next century. It is an important debate. However, it may pale alongside the debate about the linkage between county leadership and performance. Indeed, it is even plausible to suggest that leadership can make the difference in how well or poorly a county performs across a wide spectrum of tasks and responsibilities. Unfortunately, knowledge of how leadership at the county level is exercised with greater or lesser effectiveness in rural and urban counties or traditional commission and appointed manager counties is sparse and impressionistic. One widespread impression is that "more than any other level of the federal system, counties have provided barren soil for the flowering of strong executives" (Thompson 1993, 19).

This "leaderless capacity" impression is reinforced even when one examines those counties with chief executives. There are approximately 1,200 appointed or elected county executives among America's 3,043 counties. Precious few executives, however, possess the formal powers often regarded as necessary to exercise strong executive leadership. Such powers as renewable terms of office, authority to appoint and remove subordinates, the ability to control budget submissions and outlays, power to veto proposed ordinances, and the authority to issue orders changing government organization are often absent.

The need to exercise more effective county leadership has spurred some movement toward putting greater power and authority in an elected county executive. Council-elected executive governments are in place in 373 counties, with 21 more elected executives or mayors occupying top posts in city-county consolidated governments. These numbers represent a three-fold increase since 1980 (*County News* May 1995). Whether this arrangement will result in more powerful county leadership is open to debate. Nonetheless, a growing number of counties are adopting this "reform" measure.

The leadership challenge will be made more difficult by the growing diversity of the county workforce and officialdom itself. Recent statistics suggest that the county workforce will be affected by the growing diversity of the U.S. labor force as a whole. Among other things, white males will be a minority in the U.S. workplace by the turn of the century, representing 39 percent of all workers. Racial and ethnic minorities are expected to constitute 26 percent of the U.S. workforce by the year 2000 (Kelly 1993).

Similar shifts are occurring in the composition of the state and local government workforce. Kelly's (1993) research shows that the proportion of public-service employees who are white males declined from 53.5 percent to 43.3 percent between 1974 and 1990. During the same period, the minority percentage increased from 19.5 percent to 27.1 percent.

Workforce diversity is expected to be accompanied by leadership diversity. In a survey of America's 100 largest counties, Mac-Manus (1996) found that more women and racial minorities are gaining seats on county councils and occupying administrative posts. She notes, for example, that a 1988 International City/County Management Association survey found that women held 9 percent of all county board seats while her 1993 survey found that women held 27 percent of the board seats in large counties. While these figures are not entirely comparable, she concludes that "there does appear to be greater representation of women on county governing boards today than in the past" (Mac-Manus 1996, 66).

Diversity in the community and the county workforce does not necessarily bode ill for making America's counties more effective governmental entities. However, it does raise the issue of how such diversity might foster conflict or cooperation or both. The "good news," as Svara (1996) points out, is that county leaders may already have an edge in working through this challenge because many have found it necessary to become skillful negotiators, able bargaining agents, and effective conflict managers. One irony of American local government history may be that while counties were largely on the sidelines of change as the progressive reform movement swept across municipal America in the 20th century, county leaders have developed survival skills that have equipped them well for 21st century governance.

With regard to managerial leadership, the role of the county manager may have to be rethought, perhaps even reinvented. More than "neutral competency" will be required of the local government manager. The effective manager, Streib (1996) contends, will have to embrace a wide range of values, including a commitment to openness, participation, intergenerational impacts of county decision making, and a genuine interest in what people think and do. "The pursuit of 'efficiency,' the hallmark of the effective public manager of the progressive era, is no longer a singularly sufficient value. Strengthening county management will require elected and appointed leaders who have a well developed set of values that will serve as a roadmap for navigating through the frequently stormy environments that typify county rule by many masters" (Streib 1996, 136).

FISCAL MANAGEMENT CHALLENGES

Creating a government that works better and costs less is an admirable goal of the federal government, states the *Report of the National Performance Review* (1993). Such a goal is no less admirable or desirable for America's counties. Nor is the challenge of accomplishing this goal any less daunting at the local level than at the national level. The search engine for this task is dollars — incoming and outgoing, revenues and expenditures.

Like the federal government, counties face growing citizen demands for services yet unrelenting opposition to increased taxes for such services, especially in the form of higher property taxes. Some counties have resorted to imaginative revenue diversification or enhancement programs while others have resorted to risky financial investment strategies. The Economic Development and Government Equity program in Montgomery County, Ohio, is an example of the former while the spectacular bankruptcy of Orange County, California, as an example of the latter.

The Montgomery County plan is a county-municipal tax sharing scheme that seeks to "insure that each community within Montgomery County has an equal opportunity to derive some benefit from development outside its boundaries" (Pammer 1996, 186). Key to the success of this effort was the willingness of Montgomery County to dedicate $50 million to an economic development fund that villages, townships and municipalities could draw upon to attract development which, in turn, commits them to sharing future tax revenues with neighboring communities (Pammer 1996). Although it cannot be determined at this time whether this "win-win" plan is just that, this initiative demonstrates that some counties recognize that continuing to do business in the same old way by raising property taxes

will no longer suffice. They are undertaking new and imaginative efforts to keep their fiscal house in order.

Alas, not all counties have been so fortunate with perhaps the most well known being Orange County, California, which now occupies the record books for the largest municipal bankruptcy in United States history. On December 6, 1994, Orange County declared itself bankrupt, having lost nearly $2 billion in investments. The county's popular, independently elected county treasurer employed a high-risk investment strategy, one which included heavy borrowing to buy rate-sensitive derivative securities, that failed when interest rates went amok (Mydang, A14). Keeping taxes low without cutting services, which has been the preference in Orange County, apparently encouraged political and financial risk taking. Now, Orange County officials and residents face the reality of raising taxes, cutting services, and perhaps even selling county assets.

The fundamental fiscal challenge facing American counties is *how* to diversify their revenue base, not whether to diversify. Cigler (1996) offers helpful suggestions along these lines. She notes that counties continue to rely heavily on property taxes but that user charges are increasingly popular at county-owned or leased facilities such as airports, marinas, and recreation sites. Also growing in popularity are county-option sales taxes. More than 30 states have passed legislation allowing counties to use local sales taxes to enhance their revenue base. In states like Florida, heavy use is made of the local sales tax option as voters regularly decide whether to tax themselves and tourists for schools, prisons, health care and sports facilities. Local income taxes are another option, although less than a dozen states have adopted this practice (Cigler 1996).

Tax-increment financing (TIF) is also employed in some states and counties. This municipal financing tool calls for the designation of districts in which regularly assessed property taxes are earmarked for financing public improvements needed to attract new development which, in turn, is expected to generate new revenues. Tax-increment financing is dependent on potential development and uses millage rates for an entire jurisdiction (Cigler 1996). Practically speaking, this approach subsidizes new development by taxing only the value (increment) added on to the district when development occurs.

Mixing and matching these and other alternative sources of revenue to achieve the "best" arrangement for financing services in an equitable manner requires good judgment, common sense and financial know-how on the part of county leaders. It is no small challenge.

At the same time, as Cigler (1996) reminds us, revenue flexibility, as opposed to diversification, does not have to be achieved entirely through adding new revenues. Improved purchasing, contracting and financial forecasting can contribute to a county's fiscal health. Furthermore, other initiatives such as targeting state revolving funds to finance infrastructure, issuing bonds in a pool to influence credit ratings, and even establishing alternative dispute resolution centers, can yield significant financial savings.

INTERGOVERNMENTAL ROLES AND RESPONSIBILITIES

The emergence of counties as significant service providers and political entities has catapulted them headlong into the intergovernmental arena. Unlike regional councils composed of representatives of local governments, counties may be more truly intergovernmental governments because they often have multiple identities and realities. A county can be a full-service local government, a quasi-state agency and a regional actor all at once. Indeed, Berman and Salant (1996) suggest that these multiple roles and identities sometimes cause counties to engage in contradictory, inconsistent, and even irrational behavior. As quasi-state agencies, for example, they are often "good soldiers" when carrying out their state duties. And as full service local governments attempting to meet the needs and demands of residents, they often resist state and federal authorities that seek to impose their will on them, especially when that will is reflected in unfunded and unsolicited state or federal mandates (Benton 1996).

The expansive role of counties in the vertical intergovernmental system is no less expansive in the horizontal intergovernmental system. Berman and Salant (1996) assert that counties "are major collaborators with other units through contracts and agreements, important participants in regional organizations such as councils of government, and direct providers of area-wide services such as solid waste, transit and health." And, as alluded to earlier, the increasingly important role of counties as initiators of programs such as city-county-township tax base sharing underscores their ability to broker win-win relationships among natural competitors.

Perhaps the central challenge facing counties as players in the American federal system is the somewhat amorphous nature of the game itself (Benton 1996). With budget deficit reduction high on the priority list of the 104th Congress and the Clinton administration, the remaining years of the 20th century may witness significant reductions in federal intergovernmental fiscal aid which, in turn, may motivate counties to be even more aggressive players in state and local arenas. One thing seems certain — counties will not be passive pawns on a federal chessboard. Rather, they are likely to assert themselves in an effort to obtain a fair hearing, if not a fair share, of rights, responsibilities and resources.

Fiscal aid cutbacks have already compelled many counties to be more inventive in finding ways to generate new dollars or shift existing dollars so as to "do more with less." Among other things, this has meant becoming more entrepreneurial and has resulted in initiatives to broaden user fees, establish development fees and privatize numerous services.

ECONOMIC DEVELOPMENT

A number of counties are no longer waiting for economic development to happen in their jurisdictions. Rather, they are developing plans and strategies to make it happen. Some strategies are aimed at attracting, retaining, or expanding business firms. Among others, these include providing businesses with tax abatements, subsidies, loan guarantees, infrastructure investment and development, and fiscal commitments to build facilities such as a professional sports stadium. As a group, these measures can be described as supply-side incentives. One example can be found in Hillsborough County, Florida, where the Tampa Bay Buccaneers professional football ownership has vowed to relocate the team if the community does not build a new stadium. County officials once proposed to buy as many as 10,000 tickets per home game when the team attracted at least 45,000 fans. When such circumstances occurred, the county would be obligated to divert several million dollars from its revenue stream into the Buccaneers revenue stream. This particular plan faltered on the altar of public opinion and has since been replaced by a one-half cent sales tax referendum that the voters will decide on in early September 1996.

Across the Tampa Bay, similar efforts were taken by the city of St. Petersburg and Pinellas County to attract a professional baseball team when nearly two hundred million city/county tax dollars were invested in the construction of an enclosed arena. This "field of dreams" investment has netted the community a new baseball franchise. The Tampa Bay Devil Rays began play in 1998.

Strategies that employ market-like approaches or emphasize public-private partnerships are also employed by counties to help business firms develop markets or sell products abroad and at home. These strategies are often referred to as demand-side strategies and include measures such as trade missions and export-assistance programs. City-county-state initiated trade missions to Europe, Japan and other locations are increasingly commonplace. The siting of the Honda plant in Marysville, Ohio, for example, was promoted by a county-state trade mission to Japan.

County sponsored export-assistance programs are another means to foster local economic development in a global marketplace. Such programs include county financing for market research studies for small-to-medium sized business firms, technical assistance and information, and organizing meetings for foreign firms to meet with local firms wishing to do business abroad. Montgomery County, Maryland, established an export-assistance program that assisted small businesses by (1) providing funds to conduct market research studies in the foreign country identified by a local

business, (2) supplying free technical assistance through an arrangement with international trade experts retired from the U.S. Department of Commerce, (3) offering financial and staff support to firms to attend international trade shows, and (4) organizing meetings for foreign firms to meet with local firms wishing to do business overseas (Pammer 1996).

These initiatives point toward both a new attitude and a new role for counties in stimulating local public economies. Pammer (1996) astutely notes that the role of counties as agents of economic development will require county officials to adopt a different orientation than what has been accepted in the past. An orientation that embraces pro-active economic development strategies and regionalization will be necessary. Strategies that have been parochial and often resulted in fierce inter-jurisdictional competition for new businesses will have to be scrapped. Instead, the view that the "economic stability and prosperity of any single locality is critically linked to the fiscal health and attributes of its neighbors" must be adopted, concludes Pammer (1996, 185). Counties, if they choose to do so, can be catalysts for inter-local cooperation that promote local and regional economic growth and stability.

Moving Forward with an Eye on the Past?

Will America's counties transform themselves into more effective governments in the 21st century? Could they become *the* local governments of the future? Will counties be "reinvented," "re-engineered," "revitalized"— to use the "R" words of the 1990s? Or will the labels "ramshackle," "dark continent," "forgotten governments" and other unflattering phrases of the 20th century be tacked on to county governments in the decades ahead? Will counties be forced to move forward while looking backwards? The answers to these questions will depend on whether county leaders, state lawmakers, and the body politic are prepared to adopt new attitudes and strategies.

One proposed strategy advanced by the National Commission on the State and Local Public Service calls for "trust and lead" (1993, 9). High-performance government, according to the Commission, can rebuild public trust and confidence in government. Counties, as local governments that provide vital public services which touch the lives of thousands of people daily, are well-positioned to engage in this rebuilding task. The trust deficit which President Clinton noted early in his administration is real and must be dealt with by governments at all levels.

A "trust and lead" strategy will require county leaders, state officials, and the public to trust public employees to do the right things right. The demeaning of public service and the under-valuing of public employees must end. The county workforce must be treated as a valuable resource. Counties must invest in their human capital by providing education and by training and applying modern management techniques. Perhaps most importantly, county and state leaders must place confidence in and provide opportunity for the county workforce to become a high-performance workforce. Employee empowerment, the opportunity for rank-and-file employees to participate in a meaningful way in decisions affecting them and their community, is essential to the effective governance of the American county in the 21st century.

The movement to flatten organizational hierarchies should also be embraced by county boards and managers. Pushing responsibility out and to the lowest levels of the county workforce can succeed if there is a readiness and willingness on the part of all to accept that responsibility. Twentieth century management, which emphasized a culture of control, will not suffice in the century ahead.

The steady professionalization of the county workforce must also be sustained, perhaps even accelerated. In the past, counties frequently took the brunt of unflattering commentary about their lack of professionalization. This is changing rapidly but more change is needed. A more professionalized workforce will better position counties to shape policy and respond to the issues and challenges discussed in this chapter. Similarly, the movement toward electing or appointing professionally trained executives, especially if combined with reductions in the number of elected row officers, will yield greater political clout for counties and result in a more integrated executive.

Will counties meet the challenges of governance in the 21st century? This author believes they will. County leaders and state lawmakers cannot afford the luxury of weak county governments. The stakes are too high and too costly; the global challenge is real. America's communities and local governments are the bedrock on which the nation can erect a viable and prospering economy and democracy. The bumper sticker that proudly proclaims "think globally, act locally" goes to the heart of the need to insure that governing the American county in the 21st century will be a success story.

References

Benton, J. Edwin (1996). "Fiscal Aid and Mandates: The County Experience." In *The American County: Frontiers of Knowledge*, edited by Donald C. Menzel. Tuscaloosa, Ala.: The University of Alabama Press.

Berman, David R. and Tanis J. Salant (1996). "The Changing Role of Counties in the Inter-governmental System." In *The American County: Frontiers of Knowledge*, edited by Donald C. Menzel. Tuscaloosa, Ala.: The University of Alabama Press.

Cigler, Beverly A. (1996). "Revenue Diversification Among American Counties." In *The American County: Frontiers of Knowledge*, edited by Donald C. Menzel. Tuscaloosa, Ala.: The University of Alabama Press.

"NACO Surveys Elected County Executives." *County News* (May 8, 1995): 9.

Kelly, Rita Mae (1993). "Diversity in the Public Workforce: New Needs, New Approaches." In *Revitalizing State and Local Public Service*, edited by Frank J. Thompson. San Francisco: Jossey-Bass Publishers.

MacManus, Susan A. (1996). "County Boards, Partisanship, and Elections." In *The American County: Frontiers of Knowledge*, edited by Donald C. Menzel. Tuscaloosa, Ala.: The University of Alabama Press.

Mydang, Seth. "Taxes a Hard Sell in Orange County," *New York Times* (May 8, 1995): A-14.

National Civic League (1990). *Model County Charter*. Revised Edition. Denver, Colo.

National Commission on the State and Local Public

Service (1993). *Hard Truths/Tough Choices: An Agenda for State and Local Reform*. Albany, NY: The Nelson A. Rockefeller Institute of Government.

Pammer, Jr., William A. (1996). "County Economic Development Strategies." In *The American County: Frontiers of Knowledge*, edited by Donald C. Menzel. Tuscaloosa, Ala.: The University of Alabama Press.

Park, Kee Ok (1996). "Determinants of County Government Growth." In *The American County: Frontiers of Knowledge*, edited by Donald C. Menzel. Tuscaloosa, Ala.: The University of Alabama Press.

Report of the National Performance Review, Vice President Al Gore (1993). *Creating a Government That Works Better & Costs Less*. U.S. Government Printing Office, Washington, D.C., September 7, 1993.

Streib, Gregory (1996). "Strengthening County Management." In *The American County: Frontiers of Knowledge*, edited by Donald C. Menzel. Tuscaloosa, Ala.: The University of Alabama Press.

Svara, James H. (1996). "Leadership and Professionalism in County Government." In *The American County: Frontiers of Knowledge*, edited by Donald C. Menzel. Tuscaloosa, Ala.: The University of Alabama Press.

Thompson, Frank J., ed. (1993). *Revitalizing State and Local Public Service*. San Francisco: Jossey-Bass Publishers.

CHAPTER 44

REGIONAL EXCELLENCE IN THE 21ST CENTURY

William Dodge

A thousand years ago, in the late 900s, people literally feared the end of the world in some cataclysmic explosion.

Their fears caused them to consider reforms, especially of their spiritual behavior. Hoping that the end would coincide with the second coming, community leaders and citizens of the time, at least the Christian ones, dedicated themselves to a religious building campaign of colossal proportions. Their collaborative efforts resulted in constructing many of the monumental Romanesque cathedrals of Western Europe. Cluniac monk, Raoul Glaber, observed in 1003, "it was as if the whole earth, having cast off its age by shaking itself, were clothing itself everywhere in a white robe of churches."

Today, in the late 1900s, people fear the end of their local political worlds in some equally drastic change.

What used to be resolvable in their individual communities now defies resolution with neighbors across entire regions. What used to be clearly the responsibility of public, private, or nonprofit organizations now creates overlapping confusion. What used to be perceived as common — even American — values are increasingly contested by conflicted communities and interest groups.

Such fears have caused people to consider reforms, especially of their temporal behavior.

Not depending upon divine intervention for resolving their earthly challenges, community leaders and citizens are experimenting with new approaches to intercommunity and regional decision-making. These experiments have not yet reached colossal proportions, but they may preview a regional renaissance by the dawn of the 21st century.

Maybe, just maybe, our regions will be clothed with regional governance excellence in this change in millennia!

By regional governance, I do not mean metropolitan government, the one-big-government approach to regional challenges. Instead, I mean how we bring community leaders and citizens together to address challenges that cut across communities — from crime and drugs to economic competitiveness. This usually involves defining the challenge, assigning responsibility for addressing it to an existing or new regional mechanism, involving community leaders and citizens affected by it, designing a strategy for addressing it, negotiating responsibility and implementing the strategy, and monitoring and evaluating success in addressing the challenge. By excellence, I mean doing this in a more timely, flexible, and effective manner with each new challenge, so as to take advantage of regional opportunities before they are lost and prevent regional threats from exploding into crisis.

Originally published as "Regional Excellence," from *National Civic Review,* Vol. 85, No. 2, Spring-Summer 1996. Published by the National Civic League, Denver, Colorado. Reprinted with permission of the publisher.

Regional Governance Has Risen in Importance

Regions are organic systems organized in ways surprisingly similar to flowers, fish, mammals, and humans. They have evolved out of less complex — but not necessarily lower — life forms, especially in urban areas that started with small settlements that grew into cities that, in turn, expanded into regions containing suburbs and exurbs. As a result, regions have one or more vital organs — central business districts and suburban employment centers and shopping malls — tied together with the sinews of transportation, the arteries of commerce, and the protoplasm of community.

Healthy regions nurture us, their individual cells, by concentrating the resources and providing the connections to pursue a desired quality of life, locally and globally. In turn, they need our care and feeding, since, like other living beings, their health and happiness is determined by whoever or whatever shapes and controls their growth.

States and nations do not usually stir the same biological thoughts. As critical as they are to providing military security, setting uniform standards, redistributing wealth, and even supporting local and regional initiatives, they appear more to be human contrivances than living organisms.

It is not surprising, therefore, that the region has emerged again as it has repeatedly over recorded history. This time, it has become more important as the cold war, which had required nations to develop competitive armies, cooled off, and the global common market, which now requires regions to develop competitive economies, heated up.

The era of the region is already being proclaimed worldwide. In Europe, the borders between nations are dissolving in the European community and a "Europe of Regions" is taking its place. In Asia, Hong Kong shows every sign of surviving its transfer from Great Britain to the Peoples Republic of China as a relatively independent region, one that now includes a considerable part of the Guangzhou province of China. I suspect that neither ideology nor nationalism will seriously restrict the behavior of this powerful living organism in the global ecosystem.

What might be surprising, however, is that this same Global Competitiveness, and four other major developments, or change drivers — Challenge Explosion, Citizen Withdrawal, Structure-Challenge Mismatch, and Rich-Poor Community Gap — have transformed regional governance from a nicety to a necessity.

Bottom line: Community leaders and citizens need to focus priority attention on the growth development — the governance — of their own living organisms, their regions.

Pursuing Regional Governance Excellence Requires a Guiding Star

We have a long history of being easy "creationists" and reluctant "evolutionists" concerning the region.

On one hand, as easy "creationists," we have all too readily bought into the idea that a metropolitan government, in the form of a single monolithic structure that directs all decision making, would eventually be created, almost overnight, and guide regional development. It, I suspect, is doomed to be the eternal will-o'-the-wisp of regional governance.

No matter how creative we become, we cannot anticipate the range of challenges or nail down the geographic scope of the region long enough to have it governed by a single structure. Even those places that have annexed extensively, such as Columbus, Ohio; consolidated city and county government, such as Unigov in the Indianapolis region; or created two-tier governments, such as Metro Toronto, continue to be confronted with irrepressible sprawl leapfrogging across their borders into the great beyond.

Unless we are willing to pursue the highly unlikely option of making each region a state, and to then redraw state boundaries every decade to conform with the changing spheres of regional influence, we will need to build a "network" of regional decision making mechanisms — processes and structures — to address emerging challenges in each region.

On the other hand, as reluctant "evolutionists," we have resisted the evolution of regional decision making mechanisms, condemning most of them to be ineffective "footballs without laces," giving all the appearances of addressing regional challenges but being genetically flawed in their powers, participants, practices, or perseverance. Or, even worse, we have flirted with the myth that the region was divisible — that the donut (the suburbs) is not connected to the hole (the central city). To borrow a metaphor from Peter Senge, author of *The Fifth Discipline*, dividing a region into parts has no greater chance of working than dividing any other living organism, such as an elephant, into parts; all one gets is a mess.

I believe that we now need to be strategic "pragmatists" and foster a regional renaissance. We need to pursue regional governance excellence in the closing years of the second millennium if we are to compete globally and thrive locally in the third. Achieving excellence, I further believe, requires launching initiatives to improve each of five components of regional governance; that is, we need to make it Prominent, Strategic, Equitable, Empowering, and Institutionalized.

Bottom line: The pursuit of regional governance excellence needs to be empowered by community leaders and citizens in each region and enjoy the involvement and support of state and national, governmental and non-governmental, organizations.

Achieving Regional Governance Excellence Will Strengthen, and Even Save, Our Federal System of Governance

Regional decision making complements local, state and national decision making by providing mechanisms for addressing crosscutting challenges that cannot be sponsored by any one of those levels alone. It does not replace, but rather enriches and helps preserve our federal system of governance.

As regions continue to evolve, they will create a new political force in state capitals and

Washington. At times, communities within regions will come together in a collective voice that has the clout to drive almost any agenda through the legislative process and shift funding streams to regional initiatives. Witness the success of regional lobbying efforts in many state capitals.

At times, these same communities will agree to differ and offer a divided voice but still probably make state capitals and Washington their battleground. In the Washington, D.C., region, for example, the political dividing line has shifted to the Beltway, with those inside who feel they are experiencing a declining quality of life — traffic congestion and resulting pollution, loss of contact with nature, increasing economic and racial segregation, and higher taxes to try to fix these issues — increasingly confronting those outside who still want to carve out a new place in the virgin hinterlands. Resolving regional challenges now consumes a considerable amount of the agendas of a city, two states and even the national government.

It might not be unreasonable to speculate that achieving regional governance excellence will someday result in strengthening the federal system. There is an excellent historical precedent for the impact of such challenges.

In 1785, representatives from the states of Virginia and Maryland met with George Washington at Mount Vernon to deal with the regional challenge of "jurisdiction and navigation" on the lower Potomac River. Finding that regional cooperation would not suffice and that part of the problem stemmed from the limitations of the Articles of Confederation that governed relations among the fairly autonomous states, the delegates decided to invite representatives from all of the states to a meeting in Annapolis the following year. The delegates at the Annapolis conference decided that the issues had such gravity that they decided to call a constitutional convention in Philadelphia the following year. The rest is history.

Will the challenge of "jurisdiction and navigation" on the growth "streams" sprawling out of our regions have a similar impact on national, state, and local government two centuries later? And this time, will it result in the ceding of critical authorities to regional governance mechanisms?

Bottom line: Resolving regional challenges could redefine our federal system of governance and breathe life into regional governance mechanisms.

Community Leaders and Citizens Need to Act Decisively Now to Achieve Regional Governance Excellence

ACHIEVING REGIONAL GOVERNANCE EXCELLENCE IS MORE AN ACT OF THE MIND THAN THE POCKETBOOK

The real fears of addressing challenges regionally have to do with confronting unfamiliar communities and peoples, especially those that are richer or poorer or of a different ethnicity, and unpopular challenges, especially future growth, since whoever shapes it controls regional decision making.

Not that this lack of interaction has made life better or governance cheaper for any of us. When central cities decline, when crime and drugs escalate, when impoverished school districts cannot graduate productive workers, when segregated populations cannot find jobs, or when suburban communities are paved over with highways and parking lots, when the only way to get anywhere is by personal auto, when we squander resources on inefficient services, when we mourn the loss of community — then we all suffer and pay.

ACHIEVING REGIONAL GOVERNANCE EXCELLENCE NEEDS TO BEGIN DECISIVELY, NOW

We have attracted the attention of community leaders and citizens and are experimenting with regional governance initiatives. That's positive, but it raises questions: Are we handling each new regional challenge better than the last one? Are we developing individual regional decision-making mechanisms that efficiently guide community leaders and citizens through equitable and empowering processes that handle the most pressing challenges?

We have also attracted the attention of economic interests that are already jockeying for influence in each of the regional economies that constitute the global common market. That's also positive, but it raises a second set of questions: Are we shaping regional growth and development so as to compete globally and thrive locally? If we are, are we also overcoming intercommunity disparities and building regional citizenship and a sense of regional community? And are we developing a "network" of regional decision-making mechanisms that interact seamlessly to provide regional governance excellence?

Finally, we are witnessing radical changes in the responsibilities and relationships of state and national governments. It's difficult to say whether this is positive or negative for regional governance, but it helps reinforce the need for community leaders and citizens to act decisively, now.

Community leaders and citizens in some regions are already beginning to launch their regional renaissances. They have started to consider the communities of the region in the singular, as *us*, and not just in the plural, as *you and me*. Community leaders and citizens in other regions may join them. I have no doubt that those who pursue this journey will live in the most desirable regions at the dawn of the 21st century.

CHAPTER 45

HOPE FOR "SUBURBANITIS"

Thomas H. Reed

The Buffalo *Evening News* a few weeks ago coined a new word — "suburbanitis" — to describe a disease which is crippling Buffalo and its environs. Let me reassure Buffalo at once. It is in no danger of catching it. It has it already. It is endemic in every urban community in the United States and Canada and almost everywhere else for that matter. It is not a new disease. Students of municipal administration have been recording and analyzing its symptoms and suggesting means for its cure for a generation. It was discussed for the first time on a National Municipal League program in a paper I read at the 1925 meeting in St. Louis, and it has been on the League's program almost every year since.

Many better and wiser city planners and political scientists than myself have poured out millions of words by tongue, pen and typewriter on the same theme, but frankness requires me to say that so far we have accomplished little more than a world's record for words used in proportion to cures effected. This appears to be a pretty sorry performance. Can it be improved? I think it can.

A glance at the nature of suburbanitis will show why it is so hard to cure. Cities have always grown at their peripheries. Growth has to take place where there is room for it. The outward movement of city population, until very recently, has been held severely in check first by the necessity for defensive walls and later by the absence or inadequacy of trans-

portation facilities. Two great names stand out in the story of urban decentralization: Roger Bacon, whose invention of gunpowder make walls useless, and Henry Ford, whose perfection of the popularly priced automobile has made it possible for masses of men and women to live anywhere within a radius of 30 miles or more of the office, shop or factory where they work.

Urban expansion, which throughout most of human history was deliberate enough to permit the slow processes of political change periodically to catch up with it, has in the past 40 years become an avalanche which has left those responsible for local government dizzy and bewildered. Population has spread all over the countryside around large cities with utter disregard for existing political boundaries. Nucleus cities have lost many of their best citizens and have been obliged to meet ever-increasing governmental costs with withering revenues. Counties have had thrust on them functions they are ill organized to carry out.

A vast demand has arisen for the extension of water, sewers, highways and other public works which the minor municipalities, except in rare instances, have neither the energy nor the resources to provide. New schools have had to be built while old schools in the nucleus city stood empty. The whole metropolitan area has suffered intensely from the almost entire absence of planning in this vast and unruly growth. This is "suburbanitis," a

From *National Civic Review,* Vol. 83, No. 1, Winter-Spring 1994. Published by the National Civic League, Denver, Colorado. Reprinted with permission of the publisher. [This article originally appeared in the National Municipal Review in December of 1950, nearly one-half century ago.]

disease not peculiar to any unit of the metropolitan area but affecting every nook and corner of it.

Surgery Called For

It is easy to see why so little progress has been made toward the cure for suburbanitis. A genuine cure calls for drastic surgery on the present scheme of local government. For a complete cure many of the existing organs — cities, counties, town, and villages — must be removed and the body sewed together again so that it will function successfully. Most local politicians would sooner consent to the removal of their right arms than to such an operation. Average private citizens are appalled at the prospect of changes so drastic in a matter so complex and, unable to visualize the beneficial results of the operation, assume an attitude of obstinate negation. The combined opposition of the politicians and people of any substantial number of the units of government in a metropolitan area is usually enough to put a dead stop to any thorough readjustment of the number and relationships of such units.

It is not at all surprising, in fact, that public opinion has not yet welcomed the idea of metropolitan unification. To do so requires the acceptance of a wholly new conception of the city, not as a compactly built-up area in which water, sewers, paved streets, lights, police patrol, and fire protection are provided, in sharp contrast to the rural areas outside, but as a sprawling "macropolis" covering hundreds of square miles where farms and pastures mingle with intense residential developments, factories and shopping centers.

Just such a transformation is rapidly taking place, but the nature and governmental implications of the change are hardly noticed except by professional students of urbanism. Ordinary man is just too busy living to realize the character of the drama in which he plays a part. I see no reason for discouragement in the fact that a single generation has not sufficed to bring about general recognition that new social and economic conditions require a readjustment of our plan of local government. It is natural that such a reform, inevitably leading to the abolition of jobs, the destruction of vested interest and the abandonment of long-cherished traditions, should take longer to accomplish than improvements in the internal organization and procedures of existing units of government. I believe that the next ten years will see startling progress toward metropolitan integration.

That is assuming we go about it intelligently. In the first place, nothing can be gained by promoting antagonism between the city and the suburbs. The motives which have induced people to seek homes in the suburbs are laudable — cheaper land, lower taxes, more room for the children, purer air, less smoke and dirt, healthier living, a larger share in community life, a new home in place of the old, shabby and obsolete one. Suburbanites are man for man just as good as city people and entitled to every bit as much consideration. To array the city against the suburbs is to court defeat. The objective in every successful campaign against suburbanitis must be the welfare of the whole metropolitan area — the greater city of tomorrow.

The task of convincing the public (of the merits of metropolitan reorganization) is by no means a hopeless one. The facts looked at from a long-range point of view will do the job. I do not blame homeowners in the suburbs for reacting on first impression against the idea of absorption by a neighboring big city. They have gone to the outskirts in the hope of cheaper and better living. They may not have found it. The construction, maintenance and operation of a well and a septic tank, higher fire insurance rates, the fee paid to the garbage collector, and other costs incident to semi-rural life, not infrequently balance the lower price and lot and the lower taxes. All the more reason why they should balk at the higher taxes of a large city on top of these investments. You can't talk them out of their opposition by calling them parasites, chiselers or leeches. They may to some extent be getting a free ride on the backs of city taxpayers but they just can't be expected to see that without some very careful and tactful explanation.

The fact is, however, that suburbanitis is catching up with them. As the suburban population grows, wells and septic tanks become unsatisfactory. They need waterworks and sewer systems. The little towns and villages which a dozen years ago were run satisfactorily on an amateur or part-time basis, at low cost to the taxpayer, have become large towns and villages and have to pay for what they get at the same wages and prices as prevail in the neighboring city. The surge of wartime babies now pouring into the lower grades of the schools has finally demonstrated the inadequacy of the school plant everywhere, and the town and village districts, like the city districts, are going to pay through the nose to make up for the building deficiencies of the last two decades.

Suburban taxes, real taxes — the rate times assessed valuation — have been for some time on the climb and are apparently destined to scramble up so fast that the differential the suburbs have enjoyed will soon be a thing of the past. The plight of the poorer suburbs, which never had even low taxes except at the sacrifice of needed services, will be particularly forlorn in the years ahead. These are facts which can be demonstrated to any citizen with a grammar grade education.

It is now just 50 years since I was a senior at Harvard, getting my first bite of a course which dealt in part with local government. There were not then a dozen colleges in the country which thought the subject worth teaching at all. There was no textbook on American local government for student use. The proceedings of the National Municipal League's Conferences on Good City Government, then in their seventh year, contained most of the material in print on the subject. (We have made great progress in the intervening years.)

American politics is by no means spotless but let no one tell you that it is not incomparably cleaner, and American local government infinitely more honest and efficient than it was 50 years ago. When I was a senior at Harvard the subject we have been discussing today had not even been heard of except as it had already affected such great cities as London and New York. Buffalo, Cleveland, Pittsburgh, Atlanta, Birmingham, and a hundred other communities in which suburbanitis is acute today, were not even aware that there could be such a disease. The conception of the greater city of tomorrow had not even dawned on the minds of dreamers. I am confident that as we have solved so many other problems of organization and procedure in local government, in spite of the intense opposition of the politicians and the deadening pessimism of the public, we shall in good time — not too far off — conquer suburbanitis.

ABOUT THE CONTRIBUTORS

Affiliations are as of the time the articles were written.

Charles R. Adrian, Professor of Political Science, University of California, Riverside, California.

American Planning Association, Chicago-based membership organization dedicated to building better communities through planning.

Terrell Blodgett, Mike Hogg Professor in Urban Management, Lyndon B. Johnson School of Public Affairs, University of Texas, Austin, Texas.

Robert P. Boynton, Professor, School of Public Administration, American University, Washington, D.C.

Kaye Braaten, First Vice President, National Association of Counties, Washington, D.C.

Richard W. Campbell, Administrator, Research and Services Division, Carl Vinson Institute of Government, University of Georgia, Athens, Georgia.

William N. Cassella, Jr. Member, Council of Advisors, National Civic League, Denver, Colorado.

Henry G. Cisneros, Secretary, U.S. Department of Housing and Urban Development, Washington, D.C.

Victor S. DeSantis, Associate Professor, Department of Political Science, Bridgewater State College, Bridgewater, Massachusetts.

William Dodge, Principal, Strategic Partnerships Consulting, Pittsburgh, Pennsylvania.

Herbert Sydney Duncombe, Professor of Political Science, University of Idaho, Moscow, Idaho.

Julianne Duvall, Information Specialist, Municipal Reference Service, National League of Cities, Washington, D.C.

Alan Ehrenhalt, Executive Editor, *Governing*, Congressional Quarterly, Inc., Washington, D.C.

R. Scott Fosler, Vice President and Director of Government Studies, Committee for Economic Development, New York, New York, and Senior Fellow, Institute for Policy Studies, Johns Hopkins University, Baltimore, Maryland.

J. Eugene Grigsby, III, Director, Advanced Public Service Institute, University of California, Los Angeles, California.

Rob Gurwitt, Senior Writer, *Governing*, Congressional Quarterly, Inc., Washington, D.C.

Susan B. Hannah, Director, School of Public Affairs and Administration, Western Michigan University, Kalamazoo, Michigan.

C. J. Hein, Professor of Public Administration, L. P. Cookingham Institute of Public Affairs, School of Business and Public Administration, University of Missouri, Kansas City, Missouri.

Theodore Hershberg, Professor of Public Policy and History and Director of the Center for Greater Philadelphia, University of Pennsylvania, Philadelphia, Pennsylvania.

Herbert H. Hughes, Director, Finance and Administration Department, Bernalillo County, Albuquerque, New Mexico.

Karl F. Johnson, Professor of Public Administration, L. P. Cookingham Institute of Public Affairs, School of Business and Public Administration, University of Missouri, Kansas City, Missouri.

Roger L. Kemp, City Manager, Meriden, Connecticut.

John Kincaid, Executive Director, U.S. Advisory

Commission on Intergovernmental Relations, Washington, D.C.

Ann Klinger, Supervisor, Merced County, Merced, California, and former President, National Association of Counties, Washington, D.C.

Charles Lee, Assistant to the Deputy Chief Administrative Officer, City of Albuquerque, New Mexico.

Donald C. Menzel, Director, Center for Public Affairs and Policy Management, University of South Florida, Tampa, Florida.

Metropolitan Council, nationally unique government body providing services and planning for the seven-county area around Minnesota's twin cities of Minneapolis and St. Paul.

Gerald E. Newfarmer, Chief Executive Officer, Management Partners, Inc., Cincinnati, Ohio, and former City Manager, Cincinnati, Ohio.

Thomas H. Reed (deceased), was a consultant to municipal governments, long-time member of the National Municipal League, and a noted expert on urban affairs.

Tari Renner, Chair, Political Science Department, Illinois Wesleyan University, Bloomington, Ill.

B. J. D. Rowe, Assistant Professor, Department of Public Administration, Atlanta University, Atlanta, Georgia.

Tanis J. Salant, Senior Research Specialist, Office of Community and Public Service, University of Arizona, Tucson, Arizona.

Richard M. Sheehan, Accountant, Finance Department, Arapahoe County, Littleton, Colorado.

Betsy D. Sherman, Director of Member Services, International City/County Management Association, Washington, D.C.

James H. Svara, Professor of Public Administration, North Carolina State University, Raleigh, North Carolina.

Richard Sybert, Director and Chairman, Governor's Interagency Council on Growth Management, Office of the Governor, State of California, Sacramento, California.

Robert D. Thomas, Professor, Political Science Department, University of Houston, Houston, Texas.

David B. Walker, Professor of Political Science, University of Connecticut, Storrs, Connecticut.

Allan D. Wallis, Director of Research, National Civic League, Denver, Colorado, and Assistant Professor of Public Policy, Graduate School of Public Affairs, University of Colorado, Denver, Colorado.

INDEX